The Essex Gen

Volume 10

1990

*Essex Society of Genealogists, Inc.
Essex County, Massachusetts*

HERITAGE BOOKS
2008

HERITAGE BOOKS
AN IMPRINT OF HERITAGE BOOKS, INC.

Books, CDs, and more—Worldwide

For our listing of thousands of titles see our website
at
www.HeritageBooks.com

Published 2008 by
HERITAGE BOOKS, INC.
Publishing Division
100 Railroad Ave. #104
Westminster, Maryland 21157

Copyright © 1996 Essex Society of Genealogists, Inc.

Other books by the author:

Essex County Deeds, 1639-1678, Abstracts of Volumes 1-4
Copy Books, Essex County, Massachusetts
CD: The Essex Genealogist, Volumes 1 and 2 (1981-1982)
The Essex Genealogist, Volumes 1-24 (1981-2004)
The Essex Genealogist, Index to Volumes 1-15 (1981-1995)
The Essex Genealogist, Index to Volumes 16-20 (1996-2000)

— Publisher's Notice —
Several items from the inside back covers of the original journals have
been moved, in this printing, to supplementary pages after the index.

All rights reserved. No part of this book may be reproduced or transmitted in any form or by any means, electronic or mechanical, including photocopying, recording or by any information storage and retrieval system without written permission from the author, except for the inclusion of brief quotations in a review.

International Standard Book Numbers
Paperbound: 978-0-7884-0567-9
Clothbound: 978-0-7884-7250-3

The Essex Genealogist

VOLUME 10, NUMBER 1 **FEBRUARY 1990**

CONTENTS

Letter from the Editor	2
TEG FEATURE ARTICLE: "Town Records," by Ann Smith Lainhart	3
IT HAPPENED IN MIDDLESEX COUNTY: "A House Divided," by C. Nelson Bishop and Eleanor C. Bishop	13
RESEARCH IN PROGRESS:	
"Descendants of Leonard Harriman of Rowley, Massachusetts," by Lois Ware Thurston	17
"John Ramsdell of Lynn, Massachusetts" by Roselyn Listernick	25
"William Ivory of Lynn and His Descendants," by Eleanor Tucker	33
Heinrich Scherer, Hessian, alias, Henry Sherer, Gardener," by Edward T. Barnard	42
THE AHNENTAFEL: Clayton Rand Adams; Jonathan D. Enslow; William Oliver Batchelder, grandfather of Margaret Southwick; Mary Hawkes Sargent, grandmother of Anne Merrill Goulette	47
SOCIETY NEWS	51
OUR READERS WRITE	52
MISCELLANEOUS NOTES	53
QUERIES	54
Abbreviations to QUERIES	58
MOMENTS IN HISTORY: "Making Money in Colonial Days"	Back Cover

THE ESSEX GENEALOGIST is published quarterly: February, May, August, November for $13 per year, by the Essex Society of Genealogists, Lynnfield Public Library, 18 Summer Street, Lynnfield, MA 01940. Second Class Postage paid at Lynnfield, MA 01940. ISSN: 0279-067X USPS: 591-350. POSTMASTER: Send address changes to ESOG, Lynnfield Public Library, 18 Summer Street, Lynnfield, MA 01940.

Letter from the Editor

Society today is oppressed with increasing crime, and, alas, the scourge has hit our own Helen Bosworth. The week before Christmas, in the darkness of night, two men broke through the back door of Helen's house while she was sleeping upstairs. She awoke to the noise, then sat terrified until the men left, mercifully without going upstairs. After a long time, she summoned her courage to go downstairs to call the police. Stolen articles were two typewriters, a radio and some small change.

As a result of this horrendous experience, Helen suffered a nervous reaction and has been very ill, though remaining alone at home at her own request. The house has been firmly secured. We are thankful that she has recently shown signs of improvement, although she does have a touch of pneumonia. The doctor and Helen both feel it will be a slow recovery.

We know and she knows that all of you wish her well. But for now, we ask you not to call, as it is very difficult for her to make it to the telephone. Cards and letters, however, will be read and appreciated.

Meanwhile, Earle Hazelwood has agreed to handle all treasury matters for the Society. Fortunately, the great majority of members have already renewed their memberships and or subscriptions for 1990 - those checks have been deposited and credited. But there are always stragglers as well as new members who are just hearing about us.

Please address all Society mail to:

ESOG, 18 Summer Street, Lynnfield, MA 01940. You can include if you wish:

Attention: Earle C. Hazelwood, Jr. (for dues/subscriptions, memberships). or:

Attention: Marion A. MacDonald (for requests for research).

Please note also that our new Query Editor is Shirley Orr. Her address appears on TEG's Masthead (inside the front cover). We try to keep the Masthead current, so it is a good idea to check it for addresses, dues, etc.

There will be no March Newsletter with its usual revised membership list. We hope that Helen will feel like composing one in June, but we shall not rush her. If she is not up to it, we shall try to find a substitute at that time. Any volunteers?

As soon as this issue goes to the printer, Ken and I take off on January 28 for our annual Florida vacation - this year for all of February and March - then, back in Lynnfield by April 4, I start preparing the May issue of TEG. Meanwhile, our house-sitter will forward all mail to us. Since we are renting, we will use my daughter's address while we are there. You can write to:

Marcia Wiswall Lindberg, C/O Carol T. Altman, 640 Soundview Drive, Palm Harbor, FL 34683. (813) 785-5866.

Vice President, Bill Stevens, will take over the reigns for February and March, at which times we have two excellent speakers scheduled: George Sanborn will bring members up to date on New Hampshire research in March, and Jane Fiske will do the same for Rhode Island in April. Inez Dubuque will continue to provide her excellent collations. Marion MacDonald will supervise the Research Department.

Donald Doliber was unable to get his "Essex County" article for this issue, but promises to have one ready for the May issue. Meanwhile, we know you will enjoy Eleanor Bishop's article on "A House Divided."

Enjoy!

Marcia Wiswall Lindberg

TEG Feature Article

TOWN RECORDS

By Ann Smith Lainhart

[A lecture before ESOG, October 21, 1989]

Today I'm going to be speaking on Town Records other than Vital Records. What are Town Records other than Vital Records? They are the records generated by the Town Clerk or by other town officials. In the colonial period, they are known as Selectmen's Records, Proprietors' Records, or just plain Town Records. When you go into a Town Clerk, you often have to run through all the possibilities until suddenly a light flashes. "Oh, yes! We have something called that!" In the large towns such as Boston, you may even find that there are Town Records which are the minutes of the meetings of the General Town Meetings and at the same time Selectmen's Records which were the meetings of just the Selectmen. But in most of the smaller towns, there is just a single set of books in the colonial period. As you get into the late 1700s and the early 1800s, there begins to be some diversification. So instead of a single set of books recording everything in town, you begin to find Treasurer's Books, Tax Books, Poor Books, and so on.

As I've indicated, you will generally find these records in the Town Clerk's office. Sometimes you have to do a little fighting with them to get them to admit that they have such things. My famous story is calling the Richmond Town Clerk (Richmond is a small town out in Berkshire County) and "Oh no, we have nothing that goes back that far." I talked a bit longer and finally she said "Well there are some books in the vault but they're all full of creepy crawley things..." Beware that you often have to make appointments with Town Clerks particularly in the very small towns like Richmond, where the Town Clerk has hours two mornings a week - in her kitchen! So you can't just go to every New England town and expect to find an office open from 9 to 5, Monday through Friday.

You will find that some of these Town Records have been filmed by the Mormon Church. But when the Mormons were filming, they were primarily interested in Vital Records. So generally they only filmed other Town Records when they happened to have Vital Records in the same volume. Recently I was doing work on some families in Wells, Maine and at the State Archives in Augusta, I was able to do the Town Records through the 1770s because that volume also had Vital Records in it. But I found that the later Town Records were not on microfilm because at the end of that volume they went to separate volumes for Town Records and Vital Records. So all the Mormons filmed were the Vital Records. So I had to go to the Town Hall to get those. I was very pleasantly surprised to find that years ago, Wells took their original Town Books and photocopied them and then bound the copies and that's what they bring out for you to use. The original volumes are put away and preserved, but there is still a nice legible copy to use.

You will find copies of these Mormon films generally in the State Archives. Now they may not be complete for the state. For instance at the Mass. State Archives at Columbia Point, they do have many of these Mormon films for towns, but they seem to be more complete for the eastern towns and they don't have some of the western towns. For instance, they do not have Richmond. In fact, I have since learned that indeed the Mormons filmed Richmond and therefore the town was given a set of the microfilms (That's how the Mormons work - they always give a set of the microfilms to the town), and that set of microfilm records (for Richmond) has been deposited at the town library in Richmond. But, the town library in Richmond does not have a microfilm reader!

You'll find copies of the Mormon films for the New Hampshire towns at the State Library in Concord. You'll find them in the State Archives at Augusta, for Maine towns. You'll find that there is one extraordinary set of microfilm Town Records that was not done by the Mormons. This is for Middlesex County, Massachusetts. It was done in the 1960s primarily as a demographic history project. So that demographers would have access to the full records of single towns for studies of the towns. And this set of microfilms is available at Boston Public Library, the Massachusetts Historical Society and the New England Historic Genealogical Society. You can also order copies of any of the rolls from Spaulding Graphic Company. I bought the sets for Reading and Wakefield as I happen to have a particular interest in those two towns. There is a nice printed inventory of this particular set of microfilm records of Middlesex County. Now these Town Records do not include Vital Records except for those few towns in Middlesex County that at the time did not have published Vital Records. For instance, I believe, under Peperell, you will find Vital Records.

Holbrook Company is also doing a current filming of Massachusetts Records, but again they are stressing the Vital Records and probably only copy those volumes of Town Records that also include some Vital Records. These are being done on microfiche. A complete set of the Holbrook collection is being sent to Boston Public Library. They have a standing order for it as it's being produced. New England "Hist Gen" has a few towns also.

Then, finally there are some Town Records that have appeared in print that are listed on the hand out that appears at the end of this article. Many of these are books unto themselves or typescripts at NE Hist Gen. A few are Town Records that have been published in periodicals. If anyone knows any that I'm missing, please let me know. I would like to make this list as complete as possible.

Now that you know what Town Records are, and where they are, what is in them?

As I said, in the colonial period, there is usually just a single volume into which the Town Clerk would copy almost anything going on in the town. The first book in a town will generally begin with the Town Charter, which is often followed by a list of original men who settled the town - the Proprietors. That's why they're sometimes called the Proprietors' Records. The vast majority of what's in these volumes are records of the Town Meetings. Just as today, in the colonial period the town would have had meetings once a year when they would have elected their town officers for the year; the Selectmen, the Constable, the Tythingmen, the Hogreeves, the Fence-Viewers, men to lay out the highways, and so on. This meeting was often in May, often in March. Sometimes they will then have a second meeting if there was something special in the town - or some problem arising that had to be handled before the next March meeting. After these Town Meetings, you will find committee assignments. If a problem arose, generally the town would chose from two to six or seven men to be a committee to go out and resolve the problem, or report back to the town.

You'll find tallies for state and national elections, after the Revolutionary War. Sometimes the Town Records will include Tax Lists, but they vary considerably. Some towns will have a full listing for every man in town and what taxes they paid. In other towns, you can't find tax lists. It depends on the individual clerk and what he chose to enter into the town book. When the town first began, they would be given a large chunk of land by the colony and the first order of business would be to divide up some of that land into home lots, pasture and meadowland, for the original settlers (the proprietors). Then, in the Town Book you will often find the grants to each of these originaly settlers, of what land they started out with. I'm sure you've all run into the case in the County Deeds where you find a man selling land that you never can find him buying. Now in some cases, he's inherited it. In other cases, it's because it was a grant from the town, and the recording of that grant is in the Town Records, not in the County Records. Once the land is granted to a man, then the next time it changes hands when he sells it, then that deed and all subsequent deeds are at the county level. But the first one is in the Town Records. Then as the town grows, they will often come to a point where they will have a division of some of the additional common land and so you will sometimes find in the Town Records even a map showing the area of land divided into lots, which each man got in the first division or the second division or even the third division for some towns. That is nice because when you're at the County Deeds, you will often find the property many, many years later still being described as lot #26 in the 2nd division. So if you can then go back to the Town Record and find the record of that lot being granted or even one of these little maps showing here the lot was, that can be helpful.

You will find ear marks recorded in the Town Records. In the early days, all the men in town would put their cattle on the common to graze. So they had to have some way to tell the individual cows apart - which one belonged to which man. So each man would be given a certain ear mark - notches, etc. in the ears of the animal.

In the colonial period, when you're studying Town Records, you begin to realize how closely allied the church and civil governments were. In Richmond, again, I found, at certain times, committees were appointed by the town to lay out the meeting house. At this period, the higher your social rank in town, the closer your pew was to the minister. Can you imagine being on the committee to try to decide who sits where in the Meeting House? And keep friends with everybody? What was nice in the Richmond Town Records, I think it was three different times several years apart, they have drawn layouts of the Meeting House and the pews, with the people's names written in their places. So you could see how people moved forwards or backwards in the church.

You will find "warnings out" in the Town Records. In the colonial period, and even well into the early 19th century, New England towns had the responsibility to care for those people whom they considered inhabitants. If you were born to inhabitants, then you automatically became an inhabitant. But if somebody moved to town, it would take them awhile before they would be a recognized inhabitant, so that when people came into town, they were often warned out. The town was not saying "you must leave." The town was simply saying that "If you stay and fall upon hard times and can't take care of yourself, we're not going to do it for you!" So they were just giving notice to these people that the town would not take care of them. So because of this you sometimes find in the Town Record copies of these actual warnings out. This is nice, because they often mention wives' names and the names of the children. They'll often tell where the family came from. Then you'll also find bills from people who had to take someone back to another town. So Joe Brown would be billing the Town of Reading for taking Mrs. Smith back to Framingham because she was considered an inhabitant of Framingham, and Reading didn't want to have the responsibility of her.

You'll find information on school masters and what they were paid. That's one of the committees that your ancestor may have served on - to go and find a new schoolmaster and get him to come to town.

Another committee that you will find them serving on are for border disputes. When the colony government gave towns land to settle a town, they weren't always very detailed as to where the land exactly lay. So you start having two towns settled and they suddenly realize they don't know exactly where one starts and the other ends. So each town would set up a committee and the committees would meet and hopefully battle out something in the way of a boundary between them.

You'll find that they lay out highways. There are committees for that. In some Town Records they will go so far as to name the men from whose farms the land was taken for the laying out of the highways. So "eminent domain" goes way back. This may also explain why you find a man buying a 100-acre farm and then selling it several years later as a 90-acre farm. It may be that something was sliced off for a highway.

You'll get information on abated rates. This is when the town tells someone, "You don't have to pay your taxes for this year." This is often a very good indication of death, because you'll find it recorded that the widow's rates were abated. So it may be that the year after her husband's death, she was not able to come up with the money. It may be because of disability. He was wounded in the war, or injured in some other way. And they abate their rates.

You'll find military information, and the militia. In the pre-Revolutionary War era, you'll find militia rolls from the various towns. There were Indian scares. As you get to the Revolutionary times, you may find information on Committees of Correspondence being set up in the various towns, to correspond with other towns about what was happening to them, and of course information on the soldiers who fought during the war from each town.

And you may find information on fire companies. In Boston, fire companies became quite big. In fact, they became almost social organizations as well as fire companies. Paul Revere was head of one of the fire companies in Boston. So was an ancestor of mine - a Quartermaster General - Amasa Davis.

So those are the kinds of things you can find when the books were sort of all in one. When they started diversification, then these are the kinds of extra books you can begin to find.

First of all, Treasurer's Books. These are the accounts paid to and by the Town and what's nice about them is they usually give some reason why they're paying somebody. Here are some examples of information found in Treasurer's books:

"Sent to Mr. Samual Brook by his brother Thomas Brook, 4 lbs, 18 shillings, fourpence lawful money which was for his keeping school."

"Paid to James Nichols, for keeping William Boclea for the year 1754." William Boclea was probaly a pauper or an orphan and so the town paid James Nichols for taking care of him.

"Paid to Capt. Ebenezer Nichols, 17 lbs, 4 shillings to provide a nest of Troy weights for the town" ("weights" is spelled "waits").

"Paid to Joshua Nichols, 2 pounds, twopence for gathering town rates and warning town meetings." That indicates that Joshua Nichols was probably the Constable for the town, for those were two of the duties of a Constable.

"Paid Mr. Ephraim Parker 3 shillings for perambulating with Wilmington."

"Paid 9 pence to Mr. Mason for a copy of Beulah Richardson's being warned out of town." So even if the warning out of Beulah Richardson doesn't survive, this is an indication that she was warned out and someone was paid for making a copy of it.

"Paid Capt. Hezekiah Upton 17 pounds 11 shillings for planks, for bridges and a days work on the new road."

Then there are Assessor's Books, Rate Books, and Tax Books. They're all slightly different, but sort of cover the same thing. That's probably why you won't find all three in the same town. But you'll find at least one of these in most towns.

Assessors Books would have included the assessed value of animals, lands and servants. This is one book where you may find information on the poor if these are not separate Poor Books. The Rate Books covered the Rates assessed for different projects. There would be the Town Taxes, the Parish Rates - rates assessed to each person for supporting the church and minister - County Taxes, Province Taxes. And then there may be special rates every so often - such as if they were laying out a highway, building a new school or a church, there may be a single assessed rate for just that particular project. The Tax Books would include each man's taxes paid each year. This can also include non-residents who owned property in town and were allowable for taxes. These are generally divided into real estate taxes, personal taxes, poll taxes and highway taxes.

Every so often, the New England states would take more detailed taxes that are called valuation lists. The one you are probably most familiar with is the 1771 Tax Valuation List, because that was published several years ago for Massachusetts. It is not complete because at some point, somebody was wandering through the State House early in this century, I believe, and happened to see a janitor stoking the fire with some papers. These were the 1771 Valuation Lists. This person happened to be a member of "Hist Gen" and grabbed up everything that was left and deposited them with the State Archives. Then, several years ago, those that survived were published in a big red book. Valuation Lists include information on polls (males over the age of 16 with enough property to be taxed), the number of houses, barns and other buildings one has, the amount of improved land and the unimproved land, the number of horses, oxen, cows and swine, the amount of money he has at interest - if he has turnpike shares - stock in trade, and even if he owns carriages.

Starting in the 19th century, you'll also find in towns, Voters Lists - right up to the present day. The State Library Annex, which is still in the basement of the State House, has a very good collection of modern Voters' Lists for towns. They can be quite helpful. They often give people's ages. It's almost like a census in some cases, although they really are Tax Lists.

You may find books on School Records. I have not really looked into a whole lot of these. Those I've seen, unfortunately, do not give student's names. Instead, they are the records of the School Committee. They include information on the boarding of students, for the teachers, for repairs to the school. In Reading's School Book, there is even a listing of books in the school library in 1843. It's sort of interesting to read through and see what was being studied then.

You may find a book on Stray Beasts. This would be if somebody found an animal that did not have an ear mark. They would go into the Town Clerk, describe the animal, have it recorded. Then, I'm assuming someone would come along and describe an animal they had lost. They'd know where to send him. I'm also assuming that if no one came in to describe him, then that animal would become the property of whoever found it. In Reading, the title of the book is, "A Memorandum of Stray Beasts and Freed Negroes." There is one entry in the book where a man went in to the Town Clerk and wrote down an agreement that if this negro would serve him for so many years and be a faithful and dutiful servant, then he would have his freedom at the end of that period. This was well before the Revolution.

You may also find separate books for Military Records. These will be muster rolls and militia lists. Sometimes they will be pay lists - each soldier was paid for his service by the town. In Reading, they evidently decided to give each Revolutionary Soldier a blanket. There is a list titled "Blanket List." As each man received his blanket, he signed his name or made his mark. So here in the Town Records you have all these signatures.

In Dighton, there is a volume labeled, "Rebellion Record, Volume I, 1863." In the filming, I did not find a Volume II, so this may be the only one there. Across the top of the page, the headings were: "Name and Residence, Time and Place of Birth, When Enlisted, When Mustered, Enlisted for How Many Years, Resigned Company, How Much Bounty Paid, Single or Married, Names of Parents, Occupations," and a final column headed "Promotions, Resignations, Discharges, Deaths, etc." Here are some examples from that book:

"Aaron Wink, born in Germany, was mustered into the service 23 Sept 1862 for 9 months. He was in the 3rd Reg. Co. H. He was paid $200 bounty, was single, son of Frank & Katy. Occupation when he enlisted, an "ostler."
"Sylvanus B. Jones, b. 11 Apr 1826 in Dighton (Dighton does not have published Vital Records), mustered 23 Sept 1862 for 9 months. 3rd Reg., Co. H, paid $200 bounty. Married at time of enlistment. Was a merchant."
"Edward E. Wade, b. March 1843, mustered 23 Sept 1862 for 3 yrs. 40th Reg., Co. B, paid $325 bounty. Single, son of John P. & Amelia, a "Molder" by occupation. Was killed in battle, 20 May 1864."
"John H. Pitts, mustered 11 June 1861 for 3 yrs. 7th Reg. Co. C, paid $15 bounty. Single. Parents, Henry & Sarah. A shoemaker." In the final column, they have written on top: "Mortally Wounded" and written underneath it, "Reinlisted, 1864."

In this set of microfilms of Town Records, it shows Ashby, Shirley, Townsend and Pepperell have censuses in 1810 and 1821 which are in the Town Records. And Burlington has 1827 and 1837 censuses. I've not actually looked at these myself. But judging from the time period, they probably listed only the Head of Household as did the Federal Census at that period.

Finally we get to the Poor Books. All of us are going to have those ancestors we just can't seem to find. They don't appear in the land records and the probate records. We may find a marriage record for them, and it may be that they never had any real good luck in this life and ended up in the Poor House or on the Poor Farm. And these records can often give you lots of information about people. For instance, in the Town Records of Athol in 1774, they granted 8 lbs, 13 shillings, fourpence to pay Simon Goddard for bringing up Thomas Woods, a poor child put to him by the Selectmen. This may indicate that Thomas Woods was an orphan or that his family couldn't support the whole family, so that those children old enough to be put out for work were put out by the Selectmen.

Bellingham has a really nice little book on the Poor Farm, 1831-1851. The book starts out with the buying of the farm and setting it up and we can see some of the sad stories of some of these people. In 1834, it's recorded that Amy Hill, the wife of Jonathan Hill of the state of Ohio is now here and has been for nearly a month. It is also recorded that the overseers had paid the town of Barre for the above named Amy Hill, providing transportation for her here. In other words, the town of Bellingham, recognized Amy Hill as an inhabitant. Maybe she had been born there, but she had married a man either from Ohio or who was now in Ohio, and had somehow ended up in Barre and couldn't support herself. Bellingham paid to go get her and bring her to the town farm. Almost a year later, in February 1835, Amy Hill has a child born, then in July of 1835, it is recorded that her child died. Jedediah Phipps is paid to make two coffins, one for Joel Thompson and one for Amy Hill's child. In 1847, 12 years later - she's been living at the Poor Farm all that time - it's recorded that Amy Hill is at Dr. Ides and he is willing to pay her $1.25 per week. So she leaves the Poor Farm and goes out to work for Dr. Ides.

In October of 1836, they received of Stephen Metcalf, one payment of Seth Haywood's pension money, they paid Seth a little each month. At this period, pension money would have been for military service. Therefore it indicates to go look for Seth Haywood as a veteran in the War of 1812 or possibly of the Revolutionary War.

In October 1843, it's recorded that Sarah Ann Adams had a child born. In July of 1844, Sarah Ann Adams, a poor girl, is let out to Noah J. Arnold until she arrives at age 18. In July of 1847, Noah is discharged from the care of Sarah because she has now reached 18. Well, if you figure back, if she's become 18 in July of 1847, it means she was only 14 years old when her child was born in October of 1843.

The one I love best is that the Poor Farm contracted with Abijah Howard to keep his Mother in Law, Mrs. Gould!

Several deaths are recorded in the Poor Farm Book. It's understandable since many of the people at the Poor Farm are elderly. I found that all of them were recorded in the Bellingham published Vital Records, except in the Vital Records the date is always a day or two later than in the Poor Farm Book. It turns out that these deaths were all entered with a P.R. # meaning a private record kept by a doctor. So evidently he didn't record the deaths from the Poor Farm until a day or two after they had actually happened. So the Poor Farm Book which was not used for the published Vital Records has the actual death date.

And finally, at the very end of the book there was an entry on the Eccles family. It said that "William Eccles and his wife Mary and child William came to me and made application for assistance." William Eccles was age 34, born in Blackburn, England. Mary, age 30, born in Michaeltown, Ireland; William, age two, born in Frankfort, came to Mass. 11 July 1848 and then came to us from the Town of Lawrence. William Eccles children, twins, were born 24 November 1848 and William and his family left town on 7 February 1848. All that information on one page, and those twins - it doesn't give their names - are not in the Bellingham Vital Records.

In Fall River, there is a book titled "Selectmen's Letters, 1830-1840." This turns out to be copies of the letters sent out by the Fall River Selectmen (secretarial copy book). In April 1835, they write to the Overseers of the Poor of Attleboro and say, "You state that Juliette G. Davis, with her infant child, inhabitant of this town, are in Attleboro and chargeable." In other words, Juliette Davis and her child are living in Attleboro and could not support themselves. For some reason, Attleboro thinks they should be considered inhabitants of Fall River. So they've written to Fall River to say, "Come and get them!" Fall River has written back, saying, "You are misinformed as to the said Juliette G. Davis. She has no settlement in Fall River. We learn from the grandparents of Juliette (unfortunately not named) now living in Westport, that she is herself "an Illigitmate," that she was born in Tiverton, R.I.; that her mother afterwards married a man by the name of Lapham, who was then living in Cumberland, R.I. Immediately after the marriage they moved to Wareham in Plymouth County, where they lived seven or eight years until the mother died. We believe, therefore, that Julliette has a settlement in Wareham. But if not, try Tiverton, R.I."

Well, I hope that I have today made you aware of the potential of the kinds of material you will find in Town Records. They can often take a fair amount of time searching. Unfortunately, often that searching is on microfilm. But you never know what you're going to find. In some cases, particularly if you're having a real problem with a family, this may be where the only information to solve the problem will come from. I hope to see you in the Town Clerk's offices!

Ann Smith Lainhart is a professional genealogist. She has a B.A. in History from Sarah Lawrence College. She is a member of the New England Historic Genealogical Society, the Association of Professional Genealogists, the Maine Genealogical Society, the Connecticut Society of Genealogists, the Massachusetts Genealogical Council and the Massachusetts Society of Mayflower Descendants. Among her publications are "Descendants of Pax Cazneau," Register 1988; "John Haven Dexter and the 1789 Boston City Directory," Register 1986, and town-by-town abstracts of the 1855 and 1865 Massachusetts State Censuses. Her special interests include collecting information on all Lainharts/Laneharts, descendants of Alexander Gaston of Richmond, Mass., and of Abraham Bryant of Reading, Mass. She lives in Peabody, Mass.

NEW ENGLAND TOWN RECORDS IN PRINT

CONNECTICUT:

Extracts from the Records of Colchester, 1713-1730 (1864)
Town Records of Derby, 1655-1710 (1901)
The History of Enfield (1900) has published the town records
Lyme Records, 1667-1730 (1968)
New Haven Colony Historical Society: Ancient Town Records, 1649-1769, 3 vol.
Documentary History of Suffield, 1660-1749 (1879)

MAINE:

Town Meetings, 1817-1850, Brookville (1949), typescript at NEHGS
Records of the Proprietors of Narraganset Township, No. 1, Now the Town of Buxton, 1733-1811 (1871)
Records of the Proprietors of New Gloucester, Maine Historical Society, Collections, 2nd. Series, 8:263
The Pejepscot Proprietors: Records and Papers to 1768, Documentary History of Maine, 24:199
Papers relating to Pemaquid, Maine Historical Society, Collections, 1st. Series, 5:1
Records [Standish], Maine Historical and Genealogical Recorder, No. 4, 5:233, 6:359

MASSACHUSETTS:

Records of the Town of Amherst, 1735-1788 (1884)
Record Commissioners Series for Boston, 1634-1822
Boxford Town Records, 1685-1706, Essex Institute Historical Collections, 36:41
Records of the Town of Braintree, 1640-1793 (1886)
Brookfield Records, 1686-1783. In History of North Brookfield (1887)
Town Records of Brookline, 1838-1884, 3 vol.
The Records of the Town of Cambridge, 1630-1703 (1901)
Concord Town Records, 1732-1820 (1894)
The Early Records of the Town of Dedham, 1636-1766, 5 vol.
The Record of the Town Meetings of Dedham, 1887-1896 (1896)
Dorchester Town Records, 1632-1691, Record Commissioner Report, Vol. 4
Tax Payers, Town of Dorchester, 1849-1869
Town Records of Dudley, 1732-1754 (1893)
Copy of the Old Records of the Town of Duxbury, 1642-1770 (1893)
The Old Records of the Town of Fitchburg, 8 vol.
The Early Records of Groton, 1662-1707 (1880)
Ancient Records of the Town of Ipswich, 1634-1650 (1899)
The Early Records of Lancaster, 1643-1725 (1884)
The Early Records of the Town of Lunenburg, 1719-1764 (1896)
Records of ye Towne Meetings of Lynn, 1691-1783, 7 vol.
Town Records of Manchester, 1636-1786, 2 vol.
The Proprietor's Records of the Town of Mendon, 1667-1816 (1899)
Milton Town Records, 1662-1729 (1930)
Papers relating to the Island of Nantucket (1856)
The Records of Oxford (1894)
Pelham Proprietors' Records, 1738-1743, and Town Records, 1743-1897. In History of Pelham (1898)

Records of the Town of Plymouth, 1636-1783, 3 vol.
Rowley: the Early Records of the Town of Rowley, 1639-1672 (1894)
Town Records of Salem, 1634-1691, 3 vol.
First Century of the History of Springfield: the Official Records, 1636-1736 (1898)
The War Years in the Town of Sudbury, 1765-1781
Records of the Town of Tisbury, 1669-1864 (1903)
Town Records of Topsfield, 1659-1739 (1917)
Watertown Records, 1634-1829, 8 vol.
Wenham Town Records, 1642-1776, 3 vol.
Town of Weston, Records of the First Precinct 1746-1754 & of the Town 1754-1803 (1893)
Town of Weston, Records of the Town Clerk, 1804-1826 (1894)
Town of Weston, The Tax Lists, 1757-1827 (1897)
Worcester Town Records & Proprietors Records, 1722-1783, Vol 2, 3, & 4 of Collections of the Worcester Society of Antiquity

NEW HAMPSHIRE:

The Town Book of Bow, 1767-1820 (1933) typescript at NEHGS
Records of the Proprietors of Bow, 1727-1783 (1933) typescript at NEHGS
Concord Town Records, 1732-1820 (1894)
The Records of the Town of Hanover, 1761-1818 (1905)
Proprietors' Records of Lebanon, 1761-1774. In History of Lebanon (1908)
Early Records of Londonderry, Windham, and Derry, 1719-1762, 2 vol.
Early Records of the Town of Derryfield, Now Manchester, 5 vols.
Records of the Meetings of the Masonian Proprietors, 1748-1846, New Hampshire State Papers, 29:400, Pt. 2
The Records of the Original Proprietors of Peterborough. In Appendix of History of the Town of Peterborough

RHODE ISLAND:

The Early Records of the Town of Portsmouth, 1639-1679 (1901)
Early Town Records of Providence, 20 vol.

VERMONT:

Weybridge, Proprietor's Records, 1762-1811, typescript at NEHGS
Some town records, such as Guilford, are printed in the <u>Vermont Historical Gazetteer</u>

It Happened in ~~Essex~~ Middlesex County

A HOUSE DIVIDED STILL STANDS

By C. Nelson Bishop and Eleanor C. Bishop

For many years the house at 7 Avon Street in Reading, Mass. stood as a single, harmonious household. It was built by the Burnap family, and was standing in 1775 according to the will of Isaac Burnap who left the west half of the house to his widow, Susannah. The immigrant ancestor was Robert Burnap who served as a Selectman for more than a dozen years; his son, Robert, for nearly that long. The next son in line, Capt. Joseph, served for eight years. Captain Joseph was a cooper by trade, but also followed the profession of surveyor. The family grew and prospered and held many offices in the town and church and when the elder Joseph died in 1744 he left a large family that was well remembered in the distribution of his extensive lands and personal effects. The latter showed that he had acquired a sizable fortune for those days. To his son, Isaac, born in 1713 and married to Susannah Emerson in 1736, was left the homestead. When Isaac died in 1780, the use of the west half of his house went to the widow and two of the daughters. The will was drawn in 1775, so the house was known to have been standing then.

Joseph had served in the Revolution, going to Lexington as a corporal under Capt. John Batchelder. Jonathan Weston was a private at Lexington under Capt. Thomas Eaton. Both served in the Reading "train band." By 1789 they had both acquired the title of "Captain," on the town tax records, probably having continued in service with the militia. Burnap, up to then, paid a larger real estate tax.

Somehow or other Capt. Joseph Burnap got into debt to Capt. Jonathan Weston, Jr. There is no record of how it happened but it can be seen how it changed the course of life for the Burnap family. Captain Joseph tried to get out of debt but the records show him to be land poor and 206 pounds was more than he could possibly raise. In February, 1789, he tried to sell or mortgage the land and half the house to Nathan Parker, and the deed is on record, but the 210 pounds was apparently never paid over, for on March 19, Nathan deeded it all back, the consideration being not for cash but for "good and sufficient reasons." The hard-pressed man succeeded in selling off a few small tracts but he failed to raise the necessary amount and on the date that Parker returned the land, Joseph went before James Bancroft, justice of the peace, and acknowledged his debt to Jonathan Weston, Jr. and asserted he would be unable to pay it before the due date, some four days off. So the sheriff, Abijah Thompson, set off half the house, and as much land as the appraisers deemed suitable to pay the debt.

Thus Jonathan Weston came to live in the west half of the house, the part left to the use of Isaac's widow and their daughters, Tabitha and Sarah. A deal was made, however, and the widow, Susannah moved into the east end of the house. On the 24th of March it was decided: "West end of the dwelling and a small piece of land adjoining to the north side of the house, set aside to Weston. The line begins at the south side of the house in the middle running north to the kitchen then east to the end of the kitchen, then north by the kitchen to the north side of the house; then north to a stake and stones by the fence north of the garden; then west by the fence to the road; then by the road in a range with the south side of the house; then east to the place first mentioned." The agreement then gave half of the cellar and the "liberty to use the yard before the house that lyeth open to the road, and also the pantry in the north corner of the house and the chamber over the same." The owners of the east end then had reserved to them the chamber over the kitchen; "liberty to use the well on the north side of the house, liberty to pass and repass from the back door to the road."

In 1944 the Burnap House on Ash Street, which had been owned by two families from 1789 until the 1940s, still showed the dividing line on the roof and the older type small-paned windows in the westerly section.

The local history says that Joseph Burnap parted with his wife and went to New York. We find it slightly different according to the census of 1790. Listed adjacent in that tabulation are Jonathan Weston and Widow Susannah Burnap, Joseph's mother. Listed in her household is one male sixteen years of age or over and this probably was her grandson, Joseph. Also listed are four females, the other three could include her two daughters and one of Joseph's older girls. Possibly Abigail or Susanna and perhaps both of them.

We find Joseph Burnap listed in Mohawk, Montgomery County, N.Y. and listed in his household are three boys under sixteen and two females. The boys would be his three sons, Cyrus, George and Isaac, none of whom appear in later poll tax lists or the vital records of the town of Reading, and the two females would be his wife Abigail and the youngest daughter, seven-year-old Zoraday.

The local tax list shows that Captain Joseph Burnap left town in 1789, for the state tax in October assesses the property to "Capt. Joseph Burnap's successors." The same listing is carried until late in the year 1791 when Joseph Jr came of age and he took over the half of the house as his own responsibility. Susannah died in 1792.

In 1794 the assessment was in the name of Widow Abigail. This implies that Joseph, Sr. had died but he lived at least until 1813 because in September of that year he sold land in Reading to his son-in-law, Timothy Thompson. Joseph was then living in Charleston, Montgomery County, N.Y. and that is the last we can find about him. His death does not appear in the Reading vital records, nor does he appear on the rolls of the Third Parish Church. A Burnap genealogy says he died 26 August 1819 but does not give the source. His name was carried on in the Bay State by descendants of Joseph, Jr. who moved to Wilmington and died there at the age of eighty-two on 27 June 1851. The family name was further perpetuated by a brother, Jacob, who graduated from Harvard College, became a minister and settled in Merrimack, N.H. in the 1770s.

After the death of Abigail Burnap in 1850, the heirs, in 1831, by agreement, sold their half of the house "lately owned by Joseph Burnap deceased" to their sister, Susanna Winn, widow of John, and mother of George Winn. The Winns lived there with the Westons as joint owners until 1840 when the estate of Captain Jonathan was settled and the executor, Thomas Sweetser, sold that part of the house and lot to Edmund Parker who sold it two days later to Nancy Foster, who was a spinster, the 11th and youngest child of Samuel and Judith Foster who were married in Reading in 1767, then settled in Wilmington where all their children were born.

Nancy and Susanna were evidently women of some determination. Each had her own idea about a woman's home being her castle and hardly a month of their joint ownership had passed when it was recorded that "certain difficulties and disputes have arisen in relation to their respective rights." They then put into straight-laced terms the division of the house. The Westons and Burnaps had seemed to get along without further definition of the terms appearing in the indenture of 1789 but Susanna and Nancy would not go on precedent.

They specified where partitions should be built to divide off the cellar and the garrett and they worded all over again the rights each other had to certain rooms in the house, not changing at all the meaning of the words in the original indenture. And then they turned up this exact piece of agreement: In consideration that the said Susanna shall keep the east half of the roof of the house in good repair and free from leakage, the the said Nancy will keep the west half of the roof of the house in good repair and free from leakage, and the parties do hereby covenant and agree with, and promise each other, and for their respective heirs and assigns, that they will keep their respective parts of the roof and walls of the house in good repair and free from leakage."

But then they parted from the original indenture. Susanna paid $20 and gave up the use of the passage-way on the north side of the house from the back door to the road. Nancy also gave up any title to the front yard with the exception of a passageway in common of "27 1/2 feet in front of said house, extending east, to the east side of the casing of the front door, to be used in common by the parties and to remain open to the road."

Nancy also agreed to allow a pipe to run from the well through her part of the cellar so that Susanna could have a pump in her pantry. But this was only under consideration that "the said Susanna shall point the outside of her cellar wall on the east and north sides to the east end of the kitchen in the same manner that hers, the said Nancy's, is now done." Also, "the said Nancy" was allowed to pass around the north side of the house to carry out that old New England practice of banking the underpinning with evergreen boughs to keep the cellar from freezing.

From the Winn family the Burnap side of the house went to Moses Morse in 1868 and from the Morse family it went through estate settlement by the heirs of Augusta Morse to the Radulski family. Our story started with a soldier of the Revolution and on this side of the house in 1944 there was a man serving in the uniform of the United States, Lt. George Radulski being with Uncle Sam's Navy.

The other side of the house was sold by Nancy Foster's executor in 1867 to Harriet M. Crouch, and by Mrs. Crouch to Lorie A. Howard in 1897. Otis P. Symonds acquired it in 1903, and his daughter-in-law, Rose Symonds, had acquired the whole house by 1949. For a number of years it was rented.

While Nancy and Susanna put their words on paper to show their disagreement, subsequent owners gave other expression to their differences. For many years the use of paint was not a point on which both owners could agree and many older residents remembered seeing the house in two different colors with the dividing line down the middle. In 1944 there were two kinds of shingles on the roof, the separating line being very clear. Even one half of the chimney bore a coating which marked it clearly. Above the middle of the front door, and

On its new site today at 3 Avon Street two different widths of clapboards still remind us of its many years of dual ownership.

extending to the eaves was a cleat which marked the dividing line of ownership. It was placed there no doubt to aid in the application of external finish to the house. Although the entire structure was then painted white, the differences of divided ownership were still visible. The clapboards on the easterly end are older, having less surface to the weather, the windows in the west half were still made up from the small panes instead of the large ones that marked the more modern windows on the easterly end. The house, which by consecutive real estate transfers had remained in divided ownership since 1789, still stood in 1944 on Ash Street. Some ells were added, but the house still faced south and a clean white exterior did not hide the fact that previous generations lived there with their personal disagreements hedged about by legal thorn trees first planted by a sheriff's decree in the late 18th century. In 1971 the house was moved across Ash Street and now stands on the corner of Avon Street, still facing the south, and beautifully restored by Mr. and Mrs. Charles Stocker. For 160 years the house stood through divided ownership. For at least 15 years before that it was the sole property of the Burnap family. The differences in the roof tiles and siding are still visible today.

(The above article was condensed from Reading's Colonial Rooftrees, the revised and updated edition published by the Reading Bicentennial Commission in 1978. The house histories were written originally to mark the Tercentenary of the establishment of the Town of Reading. One article appeared each week in the Reading Chronicle during 1944, the anniversary year. Originally written by C. Nelson Bishop and Eleanor Bishop, these charming and informative articles were revised and updated by Eleanor Bishop after her husband's death. Mrs. Bishop has gratiously given her permission for the article given here. She informs us that she still has a few of the books left in her possession and if anyone is interested in obtaining one, they may write to her at 55 Lowell Street, Reading, MA 01867. The cost: $7.50, mailing extra.)

RESEARCH IN PROGRESS

DESCENDANTS OF LEONARD HARRIMAN OF ROWLEY, MASSACHUSETTS

By Lois Ware Thurston

The Harriman Family Association, organized just three years ago, held its annual reunion last summer at Rowley, Massachusetts in honor of the 350th Anniversary of the settlement of the town. The Association plans to publish a genealogy of descendants of John and Leonard Harriman, "two orphans" who came with the Reverend Ezekiel Rogers from Rowley, England. A detailed account of the migration of Mr. Rogers' Company and their settlement at Rowley, Massachusetts in 1639 will be found in Amos E. Jewett's Rowley, Massachusetts "Mr Ezechi Rogers Plantation" 1639-1850, hereinafter Mr. Ezechi Rogers Plantation, (Rowley 1946, reprint 1986). John Harriman settled in New Haven, Connecticut and Leonard Harriman at Rowley, Massachusetts. No attempt has yet been made to establish the English ancestry of the Harriman brothers. At this time the members of the Association are all descended from Leonard Harriman and thus the research has focused on his family.

Two brief accounts of the family appear in George Brainard Blodgette and Amos Jewett's Early Settlers of Rowley, Massachusetts, hereafter Rowley Early Settlers ([Somersworth, NH reprint 1981]:133-137) and in Mary Lovering Holman's Ancestry of Charles Stinson Pillsbury and John Sargent Pillsbury - found also as "The Harriman Line," Excerpts from The Pillsbury Ancestry, hereafter Pillsbury Ancestry, ([n.p., 1938] 905). A summary of Harrimans, found primarily in town histories, was compiled by Alta and Iva Harriman in their Descendants of Leonard Harriman of New England. The following account is based on three articles published in The Harriman Family Association Newsletter (1:1 [December, 1987]:2-4; 2:1 [December, 1988]:3-7; 3:1[December, 1989]).

1. LEONARD[1] HARRIMAN, said to have been born in Yorkshire, England ca 1622, based on his [?assumed] age of sixteen in 1638, died at Rowley, Massachusetts on 6 [sic 26] May 1691 (Pillsbury Ancestry, 905; Vital Records of Rowley, Massachusetts to the End of the Year 1849, hereafter Rowley VR, 1[Salem, MA 1928]:470). His will was drawn on 12 May 1691 and an inventory of his estate was taken on 5 June 1691 (Essex County Probate, 304:385, [original missing]). Leonard married before 16 May 1650, when their first child John was born, MARGARET _____, who died at Rowley [no date given] and was buried there on 22 October 1676 (Rowley VR, 1:470). Nothing further has been learned of her ancestry. Either she or Leonard may have been related to the family of Hugh Smith of Rowley for two of his children chose Leonard to be their guardian after their father's death in 1656 (The Probate Records of Essex County, Massachusetts, 1[Salem 1916]:237, 453; Pillsbury Ancestry, 905).

Mr. Rogers' company consisted of about twenty Puritan families who left England so that they might have freedom to worship God in a way of their own choosing. They sailed on the ship John from Hull, England, arriving at Salem in October 1638. In the spring of 1639 Mr. Rogers and his company received a land grant between Ipswich and Newbury, later organized as the town of Rowley, Massachusetts (Mr. Ezechi Rogers Plantation, 11). Mr. Jewett noted that "Leonard Harriman probably came as a minor and may have been a servant." He further noted that the servants in Rowley, who came with the emigrants, "were themselves of good families...as they came to maturity, took their places in the community and became useful citizens" (ibid., 216). As a minor and servant, Leonard likely worked in a family where he could learn a trade - probably that of a weaver as that became his occupation. A patron at John Dresser's fulling mill, he was one of the largest producers of cloth between 1673 and 1686 (ibid., 171). An inventory of his estate suggests that Leonard also was a farmer and maker of looms for it included a "barne and shopp" and "loomes and tackling and implements of Husbandry" (Essex County Probate, 304:385-386).

Land grants at Rowley were first recorded on 10: 11 mo. (Jan) 1643 when a survey was made "to Regester the seuerall lotts of all the Inhabitants granted and laid out" (Benjamin P. Migill and George B. Blodgette, The Early Records of the Town of Rowley, Massachusetts 1639-1672, hereafter

Rowley Town Records, [Rowley 1894, rep. Heritage Books n.d.], 1). Leonard Harriman was not listed as owning a house lot that year, but had been granted "seauen Acres of Meadow" at Crane Meadow, bought of William Hobson and John Harris. He also owned "one Acre & an halfe" of uplands in the field called Bradford Street plain next to Maximillian Jewett, suggesting that before 1643 he had reached his majority (ibid. 47, 49).

Before 1650 Leonard had married and in all likelihood either owned or leased a house lot. In that year the town ordered that "the fences in all Comon feilds about or belonging to the towne of Rowley shold be devided acording to proportion of land and midows" (ibid. 61). Leonard appeared on the list for Bradford Street planting lots between John Grant and George Kilburne (ibid. 66,67). The order of the list is significant for it corresponds with the order of the house lots on Bradford Street as appears on the map of original house lots from 1639-1645, and thus allows identification of Leonard's place of residence [see map, Mr. Ezechi Rogers Plantation]. Leonard's position on the list was formerly that of John Spofford, who had removed to what is now Georgetown and who was granted an acre and a half house lot on Bradford Street, bounded on the south by "an highway: part of it lyinge on the west side, and part of it on the East side of the streete" (ibid., 3). This location is now the corner of Bradford Street and Summer Street. A house of his neighbor, George Kilborn, still stands. That Leonard did in fact purchase Spofford's house lot is affirmed by the town survey, taken on 4 February 1661, of "Gates or Commonages..Now in possession haueing Beene Trancefered...since the Beginning of the Said Towne... To Leonard Harriman as belonging to the Acre and halfe lot that was John Spoferds and what was purchased of the town two Gates" (ibid. 119, 121).

Blodgette and Jewett suggest Leonard purchased Spofford's lot from John Todd as late as 1667 (Rowley Early Settlers, 133). Todd's deed to Leonard, dated 10 June 1667, was recorded in the <u>Records</u> <u>and</u> <u>Files</u> <u>of</u> <u>the</u> <u>Quarterly</u> <u>Courts</u> <u>of</u> <u>Essex</u> <u>County</u>, hereinafter Essex County Court Records, (4[Salem 1914]:51), as part of a court case disputing title to the land. Todd's deed conveyed "one dwelling house, barn, two orchards, home lot of two acres" [no street named] and several other parcels of land. Because of the dispute Leonard quitclaimed all his right to the property on 1 August 1668. There is no evidence that this deed referred to the Spofford property.

In addition to his homestead, barn and shop, Leonard owned several other parcels of land, half of which he gave to his son, Jonathan Harriman, when he married about 1685. Leonard also owned lands in Haverhill which, by his will, were given to his son, Matthew (Essex County Probate, 304:385-387).

In addition to the land grants, an early record of Leonard Harriman was his appearance as a debtor of the estate of Thomas Sandbrooke on 14: 5mo. 1649 ("Abstracts From the Earliest Wills on File in the County of Suffolk, Mass.," NEHGR, 7[Boston 1853]176). Leonard became a prominent citizen of Rowley. He was a member of the First Church of Rowley and was admitted a Freeman there in 1657 (Rowley Town Records, "First Record of the First Church," hereafter Rowley Church Records, [Rowley 1894], 81; Rev. Lucius R. Paige, "List of Freemen," NEHGR, 3[Boston 1849]:194). He also served in several civil offices - as Selectman of Rowley in 1664-1666, 1668, 1669, and 1672 and on several juries - Jury of Inquest on the death of William Scales in 1670; Grand Jury in 1671-1672, 1675; Jury of Trials in 1673, 1677, and 1679 (Rowley Town Records; Essex County Court Records).

In a time period when it was not uncommon to be sued in court for moral infringements, Leonard appeared only in his official capacity. Margaret Harriman appeared at court on 5 May 1663 as a witness, testifying that she saw the wife of John How wearing a silk scarf and silver bodkin when she was a widow (Essex County Court Records, 3:70,119).

Leonard Harriman's will, as noted earlier, was dated 12 May 1691 and probated on 29 September 1691. His estate was valued at 172:04:02. An extract of the will follows (Essex County Probate, 304:385-387 [or p. 359-361, pages are doubly marked]):

"In the name of God Amen: I Leonard Harriman of Rowley in ye County of Essex in New England being Infirme of body but of Competent understanding as formerly doe make this my last will & testament as followeth.------

Impr, I comitt my soul into ye hands of god who gave it me and my body to decent buriall In hopes of a happy Resurection...

As to my outward Estate I dispose of it as followeth.---

To my Eldest son Mathew Harriman I give and bequeath all my lands & meadows in ye bounds of Haverhill...& to his son Mathew my grand child I give my Armes & Amunition: To my son Jonathan Harriman I hereby Confirm that which I have given him by deed of gift upon marriage, & the new

Leanto built agst his Room & my shop & Loomes & all the working geers belonging to them & all my Utensills of Husbandry & half my part of the hay boat.

Also I give him the other half of my lands in Rowley provided he pay his sister hannah Boynton within six years after my decease in Corn or Cattle or both the sum Thity pounds: & to his sister Mary Harriman the sum of Thirty pounds within three years after my decease...& Suffer sd Mary to enjoy peaceably during her liuing unmarried the end of the house next the street and two apple trees by sd end, amd two more appletrees in other part of ye orchard and the garden spot before that end of ye house...

To my daughter Hannah Boynton I give the Sum of Thirty pounds to be payd by Jonathan her Brother or Lands upon nonpaym^t...

To my daughter Mary Harriman I give ye use of the end of the house next the street so Long as shee remaindth unmarried & ye use of four apple Trees as before expresst...also I giue ...Emediately upon my decease two cows and such houshold stuff as I shall leaue and Thirty pounds which Jonathan is to pay her...

Also my will is and I hereby constitute my sd son Jonathan my sole Executor...

Further my will is and I hereby desire my beloved friends Nehemiah Jewett and Joseph Jewett, sen^r, to be my overseers...; to Jonathan I give my division in the comons near Caleb Jacksons about eleven acres in the roome of that I sold to Samuel Perley that he had a share in...

In witness that this is my last will & Testament & that I revoke all former & other wills I have hereunto Set my hand & seal this twelth day of May Anno Dom: 1691--

                 Leonard Harriman
                 & a Seale

Witnesses: James Dickinson
       John Hopkinson

Children (HARRIMAN), of Leonard and Margaret (-----) born at Rowley, Massachusetts and recorded there, except Mary, who was identified as a daughter in Leonard's will (Rowley VR 1:87-88):

  i JOHN, b. Rowley 16: 3mo (May) 1650; d. in King Philip's War, in the massacre of Derryfield at Muddy Brook, thereafter called Bloody Brook, on 18 September 1675. He was a member of Captain Lothrop's Company (George Madison Bodge, <u>Soldiers in King Phillip's War</u>, [Baltimore, MD, 1976], 136). In October, 1674 "John Heriman and his wife" were "convicted for fornication and confessing, were ordered to be whipped, he twenty stripes and she fifteen, or pay a fine of 8li" (Essex County Court Records, 5:408). Such a charge usually meant the couple had a child. No record of John's marriage or the birth of a child has been found. Had a child of John's survived, as the oldest grandchild, he would have undoubtedly been named in Leonard's will. That he did not survive is affirmed by Leonard's naming of his grandson, Matthew, Jr., son of Matthew^2 Harriman,.

2 ii MATTHEW, b. Rowley 16: 6 mo. (Aug) 1652; m. 1) ELIZABETH SWAN; m. 2) MARY CALEE.

  iii HANNAH, b. Rowley 22: 3mo. (May) 1655; d. Rowley 19 February 1725/26 (Rowley VR 2:8); m. Rowley 26 May 1674 CALEB BOYNTON (ibid., 1:306), b. ca 1649, son of John and Ellen/Ellenor (Pell) Boynton (Rowley VR, 1:24). Children (BOYNTON), born Rowley (Rowley VR 1:24-29): 1. HANNAH, b. 5 September 1675. 2. MARGARET, b. 23 September 1677. 3. RUTH, b. 14 January 1681/2. 4. JEREMIAH, b. 8 January 1685/6. 5. EBENEZER, b. 17 May 1688.

3 iv JONATHAN, b. Rowley 5: 10 mo. (Dec) 1657; m. 1) SARAH PALMER; m. 2) MARGARET (ELITHORPE) WOOD.

  v MARY, b. prob. at Rowley; died there on 7 October 1736; m. Rowley, 25 June 1691 SAMUEL COOPER (Rowley VR 1:307), born 8 :12 mo. (Feb) 1646, son of Peter and Emm/Ame (-----) Cooper (ibid. 1:52). Children (COOPER) born at Rowley (Rowley VR 1:51-52): 1. SAMUEL, JR, b. 7 March 1691/2. 2.MARY, b. 10 November 1693. 3. PETER, b. 7 March 1695. 4. HANNAH, b. 10 April 1701. 5. MOSES, b. 19 April 1703. 6. LEONARD, b. 13 March 1706/7.

2. MATTHEW[2] HARRIMAN (Leonard[1]), was born at Rowley, Massachusetts on 16: 6 mo. (August.) 1652 (Rowley VR 1:88) and died at Haverhill, Massachusetts between 1 March 1731/32 and 23 January 1732 [see below] (Esssex County Deeds, 59:169, 68:143). He married first at Haverhill on 22 December 1673, ELIZABETH SWAN (Vital Records of Haverhill, Massachusetts to the Year 1850, hereinafter Haverhill VR, 2[Topsfield, MA 1910]:165), born at Haverhill on 30 September 1653, daughter of Robert and Elizabeth (Acie) Swan (ibid., 1:290). She died before 11 February 1717/18 when Mary (Calee) Harriman, as Matthew's second wife, relinquished her right of dower to land in Haverhill (Essex County Deeds, 41:31). The date of Matthew's second marriage, though obviously before 11 February 1717/18, to MARY CALEE was not recorded and her parentage has not been determined. She is not to be confused with the Mary Calee, who married at Haverhill on 31 December 1700 William Davis and died there on 5 December 1747 (Haverhill VR 2:52, 382).

Elizabeth (Swan) Harriman was deceased at the time of the distribution of her father's estate in 1724/5 and her share - the tenth lot of land - was "set apart to such as represents Elizabeth Swan alias Herriman containing seven acres" (Essex County Probate, File #26896). Two deeds concerning the heirs of Elizabeth (Swan) Harriman prove that Matthew Harriman Sr. was living as late as 1 March 1731/32 and died before 23 January 1732. In the first, dated 1 March 1731/32, their children, Matthew Harriman Jr., John Harriman, Richard Harriman, Abner Harriman, Margaret (Harriman) Gordon, Mehetable (Harriman) Whittaker, Mary (Harriman) French, Abigail (Harriman) Judkins, Thomas Gordon on his own account and for Thomas Gordon Jr, Daniel Gordon, Benoni Gordon, Dinah Macgoon, Abigail Roberts, sons and daughters of Elizabeth (Harriman) Gordon, granted Power of Attorney to their brother-in-law, Thomas Haines, husband of Hannah (Harriman) Haines, to represent them regarding land in Haverhill or Methuen which came to them "by Virtue of a Certain Deed well Executed under the Hand & Seal of Robert Swan, late of Haverhill afors[d] deceased to his Daughter Elizabeth Herriman, late of sd Haverhill dec[d] & ye late Wife of Matthew Herriman Senr of Haverhill aforsd Husbandman" (Essex County Deed, 59:169). In the second deed, dated 23 January 1732, "...Thomas Haines, yeoman & Hannah on their own account and as ye sd Haines is attorney to ye Heirs of Matthew Herriman late of Haverhill...Dec'd by his first wife...," and other heirs of Robert Swan, conveyed twelve acres of land in Haverhill (Essex County Deed, 68:143).

Matthew Harriman was among those at Haverhill who took the Oath of Allegiance on 28 November 1677 (Alonzo H. Quint, "Oaths of Freemen, Allegiance, &c. in Old Norfolk County," NEHGR, 6[Boston:1852]:201). By his father's will, probated at Essex County on 29 September 1691, Matthew was given "all my lands & meadows in ye bounds of Haverhill" (Essex County Probate, 304:385). However, Matthew was living in Haverhill as early as 1673 when he married Elizabeth Swan. He is said to have resided at "Fishing River," in a house next to Thomas and Hannah Dustin on the east side of Little River, near Primrose Street and several deeds refer to these bounds. It was not far from the New Hampshire border, established in 1741 (William Macbeth Peirce, Old Hancock County Families, [Ellsworth, ME 1933], 78). Though his occupation was given as that of a yeoman in several deeds, Matthew also operated sawmills in Haverhill and was part owner of sawmills at Amesbury (Essex County Deeds).

Matthew was a member of the First Church at Rowley, where his first three children were baptized (Rowley Church Records). He was about 65 years old at the time of his second marriage to Mary Calee, who must have been considerably younger as four children were born to them between 1718 and 1726. That these were in fact Matthew's children is confirmed by his deed, dated 18 March 1723/24, in which Matthew and his wife Mary conveyed Matthew's right in the sawmill in Amesbury to Leonard, Nathaniel and Jonathan Harriman "for the Parental Love and Naturall affection which we have and do bear towards our beloved children...all Infants and in their non age being Naturall children of me" (Essex County Deeds 43:132).

Matthew left no will, having disposed of his real property during his lifetime to his sons. In addition to the conveyance to his youngest sons mentioned above, which they would not have possession of until after his death, Matthew conveyed land to Matthew Jr. in 1702/03 and 1714; to John in 1708/09 and to Richard in 1726/27 (Essex County Deeds, 22:2, 169; 28:159; 87:178). Abner apparently remained on the homestead and several deeds conveyed in 1719-1721 seemingly settled all of Matthew's lands, culminating in the conveyance of the homestead to Abner (Essex County Deeds, 38:188-191). In this deed, dated 7 March 1720/21, Matthew made several provisions for himself and his wife Mary. There follows an extract of the deed:

"Matthew Herriman Sen[r] of Haverhill..yeoman...partly in consideration of that parentall Love & affection which I do bear toward my son Abner Herriman...yeoman and partly in consideration of ye sum of thirty pounds...convey...upon sd Abner Herriman...ye following parcels of Land and premises all situate...in Haverhill...viz. Imprimis ten acres of Land where my Dwelling house now Stands bounded by...fishing river...my son Richard Herriman...my son Matthew Herriman... Item another piece of Land or Meadow Lying in a Swamp called ye pine or Hemlock Swamp Containing Seven acres... only I reserve to my Selfe out of ye above mentioned premises ye use of four acres of plough Land next the Saw Mill path during my Naturall life and I reserve ye same to my wife if she out live me during ye time She remains my Widow, I also reserve to my Self five acres of mowing ground by the great Spring during my Naturall life, I also reserve for Mary my wife in this said mowing ground grass enough to Winter two Cows & feed them from Harvest to fodering time and ye use of my now Dwelling house During ye time She remains my widow: all which premises above reserved are to return to my Said son Abner Immediately after her Marriage onely my said Son Abner Shall have Liberty if he See Cause to build an house where my Old house now stands with ye priviledge of one Quarter of an acre of Land at said building place reserving Liberty of free passage for each of us on each others Land. I Also give to my Said son all ye Stock of Creatures that I leave at my decease..." Matthew signed the deed. Mary gave her consent and made her mark (Essex County Deed, 38:190-191).

Children (HARRIMAN) of Matthew and Elizabeth (Swan), born at Haverhill (Haverhill VR 1:172-173):

i MATTHEW, JR, b. Haverhill 26 January 1673/4, bp. First Church of Rowley 24 September 1676; d. Haverhill 28 October 1743 (Haverhill VR 2:413); m. Haverhill 19 December 1700 MARTHA PAGE (ibid., 2:165), b. Haverhill 14 February 1680, daughter of Joseph and Martha (Dow, Heath) Page (ibid., 1:239). She d. Plaistow, New Hampshire on 17 February 1767 (Priscilla Hammond, "Vital Records of Plaistow, New Hampshire 1652 - 1905" [Concord:1937], 19, hereafter "Plaistow VR"). Children (HARRIMAN), born at Haverhill (Haverhill VR 1:156,172-173): 1. JOSEPH, b. 30 January 1701/2. 2. STEPHEN, b. 25 April 1703. 3. MEHETABLE, b. 19 September 1705. 4. JOSHUA, b. 20 May 1707. 5. NATHANIEL, b. 15 July 1709. 6. MARY, b. 29 December 1712. 7. ELIZABETH, b. 26 May 1714. 8. SUSANNA, b. 20 August 1718. 9. PHILIP, b. 12 August 1720.

ii ELIZABETH, b. Haverhill 20 November 1675, bp. First Church Rowley 6 February 1675/6; d. probably at Exeter, NH after 1709 when her last child was born; m. Haverhill, 22 November 1699 THOMAS GORDON (Haverhill VR 2:138), b. Exeter, NH ca 1678, son of Alexander and Mary (Lissen) Gordon (Noyes, Libby and Davis, Genealogical Dictionary of Maine and New Hampshire [Baltimore, reprint 1976], 273 hereinafter GDMNH "7 ch., 6 rec. Haverhill"); Blanche Gordon Cobb, "The Gordon Family of Maine and New Hampshire" [Lisbon, ME, n.d.], 7-8, hereafter "Gordon Family"). He m. 2) after 10 April 1709, Rebecca Heard by whom he had seven children (GDMNH). Thomas worked at Matthew 2 Harriman's sawmill in Haverhill. His will, drawn at Exeter, NH on 2 December 1757 and probated 27 May 1761, named sons Thomas, Daniel, Benoni, Timothy, James, Benjamin, and Nathaniel Gordon, and daughters, Dinah Mugoon, Abigail Robards [Roberts], and Hannah Smith. He reserved land on the homestead for a "burying place...where my last wife was buryed and Several of my Children & Grand Children" (Probate Records of the Province of New Hampshire, hereafter NH Probate, 6[Concord, NH 1938]:186-189). Children (GORDON), first six recorded at Haverhill (Haverhill VR 1:143); Charles H. Bell,"Genealogical Register" History of the Town of Exeter, New Hampshire [Exeter 1888], 22): 1. TIMOTHY, b. 19 August 1700; d. 5 September 1700. 2. THOMAS, b. 24 August 1701. 3. DINAH, b. 26 JANUARY 1702/03. 4. DANIEL, b. 1 December 1704. 5. NATHANIEL, bp First Parish Church Haverhill, 28 April 1706 "son of Thomas." Probably died young as another Nathaniel, by the second wife, was born 25 March 1728. 6. ABIGAIL, b. 28 May 1707. 7. BENONI, b. ca 1709.

iii HANNAH, b. Haverhill 29 November 1677, bp. First Church Rowley 4 August 1678; d. Haverhill 12 February 1761 (Haverhill VR 2:417); m. Haverhill 22 December 1703 THOMAS HAINES (ibid., 2:146), b. Newbury, MA 14 May 1680, son of Jonathan and Sarah (Moulton) Haines (Hugh Grant Rowell, "The Reddingtons of Topsfield and Boxford, Mass.," NEHGR, 109[Boston:1955]:164). He was taken prisoner by the

Indians 22 February 1698 and was kept in captivity at Penacook, NH for a year (ibid.). He d. Haverhill 6 December 1771 (Haverhill VR 2:418). Children (HAINES), born Haverhill (Haverhill VR 1:151): 1. LYDIA/LIDIAH, b. 7 August 1705. 2. HANNAH, b. 26 March 1706/7. 3. MEHITABLE, b. 26 January 1708/9. 4. SARAH, b. 9 January 1710/11. 5. JONATHAN, b. 25 October 1712. 6. JOSEPH, b. 25 January 1715/16. 7. ELIZABETH, b. 4 February 1717/18.

iv   MARY, b. Haverhill 17 December 1679, d. Salisbury, MA 12 January 1748 (<u>Vital Records</u> of <u>Salisbury, Massachusetts</u> to the <u>End</u> of <u>the Year 1849</u> [Topsfield, MA:1915], 565, hereafter Salisbury VR); m. Haverhill 15 February 1704/5 TIMOTHY FRENCH (Haverhill VR 2:124), b. Salisbury on 16 June 1681 son of Joseph and Sarah (Eastman) French (Salisbury VR, 112). He died at Salisbury, MA 19 June 1745 and his will was probated 7 October 1745 (Salisbury VR, 566; David W. Hoyt, <u>Old Families of Salisbury and Amesbury</u> [Somerworth, NH rep. 1981], 168,170; Melinde L. Sanborn, <u>Essex County, Massachusetts Probate Index 1638-1840</u>, 1[Boston 1987]:340). There were two named Timothy French in Salisbury. Both having wives named Mary and having children in the same time period. See Hoyt page 170, previously cited, for clarification. Children (FRENCH), born at Salisbury (Salisbury VR, 104-112): 1. SUSANNA, b. 24 November 1705. 2. SARAH, b. 18 March 1708. 3. MEHITABLE, b. 16 October 1710. 4. RUTH, b. 9 December 1713. 5. MARY, b. 14 June 1718. 6. ELIZABETH, b. 29 April 1721.

v   MARGARET, b. Haverhill 6 October 1681; m. Haverhill on 15 September 1708 DANIEL GORDON (Haverhill VR 2:164), b. ca 1682, son of Alexander and Mary (Lissen) Gordon (GDMNH; "Gordon Family,"6). He was a brother of Thomas Gordon who married Margaret's sister Elizabeth. He also worked at the sawmill of his father-in-law at Haverhill and was a farmer and blacksmith at Kingston, NH. Daniel died before 1736. Margaret or her daughter of that name possibly married 17 February 1736 SAMUEL BRADSTREET, both of Suncook (ibid.). Children (GORDON), probably born at Kingston (ibid.): 1. ELIZABETH, b. ca 1709. 2. MARY, b. 1711. 3. ABNER, b. 1712. 4. MARGARET, b. 1714. 5. ALEXANDER, b. ----.

vi   ABIGAIL, b. 7 November 1683; d. Kingston, NH 8 October 1756 (Elizabeth L. Judkins, <u>Job Judkins of Boston and His Descendants</u> [n.p.:1962] 4, hereafter Judkins Family; "Kingston Cemetery Inscriptions," hereafter "Kingston Cem."); m. Kingston, NH 30 November 1710 SAMUEL JUDKINS (Priscilla Hammond, "Vital Records of Kingston, New Hampshire" [Concord:1936], 8, hereafter "Kingston VR"), b. Exeter, NH ca 1687 ("Kingston Cem.") son of Joel and Mary (Bean) Judkins ("Kingston VR" 8). He died at Kingston, NH 23 February 1741/42 ("Kingston Cem."). Samuel's will, dated 26 January and probated 31 March 1742, named "my beloved Wife," sons Joel and John, daughter Elizabeth, Catherine, Mary, and Abigail and grandson Samuel Judkins (NH Probate 3:93-94). He was a blacksmith at Kingston (GDMNH 396, Judkins Family 4). Children (JUDKINS), born at Kingston, ("Kingston VR" 8): 1. JOEL, b. 25 September 1712. 2. ELIZABETH, b. 27 May 1715. 3. JOHN, b. 8 February 1719. 4. CATHERINE, b. 17 November 1721. 4. ABIGAIL, b. 14 July 1725. 5. MARY, b. 8 April 1727.

vii   MEHETABEL, b. Haverhill 13 June 1686; m. Haverhill, MA [March] before 1710 WILLIAM WHITTAKER, JR (Haverhill VR 2:330), b. Haverhill on 4 December 1685, son of William and Sarah (Emerson) Whittaker (ibid. 1:313). They resided at Plaistow, New Hampshire. Children (WHITAKER), born at Haverhill (Haverhill VR 1:314-315): 1. SARAH, b. 10 November 1710. 2. DAVID, b. 2 April 1712. 3. JONATHAN, b. 31 May 1714. 4. JOSEPH, b. 23 March 1716. 5. MEHETABLE, b. 29 March 1717/18. 6. RUTH, b. 28 April 1720. 7. ANN, b. 14 September 1722; d. 19 September 1723 (Haverhill VR 2:493). 8. ANN b. 27 April 1725; d. 23 September 1737 (ibid.). 9. THOMAS, b. 1 May 1727.

viii   JOHN, b. Haverhill 16 June 1688; m. Amesbury, MA 19 November 1712 SARAH MORRILL (<u>Vital Records of Amesbury, Massachusetts to the End of the Year 1849</u>, [Topsfield, MA 1913], 374, hereafter Amesbury VR), b. Amesbury, MA 30 January 1689, daughter of Moses and Rebecca (Barnes) Morrell (Amesbury VR 174). Children (HARRIMAN) born at Haverhill (Haverhill VR 1:155-156, 172-173) 1. LEONARD,

b. 7 August 1713. 2. MOSES, b. 4 July 1715; d. 9 May 1725 (Haverhill VR 2:240). 3. SAMUEL, b. 10 November 1717. 4. MARY, b. 18 January 1719/20. 5. MEHETIBLE, b. 11 December 1721. 6. ANN, b. 9 January 1723/24. 7. JOHN, b. 6 January 1726. 8. possibly PETER, b. - April 1727. 9. ASHAEL, bp. at the North Parish Congregational Church 18 July 1731. 10. EZEKIEL, bp. at the North Parish Congregational Church 23 June 1734.

 ix LEONARD, b. Haverhill 12 March 1689/90, prob. d. before 1718 when another child of the same name was born.

 x NATHANIEL, b. Haverhill 18 June 1692, d. Haverhill December 1695 (Haverhill VR 2:420).

 xi RICHARD, b. Haverhill 9 February 1694/5; d. Haverhill, before 22 January 1782 when an inventory was taken of his estate (Essex County Probate, File #12460); m. Haverhill before 1724 SARAH HALL (Haverhill VR 2:165). She was perhaps the Sarah Hall, bp. Bradford, MA 15 September 1700, the daughter of Richard Jr. and Abigail (Dalton) Hall (Bradford VR 64). Sarah's uncle, Samuel Dalton, m. Richard Harriman's aunt, Dorothie Swan and lived at Haverhill (Rowley Early Settlers, 372; GDMNH, 180). Richard Harriman was a blacksmith at Haverhill. Harriette Eliza Noyes in her Memorial of the Town of Hampstead, New Hampshire, ([Boston, MA:1899], 19, hereafter History of Hampstead, NH) included a list of landowner's assessment rates dated 1764 on which appears "Heirs of Richard" following other Harrimans. This has been interpreted to refer to Richard Harriman, the son of Matthew^2. Richard was very much alive and residing in Haverhill when he made his will on 10 August 1772. It was probated on 5 February 1782 (Essex County Probate, File #12460). Sarah probably predeceased him as she was not named in his will. In addition to his son Joel, who was appointed Executor, Richard named his daughters Mary Harriman and Abigail, wife of William Eastman (ibid.). Children (HARRIMAN), born at Haverhill (Haverhill VR 1:172-173): 1. ABIGAIL, b. 13 May 1724. 2. SARAH, b. 19 April 1728, d. 20 November 1728. 3. MARY, b. 28 April 1731. 4. JOEL, b. 9 April 1738.

 xii ABNER, b. Haverhill 23 August 1699, d. Plaistow, NH between 14 January 1765 when he made his will and 13 April 1770 when it was probated (NH Probate 8:123); m. Haverhill 17 September 1723 SARAH MERRILL (Haverhill VR 2:165), b. Haverhill 20 May 1702, daughter of Jonathan and Mary (Brown) Merrill (ibid. 1:220). She d. Plaistow 10 September 1764 (Samuel Merrill, A Merrill Memorial 1[Cambridge, MA 1917-1928]:191; "Plaistow VR"). In his will Abner named son Jaasiel and daughters Elizabeth Hooper, Ruth Merrill, Naomi Pike, Sarah Kimball, Ana Haes, and grandson Abner Plumer (NH Probate 8:123). Children (HARRIMAN), born at Haverhill (Haverhill VR 1:172-173): 1. ELIZABETH, b. 9 July 1724. 2. RUTH, b. 5 February 1725/26. 3. JAASIEL, b. 11 March 1726/27. 4. NAOMY, b. 28 April 1729. 5. SARAH, b. 4 September 1731. 6. MEHITABLE, b. 14 June 1736, d. 8 March 1737. 7. JOAB, b. 14 February 1737/38. A John Harriman of Hampstead, NH born on this date has been identified as the son of Abner and Sarah. He died on 6 August 1822, aged 84 years (History of Hampstead, NH; Memorial of the Church of Hampstead, New Hampshire, 396,448). Abner does not name either Joab or John in his will dated 14 January 1765. More research needs to be done to clarify the identity of John of Hampstead. 8. ANNE, b. 21 April 1743.

Children (HARRIMAN) of Matthew and Mary (Calee), born at Haverhill (Haverhill VR 1:172-173):
 xiii LEONARD [called Jr. Haverhill VR], b. Haverhill 11 July 1718; d. at Conway, NH before 7 June 1786 when his widow, Ann was appointed Administrix of his estate (Helen F. Evans, Abstracts of the Probate Records of Stafford County New Hampshire 1771-1799 [Bowie, MD 1983], 75); m. Haverhill before 1744 ANN STEVENS (Haverhill VR 2:153), born ca 1723. Ann d. before 7 April 1801, when their son Leonard of Easton (sic probably Eaton) then became Administrator of Leonard's estate. They lived in Haverhill District, NH, incorporated as Plaistow in 1749. He was a carpenter, wheelwright and housewright. Leonard and Anna left Plaistow, NH on 4 November

1755 and were 'warned out' of Salem, NH on 16 December 1755 with their children Nathaniel, Philip, Abigail and Mary (Warnings Out, New Hampshire Archives, Concord, NH). Children (HARRIMAN), born at Plaistow, NH ("Plaistow VR") except as noted: 1. NATHANIEL, b. Haverhill 14 June 1744, called the "eldest brother" in the will of Moses Harriman (Haverhill VR 1:156; Grafton Co., NH Probate 1:45). 2. PHILIP, b. 3 December 1746. 3. ABIGAIL, b. 6 December 1748. 4. MOSES, b. 6 July 1751. 5. MARY, bp at Hampstead in March 1754 6. LEONARD, bp at Hampstead --- 1757; called his "youngest brother" in the will of Moses Harriman (op.cit). 7. ANN, bp. at "Pigwacket" [Concord] 5 October 1766 (Joseph B. Walker, Editor, <u>Diaries of Rev. Timothy Walker, The First and Only Minister of Concord, N. H.</u> [Concord, NH 1889], 52).

xiv JONATHAN, b. Haverhill 19 June 1721; d.? Haverhill 23 December 1792 (Haverhill VR 2:413, West Parish Church records); no further record.

xv NATHANIEL, b. Haverhill 9 October 1723. This Nathaniel, named as the son of Matthew and Elizabeth Swan in Harriette Noyes' <u>A Memorial to the Town of Hampstead, New Hamphire</u> was identified as the Nathaniel Harriman who was "sent out as one of the scouting party from Haverhill in 1722" and settled there with his brothers "John, Richard, Stephen and Abner". Since this Nathaniel was not born until 1723 it could not be he who was on the scouting party in 1722. More likely it was Nathaniel, born 15 July 1709, the son of Matthew^3 and Martha (Page) Harriman who was in the scouting party. He married in 1730/31 Sarah Page. The fact that Matthew^3 had children older than the younger children of Matthew^2 has confused these families. John, Richard and Abner were the sons of Matthew^2 and Stephen was the son of Matthew^3. Further research needs to be done on Nathaniel, son of Matthew^2 Harriman.

xvi MARY, b. Haverhill 29 December 1726, d. Haverhill 15 June 1728 (Haverhill VR 2:413) [Note that Mary^3 Harriman born 1679 (see above) was still living when this Mary was born].

Contributors to this research were Berkley Henley, Joanne Harriman and Harold Harriman. Additions or corrections may be sent to Lois Ware Thurston, RFD 4 Box 6100, Gardiner, Maine 04345. For membership in The Harriman Family Association contact: Dorothy C. Bell, 315 Setucket Road, Box 986, Dennis, MA 02638. Dues are $10.00 per year.

(to be continued)

JOHN RAMSDELL OF LYNN, MASSACHUSETTS

By Roselyn Listernick

John Ramsdell of Lynn is the only known Ramsdell who appeared in the Massachusetts Bay Colony in the 17th century. There was a Joseph Ramsden in Plymouth Colony, whose name was sometimes given as Ramsdell, but usually Ramsden (James Savage, Genealogical Dictionary of New England [Baltimore, 1969], III:503).

John Ramsdell's origins are unknown, but it is presumed he was from England. Ramsdell is a Saxon word meaning winding valley, or extremity of a valley (Frank R. Holmes, Directory of the Ancestral Heads of New England Families, 1600-1700 [Baltimore, 1980], cxcvi).

No comprehensive genealogy of the descendants of John Ramsdell has been published. Some information has been gleaned from three small typescripts at the New England Historic Genealogical Society Library at Boston: Winifred Lovering Holman, "Hudson Notes" (1950); Henry S. Gorham, "Ramsdell, Burlingame and Allied Families," (1938); and Walter K. Watkins, "Ramsdell Genealogical Notes," (1930).

This study will include the first three generations of the descendants of John Ramsdell, which will lead from Lynn to many neighboring towns in Massachusetts as well as New Hampshire and Maine. Most of the information is from vital records, probate and court records, town records and published town histories. The name is found in various records as Ramsdal(l), Ramsdel(l) and Ramsdil(l). Ramsdell will be used here unless a direct quote gives another spelling.

1. **JOHN[1] RAMSDELL** was born, probably in England, about 1602, figured from his death record and a deposition at court (see below). He died at Lynn 27 October 1688, "father of Aquilla, age 86" (Bible record cited in Lynn Vital Records) His wife's name was PRISCILLA -----; her surname has not been found. She died at Lynn, 23 January 1675/6 (ibid.).

John had arrived at Lynn as early as 1632, probably as an indentured servant. On 30 April 1657, John Ramsdell, "age 55" deposed at Salem court that "twenty-five years ago, when he was a servant of Captain Torner, his master and other inhabitants of Lynn, before it was a town, fenced in Nahant" (Records and Files of the Quarterly Courts of Essex County [Salem, Mass., 1911-1975]; hereafter EQCR, II:43).

John was a husbandman or farmer, owning property in the "Rumney Marsh" area of the part of Lynn that is now Saugus. As early as 1641, John was serving as a juror for both the General Court and on the Grand Jury (ibid., I:26, 89, 153, 169, 192; II:59, 124). He was called as a witness in a number of cases. One of particular interest was the case brought against "Robert Burgis of Lin" for "bad and coarse grinding, both of English and Indian corn" (ibid., I:196). On 25 June 1650, John Ramsdell and Jenken Davis were sworn as constables for Lynn (ibid., I:192).

John appears to have spent his entire life in Lynn, during which time he fathered at least four sons and several daughters. Unfortunately, there are no birth dates for any of the children except Jonathan.

The major source for the descendants of John is a deed-of-gift, recorded at Salem, Mass. 20 February 1679. This agreement, between John, Sr. of Lynn and Aquilla, his son, names two other sons, Isaac and John and also mentions "natural sisters" but not by name. The entire document is given here:

*These are to certifie this 12: of April, Anno: Dom: 1675 that it is covenanted and agreed betwixt **John Ramsdell Senior** of Linn in the County of Essex, Husbandman on the one part and **Aquilla Ramsdell** being the naturall sonn of the said John Ramsdell on the other part being of the same town and county: that he the said John Ramsdell, in consideration of his owne, and also of his wives inability to carry on and manage theire affairs for their comfortable livelyhoode and that by reason of age, hath with the consent of his now wife in reference to her surrendering up of her thirds ... in the housing, lands and meddowe in this writing expressed in the name of Aquilla his said sonn, hath ... by deed of gift made over unto the aforesaid Aquilla, his son and to his heirs and assignes forever to have possession of the (estate?) at the death of the said John Ramsdell and his wife, they being the natural parents of the said Aquilla, **all my house lot and housing upon it**, and orchard, the whole being **six acres** more or less, abutting easterly on the marsh and westerly on the land that was Artemus Welmans, northerly with the country highway and southerly with the land of Richard Haven; also **three acres** more or less in the same neck of land, abutting easterly on the marsh of Ensign Fuller and westerly on the lands of Mr. Cobbitt, northerly on the land of Samuel Hart, and southerly on the land of Joseph Mansfield: also **three acres** of fresh meadow ... called the great meadow lying betwixt the meadow of John Pearson and Joseph Mansfield, bounded northerly with the marsh of Isaac Hart and westerly with the upland; also **three acres** of fresh meadow lying northwesterly from the town, bounded easterly with the upland of Richard Haven, westerly with the meadow of Joseph Redknap and northerly with the meadow of Allen Bread, southerly with the upland; also **three acres** of saltmarsh lying above the bridge, bounded easterly with the creek or river, westerly with the upland; also **two acres** of saltmarsh in the first division in Rumney Marsh, being part of his three-acre lot, he reserving one acre of it for himself, only for his own disposal, the whole three acres being bounded easterly with the marsh of Thomas Wheeler, westerly on the marsh of John Burrill; also **one acre** of marsh more or less, bounded easterly with the mill creek, westerly with upland of Robert Potter, southerly with the marsh of Thomas Newhall, northerly with the marsh of Daniel Gott, and at present my old orchard adjoining to the land of Richard Hood and the lands of or lately of John Gillow, bounded southerly with the county highway, all which lands lyeth in the township aforesaid. To have and to hold all the aforesaid housing, lands and premises, with all commons, libertys and privileges belonging thereunto, unto the said Aquilla... viz: after the death of his said father and mother viz: that he shall and will manage all their businesses for them at his own cost, and that as frugally and with as good husbandry as may be and bring in one half of the hay, corn and other fruits of the aforesaid land into the barn or dwelling house of the aforesaid John Ramsdell and his now wife, yearly, during both their lives, and to keep houses and fences in good repair and also to cut and bring them all their firewood to their door at his own cost during both their lives, and whereas it is expressed the old orchard in this writing to be to Aquilla, his at present, it is to be understood that the said John Ramsdell doth reserve two of said trees in it for his and wifes use during both their lives, and also one acre of some land near the barn, which the said Aquilla doth promise to plow it, to carry dung to it and to carry in the corn of it, and that yearly at his own cost during both their lives ... and do also hereby engage to afford unto his said father and mother Christian burials and within two years next after both their deaths to* *pay unto his brother **Isaac Ramsdell** two pounds and within two years next after that to pay his brother **John Ramsdell** five pounds, and so successively to pay each of his **naturall sisters** one pound a piece, paying the eldest first and so according to their ages having two years time betwixt payment for the due and true performance of all the conditions above said .... In case any of them shall die before the time of payment as aforesaid, then their respective sum or sums is to be paid to the natural children of their own bodies. In witness whereof these parties above interchangeably put their hands and seals. Signed, sealed and delivered, John Ramsdell, Senior, in the presence of us: John Fuller, Aquilla Ramsdell, Andrew Mansfield. John Ramsdell and Aquilla his son avowed this to be their act and deed, 21: 2mo: 77, before Wm. Hathorne, Assistant."* (Essex Deeds, 5:295; the index gives page 63 in error - this document is on page 295, document #64).

Children (order of birth uncertain):

? i. PRAESILLA^2, b. early 1640s; m. at Concord, MA, 7 May 1662, JAMES ADAMS (Concord VR). "He is said to have been banished from Scotland by Oliver Cromwell and d. 2 Dec 1707 at Concord" (Lemuel Shattuck, History of the Town of Concord, Middlesex County [Boston, 1835], Appendix, III:361). Children, b. at Concord (surname Adams): 1. Elizabeth, b. 9 Feb 1665. 2. James, b. 29 Mar 1668; m. 17 Feb 1690, Priscilla Shore. 3. Hannah, b. 25 July 1670. 4. John, b. 30 Aug 1672. 5. Nathaniel, b. 19 Feb 1674. 6. Dorcas, b. 1 Feb 1677. 7. Abigail, b. 17 Apr 1681.

? ii. HANNA, b. early 1640s; m. at Concord, 11 Dec 1662, JOHN MASON (Concord VR). Shattuck states he was "supposed to be a son of Capt. Hugh Mason of Watertown," but the Watertown VRs and the Genealogy of the family of Hugh Mason, by Mary Eliza Mason [Marietta OH, 1930], page 25, shows that Hugh Mason's son John m. Elizabeth Hammond, and they had a son John b. at Watertown, 22 Jan 1676/7. Hanna (Ramsdell) and John Mason also had a son John, b. at Concord, 6 Apr 1664. (There is no proof that Praesilla and Hanna Ramsdell were daughters of John Ramsdell of Lynn. However, their brother Isaac spent some time in Concord, Mass., where his first few children were born. The Praesilla and Hanna whose marriages were recorded in Concord were very likely Isaac's sisters who were mentioned, but unnamed, in the deed of gift cited above).

2. iii. ISAAC, b. about 1646; m. ELEANOR VINTON.
3. iv. JOHN, b. about 1649; m. ELIZABETH PERKINS.
4. v. AQUILLA, b. about 1652; m. (1) HANNAH ----; m. (2) LYDIA ----.
   vi. ELIZABETH, b. about 1654; m. at Malden, MA, 12 June 1674, as his 2nd wife, JOHN SHAW, whose first wife, Hannah, d. at Malden, 8 Feb 1674 (Malden VR; Savage, III:503). Under a petition, dated 27 May 1674, John Shaw was granted a lot of land in the "new lands of Malden" in Worcester Co., near what is now Shrewsbury (Deloraine Pendre Corey, History of Malden, 1633-1785 [Malden, 1899], 305). He was a tailor and had two sons by his first wife, Hannah: John, b. 16 Dec 1667 and William, b. 25 Dec 1668. These two sons removed to York, Maine (Charles Edward Banks, History of York, Maine [Baltimore, 1967], 75).
   vii JONATHAN, b. 31 Mar 1657 (LVR); d. at Lynn, 6m: 1658 (LVR).

2. **ISAAC² RAMSDELL** (John¹) was born, probably at Lynn, about 1646 and died after 1715 when he conveyed land to his son John (see below). He married at Lynn, 12 July 1666, ELEANOR VINTON (Lynn VR). She was born at Lynn the 3rd month of 1648, daughter of John and Ann Vinton of Lynn (LVR; John Adams Vinton, The Vinton Memorial [Boston, 1858], 12-14).

Sometime before 1667 and probably around 1660, Isaac was in Concord, Mass., probably there to help with the iron works which began operations on 30 May 1660. Although there is no definite proof that he was at the iron works, his father-in-law, John Vinton, was connected with the iron works at Saugus, and Oliver Purchas and Joseph Jenks, also of the Saugus works, helped build the works at Concord (Shattuck, Hist. of Concord, 43). It is certain that Isaac and his wife Eleanor were there in 1667 when the birth of their first child, Isaac, was recorded (as Isaac Ramsden) in the Concord Vital Records. Two other children were born in Concord and a fourth child died young in Lynn in 1676. Why Isaac and his family returned to Lynn is not known.

In 1677, Isaac was among a group of men from Lynn who took the Oath of Fidelity (EQCR, VI:399).

Town records show that Isaac Ramsdell served in a number of capacities. Since there was an Isaac³, his son, it is difficult to determine which Isaac is being referred to. On 7 March 1692/3, Isaac was chosen to see that all swine were yoked and ringed. On 8 January 1693/4, Isaac "voted against a petition involving the paying of monies to the pastor" (Records of Ye Towne Meetings of Lyn [Lynn, 1949-55]; hereafter Lynn Town Records, I:16, 21). Isaac² would have been about age 47, Isaac³ about 26. In March 1698/9, Isaac was chosen a fence viewer and in March of 1701/2, Isaac was chosen to be a hayward (an official who impounds stray cattle) or field driver (ibid., I:61; II:3).

At the town meeting of 10 May 1709, it was voted "considering the necessity of Isaac Ramsdell, Sr. by reason of the miserable condition that his daughter is in, that he should have some relief as the selectmen shall see next" (ibid., II:54). On 14 May 1713, the town meeting voted that "Isaac Ramsdell, Sr. have the improvement of 80 poles of the town's land on the fresh marsh plain so-called, including his house that now stands there during his and his wives life and emediately after their decese said land to return to Town" (ibid., II:71).

On 15 April 1713, Isaac Ramsdell, Sr., with Eleanor his wife renouncing her right of dower, traded one of his lots of land in Lynn for a small dwelling house owned by Joseph Mansfield, Jr. The house, which stood near Farrington's Mill, was to be moved. Isaac's lot of land, traded to Joseph, was bounded Easterly by the lot of John Newhall, Jr., northerly on the 10-acre lot formerly Edward Bakers, southerly on land formerly Mr. Laughtons and westerly on the Town Common. It was described as land formerly belonging to his "honored father, John Ramsdell" and contained 10 acres. Witnesses were John and Mary Burrill, Samuel Baxter and Dorothy Farrington. The deed was recorded on 18 May 1713 (Essex Deeds, 25:193; 26:163).

On 29 March 1715, Isaac Ramsdell, Sr. sold to his son John, for six pounds, 7 acres, 20 poles of land in Lynn, the lot laid out to John Brintnall in the Lynn town common, the 5th lot in the 2nd range, 1st draft, 3rd division, bounded by the lot laid out to Thomas Howard on one side and Theophilus Burrill on the other side (ibid., 114:184).

Children:

5. i. ISAAC³, b. at Concord, 1 Sept 1667; m. ABIGAIL ----.
   ii. JOHN, b. at Concord, 26 May 1670; d. 3 Jan 1676.
6. iii. JONATHAN, b. at Concord, 30 Sept 1672; m. ANNA CHADWELL.
   iv. DORCAS, died young at Lynn, 16 Aug 1676.
   v. NATHANIEL, b. at Lynn, last of May 1677; m. at Lynn, 2 Nov 1698, ELIZABETH MANSFIELD, b. at Lynn 6 Feb 1679; d. bef. 1739, dau. of Joseph³ (Joseph², Robert¹) and Elizabeth (Williams) Mansfield (Geneva A. Daland and James S. Mansfield, Mansfield Genealogy [Hampton, NH, 1980], 14). No further information found.
   vi. JOHN, b. at Lynn, 19 Mar 1679/80; d. 1725; m. at Lynn, 31 Oct 1710, ELIZABETH CHADWELL, b. at Lynn, 18 Dec 1681, dau. of Moses² (Thomas¹) and Sarah (Ivory) Chadwell. Elizabeth m. (2) 16 May 1728, Joseph Bates. John Ramsdell's will, dated 2 Mar 1724/5, recorded 30 Dec 1725, left his estate to his wife "she having done much for me in this time of my weakness" and at her death, lands to be divided among the children of his brother Jonathan (Essex Probate, 23188; Marcia Wilson Wiswall, The Chadwell Family [Lynnfield, Mass., 1983], 18).
7. vii. JOSEPH, b. at Lynn, 17 Sept 1682/3; m. DEBORAH MANSFIELD.
   viii. SARAH, b. at Lynn, 8 May 1685; m. (int. at Lynn) 8 Oct 1709, JONATHAN YOUNGMAN of Roxbury, Mass., b. 9 Oct 1686, son of Francis¹ and widow Anna (Fisher) Heath Youngman. Children (surname Youngman): 1. Eleanor, b. at Roxbury, 23 July 1710; m. 19 Aug 1731, Joseph Skillins of Richmond. 2. Sarah, b. at Framingham, Mass., 9 June 1713; m. 30 April 1733, William Amos. 3. Leah, b. at Framingham, 14 Apr 1715; m. 28 Aug 1759, Richard Robinson. 4. Anna, b. at Roxbury, "Feb. the last," 1716/17; m. June 1738, Daniel Marrow. 5. Mary, b. at Roxbury, 17 Feb 1718/19. 6. Francis, b. at Roxbury, 31 July 1720. 7. Jonathan, b. at Framingham, Mass., 20 May 1722. 8. John, b. at Sudbury, Mass., 1 June 1724; d. at Brookline, Mass., Sept 1745. 9. Daniel, b. at Roxbury, 12 Mar 1725/6 (John C. J. Brown, "The Youngman Family" New England Historical and Genealogical Register, 35 [1881]:46).
   ix. ELNER (ELLINER), b. at Lynn, 8 Apr 1688; d. as Elinor Newhall, wife of Nathaniel, 12 Feb (gravestone record Old/Western Cemetery, year unreadable); m. (int.) at Lynn, 27 Dec 1718, NATHANIEL NEWHALL (LVR). The only Nathaniel Newhall eligible is the son of Nathaniel³, Thomas²⁻¹ and Elizabeth Newhall. If the above is correct, then Elinor (Ramsdell) Newhall died before 25 July 1723 when Nathaniel m. (2?) Phebe Towne. Nathaniel died shortly after that marriage, after which his widow gave birth to a daughter Phebe in 1724. Thomas Waters ("The Newhall Family" Essex Institute Historical Collections; hereafter EIHC, XVIII [1881]:239) does not give the marriage to Elinor Ramsdell but Nathaniel Newhall was 38 years old when he married Phebe Towne.

3. **JOHN² RAMSDELL** (John¹) was born, probably at Lynn, about 1651 and died at at Boxford, Mass., 23 February 1714/15 (Essex Probate, 23187). He married at Boxford, 31 May 1671, ELIZABETH PERKINS who was born at Weymouth, Massachusetts, 18 June 1643 (George Walter Chamberlain, Genealogies of the Early Families of Weymouth, Massachusetts [Baltimore, 1984], 459; "Ancient Perkins Papers" copies

by Jacob Towne Jr Topsfield Town Clerk, Essex Antiquarian, III:55). She was the daughter of the Reverend William[2] (William[1]) and Elizabeth (Wooten) Perkins.

"John Ramsdell first appeared in the village of Boxford about 1671, around the time of his marriage. He was perhaps interested in the iron works, and came from Lynn with Henry Leonard, to assist him in carrying the works on" (ibid., 69). It is assumed that John had been connected with the Saugus Iron Works, where Henry Leonard and his brother James were managing the Works (Lewis, History of Lynn, 206). In 1670, the foundry called "the works newly erected in Rowley Village" was owned by the company, Leonard and Sons, who managed the works to 1674 or after. They later moved to New Jersey. "The next manager of the iron works was undoubtedly John Vinton, and he settled in Boxford/Rowley Village." We know him as Isaac[2]'s father-in-law (see above). "John Ramsdell was a relative of John Vinton, and he, too, was a citizen of the village and connected with the iron business (Sidney Perley, "Mining, Quarying, and Smelting of Ores in Boxford" EIHC, XXV [1888]:299/300).

At a court held at Ipswich, 25 March 1673, Ambrose Makefashion, a partner with John Ramsdell, sued Henry Leonard for debt. Presumably the debt was for wages owed to the partners for "coaling" wood (converting wood to charcoal by burning) at Rowley. The verdict was for the plaintiff, but Mr. Leonard asked the court to reconsider. He claimed that Ramsdell and Makefashion did not fill the coal carts evenly, etc. The court abated 20 pounds (EQCR, V:130-31).

In 1673, John Ramsdell was one of several sending a petition to the General Court, asking "dissolution of their connection with Topsfield and praying to be annexed to Rowley" (Perley, Hist. of Boxford, 65). He was on a list of 25 families living in Boxford in 1680 and 1681 and was among those who paid a rate of 6 shillings for the minister that year (Town Records of Topsfield [Topsfield, 1917], I:37). On 16 October, John sold to Zacheus Curtis, Jr. one and a half acres of upland in Rowley Village (Essex Deeds, 6:41). In 1687, John Ramsdell was taxed 4 shillings by the Town of Boxford, for 1 house, 3 acres of land, 2 oxen, 2 horses, 3 cows, 2 young cattle (NEHG Register, 33[1879]:163).

The marriage of John and Elizabeth (Perkins) Ramsdell, and the birth of their first two children, were recorded by Elizabeth's father, Rev. William Perkins:

"Elizabeth my eldest and first daughter was by Major Hathorn at Salem the last day of May 1671, married to John Ramsdell of Lynn, with consent of parents on both sides, and had her marriage blest while I was in England with her first daughter named Elizabeth, and after my second return from thence with a second daughter named Mary born the 26th of January 1674, all which children were baptized. God grant them the baptism of his Spirit also" ("Perkins Papers," EA, III:55).

John Ramsdell died intestate, and on the 11th of April 1715, his widow and children signed an agreement for the settlement of his estate:

"This agreement made and concluded upon between the widow and children of John Ramsdell, late of Boxford in the County of Essex, deceased in respect of the real and personal estate as followeth. 1. Nathaniel Ramsdell, eldest son of the said deceased, upon consideration of what he has received out of said estate formerly, imposes no more and fully and clearly acquits and discharges the said estate from any claim upon any account whatsoever. 2. It is agreed that our mother, Elizabeth

Ramsdell, shall have all the moveables and personal estate, she paying the ten pounds to Priscilla and all the debts due from the said estate. 3. It is agreed that Timothy Ramsdell shall have all the real estate and to have full power to sell the same, yielding to his mother one third of what the real estate shall sell for, and if she should not live to waste or improve it for her necessity, it shall be to the said Timothy his heirs and assignes for ever. It is agreed that if the sisters Elizabeth Killum, wife of Daniel Killum and Mary Smith, wife of Ephraim Smith, do accept of what shall remain of the personal or moveables after our mother's decease - then this to be a final payment of the estate of the said John Ramsdell deceased. In consideration thereof, we place our hands and our seals this 16 day of April, 1715. Signed, Nathaniel Ramsdell, Elizabeth Ramsdell, Timothy Ramsdell (his mark), Elizabeth Killum (her mark), Mary Smith (her mark). On 11 April 1715, the following appeared and acknowledged the agreement: Nathaniel, Elizabeth, Timothy and Priscilla Ramsdell, Elizabeth Killum, Mary Smith, Ephraim Smith and Daniel Killum (Essex Probate, 23187).

An inventory of the estate, taken 8 March 1715, by Josiah Perkins and John Gould, included 2 cows, 3 swine, beds, bedding, table linens, cloths, cloth and yarn, money, furniture, loom, books, etc. house and about 12 acres of land. Total value was given as 53 pounds, 18 shillings (ibid.).

Children, born at Topsfield:

     i. ELIZABETH^3, b. 4 Oct 1672; d. 21 June 1751; m. at Wenham, Mass. 7 Jan 1702/3, DANIEL KILLUM ("Gleanings from the Town Records of Wenham" EIHC, VI [1864]:47). Daniel was b. 8 Mar 1676; d. 20 Mar 1745/6, s. of Daniel^3 (Daniel^2, Austin^1) and Sarah (Geare) Fairfield Killum (Austin D. Kilham, Part II, Descendants of Austin and Alice Kilham [Charlottesville, VA, 1970], Chart I). Children, born at Wenham (surname Kilham): 1. Daniel, b. 18 Oct 1703; m. at Ipswich, Mass., 4 Apr 1726, Rebecca Frost. 2. Anna, b. 16 Mar 1705; unm. in 1746. 3. John, b. 24 Apr 1710; d. 24 Jan 1774; m. (1) Sarah Patch; m. (2) Mary Poland; m. (3) Anna Dodge (Wenham VR). 4. Elizabeth, b. 11 Nov 1712; m. at Wenham, 13 Feb 1748/9, John Rogers.

    ii. MARY, b. 27 Jan 1674/5; m. at Boxford, 6 Sept 1694, EPHRAIM SMITH b. 29 Oct 1663, son of Robert^1 and Mary (French) Smith (Joseph F. Smith, Jr. Asahel Smith of Topsfield [Salt Lake City, UT], 87). Children, b. at Topsfield (surname Smith): 1. Mary, bpt. 1 Sept 1695; ?m. at Topsfield, 14 Aug 1721, Thomas Demcy. 2. Elizabeth (twin), bpt. 11 Apr 1697. 3. Hannah (twin), bpt. 11 Apr 1697. 4. Priscilla, bpt. 20 Sept 1702. 5. Hephzeba, bpt. 11 June 1704. 6. John, bpt. Nov 1706; d. 26 May 1729. 7. Sarah, bpt. Nov 1708. 8. Mary, bpt. 8 June 1729.

   iii. PRISSILLA, b. 20 Aug 1677; living in 1715 when father's estate was settled.

   iv. JOHN, b. 19 Jan 1679/80; did not sign father's estate agreement.

8.   v. NATHANIEL, b. about 1690; m. MARY LINSCOTT.

9. vi. TIMOTHY, b. about 1692; m. ABIGAIL TOWNE.

4. AQUILLA^2 RAMSDELL (John^1) was born probably at Lynn about 1652 and died after 19 February 1717/18 when he made a deed of gift to his son Benjamin (see below). He married, first, before 1672, HANNAH -----, who died 10 November 1688 (LVR). Aquilla married second, LYDIA ----.

Aquilla was a husbandman or farmer. He took the Oath of Fidelity with his brother Isaac and others, sworn by Capt. Thomas Marshall of Lynn by order of the General Court, on 26 February 1677 (EQCR, VI:399). During King Philip's War, Aquilla Ramsell was paid 1 pound 1 shilling for service on 24 November 1676 and was on a list of soldiers from Lynn who were granted land at Narragansett #3, Souhegan West, now Amherst, New Hampshire. His son Benjamin was listed as the claimant, owing to the proprieters 2 pounds 10 shillings, and also 6 shillings toward the meeting house (George Madison Bodge, Soldiers in King Philip's War [Baltimore, 1976], 422, 450).

Aquilla served the town of Lynn as member of a jury of trials on 18 May 1696 (Lynn Town Records, I:43). On the 17th of December 1701, he agreed to fence in a fresh meadow (ibid., 75-76).

On the 4th of June 1691, Aquilla and wife Lidiah sold to Benjamin Hutchinson for 5 pounds, 3 acres of land in Lynn, bounded by John Townsend, Joseph Mansfield, John Hart, and the "great meadow" (Essex Deeds, 11:220).

Aquilla was responsible for the care of his father and mother as arranged in a deed-of-gift on 24 December 1679 (see above). On the 19th of February 1717, Aquilla made a similar deed-of-gift to his son Benjamin. Declaring himself and his wife Lidia to be infirm and unable to manage their affairs, Aquilla gave to Benjamin the lands that he had received from his father in 1679; the houselot in "Ramsdell's Neck" etc. The deed was not recorded until four years later, 14 october 1721 (ibid., 38:205).

Children by first wife, Hannah ----, all born at Lynn:

    i. JONATHAN^3, b. 23 Aug 1672; d. 16 Sept 1672 (LVR).
    ii. NATHANIEL, b. 26 Sept 1673.
    iii. AQUILLA, b. last of Jan 1675/6.
    iv. JOHN, b. 25 Mar 1678.
    v. JONATHAN, b. 23 Aug 1679; d. 16 Sept 1679 (LVR).
    vi. HANNAH, b. 23 Sept 1680; d. 26 Sept 1680 (do not find...).
    vii. JONATHAN, b. 6 June 1683; d. 25 Feb 1684/5 (LVR).
    viii. SAMUEL, b. 26 Oct 1684; m. at Boston, 10 Mar 1708 ABIGAIL BEESON ("Boston Marriages," 28th Report of the Record Commissioners of the City of Boston [Boston, 1898], 20); intentions at Lynn, 22 Feb 1708/9, gives ABIGAIL MASON (LVR). Children, b. at Boston: 1. John, b. 25 Dec 1710. 2. Samuel, b. 24 Apr 1712.
    ix. PRISCILLA, b. 26 July 1687.

Children by second wife Lidia, all born at Lynn:

10. x. BENJAMIN, b. 21 Jan 1689/90; m. ABIGAIL FULLER.
    xii. MOSES, b. 10 Feb 1692.
    xiii. ELIZABETH, b. 20 Apr 1696; m. at Lynn, 16 May 1728, JOSEPH BATES, b. 25 June 1688, prob. s. of Robert & Sarah Bates. Joseph had m. (1) at Lynn, 28 Aug 1716, Elizabeth Proctor, who d. 25 Sept 1727. Children of Joseph and Elizabeth (Ramsdell) Bates, b. at Lynn: 1. Elizabeth, b. 14 Oct 1717. 2. Sarah, b. 30 Apr 1720.

(to be continued)

WILLIAM IVORY OF LYNN AND HIS DESCENDANTS

By Eleanor Tucker

William Ivory is the only known Ivory immigrant to New England in the colonial period. He was a settler of Lynn in the Massachusetts Bay Colony as early as 1638 when he was granted land (see below). William Ivory and his descendants were prominent in Lynn and they intermarried with many of Lynn's most distinguished families. The name Ivory became a popular given name in the families of married daughters.

Very little has been printed about the Ivory Family. Louis Effingham DeForest provides three pages of biographical material plus a partial chart of three generations in Our Colonial and Continental Ancestors [New York, 1939], 123-25). James Savage's Genealogical Dictionary of the First Settlers of New England (Baltimore, MD, 1969), II:526, states that William Ivory, age 28, arrived on the "Truelove" in 1635, but this has not been verified in any other source. Charles Edward Banks's 2885 English Emigrants [Philadelphia, 1937], 8-10, and Planters of the Commonwealth [Boston, 1930], 108, 171, list some passengers of the "Truelove" but William Ivory is not among those listed.

The possible English ancestry of William Ivory is given by Elizabeth French in the New England Historical and Genealogical Register, 67:339-343. A William Ivory, son of Robert, born about 1563 was lord of the manor of Westbury in Offley, Hertfordshire, England. His will, written 22 May 1619; proved 29 October 1619, names sons Edmond, Joseph, Luke, John, Thomas and William. The son William, born about 1600 may be the Lynn emigrant. Luke Ivory, a step-brother to William, had a daughter Dorcas Ivory, who came to New England and married at Ipswich, Mass., 3 Aug 1665, Sgt. John Hovey. "How Dorcas Ivory came to emigrate is not known. She may have gone to visit her Uncles Peter and Luke Hanbury, or the family of William Ivory of Lynn (if the latter was indeed her uncle) perhaps leaving London because of the plague raging there in the summer of 1665" (ibid., 343).

1. **WILLIAM**[1] **IVORY** was born, probably in England, perhaps Offley, Hertfordshire, about 1600. His death was recorded at Boston on 8 March 1652: "William Ivery, carpenter & inhabitant of Lyn, d. 3rd: 8m: 1652," (Boston Births, Baptisms, Marriages and Deaths, 1630-1699; 9th Report of the Record Commissioners of Boston [Boston, 1883], 37). He married before 1633 (eldest known child born about that year), ANN SOUTH. Ann was born in 1602, according to her deposition in 1682 (see below), and died between 1675, when her will was written, and 1689 when the will was recorded (see below). As her will names "father South," it is presumed she was the daughter of the Thomas South who was in Lynn at that time Ann (South) Ivory married, second, before 1660, William Crofts (or Crafts), who died after 1689 when his will was recorded with Ann's (see below).

The first official record regarding William Ivory, is the 1638 list of those inhabitants of Lynn granted additional land, in the so-called "six-mile" grant. William received ten acres, a modest amount granted to those who did not contribute financially to the settlement (Alonzo Lewis and James R. Newhall, History of Lynn [Boston, 1865], 172; Loea Parker Howard, The Beginning of Reading and Lynnfield Massachusetts [1937], 5-9).

On 31 October 1639, William Ivory sued Roger Scott for defamation (<u>Records and Files of the Quarterly Courts of Essex County, Massachusetts</u> [Salem, Mass., 1911], I:14). In 1644, William Ivory, Daniel King and George Burrill were presented to the Court for putting cattle in the general field before harvest. They were ordered to pay damages to Gerard Spenser, Francis Ingalls and Edward Burt (ibid., I:75). Again, in 1648, William was before the Court for stealing several different times, one-half peck of corn from Samuel Bennett's mill (ibid., I:174).

On 29: 1: 1653, Ann Ivory, relict of William Ivory, presented to the Quarterly Court at Ipswich, a "writing" as William Ivory's last will, but this document was declared invalid because no executor was named. The court granted administration to the widow. William's son, Thomas Ivory, was to have twenty pounds when he reached 21 years of age. Lois and Sarah, two of the daughters, were to have ten pounds each when they arrived at the age of 18 or were married. Ruth Baily, a married daughter, was to have 40 shillings after the death of her mother. The remainder of the estate was to go to the widow. An inventory of William's estate was taken three days earlier, 26: 1: 1653 by Edward Burcham and Richard Rooton. Listed in the inventory were: wearing apparel, 3 kine, 3 young cattell, one Asse, 3 swine, land at Boston, land bought of Mr. Laughton, House and land, broad cloth, cotton cloth, linen cloth, table linen & sheets, bedding, rugs, etc., wheat, table & chest, a musket, sword & bandeleres & powder; a feather bed, rug, pillows & bolster; pewter, warming pan and kettle, an iron pot & brass pot, carpenter tools & a grindstone, books, a cupbord, chair & table, two old chests & lumber, a bottle & leather jack, dishes, milk vessels, water pails, beer barrells, a wheele & shovel & forke, flax and bacon. Total inventory was valued at 135 pounds, 9 shillings, 10 pence. Debts against the estate were listed at two pounds (<u>EQCR</u>, I:278; <u>Probate Records of Essex County</u>, I:152-3). The above inventory suggests that William Ivory was not only a carpenter but also perhaps a clothier, since the list includes broad cloth, cotton and linen.

Widow Ann (South) Ivory Crofts testified that about 13 years ago, "William Prichard, having damnified a parcel of salt which her husband, Ivery, put on board said Prichard's boat at Boston, was arrested by her husband, Prichard being then bound for Barbadoes. Said Prichard, complying with her husband about the damage of the salt, told the latter that he had a mare that used to be about Capt. Bridges' ground, and deponent's husband should have her, if he never came back. About a year after, Prichard was reported dead at Barbadoes. Deponent's husband sold his interest in the mare to George Keaser for three pounds. But when the mare could not be found, the matter pressed on Ivery's conscience so that he abated twenty shillings of the three pounds" (<u>EQCR</u>, 2:240).

On the 15th of June 1675, Ann Crofts made a will that was signed by both herself and her husband William Crofts. William's will was written on 5 March 1688/9 and both wills were recorded together on 26 November 1689 (Essex Probate 6471 [302:182]; and 6501 [302:180-181]) Both wills have disappeared from the docket envelopes at Essex County Probate Court, but the record book copies are available, with William's will appearing first.

WILL OF ANN CROFTS

The Last Will and Testament of Ann Crofts of Lynn in the County of Essex, being weak of body but of good understanding, this 25 June 1675. Imp: I bequeath my body to the earth and my spirit to God that gave it.

It. Whereas there is a writing between my husband Crofts and I made at our marriage that touched upon that estate of houseing, lands and goods and the whole estate I brought to him should be to him during his natural life. I also with my husband's consent give to my son Thomas Ivory the house lot and housing upon it and orchard to enjoy at my husband's decease, the whole being bounded easterly with the land of Robert Driver, westwardly and northwardly with the Town Common and southwardly with the Common and land of my husband's according to a lyne that shall range with the general breadth of said field lying southward of the meeting house and so toward Mr Cobbet's lott. With all Commons and liberties whatsoever belonging unto it as his own proper right and interest.

Item: I give to my son Thomas Ivory all my right in two parcels of meadowground lying in the marsh between his house and that with my husbands cowshed(?) which meadow was given me by my father South after my husband's decease. One parcel of it being bounded eastward with the marsh that was Joseph Hows and westward with the marsh of Joseph Hall, on the sea southward and the upland northward. Another parcel bounded northward with the upland of Mr. Needham, eastward with the marsh of George Keaser and westward with the marsh of the widow Taylor and the creek.

Item: I give to my son Theophilus Bailey and his wife during their natural lives after my husbands decease 3 acres of upland out of Thomas Ivory's land and then the same to return to him again.

Item: I will, upon the consideration abovesaid that my son Thomas Ivory pay unto my son John Burrill ten pounds within two years after my husband's death.

Item: I having obtained it of my husband with his consent give unto my son John Burrill his now wife and children, viz: after my husband's death, two acres of marsh which he bought of John Dakin and one acre of marsh adjoining to it which was my husband Ivory's. This being the said meadow that my son Bailey and his wife is to have during their natural lives this one half of it.

Item: Having obtained it of my husband Crofts, do with his consent give unto my daughter Sarah Chadwell and to the children lawfully begot of her body that land he bought of Timothy Allen, viz: after my husband's death, which is about four acres lying by the meeting house, bounded eastward with the land of Robert Driver and Northwestwardly with the land of Jonathan Witt.

Item: I give unto Sarah Farrington alias Sarah Potter all my right and interest in the upland which my father South gave me which lyeth between the land of Robert Potter northward and Thomas Newhall eastward.

Item: I give to my son Thomas Ivory a ten-acre lot which the town gave my husband Ivory. Only I give the wood of it to my sons John Burrill and Moses Chadwell equally between them and give them two years time to get off the said wood.

Item: My will is that it be understood that what lands my son Thomas Ivory hath in his personal possession which was his father Ivory's, he hath it as his portion, the rest of my children having also had their portion; he is to enjoy it as his own to him, his heirs and assigns forever. He the said Thomas Ivory being the oldest child had a double portion of his father Ivory's estate, but I also have given him and his sisters each what was given them out of their father Ivory's estate. In consideration of which I give aquitance of my husband Crofts. I name Theophilus Bailey and Thomas Ivory my executors. Signed: Ann Crofts, William Crofts. Witnesses: Andrew Mansfield and Francis Burrill

This will was recorded on the 9th month of 1689 (Essex Probate, 6471). The identity of Sarah Farrington, alias Potter has not been determined.

William Crofts' will states: "as for the disposal of my outward estate my will is that my dear and loving wife have the improvement of my whole estate during her natural life, she making no strip nor waste thereof. Item: My will is that what my wife hath bequeathed away by a will made formerly by her and signed by myself it may stand good and valid provided she was faithful therein without any further demand of my estate, to be at her own absolute disposal." In addition to bequests to son [actually step-son] Thomas Ivory and daughter [actually daughter-in-law] Sarah Chadwell, he leaves legacies to "my loving cousins the eldest child of Peter Frothingham and of Nathaniel Frothingham and of Samuel Frothingham and of William Frothingham sometimes of Charlestown to the first child of each of the said Frothinghams" 20 shillings in silver to be paid after his wife's decease, and to Jonathan Thompson of Woburn the son of James Thompson five pounds, to Hannah Frothingham daughter of William twenty shillings, to son Thomas Ivory ten pounds to daughter Ruth Baily five pounds, to Jeremy Shepherd, pastor of the church at Lynn, ten pounds, all legacies after his wife's decease "together with 20 shillings to Benjamin Redknap". William Crofts' will was witnessed by John Breed, Allen Breed, tertius, and Thomas Chadwell. An inventory of his estate was taken "at his dwelling house" 11 March 1688/9 (Essex Probate, 6501).

Known children of William and Ann (South) Ivory:

    i. RUTH^2, b. prob. in England, about 1630; d. at Lynn, November 1692 (Lynn Vital Records); m. about 1649, THEOPHILUS BAILEY, b. 1627 (deposition); d. at Lynn 14 Feb 1694. In Sept of 1649, Theophilus Bailey and wife Ruth were presented for fornication, but the charge was dropped (EQCR, I:174). This charge was usually made for couples who had a child too soon after marriage; but there is no record of any child born to this couple. At the death of Theophilus, his estate was left to Lois (Ivory) Bligh, the eldest daughter of Ruth's brother Thomas (Essex Probate, 1394).

2. ii. THOMAS, b. prob. in England, about 1635; m. MARY DAVIS.

    iii. LOIS, b. prob. at Lynn, in 1640 (figured from age at death); d. at Lynn, as "Lois, wid. of Lt. John Burrill, age 80," 5 Sept 1720 (LVR). She m. at Lynn, 10 May 1656, JOHN BURRILL ("Genealogical Gleanings Relating to Lynn" in New England Historical and Genealogical Register, 5:951). He was b. at Lynn, 1631; d. there 24 Apr 1703, son of George and Mary (Cooper) Burrill (all information on Burrill family is from Frank A. Gardner, "Burrill Family of Essex County," Essex Institute Historical Collections, LI [1915]:275-277; 279-281; LII:54-56). Children, b. at Lynn (surname Burrill): 1. Capt. John, "Speaker of the House," b. 15 Oct 1658; d. 10 Dec 1721; m. 28 July 1680, Mary Stower. 2. Sarah, b. 16 May 1661; d. 27 Dec 1714; m. John Pickering of Salem. 3. Thomas, b. 7 Jan 1663; died young. 4. Anna, b. 15 Sep 1666; m. 24 July 1695, as his second wife, Josiah Rhoads. 5. Theophilus, b. 15 July 1669; m. (1) at Boston, 5 June 1695, Lydia Cathercole; m. (2) (int.) 9 Nov 1727, Hannah (Holyoke) Charnock. 6. Lois, b. 27 Jan 1671; m. Samuel Sprague of Woburn. 7. Samuel, b. 20 Apr 1674; d. 7 May 1674 (LVR). 8. Samuel, b. not given in LVR; m. 17 Sep 1682, Margaret Jarvis. 9. Mary, b. 18 Feb 1676; d. 26 Oct 1694, unmarried. 10. Ebenezer, b. 13 July 1679; d. 1 Sep 1761; m. Martha Farrington. 11. Ruth b. 17 May 1682; d. 23 oct 1771; m. 9 May 1705; Capt. Benjamin Potter (ibid.; Ellen Mudge Burrill, "The Burrill Family of Lynn", Register of the Lynn Historical Society, XI:67).

  iv. SARAH, b. prob at Lynn, in 1643 (figured from age at death); d. at Lynn, as Sarah Chadwell, 8 May 1726, age 83 (LVR). She married at Lynn, in the 12th month (Feb) 1660 MOSES CHADWELL (Court Record cited in LVR), b. at Lynn, 10 Apr 1637; d. at sea, 25 Apr 1684, at the age of 42, son of Thomas & Margaret Chadwell (Marcia Wilson Wiswall, The Chadwell Family [Lynnfield, Mass., 1983], 16). Children, b. at Lynn (surname Chadwell): 1. Thomas, b. 11 Dec 1662; m. (1) Hannah Smith; m. (2) Sarah (Brown) Breed, widow of Timothy Breed (ibid., 23). 2. Ruth, b. ca 1655; m. 24 June 1685, Joseph Hart (LVR). 3. Sarah, b. 12 Mar 1668. 4. Lois, b. 3 Oct 1670; d. unm., 28 Feb 1737 (ibid.). 5. Moses, b. 11 Sep 1673; d. 29 Sep 1676. 6. Margaret, b. 30 Sep 1676; d. 29 Nov 1693. 7. Anna, b. 17 June 1679; m. 27 Nov 1697, Jonathan Ramsdell (ibid.). 8. Elizabeth, b. 18 Dec 1681; m. (1) 31 Oct 1710, John Ramsdell; m. (2) 16 May 1728, Joseph Bates (LVR; Wiswall, Chadwell Family, 18).

2. **THOMAS² IVORY** (William¹) was born about 1635 and died at Lynn, 18 July 1690 (Lynn VRs). He married, "about 17: 3rd month: 1660," Mary Davis (ibid.), b. in 1635 (figured from age at death); died at Lynn, 15 September 1732, age 97 years (ibid.), daughter of Jenkin and Mary Davis (see below).

    Although Thomas appears to have lived in Lynn all his life, he was listed as "of Salem" on 25: 9: 1657 when he was presented with Samuell Shaducke, also of Salem, for absenting themselves from public ordinances of God. Witnesses were John Rucke, George Norton and Samuel Archer of Salem (EQCR, II:61). On 4: 27: 1659, Thomas Ivory and Francis Burrell, both of Lynn, were witnesses against Benjamin Chadwell of Lynn for smoking tobacco near a house amongst combustible matter" (ibid., I:166).

    On 4: 1: 1674, Thomas served on a jury of inquest looking into the sudden death of Edmund Rooten of Lynn, who was drowned in a brook (ibid., 6:115). On the 26th of February 1677, Thomas Ivory was one of more than 200 men of Lynn who took the Oath of Fidelity, before Captain Thomas Marshall, according to an order of the General Court.

    In 1677, Thomas Ivory accused Henry Collins, Sr., of "cutting timber trees, barking them, and laying claim to the land." A writ, dated 21 November 1677, was served by John Bullard (Ballard) constable of Lynn, by attachment of defendant's dwelling house. The suit was withdrawn.

At a court held at Ipswich, 28 March 1682, Thomas Ivory petitioned the court for reimbursement for the care of his mother-in-law, Mary Davis. Sworn testimonies of Mary Ivory, William Crofts and Ann Croft were taken at Lynn the following day, before Commissioner Thomas Laughton. Mary (Davis) Ivory, aged 43 years, testified that "her mother Davis is deprived of her senses and had been an extraordinary care and trouble. Only for natural affection she could not have undergone such care for twice as much as her husband demanded, for she is as helpless as a child...." William Crofts, aged about 70 years, testified that "about Feb. 13, 1677, the widow of Jynkin Davis, came to the house of Thomas Ivorye and had been cared for there ever since. When Ivory'e's wife went away she had someone there to tend her. He heard Thomas Ivory demand of the tenant John Daivs the rent toward the maintenance of his mother and he refused." Ann Croft, aged about 80 years, deposed that "her son Thomas Ivorye told her that John Davis had brought his mother there, and deponent told him to care for her because she and John's wife could not agree and she ought to be with her own daughter. She told her son that he would be no loser for it because authority would see that he was paid for it" (EQCR, VIII:289-90). Thomas Laiton and Francis Burrell were ordered by the court to sell enough land of the widow Mary Davis to pay her son-in-law for past maintenance of Mary, and in the future in the time of her age and weakness at the rate of 4 shillings per week during her life. They were also empowered to bring suit for any rents or debts due to her, which should be used to defray the expense. At the next court held at Salem on 27 June 1682, John Davis, "inhabitant of Lynn, brother-in-law of Thomas Ivory, and son of Mrs. Mary Davis," petitioned the court. He said that Mr. Thomas Laughton, Sr. and Francis Burrill, Sr. had sold five and a quarter acres of land which said Ivory accepted for the time past, but would not accept the 4 shillings per week for the future. He said he did not know that Ivory was going to that court at Ipswich which was not fair dealing; that his mother should be maintained by the estate and by her children, which are but two, the petitioner and Thomas Ivory's now wife; that he was and is willing to bear two parts to Ivory's one and 'am willing to do my utmost for my honored mother. And as I am the son I was willing to preserve the estate together while my mother lived if possible and so have possessed the inheritance of my father, of which lands my brother might expect a third part or pay for it after my mother's decease...and [I] have the land by lease from my mother when she was of good understanding and that for her lifetime, at a certain rate per year, which [I] paid yearly...that Thomas Ivory received fourteen pounds & twelve shillings in this four years that he declared he had maintaind my mother...[and I am] willing to joyne with [my] brother Ivory to maintain our mother two parts for one with him, and have proffered him that if he be weary, [I] would take his mother & keep her; also have proffered to refer the matter concerning his mothers maintainance to two indifferent men & will be bound to do as they should appoint, but nothing will be accepted, but the land, which is [mine] by lease, is taken away, and [I] shall be quickly bereaved of that which I had good hopes to enjoy as the inheritance of [my] father...[and I] have laid out a great deal to make a comfortable place of abode and now is greatly spoiled...and Thomas Ivory my brother has [said] he was fully satisfyed for all things concerning my mother this four years last past...and [I] emplore the court that [I] may not be driven out of the inheritance of my father, but that both as children may be ordered to do their duty, and the inheritance of our father remain together according to our deceased father's intention" (ibid., 346-47).

On 5 November 1731, widow Mary (Davis) Ivory was given her part of her husband Thomas's estate. Signing the agreement were Joseph Bass and Lois his wife, of Boston; Theophilus Ivory of Charlestown, Deborah Ivory, widow of Benjamin; Ruth Ivory, widow of John, and Ruth's son-in-law, Thomas Witt and his Wife Mary (Ivory) Witt (Essex Deeds, 63:25). On the 29th of December, the same year, Thomas Ivory's children gave to their loving "kinswoman," Mary Ivory, spinster, who has been at great expense in looking after our mother, Mary, "all land and appurtenances in Lynn belonging to their mother." Signing this agreement were Joseph and Lois Bass of Boston; Sarah Ivory, spinster, of Boston; Theophilus Ivory and Silas Ivory of Charlestown; Tabitha Rand, widow, of Lynn; Samuel and Hannah Baxter of Lynn; Thomas and Mary Witt of Lynn; Thomas, Jr. and Eunice Cheever of Lynn; Benjamin Ivory of Lynn; and Henry and Lois Blaney of Salem (Essex Deeds, 59:71).

Children, born at Lynn:

i. LOIS[3], b. 7 Feb 1661; m. (1) at Lynn, 19 Dec 1779, SAMUEL BLY (or BLIGH), who d. at Lynn, 31 Dec 1693 (LVR). Lois m. (2) Capt. EZEKIAL ROGERS, b. at Ipswich, 4 June 1667; d. at Lynn, 24 Feb 1707/8. Lois m. (3) Feb 1708, JOSEPH BASS of Braintree. Children by first husband (surname Bly): 1. Theophilus (Savage, I:206); d. at Lynn, 12 June 1681 (LVR). 2. Samuel, b. 6 June 1686 (ibid.). Children by second husband (surname Rogers): 3. Nathaniel, b. at Lynn, 18 July 1695; d. 20 Sept 1753; m. at Boston, 9 May 1717, Elizabeth Porter. 4. Theophilus, b. at Lynn, 40 Oct 1699; d. 14 Nov 1753; m. a dau. of William Hyde. Theophilus was a doctor; settled in Norwich, CT. 5. Lois, b. at Lynn, 15 July 1702; m. at Lynn, 18 Sept 1719, Phillip Britton of Boston who d. 1 Nov 1721; m. (2) Dudson Kilcup (New England Historical and Genealogical Register, 5:326-7).

ii. TALITHCUMY/TABITHA, b. 30: 2mo: 1663; m. "last of" Jan 1683 ROBERT RAND, JR. (LVR), b. abt. 1653; d. 6 Dec 1717, age 64. Children, b. at Lynn (surname Rand): 1. Robert, b. 6 Oct 1686. 2. Zachariah, b. 15 Apr 1688; bur. 26 Apr 1688. 3. Zachariah, b. 19 July 1689; d. 6 Apr 1765, age 76; bur. Old Western Cemetery; m. Elizabeth Richason. 4. Hannah, b. Sept 1691. 5. Thomas, b. 23 July 1693; d. 13 Aug 1693. 6. Mary, b. 7 Aug 1695; d. 30 Mar 1718; m. 5 Dec 1715, Thomas Rhodes. 7. John, b. 3 Feb 1698; d. 20 Jan 1700. 8. Lois, b. 19 May 1700; m. 17 Dec 1741, Stephen Phillips of Marblehead (Florence Osgood Rand, Genealogy of the Rand Family in the United States [NY, 1898], 13-14, 30).

iii. THOMAS, b. 2 Aug 1665; prob. died young.

iv. HANNAH/ANNA, b. 22 Dec 1667; m. at Lynn, 2 Apr 1684, ZACHARIAH RAND (LVR) (his estate was administered by widow in 1705/6). She m. (2) at Lynn, int. 15 Sept 1711, SAMUAL BAXTER (LVR). Children (surname Rand): 1. Daniel, b. abt. 1686; m. 18 Jan 1720, Mary Keyes. 2. Thomas, b. abt. 1700; pub. 16 Apr 1720 to Elizabeth Parker. 3. Elizabeth, m. (int.) 11 Dec 1726, David Rice of Weymouth. 4. Mary, m. (int.) 13 July 1735, Ebenezer Tarbox (LVR). 5. Anna/Hannah, b. 19 Aug 1713; m. 21 May 1730, Benjamin Eaton of Lynn (LVR). 6. possibly John, who d. at Boston, 4 June 1730, age 33; m. 24 Oct 1723, Sarah Dudley (Rand Gen., 14, 22)

3. v.   JOHN, b. 10 Oct 1669; m. RUTH POTTER.
4. vi. THEOPHILUS, b. 1 Nov 1670; m. KATHERINE ----.
5. vii. WILLIAM, b. 10 Jan 1674; m. SARAH HORTON.
6. viii.BENJAMIN, b. 22 Sept 1685; m. DEBORAH TOBEY.
    ix. MARY, b. not found. Her will, signed 10 Sept 1735, was probated 23 Sept 1734 names brothers and sisters:

WILL OF MARY IVORY

"...I, Mary Ivory of Lynn...singlewoman, being sick of body tho sound of mind...make my last will and testament: I give to Benjamin Ivory my dwelling house and all the land adjoyning thereto, he paying out thereof the sum of 30 pounds. I bequeath to my kinswoman, Mary Rand the sum of 20 pounds & also one feather bed & all the furniture thereto belonging one chest of draws & all my chairs & pewter & a looking glass. I give to Sarah Ivory daughter of my brother William Ivory deceased the sum of ten pounds & she to have my East India gown. I give to Sarah Ivory daughter of my brother Benjamin Ivory one feather bed with all the furniture thereof and also my silk crape gown. I give to the other five children of my deceased brother Benjamin five pounds to each of them. My will is that there be provided out of my estate stones for my own grave & also for the grave of my deceased mother. I give and bequeath the remainder of my estate unto my brother & sisters & to the children of my deceased brothers and sister to be divided amongst them in such ways & manner as the law doth dispose of & settle intestate estates. I appoint Deacon John Burrage to be my sole executor..." Signed: Mary Ivory. Witnesses: John Crichtin(Curtin?), Joseph Ramsdell, Matthew Breed (Essex Probate, 14662).

Attached to the will is a bill of 61 pounds 12 shillings due to Thomas Witt, for Mary Ivory's expenses for 1725 - 1730. Items include pumpkins, corn, mutton, barley, suet, malt, butter, milk, flax, cords of wood, and the pasturing of a cow.

An inventory of the estate was made 1 October 1735:

"Where there is one fifth part of two ninth parts belonging to Thomas Witt & also four sevenths parts of one ninth part belonging to four minors which never did belong to the said Mary Ivory in the house and land hereafter described that we do herein except to be subtracted from the price of the house & land. The personal estate we prise as her own:

About two acres & a half of land called ?'s lot	75-00-0
The half of the old orchard	11-00-0
One single acre of marsh & the marsh below Breed's	59-00-0
Two acres of salt marsh	22-00-0
About nineteen acres of Common Lots	<u>50-00-0</u>
	217-00-0
Waring apparell bedding & table lining & books	20-16-0
wool for floax cloth yarn & stockings	05-02-6
gold silver brass iron ? & old lumber	09-16-5

a cow a pig & a load of hay	*09-19-0*
money in the house	*02-15-8*
money at interest	*0-00-0*
	68- 5 5

*The easterly end of the old house & the land adjoining
which was given to Benjamin Ivory*   *71-00-0*

Movables given to Mary Rand	*20-00-0*
A gown given to Sarah, daughter of William Ivory	*5-00-0*
Movables given to Sarah daughter of Benjamin Ivory	*12-00-0*

    Signed by John Burrage, Exec. 29 May 1736.
    Richard Johnson, Michall Bowdon, Matthew Breed"

On 17 October 1738, John Burrage presented an account of Mary Ivory's estate. Items included were: 2 1/2 acres of marsh land sold to Henry Blaney; 1 acre of marsh sold to Nathaniel Burrill; 2 small common lots sold to Zachariah Rand. A list of payments made included money to Joseph Ramsdell for burying cloth; Silsbee for coffin; gravestones, etc. Total money brought in was 26 pounds; debts totaled 104 pounds.

On the 20th of May 1740, John Burrage, Esq. brought in the final account of Mary Ivory's estate. This included:

2 acres salt marsh sold to Isaac Smith for	38-00-0
3 acres of wood land sold to John Breed for	18-00-0
1 acres, 190 poles wood land sold to J. Brown	4--7-6
Debt due from Benjamin Ivory's acct	30-00-0
Total	90--7-6

Debts against the estate totaled 41 pounds, 7 shillings, sixpence.
Net remainder: 49 pounds, two shillings, threepence.
          John Burrage, Esquire, 20 May 1740, at Ipswich.

          (to be continued)

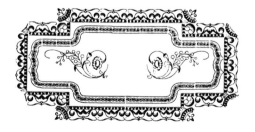

HEINRICH SCHERER, Hessian, alias, HENRY SHERER, Gardener

By Edward T. Barnard

Juliette Amanda Turner (1847-1937) was a demon genealogist, but inclined to be hasty in her conclusions. One of the family legends for which she was responsible had it that her great-grandfather, Henry Sherer, owned a farm on Manhattan Island that stretched from the Bowery to the East River. Moreover, had his granddaughter Louisa (Aunt Julie's mother and my great-grandmother) not been orphaned in childhood, and had Henry's executors not mismanaged his estate, his descendants would have been very wealthy indeed.

Few in the family gave credence to this charming thought, yet the name Henry Sherer stuck in my memory because, on her demise at age 90, Aunt Julie left me an old sea chest inside the cover of which she had written: "This chest, probably brought from Holland in the 18th Century, belonged to Henry Sherer of New York; died there about 1820. Catherine, daughter of Henry, married William Sherer, her cousin; both died in New York about 1815. Louisa Emeline, daughter of Catherine and William, married Myron Turner, and died in New York in 1899."

Among Aunt Julie's diaries and memorabilia was a scrap of paper evidently torn from an old Bible. Dated 22 July 1843, it stated, "Henry Sherrer Wass born 1783 June the 24th," which later proved to be Henry *junior*. Below this came his wife Elizabeth, born 10 October 1794, and their marriage 10 December 1812. Followed was the birth of John Henry Sherrer on 14 February 1814 and seven more children, the last born in 1827. Below these, written in the same hand, was "Louisa Emeline Sherrer Was Born August 16th, 1812."

Why Louisa, daughter of Catherine, should be listed with Henry Junior's family in 1843 when she was almost twenty-one years old, was not explained. It was, however, important in that it provided the specific date of her birth.

All of these data remained dormant until World War II when, on a day I had leave in London, the sirens began to wail and a bomb landed in the next block. Being strong on survival instincts, I ducked into the nearest solid building, which turned out to house the Society of Genealogists. A tiny bird-like woman met me in the foyer and chirped, "And what may we do for you, Captain?" She led me deeper into the building, where I found a dozen people pouring over books and manuscripts, none paying the slightest attention to the commotion outside. Before the hour was out and the all-clear sounded, my new friend had me hooked on genealogy, and I was fired up to get home to Henry Sherer, his farm, and his sea chest.

Once at it, I soon discovered that among the sources of genealogical data in New York two were most fruitful: the New York Public Library, and 31 Chambers Street in Manhattan, which houses not only Municipal Archives but also the Surrogate's Court records.

Knowing that Henry had an estate, I looked for a will, which turned up in Liber 55 of wills, pages 104-105. Written 8 June 1818 in the flowing hand of a scribe - certainly not that of a farmer - were the following bequests:

1. $100 to grandson Henry Martin (Martin likely a middle name) son of late daughter Catherine.
2. One-eighth part to granddaughters Louisa and Julia, daughters of late daughter Catherine.
3. One-eighth part to "all the children of" late daughter Margaret.
4. The remaining six equal eighths parts to sons Henry, Peter, Martin, John, Jacob, and grandson William, son of late daughter Elizabeth.

The will was probated 8 March 1819, and the executors were Rev. Frederick Christian Schaeffer and George Arcularius, baker. So I now knew who comprised Henry's family, but for his wife, and I knew that in 1818 he had five living sons and four deceased daughters. Furthermore, if Executor Schaeffer was also Henry's pastor, there might be useful information in church records.

A book on New York churchmen identified Schaeffer as pastor of Christ Lutheran Church that, in the early 1800s, stood on the corner of Frankfort and William Streets. According to the <u>Lutherans</u> <u>of</u> <u>New York: Their Story and Their Problems</u> by G. U. Wenner (NY: Petersfield Press, 1918), Rev. Schaeffer took over the pastorate from Frederick William Geissenhainer in 1814. Moreover, Christ Lutheran Church did not last as an entity beyond 1822, and the survival of its records seemed more doubtful than proved to be the case. They really did exist - at least some of them - at a successor parish at the northern tip of Manhattan, the Evangelical Lutheran Church of St. Matthew at 202 Sherman Avenue, whose pastor, Rev. Paul Schulpze, allowed me a peak at some of his treasures.

Pastor Schulze appeared not to have the records of Schaeffer's tenure at Christ Lutheran, but he did have some of those by his predecessor, Frederick Geissenhainer, which showed that on Whitsunday 1808 (June 5th), his congregation included "Henry Sherer and wife Margaretha." On 13 February 1814, there was, "Henry Scherrer jun & Elizabeth, son still born." And finally, on 10 August 1814, came "Margaret Sherer, age 54 years and 7 mos. Left husband and 10 children." So now I knew who Henry's wife was, and that his grandson, John Henry, had not survived. The will of Henry accounted for only 9 of the ten children mentioned in the church records. Pastor Geissenhainer had nothing to say about any of the other Shere/Sherrer/Sherrers.

The holdings of the New York Municipal Archives during this space of time are thin, but they seemed worth a try and three death certificates ensued:
1. Henry Sherer died 19 Feb 1851, age 68 (thus Henry junior); place of nativity New York; cemetery: removed from the City.
2. Catherine Rothermet died 1 Nov 1817, age 23, residence Forsythe St.; place of nativity New York; Lutheran German Cemetery. Could this have been Henry's dau.?
3. Margaretta Sherer died 10 Aug 1814, age 54 years 7 mos.; residence First St.; place of nativity New Jersey; Lutheran Cemetery. This, of course, was Henry's wife, and a repetition of the church records. Municipal Archives produced no vital statistics on Henry's remaining sons or on Henry himself.

The farm angle called for checking into deeds, also at 31 Chambers Street, and Liber 82, pages 99-101 showed that on 2 May 1796 Henry had, for 1,000 pounds, bought four lots from one Frederick Westfall, gardener, which, when the streets became numbered in 1808, turned out to be #66 and #68 First Street (later Chrystie) and #53 and #54 Second Street (later Forsythe). Following his death in 1819, all these were disposed of for a total of $4,500 (Lib. 143, pages 178-189). So much for the big farm and the lost millions - perhaps both Westfall and Henry did their farming on the four lots which at one time had been part of the Delancy Estate.

But where did Henry live? Once again N.Y.P.L. came to the rescue with the New York City Directories. These began in 1791, but Henry did not show up until 1793. Between then and his demise in 1819, this is what the directories revealed about Henry Sherer:
1793, grocer, Greenwich do (domicile) opposite the market.
1794 & 1795, grocer, 89 Greenwich Street do.
1796, grocer, First do.   1797, gardener.   1798-1802, gardener, First.
1803, gardener.   1804-1807, gardener, First.   1808-1810, gardener, 68 First.
1811, gardener.   1812, Fourth near Stanton.   1813, gardener.
1814, gardener, First near Hester.   1815-1816, gardener, 68 First.
1816 also, gardener, 72 Second. (later remaned Forsythe).
1817-1818, gardener, 68 Chrystie. (First having been renamed).

These addresses were valuable in that they revealed the domiciles of other Sherers/Sherrers, likewise listed in the directories. For example, in 1814 "Catherine Shere, marketwoman" also lived at 68 First, the only citation of Catherine. And whereas Henry lived at Fourth near Stanton in 1812, son Peter lived there in 1813 and 1814. And while Henry lived at 72 Second/Forsythe in 1816, so did Peter, as did his brother Henry junior the next year. In addition, two Sherer/Sherrer women, whose relationship remains unknown, inhabited Henry's property: Widow Lucretia Sherer, "huxter," in 1816/1817 lived at 55 Second/Forsythe, and in 1818 was at #53. And in 1818 Widow Ann Sherrer lived at #55.

At this juncture, a Great Disheartening set in. I knew nothing about Henry's origin, except for Henry junior nothing about his children beyond where a few of them had lived, nothing about his Jersey-born wife but her name and death, and nothing whatever about Catherine's alleged husband or her second daughter, Julia. I had received from Surrogate's Court the news that as of 19 June 1820, Louisa Sherer, "daughter of the late Catherine Rhodeamille," was put under the guardianship of a physician named Peter van Arsdale, but all this revealed was a second marriage by Catherine, and, sadly, not only did Rhodeamille not look much like Rothermet but neither name showed up in Municipal Archives or the city directories except for the Rothermet death.

Loudly expressing my frustrations one day at N.Y.P.L., a genealogy research librarian disappeared and returned with a large book, remarking, "We sometimes have records that Archives doesn't." In it, I found matching data on Margaretta and on Catherine Rothermet, and also, "16 February 1819, Henry Sherer, Chrystie Street, born Cassel Germany; 78 years; died old age, Lutheran Cemetery."

Henry was German! And since Margaretta was born in New Jersey, obviously all their children were also born in America. And wouldn't Henry himself have opted to become an American?

Minutes of the District Court, Southern District of New York, 5 June 1800: "Henry Sherer, at present of the City of New York xxx but late of Murberk in Germany, gardener, age 55 years and upwards, came into Court and, being duly sworn, declared that it is bona fide his intention to become a citizen of the United States and to renounce forever all allegiance and fidelity to any foreign Prince, Potentate, State, or severeignty whatever, and particularly to the Emperor of Germany whereof he is now a subject...."

On 7 April 1807, Henry's U.S. citzenship was finalized in Mayor's Court (Common Pleas, N.Y. County, Bundle 5, record 4331), his sponsor being a dentist named Leonard Fisher. Henry had indeed become an American, but what of his past? Perhaps the court clerk mistook his German accent and heard Murberk instead of Marburg in Cassel.

Since Henry was a German, his native name was surely Heinrich Scherer, but where next to turn? The answers came from Mark Schwalm of the Johannes Schwalm Historical Association, and from Herman Radloff of the St. Louis Genealogical Society, who, between them, turned up a candidate who fit the requirements perfectly. From HETRINA (Hessische Truppen im Amerikanishen Unabhaengigkeitskrieg, by Auerbach & Froehlich, Marburg 1974) Vol. III, Mr. Radloff supplied, "Henrich (spelling adopted by HETRINA) Sherer, both 1742/43, from D3551 Elnhausen, a corporal in the Regiment Erbprinz commanded by Lt. Marrh. von Fuchs of the Fifth Company, deserted July 1778." Mr. Schwalm, citing Marburg Pruess, Staatsarchiv OWS 1513 in the Library of Congress, advised that "Corporal Heinrich Scherer from Elnhausen, age 35, deserted from Fort Independence (N.Y.C.) on 22 July 1778 with complete uniform, sword belt, and side arms." Elnhausen is a village near Marburg.

Subsequent correspondence with the Evangelishces Pfarramt in Elnhausen produced four sons and eight daughters born to Johann Jost Scherer and Anna Catharine Steinhauser: 1734, Catharina; 1736, Elizabetha; 1738, Margaretha and Anna; 1739, Anna Catharina; 1742, Elizabetha; 1744, Johann Heinrich; 1746, Johann Christian; 1749, Johann Conrad; 1752, Elizabetha; 1754, Anna Catharina; 1757, Jacob.

A further check with the church in Elnhausen indicated Henry's Catherine had male cousins and second cousins, but none born in that village by the name of Wilhelm between 1766 and 1810.

There are discrepancies in the origin and birth dates of Henry/Heinrich. The death notice of Henry born in Cassel likely referred to the principality of Hessen Cassel rather than to the modern city of Kassel, and the implied birth date of 1741 surely stems from how old Henry's American-born children thought their father was at his demise. The naturalization intention cites Murberk, which does not exist, whereas Marburg is the nearest metropolis to Elnhausen. HETRINA has Henrich born in Elnhausen in 1742/3, the latter being a computerized calculation based on his stated age at the time of muster. The church records at Elnhausen shows a birth year of 1744, presumably the most reliable.

There remain some teasing gaps.

1. No non-commissioned Hessian soldier could possess bulky equipment like the sea chest, or desert with it, but of course Henry could have bought it after his desertion.

2. Where could Heinrich have holed up between 1778 and 1793? During World War II, I was heavily involved with Escape and Evasion, and drummed into American pilots two vital rules if they landed in enemy territory: leave the area quickly and get into civilian clothes as soon as available. I do not doubt Heinrich knew this without my help. After all he spent almost two full years on Staten Island, Long Island and Manhattan, during which time as a corporal he must have had some responsibility for patrol activity and periodic foraging missions. He had three places to go: south right into Manhattan in full

uniform as though he had business there, and find refuge among the resident Germans (the British did not leave until 1783); head north into Dutchess or Columbia County, where there were many resident Germans; paddle across the Hudson River into New Jersey and find his Margaretha there somewhere. Henry junior, who may not have been his first born, arrived in 1783, ten years before Henry surfaced in Manhattan.

3. Nothing has been discovered about Catherine's husband, William. Further probing may reveal him as the son of one of Heinrich's brothers or cousins who may have had a family after he left Elnhausen. Failing that, it is possible that young Louisa was what Downeast Yankees term a "wood filly," the product of a mare who escaped from the barn for romance afield. Moreover, there is no trace of Julia, perhaps the daughter of Catherine and Mr. Rhodeamille. i cannot find any of Aunt Julie's papers where she got the name Juliette. She had no ancestors with a similar name on either side of her family other than her aunt, Catherine's daughter Julia.

One of the more interesting discoveries on this genealogical adventure was that Pastor Geissenhainer's Whitsunday journal came to rest less than a mile from where Fort Independence stood, the site from which Heinrich chose freedom. But there is still work to be done. Will all of the descendants of Rhodeamille, Rothermet, and Sherer/Sherrer please stand up?

DESCENT OF EDWARD T. BARNARD FROM HENRY SHERER

Heinrich Scherer, b. 18 Apr 1744 (D3351 Elnhausen, West Germany)
Catherine Sherer
Louisa Emeline Sherer, b. 16 Aug 1812; m. Myron Turner 15 Apr 1845
Adelaide Louisa Turner, b. 26 Sept 1850 NYC; m. Edward Townsend 2 June 1874
Therina Townsend, b. 14 Apr 1875, NYC; m. Everett L. Barnard 1 June 1901.
Edward Townsend Barnard, b. 10 Oct 1910 New Rochelle, NY

> Edward Townsend Barnard, son of a Downeast Yankee and a descendant of Heinrich Scherer, was born in New Rochelle, N.Y. on 10/10/10 so he could remember the date. After four years at the feet of great Yale teachers, he worked for various magazines until joining the United Press foreign department, resigning to enlist in the Army Air Force from which, after serving in Military Intelligence, he emerged as a Lt. Col. Invited to join the C.I.A. at its inception, he remained there until retirement in 1970, and then served his home town of Guilford, CT in various capacities. For the past 15 years, he has been a volunteer driver for the Red Cross. Following the departure of his three grown children, his main interests have been genealogy, supporting the IRS, and anticipating the daily arrival of junk mail. Author of thousands of reports, all blessedly classified, this is his first attempt at one that isn't, but he is already working on another to be titled "How I coached Bill Tilden to the 1990 Wimbledon Championship."

The Ahnentafel

Ahnentafel of Clayton Rand Adams, 6 Laurel Road, Brunswick, ME 04011

I	1	Clayton Rand Adams	1925-	Westbrook, ME
II	2	Ernest Clayton Adams	1888-1941	Westbrook, ME
	3	Harriet Moulton Pettingell	1895-	Amesbury, MA
III	4	Franklin Adams	1839-1903	Westbrook, ME
	5	Elizabeth Trask Rand	1849-1915	Portland, Westbrook, ME
	6	William Fisher Pettingell	1856-1921	Newburyport, MA
	7	Elizabeth Maria Moulton	1854-1944	Newburyport, MA; Manchester, NH
IV	8	Mark Adams	1802-1883	Limerick, North Yarmouth, ME
	9	Amanda Hall	1811-1867	Westbrook, ME
	10	Woodbury Rand	1804-1865	Windham, Westbrook, ME
	11	Lucy Ann Small	1814-1893	Westbrook, ME
	12	Andrew Haskell Pettingell	1827-1898	Newbury, Newburyport, MA
	13	Mary Nash	1836-1917	Carridoc, Ont; Newburyport, MA
	14	Moses Benjamin Moulton	1826-1858	Newburyport, MA; At sea
	15	Elizabeth Winn	1827-1914	Newburyport, MA
V	16	Thomas Adams	1770-1827	Biddeford, Limerick, ME
	17	Mary Perry	-1808	Scarboro, Limerick, ME
	18	Israel Hall	1774-	Gorham, Westbrook, ME
	19	Abigail Hutchinson		Windham, Westbrook, ME
	20	Roland Rand	1771-1840	Portland, Windham, ME
	21	Elizabeth Woodbury	1778-1856	Cape Elizabeth, Windham, ME
	22	James Small	1781-1858	Falmouth, Windham, ME
	23	Anna Staples	1790-1853	Falmouth, Windham, ME
	24	Moses Pettingell	1795-1874	Newbury, Newburyport, MA
	25	Mary Haskell	1793-1868	Deer Isle, ME; Newburyport, MA
	26	James Nash	1803-1839	Trenton, NY; Chatham, Ont.
	27	Keziah Lockwood	-1899	Ont.; Mount Bridges, Ont.
	28	Moses Emerson Moulton	1805-1826	Newburyport, MA
	29	Ruth Somerby	1806-1859	Newburyport, MA
	30	Moses Winn	1783-1861	Wilmington, Newburyport, MA
	31	Mary Rogers	1790-1871	Hopkinton, NH; Newburyport, MA
VI	32	John Adams	1737-1819	Kittery, Limerick, ME
	33	Mary Hill	1737-	Kittery, Biddeford, ME
	34	John Perry	-1787	Scarboro, Limerick, ME
	35	Mary Runnells		Scarboro, Limerick, ME
	36	Ebenezer Hall	1741-1807	Dover, NH; Gorham, ME
	37	Hannah Anderson	1743-	Windham, Gorham, ME
	38	Stephen Hutchinson Jr.	1741-1826	Salem, MA; Windham, ME
	39	Sarah Sawyer		Cape Elizabeth, Windham, ME
	40	John Rand	1739-1807	Amesbury, MA; Windham, ME
	41	Jerusha Bradbury	1738-1817	Portland, Windham, ME
	42	John Woodbury	1735-1806	Cape Elizabeth, ME
	43	Joanna Mitchell	-1818	Cape Elizabeth, ME
	44	John Small	1732-1820	Durham, NH; North Yarmouth, ME
	45	Bethia Wyman	1733-	Falmouth, ME
	46	Joseph Staples	1762-1800	Topsham, Falmouth, ME
	47	Miriam Pote	-1798	Falmouth, ME
	48	Eleazer Pettingell	1752-1825	Newbury, MA
	50	Caleb Haskell Jr.	1754-1829	Ipswich, Newburyport, MA
	51	Edna Hale	1761-1841	Newbury, Newburyport, MA

52	Ephraim Nash	1769-1809	Braintree, MA; Brockville, Ont.
53	Mary McDonald	1768-1849	Scotland; Thurlow, Ont.
54	Benjamin Lockwood	1770-1857	Westchester Co., NY; Delaware, Ont.
55	Keziah Springer	1776-1860	Albany, NY; Delaware, Ont.
56	Joseph Moulton	1760-1813	Newbury, Newburyport, MA
57	Hannah Eaton	1775-1821	Newburyport, MA
58	Henry Somerby	1773-1830	Newbury, MA
59	Hannah Goodwin	1776-1852	Newburyport, MA
60	John Winn	1751-1783	Wilmington, MA
61	Abigail Rogers	1748-1819	Tewksbury, Wilmington, MA
62	Paul Rogers	1766-1830	Newbury, MA
63	Miriam Rogers	1768-1824	Hopkinton, NH; Newburyport, MA

****

Ahnentafel of Johnathan D. Enslow, P.O. Box 1852, Gloucester, MA 01930

I	1	Johnathan David Enslow	1965-	Gloucester, MA
II	2	William David Enslow	1941-	Gloucester, MA
	3	Diana Marie Houde	1944-	Gloucester, MA
III	4	Clayton Nehemiah Enslow	1907-1971	W. Green Harbor, N.S.; Gloucester, MA
	5	Elizabeth Pool	1906-1942	Gloucester, MA
	6	Roland M. Houde	1920-1982	Montmagny, Que; Gloucester, MA
	7	Beulah Burgess	1920-	Queensland, N.S.; Gloucester, MA
IV	8	William Howard Enslow	1872-1953	W. Green Harbor, Nova Scotia
	9	Ann E. Williams	1875-1934	W. Green Harbor, Nova Scotia
	10	Waldo E. Pool	1873-1934	Gloucester, Beverly Farms, MA
	11	Alice Chester Middleton	1879-1946	Gloucester, MA
	12	Hector H. Houde	1873-1943	W. Boylston, Lowell, MA; Montmagny, Quebec; Gloucester, MA
	13	Matilda Houde	1876-1946	Louisville, Que; Lowell, MA; Montmagny, Que; Gloucester, MA
	14	Reginald Burgess	1894-1940	Queensland, N.S.; Gloucester, MA
	15	Lillian Dorey	1903-1986	Hubbards Cove, N.S.; Gloucester, MA
V	16	James Cox Enslow	c1835/36-	W. Green Harbor, Nova Scotia
	17	Hannah I. Williams	c1840/41-bef 1917	W. Green Harbor, Nova Scotia
	18	Paul Williams	c1830/31-	W. Green Harbor, Nova Scotia
	19	Agnes Belong	c1830/31-	W. Green Harbor, Nova Scotia
	21	Ann Eliza Pool	1853-	Gloucester, MA
	22	Charles W. Middleton	1861-1900	Gloucester, MA
	23	Anna E. Lane	1859-1947	Gloucester, Attleboro, MA
	24	Anthony Houde		Quebec
	25	Julianna Heureux		Quebec
	26	Alfred Houde		Quebec
	27	Matilda Boulanger		Quebec
	28	Reginald Burgess		Queensland, Nova Scotia
	29	Flora Williams		Queensland, Nova Scotia
	30	James Dorey	c1850-	Hubbards Cove, Nova Scotia
	31	Melissa Boutilier	c1860-	Hubbards Cove, Nova Scotia
VI	42	Thomas Saville Pool	1829-1917	Gloucester, MA
	43	Harriett Babson Figgies	1828-1913	Gloucester, MA
	44	Watson Middleton	c1814-1892	Mariah (Elmira?), NY; Gloucester, MA
	45	Elizabeth Allen	1822-1907	Gloucester, MA
	46	George W. Lane	1834-1879	Gloucester, MA; "died at sea"
	47	Ann Elizabeth Andrews	1837-1913	Guysborough Co., N.S.; Gloucester, MA

Ahnentafel of William Oliver Batchelder, Grandfather of Margaret Batchelder Southwick, 529 Plantation Club Villas, Hilton Head Island, SC 29928

I	1	William Oliver Batchelder	1845-1920	Danvers, Peabody, MA
II	2	Oliver Felton Batchelder	1815-1887	Danvers, Peabody, MA
	3	Sally Osborn	1825-1896	South Danvers, Peabody, MA
III	4	Andrew Batchelder	1772-1845	Andover, Danvers (?), MA
	5	(2) Sally Felton	1787-1855	Brookfield, Danvers, MA
	6	Kendall Osborn, Esq.	1796-1875	Danvers, S. Danvers, MA
	7	Sally Bushby	1798-1849	Danvers, MA
IV	8	Ezra Batchelder	1741-1809	Salem, Danvers, MA
	9	Mrs. Mary Woodbury Ober	1737-1821	Beverly, Danvers (?), MA
	10	Capt. Benjamin Felton	1739-1820	Salem, Brookfield, MA
	11	(2) Ruth Hamilton	1752-1819	Brookfield, MA
	12	John Osborn, 3rd	1765-1845	Danvers, MA
	13	Lydia Southwick (her 3m)	1766-1864	Danvers, South Danvers, MA
	14	Asa Bushby	1770/1-1833	Danvers, MA
	15	Lydia Willson	1766-1844	Danvers, MA
V	16	John Batchelder	1697-1753	Salem, Beverly
	17	Jemina Conant	1701-	
	18	Capt. Andrew Woodbury	1712-1757	Beverly, MA
	19	Joanna Dodge	1717/8-1756	Beverly, MA
	20	Joseph Felton	1715-1803	Salem, Rutland, Oakham, MA
	21	Mary Trask	1716-1801	Salem (?), MA
	22	Nathan Hamilton		Brookfield, MA
	23	Ruth Wheeler	1752-1819	Brookfield, MA (?)
	24	Joseph Osborn	1726-1808(?)	Danvers, MA
	25	Mary Proctor	1733-1791	Danvers, MA
	26	Ebenezer Southwick	1736-1812	Danvers, MA
	27	Susann (Orr) Foster	1734/5-1811	Yarmouth, ME; Danvers, MA
	28	John Bushby	1741-	Medford, Danvers, MA
	29	---- Brown		
	30	Benjamin Willson	1734-1818	Danvers, MA
	31	Lydia Bancroft	1738/9-1811	Lynn, Danvers, MA
VI	32	John Batchelder	1675-1748	Salem, Beverly, MA
	33	Bethiah Woodbury	1673-1708	Beverly, MA
	34	John Conant	1652-1724	Beverly, MA
	35	Bethiah Mansfield	1658-1720	Beverly, MA
	38	Dea Joshua Dodge	1694-1771	Beverly, MA
	39	Hannah Raymond	1699-1783	Beverly, MA
	40	Skelton Felton	c1680-1749	Salem, Rutland, MA
	41	Hepsibah Shelton		
	42	John Trask	1678-1737	Salem, MA
	43	Hannah Osborn (2)		
	50	Joseph Osborne	1702-1780	Salem, MA
	51	Rachel Foster		
	52	John Proctor	1705-1773/5	Salem Village, MA
	53	(1) Lydia Waters	-1769	Salem Village, MA
	54	Ebenezer Southwick	1690-	
	55	Mary Whitman		
	56	John Orr (?)		North Yarmouth, ME
	57	Susan Skofield (?)		
VI	62	Robert Wilson		
	63	Mary Shillaber		
	64	John Bancroft	1708-1777	Lynn, MA
	65	Ruth Newhall	1712-1745/6	Lynn, MA

Ahnentafel of Mary Hawkes Sargent, GG Grandmother of Anne Merrill Goulette, R.R. 3, Box 120, Dexter, Maine 04930

I	1	Mary Hawkes Sargent	1827-1880	Lynn, Lynnfield, MA
II	2	Benjamin Sargent	1788-1845	Lynn, MA
	3	Isabella Newhall	1797-1833	Lynn, MA
III	4	Nathaniel Sargent	1760-1798	Lynn, MA
	5	Sarah Massey	1764-1833	Lynn, MA
	6	John Brown Newhall	1773-1833	Lynn, MA
	7	Susannah Lewis	1774-1837	Lynn, MA
IV	8	Nathaniel Sargent	1732-1766	Lynn, MA
	9	Sarah Jenks	1730-1808	Lynn, MA
	10	Benjamin Massey	1736/7-1787	Salem, Lynn, MA
	11	Sarah Hart	1733-1797	Lynn, MA
	12	Andrew Newhall	1730-	Lynn, MA
	13	Susannah Brown	-1789	Lynn, MA
	14	John Lewis	-1792	Lynn, Boston, MA; Halifax, N.S.
	15	Sarah Lindsey	c1744-1780	Lynn, MA; New York
V	16	Nathan Sargent	1706-1774	Chelsea, Malden, MA
	17	Mary Viall	1711-1795	Boston, Chelsea, MA
	18	John Jenks	1697-1764	Lynn, MA
	19	Elizabeth Berry	1701-1736/7	Rumney Marsh, Lynn, MA
	20	John Massey	1712-1740	Salem, MA
	21	Jane Vining	-1767	Salem, Lynn, MA
	22	Samuel Hart	1707-1807	Lynn, MA
	23	Phebe Ivory	-1768	Lynn, MA
	24	Joseph Newhall	1684-1742	Lynn, MA
	25	Elizabeth Potter	1691-1743	Lynn, MA
	26	John Brown	1704-1771	Salem, Danvers, MA
	27	Susanna Masury		Salem, MA
	30	Eleazar Lindsey	716/7-1791-3	Lynn, MA
	31	Lydia Farrington	1721-	Lynn, MA
VI	32	Joseph Sargent	1663-1717	Barnstable, Malden, MA
	33	Mary Green	1668-1759	Malden, MA
	34	Nathaniel Viall		Boston, MA
	35	Sarah Bennett		Boston, MA
	36	John Jenks	1660-1698	Lynn, MA
	37	Sarah Merriam	1665-1740	Lynn, MA
	38	Thomas Berry	1670-c1736	Rumney Marsh (Lynn/Saugus), MA
	39	Elizabeth Divan	1672-	Lynn, MA
	40	Nathaniel Massey	1679-1739	Salem, MA
	41	Rebecca Tomkins	1676-1735	Salem, MA
	44	Joseph Hart	1659-1736/7	Lynn, MA
	45	Ruth Chadwell	c1665-	Lynn, MA
	48	Joseph Newhall	1658-1705/6	Lynn, MA
	49	Susanna Farrar	1659-1733	Lynn, MA
	50	Robert Potter	1661-1709/10	Lynn, MA
	51	Martha Hall	1660-1709	Lynn, MA
	52	James Brown	1675-	Salem, MA
	53	Elizabeth Pickering	1674-	Salem, MA
	60	Ralph Lindsey	1684-1746/7	Lynn, MA
	61	Mary Breed	1684-1748	Lynn, MA
	62	John Farrington	1698-	Lynn, MA
	63	Abigail Fuller		Lynn, MA

****

Society News

FORTHCOMING MEETINGS

February 17   Saturday. Centre Congregational Church, Lynnfield, Mass.
                Social Hour: 12:00. Lecture promptly at 1:00
                Speaker: **GEORGE F. SANBORN, JR.**, Dir. of Libr. Operations
                       for New Eng. Hist. Gen.; Pres. N.H. Soc. of Genealogists.
                Topic: **Genealogical Research in New Hampshire**

March 17   Saturday. Centre Congregational Church, Lynnfield, Mass.
                Social Hour: 12:00. Lecture promptly at 1:00
                Speaker: **JANE FISKE**, F.A.S.G., Editor, <u>The Register</u>.
                Topic: **Rooting Around Rhode Island**

April 21   Saturday. Haverhill Public Library. All day Work Meeting.
                       Lecture at **2:00**
                Speaker: **ROBERT C. ANDERSON**, F.A.S.G. of Salt Lake City.
                Topic: **Essex County in the Great Migration**

May 19   Saturday. Centre Congregational Church, Lynnfield, Mass.
                Social Hour: 12:00. Lecture promptly at 1:00
                Speaker: **RON TAGNEY**, author.
                Topic: **Essex County 200 Years Ago**

REPORTS OF PREVIOUS MEETINGS

DECEMBER

    The December Covered Dish Luncheon and "Show and Tell" was cancelled for the first time in 15 years (the first was in 1975)! The forecast of a possible (or probable) large storm encouraged the decision to abandon the affair. Since the table and decorations had to be set up the day before, the decision had to be made at that time. We could not wait until meeting day as we can in other "snow" months. The cancellation announcement could not reach the newspapers in time, so radio/TV was the only public means available. Unfortunately, many stations now have a policy whereby a society has to enroll in their "storm alert" program to get "on the air." Imagine! We hoped that members would check at the library if in doubt before baking or coming, but we have heard of at least three stalwart members who never even thought of cancellation, and were therefore inconvenienced. We are certainly sorry about that. The Board will be discoussing this issue and will have more on the subject later.

JANUARY

    The January all-day work meeting at the Lynnfield Public Library was well attended in spite of the fact that we couldn't hold the Book Auction. The books were at Helen's house and had not been analyzed, priced, etc. Meanwhile, Marcia introduced board members, and gave a review of new acquisitions to the library's Genealogy room. Ann Lainhart entertained the group with amusing names she has found in preparing her state censuses for 1855/1865. Inez Dubuque and her committee had a splendid collation; Dorothy & Frank Brooks and Edith Choate kept attendance and registered three new members.

Our Readers Write

"Of all the publications I subscribe to, I always look forward to receiving TEG the most. You are informative without being officious, and have a human side exhibited by few other journals and newsletters. You're really in tune with the members. Keep up the great work." ...Bailey Rogers. Cincinnati, OH

"Suggestion: I would like to see more (some) articles on 1850-1900 Essex County. The Colonial period is fine, but a lot of Essex County was post-1850 immigrants. The Society should offer a little something for everybody."
...Richard J. Wall, Upper Marlboro, MD

(Editor's note: We agree, but use only what contributors send. Perhaps your suggestion will prompt material on later dates.)

"I am at a loss to understand these records found in "New Brunswick Royal Gazette" under Marriages (at Lynnfield Library). '#260: 25 Mar 1800, marr. Middletown, Monmouth NH 5th last - Thomas Tilton, age 70, to Mary Lucar, age 13, dau. of Thomas Tilton's former wife...' '#261: same place, few weeks later, John Lucar, brother of the bride, marr. to his aunt Catherine Clinton, widow, and daughter of Thomas Tilton, above groom.' My Tilton branch were Loyalists who fled to New Brunswick in 1783. This is the only such "marriage" (bigamy?) I have ever encountered. Can anyone help me?"
...Mildred D'Ambrosio, 25 Pleasant St., No. Reading, MA 01864

"I want to let you know how much I enjoy The Essex Genealogist and also how happy I was to see my husband's work on the "Brantry" Needhams included. I'm curious as to the copy being in the Allen County Public Library, Fort Wayne, IN. We do not have relatives there as far as I know. I do have the copy from NEHGS accepting it in 1934, but may be they no longer have it. Bob died in June of 1985. Before he became ill he sent xerox material to members of his family. I have all the correspondence and material he gathered. Bob was living in Arlington at the time he gathered his material, but he and I were married in 1951 and moved to Concord in 1952. He got me interested in history and genealogy. I think the Lynnfield library is great, and I encourage the Concord genealogical group to go there." ...Lucile Needham, Concord, MA

"I would like to start a chapter of the Essex Society here in Ontario, California. I notice there are numerous members in the western states and most of them are unable to attend meetings in Lynnfield. It would build the membership and possibly start other chapters in other parts of the country."
...Howard E. Wescott, Jr., 3031 Fairfield St., Ontario, CA 91761

(I'm afraid the Society's officers have as much (or more) than they can handle now, with 700 members. However, getting together with others in your state who have Essex County roots, might be worth a try. Let us know if you do, and we will publish your results in TEG or the ESOG Newsletter.)

"I believe an error appears in Donald Doliber's article on Rev. Thomas Wells. Mrs. Dorothy Trull was the wife of Luke Wells, not Titus Wells. Titus, b. 15 Mar 1675-6, Amesbury, m. Joanna Rowell, ca 1697-8. Sources: David Hoyt, Old Families of Salisbury..., 348-52; 808-11; and Clarence Almon Torrey, New England Marriages Prior to 1700, 795." ...Bailey Rogers, Cincinati, OH

Miscellaneous Notes

SUFFOLK COUNTY EARLY PROBATE RECORDS (1636-1894) (Files, Record Books and Docket Books) have been transferred from their former location at the Suffolk County Courthouse to the Judicial Archives located in the new Massachusetts State Archives, 220 Morrissey Blvd., Boston, MA 02125. (617) 725-2816.

INDEX TO MASSACHUSETTS VITAL RECORDS TO 1971 is also now at Mass. State Archives. One can find vol. & page number before going to 150 Tremont St.

MASSACHUSETTS VITAL RECORDS OFFICE at 150 Tremont Street has announced new cutback hours due to budget restraints. Mon & Fri 2-4; Tues & Thurs 9-11. No Wed.

THE GEORGE LITTLE FAMILY ASSOCIATION (est. 1989) is planning a 350th Anniversary Celebration in August 1990. George Little settled in Newbury, Mass. in 1640. The farm he established is the oldest farm in the U.S. continuously cultivated by the same family and will be the site of the reunion. For information write to the George Little Family Association, Stone Road, Hebron, IN 46341.

THE ORPHAN TRAIN HERITAGE SOCIETY OF AMERICA, INC., 4912 Trout Farm Road, Springdale, AR 72764 (501) 751-7830, has started a quarterly newsletter called **CROSSROADS**. For the orgainization membership ($25) one will receive the back issues for 1989 and the index to the first nine issues plus all four issued for 1990. (Mary Ellen Johnson, Executive Director, OTHSA)

PROLOGUE is the name of the quarterly of the **NATIONAL ARCHIVES**. For 20 years it has brought the programs and holdings of the Archives to national attention. Starting in September 1989, it brings a new regular feature - "Genealogy Notes. offering practical advice on how to use the rich resources of the National Archives for research in genealogy and local history. The Archives has custody of billions of records that relate to individuals who have had dealings with the federal government. To help you get the most out of your visit, the first column in this new series, featured in the Summer 1989 issue, describes policies and procedures at the National Archives Building in Washington, DC. An introduction to National Archives finding aids will appear in the Fall 1989 issue. Guides, catalogs of select microfilm publications, and descriptive pamphlets useful for genealogical research will all be discussed. Other scheduled topics include genealogical research in the regional archives (Winter 1989), St. Albans manifests for Canadian crossings (Spring 1990), and preservation of family documents (Summer 1990). To order your subscription to **PROLOGUE** send $12 for one year to **PROLOGUE**, National Archives,
NEPS, Dept. 810, Washington, DC 20408.

EARLY MARRIAGES OF STRAFFORD COUNTY, NEW HAMPSHIRE, 1630-1850, a four-volume set compiled by local researcher and avid genealogist Robert S. Canney of Berwick, Maine (ESOG member), was recently presented to the **DOVER PUBLIC LIBRARY**. Noting the fragile state and informational gaps of Dr. John Ham's Dover, NH Marriages, 1623-1823, Canney spent three years expanding 4000 entries to over 12,000 and includes all of Strafford County. Robert Canney is an 11th generation descendant of Thomas Canney who settled at Dover Point in 1630, and admits he "got carried away with the project." Jennie Leathers, Sec. of the NH Soc. of Geneals. typed the manuscript. (Foster's Daily Democrat Dover, NH, 22 November 1989, p. 30).

Queries

> **GUIDELINES FOR SUBMITTING QUERIES**
> Readers may submit free queries. No query to exceed 50 words. No limit on number of queries. Ask specific questions re parentage, birthplace, marriage, children, etc. Use identifying detail such as name, date, or place. *Type* or *print* on 3x5 card. Use abbreviations listed at end of February Query section. Deadlines for queries: Jan 1, Apr 1, July 1, Oct 1. Send queries to: Teg query editor, Lynnfield Public Library, 18 Summer St., Lynnfield, MA 01940

MILLS
Seek info b & par; Jane MILLS b Scotland; d 1750 Hempstead, NH; m 1739 Haverhill.

DOUGLASE
Was James Douglase m 1731 York, ME, fa of James & John settlers in Brooksville, ME or of James in Castine?

JOHNSTON
Need all info for mo James Jr; and for Jane w of James JOHNSTON (1690-1774)

TUTTLE
Who were w & ch Trueworthy TUTTLE bpt 11 May 1766 No Yarmouth ME?

GETCHEL/BLETHEN
Seek all info Miriam BLETHEN, m 6 Dec 1781 Nathaniel GETCHELL. Was she dau of Joseph & Elizabeth BLETHEN?

AVERY (AVERILL)/BARNS
Need dts, par Lydia. Was Solomon AVERY (AVERILL) of York ME hus to Lydia? He m 25 Dec 1772 Hannah BARNS.

ANDERSON
Were Betsey and Joseph ch of Agnes ---- who m 1745 Jacob ANDERSON of Flying Pt (Freeport) ME? Elizabeth C. Wescott, RFD 2 Box 920, Apt 202, Bucksport, ME 04416.

****

CHAMBERLIN/WHEELER
Seek all dts, anc Elizabeth CHAMBERLIN who m 5 May 1673 Charlestown, MA Thomas^2 WHEELER who d 1678, s of Isaac^1 & Frances WHEELER.

JOHNSON/PROCTOR/BUTTERFIELD
Seek dt, anc both William JOHNSON who m Martha PROCTOR; and dau Sally JOHNSON who m 20 Apr 1817 Saugus, MA, Ebenezer BUTTERFIELD; res North Saugus, MA.

BECK/HYDE/DANA
Seek anc & dt for Mary BECK who m 23 Apr 1746 Boston MA or 5 Apr 1746 Attleboro MA, Samuel^4 HYDE, s of Jonathan^3 & Hannah (DANA) HYDE.

FULLER/FARRINGTON/MANSFIELD
Need dt and par for Abigail FULLER who m 8 Dec 1720 at Lynn, MA John^4 FARRINGTON, s of William^3 & Lydia (MANSFIELD) FARRINGTON.

BULLARD (BULLOCK)/DANA
Need all info and anc for Anna BULLARD (BULLOCK) who d 1711; m March 1648 at Cambridge MA, Richard DANA.

MASURY/BROWN/PICKERING
Seek all info and anc for Susanna MASURY who m 2 Apr 1728 John^4 BROWN of Salem, MA, s of James^3 & Elizabeth (PICKERING) BROWN.

WHITMAN/SOUTHWICK/ROSS
Need anc & dt for Mary WHITMAN who m 18 Oct 1727 as w/2 Ebenezer^4 SOUTHWICK, s of Samuel^3 & Mary (ROSS) SOUTHWICK of Salem MA.

FOSTER/FRENCH/CHAMBERLAIN/DYKE
Need anc & dt for Ezperience FOSTER who m/1 Joseph^2 FRENCH, s of John of Cambridge; m/2 bef 1694 Jacob^2 CHAMBERLAIN s of William of Billerica; m/3 aft 1716 Jonathan DYKE. Experience d 1749. Anne Merrill-Goulette, RR 3, Box 120, Dexter, ME 04930.

****

CAMMITT/BODFISH/BATES
Seek par of Peter CAMMITT b 1719 Lynn, MA; mov to Barnstable; m Thankful

BODFISH 1741. Ch: David; Hannah m John BATES.

CAMMITT/HALLOWELL
Seek anc of Thomas CAMMITT who m Margaret HALLOWELL 22 June 1720 at Nantucket, MA; mov to Salisbury, MA. Ch: Paul, b 1722 Casco Bay, ME; Silas, Abraham, Isaac, Mary, Ann, Judith, all b Salisbury.

CAMMITT
Seek info on par of Robard CAMMITT of Arrosic, ME. Warned out of Lynn, MA in 1722. Was he bro of Thomas? June Schoenfeldt, 112 S. Knox, Topeka, KS

****

LINCOLN/HASKINS
Seek anc of Rebecca LINCOLN who m William HASKINS at Taunton, MA.

COBB/NASH
Seek anc of Bethia COBB of Taunton, MA, b early 1700s and Sarah NASH, of Weymouth, MA, b 1669.

FELLOWS/RING
Seek anc of Samuel FELLOWS who m Molley RING 1761 at Hampstead, NH.

GRACIE/FORTUNE/AD(E)SHADE/MCLEOD
Seek anc of GRACIE, FORTUNE, AD(E)SHADE, MCLEOD of Sydney, Ragawas, Wallace, Nova Scotia. Eleanor E. Gracie, 201 Rodes Blvd #36, Melbourne, FL 32934.

****

GOODWIN
Need par of James GOODWIN, tailor, of Hopkinton, Framingham, Reading, MA area. Poss b 1700-1714; m Judeth --- bef 1732. Ch: Lois b 1732, James b 1738. Justin E. Morrill, 5185 Downwest Ride, Columbia, MD 21044.

****

HENRIKSSON (HENDRICKSON, HENRICKSON)
Where in US did they settle: Carl Wilhelm HENRICKSSON b Saterba, Sweden 30 Jan 1847; emigr 3 Oct 1874; Hulda Maria b Saterba 8 MAr 1849; Adolph Herman b Saterba 7 Dec 1852 emigr 29 June 1882/3. Inez Dubuque, 9 Beede Ave., Lynn, MA 01902.

****

NORTON/GUNNISON
Samuel NORTON b 18 Dec 1756 at Greenland, NH; Capt in RevW; mov to Kittery, ME; m there Eunice GUNNISON 19 Aug 1784. Eunice b 4 July 1762 dau of John & Rebecca. Need data/par Samuel, mo of Eunice.

BARNARD/HOLT
John BARNARD, Jr b 16 Apr 1697 Andover, MA; m there Alice HOLT 13 Mar 1740. Need anc of Alice.

SHEARER/ATWOOD
Need anc of Nancy SHEARER b 1818 NY State; m Orsamus ATWOOD b 1810 NY State. They liv Royalton, Pembroke, Lockport, NY.

LUMBERT/ISHAM
Need data on David LUMBERT who m 1750/1 Abigail ISHAM, b 1731/2 at Barnstable, MA, dau of Isaac & Abigail.

ATWOOD/BAKER
Isaac ATWOOD d ca 1811; liv Rensselearville, NY; m ca 1790 Cynthia BAKER, who d 1841, dau of Rev Isaac BAKER. Need anc Isaac ATWOOD & Isaak BAKER.

BOSWORTH/SHATSWELL
Need anc Susanna BOSWORTH who d 1672 at Haverhill, MA; m 1642 Theophilus SHATSWELL in Haverhill. He was b 1617 in England; d 1663 at Haverhill. Edward W. Crutchley, Greystone 16, Rt. 4, Boone, NC 28607.

****

BOYCE/HARWOOD
Was Sarah BOYCE b 1705 at Salem, MA; m Jonathan HARWOOD 18 Aug 1726, dau of Benjamin BOYCE & Susanah ---? If so, need par of Sarah.

ELKINS/GUTCH/HOLGRAVE
Need anc of Thomas ELKINS who m Sarah

GUTCH ca 1673, poss at Salem, MA. Thomas d 1705 at Salem. Sarah bpt 4 June 1654; d aft 1734, dau of Robert GUTCH & Lydia HOLGRAVE. Need anc of Sarah.

SPENCER/BRAINARD
Need anc of Jared (Gerrard) SPENCER who res Cambridge, MA 1634; rem to Lynn; rem to Haddam, CT bef 1660; w Hannah ----. Dau Hannah b Lynn; m Daniel BRAINARD 1633/4 at Haddam.

BURNAP/NEWHALL/BARTRAM
Need anc of Benjamin BURNAP who m 19 June 1700 at Reading, MA, Elizabeth, dau of John NEWHALL & Esther BARTRAM.

POTTER/NEWHALL
Need anc of Elizabeth POTTER dau of Robert & ---; who m Thomas NEWHALL 19 Dec 1652 at Lynn, MA.

BARTRAM/NEWHALL
Need anc of Esther (Estar) BARTRAM, b 3 Apr 1658 at Lynn, MA, dau of William & ----; m John NEWHALL, 18 June 1677 at Lynn. Harwood C. Palmer, Royal Greens, 2075 NE 19th, Gresham, OR 97030.

****

ROBINSON
Did Daniel ROBINSON, b 1740 on the Shoals have siblings?

CLOUGH
Need anc of Marshall H. CLOUGH, Lowell Librarian, whose w was b ca 1850.

GROVER/RICHARDSON
Who was Mr. GROVER who m Mary RICHARDSON b Yarmouth, ME? Dau Jane b 1808. Other Ch? Need anc of Mary.

ATWOOD/CLOUGH/VARNUM
Abigail ATWOOD m 15 May 1785 at Bradford, MA, Daniel CLOUGH. Was he s of Daniel^5 CLOUGH & Abigail VARNUM of Dracut? Printed CLOUGH gen shows his s of Jabez^4.

TAPLEY
Did Samuel & Mary TAPLEY have more ch than printed TAPLEY gen shows? Only Margaret Howard b 1770 listed. Do Samuel & Francis belong? Others? Elizabeth C. Wescott, RFD 2, Box 920, Apt 202, Bucksport, ME 04416.

****

ANDREWS
Seek anc of John ANDREWS b ca 1747; m Deborah ----. Known ch: Jerusha b 1773, Hulda b 1775, Dorcas b 1778, John, Jr b 1783, Stephen b 1785, Elizabeth b 1787. Res Brunswick, ME.

LORD/SWIFT
Seek anc Mary LORD b 1782 NH; m Elnathan SWIFT 6 Apr 1805 at Wayne, ME; d 1870. Ch: Enoch b 1805, Hasadiah b 1807, Mary b 1808, Betsey b 1810, Dean b 1812, Rebecca b 1814, Rufus b 1816, Elnathan b 1818, Sarah b 1822. Res Winthrop & Sidney, ME. Mary A. Wilhelm, 28 Western Ave., Essex, MA 01929.

****

HALE/KEITH/COON
Seek info on Adolphus HALE who m Achsah S. KEITH 16 Apr 1839 at Palmer, MA. Ch: F.D., E.M., Sarah Jane. Achsah m W. H. COON 1847; had 6 ch.

PENNOCK/POOL
Seek par of George Merle PENNOCK b 28 Jan 1828 at PA (Lancaster Co.?); m Elizabeth POOL on 18 July 1850 at Lancaster. Ch: William, Franklin, Charles, Mary, Emma, Anna, George, Alice, Albert. Fam mov to Coffey Co., KS 1880.

MCREYNOLDS/SNODDY
Would like to corr with desc of Hugh MCREYNOLDS, b 1750 at Belfast, N. Ireland, who d 28 Feb 1797 near Watsontown, PA; w Elizabeth SNODDY. Ch: Esther, Andrew, John, Matthew, Robert, Eliza, Isabella, Samuel. Richard L. McReynolds, 1901 Arnold, Topeka, KS 66604.

****

GRAFFAM/WILLIAMS/WATERHOUSE/PURRINGTON/DEERING/DUNN/STEVENS
Need to identify: Sarah GRAFFAM who m John WILLIAMS s of Peter at Gorham ME 1850; Sarah GRAFFAM who m Sargent WATERHOUSE b ca 1700 at Gorham, ME; Elmira GRAFFAM who m Charles PURRINGTON of "Moderation," who d at Cumberland Mills, ME; Samuel GRAFFAM who m Lydia DEERING b Gorham, ME 24 July 1800; Elias GRAFFAM who res Limington, ME & m 9 Sep 1852 Lydia DUNN who res Gorham, ME; Hannah GRAFFAM who m Aug 1836 William H. STEVENS of Windham, ME & settl at Waterville, ME. Merle G. GRAFFAM, 2827 Westbrook Dr., Bldg 3/4 Apt. 513, Ft. Wayne, IN 46805.

****

DAVIS/BARTLETT/BLAISDELL
Would like corr. ca Jonathan DAVIS b 17 Sept 1773, Essex Co., Mass.; m. 15 Apr 1798 Andover, NH, Miram BARTLETT, b 10 Jan 1780 Northwood, NH. Miriam was dau. of Nathan BARTLETT & Molly BLAISDELL from Newbury, Mass. & Northwood NH. Any in. on this DAVIS lineage will be greatly appreciated. Hazel Davis Haselton, P.O. Box 125, Lyndon Center, VT 05850.

****

BADGER
Need anc Rev John BADGER of Old North Church, Boston, Loyalist to Nova Scotia 1778.

HOLMES/PEARL/DURKEE/HANKEY
Need anc of John PEARL & w Elizabeth HOLMES; liv 1650 at Skidby, 1660 at Yorkshire, Eng; mov to Brimfield, MA? Phineas DURKEE (Sept 1730-Nov 1801) m Phebe PEARL; they were Nova Scotia parents to Capt. Pearl DURKEE of ship "Chasseur" in Baltimore, MD, who m Mary HANKEY 1797.

CUNNINGHAM/MORRISSEY
Desire other early data: At Rock of Cashel and Emly, county Tipperary, Ireland were m. Edmund MORRISSEY to Mary CUNNINGHAM in 1723. John MITCHELL married Mary MORRISEY 1708 at Roscommon.

WANTON
Need wife of Rhode Island governor, Joseph WANTON, 1770.

STEVENS/PARKER/BARNARD
Wish to connect Leftenant John STEVENS Jr who m. Hannah BARNARD, Andover, MA to John STEVENS who m April, 1638 to Elizabeth PARKER. They came from Caversham, Oxfordshire, England. Died in Andover.

ATKINS/ABBOTT/BARNARD/STEVENS
Wish to trace Nathan STEVENS (1665-1740) and Elizabeth ABBOTT (29 Jan 1673-23 Apr 1750) Andover, MA; Left. John STEVENS & Hannah BARNARD back to Caversham, Oxford, Eng. John STEVENS m 27 Feb 1597 Alice ATKINS of Caversham, Oxford, Eng.

ATKINS/STEVENS/PEARL
Timothy PEARL m Elizabeth STEVENS, b 14 Oct 1697 Andover, MA. From Nathan STEVENS & Elizabeth ABBOTT (Jan 1673-Apr 1750) connect?

DeLANO/PETERSON/PRINCE/DREW/
Want information on Joshua DeLANO & Hopestill PETERSON (1703-1773). Dau. Lydia DeLANO m. Thomas PRINCE in Kingston, MA. Thankful PRINCE (1750-1840) m. Serg. Job DREW (1744-1833)

HALLAHAN/MORRISEY
Seek "Acadian Recorded News" obit. for Richard MORRISEY, b. 1793; came to Boston 24 Dec 1823, age 30; was a merchant; m. Johanna HALLAHAN, nee KRAMER, by Father Dumphy of St. Malachy Church, St. John's, New Brunswick, Canada. Johanna d 13 June 1826. John MORRISSEY m. Mary HEELEY 25 Nov 1833 at St. Malaki.

STEVENS/ABBOTT/ATKINS
Is there a connection between Elizabeth STEVENS, b 14 Oct 1697 Andover, MA; m. Timothy PEARL and Nathan STEVENS and Elizabeth ABBOTT, b Jan 1673; d April 1750, and John STEVENS who m 27 Feb 1597 Alice ATKINS of Caversham, Oxford, England. Richard Morrissey, 28656 Murrieta Rd., Sun City, CA 92381.

****

ABBREVIATIONS FOR QUERIES

about (circa)	ca	father	fa	parents	par
age	ae	family (-lies)	fam	place	pl
after	aft	female	f	possible	poss
ancestors	anc	first	1st	probated	pro
arrived	arr	first husband	1/h	record(s)	rec
and	&	first wife	1/w	regarding	re
answer	ans	following	fol	relative	rel
baptised	bpt	from	fr	removed	rem
before	bef	genealogy	gen	requested	req
between	bet	grand	g	reside	res
birth date	bdt	grandchild	gch	Reverend	Rev
birthplace	bp	granddaughter	gdau	Revolutionary War	RevW
born	b	grandmother	gmo	Self-addressed,	
brother(s)	bro	grandparents	gpar	stamped envelope	SASE
buried	bur	grandson	gson	second	2nd
cemetery	cem	great	gr	siblings	sib
census	cen	great grand-	gg-	sister	sis
certificate	cer	husband	h	soldier	sol
child(ren)	ch	identity	iden	son(s)	s
Civil War	CivW	information	info	territory	terr
correspondence	corr	in-law	/law	tradition	trad
County	Co	i.e.	mo/law	township	twp
cousin	csn	intention of mar.	int	unknown	unk
date(s)	dt	known	kn	unmarried	unm
daughter	dau	lived (living)	liv	verify	ver
Deacon	Dea	location	loc	vicinity	vic
death date	ddt	male	M	volume	vol
descendant(s)	desc	manuscript	Ms	wife	w
died	d	marriage (-ried)	m	widow(er)	wid
died young	d.y.	marriage date	mdt	Vital Records	VR
divorced	div	married first	m/1	year(s)	yr(s)
emigrant (-grated)	em	mother	mo	World War I	WWI
enlisted	enl	moved	mov	World War II	WWII
estate	est	no date	ndt		
exchange	xch	obituary	obit		

The Essex Genealogist

VOLUME 10, NUMBER 2   MAY 1990

CONTENTS

Letter from the Editor	60
TEG FEATURE ARTICLE: "Research in New Hampshire," by George Freeman Sanborn, Jr.	61
"Jacob Lurvey (1761-1853) - What is Your Ancestry?" by Agnes D. Carr	75
"Two Coincidences Lead to Family Connections," by Joann Coombs	77
RESEARCH IN PROGRESS:	
"John Ramsdell of Lynn and His Descendants," - continued, by Roselyn Listernick	79
"William Ivory of Lynn and His Descendants," - continued by Eleanor Tucker	85
"The Tilton Family" - continued, by Barbara Marden, C.A.L..S.	91
"Descendants of Leonard Harriman of Rowley, Massachusetts" - continued, by Lois Ware Thurston	100
THE AHNENTAFEL:	
John Abbot, GGG Grandfather of Lyman Drewry Coombs	106
Elizabeth Moulton, Grandmother of Clayton R. Adams	107
Anna Ellis (Wise), Mother of Robert E. Wise	108
SOCIETY NEWS	110
QUERIES	112
MOMENTS IN HISTORY	
The Perils of Disease in the 17th Century	Back Cover

THE ESSEX GENEALOGIST is published quarterly: February, May, August, November for $13 per year, by the Essex Society of Genealogists, Lynnfield Public Library, 18 Summer Street, Lynnfield, MA 01940. Second Class Postage paid at Lynnfield, MA 01940. ISSN: 0279-067X USPS: 591-350. POSTMASTER: Send address changes to ESOG, Lynnfield Public Library, 18 Summer Street, Lynnfield, MA 01940.

Letter from the Editor

There is good news to relate. Helen Bosworth, after three months of being "in limbo" (her words), is now "up and at 'em." She is driving her car, answering mail, and has reassumed her duties as Treasurer/Membership Chairman of ESOG. She is busy at work composing her Newsletter for June, and at that time, will give her ESOG friends an account of her trials and tribulations in her own inimitable style.

The Society is very grateful to Earle Hazelwood, who so willingly took over the reigns while Helen was so ill. Also thanks are extended to Shriley Orr and Marion MacDonald for assisting with mail and personal matters while Helen was out of commission and I was in Florida.

We welcome our many new members and subscribers across the country, and hope they will find the Society and its journal to be of assistance to them as they pursue their family roots. We remind them that ESOG offers four services to benefit out-of-state members. One of those services is the publishing of transcriptions of important lectures, the latest of which, "Research in New Hampshire," by George Freeman Sanborn, appears in this issue. The second service we provide out-of-staters is the Query section of TEG, usually five pages at the end of each issue, with an index in the November issue each year. We urge new members to read the introductory block at the beginning of the Query section and also read the queries themselves. This will act as a guideline for those wishing to submit queries to our Query Editor, Shirley Orr, whose address appears on the Masthead of each issue of TEG. To all our "older" members, we urge you to answer queries whenever you can. In this way, TEG will continue to serve its subscribers.

A third service is provided by our Research Committee, which meets bi-weekly at the Lynnfield Library to answer mail from out-of-staters. The Research Committee will search the various indexes, genealogies and histories in "our" collection and will make copies of any material found, for a minimal rate. For details, see page 111.

A fourth service useful to out-of-staters, is the Surname File, which is kept in the old wooden file cabinet in the Genealogy Room. This is a card file of ancestors of members, with the researchers (members) name and address on each card. For instructions on filling out cards, see page 78 of this issue. The usefulness of this file is only as good as the number of members who add their ancestors to the file. Out-of-state members can send their cards in for filing, and requests for print-outs of surnames being researched can be mailed out upon request. There is a small copying fee. Write to the ESOG Research Committee.

Marcia W Lindberg

RULES FOR SUBMITTING ARTICLES FOR TEG

1. Articles should be typed, preferably with double spacing.

2. Articles should be properly documented according to Cite Your Sources, The MLA Handbook or similar research manual, copies of which may be found in local libraries.

3. The Editor reserves the right to accept or reject any article.

4. Neither the Editor nor the Society assumes responsibility for the content of articles published.

TEG Feature Article

NEW HAMPSHIRE RESEARCH

By George Freeman Sanborn, Jr.

(A Lecture before the Essex Society of Genealogists, 17 February 1990)

One of the things that has amazed me over the years since I started taking an interest in my own family, is how different each state in New England is, and even regions within each state. You would think that in a small geographical area such as New England, compared to the other parts of the country, that there would be similarity. Of course, there is some, but there's still a great deal of difference. If you're going to effectively research any of these states, or even an area within one of these states, you really have to become familiar with local peculiarities of the records - migrations of the people, the family names, and the history of the towns and counties that make up each area. People like to lump us all together as New Englanders, but of course, we know that doesn't mean much, as we are all different in our accents, our ethnic cultures, our backgrounds. We are a very varied area, and the records are varied, too.

It helps to take a quick overview of the population of New Hampshire. New Hampshire may contain some surprises for you when you begin to look at the history of the place. The history of migration into New Hampshire is an interesting chapter all of its own. All of the early people came from three or four different areas. There was some migration directly to New Hampshire starting at Hilton's Point in Dover. The first settlement there was 1623, just three years after the Pilgrims settled Plymouth. There had been some brief settlement and people coming to the Isles of Shoals - fishermen, largely from Devonshire and the points around Barnstable and Plymouth in Devonshire. Some of those people stayed and eventually moved over to the mainland. There are no permanent residents now on the Isles of Shoals. But there was an early trickle of people moving over to Portsmouth and Kittery just opposite the Islands. Then there was migration up from the Bay Colony. Now this is still going on. If any of you have tried to travel Route 93 lately, around evening rush hour, you will see that people still are moving north into New Hampshire from the Bay Colony. The largest percentage of our people in New Hampshire came up from the Massachusetts Bay Colony. And then later on, we had the Scotch Irish who came into New England. They were a very interesting group of people, because they kept in touch with other Scotch Irish settlements for generations, preferred to marry their own kind, and moved from one Scotch Irish settlement to another, even if they were hundreds of miles apart. The Scotch Irish have their own peculiarities. You've heard of Londonderry, the big New Hampshire Scotch Irish settlement. They really settled in Derry; the old part of Londonderry where the Scotch Irish people settled is now East Derry. One group came into the state around 1718, and another wave around 1721 to 1723.

The next group of people we need to take into consideration are those that came up largely from Connecticut through Western Massachusetts and into the Cheshire County area of New Hampshire. Cheshire County is very different from the rest of the state, both in the people it received and in its history. In fact, for a long time, even though it was part of the state of New Hampshire, Cheshire County preferred to do business with western Massachusetts and Connecticut, and so many of the early records will actually be found there.

These were the four groups of people that gave us our early population. It mixed for another couple hundred of years until we had a very significant change in our population, starting about 1880 - a little later than Vermont. About 1880, large numbers of French Canadians started coming down, mostly from Quebec. After the turn of the century there were some from New Brunswick as well, so when you're dealing with a French name, you can't just assume that they're from Quebec. So there was an overlay of French Canadians in the population. And then, in certain locations, although they appeared everywhere, Maritimers, the Scottish and the Irish people, descendants of Loyalists and others, started coming down (or "up," as they say) from the Maritimes, into New Hampshire. The result is that nowadays it is said that roughly one-third of the population of New Hampshire is French Canadian. They came largely to the mill towns but there were French Canadians everywhere, even in the small towns. Of course, most people are mixed. There aren't many of us these days who are pure anything. There's a very significant group of French Canadians in the New Hampshire population. Today, we have the phenomena of people moving directly to New Hampshire from California, from the South, the Midwest, etc. They wouldn't have done that 100 years ago. Everyone was moving west or north, but nowadays, the old migration patterns are falling by the wayside.

Getting started in research in New Hampshire is just like getting started anyplace else. You make initial inquiries of your family. You work from the known to the unknown, and you start poking around at local records where the people lived - cemeteries, the Vital Records, newspaper obits, and so on. I want to touch upon today some of the unknown or little known places in New Hampshire where material might turn up - (This will not be an exhaustive list) - some of the things that I've encountered which may pique your interest to see if you can find similar things for the areas in which you're interested.

There are major libraries both in the state and out of the state that we can't fail to pass up. After you've found out information from your family, and looked at family papers and records, probably one of the first things you do is to head for a major library that has a genealogical collection to see if there's been anything written up on the families you're interested in, or the areas in which they lived. The single major repositories are the State Library in Concord, the New Hampshire Historical Society in Concord, the State Archives in Concord, the Vital Records office, also in Concord, the Baker Library at Dartmouth College, the Dover Public Library in Dover, the Exeter Library, at Exeter, the Dimond Library at the University of New Hampshire in Durham, the American Canadian Genealogical Society, which, in spite of its name has until recently concentrated on French Canadian material. They're now trying to expand and broaden that so that there may be information for you there even if you're not particularly interested in French Canadian research. Then there are the LDS libraries in Concord and Nashua.

Then there are the major repositories outside of New Hampshire that you shouldn't fail to investigate. Sometimes the exact information you're looking for could be outside the state. The New England Historic Genealogical Society in Boston has many very unique items pertaining to New Hampshire. The Rhode Island Historical Society in Providence, the Maine Historical Society and the Vermont Historical Society. As you know, most (or all) of the Quaker Records for New England are found on microfilm (and the originals are also there) at the Rhode Island Historical Society, except for the Hicksite splinter group of Quakers whose records are located in New York. All the early ones are at Providence, Rhode Island, and we're trying to get copies of all of them at Hist

Gen in Boston. The reason I mention the Maine Historical and Vermont Historical societies, is that although they would not necessarily specialize in unique items on New Hampshire - I found one day at the Maine Historical Society, in the manuscript collection, one of the early volumes of Proprietor's Records for a New Hampshire town. It was actually in the back of a ledger of other records. Evidently someone carried the book to Maine and not wanting to waste the blank pages, turned it upside down and started at the other end. So you never can tell what's going to turn up outside the state.

There are also small treasure troves in local historical societies and libraries. You don't want to overlook what's right under your nose. People think "Oh, there couldn't be anything in my little one-horse-town library," but there may be something there you wouldn't find anywhere else. I found a trunk of papers a few years ago, for example, at the Laconia Public Library. I had been reading an old book, which, in its bibliography, mentioned that these papers were there. A former library trustee, Erastus Perry Jewell, who was a local wheeler-dealer, had come from the Tamworth Intervale area. After Mr. Jewell's death, his heirs had deposited a trunk full of old papers at the Laconia Public Library. Since this was written back at the turn of the century, I wondered if these papers would still be there. So I went to the library and, of course, no one there knew anything about them. I stood at the counter and kept on talking about it, until someone said, "All right, I'll take a key and go down in the cellar and look, but don't get your hopes up." But they came back and said, "Yes, there's this filthy metal trunk and I don't want to handle it, but I'll get one of the 'boys' who works here to go down and get it." They told me I could take it into the other room and go through the papers. There were all kinds of old letters from the 1790s into the 1800s, and business contracts, but many letters from Jewells back and forth, saying that people had died, and so and so had done this and someone else had moved somewhere - all sorts of information. I found reference to people's deaths there that I wouldn't have found anywhere else. And that can be useful if you're separating people of the same name. Anyway, that is just an example of what might turn up in a small library.

I also would mention if you're interested in the Moultonborough area, which is my home town, that there is a series of account books kept by one of the early settlers, named Bradbury Richardson. They begin in 1771, which is about two and a half years after the very first white man ever set foot in Moultonborough, and they go, without a gap, up into the early 1800s. Mr. Richardson recorded all kinds of local events, and you really get a feel from looking at account books, for what people did in their day-to-day life, the kinds of activities they were involved in and where they went to do business. This can open up all sorts of possibilities to you as you're trying to figure out where the unnamed wife may have come from, and so on. Many of them include actual autographs. Some of the people who kept account books insisted that everyone sign off on their accounts. As you know, autographs can help you to identify people of the same names. Just about everyone had account books in the old days, not just store keepers. With the scarcity of money, neighbors helped each other, and kept track of the time and goods and expense of helping each other. Just about everyone had account books. When you can find family account books they can be fabulous. There are a lot of account books languishing in various places. We have a ton of them at Hist Gen in Boston. You go to the Manuscript Catalog File and look under Account Books, and you'll find them all. The same is true at the Maine Historical Society.

The Folsom Papers are papers kept by Elizabeth Knowles Folsom, who did the Folsom Genealogy back in 1938. She worked on every family in old Exeter, and her papers are at the Exeter Historical Society. You're lucky if you can catch them open. But if you go to the library, whenever the library's open, and tell them you want to use those papers, they will actually throw on a coat and walk down the street to the Historical Society, get them for you, and bring them back so you can use them at the library. You just tell them what family you're interested in, and have an alternate two or three families, in case the papers don't have anything on the first one mentioned. It is well worth the time to look at them. They also have a very good collection of genealogies and local histories.

A few years ago, I thought I would try to track down the early town record books of Kensington, near Hampton Falls. Roland Sawyer was a minister in Kensington in the first half of this century, Mr. Sawyer decided that he would make a typed copy of all existing Town Records he could find, and the Town Clerk, a trusting soul, let Mr. Sawyer take them home. He'd work on some of the books and take them back. Now, you might wish that Mr. Sawyer had been a better typist, or at least had invested in a better typewriter. Sometimes he typed one line on top of another, put the carbon in backwards, and did all kinds of things. The result is a little disappointing sometimes. There were town books still left in his house when he suddenly died. According to the story, they were burned when lightening struck the house sometime after he died. Now, a local wag gave me a different story, saying that the minister's daughter arrived one day with a truck to clean out the house, and tossed the books into the truck and took them off, and no one knows what happened after that. I don't know which story is true, but the books he had at the time of his death disappeared. The books he had taken back to the Town Clerk are kept in a little brick hole-in-the-wall in the town library behind the big wooden entrance door. That's where the old Kensington town books are kept.

The Sandwich Historical Society is one of the best historical societies I know of in the state because of its physical features. They have a fire-proof vault. The people who run the society are also passionate about genealogy, which isn't always the case. They have made indexes, and they've stored things in the vault, and they're open frequently. So, if you're interested in the Sandwich area, don't hesitate to go to the Sandwich Historical Society.

A few years ago, I went to the Amesbury, Mass. Public Library, because I had heard that one of the former members of the library board had taken an interest in some families in Seabrook, New Hampshire, an area I'm interested in. I thought maybe his papers might be at the library. I found a number of things, including the best information I've seen anywhere on Henry Elkins of Hampton, New Hampshire and his descendants. As I recall, there were some original papers from the 1600s with Henry Elkins's signature on them.

Let's go back and take a closer look at some of the resources I mentioned. At the State Library in Concord, you're going to find copies of the state census, the large manuscript ledger books. They now like you to use microfilm because people were tearing the pages and changing entries that didn't agree with their records, and so on. At any rate, the census is there up through 1910. They also have copies on microfilm of the books, not the actual original papers, but the bound record books of Grafton, Strafford and Merrimack County Court Records, including the Court of Common Pleas, the Court of General Sessions of the Peace, and the Supreme Judicial Court. They also have a real treasure for us since restrictions were imposed on birth records since 1901 and marriage, death and divorce records since 1938 in New Hampshire a few years ago. The State Library in Concord has a complete collection of Town and City Reports for the whole state - every community. Usually they begin in the 1880s, but the town of Guilford, for example, has Town Reports from 1846, but they didn't include Vital Records that early. I don't think any included Vital Records until the very early 1880s. The city of Manchester never did record its Vital Records in their city reports because the city is so large. But every other city did, up until the 1920s or 30s. Each city stopped doing that when the volume of records got out of hand. But the small towns, for the most part, still do. Of course, Derry doesn't. But most of the other small towns in the state do. Here you will find most of the same information that would be on the state copy of the Vital Records. Sometimes the detail is lacking, particularly in recent years. They give you an abbreviated form of the Town Records but it would give you a date and for the most part, parents' names, places of birth and so forth. There is, thus, a lot of information you can't get any more readily by going to the Vital Statistics Office.

The State Library also has the Town Records on microfilm for all the towns in the state, and there's a WPA index on cards to the Town Records there. Some people erroneously refer to that index as the Sargent Index, but the Sargent Index is something else altogether. The index to the Town Records is the WPA Index. They failed to index the 11 rolls of microfilm of the Exeter town records, however. If you're looking for Exeter, you won't find a single reference to it in the card index. It was overlooked. We're in the process now of getting a copy of both the index and the various town records at the Hist Gen in Boston. We have recently gotten all the Vital Records up to 1901.

Also at the State Library are newspapers since 1900, only some of which you can get at. They imposed a ridiculous rule in 1971 or 1972 that only newspapers since 1900 *that* *had* *been* *microfilmed* can be seen. Anything that has not been microfilmed can not be seen. But if you go to the Historical Society where they have newspapers before 1900, you can look at any of them. Anyway, in several letters over the years from the librarian at the State Library, I keep being told that the legislature is not appropriating enough money, so that we can carry on with the microfilming. So, there the newspapers sit. I did talk my way last summer into looking at the Pittsfield newspapers - the Suncook Valley Times - for the 1910s and 1920s, but it took a while. The librarian insisted on standing there and turning the pages herself and she proceeded to tear two or three of them, which I wouldn't have done, I can assure you. It's quite a hassle to get to see the unmicrofilmed post-1900. The pre-1900 newspapers are at the Historical Society just across the street.

At the New Hampshire Historical Society, you will find reference works on local history. The Historical Society is really the best library in the state to go to. They have the best historical and genealogical collection of published material, typescripts, some manuscript material as well, which they're now getting a handle on for the first time. Many of us have been grappling with manuscript material for years, and at Hist Gen, we don't have ours under control yet, either, but we're working on it. And the New Hampshire Historical Society is doing the same thing. They also have seven boxes of militia records many church records, original books as well as copies of them (the copies are usually indexed). There are microfilms of town records, duplicates of the films that are at the State Library, but they don't have the card index. Since they're open at slightly different hours, you can use the card index at the State

Library, then go over and use the films at the Historical Society on Saturdays when they're open from 12 to 5. They also have a series of Revolutionary War Pension Abstracts, covering any soldier that served from New Hampshire, regardless of where they ended up, and applied for a pension - abstracts made of pension cases from original records in Washington. Of course, there are microfilm of <u>all</u> the Revolutionary War pensions and military records now in Waltham, and we have microfilm copies at Hist Gen of these New Hampshire pension abstracts. So there are many places you can access this information. They also have some of the original proprietors' records, which in New Hampshire tend not to be very informative. Proprietors' records in Massachusetts are much more interesting to look at than those in New Hampshire, but nevertheless, it may give you an earlier time that your family was in a particular town than you thought, and so on.

They also have a microfilm of the New Hampshire Province Deeds with the index, and copies of many family Bibles. Many times people just took out the sheets from Bibles and sent them in. In other cases there are typed copies, and, as I mentioned, typescripts of church records and cemetery records, some of Town Records, and these are usually indexed. They have some of the famous Weare Papers. Judge Nathaniel Weare, his son, Nathaniel, his grandson, Nathaniel, and great-grandson Mesach Weare of Hampton Falls, were all judges and magistrates. They kept copies of all the papers they drew up, notary public papers, minor court records, and the like, for local residents on both sides of the border. These papers, for the most part, are all in Concord. There are some at the Massachusetts Historical Society, and I'm about to get a copy of that microfilm for Hist Gen. But these others are at Concord. Some were at the Historical Society and some at the State Archives. There's a new index that the State Archivist has made to those in his possession. We have a microfilm copy of them at Hist Gen. I've looked at papers referring to the same cases that appear also in the county court records, and there is usually additional information in the Weare Papers. So it's worthwhile looking at both.

There's a large manuscript collection at the New Hampshire Historical Society. Some selected items are on the open shelves. You'll find that at Hist Gen also. We're trying to get these all back in the manuscript collection as we find them. They have the Charles H. Batchelder papers, reflecting many years of work on all the descendants of Rev. Stephen Batchelder of Hampton. Mr. Batchelder's papers, in 23 boxes, are in the basement of the New Hampshire Historical Society. Also, the Harry Dana French papers concerning the descendants of Edward French of Salisbury, Mass. I knew Mr. French since about 1960. He had been collecting his material for years on Frenches and other families that married into the Frenches, particularly in his own line, around Loudon, Canterbury and so forth. There are extensive write-ups on those other families as well. These far surpass the French Papers at the Amesbury Public Library. After Harry died, I looked up his elderly sister with whom he had lived. The papers were still there in her house, all over the place in boxes. I tried and tried to get her to give the material to the Historical Society, but she was real suspicious of that, so finally, I sicked some other people onto her, and eventually we prevailed. So all the papers now are down there at the Historical Society. But somehow or other, they only transferred the stuff he had <u>compiled</u>. There were several boxes of correspondence, including letters I had myself sent to him. Those evidently got lost along the way. They may have gotten lost forever. They probably would have added some biographical material if nothing else.

Also at the New Hampshire Historical Society are Plumer's Deaths. William Plumer of Epping, first Governor of New Hampshire, kept a record of deaths from the late 1700s into the 1800s. He moralizes a great deal, and goes on and on about who was lazy, who abused his wife, etc. You'll find a lot of information about these people in addition to just the dates of their deaths. You have to be careful of the early period which was really before his time, as he was reconstructing the dates of people's deaths. He tried to reconstruct several years before he actually started keeping the records, so the dates may be off slightly. But his original records are there, as well as a typed version with an index. Epping is a terrible place to research because of poor records, but these death records may help.

Now the Baker Library at Dartmouth may be a place that you've overlooked if you're interested in the Connecticut Valley. The Dr. Gilman D. Frost Collection is a card file of early Hanover, New Hampshire families from the town's founding to the early 1900s. It's now on 15 roles of microfilm. The papers of Vernon Hood of Plainfield, New Hampshire, files on the families of Plainfield and Cornish, and the Dartmouth Cemetery Records, compiled by Reverend Arthur Chivers, known as the Chivers Collection, cover all the cemeteries in that area. There are also four boxes of material known as the Kenerson-Miles Collection, which are the papers of the late Mrs. Byrd E. Miles of Hartland, Vermont, who was endeavoring to compile a genealogy of the descendants of John Keniston of Greenland, New Hampshire. His descendants loved to live in small towns where there are no records. Mrs. Miles proceded to botch the business up even worse than it already was. So, if you're going to use her papers, which you should for clues, be real careful, because her stuff is full of wild things. She typed up some of her material - we have a copy in Boston - there's a copy in Concord, also, but use it at your own risk.

There are also letters, diaries, journals, personal things at the Baker Library. You have to go to Special Collections, which is one of those places under lock and key, but if you go there during normal business hours, you can view their material. It is helpful to call ahead and make an appointment. They also have a manuscript catalog there - arranged by author and subject, and a calendar arranged by date, a sort of accessions list of what they have.

The Dover Library in Dover has an excellent collection of printed material, Dover newspapers on microfilm, and a real treasure, known as the Place Diaries. Elder Enoch Hayes Place, one of the early Free-will Baptist ministers, lived most of his life at Crown Point in Strafford. He labored there, in Barrington and at Strafford Bow Lake, and indeed in that whole area where the records are terrible. He kept a collection of 151 diaries. I've read them all with the exception of two that are now missing, number six and number 82. He went into great detail about funerals and who died, and how they were related, and how the deceased person may have been married two or three times, and who the other spouses were, and how many children they had, where they all lived, and so forth. Now he kept as well a list of marriages which he had performed, and a list of deaths and funerals in Strafford. I'm talking here about the diaries. We have them at the Hist Gen in Boston on five rolls of film. It takes a while to go through them, and of course they are hand written. But it's worth the effort if you find what you're looking for - especially in that area where there's not much else in the way of public records.

The Dimond Library at the University of New Hampshire, particularly the Special Collections Department (another of those places where you can hardly ever catch them home) is a good place to go. They have something called the Lamson Papers - a nice collection of genealogies and local histories and local papers. They have the Piscataqua Pioneers Collection - all the papers people filed when they joined the Piscataqua Pioneers society, reciting their ancestry. They have the Durham Historic Association's collection, including any original Town Papers that may have turned up, in folders, arranged chronologically year by year. They begin in 1791, which is a little disappointing. But nevertheless, you'll find some signatures, etc. there that may be of interest. And they have something many of us may not have looked at, but you should sometime, the New Hampshire Reports - not the Town Reports I was talking about before. These are the published judgements of the State Supreme Court. Now, you'd be surprised how many of your ancestors will turn up in the State Supreme Court, doing one thing or another. As you know, back before lawyer's fees got as high as they are now, old people were very litigious, suing each other, their brothers, sisters, next-door neighbors, etc. for small amounts of money. If they had had to pay a lawyer at the same rate we do today, they wouldn't have bothered. Many of these things got to the Supreme Court, particularly when it was one town squabbling with another town over who was to support a pauper.

The American Canadian Genealogical Society in Manchester, New Hampshire has an unsurpassed collection of Catholic Church records, largely French parishes - but that doesn't mean that other Catholics don't show up there too. These cover all of New England and Quebec, and parts of upstate New York and so on. We have lots of those records now in Boston at the Hist Gen. We're trying to complete our collection. They also have a nice collection of books - anything relating to Canadian research. It does have a strong French Canadian and Acadian emphasis, but they wish to broaden their collection to include all Canadians from all ethnic backgrounds..

In New Hampshire, when you say Canadian, what you really are saying is French Canadian. If they were from the Atlantic Provinces, where many people also came from, they get referred to as "Nova Scotian" - whether they were from Nova Scotia or not!

The State Archives is a place you may not have gone to. They were closed for reconstruction, and they now have reopened. There are records there you don't find anywhere else. They are located on the west side of Concord, off a street called South Fruit Street, near the Memorial High School. It's on the grounds of the State Hospital in a small building. You go up Pleasant Street from Main Street. Do keep your car locked when you're there, because it has been known that State Hospital patients may get into people's cars. But it's perfectly safe. The State Archives has the old Province Records. Now, New Hampshire had no counties until 1771. Before that, the records are referred to as Province Records - Province Deeds, Province Probate Records, Province Court Records. They have all the original Old Province Records. The Province Deeds with the Sargent Index - the index to the deeds, which is also an index to the probate records. They also have the probate files with the original documents before 1771. These have recently been microfiched and we have a set of those in Boston now at the library, so if you would like to see the original probate records with people's signatures, you can come into Boston. Of course, the Province Probate Records were published in Volumes 31 - 39 of the New Hampshire State Papers series - wills are reproduced in extenso (every word) - supporting papers and inventories are just summarized. You will notice, if you're dealing with Cheshire County in southwestern New Hampshire, that the deeds which should be there are not. I am told that many of the early deeds for the Keene, Swanzey, Fitzwilliam, Walpole, Chesterfield area, were recorded in Springfield, Mass., because the people felt more akin to western Massachusetts, many of them having lived there before they went into southwestern New Hampshire. They also thought it was rather nervy that they would have to travel east all the way over to Portsmouth and later Exeter to record a deed. New Hampshire is still a north-south state (look at all the highways).

The Province Court Records have a separate index made by Mr. Sargent, a retired judge who liked to make indexes. This is also at the State Archives. The early Dover/Portsmouth Quarterly Court Records are published in Volume 40 of the New Hampshire State Papers. You're all familiar with the Essex County Quarterly Court Records. That's only three of the Old Norfolk County Quarterly Courts. The records of the fourth Quarterly Court - Dover/Postmouth - such as exist - are published in Volume 40 of the New Hampshire State Papers. So if you take that and the nine volumes of Essex Quarterly Courts, you've got the whole line of existing records of the Old Norfolk County court records. The Sargent Court Records index also includes the "Warnings Out." In that period of time up to the beginning of the second half of the 1700s, people were "warned out" of town if it looked as though they were going to become town charges (the old welfare system - get them out and back to wherever they came from).

The Province Probate Records, which I mentioned, with an index by Sargent, being the original copies of those in the State Papers, and the Rockingham County Deeds from 1771 are now there up to Volume 300, with the indexes as well. And the Court Records for Rockingham County, Hillsborough County and Strafford County are there. The Strafford County Court Records, we had once been told, were lost (another of those fire stories), and all of a sudden, about three years ago, the State Archivist got a phone call from somebody poking around in the basement of the new court house in Dover, saying that there were a number of crates of old papers there. He was asked to come and take a look at them. Strafford County Records go back to 1773. Strafford was set up in 1771 like the other original counties, but it didn't get its act together and start record keeping until 1773. There's a two-year gap. During that two-year gap, records were filed in Rockingham County, because they kept on recording deeds and probates and court records in Rockingham County down to the last second, until the courthouse got going in 1773 in Strafford County. Many problems are solved in that two-year period by going to Rockingham County records.

There's a guide to the Archives Collection. There's one on the desk at the Archives if you go there - so you have some idea of what they've got and what the collection numbers are, so you know what to ask for. Legislative petitions - many are in the State Papers - is a source we don't use very often - not all are in the State Papers, even for the period covered, but many of them are. They are in a series of about 100 boxes. There are all kinds of things there. The legislature changed names, decreed divorces in some cases, and oversaw granting pardons to people in prison, and if you wanted to build a bridge or divide your town up into more parishes (because it was hard on people to get to church) so you could establish another parish and get a minister for your area of town - you fill find records in the Legislative Petitions. We're going to be getting a complete set at Hist Gen on microfiche for the entire period up to 1785. Those have been microfiched by the State Archives. After that, you'll need to consult the originals.

Some of the other kinds of Court Records may be transferred to the State Archives as well. When they transferred the Hillsborough County records a couple of years ago - these were at the Court House in Nashua, which is rather small - they loaded them all on a truck and they started up Route 93. Somebody didn't fasten the back door of the truck too well and two crates of Court Records bounced out onto Route 93, and broke open and it was a windy day and the papers started blowing down into the woods near the highway. Luckily, whoever was driving the truck saw this before he got too far and he jammed on the brakes and they all got out and went running down and they think they found all the papers in the woods. The papers are now at the Archives in Concord, although they haven't had a chance to do anything with them yet, so they're not arranged yet for people to see. However, if you go in there and say you want to see the Court Records for the Court of Common Pleas for Hillsborough County from 1780 to 1785, they probably can find them. They have the boxes labeled somehow.

They also have, as I said, the Strafford Court Records, and I'm trying to persuade them to go after the Cheshire County Records. A few years ago, the previous Archivist, went over to Keene one day and went down to the basement of the court house. It was damp, as some of the old basements can be, rather poorly lit - and he noticed he was walking on a lot of old papers. He picked up some of the papers to look at them, and they were the old Cheshire County Court Records. They had been in boxes but some of the boxes had tipped over, and the papers had fallen on the floor. The area wasn't used much. Most of the current papers were somewhere else. Anyway, he raised a bit of a fuss, and they managed to get the papers all scooped up off the floor and put back in the boxes. But they're still in Keene, and I think they belong in Concord in the State Archives. Eventually, what they do plan is to have most of the early records in Concord at the State Archives. New Hampshire, as you know, does not have a broad-based income tax, and as a result, the critics say, we don't have some of the available funding that we might have for such projects as enlarging the Archives and bringing things like this to the Archives and sorting and arranging them, or for microfilming the old newspapers at the State Library. But we do intend to get the old records centralized sooner or later.

There is an index now at the State Archives - it used to be in the basement of the Historical Society, but not many people knew about it - to all name-changes and all adoptions in the State of New Hampshire from the beginning up to the 1940s. It's available and its open to use. It doesn't give all the details, but it does tell briefly what happened, and gives the date and the term of court. You still would have to run the gauntlet at the county court if you wanted to see the original.

State Vital Records are sketchy. In 1905, when they decided to collect vital records, they asked the Town Clerks to copy off whatever they could find in the old books and send them in on cards. Well, as you know from looking at old Town Books, there's a record here and a record there, and the Town Clerks may have missed some of those, I know that they did - and not just the early ones. I know of several in the late 1800s. These have been curiously arranged in a crude type of soundex system; that is to say, the first and third letter of the surname. Now, New Hampshire isn't the only place that devised this weird system. When I was at Ft. Lauderdale, I decided to go to the deeds office (rather than the beach) and while I was there, I noticed all the land records in Broward County, where Ft. Lauderdale is, were all recorded by the first and third letters. And I thought that we were the only strange people. It's an awkward system, but once you're onto it, it works. We now have microfilm copies up to 1901 - births marriages, deaths, divorces, and bride's index - at New England Hist Gen. In fact, the divorce records go up to 1937, but they only begin in the 1880s. There are divorces before that, but they're in the County Court Records. None were carded and kept by the Registrar of Vital Records.

Unlike Massachusetts, where two-thirds or so of the towns have published VRs, only a few towns in New Hampshire have published VRs, such as Keene (one of the earliest, done in 1905), Hampton Falls, So. Hampton and Danville (which used to be called Hawke). Nancy Dodge is now doing one for Colebrook, and a few of the towns way up in the North Country - the old Indian Stream Republic. Londonderry records were published as Volume VII in the Manchester Historical Association Collection. There are a few others - particularly typescripts which you'll find at the New Hampshire Historical Society. Usually these are just the town (civil) records. My wife and I are involved in compiling the VRs for the town of Hampton, up to the end of 1900, which will be published by the Hist Gen. Volume 1 is due out late this summer, volume 2 will be out next year. Each volume is about 600 pages. We're including VRs from any source whatsoever, cemetery, church records, private records, the old Norfolk County Court records that contain VRs, town VRs, family Bibles, anything we can lay our hands on, will be in those 2 volumes. We are purposely omitting newspaper records, however. I'm hoping that the format, the procedure and the modus operandi of doing the Hampton VRs will be the start of a state-wide town VR publication program that maybe the Hist Gen will carry on. I'm hoping this will set the tone and get the ball rolling, so we can do this for all the towns in the state. I'm not going to live to see it done - it'll be a long while, but I'm probably going to be rash enough to say that I'll work on some more towns. It's quite a struggle, especially with two small children. We've had several delays. We thought it was going to be done two years ago.

I did mention other repositories outside the state. First of all, of course, the New England Hist. Gen. Soc. in Boston. Particularly our manuscript material; there are many unique items. Some of the things we have are "Master Tate's Diary" - Master Tate was a schoolmaster in what is now Rollinsford, near Somersworth and Dover. He kept a record of vital events and other things such as earthquakes, etc. for the Rollinsford, Somersworth, Berwick, Maine area on both sides of the state line there. He also decided that he would go around from family to family and record family groups (this must have raised a few eyebrows) with births of all the children and so on. I can just imagine the reception he got from some homesteads! We have the original in Boston. It's a beautiful thing. It was published in *The Register* in volumes 73 and 74. There's a criptic footnote in *The Register* saying the person who abstracted these from the original - he did it verbatim - had, in the interest of good taste, left out certain things. Well, of course, I couldn't wait to compare the two and see what it was he left out. I compared the published version word for word with the original, and it's exactly the same, so I don't know what he was talking about.

We also have Seaborn Cotton's waistbook. He was one of the early ministers in Hampton, and kept a diary in which he recorded the baptisms, marriages and other things he officiated at. As you know, Hampton families kept marrying each other. In many cases, you will need something like Seaborn Cotton's waistbook to straighten out people of the same name. I can think of a couple of baptisms and marriages where he says "John so and so, son of so and so, married Mary so and so, daughter of so and so," thus there can't be any mistaking who got married. He does this frequently and it's very helpful.

We also have the Samuel Burnham Shackford Collection. S.B. Shackford was an important New Hampshire genealogist many years ago who worked on a number of families in the Strafford County/Piscataqua area, and we have all his papers. They're beautifully done, particularly his typed genealogy of the Shackford family and all their descendants. It's the only genealogy on the Shackford familiy. Then he went back and annotated his typed copies as he found more information or got a letter from somebody giving more dates and so on. It really should be published. It could be published in the form it is in right now. We have beautiful manuscript collections on the Webster families, the descendants of John Webster of Ipswich, many of whom went to New Hampshire. And the descendants of Thomas Webster of Hampton and to a certain extent, the descendants of James Webster, a Scottish man who came into Boston. His descendants got to New Hampshire, and lived in the same towns as the descendants of the other two Websters, and, of course, that adds to the excitement. There are beautiful manuscripts of these families at the Hist Gen and I'm about to propose to the Publications Committee that I edit one of those for publication. I haven't learned, you see. I keep getting into these things. It's too bad to let it sit there almost ready to be published, and collect dust. There are many of these beautiful family manuscripts there. We also have the Katharine Hayes Richmond papers. She is the lady who did the beautiful two-volume genealogy on the descendants of John Hayes of Dover. I think it's the nicest genealogy that ever came out of New Hampshire of a New Hampshire family. She collected material in a most difficult area for many years. We have all of her papers, her annotated copies of the book with additional material, corrections and changes, as well as many original records she had dug up over the years. And it's clear from looking at the volume of material that Mrs. Richmond went from door to door in Madbury, New Hampshire, which is a small pie-shaped place down near the Great Bay, near Dover, Durham and Newington. It's one of the most difficult areas in New Hampshire to do any kind of research. There are very, very few early records. Many of the records that exist were published in *The Register* some time ago. A lot of early families settled there from Oyster River (Durham) and Dover. Mrs. Richmond went around asking people what they had in their attics. She had a huge collection of account books, mentioning many different families, and we have them all at Hist Gen. It would take a while to go through them. I've looked at some of them. They're wonderful things. They don't go back to Adam and Eve, but a lot of them to the late 1700s - a very difficult period to work in.

There are many other collections of genealogists' notes and papers, for example, the Holman Collection, compiled by Winifred Lovering Holman Dodge. We have all her working papers on various families. The Cram Papers, by Elmer H. Cram, are a genealogy of the descendants of "good old John Cram." This collection has recently been indexed by a wonderful volunteer at Hist Gen, Mrs. Ardis King. Copies have been made, and the index has been bound, so now you can find things quickly in that collection at last. And the collection of Buzzell family papers, relating to the descendants of John Buss/Buzzy of Dover, as well as those of Isaac Buswell of Salisbury and other variant names, is presently being indexed by Mrs. King. She's almost finished. There's also a collection of material relating to Enfield, New Hampshire families at Hist Gen, and other collections too numerous to mention.

We have a bit of an emphasis on New Hampshire these days at the Hist Gen because Mrs. Ethel Farrington Smith, a former Trustee, and a native of Manchester, New Hampshire, gave us a large financial contribution a few years ago with the idea it would be used for collection development and publication projects relating to New Hampshire. Of course, I was pleased with that. We'd like this for every state. So we are doing what we can in acquiring material for New Hampshire.

There's a lot of information on New Hampshire in the various volumes of The Register. We're now in our 144th year of publication. If you spend some time going through The Register, particularly back around volumes 70 through 90, you'll find a lot of material on New Hampshire families. And Torrey's Marriage Index will give you some clues - if you use the original one at Hist Gen that has the references, not the published volume without the references to material in printed sources and in some of the manuscript collections on New Hampshire.

So I'll summarize all this by saying: Where might we look for some of the records? Cheshire County records and deeds might be in Springfield. Belknap County, founded in 1841, has a typed WPA copy of Strafford County deeds referring to land that is now in Belknap County, so you needn't drive back and forth between Laconia and Dover if you're doing a title search. Early records of the Hampton Quarterly Court were published in the nine volumes of the Records and Files of the Quarterly Courts of Essex County, but the records of the Dover/Portsmouth Quarterly Court are in volume 40 of the New Hampshire State Papers. Old Norfolk County deeds (4 volumes) in Salem at the Essex County Court House, have many New Hampshire deeds. And so do the Ipswich Deeds, surprisingly enough, at the same court house. And many of the early Essex County, Mass. Deeds and probate records have New Hampshire material in them, for some reason. A lot of estates were filed in Essex County. Those were pulled out and were put into the probate records, published in the State Papers series that I mentioned. The Essex Quarterly Court Records now at The Essex Institute should also be checked for the odd court case that would refer to New Hampshire people. Many deeds and probates relating to Strafford County from the confusing 1771-1773 period were recorded in Rockingham County, because, as I mentioned, in 1771, the five original counties were set up and there was some delay in getting the court house in Dover going. Sullivan County's Deeds burned. Sullivan County broke off from Cheshire County in 1827, and their early deeds were partially burned. People grabbed them and threw them out the windows, and the portions that are left are bound up in a series called "The Burned Deeds." They're separate from the regular series of deeds.

I've mentioned to you some of my favorite sources. Is anyone interested in Pittsfield? You might be interested in Jonathan Perkins's book, covering the period of 1762 to 1844 at the New Hampshire Historical Society. He came from Hampton Falls and settled in Pittsfield, and kept a valuable record of deaths that you won't find anywhere else. The Lane family of Stratham kept volumes of vital records, among other things, and the papers are now all at the New Hampshire Historical Society, which is in the process of readying them for publication, edited somewhat.

The wife of Samuel Locke (that's how she'll always be known to us, poor soul; we don't know what her name was) lived in Seabrook, and she kept a manuscript record of all the deaths in Seabrook 1807-1828, and she also decided to keep, in her spare time, a list of all the removals from Seabrook, for whatever reason, for about the same time, saying who they were and where they had gone. She didn't just record the deaths, she recorded the manner of their deaths, and often who their father was and where the person died. When we find a death record, we assume the person died there, but not necessarily so. He or she could have died somewhere else, even though the death got recorded in a particular town. Anyway, Mrs. Locke kept these records for Seabrook, which is a tough place to do research, not just because of the traffic jam on Route 1, but because the records are poor for the early period.

One of my contacts in Long Island, NY, a rare book and manuscripts dealer, turned up, a few years ago, a large volume of old Seabrook records in upstate NY somewhere, and he approached the town selectmen to see if they'd like to buy it. Obviously he's not going to give it to them. He's in business. They said, "No!" So he approached the Historical Society, which is a little more enlightened, and they said, "Yes." So they scraped up the money, and bought the volume of early records, and I'm anxious to get over there and see what they are.

Rev. Jeremiah Fogg kept records for the Kensington area, and Rev. Sawyer, with his faulty typewriter, tried to type them up. The original Fogg records are momentarily missing - there's a copy of them at the New Hampshire Historical Society.

How many of us have ancestors who were carried off to Canada, as captives, during the French and Indian Wars? If you do, you'll be interested in Nehemiah Howe's Captivity. Nehemiah Howe was a farmer on the Great Meadows in Westmoreland, New Hampshire. He was "captivated," as they used to say, and taken off to Canada for about two years and kept in the jail at Quebec City, where he died. Prisons were not as spiffy as they are now, and people often died in them. While he was there, for something to do (he was an educated man), he kept a record of everybody brought to the prison in Quebec from anywhere in New England, or New York, or Pennsylvania, or anywhere - who they were, their ages, when they died, and if he knew anything about their family, he put that in also. There's also a similar journal called "Pote's Journal." Pote was "captivated" as well from the Falmouth-Portland, Maine area, and it's interesting reading because he was there at the same time Nehemiah Howe was. One should compare what they say. Fabulous reading! In fact, there's a whole published list of printed captivities, and three wonderfully complete reference works on the captives. If you can get your hands on any of those for that period, you should look at them. We have most of them at Hist Gen in Boston.

So, as you can see, in New Hampshire, the records are scattered. You need to search high and low, and inside and outside the state. Don't leave a stone unturned, and never give up!

###

George Freeman Sanborn Jr. was born in Laconia, NH 18 Jan 1944, but considers Moultonborough, NH his "home town." He is married to the former Melinde Laura Lutz, herself a well-known New England Genealogist, and with their two children, live in Derry, NH. George has an A.B. in Romance Languages and Literature from Boston University, an A.M. in Portuguese from the U. of Illinois, an M. Ed. in Counseling from U. of NH. He is Director of Library Operations at New England Historic Genealogical Society in Boston. George is a recognized genealogist, and author of several articles in The Register, The American Genealogist, etc. He is preparing genealogies of the Caswell, Dow, Avery and Adams (Prince Edward Island) families and is conducting English research on the Dearborn, Chadbourne and Mudgett families.

JACOB LURVEY (1761-1853) - WHAT IS YOUR ANCESTRY?

By Agnes D. Carr

Jacob Lurvey, immigrant settler at Mount Desert Island, Maine, is quoted as being born 14 October 1761 at Gloucester, Mass., son of Samuel and Mary (Graham) Lurvey[1]. Samuel Lurvey is reputed to be the son of Jacob and Sarah (Bennett) Lurvey of Gloucester, Mass.[2] The story continues that Jacob's father, Samuel, died when Jacob was very young, and his mother, finding herself in desperate circumstances, "bound out" her young son at the age of six years to Enoch Boynton, a farmer of Newburyport, Mass. Sources also cite that Jacob's mother, Mary, married secondly, William Nathaniel Hadlock, and in her later years she married "old" Mr. Bunker of Mt. Desert Island, Maine and came to Maine to live[3].

Jacob enlisted in Washington's Army at age 14 and served 13 1/2 months, receiving an honorable discharge the last of February 1777 and returning to Mass. with Capt. Nathaniel Wade's company as a free man. By enlisting in the Army, the apprenticeship, that otherwise would have lasted until he was 21 years of age, was cancelled and he was "his own man" at a little past 16 years of age.

After his military enlistment, Jacob shipped out on fishing vessels and cargo trading trips for several seasons.[4] On 26 February 1782 Jacob Lurvey married Hannah Boynton, daughter of his former employer. Jacob had been on the coast of Maine on fishing trips and in 1789 he purchased some land at Southwest harbor. In the spring of 1791 he sailed to Mt. Desert where he built a log house on his land and in November 1791 he brought all his household goods and family to Maine which was to be their home forever more.

This writer could go on at length about the virtue, honesty and bravery of this family who decided to forsake what luxuries they had in Massachusetts to scratch out their livelihood from the wilderness of Maine, but this is a search and plea for answers to Jacob's ancestry. This man helped settle Southwest Harbor, and all his descendants are extremely proud. This article is an attempt to resolve the issue of his parentage from what has been reported in articles to what can be found in vital records.

1. I can NOT find any Jacob Lurvey listed for 24 October 1761 as being born in Gloucester, Mass. to Samuel and Mary Lurvey or to any Lurvey, neither can I find any children listed in Gloucester, Mass. vital records as children of a Samuel and Mary Lurvey.

2. Jacob and Sarah (Bennett) Lurvey DID have a son, Samuel, listed as follows in the Gloucester VRs: LOUVE, Samuel, s. Jacob and Sarah b. 14 June 1733; however under deaths is listed: LOUVY, Samuel, s. Jacob and Sarah d 2 July 1733 which would make this Samuel only a little over two weeks of age at his death. This is the only Samuel Lurvey I can find listed as dying in the Gloucester VRs. Neither can I find any marriage for Samuel Lurvey and Mary Graham in the Gloucester VRs nor can I find any Samuel Lurvey at all who married in Gloucester.

Armed with these disappointments I decided to pursue the Graham family through VRs and histories. On searching for Graham I also found that the name was very often Grimes and there appears to be very few by that name in

Gloucester. There was listed a family of Andrew and Mary Graham/Grimes and they did have a daughter named Mary, b. 12 Oct 1731; m. Feb 1752 David Elwell. I could find nothing further on the David Elwell/Mary Graham union so I proceeded to try to get some clues from the Hadlock family.

Here was where I first found what seemed to be an answer if all the written articles were, in fact, accurate to a degree. Not finding any marriage listed for a Mary Lurvey and William Nathaniel Hadlock, I searched the male name only and it does appear from various sources that William Nathaniel Hadlock was most often listed only as Nathaniel Hadlock. I did find a Nathaniel Hadlock and Mary MARSHALL of Ipswich m. at Ipswich 13 Dec 1750 who appears to be the right Hadlock but then I noticed a Nathaniel Hadlock and Hannah RAL/RALL m 6 Dec 1764 at Gloucester. I then remembered that I had seen where Mary Graham's sister, Hannah, had m. a Mangel Rall, listed as a sojourner, and I returned to the Graham/Grimes family. Hannah Graham/Grimes m. Mangel Rall (int.) 12 Feb 1757 and there is listed one child, Hannah Ralls, d. Mangell bpt. 6 Nov 1757. I cannot find any death listed for Mangell or any other children born to Mangell and Hannah in Gloucester. However, Hannah Rall and Nathaniel Hadlock m 6 Dec 1764 at Gloucester and there is listed three daughters, Lucy, Mary and Hannah, born to them, the same three daughters that have been cited to be half-sisters to Jacob Lurvey. I find no death record for Nathaniel Hadlock.

3. In desperation I checked the Hadlock/Bunker marriages to see if a Mary m some Bunker from Mt. Desert Island and what I found was Hannah Hadlock m John Bunker of Mt. Desert, Lincoln County, Maine on 7 August 1785.

4. In an article entitled "The Venturesome Youth of Jacob Lurvey," by the Pemaquid Chapter, Maine, DAR, it is cited that during one of the cargo trading trips that Jacob had shipped on, the crew had met with a storm and had been feared to be all dead but upon his return he went to the home of William Nathaniel Hadlock, his stepfather. This trading trip had to occur between 1777, the date of Jacob's discharge from the military, and 1782 when Jacob Lurvey m. Hannah Boynton. Hannah Graham/Rall m. Nathaniel Hadlock in 1764 and children were listed as being born and baptized in 1770, 1772 and 1775 and therefore one has to assume that the reference is to Nathaniel Hadlock and Hannah Graham/Rall.References to written articles have been from the "Venturesome Youth of Jacob Lurvey," from Hadlock Family, Cranberry Island-William Otis Sawtelle; The Gilley Family of Mt. Desert-William Otis Sawtelle who cites in this reference "Hence, Jacob Lurvey may be recorded as the son of Samuel Luvey. It is well known that his mother was Mary Graham;" Lurvey Family, Cranberry Island Families-William Otis Sawtelle; Carroll Genealogy-Nell Thornton and articles by Robert Smallidge.

If Jacob Lurvey's mother was Mary and if she married (2) William Nathaniel Hadlock and (3) Mr. Bunker why can't at least one of these facts be substantiated in vital records. If Jacob's mother did, in fact, marry (2) William Nathaniel Hadlock and (3) Mr. Bunker it would appear that his mother was Hannah. If his mother was Hannah Graham why isn't there a Lurvey marriage between Hannah Rall and "Samuel" Lurvey and if that marriage took place, why did Hannah marry William Nathaniel Hadlock as a Rall and not a Lurvey. I can NOT find any reference that Jacob's mother was named Mary but from other related articles it appears that it might have been Hannah but that does not explain for his father. I would appreciate information or help that anyone can offer.

Agnes D. Car, RFD#3, Box 200, Ellsworth, Maine 04605

TWO COINCIDENCES LEAD TO ABBOT(T) FAMILY CONNECTIONS

By Joann Coombs

Our family moved to Andover, Mass., from Maplewood, Minnesota (near St. Paul) in July of 1974. Shortly thereafter, my daughter Laura and I decided to pursue a search for our ancestors. I had made a couple of feeble attempts in the past, but now we were living in New England near so many repositories of early American history, so surely this would be the time to get serious about family history. We knew that many of my husband's ancestors traced back to New England; some were even of Mayflower vintage. In fact, we had even noticed that the name "Abbott" was prevalent in Andover - and wouldn't it be a coincidence if we could make some connection to my husband Lyman's grandmother, Lavanda Laura Abbott?

Our search began, and with a little bit of work, we determined from family papers that Lavanda's grandfather was John Bennett Abbott of Ohio. Try as we might, however, we could find nothing on his parentage.

One day while doing research at the Andover library, the librarian suggested we extend our research to the New England Historic Genealogical Society in Boston, which we did, and soon thereafter, David Dearborn, NEHGS librarian and ESOG member, told us about the New England Branch of the National Archives in Waltham and the LDS Library in Weston. Not long thereafter, I journeyed to the LDS Library to see what I could find. While waiting to talk to the librarian, I started paging through a recent copy of The Genealogical Helper. I turned to the Query Page and couldn't believe my eyes! The very first query was in reference to a John Bennett Abbott. How lucky can a person be! I learned about the library that night, but I could hardly wait to get home to write to the author of the query.

My correspondent was able to give me a clue which led to Massachusetts, and from then on, it was just a matter of time until I had connected our Abbotts to George Abbot, immigrant, and a founder of Andover, Mass., as shown in my Ahnentafel in this journal.

While researching, I uncovered an important error in both The Essex Antiquarian of March, 1897, and The Genealogical Register of the Descendants of George Abbot. They stated that Joseph[4] Abbott went to Lancaster, Mass. and then moved to Chester, Vermont. In fact, Joseph moved to Lancaster and then to Chester, Massachusetts.

The Lancaster Vital Records show that on 29 November 1743, was born "Hannagh, daughter of Jos. A. and his wife, both of them having owned the Covenant in Mr. Phillips's church in Andover." The Abbot family moved from the Lancaster Vital Records to the Chester Vital Records in the late 1700s. Joseph died in Chester in 1790 at the age of 71; he had been born in Andover in 1719. Hannah, wife of Joseph died in 1805 at the age of 85; she had been born in Andover in 1721. Joseph and Hannah's son, John, and his wife, Lois Bennett Abbot, lived in Chester; John's death is recorded under Chester deaths in 1798. We do not know where Lois died. John and Lois's son, John (our line), disappears from Chester records about that time, but in 1802, we find John and other Abbots listed in a ledger of Ruth Ives (at the Mason Public Library in Great Barrington) as original members of the First Baptist Society of Great Barrington. it appears that some members of the Abbot family left the Congregational Church in Chester and joined with the Baptist Society in Great Barrington. The Baptist Church in Chester was formally organized in 1811, and at that time Abbots and other relatives (Sizers and Wilcoxes) were on the Baptist rolls there in Chester.

From Great Barrington, John and his wife, Clarissa Sizer Abbot, went west with son, John Bennett Abbott, and the rest of the family to Greene County, New York, then on to Huron County, Ohio.

Sources:
1. *Annals of Lancaster, MA (Nashaway Plantation), 1643-1725*.

2. *Vital Records to 1850, Chester, MA*.

3. *Vital Records to 1850, Andover, MA*.

4. *Ledger of Ruth Ives* (regarding the First Baptist Society of Great Barrington, MA) in folder entitled "Congregational Church Records, Great Barrington, MA, and other records," Research Room, Mason Public Library, Great Barrington, MA.

SURNAME FILE

ESOG's Surname Index File was started in 1978 by David Kelley of Middleton who donated the 9-drawer cabinet in the Genealogy Room. The file now contains over 2000 cards and has put many "cousins" in touch with one another. Out-of-state members should also contribute their cards to the file; the larger the file, the more useful it become for everyone. A print-out of particular surnames will be mailed upon request, for a small photocopying charge.

DIRECTIONS: START AT TOP OF CARD WITH MOST RECENT ANCESTOR & WORK DOWN.
USE ONLY 3 X 5 CARDS.
ONLY ONE SURNAME PER CARD.
PUT YOUR NAME & ADDRESS ON BACK SIDE OF CARD.

Example:
Pierce, May Lizzie	1875-1956	Lynnfield/Lynn, MA
Pierce, William H.H.	1837-1884	Woodstock, VT/Lynnfield, MA
Pierce, James	1803-1868	Woburn, MA/Reading, VT
Pierce, Heman	1768-1818	Woburn, MA/Reading, VT
Pierce, Jacob	1724-1774	Woburn, MA
Pierce, James	1690-1773	Woburn, MA
Pierce, James	1659-1742	Woburn, MA
Pierce, Thomas, Jr.	1608-1683	Woburn, MA
Pierce, Thomas	1583-1666	Norwich, Eng/Woburn, MA

Research in Progress

JOHN RAMSDELL OF LYNN, MASSACHUSETTS - continued

By Roselyn Listernick

5. ISAAC[3] RAMSDELL (Isaac[2], John[1]) was born at Concord, Mass., 1 September 1667 and died at Lynn, Mass., 9:1m:1741 (Concord & Lynn VRs). He married, probably at Lynn, before 1690 (first child born 16 September 1690), ABIGAIL ----, whose last name is unknown. Her death date is uncertain, as two widows listed as Abigail Ramsdell, are recorded in the vital records; one, buried 15 November 1756 and the second buried October 1762 (Lynn VRs).

Isaac was a weaver, according to deeds on file at Essex County Registry of Deeds (see below). He served the town of Lynn in a number of capacities: as a jury member at Salem Superior Court on 6 November 1705; as a "hayward," or "howard" in 1709/10; as a fence viewer on 5 March 1710/11 (Lynn Town Records, II:33, 54, 61). On 3 November 1704, he and others agreed "that each proprietor shall make and maintain his proportion of fence according to the number of acres of land...and the fence to be kept all year...and put in their proportionable part of cattle into said field...." (ibid., II:27-28).

On the 18th of June 1708, Isaac Ramsdell, Jr. sold to Benjamin Potter, one acre, 42 poles of land laid out in Lynn Town Commons, the 3rd lot, 7th range on Great Nahant, part of the 7th division (Essex Deeds, 51:12). On 11 April 1712, he sold to Joseph Mansfield, Jr., 81 poles of land in Lynn in the field not far from the dwelling of Nathaniel Hathorn (ibid., 26:163). On 24 December 1714, he sold to Ebenezer Hawks, 3 acres of land laid out on Lynn Town Commons, the 5th lot, 9th range in the 2nd draught in the 2nd division (ibid., 43:159). And on 16 May 1722, he sold to Daniel Mansfield, three acres of land laid out on Lynn Town Commons, 4th lot, 16th range, 2nd division (ibid., 50:110).

Children, born at Lynn:

11. i. JONATHAN[4], b. 16 Sept 1690; m. SARAH HATHORN.
    ii. ANNA, b. 30 Apr 1691.
12. iii. NATHANIEL, b. 14 Sept 1694; m. JOANNA DOWNING.
    iv. ABIGAIL, b. 17 Aug 1698; d. aft. 1747; m. (1) int. at Lynn, 4 Apr 1718, THEOPHILUS MERRIAM, b. at Lynn 16 July 1688; "found dead on the ice" 31 Oct 1744 ("Zaccheus Collins Diary" in LVRs), son of Joseph[4] (William[3], Joseph[2], William[1]) and Sarah (Jenkins) Merriam (Charles Pierce Merriam, Genealogical Memoranda relating to the Family of Merriam [London, 1900], 48-49). Abigail (Ramsdell) Merriam is prob. the "Abigal Miriam" who m. (2) at Lynn, 7 July 1747, JAMES BUTLER, "a stranger" (ibid.; LVR). Children of first husband, b. at Lynn (surname Merriam): 1. Sarah, b. 22 Jan 1719/20; m. at Lynn, 14 Jan 1738/9, Samuel Rhoads. 2. Esther (Easter), b. 24 Nov 1722; m. at Lynn, 15 Oct 1751, Joseph Brown (LVR). 3. Ebenezer, b. 6 Sept 1724; m. at Lynn, 27 Nov 1760, Sarah Daniels (Family of Merriam, 79). 4. Joseph, b. 21 July 1728; m. at Lynn, 7 Oct 1762, Ann Mason (ibid., LVR). 5. Abigail, b. 19 Mar 1732/3. 6. Jerusha, b. 18 Mar 1735; m. at Lynn, 7 Dec 1761, John Hawks (ibid.). 7. John, b. 24 May 1738. 8. Ezekiel, b. 29 July 1744.

v. ISAAC, b. 12 Sept 1700; m. (1) at Lynn, 18 Mar 1722/3, MARY RHOADES (LVR), b. 23 Jan 1703/4, dau. of Joseph³ (Josiah², Henry¹) and Priscilla (Smith) Rhoades (ibid.; "Genealogy of Henry Rhodes," MSS at New England Historic Genealogical Society). She is prob. the Mary Ramsdell who d. 29 Sept 1724 a. 21 y. (LVR). Isaac m. (2) at Lynn, (int.) 15 Oct 1727 MARY RICH (ibid.). No further information found.

13. vi. EBENEZER, b. 9 Apr 1705; m. TABITHA RHOADES.
vii. ESTER, b. 2 Aug 1707; d. at Lynn 8 Aug 1707 (ibid.).
viii. EPHRAIM, b. 20 Feb 1708/9; d. 23 Nov 1709 (ibid.).
ix. TIMOTHY, b. 1 Aug 1711; m. at Lynn, 12 Nov 1732, MARGERITY WILLIAMS (ibid.). Nothing further found.

6. **JONATHAN³ RAMSDELL** (Isaac², John¹) was born at Concord, Mass., 30 September 1672 and died at Lynn, Mass., 26:6 mo: 1742 (Concord and Lynn VRs). He married, at Lynn, (int.) 27 November 1745, ANNA CHADWELL, born at Lynn, 17 June 1679; died after 1745 when she signed a deed with Henry and Ruth West (Essex Deeds, 93:271). She was the daughter of Moses² (Thomas¹) and Sarah (Ivory) Chadwell (Marcia Wilson Wiswall, *The Chadwell Family* [Lynnfield, Mass., 1983], 17-18; Mary E. N. Backus, *The New England Ancestry of Dana Converse Backus* [Salem, 1949], 141-42).

Jonathan lived on his father Isaac's land and had a house there (Essex Deeds, 33:194). At the town meeting, 2 March 1723/4, he requested a piece of land to set a house on, but after some debate, his request was refused (*Lynn Town Records*, III:68). He asked again on 15 September 1725:

"The petition of Jonathan Ramsdell Sr, to the Town of Lynn, your poor petitioner being under very low circumstances and no place of abode when turned out [of] where he now lives as he is like to be in a short time; and his aged mother living alone is exposed to many difficulties, and under her bodily weakness not fit to live alone any longer, your petitioner humbly prays that for his owne releaf as well as his said mothers, you would please to grant to him a small piece of land somewhere near the burying place, and what small right said town may have in the house...to do something towards the repairing and fitting up said house whereby it may be something comfortable: and in consideration thereof, your petitioner will receive his said mother into his family and look after her and do what he can for her whereby the town may be at as little charge as may be...."

In answer to the petition: "It was voted that...Ramsdell should have all the right the town hath in the house where his mother now lives, and that he shall have five pounds of that money that the committee has sold land for to fence in the burying place if there be so much left after said burying place is fenced in.... Ramsdell should have between ten and twenty poles of land near the burying place to set said house upon and his barn and he to have the improvement of said land during the Town's pleasure, and Major Burrill, Joseph Mansfield, sr., Capt. Breed, Richard Johnson and Richard Mower are appointed to lay out said land as they shall think convenient" (ibid.).

In a deed recorded 30 May 1726, Jonathan's mother-in-law, Sarah Chadwell, put forth directives to her two daughters, Elizabeth Ramsdell, widow of John

Ramsdell, and Anna Ramsdell, wife of Jonathan Ramsdell and their heirs. She requested that Elizabeth take care of her funeral (Essex Deeds, 47:32). Little else is known about Jonathan. No probate is recorded.

Children, b. at Lynn:

14. i. JONATHAN^4, b. 23 Mar 1698/9; m. ANNA FOSDICK.
    ii. LOIS, b. 19 Nov 1700; m. at Lynn, (int.) 26 May 1728, GEORGE CAIN, but prob. did not marry him, as she m. at Nantucket, 9 June 1732, GRINDAL GARDNER, s. of Joseph & Ruth (Coffin) Gardner. She m. (2) at Nantucket, JEREMIAH GARDNER (Nantucket VRs).
    iii. MARY, b. 18 Dec 1702; d. at Lynn, Sept 1724 (LVR).
    iv. JACOB, b. 4 Jan 1704/5; d. at Lynn, 25 Mar 1705 (ibid.).
    v. MARGARET, b. 18 Feb 1706/7; m. at Lynn, 31 Mar 1726, as his 2nd wife, JOSEPH COATES, b. at Lynn, 20 Mar 1695/6, s. of Robert^2 (Robert^1) & Mary (Hodgkins) Coats, who had m. (1) 7 Nov 1723, Hopestill Eliot of Preston, CT. There is no record of children by either marriage. Joseph was a carpenter of Lynn in 1752 ("Coates Family of Essex County Mass, 1645-1845," NEHG Register, 111 [1957]:223).
    vi. ANNA, b. 27 Feb 1708/9; m. at Lynn, 27 Nov 1729, NATHAN^3 ATWELL, son of John^2 (John^1) and Margaret (Max) Atwell (Lewis, Hist. of Lynn, 116). Children, b. at Lynn (surname Atwell): 1. William, b. about 1730; d. at Lynn, 5 Nov 1806 (LVR). 2. Nathan, b. 16 Oct 1744; m. at Lynn, 24 Nov 1806, Mary Stone (ibid.).
    vii. HEPSEBA, b. 18 Oct 1711; m. at Lynn, (int.) 30 Mar 1735, JOSIAH RHODES, b. 2 Mar 1705/6, s. of Josiah^3 (Josiah^2, Henry^1) and Priscilla (Smith) Rhoades ("Genealogy of Henry Rhoades of Lynn," [MSS at NEHGS]).
    viii. SARAH, b. 15 Apr 1714.
    ix. EUNICE/UNIS, b. 15 Feb 1716/7; m. at Lynn, 5 Feb 1735/6, JACOB BURRILL. Jacob is not listed in Ruth Burrell-Brown, Burrill Genealogy (New York, 1990), or any other Burrell published work.
    x. DORCAS/DAKIS, b. 5 Jan 1718/19; m. at Lynn, 5 Apr 1738, JONATHAN MANSFIELD, b. 29 Apr 1717; d. at Salem, 9 Mar 1791, s. of Jonathan^4 (Joseph$^{3-2}$, Robert^1) and Martha (Stocker) Mansfield of Lynn (LVR; Geneva A. Daland & James S. Mansifled, Mansfield Genealogy [Hampton, NH, 1980], 18, 26). Children, b. at Lynn (surname Mansfield): 1. Jonathan, b. 11 May 1744; d. bef. 1791; m. 27 Oct 1762, Anna Ward. 2. Amos, b. ab. 1746; d. at Salem, Mass., Apr 1781; m. Mary Palmer. 3. James, b. ab. 1748; d. bef. 1791; m. Hannah ----. 4. William, b. at Salem, ab. 1750; d. 22 July 1839; m. 9 Dec 1775 ----? (ibid.).
15. xi. JOHN, b. 28 Jan 1721/2; m. REBECCA HAZLTON.

7. **JOSEPH^3 RAMSDELL** (Isaac^2, John^1) was born at Lynn, 17 September 1683 and died there, 8 March 1756 (LVR). He married at Lynn, 21 October 1712, Debora Mansfield (ibid.) who was born at Lynn 21 April 1686, daughter of Joseph, Jr. and Elizabeth (Williams) Mansfield (ibid.). Deborah's marriage intentions were published, 10 June 1710, to her first cousin, Moses Wheat, but she evidently did not marry him.

Joseph³ Ramsdell was active in town affairs. At the town meeting, 2 March 1723/24, he was chosen titheman; on 1 March 1724/25, hogreave; and in March of 1728/29, titheman (Lynn Town Records, III:53, 65, 85).

On 10 March 1711/12, "it was desired to let John Ramsdell, James Mills, Joseph Ramsdell, and Jonathan Johnson, each of them have a bit of land to set a house upon (ibid., II:67). In a deed, dated 11 February 1716, Joseph Ramsdell, "husbandman" sold two acres and forty poles for three pounds, to Benjamin Potter, "a tanner" (Essex Deeds, 50:220). On 9 March 1730, he sold land to Joshua Felt, a cooper, of Boston, for two pounds, ten shillings (ibid., 58:101).

Following his death, on 5 November 1757, his widow, Deborah, "released and surrendered unto my son, Silas Ramsdell, of Lynn...a joiner, all real estate, both buildings and lands of every denomination wheresoever situated and butted and bounded...that my late husband, Joseph Ramsdell, possessed and I give up all my rights of dower power of thirds" (ibid., 105:26).

Child, born at Lynn:

16. i. SILAS⁴, b. 31 July 1713; m. LUCY KEMBAL/KIMBALL.

8. **NATHANIEL³ RAMSDELL** (John²⁻¹) was born, probably at Topsfield, Mass., about 1690 and died most likely at York, Maine, death date unknown. He married in 1710/11, at York, Maine, MARY LINSCOTT, born 1691, the daughter and sixth child of John and Lydia (Milbury) Linscott of York (Sybil Noyes, Charles Thornton Libby and Walter Goodwin Davis, Genealogical Dictionary of Maine and New Hampshire [Baltimore, 1972], 573).

Sometime around 1709, Nathaniel was at York, Maine. At the General Court session on 3 January 1709/10, a case came before the court concerning Mary Linscott and an alleged child conceived out of wedlock. Earlier, on 17 December 1709, the constable was asked "to apprehend...Mary Linscott...on suspicion of her being with child and making away with it and bring her before me...and to summon Nathaniel Ramsdell to give evidence." Nathaniel Ramsdell, "full of age" testified that December 16th at night, "Mary Linscott told me that she was carrying in a lodge at Grovers and hurt herself and then lifting of a pot of soup and then she went into the field and had a child. I asked her if it was dead when it was born and she told me yes. I told her I was afraid that she had made away with it. I asked her further whether she did not put her hand to hurt it and she said no. I asked her what she did with it and she told me she buryed it in the field. She also told me that she did this a month ago." On the same date, 17 December 1709/10, "Mary Linscott appeared before me, Abraham Preble, justice...and being searched by three midwifes, they say to the best of their judgments that she never had a child." She then stood bound to the next session at York.

At the court session, 3 January 1709/10, Mary Linscott denied "the said accusation but owning herself guilty of committing fornication with said Ramsde.. It's therefore considered by the court that she receive seven stripes on her naked back at the post and pay fees of court thirteen shillings and two pence or to pay a fine of 25 shillings to her Majesty...and by her humble petition her fine is abated to 10 shillings, her bond continued to the next court" (Province and Court Records of Maine Court of General Sessions [Portland, 1709/10], IV:373-74).

In spite of these events, Nathaniel Ramsdell did marry Mary Linscott. That same year he received a grant of twenty acres on the north westward of Agamenticus Great Hill (Charles Edward Banks, History of York, Maine [Baltimre, 1967], I:77). Several other parcels of land are recorded in several deeds. On 16 May 1711, 30 acres on the west side of the head of the NW branch of the York River, and also a half parcel of fresh meadow NW of Agamenticus Hill in York were purchased from Arthur Bragdon (York Deeds [Portland, 1892], VII:124, Folio 233). in a deed, grantors Arthur Bragdon and Peter Nowell sold 20 acres of land bounded on one side by the cartway to the sawmill of Capt. Preble, to Nathaniel Ramsdell (ibid., Folio 226). According to C. E. Banks (II:77), "Nathaniel was the son of John Ramsdell of Boxford. His descendants have lived in York ever since, and a genealogy of the family will appear in Volume III of this history." Mr. Banks did not complete this third volume before his death; his notes and manuscripts are on file at the library of Congress, Rare Book Room, in Washington, D.C. (The Essex Genealogist, II:149).

In the Court of General Sessions, 4 January 1714/15, Nathaniel appeared "to answer for his pulling down Arthur Bragdon's fence and destroying his hay... By consent of said Bragdon, he was acquitted, paying fees of court, 18 shillings..." (Maine Court Records, IV:155).

Between 1710 and 1724, Nathaniel returned to Topsfield, and in 1724, he was warned out of town along with Francis Johnson (George Francis Dow, History of Topsfield (Topsfield, 1940), 347). He was of Topsfield in 1726, but of York in 1728, when he and his wife deeded land to her brother, John Linscott (Gen. Dict. ME/NH, 573).

In 1730, "Preble brought suit against Nathaniel Ramsdell for throwing stones or brick-bats against the plaintiff's sign, known by the name of the Green Dragon (a local tavern), claiming damages...of five pounds. He said it had been split in several places and otherwise defaced. Mr. Justice Pepperall gave judgement for the defendant, which was sustained on appeal" (Banks, History of York, II:324).

No probate papers of Nathaniel's estate have been found.

Children, born probably at York, Maine (1st 3 from Noyes, 573; last 2 from a Ramsdell Typescript at York Public Library):

    i.   NATHANIEL[4], m. SARAH WITTUM.
    ii. LYDIA, m. 31 May 1733, JOHN WITTUM, JR.
    iii. A child, d. 4 Sept 1721.
    iv. TIMOTHY, d. 1746.
    v.   JOHN, d. 1730.

Child, born at Topsfield:

    vi. ELIZABETH, bpt. 12 July 1724 (Topsfield VRs).

9. **TIMOTHY[3] RAMSDELL** (John[2-1]) was born, probably at Topsfield, about 1692 and died, probably at York, Maine, 18 December 1772. He married at Topsfield/Boxford, 12 March 1712/13, ABIGAIL TOWNE, who was born at Topsfield, 10 December 1687, the third child of Jacob[3] (Jacob[2], William[1]) and Phebe (Smith) Towne (Edwin Eugene Town, The Descendants of William Towne, [Newtonville, MA,], 901).

Timothy was a resident of Boxford, and was taxed there from 1711-1723 (Sidney Perley, History of Boxford [Boxford, Mass., 1880], 69).

On 18 October 1722, Timothy Ramsdell came into agreement with John, Thomas, Zacheus, and Joseph Gould all of Topsfield and Samuel Gould of Boxford, all husbandmen and sons of Capt. John Gould, late of Topsfield, deceased. In consideration of five shillings he shall now lawfully possess a piece of land amounting to 12 acres, which at an earlier time was sold by John Gould deceased to John Ramsdell, late of Boxford, deceased, but which had not been lawfully conveyed. The land, "now is in the possession of Timothy Ramsdell of Boxford, husbandman, son of John Ramsdell," was bounded north and west by the Gould family, east and south by land of James Curtice (Essex Deeds, 41:213).

The following year, on 12 December 1723, Timothy sold to his neighbor, James Curtice, for 150 pounds, "a parcel of land with dwelling house, situated in Boxford," and by description probably the same 12 acres mentioned in the deed with the Gould family (ibid., 43:191). It is likely that he left the area and went to York, Maine where his brother Nathaniel had settled.

Children, born at Topsfield:

    i.   ABIGAIL^4, b. 2 Feb 1713/14; bpt. 1716/17 (EIHC, XXIV [1887]: 200-1).
    ii.   JOHN, b. 3 Feb 1714/15; bpt. 1716/17 (ibid.).
    iii. KATHERINE, b. Nov 1718.
    iv.   TIMOTHY, bpt. 7 Aug 1720 (ibid.).
    v.   JOSEPH, bpt. 1 Apr 1722 (ibid.).

10. **BENJAMIN^3 RAMSDELL** (Aquilla^2, John^1) was born at Lynn, 21 January 1689/90 and died there after 1730/1 (birth of last known child). He married at Lynn, 8 December 1719, ABIGAIL FULLER, who was born 14 Jan 1692/3, the daughter of Benjamin and Susanna (Ballard) Fuller. He was probably the Benjamin Ramsdell whose intentions of marriage to Sarah Jenks were published at Lynn on 22 April 1716. It appears that Sarah Jenks never married Benjamin, for on 26 October 1720, a Sarah Jenks married Henry Stanton and had a child, Benjamin, born 15 September 1725 (LVR).

In March 1718/19, Benjamin was "chosen to see swine be yoked and ringed as the law directs (Lynn Town Records, III:15). He was the tenth child of Aquilla, and the first child by Aquilla's second wife, Lydia. He was called "husbandman" on 19 February 1717, when he signed a deed-of-gift with his father (see details under Aquilla, TEG, X:32).

Children, born at Lynn:

18. i.   MOSES^4 (twin), b. 20 Dec 1720; m. MARY WARES.
    ii.   MARY (twin), b. 20 Dec 1720; died young.
    iii. ABIGAIL, b. 10 Sept 1723; m. at Lynn, 17 July 1749, THOMAS NEWMAN b. 31 Mar 1727, son of Thomas & Hannah (Downing) Newman (LVR).
    iv.   MARY, b. 25 Jan 1726/7; m. at Lynn, 12 July 1744, JOHN NEWMAN, b. 13 Mar 1721, son of Thomas & Hannah (Downing) Newman (ibid.)
    v.   ELIZABETH, b. 10 Feb 1731/32.

(to be continued)

WILLIAM IVORY OF LYNN AND HIS DESCENDANTS - continued

By Eleanor Tucker

3. JOHN[3] IVORY (Thomas[2], William[1]) was born at Lynn, Mass., 10 August 1669 and died there 11 February 1718/19 "in his 50th year" (LVR). He married (int.) 2 July 1698, RUTH POTTER (ibid.), who was born 27 February 1673 and died as "wid. Ivory, 26 October 1756" (Zacheus Collins Diary; LVR). She was the daughter of Robert and Ruth (Driver) Potter (LVR: Harriet Ruth [Waters] Cooke, The Driver Family... [Cambridge, Mass., 1889], 52, 65).

John Ivory was active in the affairs of the Lynn community. In 1700 he was chosen to see that the law against carrying shale and lime out of the town was followed. The same year he was chosen to prosecute the persons who kept geese on the common. Between the years 1701 and 1718, he served as selectman, surveyor, constable, on the Grand Jury and the Jury of Trials. During 1717, he was on the committee to consider rates for the church pews. His name was on a petition for land where the meeting house stood, and he was on a committee to lay out a highway through Belcher's land (Records of the Town Meetings of Lynn [Lynn, 1695-1730], I:41, 67-68; II:8, 45, 56, 66, 87, 91; III:9, 10).

On the 17th of July 1707, John and Ruth Ivory sold to Matthew Eustis, for four pounds, ten shillings, one acre of salt marsh in Lynn, in the town marsh, so called, bounded north by Whitings, west by David Browne, south on a creek and east on Withers. The deed was witnessed by Mary Hawthorn and Mary Farr (Essex Deeds, 20:52). On the same date, they sold to William Brintnall one lot in Lynn, laid out to John Ivory in Lynn Town Common, described as the 2nd lot in the 5th range, 2nd division, bounded east by John Ivory's land, west by John Brintnall, north and south by range lines, containing eight acres, seventy poles. Witnesses were Abraham and Hannah Hill (ibid., 21:52).

In a deed recorded 29 June 1710, John Ivory sold to Mary Jeffords, three acres and 40 poles of upland in Lynn near Jeffords house, bounded east and west by Mary Jeffords, south by Hugh Alley and north by the Town Common. Witnesses were Ephraim and Sarah Potter (ibid., 23:153). In another deed, dated 3 June 1699, but not recorded until the 18th of February 1714, John sold to Thomas Burrage for ten pounds, two acres in Lynn bounded east by Theophilus Bayley, north by Matthew Farrington, south and west by Thomas Burrage. Witnesses were Ruth Driver and Ruth Bligh (ibid., 28:160).

John Ivory died on the 11th of February 1718, without making a will. On 1 July 1720, widow Ruth Ivory, having given her bond, presented an inventory of her husband's estate, signed by Ebenezer Burrill, Richard Johnson and Joseph Jacobs (Essex Probate, 14661):

One Dwelling House and Barn and 9 acres of land joining it	188 pounds
12 acres, part upland & part salt marsh lying below the homestead and joining to it	80 pounds
One acre of upland lying in Lindsey's field so called	80 pounds
2 Ten-acre lots lying near Collins pond so called	100 pounds
One common lot lying near Newman's house	20 pounds
One common lot lying in the second division	10 pounds
One common lot lying near Flagg's Hole so called	17 pounds
One common lot lying near Bancrofts marsh so called	9 pounds

One common lot lying in the six hundred acres so called	5 pounds
One common lot lying near Farrs	2 pounds
3 common lots lying in Nahant so called	60 pounds
One common lot lying in the Ox Pasture	5 pounds
About 15 acres of salt marsh	115 pounds
Total	619 pounds

His personal estate included wearing apparel, books, money, plate, looking glass, 4 beds, 3 dozen chairs, tables, etc. for a total of 195 pounds

On 6 July 1720, a division of the estate was made by the same three men. The widow received one-third, including the lower room in the house's west end, the kitchen and cellar under it, and 1/3 part of the southerly end of the barn. She also received six acres of land adjoining the house, 2 acres of salt marsh in the town marsh and 2 acres, 120 poles of salt marsh at Rumney Marsh, one-half of the ten-acre lot lying between Burrills ten-acres and William Collins; also 5 acres, 120 poles of salt marsh at Seldom Good Pasture, so-called, joining Joseph Collins; and 3 acres pasture at Nahant. The widow's share was valued at 242 pounds.

The remaining two-thirds of John Ivory's estate was divided into five equal shares; one share to Thomas Witt (husband of the eldest daughter, Mary Ivory), and one share each to Ruth Ivory, Lois Ivory, Elizabeth Ivory and Eunice Ivory. The unmarried daughters, who were 18, 16, 12 and 10 years of age, were each given "her part in the house and barn" in addition to shares in each parcel of land, including Nahant. The shares of the oldest four sisters was valued at 82 pounds each. Ten-year-old Eunice's part was valued at 75 pounds. Several years later, two of the sisters sold part of their inherited land to their brother-in-law, Capt. Thomas Witt; on 22 November 1727, Ruth Ivory, "spinster" sold part of her portion for 171 pounds, 10 shillings. On 11 December the same year, Lois Ivory, "spinster" sold part of her portion for the same amount; Lois's intentions of marriage to Henry Blaney had been published on 12 October that year (LVR).

On the 11th of June 1733, Thomas Witt bought all the remainder of his sister-in-laws' land, as well as interest in the homestead, for 400 pounds - 100 pounds to Benjamin Ivory (husband of Ruth), 100 pounds to Henry Blaney (husband of Lois), 100 pounds to Elizabeth Ivory "single woman," and 100 pounds to Thomas Cheever (husband of Eunice) (Essex Deeds, 63:100).

Children, born at Lynn (Lynn VR, unless noted):

  i. MARY[4], b. 8 Feb 1699; bur. 3 May 1764; m. (int.) 21 Nov 1719, CAPT. THOMAS WITT, b. at Lynn, 30 Jan 1688; d. there, 19 Sept 1754, "in his 65th year" (Z. Collins Diary, LVR). He was the son of Thomas[2] (John[1]) and Bathia (Potter) Witt (LVR; Frank W. Balcomb, Witt Genealogy [Peabody, Mass., 1943], 2, 4). Thomas Witt died intestate, and on 14 Apr 1755, the court appointed William Collins, Daniel Mansfield, Zacheus Collins, John Lewis and Samuel Johnson to divide the "estate of John Ivory, dec'd" into five equal parts (Essex Probate, 30228). Each parcel included a 5th part of the former Ivory homestead. Debts against the estate included "Widow Ruth Ivory's yearly annuity, now due, 4 pounds, 10 shillings." Widow Mary Witt received her dower's thirds; Gedney, John and Benjamin Witt received shares, as did the heirs of Ivory Witt (the eldest son), deceased (ibid.). 17-yr-old Benjamin was placed under guardianship of his brother John (Essex Probate, 30219; Cooke, Driver Family, 67). Widow Ruth Ivory died the following October. Children, b. at Lynn (surname Witt): 1. Ivory, b. 6 May 1721; d. 19 Mar 1752; m. 1 Dec 1747, Ruth Breed. 2. Mary, b. 26 May 1726. 3. John, b. 17 Sept 1729. 4. Gedney, b. 17 Sept 1731; m. (1) (int.) 23 Nov 1755, Elizabeth Cheever; m. (2) (int.) 26 Sept 1756, Hannah Hawkes; m. (3) (int.) 7 Apr 1765, Elizabeth Merry. 5. Daniel, b. 2 Mar 1734; d. 25 June 1755, age 23. 6. Lydia, b. 20 Apr 1736; m. 21 Dec 1780, Joseph Richard. 7. Benjamin, b. 9 Feb 1739; d. 29 Nov 1820; m. Abigail (Rust?) (LVR; Balcomb, Witt Genealogy, 4, 5, 9).

ii. RUTH, b. 17 Sept 1702; m. 2 Mar 1732 BENJAMIN IVORY (see below).

iii. LOIS, b. c1704; d. bef. 1748; m. (int.) 15 Oct 1727, as his 1st wife, HENRY^3 BLANEY, b. at Salem, 6:20:1698, son of John^2 (John^1) and Elizabeth (Purchis) Blaney (Salem VR). He m. (2) Hannah (Rand) Graves (2 children). Child by 1st wife Lois Ivory, b. at Salem (surname Blaney): 1. Ivory, m. at Salem, 25 Oct 1753, Mary Browne of Lynn ("Blaney Genealogy," Essex Antiquarian, IX:32).

iv. ELIZABETH, b. 1708 (figured from age at death); d. 3 Aug 1754, age 46 yrs, 4 months; m. 8 Oct 1735, RICHARD PAPOON of Lynn, who d. abt. 5:4m:1741, age 44 (Z. Collins Diary, LVR). Marriage intentions published 3 May 1730, but Elizabeth "forbid the banns" (Essex Institute Historical Collections, 16:130). Children, b. at Lynn (surname Papoon): 1. Richard, b. 17 Sept 1736; m. 5 Feb 1767, Mary Newhall. 2. Joseph, b. 16 Aug 1738; d. 26 Sept 1740. 3. Mary, b. 20 July 1741; d. 5 May 1744. 4. Joseph, b. 19 Apr 1745; d. 6 May 1744 (1745?). 5. Elizabeth, b. 3 Apr 1748; m. 5 Oct 1785, John Andros.

v. EUNICE, b. c1710; m. at Lynn, 5 Mar 1729/30, THOMAS CHEEVER, b. at Lynn, 25 Feb 1704; d. there 14 Mar 1734, son of Thomas^3 (Thomas^2, Ezekial^1) and Mary (Boardman) Cheever (LVR; John T. Hassam, Ezekial Cheever and Some of His Descendants. Part II [Boston, 1884], 180). Eunice m. (2), at Lynn, 8 Jan 1740/1, JOHN BOARDMAN, b. at Lynn, 26 Aug 1712; d. Feb. 5 Nov 1800 (Essex Probate, 2697), s. of William^3 and Abiah (Sprague) Boardman (LVR; Thomas Bellows Wyman, Genealogies and Estates of Charlestown [Boston, 1874], 888). Children, by 1st husband, b. at Lynn (surname Cheever): 1. Mary, b. 4 May 1732; d. 14 Sept 1803; m. at Lynn, 26 Sept 1754, Aaron Boardman. 2. Thomas, b. 20 Feb 1733/4; d. at Lynn, 28 Jan 1823; m. Mary ----. Children by 2nd husband, b. at Lynn (surname Boardman): 3. Abiah, b. 23 Sept 1741; d. bef. 1799. 4. Eunice, b. 29 Mar 1743; d. bef. 1799. 5. John, b. 18 Aug 1745; d. bef. 1799; m. at Lynn, Susanna Norwood. 6. Lois, b. 13 Aug 1747; m. at Lynn, 3 May 1767, Benjamin Goldthwaite of Malden. 7. Ivory, b. 5 Aug 1749; d. bef. 21 Oct 1807 (Essex Probate, 2687); m. at Lynn, 3 Jan 1774, Mary Jenks (LVR). 8. Sarah, b. 12 Jan 1752; named in father's will.

vi. JOHN, b. May 1713; d. 1 Oct 1716, 3y. 5m. (ibid.).

4. **THEOPHILUS³ IVORY** (Thomas², William¹) was born at Lynn, 1 November 1670 and died at Charlestown, Mass., 11 February 1747/8, in his 77th year (gravestone). He married, KATHERINE (MITCHELL?), probably the daughter of Alexander and Susanna (Burrage) Mitchell. Alexander's will, 30 December 1717, named "six children of Theophilus Ivory" [Wyman, Charlestown, 548]). Katherine Ivory died at Charlestown, 14 September 1745, age 70 years, 6 months (gravestone). She owned the covenant at the Charlestown church 19 (5) 1696, and was admitted to the church 21 November 1708 (ibid.).

Theophilus was a joiner by trade (ibid.). His will, dated 7 October 1745, probated 27 February 1747, devised to daughter Mary Frothingham, the southwest end of the house occupied by Joseph Collins; the shop in front to grandson John Ivory; the other end, except the yard in common for daughter Mary; to daughter Hannah Brasier, the house where she lived and barn land; to daughters-in-law Ann and Mary Ivory, one acre in the field. The inventory of personal property, including one-half pew, totaled 353 pounds (Middlesex Probate, 12394).

Children, born at Charlestown (all information from Wyman, Charlestown), unless otherwise noted):

- i. ELIZABETH⁴, b. 16 June 1695; d. 31 July 1695.
- ii. THOMAS, b. 28 Sept 1696; d. at Antigua, "a young man," 1723; m. at Charlestown, 7 Feb 1722/3, ANN(E) CALL, b. there, 18 Feb 1699/1700, dau. of Caleb & Ann (Wharff) Call. No issue. Ann was named in Theophilus Ivory's will.
- iii. KATHERINE, b. 22 Dec 1698; d. at Charlestown, 10 Dec 1721 of small-pox; m. George Barrow, a Sea-Captain of Monmouthshire, who was lost on a voyage from England in 1748. He m. (2), 23 Aug 1723, Relief Rows; m. (3) Hannah Chandler. One child by Katherine (surname Barrow): 1. George, b. 11 Oct 1720; d. of smallpox, 18 Dec 1721.
- iv. THEOPHILUS, b. 27 May 1701; d. at Charlestown, 30 Sept 1745, age 45 (gravestone); m. at Charlestown, 27 June 1728, MARY HILL, b. at Charlstown, 17 Apr 1709; d. at Littleton, Mass. abt. 1782, dau. of Capt. Abraham & 2nd w. Martha (Cary) Hill. Mary (Hill) Ivory m. (2) at Charlestown, 20 Sept 1759, Joseph Rand. Mary was named in Theophilus Ivory's will).
- v. JOHN, bpt. 16 June 1703; d. 13 July 1703.
- 7. vi. JOHN, b. 26 July 1705; m. MARTHA THWING.
- vii. MARY, b. 4 Dec 1711; m. at Charlestown, 6 Nov 1729, as his 2nd w. JOSEPH FROTHINGHAM, b. at Charlestown, 15 July 1703, son of Nathaniel & Hannah (Rand) Frothingham. Joseph had m. (1) Elizabeth Call, and had a daughter, Elizabeth. Mary (Ivory) Frothingham m. (2) at Charlestown, 11 Dec 1735, as his 3rd wife, Deacon THOMAS SYMES; m. (3) 2 Sept 1756, SAMUEL PRESTON of Littleton. Child by 1st husband, b. at Charlestown (surname Frothingham): 1. Joseph (Jr.), b. 20 Jan 1730/1; d. at Charlestown 4 Dec 1762; m. there, 22 Aug 1753, Mercy Stearns.
- viii. HANNAH, b. 11 Mar 1714; d. 2 Sept 1758 in 44th year (gravestone); m. 12 Nov 1741, THOMAS BRASIER, housewright, b. at Charlestown, 25 July 1714; d. there (will probated) 30 Dec 1754. He was son of Thomas and Hannah (Webb) Brasier. Hannah (Ivory) Brasier's will, dated 22 Aug 1758, divided her estate in thirds: 1/3 to her sister Mary, wife of Samuel Preston; 1/3 to John Ivory.

Others named were Sarah, wife of John Ivory (Jr.); John Ivory, Jr. and to Mary & Catherine Frothingham, daus. of Joseph Frothingham (Jr.) (Wyman, Charlestown, 117-118).

5. **WILLIAM³ IVORY** (Thomas², William²) was born at Lynn, 10 June 1674 and probably died before 10 July 1720, as he is not named in his mother's agreement with her children (Essex Deeds, 63:25). He married, at Boston, Mass., 6 January 1701, SARAH HORTON (Boston Marriages, 1700-1751).

Child, b. at Boston:

    i. SARAH⁴, b. 28 Oct 1702. She is probably not the Sarah Ivory who married John Witt of Lynn (see Sarah, daughter of Benjamin listed below).

6. **BENJAMIN³ IVORY** (Thomas², William¹) was born at Lynn, 22 September 1685 and died before October, 1721 when his widow remarried. He married at Boston, Mass., 20 January 1707, DEBORAH TOBEY (Boston Marriages, 1700-1751). She married (2) at Lynn, 17 October 1721, as his second wife, William Ballard, son of Nathaniel and Rebecca (Hudson) Ballard (LVR; Charles Frederic Farlow, Ballard Genealogy [Boston, 1911], 24). William had married (1) Sarah Burrill. William and Deborah (Tobey) Ivory Ballard removed to Framingham, Mass. and had 10 children born there between 1722 and 1733: Mary, Nathaniel, Ebenezer, Stephen, John, Esther, Timothy, Zaccheus, Sylvanus and Joseph (Farlow, Ballard Genealogy, 24).

At Benjamin Ivory's death, his two youngest children, Deborah and William, were placed under the guardianship of John Burrage (Essex Probate, 14664). On 26 August 1736, John Burrage was granted a "faithful discharge" of that trust by John Appleton, Judge of Probate.

Children named in Benjamin's sister Mary Ivory's will (Essex Probate 14552):

    i. BENJAMIN⁴, b. c1707; d. at Boston, bef. 28 Sept 1739; m. at Lynn, 2 Mar 1732, RUTH IVORY, b. 17 Sept 1702. dau. of John & Ruth (Potter) Ivory. Benjamin and wife Ruth signed a receipt for part of her father, John Ivory's, estate (see above). On 28 Sept 1739, Henry Pigeon of Boston, "mariner, administrator to the estate of Benjamin Ivory, late of Boston, courier, deceased intestate," sold to John Fayerweather for 117 pounds all the real estate of Benjamin Ivory to pay the debts of the deceased; 87 pounds to Henry Pigeon as administrator and 30 pounds to Deacon John Burrage to clear the estate from encumberances it was subjected to "by virtue of the power granted by the State Superior Court." John Fayerweather had made the highest bid at a public auction for the estate, which included land in Lynn, near the meeting house, formerly Thomas Ivory's, bounded by Matthew Breed and Robert Rand; plus two dwelling houses with barns and fences, now occupied by Ruth Ivory, widow of said Benjamin, reserving to the widow her thirds, or dower rights (Essex Deeds, 78:204). No known issue.

    ii. SARAH, b. c1708; named in Aunt Mary Ivory's will. She is probably the Sarah Ivory who m. at Lynn, 16 Oct 1734, LT. JOHN WITT,

b. at Lynn, 24 Oct 1705; d. at New Braintree, Mass., 16 Nov 1754; settled at North Brookfield, Mass. (Balcomb, *Witt Genealogy*, 5). Sarah and John Witt named two children Benjamin and Deborah (her parent's names). Children (surname Witt): 1. Rebecca, m. at N. Brookfield, 23 June 1760, Joseph Lane. 2. Sarah, m. (int.), at Brookfield, Sept 1762, Aaron Woods. 3. Deborah, m. at New Braintree, 25 Nov 1773, John Fisher. 4. Benjamin, b. at Brookfield, 15 Aug 1750; m. at Oxford, Mass., 22 Jan 1787, Olivia Campbell. 5. Ivory, b. at Brookfield, 20 Oct 1752; m. 1779, Abigail Montague. 6. Stephen, b. at Brookfield, 15 Aug 1754; m., as her 2nd husband, 4 Oct 1791, Sally Patten (ibid., 5, 10, 11).

iii. BATHSHEBA, b. 1710 (figured from age at death); d. at Petersham Mass., 18 Oct 1764, age 54 (Petersham VRs); m. as his 2nd wife, 1 Feb 1738, JONAS HOLLAND of Marlboro, Mass., b. 12 May 1711, s. of John & Elizabeth (Park) Holland. Children of Jonas & Bathsheba (surname Holland): 1. Ivory, b. 27 Dec 1739; m. 1762, Martha Rogers (ibid.); rem. to Dublin, NH. 2. Park, b. 7 Aug 1740; d. 1745. 3. Esther, b. at Shrewsbury, Mass., 7 Mar 1744; m. at Petersham, 20 Nov 1781, Abraham Robinson. 4. Park, b. 15 Apr 1748; d. 1750. 5. Luther, b. 29 May 1750; d. 5 Jan 1821; m. at Petersham, 10 Dec 1775, Elizabeth Spooner (PVR). 6. Park, b. 19 Nov 1752; d. 21 May 1844. 7. Deborah, b. 3 Mar 1756; d.y. (ibid.). 8. Jonas, b. at Petersham, 2 Oct 1758; m. there, 25 Feb 1787, Hannah Spooner. 9. Vashti, b. 4 May 1761; m. 2 Dec 1783, Benjamin How (Private Records of Col. John Jones Sr., ibid.).

8. iv. SILAS, b. c1716; m. HANNAH MORGAN.

v. DEBORAH, b. 1718, according to her age given as 18 in 1736 when she was released from the care of guardian John Burrage (Essex Probate 14664); d. at Sherborn, Mass., 12 June 1766; m. there, 17 Feb 1742, MOSES PERRY of Sherborn, b. there, 28 July 1719; d. there 18 Mar 1809, age 90, s. of Nathaniel & Abigail (Adams) Perry (Framingham VRs). He m. (2) Susanna Child of Newton. Children by 1st w. Deborah (Ivory), b. at Sherborn (surname Perry): 1. Ivory, b. 10 Nov 1743; m. 3 Sept 1767, Kaziah Broad of Natick. 2. Mary, b. 2 Apr 1745; m. 26 Feb 1766, Reuben Partridge. 3. Abigail, b. 31 Jan 1746; m. Moses Perry of Brush Hill. 4. Deborah, b. 2 Dec 1748; d. 27 oct 1754. 5. Moses, b. 15 Dec 1750; d. 30 Oct 1754. 6. Elizabeth, twin, b. 15 Oct 1752; m. ---- Cleveland. 7. Phebe, twin, b. 15 Oct 1752; d. 15 July 1754 (Rev. Abner Morse, *Genealogical Register of Inhabitants and History of the Towns of Sherborn and Hollister*, [Boston, 1856]).

vi. WILLIAM, b. 1719, according to his age given as 17 in 1736 when he was released from the care of guardian John Burrage (Essex Probate 14664). No further record.

(to be continued)

THE TILTON FAMILY - continued

By Barbara B. Marden, C.A.L.S.

FIFTH GENERATION

With the passage of time, the young men of the fifth generation of the Tilton family began to spread out from the towns of their forefathers. We now find them marrying women from Deerfield, Bristol, Chester, and Raymond; or perhaps bringing their wives from the places of their births to these outlying towns. While some of the men were still farmers and working with their hands, we occasionally find a doctor, a lawyer, an innholder. There is a new sophistication in this generation; most of the Tilton men could read and write, as evidenced by their signatures on their land transactions and when they drew their wills. The Indians were no longer a threat; the Revolutionary War had been fought and won; now these men had come home to go on with their lives and raise their families in a time of peace.

Sons of Samuel and Abigail (Batchelder) Tilton:

19. **SAMUEL^5 TILTON** (Samuel$^{4-3}$, Daniel^2, William^1) was born probably at Hampton Falls in 1734; died at Hampton Falls, 4 Dec 1796. He married there, 4 Dec 1767 JOANNA BATCHELDER (VSHF:58). Joanna was born 10 Aug 1741, oldest child of John and Esther Batchelder (ibid., 1; also Batchelder Gen, 140).

Samuel Tilton, Jr. of Hampton Falls, husbandman, sold to Caleb Tilton "a certain parcel of land situate in Hampton Falls, being part of the land which I bought of my honoured father Samuel Tilton, which was part of the home place where he now lives, containing 5 acres" (Rockingham Deeds, 96:487). The consideration was 400 pounds, old tenor; dated 13 May 1765. Jeremiah Lane and Ephraim Batchelder witnessed this transaction.

Joanna was named administratrix of the estate of Samuel Tilton, yeoman, of Hampton Falls (Rockingham Probate, 6293) in 1797. The inventory of the estate totalled $260.77, signed by Ebenezer Tilton 22 Mar 1798. Joanna received a dower of 11 acres, land and buildings (one-third of the estate)... "reserving for the other heirs (not named) liberty of the use of the house and barnyards." This was signed by Jeremiah Lane, James Prescutt, Jr., Peter Tilton, Levi Healey, and Jonathan Cram, Jr.

The will of Joanna Tilton, widow, of Hampton Falls, was drawn 7 Dec 1814 and proved 12 Jan 1826 (Rockingham Probate, 11154). She bequeathed to her sons John and David $1.00 each; to her daughter Joanna Morse she gave her wearing apparel and household furniture. To her son Ebenezer she gave "all my real estate which was given to me by my son Joseph in his last will and testament, along with my barn." She also gave him a bed and bedding, a chest and warming pan. To her granddaughter Charlotte, she gave one cow. Joanna named Jeremiah Blake, gentleman, of Hampton Falls, as Executor; Peter Tilton, Joseph Tilton and Levi Lane witnessed her signature. Included in this file was a request from Ebenezer asking that Levi Lane of Hampton Falls, Esq. be appointed administrator, with the will annexed to said estate.

Children, all born Hampton Falls (VSHF. 35-37; Granite State Mag., 33):

    i.   MARY^6, b. 2 Jan 1768.
    ii.   SAMUEL, b. 11 Apr 1769; d. young.

```
iii.   JOHN, b. 4 Nov 1770; m 30 June 1791 PATTY ODLIN, dau. of Winthrop.
iv.    EBENEZER, b. 12 May 1773.
v.     JOANNA, b. 29 Aug 1775.
vi.    DAVID, b. 17 Aug 1777.
vii.   SAMUEL, b. 24 Aug 1779.
viii.  JOSEPH, b. 2 Mar 1781.
```

20. **JETHRO BATCHELDER**[5] **TILTON** (Samuel[4-3], Daniel[2], William[1]) was born at Hampton Falls, 9 Oct 1736 (VSHF, 35; DAR P.I., 680), and died at Epping, 16 Mar 1817 ("Baptisms and Deaths in Epping, N.H.," [MSS, NH Hist. Soc.]; hereafter B/D Epping, 60). He married BRIDGET ---- (DAR P.I., 680). Mrs. Jethro Batchelder died at Epping, 17 May 1782, age 48 (B/D Epping, 60). Jethro signed the Association Test at Epping (Misc. Rev. Doc., XXX:50) and was credited with Patriotic Service in the Revolutionary War (DAR P.I., 680).

Children, b. or bpt. at Epping (VTNH; B/D Epping, 31-32):

```
i.     LEVI[6], bpt. 24 Feb 1760.
ii.    SAMUEL, b. 17 Dec 1761.
iii.   BETTY, bpt. 11 Mar 1764.
iv.    ABIGAIL, twin, b. 21 Aug 1766.
v.     NANNY, twin, b. 21 Aug 1766.
vi.    ESTHER, bpt. 15 Sept 1771.
vii.   JESSE, b. 26 Feb 1772.
viii.  MOLLY, twin, b. 15 Feb 1773.
ix.    OLLY, twin, b. 15 Feb 1773.
```

21. **REUBEN**[5] **TILTON** (Samuel[4-3], Daniel[2], William[1]) was born at Hampton Falls, 12 Sept 1743 (VSHF, 37) and died at Raymond 17 May 1826 (H. Raymond, 292). He married MARY PEVEAR at Hampton Falls on 12 Feb 1767 (VSHF, 58), probably the daughter of Phillip and Mary (Emmons) Pervear (H.H. Falls, 599). Reuben moved to Raymond from Hampton Falls about 1771 (ibid., 451) and settled on land a mile north of the Baptist Chruch. He built a log house in the wilderness and lived there until his death in 1826. For several of his last years he walked to church on crutches, accompanied by his aged wife (H. Raymond, 292).

Reuben's will was written 16 July 1813; proved at Raymond, 15 Jan 1826 (Rockingham Probate, 11246) with his son Samuel named as Executor. In the custom of the men of his time, he provided for his unmarried daughter Mary by stating that she was to have 6 bushels of Indian corn, 2 of rye, 6 of potatoes. She was to receive 50 lbs. of pork, 25 lbs. of beef and 10 lbs. of flax. She was to have 1 barrel of cider and the barrel to hold same; 3 bushels of winter apples annually; one cow and two sheep. She was to be furnished with wood cut at her door sufficient for a fire as long as she remained single. Should she marry, she was to receive $30 in household furniture and one cow to be paid at her marriage day. The testator bequeathed $2 to his sons Daniel and Josiah, his daughters Susanna Hardy and Abigail Harriman. The remainder of the estate was apportioned to Samuel. Sherburne Blake, Joseph Blake and Louisa Smith witnessed the signature on this document.

Children, all born at Raymond (H.Raymond, 292-93):

```
i.    JOSIAH[6], b. 7 Dec 1767; d. 4 Oct 1776 (ibid.).
ii.   MOLLY, b. 10 Mar 1770; lived and d. at home (ibid.).
iii.  DANIEL, b. 23 July 1772.
iv.   SAMUEL, b. 15 Sept 1774.
```

    v.   SUSANNA, b. 27 Mar 1777.
    vi.   ABIGAIL, b. 23 Oct 1779; d. 23 Dec 1779.
    vii.   ABIGAIL, b. 12 Nov 1780; m. JESSE HARRIMAN.
    viii.   JOSIAH, b. 22 Apr 1783; m. SARAH MOULTON (VRNH).

22. **EBENEZER^5 TILTON** (Samuel$^{4-3}$, Daniel^2, William^1) was born at Hampton Falls, 11 Apr 1752 (VSHF, 35) and died at Andover, NH Jan, 1835 (DAR P.I., 680). He married LEAH LOVERING who died at Andover, Jan 1840 (John R. Eaastman, History of the Town of Andover, NH [Concord, 1910], hereafter H. Andover, 359). Ebenezer served as a private with Gen. John Stark at Bennington and Stillwater (ibid.).

Children, born at Andover (H. Andover, 359):

    i.   CALEB MORSE^6, b. 20 Jan 1777; m. RUTH T. COOPER.
    ii.   SAMUEL, b. 13 Nov 1779; m. HANNAH ROWE.
    iii.   ABIGAIL, b. 13 Sept 1781; m. STEPHEN DUDLEY of Hawke.
    iv.   JOHN, b. 27 Feb 1783.
    v.   JOHN, b. 18 Apr 1784.
    vi.   WILLIAM, b. ----; m. ELIZA ASH.
    vii.   EBENEZER, b. 22 Dec 1787; m. DEBORAH CILLEY.
    viii.   JONATHAN, b. 1791; m. (1) NANCY ROWE; m. (2) ABIGAIL (PARKER) HALL
    ix.   JOSEPH, b. 6 Sept 1793; m. MARY ROWE.
    x.   SILAS BARNARD, b. 25 Aug 1795; m. ABIGAIL SANBORN.
    xi.   LEVI R., b. 1797; m. PHEBE SANBORN.
    xii.   HULDA.
    xiii.   HANNAH, m. STEPHEN BROWN.
    xiv.   MEHITABLE, b. ca 1805; d. Boscawen 24 Mar 1885.

23. **DANIEL^5 TILTON** (Samuel$^{4-3}$, Daniel^2, William^1) was born at Hampton Falls, 20 Oct 1754 (VSHF, 35) and died at Sanbornton, NH, 8 Apr 1826 at the age of 71 (H. Sanbornton, 805). He married 7 Dec 1780 MARY LOWD who was born 10 May 1760 and died there 30 June 1829 (ibid.).

Daniel came from Hampton Falls to Sanbornton, 3 Feb 1781. He owned 50 acres of Lot #31, 2nd Division and 50 more on the next lot west. He was a tanner and shoemaker as well as a farmer, and used to go back to Hampton Falls for work and provisions during the early years of his settlement in Sanbornton (ibid.). Daniel served as a private in the Revolutionary War (DAR P.I., 680).

Children, born at Sanbornton (H. Sanbornton, 805):

    i.   CALEB^6, b. 13 Aug 1782; d. unmarried 22 Feb 1853.
    ii.   ABIGAIL, b. 21 Dec 1784; m. STEPHEN WALLIS.
    iii.   JOHN LOWD, b. Apr/Aug 3, 1787.
    iv.   DANIEL, b. 4 Mar 1789.
    v.   MOLLEY, b. 21 July 1791; d. 7 Nov 1832; m. 9 May 1811, JONATHAN
           SIMPSON of Billerica, MA.
    vi.   SAMUEL, JR., b. 18 Aug 1793.
    vii.   ABRAHAM HAYWARD, b. 2 May 1795.
    viii.   LEVI, b. 9 Mar 1797.
    ix.   ELIZABETH, b. 11 May 1799; m. GUY HANAFORD.

<u>Sons of Josiah and Sarah (Flanders) Tilton</u>:

24a. **SAMUEL^5 TILTON** (Josiah^4, Samuel^3, Daniel^2, William^1) was born at Kingston, 1 Dec 1733 (Kingston TR [Microfilm, NH State Library], 1:651) and died circa 1778 at Deerfield, NH. He married REBECCA PRESCOTT, the daughter of Hon. Benjamin Prescott (Gen. of NH 4:1653) and they made their home at Deerfield. Widow Rebecca married (2) as his second wife, John Prescott.

Samuel Tilton of Deerfield, husbandman, wrote his will 29 Apr 1775, stating that he was "sick and weak in body." It was proved 31 Dec 1777. He named his wife Rebecca as Executor, leaving her his lands and tenements, together with household goods and moveables. "I have no issue" he wrote, "I give to my said wife one pew that I own in the South Deerfield Meetinghouse." This was signed by Samuel and witnessed by Josiah Sawyer, James Brown, and Benjamin Butler (Rockingham Probate, 4409).

24b. **DAVID**[5] **TILTON** (Josiah[4], Samuel[3], Daniel[2], William[1]) was born at Kingston, 27 Oct 1735 and died at E. Kingston, 27 Aug 1825 (DAR P.I., 680); Greeley Gen, 98). He married at Kingston, 26 Mar 1760 JANE GREELEY, born at Kingston 16 Mar 1739; died there, 8 Mar 1814, daughter of Jonathan Greeley (ibid.). David was credited with Patriotic Service in the Revolutionary War (DAR P.I., 680).

David Tilton, husbandman, wrote and signed his will (Rockingham Probate, 11071) 18 Nov 1817; recorded 15 Sept 1825. His son Aaron was named Executor; witnesses were John Webster, Dearborn Blake, Jonathan Webster and Joseph Tilton, Jr. He devised to his son Jonathan the notes in hand held against him, plus $5.00. His son Daniel inherited all lands and real estate in Deerfield, with he (Daniel) paying the legacy of $30 "hereinafter given to my son Richard." The same sum was to be given to his grandson, the oldest son of son Josiah, and also the son of son Samuel "which legacies I charge upon the above real estate devised to my son Daniel." Son Richard received $30 "to be paid one year after my decease; also my great Bible." To son Josiah $200, with the same stipulation; he had already received most of his portion. To son Aaron all the salt marshland situated in said county of Rockingham. He also gave his clock to son Aaron. To his grandchildren, the children of son Jacob deceased, a note of hand of $100 signed by "my said son Jacob in his lifetime, to me." Also $1.00 to each of his grandchildren, the said children of son Jacob. To "beloved son" Samuel he gave $30; he having had the most of his portion out of the estate before; plus all demands against Samuel were to be cancelled. To his grandson, the oldest son of his son Josiah, was given $30 to be paid by the testator's son Daniel six months after his decease. To children Daniel, Richard, Josiah, Aaron and Samuel, he devised "all my real estate situated in Kingston, being 12 acres of woodland to be equally divided among them." The rest, residue, and remainder was devised to Aaron, the Executor.

Children, all born East Kingston (Greeley Gen., 98):

    i   JONATHAN[6], b. 26 Apr 1761.
    ii.   DANIEL, b. 30 Mar 1763 (VRNH).
    iii. RICHARD, b. 17 Oct 1764.
    iv.   JOSIAH, b. 18 Aug 1766; m. MARTHA GREELEY.
    vi.   AARON, b. 9 Nov 1768.
    vii. DAVID, b. 19 Jan 1771; d. at E. Kingston, 12 Aug 1786.
    viii. JACOB, b. 13 June 1773.
    viii. SAMUEL, b. 3 July 1776 (VRNH).

24c. **PHILLIP**[5] **TILTON** (Josiah[4], Samuel[3], Daniel[2], William[1]) was born at Kingston, 10 Apr 1741 (Kingston TR [Microfilm, NH State Library], 1:651) and died at Kingston, 26 Jan 1835. He married (1) 11 Sept 1766, MOLLY/MARY BATCHELDER; (2) 4 Oct 1809, EUNICE DODGE born ca 1760 (Edith Flanders Dunbar, The Flanders Family *from Europe to America* [Rutlant, VT, 1935], hereafter Flanders Family, 75).

Phillip served as a Captain in the Revolutionary War (DAR PI, 680). In Pension S18250 (NH DAR Pension Records [NH Historical Society]), on 20 Apr 1818, Phillip Tilton of East Kingston deposed that on 1 July 1775 he was appointed and commissioned a Captain of the 11th Regiment and served until Nov or Dec 1776.

On 5 July 1820, still of East Kingston, Phillip testified that he had in his family a wife about 60 years of age; mother 88 years of age and a grandchild 11 years of age (ibid.).

Captain Phillip served at Winter Hill, MA under the command of Col. Enoch Poor; as Captain of the 11th Regiment he served at Ticonderoga, NY; and also in Rhode Island as a volunteer with the regiment of NH Militia under the command of Col. Gale (ibid.).

In Certificate #121892 (Rockingham Probate) dated 10 Mar 1835, John Kimball of Exeter and Dearborn Blake of Kensington deposed that "Phillip Tilton, late of East Kingston, died 26 Jan 1835; that he was a Revolutionary pensioner. He left no widow at his decease but left the following children: Nathaniel, Nathan, Joseph Tilton, Jr., Levi Tilton" ... and no more.

Children, all born E. Kingston (TR E. Kingston 1:122):

    i.   NATHANIEL, b. 24 July 1767.
    ii.   MOLLY, b. 28 Feb 1770; d. 23 July 1776 (VRNH).
    iii. NATHAN
    iv.   JOSEPH, b. 10 Aug 1774.
    v.   LEVI, b. 18 Sept 1777.
    vi.   MOLLY, b. 3 July 1781.

25. **JOSIAH^5 TILTON** (Josiah^4, Samuel^3, Daniel^2, William^1) was born at Kingston, 22 Oct 1743 (Kingston TR 1:651) and died at Cornville, ME, 13 Feb 1820 (Flanders Family, 76). Josiah settled in Deerfield, but in 1820 removed to Cornville. His first wife was SARAH TRUE, daughter of Deacon Abraham True. He married (2) 25 Oct 1798, ABIGAIL NUDD of Kingston (ibid.). Josiah served as an Ensign in the Revolutionary War (DAR PI, 680), 1).

Children by Sarah True (H. Deerfield, 476, unless noted):

    i.   SAMUEL^6, b. 1771; m. 30 Sept 1795 SARAH BATCHELDER (Batchelder
          Gen, 134).
    ii.   MERIBAH, b. circa 1775; m. 6 Jan 1795 DANIEL CURRIER (Deerfield
          VR [Family Records; typed MSS at NH Hist. Soc.], hereafter
          Deerfield VR, 24).
    iii. JOSIAH, b. 28 Feb 1778; m. SARAH DEARBORN (G.S.I.).
    iv.   SALLY.
    v.   HULDA.

Children by Abigail Nudd (H. Deerfield, 476):

    vi.   ABRAHAM.
    vii. DANIEL.
    viii. HORATIO GATES.

26. **EBENEZER**[5] **TILTON** (Josiah[4], Samuel[3], Daniel[2], William[1]) was born at Kingston, 3 Oct 1754. He married at Kensington, 23 Jan 1777 LUCY PRESCOTT (VRNH), born 3 Jan 1751, daughter of Jonathan and Rachel (Clifford) Prescott of Kensington and Gilmanton (Prescott Memorial, 267). Jonathan and Lucy resided at Deerfield near his brother Josiah (H. Deerfield, 480). He signed the Association Test there (Misc. Rev. Doc. XXX, 42).

Children, born at Deerfield (H. Deerfield, 480):

    i.   JOSEPH[6], lived at Exeter.
    ii.   DANIEL, m. ELEANOR NORRIS, dau. of Major William Norris of Nottingham.
    iii. SALLY, m. JONATHAN STEVENS of Deerfield.

<u>Sons of Sherburne and Ann (Hilliard) Tilton:</u>

27. **SHERBURNE**[5] **TILTON** (Sherburne[4], Joseph[3], Daniel[2], William[1]) was born at Kensington, 20 July 1735 (TR 1:337) and died at Wheelock, VT, 20 Sept 1813 (H. Bristol, 426). He married HULDAH PRESCOTT, who was also born at Kensington, 14 Nov 1738 and died at St. Albans, VT on 11 Apr 1823 (ibid.).

In July of 1776, Sherburne enlisted in Capt. David Quimby's Company of Col. Josiah Bartlett's regiment; in 1777 he marched from Sandown to join the Northern Army at Saratoga (ibid.).

Sherburne and Hulda settled in Sandown but removed about 1780 to Bristol, NH where he built a log cabin on South Main St. He operated a saw mill and grist mill which he later sold and moved to Hemp Hill in Bristol. Later he moved to Wheelock, VT where he died.

Children, all born at Sandown, except the last (ibid.):

    i.   JOHN[6], b. 24 Sept 1761.
    ii.   ANN (twin), b. 11 Aug 1763; m. DANIEL SLEEPER.
    iii. DOROTHY (twin), b. 11 Aug 1763; d. unm. 1857 age 94.
    iv.   ELIZABETH, b. 26 June 1765; m. JOHN SLEEPER.
    v.   SHERBURNE, b. 12 May 1768.
    vi.   DANIEL (twin), b. 20 Apr 1770.
    vii. SARAH (twin), b. 20 Apr 1770.
    viii. REBECCA, b. 29 July 1772; d. 11 July 1773.
    ix.   BENJAMIN, b. 12 Sept 1774.
    x.   THEOPHILUS, b. 15 Jan 1777; m. COMFORT POWELL.
    xi.   JONATHAN, b. 22 Aug 1779.
    xii. TIMOTHY, b. at Bristol, 30 Apr 1783.

28. **BENJAMIN**[5] **TILTON** (Sherburne[4], Joseph[3], Daniel[2], William[1]) was born at Kensington, 26 Dec 1740 (Kensington TR 1:337) and died there 1807. He married there on 30 Oct 1765 SHUAH PERKINS (ibid., 1:356). Shuah was also born at Kensington, 20 Dec 1746, daughter of James and Shuah Perkins (H. Kensington, 332).

Benjamin wrote his will (Rockingham Probate, 7714) 29 May 1806; it was proved 19 Oct 1807. To his wife Shuah, he left one-third of his land and buildings, plus two cows and one sheep. To sons Daniel, Sherburne and James, he bequeathed $50; to son Abraham he gave one third part of his real estate, undivided. He gave $1.00 each to daughters Ann, wife of Theophilus Sanborn; Betty, wife of Jonathan Godfrey, and Huldah, wife of Simeon Lane. To son Benjamin, whom he named as Executor, he gave 3/4 of all his real estate and buildings, stock of cattle, sheep and swine. Elijah Shaw, John Tilton and Moses Shaw witnessed his signature and will. (The writer wonders at Benjamin's arithmetic. One-third plus one-third plus three-quarters equals trouble!)

Children, born at Kensington (TR, 1:356, 386):

 i. BENJAMIN, b. 22 Apr 1767.
 ii. DANIEL, b. 24 Oct 1770.
 iii. ANN, b. 27 Feb 1773; m. THEOPHILUS SANBORN.
 iv. HULDAH, b. 6 Mar 1774; m. SIMEON LANE.
 v. ABRAHAM, b. 8 July 1775.
 vi. SHERBURNE, b. 17 Aug 1777.
 vii. JOHN, b. 4 Nov 1781 (VRNH).
 viii. BETTY, b. 31 Aug 1779; m. JONATHAN GODFREY.
 ix. JAMES, b. 4 Nov 1781.
 x. MERCY, bpt. 21 Jan 1787 (Rev. Roland D. Sawyer, Kensington Vital Statistics [MSS, 1943, at NH Hist. Soc.]; hereafter Kensington VS, 35).

29. **TIMOTHY^5 TILTON** (Sherburne^4, Joseph^3, Daniel^2, William^1) was born at Kensington on 1 Jan 1748 (Kensington TR, 1:337) and died at Sandown, 11 Jan 1831 (Pension Record, W16080 [DAR Pension Records at NH Hist. Soc.]. He married at Kensington, 5 Dec 1771, SARAH PRESCOTT (ibid.). From the same source: on 7 Mar 1818, Timothy Tilton of Sandown deposed that he received a commission as Ensign in the NH Militia in 1776 and served in that rank until his company was disbanded a year later. On 11 July 1820, aged 72, Timothy testified that he was a cordwainer and his family consisted of his wife of 71 years and himself. On 19 Sept 1836, Sarah Tilton at 86 years of age, deposed that she was the widow of Timothy, to whom she was married 5 Dec 1771, and that her husband died 11 Jan 1831. Sarah was b. 1 July 1750, the daughter of Jonathan and Rachel (Clifford) Prescott of Kensington & Gilmanton. Her sister Lucy married Ebenezer Tilton of Deerfield (Prescott Memorial, 267).

In his will (Rockingham Probate, 12169) received and filed 25 Jan 1831; proved 16 Mar 1831, Ensign Timothy named his wife Sarah, giving her the household furniture and bedding belonging to his house. To son Timothy he bequeathed $40 "to be paid by my creditors one year after my decease." To son Joseph C. was given $20 with the same stipultaion. He appointed his sons Sherburne and Jonathan to be Executors, giving them "all my other estate of whatever name or nature not herein disposed of." Witnesses were Eliphalet Hunt, Joseph G. Wood, and Albert G. Wood. The beautiful colonial house where Timothy and Sarah Tilton lived is still standing and occupied in Sandown today.

Children, born at Sandown (VRNH):

 i. TIMOTHY^6, b. 23 Dec 1776.
 ii. JOSEPH, b. 17 Apr 1779.
 iii. SHERBURNE, b. 18 Aug 1786.
 iv. JONATHAN, b. 8 Mar 1791.

<u>Sons of John and Hannah (Robie) Tilton:</u>

30. **JOSEPH^5 TILTON** (John^4, Joseph^3, Daniel^2, William^1) was born at Kensington, 21 Oct 1735 (Kensington TR 1:236-37) and died at Sandown 1823 (WP, 11 Dec 1823). He married MARY ----.

(Rockingham Deeds, 159:120) John Tilton of the parish of Kensington, gentleman, "for and in consideration for the parental love and good will that I have and do bear towards my well beloved son Joseph Tilton of Sandown" gave Joseph a tract of land in Sandown containing 48 acres. Dated 29 Mar 1765; witnesses were Nathaniel and Ebenezer Dow.

Joseph Tilton of Sandown wrote his will (Rockingham Probate, 10749) 12 Feb 1816; proved 11 Dec 1823. He devised 30 acres of land to his son Isaac. To his daughter Mary, wife of Samuel Davis, he gave one-half of the household furniture and her mother's wearing apparel after her decease. To granddaughter Sally Brown, wife of Daniel Brown, was given the other half of the furniture "and also my chaise." To grandson-in-law Daniel Brown, Joseph gave "my home, containing about 38 acres of land." To his son-in-law Samuel Davis he left "my clock and my share in the cider mill." He named Samuel Davis as Executor. He signed his will which was witnessed by James Sawyer, James Sawyer, Jr. and John Scribner.

Children (order of birth uncertain):

    i.   ISAAC^6, b. 10 Aug 1760 at Kingston (IGI).
    ii.   MARY, m. SAMUEL DAVIS (mentioned in will).

31. **JOHN^5 TILTON** (John^4, Joseph^3, Daniel^2, William^1) was born at Kensington, 7 Sept 1737 (Kensington TR 1:325-27) and died there, 18 Jan 1818 at age 82 (VRNH). He married there, 19 may 1761, HANNAH CLIFFORD, who died 28 Mar 1829 (H. Gilmanton, 289). John and Hannah resided at Gilmanton. He saw service during the Revolutionary War as an Ensign (DAR P.I., 680).

Children (H. Gilmanton, 289; first five found in IGI):

    i.   SAMUEL^6, b. 7 May 1762 Weare Twp (VRNH).
    ii.   ELIZABETH, b. 12 Mar 1764 " "
    iii. NATHANIEL, b. 16 Oct 1766 " "
    iv.   JUDITH, b. 22 Aug 1769 " "
    v.   HANNAH, b. 18 June 1771 " "
    vi.   ABIGAIL.
    vii. MARY.
    viii. JOHN.
    ix.   RICHARD
    x.   DAVID.
    xii. SARAH.
    xiii. DOLLY.

32. **SAMUEL^5 TILTON** (John^4, Joseph^3, Daniel^2, William^1) was born at Kensington, 4 Feb 1741 (TR, 1:326-27). He was not mentioned in his father John Tilton's will, written 1 June 1872, nor has any record of him been found with the exception of his birth record as given. The Batchelder Genealogy, 140, has the Samuel who married Joanna Batchelder as the son of John and Hannah Robie. However, the deed of Samuel, #19, who married Joanna, refutes this as he mentions in that deed "my honoured father Samuel Tilton of Hampton Falls" The author would appreciate any existing information on this Samuel.

33. **JEREMIAH^5 TILTON** (John^4, Joseph^3, Daniel^2, William^1) was born at Kensington, 2 Feb 1743 (TR 1:326-27) and died there, 11 Aug 1832, age 89. His widow died in 1834, age 87; they were both buried in the Tilton burial lot on North Road, established by his father John (H. Kensington, 286). He was called a farmer; cause of death was palsy (VRNH). He married at Kensington, 25 Nov 1766 MARY

BROWN, born 4 Mar 1737, daughter of Benjamin and Mary Brown (Kensington VS [Birth Records in Parish Book, 361], 5). Jeremiah is listed as not signing the association Test at Kensington by reason of being a Quaker (Misc. Rev. Doc., XXX:76).

Jeremiah Tilton of Kensington drew his will (Rockingham Probate, 12423) 20 Dec 1820; recorded 12 Sept 1832. He devised to his oldest son Nathaniel "all the land that I own in the town of Epping, plus $50 and $25 cash within one year of my decease." To Jeremiah: $200, also a bedstead and bedding. To John: "one half of all the lands I own in Kensington except that piece of land which formerly belonged to Capt. James Leavitt, and also the westerly half of my house and barn. To Jonathan: "all that piece of land which was once owned by Capt. James Leavitt, and also half of all the other lands I own in the town of Kensington, and the easterly half of my house and barn. To his wife Mary he gave the use of the front room of his house during her widowhood; after which the same is to revert to my son Jonathan. Also to Mary all the household furniture, a chaise and sleigh. "My executors shall supply my wife with everything necessary for her support and comfort so long as she continues to be my widow." He left his wearing apparel to be equally divided between Nathaniel, Jonathan, Jeremiah and John. To John and Jonathan he gave his stock of creatures, farming utensils, husbandry tools. He named John and Jonathan as Executors; witnesses were John Blake, Jeremiah Sanborn, and Edward J. Sanborn.

Children (Kensington TR, 1:365):

   i.   NATHANIEL^6, b. 8 Aug 1769.
   ii. JEREMIAH, b. 9 Apr 1771.
   iii. JOHN, b. 2 Sept 1773.
   iv. JONATHAN, b. 23 Sept 1777.

34. **DAVID^5 TILTON** (John^4, Joseph^3, Daniel^2, William^1) was born at Kensington (TR 1:326-27) on 5 May 1745 and died at Sandown before 25 June 1783. He married at Kensington, 13 July 1768, MIRIAM CLOUGH. David saw considerable action in the Revolutionary War (Isaac W. Hammond, Revolutionary Rolls, XIV [Concord, 1885]:11, 146, 195, 226). David was listed as a miller, residence Sandown, age 30, when he served in Capt. Phillip Tilton's company 12 June 1775 (ibid., 112).

David Tilton of Sandown, yeoman, wrote his will (Rockingham Probate, 4913) 3 May 1783; proved 25 June 1783. He named his wife Miriam as Executrix and gave her one third of his real and personal estate and household goods. To his son John he devised one half of his real and personal estate "when he arrives at the age of 21 years." To son Joseph, the other half of same." To daughter Molly he gave 10 pounds of lawful silver money and one cow of middling size "when she arrives at the age of 21 years," to be paid by son John. To Margaret, the same, to be paid by son Joseph. Witnesses were Joseph, John and Jeremiah Tilton.

Children:

   i.   JOHN^6, b. 29 Feb 1768 (Kensington TR, 1:361).
   ii. MOLLEY, b. 17 Feb 1770 as Sandown (VRNH).
   iii. JOSEPH, b. 7 Sept 1771 at Sandown (ibid.).
   iv. MARGARET, b. 29 Aug 1773 at Sandown (IGI).

(To be continued)

DESCENDANTS OF LEONARD HARRIMAN - continued

By Lois Ware Thurston

3. JONATHAN^2 HARRIMAN (Leonard^1) was born at Rowley, Massachusetts on 5: 10 Mo (December) 1657 (Rowley VR 1:87) and died there on 15 February 1741/42, aged 84 years (Rowley VR 1:469, P.R.2 Records of the Second Church). Jonathan resided in that part of Rowley that was established as Georgetown in 1838. His gravestone in the Georgetown cemetery still stands and reads:

"Here Lies Burried the Body of Mr Ionathan Herremen who died Feby 15 1741 in ye 85th Year of his age.".

He married first, before 19 August 1686 when their daughter Margaret was born (Rowley VR 1:87), SARAH PALMER, born at Rowley on 13: 11 mo. (January) 1661, daughter of Sergeant John and Margaret (Northend) (Cross) Palmer (ibid. 1:150). She died at Rowley on 30 June 1688 (ibid. 1:470). That Jonathan's wife, Sarah, was in fact the daughter of John Palmer is proved by Palmer's will, dated 23 August 1693, in which he named his "son-in-law Jonathan Harriman," (Essex County Probate, #20430; Early Settlers of Rowley, hereinafter Rowley Early Settlers, p 262). Jonathan married second at Rowley on 19 August 1691 MARGARET (ELITHORP) WOOD (Rowley VR 1:307), born at Ipswich on 24 July 1672, daughter of Nathaniel and Mary (Batt) Elithorp (Ipswich VR 1:127). Margaret, the widow of Samuel Wood of Rowley, was also left with an infant child, a son Thomas Wood, born at Rowley on 4 November 1689 (Rowley VR 1:235; Rowley Early Settlers, p 413). Margaret died at Rowley on 25 January 1754 "aged" (ibid. 1:470).

Jonathan Harriman and his family has been adequately addressed in the Early Settlers of Rowley (pp. 134-137; 30;147-148) and by Mary Lovering Holman in her Ancestry of Charles Stinson Pillsbury and John Sargent Pillsbury - found also as "The Harriman Line," Excerpts from the Pillsbury Ancestry ([n.p., 1938] 905-909), which follows the line of Jonathan's daughter, Margaret, who married Jonathan Boynton.

Leonard^1 Harriman, by his will dated 12 May 1691, noted that he had already given his son Jonathan, land "by deed of gift upon marriage, and the new Leanto built agst his Room and my shop and Loomes & all the working geers belonging to them & all my utensills of Husbandry & half my part of the hay boat." By his will he gave Jonathan "the other half of my lands in Rowley... [and]...my division in the commons." Jonathan was named Executor of his estate (Essex County Probate 304:385).

Mrs. Holman noted that the earlier transaction was not recorded at Essex County. She then summarized several deeds recorded there concerning Jonathan Harriman as follows:

"..I Jonathan Herriman yeoman in ...Rowley... with consent of Margarett my wife concerning her Right of Dower sells to Samuel Smith husbandman of Ipswich land in Rowley formerly Laid out unto my Father Leonard Herriman", 15 Oct 1708 (Essex Co., Deeds, 43:47).

Thomas Wood, son of Samuel Wood, deceased, sells land to Collins Fraser, Jonathan Harriman and his wife Margaret quit their rights in the same, 10 Nov. 1710 (ibid., 32:157). Margaret was the mother of Thomas Wood and hence had her dower right in the estate of his father, which on her second marriage became the property of her second husband. This is explained in the next deed of theirs.

Thomas Wood, son of Samuel Wood, deceased, sells land in Rowley to the Inhabitants of Byfield and 'Jonathan Herriman & Margaret his wife Relict of the parent of said Thomas vizt Samuel Wood,' quits any right of dower in the premises, 2 May 1711 (ibid., 24:167).

Jonathan Herriman, yeoman of Rowley for love and affection for son John Herriman gives to him land in Rowley bounded on Samuel and Jeremiah Herriman, Margaret signs the acknowledgement, 6 Mar 1720 (ibid., 63:116).

'I Jonathan Herriman yeoman for... Love goodwill & affection that I...bear towards my well beloved son, Nathaniel Herriman...do...grant...to the abovesd Nathaniel Herriman... forty Acres upland & Swampy Ground in... Rowley which is part of the Farm I purchased of Thomas Lambert... also third part of my meadow called Crane meadow...also one Eighteenth part of the Saw Mill... with consent of Margarett my wife,' 21 Jan 1720/21 (ibid., 44:222).

He makes a similar deed to his 'beloved son Leonard Harriman' 10 Jun 1720 (ibid., 44:223). He gives land partly in Bradford and partly in Rowley to his sons Leonard and Nathaniel, 2 Aug 1725 (ibid., 47:111) and more land to his son John, 2 Aug 1725 (ibid., 63:117). He gives a salt marsh in Rowley to his son Nathaniel, 1 September 1729 (ibid., 61:108). On 17 September 1729, for 'Parental love and affection,' he gives to his son Samuel, 2/3 of all land he has in Rowley, Margaret signs with him. (ibid. 63:118).

And on this same date, he gives 45 acres of land to his son Jeremiah, Margaret signing with him. He signs this deed by mark, witnessed by Thomas Wood and John Heriman (ibid., 61:112) See also, 65:99; 56:180; 28:4; 26:182; 31:176."

Jonathan Harriman served in the Rowley Militia and was among those listed as "foot soldiers" who petitioned the Court about 1677 to have Lieutenant Phillip Nelson named as Commander in Chief of the Rowley Company. Holman states Jonathan was a Sergeant in this company. Also listed is an unidentified Abraham Harriman of whom no further information has been found (<u>Mr. Ezechi Rogers Plantation</u>, p 54). Jonathan attended the First Parish Church in Rowley, where most of his children were baptized. He apparently also attended the Byfield Church as his youngest son, Jeremiah, was baptized there in 1709. The record of Jonathan's death in the records of the Second Church of Rowley [now Georgetown] indicate he later attended that church.

Jonathan Harriman's will, dated 12 June 1734 and proved on 19 April 1742, is excerpted as follows (Essex County Probate, #12447; 325:34):
"Item I give to my beloved wife Margaret Herreman the use of all my Household Stuff during her natural life & whereas I have before disposed of most of My lands & of part of ye house y^t I now dwell in & a part of my Barn I now hereby Give to my s^d Wife the use & improvement of my Lands yt remain in my possession & of my House & barn so long as she Shall remain my Widow I also give unto Her two Cows and I give to Her Sufficient firewood for one fire yearly to be cut & bro't to the house... & if what is here mentioned be not Sufficient for Her Comfortable Support then my Will is that She have a Comfortable support out of my Estate so long as She shall remain my widow...

Item I give to my son Leonard Herriman besides w^t I have given him by Deed or otherwise the sum of five shillings.
Item I give to my son Nathaniel Herriman besides w^t I have...given him the Sum of five shillings.
Item I give to my son John Herriman besides w^t I have... given him the Sum of five shillings.

Item I give to my son Samuel Herriman besides w^t I have...given him the sum of five shillings.

Item I give to my son Jeremiah Herriman besides w^t I have...given him all my lands y^t remain in my possession & also my House & barn after his Mothers decease, if He shall provide for his mother ye firewood which I have above given to her, & shall also make w^t provision is needful for his Mother's support...& shall also bury her...and w^{t}ever estate I now have that is not yet disposed of... I give it to my son Jeremiah.

Item I give to each of my three Daughters (viz) Margaret Boynton & Mary Nelson and Sarah Hazzen besides w^t I have already given them the sum of ten shillings... and all my Household Stuff which shall remain after my wife's decease...

And I hereby Constitute & appoint my son Jeremiah Herriman Sole Executor." Signed by the mark of Jonathan Heriman and witnessed by Thomas Lambert, John Brocklebank and James Chandler.

Child (HARRIMAN) of Jonathan and Sarah (Palmer), born at Rowley (Rowley VR 1:87):

    i. MARGARET, b. 19 August 1686, bpt. at the First Churchof Rowley on 22 August 1686 (Rowley Church Records, p 213); d. Rowley on 16 October 1752 (Rowley VR 2:27); m. 1) Rowley on 6 June 1711 JONATHAN BOYNTON (ibid. 1:307), b. 19 August 1684, son of Captain Joseph and Sarah (Swan) Boynton (ibid. 1:27). He d. Rowley on 16 March 1740 (ibid. 1:444). Margaret m. 2) Rowley 12 May 1742 DANIEL GAGE of Bradford (ibid. 1:252). He was probably the Daniel Gage b. Bradford on 12 March 1675, son of Daniel and probably Sarah Kimball (Bradford VR p. 51). He d. Bradford on 14 March 1747/48, aged 73 years (ibid. p. 313). Margaret m. 3) Rowley 5 September 1749, as his fourth wife, JOHN STEWART (Rowley VR 1:298), b. Newbury in 1766, son of Duncan and Anne (Winchurst) Stewart of Newbury and Rowley (Rowley Early Settlers, p. 356, 358).

        Children (BOYNTON) born at Rowley (Rowley VR 1:24-26; Rowley Early Settlers, p. 30): 1. Margaret, b. 5 April 1712. 2. Sarah, b. 10 December 1713. 3. Elizabeth, b. 21 May 1715. 4. Jonathan, b. 16 March 1716/17. 5. Benjamin, [twin] bp. 12 April 1719; prob. died young. 6. Ellenor, [twin] bp. 12 April 1719; prob. died young. 7. Mary, b. 21 August 1720. 8. John, b. 22 May 1723. 9. Anne, b. 29 October 1726.

Children (HARRIMAN) of Jonathan and Margaret (Elithorp), born at Rowley (Rowley VR 1:86-88) and baptized at the First Church of Rowley (Rowley Church Records, pp. 217, 218, 221, 223, 225, 227):

    ii. JONATHAN, b. 15 July 1692, bpt. 17 July 1692; d. Rowley 20 November 1711 (Rowley VR 1:469). Unmarried.

    iii. CAPTAIN LEONARD, b. 5 October 1694, bpt. 7 October 1694; d. Rowley 18 February 1785, aged 92 years (Rowley VR 1:470); m. Newbury 5 July 1715 MARTHA PLUMMER (ibid. 1:307), b. Rowley 2 March 1696/97, daughter of Benjamin and Ann (Wood) Plummer (ibid. 1:174). Martha d. Rowley 6 August 1733, aged 36 years, 5 months (ibid. 1:470; gravestone, Georgetown Cemetery). Leonard resided in that part of Rowley that became Georgetown in 1838. No probate records were found concerning Leonard Harriman.

        Child (HARRIMAN), born at Rowley (Rowley VR 1:87): 1. Jonathan, b. 2 April 1715, bpt 8 April 1716 (Newbury VR 1:219, Byfield Church).

iv. LIEUTENANT NATHANIEL, b. 31 December 1696, bpt. 3January 1696/97; d. Louisburg, Nova Scotia 13 October 1744/45 (Rowley Early Settlers p. 184); m. Rowley 25 August 1720 MEHITABLE SPOFFORD (Rowley VR 1:307), b. Rowley 29 October 1697, daughter of Samuel and Sarah (Burpee) Spofford (ibid. 1:203). She d. between 16 August 1753 when she made her will and 19 January 1756 when it was proved (Essex Co. Probate, #12453, 333:340). Lieut. Nathaniel Harriman's will, dated 13 March 1744/45 just before he left for Louisburg, was proved on 18 November 1745 and named "my beloved wife", [unnamed], who was Executrix of his estate; sons Samuel and Moses; daughters Abigail, wife of Samuel Kezer, Mehitable, wife of Jonathan Plummer, and Margaret Harriman; grand-daughter Rossamon Harriman [Rosamond5, b. 6 January 1744-5], daughter of son Nathaniel Harriman, late of Bradford, deceased. His son, Moses, chose Captain Leonard Harriman for his guardian on 26 March 1753 (Essex Co. Probate, #12458; 333:340; #12454). Mehitable's will, dated 16 August 1753 and proved on 19 January 1756, named sons, Samuel and Moses; daughter, Margaret Harriman; grandson Nathaniel Plummer; and "ye rest of my Dafthers"; son Samuel was named Executor. (Essex Co. Probate, #12453, 330:340).

Children (HARRIMAN) born at Rowley (Rowley VR 1:86-89; Newbury VR 1:218-219, bpt. Byfield Ch.): 1. Abigail, b. 8 October 1721, bpt 15 October 1721. 2. Nathaniel, b. 22 March 1722/23, bpt. 24 March 1722/23. 3. Mehitable, b. 10 March 1726/27, bpt. 12 March 1726/27. 4. Samuel, b. 23 May 1732. 5. Margaret, b. 23 February 1734/35. 6. Moses, b. 28 April 1737.

v. MARY, b. 11 November 1698, bpt. 13 November 1698; death date and place unknown; m. 1) Rowley (int) 11 May 1728 JACOB HALE (Rowley VR 1:307), b. ca 1695/96, son of Joseph and Mary (Watson) Hale of Newbury and Boxford (Boxford VR 1:43). He d. Boxford 17 April 1731 (ibid., 1:240; see Des. of Thomas Hale, p. 60-61, 100-101). Mary m. 2) Rowley 1 February 1732/33 JEREMIAH NELSON (Rowley VR 1:303), b. Rowley 23 June 1707, son of Joseph and Hannah (Brocklebrook) Nelson (ibid. 1:143; Rowley Early Settlers, p. 245, 247). Jeremiah was admitted to the Second Church in Rowley on 10 February 1734 and dismissed to the Second Church of Ipswich on 14 April 1765. He d. Ipswich 26 February 1773 (Ipswich VR 2:636). His will, dated 27 June 1761, named his wife, Mary; daughter Hannah Pickard; and sons Jeremiah and Jacob Nelson, who were named his Exectutors (Rowley Early Settlers, p. 247).

Child (HALE) born at Boxford (Boxford VR 1:43, 240): 1. Jacob, b. 3 April 1730; d. 27 September 1730.

Children (NELSON) born at Rowley (Rowley VR 1:140-146,496): 2. Jeremiah, b. 5 February 1733/34; d. 22 November 1736. 3. Hannah, b. 16 March 1736/37. 4. Jeremiah, b. 28 April 1739. 5. Jacob, b. 27 November 1742.

vi. SARAH, b. 19 March 1700/01, bpt. 23 March 1700/01; d. Shirley 1 August 1794, aged 96 [sic] years (Shirley VR 1:192); m. Rowley (int) 14 September 1723 [m. 1 October 1723, Rowley Early Settlers] SAMUEL HAZEN of Boxford (Rowley VR 1:92), b. Rowley 20 July 1698, son of Edward and Jane (Pickard) Hazen of Rowley and Boxford (ibid. 1:92). Samuel and Sarah moved to Groton in 1738 and then to Shirley where he died 20 September 1790, aged 94 years 1 month 2 days (Shirley VR 1:192). Several of their children died of the "throat distemper" that spread throughout Essex County in 1736.

Children (HAZEN) first six born at Rowley (Rowley VR 1:91-92, 471-472; Rowley Early Settlers, p. 147-148): 1. Edward, b. 26 May 1724; d. 10 January 1736/37, aged 12 years 8 months. 2. Samuel, b. 31 January 1726/27; d. 25 November 1736, aged 9 years 10 months. 3. Margaret, b. 23 January 1729/30; d.

24 December 1736, aged about 8 years. 4. Sarah, b. 9 April 1731; d. 20 December 1736, aged 5 years 8 months. 5. Benjamin, b. 22 April 1734; d. 6 January 1736/37, aged 2 years 8 months 14 days. 6. Unice/Eunice, b. 8 August 1736. 7. Edward, b. at Groton 2 May 1738 (Groton VR 1:108). 8. Samuel, b. at Shirley 24 May 1740 (Rowley Early Settlers p. 147-148).

vii. JOHN, b. 13 June 1703, bpt. the same day; d. Rowley 25 January 1753, aged "about 50 years" (Rowley VR 1:469); m. Rowley (int) 7 May 1726 JANE BAILEY (ibid. 1:306), b. Bradford on 4 February 1706, daughter of Thomas and Eunice (Walker) Bailey (Bradford VR 1:14). Jane m. 2) Rowley 18 June 1761 Israel Hazen of Rowley and Boxford (Rowley VR 1:306; see Rowley Early Settlers, p. 148) and d. Rowley 8 July 1803, aged 97 years (Rowley Early Settlers, p. 148). John resided in that area of Rowley that later became Georgetown. Two children died in 1736, probably from the "throat distemper." John's will, dated 10 September 1751 and proved 19 March 1753, named: "my beloved wife, Jane Harriman"; sons John, Enoch, Leonard, and Thomas; and daughters Jane, Margaret and Anne; his wife and son John were named Executors of the estate. His "brother [half-brother] Thomas Wood" was named Exectutor of the sale of lands he bought of Jonathan Hopkinson. In addition to lands owned in Rowley, John mentioned lands he owned in Newbury, MA and Contoscook, NH [now Boscawen]. His son Enoch chose his brother, John Harriman, to be his guardian on 17 December 1753. Leonard also chose his brother, John Harriman, for his guardian on 14 October 1754. On 30 January 1758 Jane and Thomas Harriman chose John Adams of Rowley to be their guardian (Essex Co. Probate, #12445, 331:200; #12437; #12452; #12443).

Children (HARRIMAN) born at Rowley (Rowley VR 1:86-88, 469-470; gravestones, Georgetown Cemetery): 1. Enoch, b. 18 May 1727, bpt. 28 May 1727 (Newbury VR, 1:218, Byfield Ch.); d. 24 August 1736, 10 years 3 months. 2. Jane, b. 24 June 1729; d. 23 August 1736, 7 years 2 months. 3. John, b. 17 October 1731. 4. Leonard, b. 14 June 1734; d. 1 September 1736, 2 years 2 months. 5. Enoch, b. 5 October 1736. 6. Leonard, b. 12 March 1738/39. 7. Jane, b. 27 March 1741. 8. Thomas, b. 12 January 1743/44. 9. Margaret, b. 9 March 1745/46. 10. Solomon, b. 12 June 1749; d. 17 June 1749, 5 days. 11. Anna, b. 13 August 1750.

viii. SAMUEL, b. 12 [sic] November 1705 by Rowley VR's, but according to Rowley Chruch records he was baptized on 11 November 1705; d. between 25 January 1758 when he made his will and 3 April 1758 when it was proved. He died as a result of a fall from a beam in his barn (Descendants of Leonard Harriman of New England, p. 95). Samuel m. Newbury 16 October 1729 JANE COLMAN (Newbury VR 2:221), b. Newbury 20 March 1712, daughter of Thomas and Phebe (Pearson) Colman of Rowley and Newbury (Newbury VR 1:122). Jane, m. 2) Newbury 23 November 1758 Timothy Toppan (Newbury VR 2:492). Her death date and place unknown. Samuel resided at Newbury. His will, dated 25 January 1758 and proved 3 April 1758, named his wife Jane; son Asa; and daughter Jane. His wife and son Asa were named Executors of the estate. Asa and Jane, "over fourteen years of age" chose Benjamin Colemen of Newbury for their guardian on 3 April 1758 (Essex Co. Probate, #12461, 335:240; #12430). Several of John's children died in 1736 - probably from the "throat distemper."

Children (HARRIMAN) born at Rowley (Rowley VR 1:86-89, 469-470; Rowley Early Settlers, p 135): 1. a child bp. -- March 1730/31 (Newbury VR 1:219, Byfield Ch.); died young as Jane, who died in 1736 was then the "only child." 2. Samuel, b. 23 February 1731/32; the first child baptized at the West

Parish Meeting House in Rowley; d. 13 September 1736, aged 4 1/2 years. 3. Jane, b. 10 November 1733; d. 28 September 1736, "only child" aged 2 years 11 months (Rowley VR 1:469; gs Georgetown Cem.) . 4. Dudley, b. 9 March 1734/35; d. 27 September 1736, aged 1 1/2 years (gs Georgetown Cem.). 5. Phebe, b. 2 August 1737; d. 29 July 1745, aged 8 years. 6. Jane, b. 8 October 1739. 7. Asa, b. 30 January 1742/43. 8. Nathaniel, b. 17 September 1747; d. 1 October 1747, aged 14 days.

ix. JEREMIAH, b. 22 [sic] September 1709, bpt. 4 [sic] September 1709 (Newbury VR 1:218, Byfield Ch) ; d. Rowley 30 January 1753, about 40 years (Rowley VR 1:469) - just five days after the death of his brother John Harriman; m. Rowley 17 April 1735 PATIENCE PERLEY (Rowley VR 1:306), b. Rowley 20 March 1704/05, daughter of Samuel and Abigail (Cummings) Perley (Rowley VR 1:160). Blodgette and Jewett suggest this was perhaps his second marriage, but no evidence has been found to confrim that. His age of 26 years at the time of his marriage was the customary age to marry in that time period. His will, dated 3 August 1749 and proved on 19 March 1753, named wife, Patience, who was the Executrix of his estate; only daughter, Lucy; sons Jonathan, Jeremiah and William - all under 21 years of age. His son William chose Jonathan Harriman of Rowley, probably his brother, to be his guardian on 30 October 1758 (Essex Co. Probate, #12444, 331:203; #12467). Patience died at Rowley on 20 May 1772 "in her 72d year" (Rowley VR 1:470).

Children (HARRIMAN) born at Rowley (Rowley VR 1:86-89, 470; Rowley Early Settlers, p 136-137): 1. Lucy, bp. 22 August 1736; d. 25 February 1755, aged 18 1/2 years. 2. Jonathan, b. 26 November 1737. 3. Jeremiah, b. 25 July 1740. 4. William, b. 8 January 1742/43 (dy or an error for William b. 1747/48 - see below). 5. a son, b. 21 September 1745; d. 29 September 1745, 8 days. 6. William, b. 7 January 1747/48.

The Ahnentafel

Ahnentafel of John Abbot, GGG Grandfather of Lyman Drewry Coombs, 14367 Embry Path, Apple Valley, Minnesota 55124

I	1	John Abbot	1783-c1844	Chester, Great Barrington, MA; Hunter, NY; Huron Co., OH
II	2	John Abbot	1751-1798	Lancaster, Chester, MA
	3	Lois Bennett	1757-	Lancaster, Chester, MA
III	4	Joseph Abbot	1719-1790	Andover, Lancaster, Chester, MA
	5	Hannah Abbot	1721-1805	Andover, Lancaster, Chester, MA
	6	Elisha Bennett	1728-1769	Lancaster, MA
	7	Lois Wilder	1733-1759	Lancaster, MA
IV	8	John Abbot	1674-1754	Andover, MA
	9	Elizabeth Harnden	1683-1756	Andover, MA
	10	Ebenezer Abbot	1689-1761	Andover, MA
	11	Hannah Furman		Andover, MA
	12	John Bennett	1693-1761	Lancaster, MA
	13	Bathsheba Phelps	1695/6-1762	Andover, Lancaster, MA
	14	Oliver Wilder	c1694-1765	Lancaster, MA
	15	Mary Fairbank	c1695-1748	Lancaster, MA
V	16	John Abbot	1648-1720/1	Andover, MA
	17	Sarah Barker	1647-1728/9	Andover, MA
	18	Richard Harnden	-1693	Reading, MA?
	19	Mary ----		
	20	John Abbot	1648-1720/1	Andover, MA
	21	Sarah Barker	1647-1728/9	Andover, MA
	24	Samuel Bennett	1665-1742	Lancaster, MA
	25	Mary ----		
	26	Edward Phelps	c1663-1748	Andover, MA
	27	Ruth Andrews	1664-	Topsfield, Andover, Lancaster, MA
	28	Nathaniel Wilder	1655-1704	Charlestown, Lancaster, MA
	29	Mary Sawyer	1652/3-btw1709/1713	Charlestown, Lancaster, MA
	30	Jonathan Fairbank	1666-1697	Lancaster, MA
	31	Mary Hayward	c1667-1733/4	Concord, Lancaster, MA
VI	32	George Abbot	c1616-1681	Hertfordshire, England; Roxbury, Andover, MA
	33	Hannah Chandler	c1629-1711	Hertfordshire, England; Roxbury, Andover, MA
	34	Richard Barker	-1693	Andover, MA
	35	Joannah ---		Andover, MA
	40	same as #32		
	41	same as #33		
	43	same as #34		
	44	same as #35		
	48	George Bennett	-1675	Lancaster, MA
	49	Lydia Kibby	c1637-	Lancaster, MA
	52	Edward Phelps	c1625-1689	Salem?, Andover, MA
	53	Elizabeth Adams	c1627-1718	Andover, MA
	54	Robert Andrews	-1668	Berkshire, England; Topsfield, MA
	55	Grace Melburn?	-1702	Topsfield, MA
	56	Thomas Wilder	1618/9-1667	England; Lancaster, MA
	57	Ann (Anna, Hannah) ---	-aft 1667/8	

	58	Thomas Sawyer	c1616-1706	Lincolnshire, England; Rowley, Lancaster, MA
	59	Mary Prescott	c1629-c1716	Sowerby, Yorkshire, England; Lancaster, MA
	60	Jonas Fairbank	-1676	England; Boston, Dedham, Lancaster, MA
	61	Lydia Prescott	1641-	Watertown, Lancaster, MA
	62	Joseph Hayward	1643-1714	Concord, MA
	63	Hannah Hosmer	1644-1675	Concord, MA

****

Ahnentafel of Elizabeth Moulton, Grandmother of Clayton R. Adams, 6 Laurel Road, Brunswick, Maine 04011

I	1	Elizabeth Maria Moulton	1854-1944	Newburyport, MA; Manchester, NH
II	2	Moses Benjamin Moulton	1826-1858	Newburyport, MA; At sea
	3	Elizabeth Winn	1827-1914	Newburyport, MA
III	4	Moses Emerson Moulton	1805-1826	Newburyport, MA
	5	Ruth Somerby	1806-1859	Newburyport, MA
	6	Moses Winn	1783-1861	Wilmington, Newburyport, MA
	7	Mary Rogers	1790-1871	Hopkinton, NH; Newburyport, MA
IV	8	Joseph Moulton	-1813	Newburyport, MA
	9	Hannah Eaton	1774-1821	Newburyport, MA
	10	Henry Somerby	1773-	Newbury, MA
	11	Hannah Goodwin	1774-	Newburyport, MA
	12	John Winn	1751-1783	Wilmington, MA
	13	Abigail Rogers	1748-1819	Tewksbury, Wilmington, MA
	14	Paul Rogers	1766-	Newbury, MA
	15	Miriam Rogers	-1824	Newburyport, MA
V	16	Stephen Moulton	1733-	Newbury, MA
	17	Abigail Williams	1737-1802	Newbury, Newburyport, MA
	18	Benjamin Eaton	1745-1777	Lynn, Newburyport, MA
	19	Hannah Pearson	1751-	Andover, MA; Hawke, NH
	20	Henry Somerby	1738-	Newbury, MA
	21	Joanna Cheney	1735-	Newbury, MA
	22	Amos Goodwin	1746-	Newbury, MA
	23	Esther Pierce	1746-	Newbury, MA
	24	Hezekiah Winn	1706-1772	Wilmington, MA
	25	Bethiah Parker	1714-	Reading, MA
	26	Timothy Rogers	1717-	Billerica, MA
	27	Rebecca French	1724-1750	Billerica, Tewksbury, MA
	28	Silas Rogers	1736-1820	Newbury, Newburyport, MA
	29	Abigail Chisimore	1735-	Brunswick, ME
	30	Simeon Rogers	1739-1811	Newbury, MA; Henniker, NH
	31	Hannah Turner	1741-	Newbury, MA
VI	32	Joseph Moulton	1694-1756	Newbury, MA
	33	Mary Noyes	1693-	Newbury, MA
	34	Benjamin Williams	1708-1766	Newbury, MA; Hawke, NH
	35	Jemima Robinson	c1705-	Newbury, MA
	36	Benjamin Eaton	1705-1753	Lynnfield, MA; Londonderry, NH
	37	Anna Rand	c1705-	Lynn, MA
	38	John Pearson	1710-	Lynn, MA
	39	Rebecca Osgood	1714-	Andover, MA
	40	Samuel Somerby	1712-c1775	Newbury, Newburyport, MA

41	Sarah Adams	1713-c1770	Newbury, Newburyport, MA
42	John Cheney	1702-1738	Newbury, MA
43	Joanna Pike	1711-	Newbury, MA
44	Major Goodwin	1706-	Newbury, MA
45	Mary Atkinson	1708-	Newbury, MA
46	Moses Pierce	1715-	Newbury, MA
47	Abigail Brown	1724-	Newbury, MA
48	Joseph Winn	1671-1718	Woburn, MA
49	Martha Blodgett	1673-	Woburn, MA
50	Nathaniel Parker		Reading, MA
51	Elizabeth Wright	1685-	Andover, MA
52	John Rogers	1680-1736	Billerica, Woburn, MA
53	Abigail Winn	1680-	Woburn, MA
54	Jacob French	1696-	Billerica, MA
55	Elizabeth Davis	1699-	Billerica, MA
56	Jonathan Rogers	1702-	Newbury, MA
57	Hannah Brown	1699	Newbury, MA
58	Jacob Chisemore	c1705	Newbury, MA
59	Martha Smith	-1808	Dunbarton, NH
60	Daniel Rogers	1698-	Newbury, MA
61	Abigail Chisemore	1699-	Newbury, MA
62	William Turner	1705-1755	Newbury, MA
63	Joanna Goodridge	1707-1781	Newbury, MA

****

Ahnentafel of Anna Ellis (Wise), Mother of Robert E. Wise, 54 Ellis Farm Lane, Melrose, MA 02176

I	1	Anna Ellis	1883-1963	Braintree, MA; Winter Park, FL
II	2	Frederick O. Ellis	1836-1929	Orono, ME; Braintree, MA
	3	Emma Jane Hale	1852-1896	So. Royalston, MA
III	4	Orin Ellis	1810-1841	Orange, Boston, MA
	5	Mary Brown	1808-1890	Portland, ME; Braintree, MA
	6	John Waldron Hale	1804-1878	So. Royalston, MA
	7	Betsey Evans	1818/9-1901	Rockingham, VT; So. Royalston, MA
IV	8	Seth Ellis, Jr.	1784-1855	No. Orange, MA
	9	Susannah Cheney	1786-1870	Orange, MA
	10	Aaron Brown	1782-1846	Bow, NH; Brewer, ME
	11	Olive Mitchell	1787-1849	Portland, Brewer, ME
	12	Stephen Hale	1779-1855	Athol, So. Royalston, MA
	13	Susan Waldron	1782-1835	Dover, NH; So. Royalston, MA
	14	Randall Evans	1784-1825	Rockingham, VT
	15	Betsey Walker	1786-1869	Langdon, NH; Rockingham, VT
V	16	Seth Ellis	1760-1840	Medfield, Orange, MA
	17	Elizabeth Rawson	1763-1818	Warwick, Orange, MA
	18	Ebenezer Cheney	1741-1828	Mendon, Orange, MA
	19	Hannah Gould	1758-1828	Framingham, Athol, MA
	20	John Brown	c1745-1795	Ipswich, MA; Bow, NH
	21	Mary Burnham	1753-1795+	Ipswich, MA; Bow, NH
	22	Robert Mitchell	1751-1820	Cape Elizabeth, Portland, ME
	23	Mary Ingersoll	1760-1852	Scarborough, ME?; Boston, MA
	24	Silas Hale	1748-1832	Stow, So. Royalston, MA
	25	Lydia Stow	1754-1800	Marlborough, So. Royalston, MA
	26	Col. John Waldron	1740-1827	Dover, NH; Bath, ME

	27	Mary Winn	1743-1599	Woburn, MA; Dover, NH
	28	Eli Evans	1754-1840	Northfield, MA; Rockingham, VT
	29	Hannah Larcum	1752-1819	Enfield, CT; Rockingham, VT
	30	Samuel Walker	1762-1813	Rehoboth, MA; Saxtons River, VT
	31	Anna Carpenter	1762-1815	Attleboro, MA; Charlestown, NH
VI	32	John Ellis	1723-1816	Medway, Orange, MA
	33	Mary Baker	1724-1804	Medfield, Orange, MA
	34	Josiah Rawson	1727-1812	Braintree, Warwick, MA
	35	Hannah Bass	1732-1813	Braintree, Orange, MA
	36	William Cheney	1704-1756	Dorchester, Mendon, MA
	37	Joanna Thayer	1706-1766	Braintree, Mendon, MA
	38	John Gould	1719-1759	Sudbury, Framingham, MA
	39	Hannah Learned	1740-	Framingham, MA
	40	John Brown	1716/7-1777	Ipswich, MA
	41	Sarah Emmerson	1718-1795	Ipswich, MA
	42	Thomas Burnham	1720-c1758	Marblehead, Ipswich, MA
	43	Mary Lane	1723-1760+	Gloucester, Ipswich, MA
	44	Robert Mitchell	1710-1769	Kittery, Spurwick, ME
	45	Miriam Jordan		Spurwick, ME
	46	Nathaniel Ingersoll		Scarborough, ME?
	48	Jacob Hale	1721/2-1782	Stow, MA
	49	Elizabeth Holman	1730-1803	Concord, Stow, MA
	50	Stephen Stow	1724-1811	Marlborough, Stow, MA
	51	Abigail Smith	1727-1808	Stow, MA
	52	Richard Waldron	-1771	Dover, NH
	53	Hannah Smith	1716-	Durham, Dover, NH
	54	Timothy Winn	1712-1800	Woburn, Burlington, MA
	55	Mary Bowers	1715/6-1807	Chelmsford, Burlington, MA
	56	Peter Evans	1713-1793	Deerfield, MA; Rockingham, VT
	57	Ruth Petty	1716-1789	Northfield, MA; Rockingham, VT
	58	Job Larcum	1726-	Enfield, CT; Rockingham, VT
	59	Mary Bush	1721-	Enfield, CT; Rockingham, VT
	60	Aaron Walker	1728-1775	Rehoboth, Boston, MA
	61	Esther Carpenter	1735-1763	Rehoboth, MA
	62	Oliver Carpenter	1734-1809	Rehoboth, Brookfield, MA
	63	Sarah French	1736-1815	Attleboro, Brookfield, MA

****

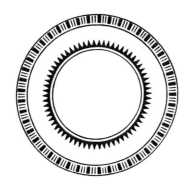

Society News

FORTHCOMING MEETING

19 May 1990 Saturday. Centre Congregational Church, Lynnfield, Mass.
Social Hour: 12:00. Lecture promptly at 1:00
Speaker: **RONALD N. TAGNEY**, author of <u>The World Turned Upside Down</u>; Essex County During America's Turbulent Years, 1763-1790 [1989].

JUNE, JULY, AUGUST   SUMMER RECESS

ESSEX COUNTY CEMETERY PROJECT

The Essex County Cemetery Project will result in a published book, softbound with spiral binding, of about 150 pages. The book will identify and describe every cemetery, town-by-town, in Essex County, with information on what agency has jurisdiction over the records. If a given cemetery has been transcribed, stone-by-stone, the whereabouts of that transcription will also be given. The format will be patterned after Pittsburg County's <u>A Guide to Berkshire County Massachusetts Cemeteries</u>, published in 1988 by the Berkshire Family History Association, and will contain location maps for each town. Barbara Holden has acted as Coordinator for the research.

To date, information for all 34 towns by 29 volunteer researchers has been completed. Working on the project were Dot and Russ Battersby, Helen Cammett, Ann Conwell, Hazel Downing, Harold Everett, Don and Barbara Glencross, Rosalie Godfrey, Marion Gosling, Betty Green, Mary Hagen, Phyllis Harvey, Jan and Earle Hazelwood, Barbara Holden, Gregory Laing, Robert Lovett, Natalie Marshall, Rose Morrison, Noreen Pramberg, John Reiley, Irene Robertson, Celestine Sager, Eleanor Spiller, Bill Stevens, Eleanor Tucker, Bill Twiss, Margaret Walsh and Theresa Whitney. Bill Stevens has agreed to prepare maps.

Now, all that is needed is typing, or keying onto disk, the compiled information from the questionnaires. **ARE YOU A TYPIST? WILL YOU HELP?** Marcia Lindberg now has all the completed questionnaires, but she cannot undertake the final typing and still continue to prepare each quarterly issue of TEG. Therefore, we must have **YOU**. If you can help, please contact Marcia at 3 Russet Lane, Lynnfield, MA 01940 (617-334-3406). Help your society bring this worthwile project to reality.

EARLY LYNN FAMILIES PROJECT

The Early Lynn Families Project will result in a work of probably two to three volumes, projected to be published in five years. It will consist of 5-generation studies of all the families who settled in Lynn before 1700. Started two years ago by Marcia Wiswall Lindberg, whose ancestors include 35 of the 200 or so early Lynn families, the project is well underway. Marion MacDonald, Eleanor Tucker and Roselyn Listernick are the prime assistant researchers for this undertaking; with Bea Dalton, Jane Friedman and Carolyn Martino also contributing research on one family. Others who have assisted in the project so far are members of Advanced Genealogy classes, which are given each fall - Hope

Carter, Marilyn Fitzpatrick, Rosalie Godfrey, Barbara Holden, Mary Koen, June Miller, Marjorie Owen, Dorothea Powers, Eleanor Sproul, Margaret Walsh and others. Barbara Marden's work on the Tilton family, that originated in Lynn, but shortly moved to New Hampshire, is being published currently in TEG.

As an interim measure for the project, the five-generation studies are being pre-published in TEG in hopes that readers will add information or correct errors before final publication in book form. To date, eight families have been published: Berry, (Nicholas) Brown, Gowing, Ivory, King, Lindsey, Needham and Ramsdell. Ready for publication are Bachelder, Bennett, Boardman, Breed, (Robert) Bridges, Collins, Marshall, Raddin/Redding, Stocker, (Thomas) Townsend, and Witter. In progress, are Aborn, Alley, Atwell, Bachelder, Boutel/Boutwell, Edmunds, Farr, Farrington, Hathorne, Hudson, Johnson and Norwood.

As part of the project, a careful search has been made for existing manuscript material. Many manuscripts have been located at Essex Institute, New England Historic Genealogical Society, The Lynn Historical Society, The Boston Athenaeum and other places. Copies have been made of these manuscripts and additional research will be prepared. Published works, both monographs and articles in journals, have been collected and are now at the Lynnfield Library. In many instances, the published works, often done in the early 1900s, have not met current standards, as described in the new _Guidelines for Genealogical Writing_, by Margaret Costello and Jane Fiske (Boston: NEHGS, 1990). The Early Lynn Families project will include all court records - probates, land deeds, records of the quarterly courts, etc.

Anyone with a special interest in an early Lynn family - who would like information, or would like to contribute information - may write to Marcia Lindberg, 3 Russet Lane, Lynnfield, MA 01940 (617-334-3406).

ESOG GENEALOGICAL RESEARCH COMMITTEE

The Genealogical Research Committee of the Essex Society of Genealogists meets bi-weekly under the chairmanship of Marcia Lindberg, and consists of Marion MacDonald, Eleanor Tucker, and Roselyn Listernick. Rules for submitting questions to the Committee, are as follows:

1. Queries will be answered only if the information can be found at the Lynnfield Public Library Genealogy Room, whose main emphasis is on Essex County, Mass., but also contains general genealogical works published or reprinted since 1980 for New England and the Maritime Provinces of Canada.

2. The Research Committee cannot supply Vital Records after 1850. For Mass. VRs from 1850 to 1890, write to the Massachusetts Archives at Columbia Point, Dorchester, MA 02125. For Mass. VRs from 1891 to the present, write to the Registrar of Vital Statistics, 150 Tremont St., Room B-3, Boston, MA 02111. There will be a fee of $3 (or more) per record searched at these institutions.

3. The Committee cannot provide copies of wills or deeds. For these, write to the Registry of Deeds (or Probate Court), 32 Federal Street, Salem, MA 01970.

4. Copying fees: 10 cents per page, plus postage; minimum charge, $2.00. Checks should be made out to ESOG Research Committee. Mail to ESOG Research Committee, C/O Lynnfield Library, 18 Summer St., Lynnfield, MA 01940.

Queries

> **GUIDELINES FOR SUBMITTING QUERIES**
>
> Readers may submit free queries. No query to exceed 50 words. No limit on number of queries. Ask specific questions re parentage, birthplace, marriage, children, etc. Use identifying detail such as name, date, or place. *Type* or *print* on 3x5 card. Use abbreviations listed at end of February Query section. Deadlines for queries: Jan 1, Apr 1, July 1, Oct 1. Send queries to: Teg query editor, Lynnfield Public Library, 18 Summer St., Lynnfield, MA 01940

CLARKE/MOULTON
Wish data Stephen CLARKE who m Mrs Abigail MOULTON 18 Sept 1786 at Newburyport, MA.

MOULTON/DENNIS
Seek iden Joseph MOULTON of Charlestown, MA who m Mary E. DENNIS 7 Nov 1838 at Newburyport, MA.

DUSTIN/JOHNSON
Seek iden Ruth, w of Samuel DUSTIN, physician. Samuel b 10 Feb 1719/20 Haverhill, MA, s of Timothy & Sarah (JOHNSON). He d 1760 Plaistow, NH. Clayton R. Adams, 6 Laurel Rd., Brunswick, ME 04011-3420.

****

BAILEY/DINGLE/FULLER
Who were par of Caleb BAILEY, m 8 Jan 1782 Duxbury, MA; d 3 Oct 1840 Marshfield, MA; w was Susanna DINGLEY b 26 Apr 1764 Duxbury, dau Jacob & Susanna (FULLER) DINGLEY, Jr.

FRIZZELL/THOMPSON/FISHER
Need all info John FRIZZELL, b 14 Sept 1802 Walpole, MA & w Annie THOMPSON, d 16 Feb ---, Walpole. His par John Allen FRIZZELL & Molly FISHER of Dedham or Walpole, MA. Pls give sources.

STODDARD (STODDER)/LOW
Need all info Abner STODDARD (STODDER) b 14 June 1768; m 22 Nov 1789 Elizabeth (Betsy) LOW of Boston.

PUTNAM/STODDARD
Need any info PUTNAM family, res Chelsea, MA in 1800s, esp. Ephraim & w Rachel STODDARD.

BAILEY
Need info David BAILEY b Falmouth, ME 28 Oct 1737. Was w Mary ---? Where did they res/d? Other ch than Mary b 1769?

HATCH/RIDER
Seek pos iden Jeremiah HATCH & w Ann RIDER, m 5 June 1716, Truro, MA.

HAWKES/NEWHALL/FARRINGTON
Need ddt, pld Sarah (NEWHALL) HAWKES 1/w Jonathan HAWKES of Lynn, MA. He m/2 Abigail FARRINGTON 1743. Merle G. Graffam, 2827 Westbrook Dr., Bldg 3/4 Apt. 513, Ft. Wayne, IN 46805.

****

DAVIS/TUCKER
Need anc Alice DAVIS, m Benjamin TUCKER 16 Dec 1714 Salisbury, MA.

BODWELL/EMERY
Need anc Henry BODWELL b ca 1651; m 4 May 1681 Newbury, MA Bethia EMERY, d 1 June 1745 Methuen, MA.

FARREN (FERRIN)/WELLS
Need all data Jonathan^2 FARREN (FERRIN) b 7 Feb 1735/6 Amesbury, MA & Sarah FARREN (FERRIN) b 5 Oct 1737 Amesbury. Both ch of Jonathan^1 & Sarah (WELLS) FARREN of Amesbury & Newton, NH.

HILTON/SEARS/HUSE
Need anc Mary (HILTON) SEARS who m Abel HUSE 25 May 1663, Newbury, MA.

WILLIAMS/LOWELL/WOODMAN
Need anc Thomas WILLIAMS, Newbury, MA, who m (1) Mary^4 LOWELL 15 Jan 1695/6; m (2) Ruth^3 WOODMAN 30 Dec 1713.

FARREN (FERRIN)
Need anc Hannah ---, 1/w Aquilla^2 FARREN (FARRIN). She d 18 July 1791, Newton, NH. Aquilla b 1 June 1741 Amesbury, MA; d 17 Apr 1825 Concord, NH. They had 9 ch b Newton, NH.

HEMINGWAY/DENNISON/FARREN (FERRIN)
Need anc, dts Samuel HEMINGWAY & w Mehitable DENNISON, par of Desire b 19 Feb 1741/2, E Haven, CT; m there 3 Mar 1768 Zebulon FARREN (FERRIN).

BARETO (BARSTOW)
Need any info Nicholas BARETO & w Eliz. --- of Amesbury. Had 6 ch b there 1711-23. Hoyt gives 12 spellings for surname, incl BARSTOW.

NICHOLS/TUCKER/MOULTON
Need all info Thomas NICHOLS of Salisbury, MA. His s Ebeneazer m Benoni TUCKER June 1685 or 6, Salisbury. Was Thomas's w Mary MOULTON? Need her info.

HILTON/PARSONS/SHEPARD
Need info William[1] HILTON of NH, w Frances ---, s William[2] & w Ann PARSONS, their dau Hannah[3], who m/2 Mark SHEPARD. Also need anc Mark SHEPARD b ca 1700, liv York & Biddeford, ME. Bailey Rogers, 10018 Regency Ct., Cincinnati, OH 45251.

****

HOWLETT (HOLLET, HALLET)/ABBOTT
Need any info Martha Manning HOWLETT (HOLLET/HALLET) who m John Bennett ABBOTT 1841, Huron Co., OH.

GROVER/BROWN
Need par Emily H. F. BROWN, m 1872 Thomas GROVER in ME. Need exact mdt & pl.

GROVER/COBB
Need exact mpl in ME: James GROVER & Helen (Nellie) Elizabeth COBB, m 17 Aug 1865. Need anc of bride. Joann Coombs, 14367 Embry Path, Apple Valley, MN 55124.

****

BARTLETT/PHILBRICK
Seek par/anc Perley BARTLETT; filed int Hannah PHILBRICK 10 July 1825 Salisbury, MA; d 8 June 1870 Kensington, NH, bur Salisbury; 5 ch, 2 w/middle name Norton. Donald B. Stevens, 25 Gardner Ter., Delmar, NY 12054.

PRATT/FELTON/MILLET/POWER
Joseph PRATT m Margaret FELTON 20 Sept 1792, Marblehead, MA. Seek bdt, bpl, par Joseph. Also ddt Margaret who m/2 Joseph MILLET & m/3 Thomas POWER.

MILLET/POWER/PRATT
Joseph MILLET b Bilbao, Spain m Hannah POWER Aug 1789 Salem, MA. Seek bdt, ddt, par of Joseph; ddt Hannah. He m/2 Margaret Felton PRATT 1809.

POWER/MIRES
Richard POWER m Mary MIRES 6 Jan 1763 Salem, MA. Seek bdt, ddt, dpl of both; also info on par.

REVIL (REVELL/RAVALL/ROWEL)/POOR (POWER)
Seek anc & all dts William & Mary REVIL, Marblehead, MA; dau Mary m Thomas POOR (POWER) 27 Oct 1754.

SAVAGE/RUSSELL/GROE
Mary SAVAGE dau John & Hannah, m Louis RUSSELL 24 Dec 1727, Marblehead, MA. Seek anc & all dts John & Hannah. Was she a GROE?

STEVENS/FELTON
Sarah STEVENS m Daniel FELTON ca 1714, d 4 May 1763, ae 93, Marblehead, MA. Seek bdt, mdt, par Sarah & ddt Daniel.

PEDRICK (PEDERICK/PETHRICK)
Marblehead rec show John PEDRICK ae 25 in 1663 & John PEDERICK ae 40 in 1664. Error? Or were there 2 Johns? Which was "of the Neck" & did he own prop. on mainland? Any relationship? Cora S. Leukhart, 1850 Columbia Pike, Arlington, VA 22204.

CARLETON
Richard A. CARLETON b 5 Aug 1796 Kent Co., DE, d 10 June 1847 Sharon Twp, PA. What was his conn to CARLETON fam of Rowley, MA? Shirley A. Orr, 12 Moran Rd., Lynnfield, MA 01940.

****

MEARS
Seek corr w/any searcher of MEARS fam. Any line.

MEARS/POLAND
Alexander MEARS b 1750 London, Eng., m 22 Apr 1773 Wenham, MA, Mrs. Martha POLAND b 1753; d 17 Feb 1843 Essex, MA. Need exact dts, par, sib of both, maiden name of Martha. Linda B. Blood, 8 Amesbury Rd., Kensington, NH 03833.

****

WILEY/SANBORN
Charles Edwin WILEY m 1869 Louisa Hoyt SANBORN. Ch: Mary Sanborn, Emily Louisa, Alice Jennie, Ruth Benton. Res Lynn, MA aft 1880. Wish corr w/any desc.

JONES/LEWIS
Need par Hannah JONES of Malden & Woburn, MA, m 1700 Joseph LEWIS s Joseph & Mary (JONES) LEWIS. She d 1760 Wilmington, MA.

INGALLS/EATON
Was Edmund Ingalls 1598-1648 (w Anna) f of Mary who m 1664 Daniel EATON at Reading, MA? Need proof.

LEWIS
Need w, anc Edmund LEWIS 1601-1650 Lynn, MA. Need info s James b 1635, prob Watertown, MA & 2 ch b aft 1642.

GOODRICH (GOODRIDGE)/BOWMAN
Need ddt/pl Capt William^5 GOODRICH (GOODRIDGE) b 1757 Lunenburg, MA, m Hannah BOWMAN 1791 Bedford or Concord, MA. Ch: Sophia, Charlotte. Francis Bowman b 1800. Did he have prev w in VT?

KNIGHT/COLE/JACOB/BALLARD/BREED
Need b & d Mary KNIGHT dau Wm. & ----, m John COLE 1667, Salem, MA. Was she dau Elizabeth JACOB who m/1 William BALLARD & m/3 Allen BREED of Lynn" Need b, d, par Elizabeth.

JONES/CURTIS/SOANE/LEWIS/JENKINS
Need bdt of Robert^1 & Robert^2 JONES of Hingham & Hull, MA. Also ws Robert^1, May be CURTIS or SOANE. Need b, c Mary^3 JONES, w Joseph LEWIS b 1675 Swansea, MA, & Obadiah JENKINS d 1720. M. J. Lewis, Box 676, Balboa, CA 92661.

COLBY/WEBB
Seek anc Frances WEBB(?) b 1677 Amesbury, MA; m 1699 at Amesbury Thomas^3 (Thomas^2, Anthony^1) COLBY 1675-1741.

WILLIAMS/KNIGHT
Seek all info John WILLIAMS, m 4 Oct 1674 Beverly, MA Martha KNIGHT b 1 Sept 1653; d 1744 Beverly. Was she dau Robert KNIGHT d 27 Feb 1655 Boston, MA?

CHADWICK
Seek anc Hannah ----, b 1739; d Hopkinton, NH; m John^3 (Jonathan^2, John^1) CHADWICK, b 7 July 1728, Bradford, MA; d ca 1795, Hopkinton, NH.

CHANDLER/FOWLER/LORD/CARTER/LOWELL
Seek anc William CHANDLER d 5 Mar 1702 ae ca 85 Newbury, MA. He m/1 Mary FOWLER; m/2 1667 Mary LORD; m/3 Mary CARTER. Dau Mary m 1664, Newbury, MA, Percival^3 (Richard^2, Percival^1) LOWELL.

FRENCH
Seek anc Elizabeth ---, b 6 Apr 1730, Norwich, CT; m at Topsfield, MA, John^4 (John^3, Thomas$^{2-1}$) FRENCH b 26 Aug 1671, Topsfield; d 20 Apr 1730, Norwich, CT.

LEE (LEIGH)/COY/ROBERTS
Seek par Richard LEE 1644-1713, gson & heir Thomas LEE (LEIGH) of Ipswich, MA who d Ipswich 23 Mar 1622. Richard m Sarah COY, dau Matthew & Elizabeth (ROBERTS) COY. They d Norwich, CT.

PHILLIPS
Seek anc James PHILLIPS d Bradford, MA 17?? & Mary (Molly/Elinor?) LORD "of Ips." They m 18 May 1717 Ipswich. Glen L. Bachelder, 5385 Wild Oak, E. Lansing, MI 48823.

****

HASTINGS
Seek info Solomon C. HASTINGS m 17 Apr 1843 Harriet E. ---, Morristown, VT; s Charles S. b 1844 Wolcott, VT.

TOLBERT (TALBERT)/LOOMIS
Seek anc, par, bpl James Clinton TOLBERT (TALBERT) b ca 1833 MA?, m Lucy LOOMIS 9

June 1852 Waterbury, VT or Chateaugay, NY. Where was he aft 1870?

GOODELL/CLEVELAND
Seek info Alfred GOODELL & w Jerusha CLEVELAND; s William b 1816 Morristown, VT.

DUNHAM
Seek anc par, bpl Thomas DUNHAM b ca 1767 MA, d 5 June 1853 Hebron, ME; m Sylvina or Sarah ---. James A. Streeter, 8313 Los Altos, Buena Park, CA 90620.

****

MERRILL/OSBORN
Need bdt, mdt, ddt John^6 (Paul^5) MERRILL, res Gilmanton, NH, m Hannah^5 OSBORN b 1795 Loudon, NH. Also need bdts, mdts, ddts, Joseph^6 (Paul^5) MERRILL, res Gilmanton, NH, m Margaret^6 OSBORN b ca 1810. Ch? Also need bdt, ddt Eliza^7 (Bela^6, Paul^5) MERRILL, m June 1854 Thomas F.^{6} OSBORN b 28 May 1825, Gilmanton, NH.

BARTON/OSBORN
Seek par Mehitable BARTON b 1807; d 1844; m Green^6 OSBORN b 1807. Res Loudon & poss Gilmanton, NH. Need dts, m info on 7 OSBORN ch.

OSBORN/MOORE/OSGOOD
Jacob^5 OSBORN of Loudon, NH m/1 1810 Betsey MOORE; m/2 1851 Betsey's sis Martha or Patricia (MOORE) OSGOOD who had s Jacob Dyer OSGOOD. Need anc & dts MOORE & OSGOOD.

BROWN/OSBORN
Need anc & dts Jane BROWN, Loudon, NH; m John Simpson^6 OSBORN b ca 1808; res Loudon; 1st ch b 1846.

LOWELL/OSBORN
What LOWELL m Mehitable^6 OSBORN b ca 1810, Loudon, NH? Were par Elijiah O. LOWELL of Orange, NH. Need LOWELL data, dts, any sib Elijiah.

SAWYER/OSBORN
Alan SAWYER, Weare, NH, s Humphrey & Mary --- SAWYER m Anna^6 OSBORN b ca 1814-20, Loudon, NH. Need SAWYER ch, Alan's dts, Mary's maiden name.

GREEN/OSBORN
Russell GREEN m Eliza^6 OSBORN b 1819, Loudon, NH. Russell's bro Loami m Eliza's sis Hannah^6 b 1816, Loudon. Need GREEN par, all dts, GREEN ch.

HUSSEY/OSBORN
Lydia HUSSEY m James L. OSBORN b 1833, Loudon, NH. Need HUSSEY anc, dts, OSBORN ch. Anne Merrill-Goulette, RR3, Box 120, Dexter, ME 04930.

****

COBB/DREW
Need exact dts ca 1743 for m Ebenezer DREW & Martha COBB, Kingston, MA.

MORRISSEY
Need ae & w Michael MORRISSEY, Charlestown, MA 1830.

ABBOTT/KIMBALL/JOLLS/DREW/CHURCHILL/ STEVENS/DELANO/CHILTON
Seek Elizabethan era family portraits and keepsakes.

KIMBALL/JOLLS
Christopher KIMBALL & Sarah JOLLS had dau Babgail, b 28 Jan 1803, Boston, MA. Need data on fam portraits. Richard Morrissey, 28656 Murrieta Rd., Sun City, CA 92381.

****

KILBURN/SOUTHWICK
Lucy KILBURN b 10 Jan 1755, Rowley, MA; m William^6 SOUTHWICK So. Danvers, MA 3 Sept 1809. Need anc & dts.

MASON/TARBELL/CROSBY
Need anc & dts John L. MASON b 10 Dec 1808, Chichester, NH; m 15 May 1828 Sally TARBELL, d 22 Jan 1846 near now Winnetka, IL. Mother's Maiden name poss CROSBY.

TARBELL/KEMP/NURSE
Jesse TARBELL b 1 Nov 1778, Hillsboro, NH, s/o David & Esther (KEMP?) TARBELL, Groton, MA. Need anc, dts esp TARBELL

to John m Mary NURSE 25 Oct 1678, Salem, MA.

NEWHALL/MANSFIELD/BANCROFT
Mary NEWHALL b Lynn, MA m Andrew MANSFIELD 22 Sept 1737; m/2 Timothy BANCROFT. She d 6 Feb 1791. Need anc, par, d.

ALLEN/HOOPER
Lydia ALLEN m William HOOPER b 23 Dec 1698, Marblehead, MA. Need her anc, dts.

OSBORN(E)/BURTON
William OSBORNE b 1640 Braintree, MA, bpt 44/5 Dorchester, m 17 Mar 1672 Hannah BURTON, Salem, MA. Need his par, dts, pls.

BARKER/GOODRIDGE
John BARKER, Jr, b Andover, MA, m 11 June 1747 Boxford, MA, Mehitebel GOODRIDGE(?) b Boxford, MA. Need par, anc, dts. Margaret B. Southwick, 529 Plantation Club Villa, Hilton Head, SC 29928.

****

ROPES
Salem VR sho John ROPES b 4 July 1647 s George & Ruth. <u>Hist. of Salem</u> & <u>The Wells Family</u> name mary, w of George who d June 1670. Was George m twice? Who was mo/of John?

RAMSEY/SARGENT/CHALLIS/PRESSEY
Charles RAMSEY b 1775, Newburyport, MA, s William & Elizabeth (SARGENT) m 1799 Anna (Miriam) PRESSEY dau Hezekiah & Mary (CHALLIS). Need mo Mary PRESSEY & anc William. William RAMSEY may desc fr Londonderry, NH settlers. Donald R. Sutherland, 162 Foxwood Dr., Guilford, CT 06437.

****

JEWETT/BERRY
Seek all info anc Sally JEWETT m Henry BERRY (b Middleton, MA ca 1778, d Denmark, ME 11 Nov 1836). Sally d 1 June 1852 Denmark, ME ae 74.

BERRY/BIXBY
Isaac BERRY m Anna (Nancy) BIXBY, res Middleton, MA, until ca 1785/96. Seek info ddt, dpl of each.

BERRY
John BERRY b ca 1660 m Rachel ---, res Wenham, MA ca 1695-1722; rem to Middleton, MA. Seek all info & anc Rachel; bp, bdt for John who d by 1738, believed to be s Thadeus (Teague) BERRY, Rumney Marsh.

BERRY (BARRY)/FARRAR
Thadeus (Teague) BERRY (BARRY) m Hannah FARRAR of Lynn, MA by 1665. Seek mdt & mpl, her ddt & dpl. bur pl of both.

BOSTON (BASTON)/JEWETT
Need all info/anc Sophia BOSTON (BASTON) m Spofford JEWETT, Denmark, ME 7 May 1849, ae ca 60. Michael E. Hager, 45 School St., Boston, MA 02106-3204.

****

The Essex Genealogist

VOLUME 10, NUMBER 3　　　　　　　　　　　　　　　　**AUGUST 1990**

CONTENTS

Letter from the Editor	118
TEG FEATURE ARTICLES	
"Rooting Around Long Island," by Jane Fletcher Fiske, F.A.S.G.	119
"Warnings Out in Reading," by Ann Smith Lainhart	130
"The High Road to Scotland," by Sherrill Yates	138
"The Making of a Nation," by Terry	142
RESEARCH IN PROGRESS	
"Henry Collins of Lynn," by Carolyn Martino and Marcia Lindberg	145
"The Ivory Family" - continued, by Eleanor Tucker	153
"The Stocker Family of Lynn," by Marcia Lindberg	155
MISCELLANEOUS NOTES	161
AHNENTAFEL	162
BOOK NEWS	167
SOCIETY NEWS	169
"Waltham Archives Threatened"	170
QUERIES	171
MOMENTS IN HISTORY	Back Cover

THE ESSEX GENEALOGIST is published quarterly: February, May, August and November for $13 per year, by the Essex Society of Genealogists, Lynnfield Public Library, 18 Summer Street, Lynnfield, MA 01940. Second Class Postage paid at Lynnfield, MA 01940. ISSN: 0279-067X USPS: 591-350. POSTMASTER: Send address changes to ESOG, Lynnfield Public Library, 18 Summer Street, Lynnfield, MA 01940.

Letter from the Editor

This issue marks the beginning of a NEW LOOK for TEG. A Hewlett Packard Laserjet IIP printer, with add-on type-font cartridge now graces the desk in the loft-study of my new house. Actually, ESOG purchased this printer, because 90% of the work done on it is for the Society. It was Gary Boyd Roberts, Publications Director for NEHGS, who urged me to switch to the new laser jet technology, since ESOG will be publishing not only TEG but other works in the future. According to Gary, the quality of print is so good, and so similar to typesetting, that no future changes should be necessary. Do you agree?

Only computer people will be interested in the crazy domino-effect this new printer caused. Foolishly, I just bought the printer, took it home, plugged it in and tried to install it on my computer. It wouldn't work! "Oh!" they said, "You need to increase the RAM on your computer to 640K." So I lugged my CPU over to Computerland and had 2 circuit boards put in ($300). It still wouldn't work. "Oh!" they said, "Probably, your software (Wordstar) is out of date. You should upgrade to Wordstar 5.5!" So, I went to "Egghead" (that's the name of the store, so help me!) and bought Wordstar 5.5 ($300). It still wouldn't work! "Oh!" they said, "You need a hard-disk drive to support Wordstar 5.5!" (I had two floppy disk drives.) I lugged my CPU over again (meanwhile, the first computer store in Reading had closed, so I had to go to another one in Peabody), and they replaced my right floppy drive with a hard drive ($400). This hard drive wouldn't work consistently - sometimes yes, usually no. "Bring it back in," they said. It seems they had taken out the wrong floppy drive. They then took my left floppy out, replaced that with my old right floppy (no charge), and back home I went. Voila! Everything worked! This whole process, including learning the new Wordstar 5.5 commands, and installing the new printer and all its type fonts, took me about 8 or 9 full days of work over a 5-week period, plus $2,000 cold cash! A word of advice for anyone starting in with home computers - be prepared for a lifetime of keeping up, revamping, learning new systems, techniques, etc. You cannot stay static in this field. My basic IBM PC is 7 years old, and that is <u>ancient</u> when you're dealing with computers. On the bright side, I must say, the improvements in the new printer and hard disk drive and new Wordstar capabilities are spectacular, and (I think) well worth the effort and expense.

There are other type fonts available but we do not see the need for them at this point. We now have 3 groups of fonts: Courier, Helvetica and Times Roman (so-called because the *New York Times* uses it). Each of these type fonts have four sizes: 14 point, 12 point, 10 point and 8 point (this is 10 point), and each also has italic type as well as regular. Now we can put book titles in italics instead of having to underline each title (see BOOK NEWS).

This has been a busy time for me, and probably the most difficult issue of TEG I've yet had to prepare. In addition to learning all the new technology to prepare TEG, Ken and I put our home in Lynnfield on the market in January, found a buyer in May, contracted to buy a Town House at the Thomson Club in North Reading, and on 18 July, passed papers on both properties, moved out of one house and into the other. This was just one week ago. As anyone who has moved knows, the myriad details of establishing a new home are overwhelming. It was interesting to me that, although we moved only 2 miles away from our former home, we are in a different town, a different county (Middlesex) and have a different area-code telephone (see Masthead for details). At any rate, we are now comfortably ensconced and the open upstairs study, complete with computer, typewriter, file cabinets and bookcases is enough to keep me happy and productive. Another plus feature: we can walk out of our door and, in minutes, be on the first tee of a very challenging golf course, and we can hear the geese honking on the 18th fairway that runs by our back decks. Now Helen B has another "change of address" to plague her! I can hear her mumbling from here!

We extend a hearty welcome to three new contributors: Jane Fiske, who needs no introduction; teenager Tammy Terry, whose "Making of a Nation" appears on page 142; and Sherrill Yates, who gave us permission to reprint her excellent "High Road to Scotland, " which first appeared in *Middlesex [Connecticut] Genealogical Society Newsletter*, Darien, Connecticut - Sherrill is the Editor.

We hope you all had a fine and productive summer and we look forward to receiving your research for publication in TEG.

Marcia W. Lindberg

TEG Feature Article

ROOTING AROUND RHODE ISLAND

By Jane Fletcher Fiske, F.A.S.G.

(A lecture to the Essex Society of Genealogists, 17 March 1990)

I should probably explain the title of this lecture. The Rhode Island Historical Society publishes a journal called *Rhode Island Roots*. Back before the FGS Conference in Boston, Bill Schoeffler and I were throwing titles around. "What do you want to call your lecture on Rhode Island," he asked. "Oh, I don't know, just 'Research in Rhode Island,' I guess." and he said facetiously, "How about 'Rooting Around Rhode Island?'" - and for lack of a better idea, that title stuck.

First of all, people ask me "Where do you live in Rhode Island?" When I tell them I live in Boxford, Massachusetts, they ask, "What are you doing working in Rhode Island?" It all started about 20 years ago when we moved here from Corning, New York. My mother had recently died and I was trying to trace some of her ancestry that I hadn't worked on before very much. She had a grandfather, David Cook, with a wife, Ruth Sanford, who had settled over in Berne, New York, Albany County. In the course of tracing that couple, I was drawn right back to Rhode Island. One thing led to another and I found it was easy to go down there. I enjoyed it so much, I just kept on doing it. One of the results was the book, *Thomas Cooke of Rhode Island*.

I think that a lot of people feel that working in Rhode Island is difficult. I've been asked to speak at the conference coming up in June in Washington, and the title that was given me was "Banished to Rhode Island." I thought, "Now, who was banished to Rhode Island?" No one was "banished" there, but a lot of people went there. Do you suppose they're talking about the genealogist who has to work there? But really, it's not bad once you know what you want to do. Do your homework - that's the one thing that's terribly important anyplace. But in Rhode Island, if you just go there, first, to the town your ancestor came from or the Archives or the Historical Society, you can be in deep trouble. You can spend lots and lots of time without learning a thing. So, the first thing is to do your homework.

Part of that includes getting a background. I know a lot of genealogists don't like history very much. I won't bore you with a lot, but you need a little bit to give you a context. There's a kind of spirit in the past of Rhode Island when you work there and it's very different from what you find here in Massachusetts or Connecticut or the other early colonies. And a lot of that has to do with the way Rhode Island was founded. It was a place where from the very beginning, church and state were separate - totally different from Massachusetts and Connecticut. Just think of Rhode Island as a tiny, tiny area that was surrounded, in the early days, by colonies where religious conformity was the rule. On one side was Massachusetts and on the other sides Plymouth Colony, which in the early days was separate from Massachusetts, and Connecticut, and all other edges by the ocean. The ocean was important too, in determining the character of Rhode Island. Many people took to the sea at one time or another in their lives. This had an effect on the kinds of records that were kept there, and what they didn't keep, and what we can expect to find.

Originally, there were just four separate towns. The first settler was William Blackstone, but not much of William Blackstone remains in Rhode Island, except the river which was named for him. He left Boston because it was getting too crowded - this was in 1636 or so. A plaque is on the place where his house stood on Beacon Street opposite the Common. Eventually, in 1636, Roger Williams was forced to leave Massachusetts because he did not see things quite the way the authorities did. So where did he go? He went down and founded Providence. He became the leading spirit in what became the Baptist Church which was one very important stream of thought in Rhode Island history. He was perhaps banished from Massachusetts, but he wasn't banished to Rhode Island. He went there because he knew there were opportunities there to be developed, and also he got along well with the Indians. He treated them very fairly. He learned their language. This was very important in the development of Rhode Island.

There was a second stream of thought (the first was Baptist) - provided by a woman named Anne Hutchinson, whom I'm sure you've heard of. She was preaching in Boston and was encouraged to leave. She and her followers believed in the continual revelation from God - the spirit within. About a generation later when the first Quaker missionaries arrived, they found that the followers of Ann Hutchinson received their message very readily. It gave a structure to what they already believed. She and her group went to Portsmouth on the Island of Aquidneck which gave its name to Rhode Island. A few of the followers of Anne Hutchinson split off and settled in Newport which is at the other end of the island - Portsmouth at one end and Newport at the other. Warwick, which runs right into Providence, is the fourth original town, where Samuel Gorton was one of the most prominent early settlers. He was a very contentious character who had been thrown out of a number of different colonies including Plymouth. He finally went over to Warwick where he had his own brand of Christianity or Puritanism or whatever. It caused a great deal of difficulty until he found a place where he could settle down and do his own thing. So that was Rhode Island originally - four separate towns.

And what do you find when you go looking for early records? Lots and lots of diversity. Everyone kept records their own way. It wasn't like here in Massachusetts where there were rules laid down as to how it was to be done. So if you don't ever go any deeper into Rhode Island history than this, just remember it was a collection of towns formed by individual nonconformists, surrounded on three sides by Puritan colonies and every place else by water.

A man named Thomas Robinson Hazard was born in South Kingstown, Rhode Island in 1795. There were a lot of Tom Hazards and so they were given nicknames. This one was called Shepherd Tom. Another was College Tom and a third was Nailer Tom who left a wonderful diary I'll talk about later. Shepherd Tom, among other things, wrote a series of essays called "The Johnny Cake Papers." It was published as a book in 1915. In the introduction, his nephew, Roland Gibson, said of his uncle,

> *He was bred in the strictest school of the Quaker doctirne and so used the plain language as long as he lived. And yet he quotes three articles of faith to nearly every well-ordered family found in Narraganset when he was a child: first, that you love one another and your neighbors as yourself; Second, that you hate the Puritans of Massachusetts with a perfect hatred; And third, that you hold the Presbyterians of Connecticut in like contempt.*

What I'd like to do today is to suggest to you a practical approach to research in this place of varied and diverse public records. As I said before, it doesn't do any good to head straight for the Rhode Island Archives. Although there are lots and lots of treasures there, you won't find the things you need to begin with.

The first thing you remember in Rhode Island research is think Town. This can be a stumbling block for people from Massachusetts, New York, New Hampshire or wherever because most states keep records on the county level. The only county records of any significance are the court records. These are all in one place now, so unless you're looking for recent court records, you don't even have to go to the county for those.

I edit the quarterly called "Rhode Island Roots" and recently one of our members submitted an article for publication. It was based largely on the story of how he had found a "missing" will on microfilm in Salt Lake City that should have been in the Kent County court house in East Greenwich. He didn't realize that wills were never kept in the county court house in East Greenwich. He was looking in the wrong place. The will he needed was right there in the Town Hall of East Greenwich the whole time. This is one of the most common mistakes that people make when they are not familiar with Rhode Island and trying to work there. If you know the town your ancestor came from you're lucky. If you don't, you have a problem. In Massachusetts or New York, if you are looking for an ancestor and you just want to find out more about him - as to where he might be - and you've done the vital records - you'd probably head for the court house and check out wills and deeds. But you can't do that in Rhode Island unless you know the town the ancestor came from.

So my technique is to start out with the printed sources in the library. Lets review some of those. You can sometimes develop a beautiful ancestral chart just by using printed sources in the library. I've done that for people. Gary Roberts at New England Historic Genealogical Society in Boston just recently did one that will be in *Nexus* next issue - the possible ancestry of a famous person. It's a lovely Rhode Island chart.

The standard reference books for Rhode Island, as anybody who's worked on Rhode Island knows, are "Arnold" and "Austin." John Osborn Austin's *Genealogical Dictionary of New England* is a large book, first published in 1887 and reprinted several times. It covers the first three or four generations of over 400 Rhode Island families. Obviously if it only comes up to three or four generations it doesn't get far into the 1700s. In many cases it just barely gets there. But if you know the surname in Rhode Island, go first to Austin and see what he has to say about that family. It may be too early for what you're doing, but chances are the family you're working on will tie back in eventually. And Austin may give you some clues as to where you should be working. The worst problem with Austin is, he never gave any references. He'll say "in 1635 so and so left a will," and you have to find it. But the deeper I've gotten into Rhode Island records, the more I find that he really combed everything. He went through the Court Records, I'm convinced, at least up to 1740. A lot of the things he quotes are there in the court records.

The other basic source for Rhode Island is James Newell Arnold's *The Vital Record of Rhode Island; a Register of the People*. He was the publisher of the *Narragansett Historical Register*, and when it ceased publication, he started this series of books which were brought out around the turn of the century. There are 21 volumes but only the first six are Vital Records from the towns. Deaths were almost never recorded. You find a lot of deaths in inventories in the probate records, and of course cemetery records sometimes. Arnold's Volume 7 includes the Quaker records. The rest of the volumes are mostly other church and newspaper records. Arnold was the same man who did the Rehoboth, Mass. Vital Records, and he also did all the work for many of the volumes of the Barbour Records in the Connecticut State Library. He was tremendously productive. He got around with great difficulty; he limped badly. There are a lot of mistakes in what he did but he certainly did an enormous amount. Arnold's volumes are separated by county - one per county. Volume one is Kent County; two and three are bound together for Providence County. Four is Newport County and five is Washington County, which is North and South Kingstown and the towns that were set off from that.

The little numbers to the left of the entry such as (1-34) means the entry was on p. 34 of the first record book found in the Town Hall. A month or so ago I received and SOS from a friend I had done some work for, in Illinois, and he had found the record of a marriage - I think it was another Thomas Hazard and a Patience Woodmansee in the town of Richmond in 1740. He thought there might be more to that record than was given in Arnold. He had written to the Town Clerk in Richmond and asked for a copy of the record. He wanted a certified copy. She wrote back that she didn't have it and he should write to the Archives for it. He did and the Archivist wrote back and said she didn't have it. It was in the Town. So he wrote back to the Town Clerk, and you know what happened, she said she didn't have it. So he just copied everything and sent it along to me. I looked first in Arnold and found it was 1-34 and I wrote back and said "Write the Town Clerk again and say you want a photocopy of page 34 in the first book of Town Records." He did and got it right back by return mail. These are the kinds of problems you can run into if you don't know what you're doing.

You have to be prepared for the possibility that the first book of Vital Records is actually part of the Town Council Book or even a deed book in some cases. Someone had written into *Rhode Island Roots* with a query. She had been looking for the wife's name of a marriage - James Tefft's wife Martha - who was she." Finally someone answered the query who had been looking at Town Meeting Records on microfilm out in Montana and noticed half way down the page it gave the birth information...James Teffts, son of so and so, born on such and such a date; his wife Martha, dau of Joseph Sheffield, born .... This was buried in such a way it had just gone unnoticed by Arnold, and a lot of people had been looking for it for quite a while.

Another thing to remember in using Arnold is that in marriages, there's frequently more information in the entry that is alphabetized under the groom's name than that under the bride's name. For a marriage between Mary Jones and John Smith, always check the entry under John Smith to get all the information given. It may look fine under Jones, but the parents' names may be given under the man's entry.

Austin and Arnold have both been around for a century now. There's one new source in the library to help you locate ancestors. Alden G. Beaman, who just recently died, of East Princeton, Rhode Island, had been publishing Rhode Island material for about 15 years before his death. Incidently, his daughter, Nellie Beaman Mosher is continuing to do so. One of the things he did is called the *Rhode Island Genealogical Register*. It was a quarterly, but the last three volumes have been brought out annually as one hardbound book, rather than in four separate journal issues. Anyway, in that he has included abstracts of wills from almost every Rhode Island town. The trouble is, they're serialized. You get just a few pages in one issue, and maybe two or three in another later - or maybe a year or two later before you get the next installment. So it's a little difficult to locate, but it's worth doing. If you're looking for someone in Smithfield, you should go back and read all the Smithfield wills - and you'll find them all in Beaman right up to a recent date. The other thing that Beaman did was a series of books called *Vital Records of Rhode Island - New Series*. They're red-bound books - 13 volumes. These cover Washington County, which is the old area called South County. It never was officially South County, but it's always called that. That's been pretty well covered, and part of Kent County and Newport County. He didn't do anything on Providence County. For instance, the title will be *Newport Marriages from Probate Records*. What you will find here is marriages that are <u>inferred</u> from information in wills or probates. There's another volume called *Newport Births*. A lot of marriages and births in these were never recorded. Rhode Island is worse, probably than Massachusetts on that score. Most people have trouble understanding the format that Beaman used, so I'll go into it. It's important to remember how he got the information - not from Town Record Books, but out of a will in most cases. For example: a man named Peter Parker may have died in East Greenwich and left a will naming his wife Mary, and his children George, Elizabeth and Mary, wife of Joshua Green. What does it really tell us? It tells us Peter Parker had a wife Mary and that he was the father of children George, Elizabeth and Mary, who was the wife of Joshua Green. It doen't prove that any of those children were born in East Greenwich. It just proves the father was living there when he died. The marriage of the daughter Mary to Joshua Green may have taken place somewhere else entirely. They may never have lived in East Greenwich. It doesn't even prove that Peter Parker's wife, Mary, was the mother of these children. So you have to use Beaman with caution. It's wonderful for clues, because he's combined the records by county in most places, so you can zero in on a bunch of towns at once. And he gives his references - for the wills he cites probate numbers and far more information.

One other problem with Beaman's work is that he abbreviates everything to the point where a lot of people have trouble making sense of it. For instance, a birth index might list the marriage of George Smith to Mary Jones, with a notation in small letters "m w w f Jan 4th 1767." In this case, the "m w w f" mean "mentioned in the will of the wife's father, dated 4th of January." I've had town clerks ask me how to use those records. But once you catch on - and he does explain it in the beginning - once you realize what it's all about, it's a tremendously helpful source. You should do this before you go down to Rhode Island.

Rhode Island had censuses in 1774 and 1782. And there was a military census taken of all men over 16 years in 1777. The first federal census as you all know was taken in 1790 and every ten years thereafter. In 1865, the state began taking censuses in the half decade. The state censuses of 1774 and 1777 and 1782 are in print, and the 1790 and 1800 Federal censuses. The indexes of the other federal censuses, 1810-1870, are available now in libraries. You can easily make an analysis of the census records for the person you are interested in or other people of the same surname. It's a good idea to do that too before you head down to Rhode Island.

The 1865 State Census is a wonderful resource but you do have to go to the Rhode Island Historical Society - or I suppose its on Mormon microfilm, although I haven't used it - but the Historical Society has a card index to that. Every single person who was living in the state - not just heads of housholds but everyone in 1865 is listed in the index. Then you go back to the microfilm of the census itself which they also have. It gives the town of birth if they were born in Rhode Island. If they were born in another state it will just give you the state or country. If you're looking for someone who was alive at that date, that's the first place to go, really.

There are other things that you can do at a library. You might want to check some of the published genealogical books of other families that lived in the same general area as your ancestors, like my "Tom Cook." There are lots of great books on Rhode Island families. Some of them are old and contain errors - even new ones like mine contain errors; others are out of date. I was speaking with someone a little while ago about the Slocum Genealogy. I found a will a couple of years ago in the Taunton Town Hall - just loose - of a second Giles Slocum that completed a picture of his family. So new things are still being found. But do check some of these old books. The Durfee genealogy is particularly good - and the Hathaway - families who lived east of the Bay.

There are a couple of wonderful sets on Rhode Island Families published by the Genealogical Publishing Company. They're two volumes each. Unfortunately, they're bound in the same color and have the same title. The first one was published a few years ago and it includes genealogical articles from all the old periodicals that were published in Rhode Island in years past, like the *Narragansett Historical Register*, the *Rhode Island Historical Society Collections* - those things that are now very hard to find.

The second set was published last year, of articles on Rhode Island families that had been published in the *New England Historical and Genealogical Register* goes right up through volume 142. And there are also good source records. It does not include my article on how to do research in Rhode Island, and does not include families or articles that already appeared in the Society's *English Origins* series. There are quite a few of those, too. So if the English origin is known, it's probably in that set.

The journal we call TAG - *The American Genealogist* - has also had a lot of articles on Rhode Island families over the years. There is a new subject index available for that so you should check that too.

At this point you probably have collected a lot of information on the family, even if you haven't found your particular ancestor. So you should have some idea of what towns you want to go to. When you go, take copies of the relevant pages you found in Arnold and Beaman especially - even Austin. This will short-cut your search considerably, and without them, you can spend all day searching for something you know is there, but can't find it because the the records aren't indexed, and the town halls often don't have the published indexes.

The indexes in towns vary tremendously. Some of them have good indexes to their deeds A few have indexes to their probates but don't count on it! A lot don't. If you have in your hand a copy from Arnold or Beaman giving book and page, you can go right to that.

Now that you're through in the library for a while, you're going to want to look up deed and probate records too. And even if you have developed a whole ancestry from secondary sources in print, you're still going to want to go back and look up more and find out what these ancestors were really doing. You can do some probate work in sources like Beaman's journal and also in *Rhode Island Roots*. We have, over the fifteen years that we've been printing it, published abstracts of wills from some towns. The early Town Records for Portsmouth and Warwick are in print. You can find these in a library, and a new one on South Kingstown, covering the revolutionary period, I think 1771 to 1795. A lady by the name of Jean Stutz who lives in South Kingstown copied this. She went to the Town Clerk, who let her make xerox copies of the Town Council Book and she transcribed it. She published it last year and it's wonderful. If you have any interest in that area at that time you'll find a lot in it.

Now I guess we've finished with the library and it's time to go on a field trip. Take a map. The Highway Maps are great. You can get them free from the Historical Society, and many town halls have them. I suspect if you write to the State Highway Department you can get one free. They're marvelous because the scale is so great. At this point you're going to have to worry a little bit about geography - not only where the Town Hall is and how to get there, but where did your people really live. Maybe you think they lived in Coventry, but you'll soon find that Coventry was set off from Warwick, so you may have to go back to Warwick records, and so forth. There were a lot of geographical changes in Rhode Island over the years. The big obvious one is Bristol County, Massachusetts. Up until 1747, the Rhode Island towns that are now Tiverton, Little Compton, Barrington, Warren, and Bristol, were all in Bristol County, Mass. Before that date, you have to go to the County Court House in Taunton to find records for these people All of what is now Providence County, was the Town of Providence until 1731 and then it was split up into several towns like Smithfield and Scituate and Glocester. Later some of those towns were divided. Glocester was set off from Providence in 1731; Burrillville was set off from Glocester in 1806. You may find an ancestor, for instance, who was living in Burrillville in 1815, who had been there for years, living on the same farm, but you'll have to go back to Glocester, and from Glocester, you'll have to back to Providence as you go backwards in time, to find all the records you need for him.

Rhode Island Roots has a listing in the inside of its front cover giving the dates of all these geographical changes, and on the inside of the back cover is a map showing each town. I think it also gives the date. I like the map from Bowen's book, *Early Rehoboth*, because it shows the names of towns that were adjacent. You have to be aware that a lot of people from, say, northern Providence County, wandered over into Worcester County, Mass. at one time or another. And a lot of people in towns on the western border show up in Connecticut towns too. On the eastern side, New Bedford and Fall River records are full of Rhode Island people, who sometimes were recorded in both Tiverton and Fall River. You have to realize this was all fluid and people moved back and forth. Include these areas in your search if you're having problems. There are various maps showing the towns at different dates or showing what the state looked like at different times, included with the census indexes published by Accelerated Indexing. The state published a book of these too, which you can find at libraries.

Most of the town halls in Rhode Island are open week days for normal office hours. A couple may still close for lunch. One town clerk, in Richmond, was going home for lunch and she offered to lock us in (my husband was with me) for the hour she was gone. It's important to keep a perspective in your research in town halls. The clerks have so much to do with dog licenses, recording of deeds, and so many things that are going on today, and many do not understand about old records and they don't want to be bothered with questions about them. A few years ago, I was in Scituate getting copies for someone I was doing work for. There was a clerk in the office who copied them for me, and she and asked, "Can you read these things?" I said yes, and she said, "Would it be all right if we send your name out when we get inquires?" I said "Sure!" I'm still getting inquiries from people saying, "I wrote to Scituate for records and they say you have the Scituate records." I guess it's typical. On the whole, they try to be cooperative, and a lot of them, if you write for copies, will send you what you want.

There is in some places, a reluctance to let people look at vital records after 1850. I guess it's no different than anywhere. I think there is more and more a tendency for the clerk to ask for a membership card, and if you have a membership card in an organization, then you can go in. It doesn't much matter what, in some cases. The main thing is, go prepared with your copies and your references. Don't expect anyone there to help you out. Just ask them to point you in the right direction. Then use your own eyes to find the books that you need.

If you're having trouble getting in to look at vital records, an old ploy that works pretty well - I was told this many years ago - is to say you want to see the deed books. Once you're in there, you can look around and find other things. Some town clerks will deny that they have the oldest record books. There is a report, The Brigham Report, that was put together in 1904 or 1905 - it's in print, but it's not easy to get hold of. I discuss it at more length in the article I wrote on Rhode Island in the *Register*. Brigham did a thorough inventory of the records in every town hall. I understand the state is doing one now. We'll have a chance to compare them before too long. If you really are stuck with something, you can go back and look at that report and say, "These records were here in 1904. Where are they? What's happened to them?" It will stir them up a little.

A few years ago in Coventry, I was looking for the early Town Council Records. The Clerk said, "We don't have them.." I kept insisting. Finally she admitted that they did, and she brought out archival boxes full of loose sheets. They had sent them out to be restored back at the time of the Bicentennial - it was somebody's project - and they had come back, unbound, in loose sheets. And the problem was they had gotten out of order and were a mess, and she was understandably reluctant to let anyone look at them. But once you convince someone that you are responsible and know how to be careful with records, they may relent.

I've already spoken about indexes. Some towns have good indexes to their deeds - grantor and grantee indexes - but very often you'll find an index that is just by the first initial. So, if you're looking for Smith you have to go through them all and sort out the ones you want. You can't even be sure they're in chronological order. Sometimes they will have found a deed and put it at the end. So this can be a little time-consuming, unless you have a rare name. A few towns, like East Greenwich, for instance, have very good indexes. All the deed books and vital records, everything in East Greenwich is very well done. The early probate records - wills and administrations - were usually kept in with the Town Council records, because the Town Council was also the Probate Court. They would go on from one business to the next and record each matter as it came up, and it's all in the same book. The wills that Beaman abstracted in the *Rhode Island Genealogical Register* don't include records of people who died intestate (without wills). For most towns, the only way to find these records is to go through the Town Council books yourself.

The Town Council records can be a gold mine - especially if you're looking for a family that was poor or had a problem of some kind. The Overseers of the Poor made regular reports and you may find in these an ancestor that appears in no other records. It doesn't necessarily mean they were poor - they may have had a problem in the family. A husband may have died leaving a lot of small children and if the wife didn't marry again right away, the town might have bound those children out. I've found records of this being done as early as age three. It might say this child would be three on the 3rd of April - it gives you an exact birth date. The same thing would happen if a man couldn't support his family. If the wife asked the Town Council for help, which is what somebody named Phebe Mitchell did in Scituate, the Town Council would take the family under its care and see that they got the help they needed. Any children that were old enough would be bound out. You might find a record of payments for keeping various members of the family in food and clothing, etc. And sometimes for coffin and funeral expenses. Sometimes this is the only record of a death that you can find. There are a lot of sad stories in the Town Council records. I wrote one up several years ago. John Pitcher in East Greenwich evidently deserted his family and his wife eventually died. His son Andrew was bound out at age three to a weaver. You find very sad stories sometimes. But it can be the place you find someone you're looking for. I was reading through Town Records in Middletown last fall looking for a Phillips family member. It was a last-minute effort to trace some family members I couldn't account for and sure enough, I found an Israel Phillips and his wife. First of all they were given certificates of residence to go and settle in North Kingstown. Then later they came back. A town would give a man who belonged to a town a certificate to move from their town to another town saying they would receive them back - meaning they would be responsible for them if anything happened. And the Town Council in the new town would want to see this before they'd let them settle. The reasons was, if they got sick or if anything happened to them, the new town didn't want to take care of them. They had the legal right to send them back to the old town. This happened regularly. You find people being "warned out" and told to go back to the town where they came from. If they didn't and they couldn't prove residence in the new town, if they didn't own land or whatever, they were often taken back. You find all this kind of thing in the Town Coucil Records. They're a wonderful resource but you have to have the time to read them.

Well, even if you haven't found your ancestor after you've gone through the Town Records, there are some other places to look. A third line of attack might be the State Archives. The State Archives, incidentally, is moving next October. For years it has been in the basement of the State house in Providence, but it's being moved to a new building downtown, near the Westminster Mall. There is parking in an adjacent public lot. Anyway, they have indexed lists of freemen and Deputies, and petitions to the General Assembly. These are wonderful. You get a chance to comb the whole state at once. They have an index to Rev. War records, to French and Indian War service and such things. You really have not researched your ancestors in Rhode Island until you've checked all these.

If your ancestor lived in the Newport area, it's worth a trip to the Newport Historical Society. Do you know the story of the Newport records? Newport was captured by the British during the Revolution, and when they retreated in 1779 - the Town Clerk, who was a Tory, took all the Town Records with him. The ship sank on its way to New York and the records went down in New York Harbor. Through the efforts of Washington and General Nathanial Green, they were saved after awhile. They were left in a warehouse in New York for a long time. Finally, they were returned to Newport but nothing was done about that for years. People were allowed to go through them. The Newport Historical Society has a couple of boxes of little tiny fragments that nothing can be done with. They did eventually get around to restoring what could be restored, using the Emery Process, where you put records between layers of fine silk. But many of them are fragmentary. Many are faded. I have sat there for a long time trying to make out a name on an old inventory or accounting. You know it's there, but you just can't make it out. That type of thing. But they do have what's left of all the old Vital Records, the Town Council Records which include the early probates, and deeds, and they have card indexes to them. You can find a lot in those records. They're fascinating.

If you're looking for someone in the Providence area there's something that is well worth looking into at the Rhode Island Historical Society. They have the Town Papers in the manuscript collection there. But there are a couple of books indexing them. It's not an every name index but a subject index. We have a copy of that index at Hist. Gen. I've not seen a copy anywhere else around. It's great because you can look, for instance, under "Overseers of the Poor," go through it and it will give you names. It doesn't include every name in every record, but it will give you enough to help you find someone. I was looking for a family named Townsend. We had a Jerusha Blowers who married a man named Townsend in Newport. Jerusha is, we think a descendant of the Fayerweather family. (In the *Register*, we've just started printing a large genealogy by John Carney, of the Fayerweather Family of Boston.) This was a mercantile family and they spread out all over the place. Jerusha was a descendant of that family and she married William Townsend. We had some children a couple generations down the line that we thought belonged here but we couldn't tie them in. Well, among the Providence Town Records, I found Jerusha Townsend's name. So I went down there and looked up the record and found a long, hand-written page. It seemed that William Townsend, goldsmith, and his wife Jerusha died - William had died in Ireland. What he was doing in Ireland nobody knows. This was in the 1770s. Anyway, they had left in the Town of Providence, four small children named Jerusha, Lydia, Abigail and Anna Townsend, and these children had no means of support. The last legal place of settlement was Newport, and therefore, they were to be returned to Newport. This was the only place we have found those children. We still don't know exactly what happened, but this was an important link to connect these people in Newport with people in Providence.

The Rhode Island Historical Society also has a notebook that John Osborn Austin kept. He was thinking of a second volume for his *Genealogical Record of Rhode Island* but he never published it. They also have an index for a lot of his notes there. So if you're trying to make that link between your ancestor and families that Austin treated, go look at his notebook and see what you can find.

Finally there are diaries and journals that may hold clues that you need. There's a marvelous thing called *Peleg Burroughs Journal, 1778-1798*. Peleg was a minister in Tiverton for about 25 years during the period of the Revolution. I was instrumental in getting that printed. It's a fascinating story. Anyway, if you have an ancestor that lived in Tiverton in that time period, look up *Peleg Burrough's Journal* at Hist. Gen. or other libraries. Another marvelous thing if you have ancestors in South Kingstown is *Nailer Tom's Diary*, kept by "Nailer" Tom Hazard from about 1770 right into about 1840. I found there some records of my own great great grandfather, John Bull, who moved from South Kingstown to Lebanon Srpings, New York, then settled in southern Albany County which is where my own grandfather came from. Anyway, Nailer Tom mentions John Bull as visiting from the "new country." There's a recent index to that book. The late Joseph Blaine indexed everything in sight and he did it not on a computer, but with little slips of paper which he pasted in telephone books and then got someone to type it up for him. One of the things he did was *Nailer Tom's Diary*, which is a big, thick book. We have a copy of the index at Hist. Gen. Newport Historical Society let us copy it.

I've got to say just one word about the court records. For about eight years, I've been working on and off, abstracting county court records. The court records of course were originally kept in the county court house, but then the state tried to gather them all together in the Record Center which is under the Veterans Auditorium in Providence, where they were all over the floor. It was a real mess. They gathered them up a few years ago and moved them all to Providence College Archives. The Archivist at Providence College at that time was a brother to the Speaker of the house and there was definitely a political connection. They wanted to keep them in Providence, but nobody else wanted them. And so there they were. I used to go down there a day a week and you couldn't find anything you were looking for. If you just sat there and browsed through them, however, you found all sorts of wonderful things. I found copies of Newport wills that had been lost in the harbor that had been copied before that date because they were needed in court cases. They were really a gold mine. Now the Archivist has left and he is in charge of the court system for Rhode Island. So he promised Providence College that he'd get them out of there. He did and they moved them to the pipe room in the Providence Superior Court House and there they have been for a couple of years. The state has just opened a new facility at 1 Hill Street in Pawtucket and they have moved a lot of the court records over there. I understand some of the early ones are not there yet but they will be and if you are interested in a particular case, the Archivist there can get it for you.

Well, I could go on but I think I've come to the end of the time allotted me, so let me say that although there may not be a central archives in Rhode Island (something like Columbia Point is still just a dream down there - I hope it gets done because they've been altogether too careless with their records), but there's a lot of satisfaction in finding bits and pieces here and there, and the key to doing it is simply do your research at home and at the library and go down there with your references so you don't waste time looking for things.

I think the article I published in the *Register* back in 1982 may suggest some other sources and it provides a good overall background. A few of the physical situations like the court records have changed, but I think I have given you up-to-date information. So don't hesitate to try to solve problems in Rhode Island and enjoy it!

JANE FLETCHER FISKE is a Fellow of the American Society of Genealogists, and is Editor of the *New England Historical and Genealogical Register*. She has a B.A. (English and History) from Swarthmore College. She is a member of the Rhode Island Genealogical Society (Past President and Editor of *Rhode Island Roots*), the Rhode Island Historical Society, and the National Genealogical Society. She is the author of *Thomas Cooke of Rhode Island* (1987), which received the Connecticut Society of Genealogists' First Literary Award for the best book on a New England family since 1980. She also is the author of "Genealogical Research in Rhode Island," the *Register*, 1982. She is currently preparing for publication abstracts of Newport (Rhode Island) court records. Her special interests include Rhode Island, and English origins of early New England settlers. She lives in Boxford, MA.

SELECTED BASIC BIBLIOGRAPHY FOR RHODE ISLAND RESEARCH

Reference - General Guide:

Fiske, Jane Fletcher, "Genealogical Research in Rhode Island," in the *New England Historical and Genealogical Register*, 136[1982]:173-219; reprinted as a chapter in *Genealogical Research in New England*, Ralph J. Crandall, ed. (1984), temporarily out of print.

Sperry, Kip, *Rhode Island Sources for Family Historians and Genealogists* (Logan, Utah, 1986). Available from Everton Publishers, Inc., P.O. Box 368, Logan, Utah 84321.

Families

Austin, John O., *Genealogical Dictionary of Rhode Island* (Albany, 1887; repr. Baltimore, 1969, 1982; includes additions & corrections published in *The American Genealogist* 1943-1963; temporarily out of print.

Genealogies of Rhode Island Families, from Rhode Island periodicals, 2 vols. (Baltimore, 1983). GPC, $90 per set or $45. per volume.

Genealogies of Rhode Island Famlies, from New England Historical and Genealogical Register, 2 vols. (Baltimore, 1989; includes source material published, but not J. Fiske's article cited above. GPC, $95. per set or $45. per volume.

Vital Records

Arnold, James N., *The Vital Record of Rhode Island*, 21 vols. (Providence, 1891-1912).

Beaman, Alden G., *Rhode Island Vital Records, New Series*, 13 vols. (Princeton, Mass., 1975-date). Washington County, Newport County, and part of Kent County are covered. Available from Nellie Beamin Mosher, P.O. Box 585, East Princeton, MA 01517; prices vary.

Diaries

Peleg Burrough's Journal, 1778-1798: The Tiverton, R.I., Years of the Humbly Bold Baptist Minister, Ruth Wilder Sherman, ed. (Warwick, R.I., 1981). Out of print, but it may be possible to arrange to buy a second-hand copy, by writing to Mrs. Sherman, 128 Massasoit Drive, Warwick, RI 02888.

Nailer Tom's Diary (Boston, 1930) covers South Kingstown from 1778 to 1840. Not indexed, but the late Joseph Blaine of Newport compiled a complete name index (by date), copies at Newport Hist. Soc., R.I. Hist. Soc., and NEHGS. Out of print.

Journals

Beaman, Alden G., *The Rhode Island Genealogical Register*, published quarterly 1978-1986, annually 1987-1989. Back issues available at $30 per annual bound volume.

Rhode Island Roots, see Rhode Island Genealogical Society.

Societies and Repositories:

Newport Historical Society, 85 Touro Street, Newport, next to Touro Synagogue.

Rhode Island State Records Center, 1 Hill Street, Pawtucket, has County Court Records.

Rhode Island Archives, State House, Providence. Military records for the Revolution; indexed lists of freemen; some early deeds and notarial records; petitions to the General Assembly; French and Indian War records; maritime records.

Rhode Island Genealogical Society, 13 Countryside Drive, Cumberland, RI 02864. $10 per year ($15 per couple); includes quarterly, *Rhode Island Roots*.

Rhode Island Historical Society, Providence. Library is at corner of Hope and Power Streets. Membership, $25. per year, but non members may use library free.

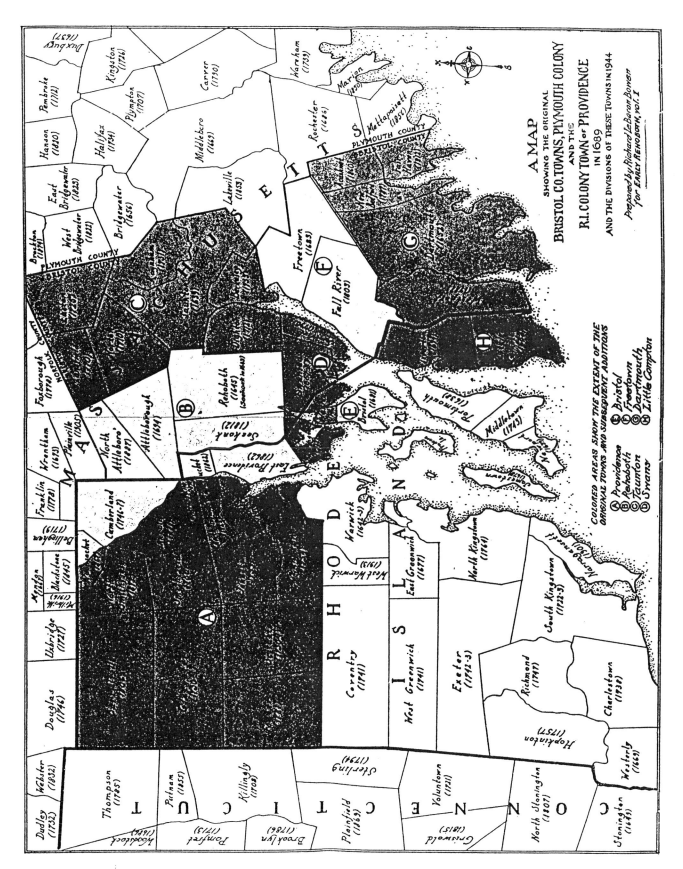

WARNINGS OUT 1757 TO 1791 FOR READING, MASSACHUSETTS

By Ann S. Lainhart

These warnings out are taken from a volume of Reading Town Records that also includes town rates from 1750 to 1852 and warrants for strays 1756 to 1852. This volume is item #12, reel #3 of the Reading records from the microfilm collection "Early Massachusetts Records, Inc. Records of Middlesex County, Mass. Towns through 1830" available at the New England Historic Genealogical Society, Massachusetts Historical Society, and the Microtext Room at the Boston Public Library.

Reading December 13^{13} 1757
Samuel Read wife & one child Samuel Badger his wife & two children Josiah Green & wife: Ruth Chaddle and Child: Elisabeth [Tuttell?] ware warned to Depart out of this town

March 1759: the persons hearafter named ware warned to Depart out of this town of Reading to the Several towns to which they Severally Belonged and the warrant Returned to the court (viz)
Nathan Eaton to pepprell
Andrew Sherron to Marblehead
Mary Pool to Andover
Elener Larabee to Lynn
Alles Flood to Tuksbary
Benjamin Peale to Salem
Daniel Williams to Concord
Joshua Bancroft to Worster
May Hitchens to Lynn
Ephraim twist to Lynn
Ruben Bourwell and 2 children to Willmington
Kendall Townsend to Willmington
Elisabeth Doge to Dorchester Canada
Benjamin ye child of Aaron [Eatons] wife to Tompson
Joshua Danforth and wife & three Children to Andover

may 1760 the persons hearafter named Being warned out of town ware Returned to the Sessions of ye Peace a Child of ye wife of thomas Richardson from Boston

June 26:1771 Elisabeth [Buck?] Warned out of Reading to Wilmington

June 26:1771 Timothy Hutchinson and familie...to Salem

July 10:1771 Samuel Buck Lydia Buck Dolley Buck Ebenezer Buck and Willard Buck...to Wilmington

Decem^r 1771 Neholis Conley & Wife & Children...viz Catherine Conley Solomon Conley & Benj^a Conley

February 24:1772 Betty Alious Elisabeth Brown...to Stonhan

February 28 1772 Ichabod Whitney & John William

March ye 2:1772 Micael Dolton Abigail Cross: Jacob Fould William Macksfield & Swain Laton

July 16th 1772 Thaddeas Bancroft...to Worsester...Septem^r 7th 1772 Robert Daland...to Salem...Said Daland taken in by John Nichols ye 4th said Bancroft taken in by Jonath^n Parker

Septem^r 21-1772 Jabez Carter & Lydia his Wife with their Children hereafter named that is Benjamin: Enock: Lydia: Mary: Martha: Amos and Kezia...to...Woburn...Familie was taken in By Deacon John Smith

Septem^r 3:1772 John [Casie]...to Middleton

Septr 29:1772 John Mead...to Lynn - Ammaziah Cade...to Oxford: William Cole...to Woburn

Decem^r 26:1772 Thos Hay...to Stonham

January 4th 1773 Margret Johnson & David Johnson...to Andover
Hannah Williams...to the town from where She Last Came

David Wright & Sarah his Wife...to Middleton...January the 4th 1773

Jonas Green Junr...to Maldin Jany 1773; James Barrit his Wife and Son...to Maldin February 1773

Ephraim Jonson & his family James Pool & Ebenzer Richerdson to the plase they last Came...april ye 8th 1773

august ye 3^d:1773 Sarah andros...to Boxford Sarah Wright to Mideltown Jeduthan Upton to fitchburge

august 21:1773...Obed Jonson abigal Jonson & Samuel Straton to andevour Susanna [Beueredge?] to maruelhed Steeven Ralfe Luse Ralfe his wife & Luse Ralfe & Patte Ralfe their Children to Boxford Jesse Ralfe to oxford & abigal Ralfe to the Place of her last Residence

September ye 3^d:1773...John [crumbled page] Mary Crocker John Crocker Sarah Crocker & Elizabeth Williams to Stoneham Abiather Perkins to New ipswitch

March 12th 1774...James Hay and his Wife & Eight Children...to Watertown their names are these [viz] James Hay Elizabeth Hay their Children abigal, James, thomas, Sarah, anna, Luce, John, & Lucrece

Feb^r 1774 thankful Brown & abial & John her Children and a young man Named Luis that lived with mr Cornelius Sweetser...to Stonham

May 12th 1774 John Clemmons and his wife abigal Hannah Clemmons John Clemmons Jonathan Clemmons Ruth Clemmons & Eli Clemmons their Children to Danvers Doc^t John Hart to Woolwich, Perhas Gardner to ye Town from whence he last Came

april 25th 1774 Persiluh How...to Lineborow & Nathan Mason to Maruelhed

may 31:1774 Lois Dodge...to the Plase from whence She last Came & Winthrop Dodge her Child to Concord where he was Born

may 20th 1774 Jane Gill...to Maldin

july 27 William Ston...to Danvers...he was taken in by Hezekiah Flint

September 8th 1774 Hannah Haywood...to Salem...Taken in by Ebenezer Mackintire

Sept 23:1774 Steephan Thomson Dorcis his wife and William their son to wilmingtown Sarah Bancroft to worsester

November 10th...John Colman Lois his wife Eunis Joseph & Thomas their Children

December ye 25th 1774...John Bragg and Sarah his wife their Children Elizabeth Bridget & Sarah to Andover Adino Carter Abigal his wife their Children Ephraim Isaac Sarah Elijah Abigail to woborn george Upton & Eunis his wife to Danvers

December 23^d 1774...Ebenezer Dealon to Salem

Joseph Dalton...to Marblehead

april 3ᵈ 1775 Benjamin Butters Elizabeth his wife with mahetable & Elizabeth their Children...to Wilmingtown

February 7:1776 Rebecah Pike...to Wilmingtown

Abigal Bray alis Burk...to Leomester...February 19:1776

Joshua Upton...to Middeltown...may 17ᵗʰ 1776

Mary 27ᵗʰ 1776...Joseph Holdin Mary his wife Joseph their Son to Stoneham

February 20ᵗʰ 1777. Jethro Kenney a Minor...to Middleton

May 2ᵈ 1777. Benjamin Newhall...to Lynn

July 30ᵗʰ 1777. John Cutler [Cutter?] to Lynn

October 20ᵗʰ 1777. Hephezibah Fisk and her Child Moses Pearsohn...to Andover

February 19ᵗʰ 1777. Mary Going...to Lynn, Samuel Pierson Wife Lois Chidren Lois Timothy Kendal Hannah and Jonathan...to Woburn, and Samuel Rucks...to Salem

November 18ᵗʰ 1777. Benjamin Johnson...to Exeter, and Richard Mason...to Marblehead

[November] 28ᵗʰ [1777] Stephen Greenleaf Wife Mary and Son Stephen...to Woburn

April 15ᵗʰ 1778. Susanna Nichols and Hannah Turner...to Merrimack in New Hampshire State
Deborah Mason and her Children Elizabeth and Mary...to Marblehead

[April] 30ᵗʰ [1778] Ebenezer Nichols his Wife Sarah and their Children Sarah, Susanna, Mary and Ebenezer...to Merrimack in New Hapshire State

September 1ˢᵗ 1778. Tabitha Allen...to Marblehead

[September] 30ᵗʰ [1778] Phinehas Sweetser...to Stoneham

November 10ᵗʰ [1778] Deborah Mackentire...to the Town from whench she last came

December 15ᵗʰ 1778. William Beers and Mary his Wife...to Boston

April 2ᵈ 1779. Jeremiah Winn his Wife Mehetabel, and Children Jeremiah and James...to Willmington

May 22ᵈ 1779. Stephen Russell, his Wife Sarah, their Children - Jedediah and Stephen...to Andover

March 31ˢᵗ 1779. Humphry Case, his Wife Elisabeth, their Child Betsey...to Middleton

May 3ᵈ 1780. Sarah Chadwell...to Concord

Mary 15ᵗʰ 1780. Sarah Cheever...to Lynn

March 5ᵗʰ 1781. James Holden and Wife and Naomi Holden...to Stoneham
March 12ᵗʰ 1781. Ebenezer Pope, Wife Sarah, Children - Lucy, Oliver, Polly Betsy, Jesse, Gould; and John Pope, Wife Ruth...to Danvers

January 22ᵈ 1781. Robert Mason...to Marblehead

February 13th 1781. Abraham Upton, Wife Susanna, Children - Abraham, Elias, Sarah, Rebecca, Molly, Isaac...to Lynn

February 13th 1781. John Cutler, Wife Lydia, Children - John, Lydia...to the Town from whence they last came

February 17th 1781. Asa Case, Wife Hulda - and Mary Kinney...to Middleton

February 5th. Richard Thomas and Wife Joanna...to Lynn

January 25th 1781. Lydia Thoits...to Lynn

February 13th 1781. Dudley Porter, Wife Sarah and Sarah Patch Children Sarah Dudley Samuel Greenleaf & Maho Greenleaf patch and Cate...to Danvers

April 20th 1781. Henry West...to Danvers

December 3d 1781. Dinah a Molatto Woman with Venus her Child...to the Town from whence they last came

February 26th 1782. Benjamin Laythe...to Lynn

December 3d 1781. Jonathan Wardwell and Hannah Wardwell...to Andover

December 3d 1781. Elisabeth Read...to the Town from whence She last came

December 3d 1781. Eunice Dudley...to Sudbury

December 24th 1781. Samuel Fisk...to Salem

December 24th 1781. Francis Hutchinson...to the Town from whence he last came

Febr 26 1782. Benjamin Laythe...to Lynn

September 30 1782. Phebe Hay...to Woburn

October 10. 1782. Phebe Hay...to Woburn

December 7. 1782. Gamaliel Jerrill & Wife Jemima & Child Rebecca...to Stoneham

March 6. 1783. Edmond Upton...to Andover, Asa Mackintier & Wife Sarah & Child Asa to Beverly, and Sally Wright to Hillsborough in the State of New Hampshire

April 23. 1783. Elisabeth Newhall...to Malden

April 23. 1783. Samuel Call and Wife Esther & Child Esther Call...to Malden

March 3. 1783. Dean Francis Smith & Wife Sarah...to Lynn

March 25. 1783. Francis Shelden & Anna Shelden & her Daughter Anna and Elisabeht Hitchinson...to Danvers, & Amos Smith to Lynn

May 18. 1783. Hannah Winship...to the Town from whence She last came

October 13. 1783. Samuel Bancroft Junr...to Warwick

October 13. 1783. Joshua Danforth & Wife Lydia to Lynn

October 15. 1783. Joshua Danforth & Wife Lydia...to Lynn

May 3. 1784. John Dinon...to Medford

May 4. 1784. Patience Mellindy...to the Town from Whence She last came

August 14. 1784. Sarah Smith Wife to Isaac Smith of Amherst in the State of New Hampshire and Sarah their Daughter...to Amherst

July 26. 1784. Sharper Freeman & Phillis his Wife with Dos and Sharper their Children...to the Town from whence they last came

October 9. 1784. John Newhall...to the Town from Whence he last came

December 2. 1784. Abigail Johnston...to the Town from whence she last came

December 18. 1784. Reuben Garey & Joanna his Wife with Robert & Anne their Children...to the Town from whence they last came

March 22. 1785. Jonathan Farwell...to the Town from whence he last came

April 26. 1785. Capt[n] Phinehas Parker & Elisabeth his Wife...to the Town from whence they last came

April 26. 1785. Jonathan Kiddar & Mary his Wife with Nancy Kiddar, Sarah Kiddar, William Lambert Kiddar, & Calatine Kiddar their Children, & Polly Butler their Grand-child...to the Town whence they last came

April 30. 1785. William Mellendy & Abigail his Wife, & their Children William, Daniel & Nabby...to the Town whence they last came

July 5. 1785 Mary Tay... to the Town whence She last came

July 20. 1785. Peter Freeman & Chloe his Wife with their three Children Jenney, Peggy & Phebe..to the Town whence they last came

August 22. 1785. Hannah Lewis..to the Town whence She last came

September 14. 1785. Timothy Lewis & Martha his Wife with Martha, Timothy, Ede, William, Pearson, Charles, Lydia & Polly their Children...to the Town whence they last came

September 14. 1785. Timothy Stearns & Sarah his Wife...to the Town whence they last came

September 26. 1785. Joshua Danforth, Keziah his Wife, their Children, Polly, Piercy, Sarah, Elisabeth & Benjamin...to the Town whence they last came

December 9. 1785. Dudley Woodbridge & Sarah his Wife, & the Wid[w] Rebecca Johnson...to the Town whence they last came

December 19. 1785. Thomas Hadley & Thomas his Child, & the Wid[w] Abigail Hayward...to the Town whence they last came

January 19. 1786. Cesar Mason...to the Town whence he last came

March 3. 1786. John Parker & Lucy his Wife with John & Lucy their Children & Polly Stephens...to the Town whence they last came

March 20. 1786. Mary Beers & her Children William Jesse, Joseph & John...to the Town whence they last came

March 27. 1786. John Marshall...to the Town whence he last came

August 25. 1786. Hannah Johnson...to the Town whence She last came

December 30. 1786. Benjamin Peters, his Wife Hannah, his Daughter Hannah & his Son Samuel...to the Town whence they last came

February 29. 1787. Sin Annis...to the Town whence he last came

March 1. 1787. John LeFavor...to the Town whence he last came

March 5. 1787. Josiah Brown, his Wife Judith, their Children - Josiah, Judith, Jephtha, Mehetabel, Patience, Jesse & Jedidiah - and Loammi Richardson...to the Town whence they last came

June 27. 1787. Enoch Stocker...to the Town whence he last came

July 6. 1787. John Favour...to the Town whence he last came

April 18. 1788. Jane Castle, Polly Mackintier, Abigail Bancroft, Alice Bancroft, Alpheus Bancroft, Solomon Mackintier Junr...to the Towns whence they last came

May 28. 1788. Mary Gilyan...to the Town whence she last came

John Hadley his Wife & Child of Stoneham...Labourer...twentieth day of October A.D. 1789

Ephraim Buck and Dorcas his Wife...of Wilmington...Labourer...with their Children...Ephraim & Cleaveland...30th Day of November [1789]

Peter Richardson & his Wife of Woburn...Labourer...with their Children whose Names are as follows, Patty, William, Grover & Mary...thirtieth Day of November [1789]

Abel Beard & his Wife Mary Beard of Woburn...Labourer...with their Child Abel...thirtieth Day of November [1789]

Kemer Freeman & Dinah his Wife & Chloe his Daughter Negroes of the Town of Lynnfield...Labourer...Nineteenth Day of November [1789]

John Nelson & Ann his Wife & children Sarah & James & Jane & Elisabeth & John & Esther...Labourer...Twelfth Day of November A.D. 1789

Joseph Atwell & Pann his Wife of Lynn...Cordwainer...with their Children, Namely, Elisabeth, Joseph, Rebecca, Hannah & John...seventh Day of December [1789]

Leonard Thompson of Wilmington & William Bullard of Ashby...Cordwainers...26th Day of January A.D. 1790

William Bennet & Susanna Bennet his Wife & William, Thomas & David their Children of Merimack...New Hampshire Blacksmith...Eighteenth Day of January A.D. 1790

David Sweet of Malden...Gentleman...with his Wife Sarah, & Child Betsey...Twenty sixth Day of January A.D. 1790

Benjamin Pool & Mehetabel his Wife of Boston...Eighteenth Day of January A.D. 1790

Robert Conners of Stoneham...Labourer...with his Wife Mary, & Children, Josiah, Ebenezer & Rebecca...1st Day of February A.D. 1790

Eli Mead of Bedford...Blacksmith...1st Day of February A.D. 1790

Nathaniel Bancroft supposed to be of Nova Scotia or transient Person Cordwainer...1st Day of February A.D. 1790

Caleb Bouttell of Amherst...New Hampshire Labourer...1st Day of February A.D. 1790

Deacon Francis Smith of Lynn...yeoman...with his Wife Sarah, & Amos Smith under his Care...and also...Enoch Stocker of Lynn...Cordwainer...with his Wife Hannah, & Child Sally...8th Day of February A.D. 1790

Samuel Larrabee of Salem...Cordwianer...with his Wife Hannah, & their Children viz, Hannah, Samuel, Polly, Betsey, John, Thomas, William, Nancy & Sarah...Eighth Day of February A.D. 1790

Benjamin Peters of Andover...Labourer, with his Wife...with their Daughter Hannah...and also...Samuel Peters of Andover...Labourer...1st Day of February A.D. 1790

Benjamin Peters Junr of Andover...Yeoman, with his Wife Patty & Child Patty...8th Day of February A.D. 1790

William Dedman Labourer, his Wife Mary with their Children, namely, Mary, Nancy, William & Lydia, of the Town of Salem...8th Day of February A.D. 1790

Peter Freeman...of Stoneham...Labourer...with his Wife Chloe, & their Children viz, Jenney, Phebe, Chloe, Anna & Lucy...8th Day of February A.D. 1790

Jabez Carter of Woburn...Yeoman...with his Wife, & Children, Martha, Keziah & Amaziah...1st Day of February A.D. 1790

Mayo Greenleaf Patch Cordwainer, his Wife Abigail, & their Child Polly of Danvers...& Abigail Johnson of Andover...& Sampson Whiting Labourer of Tewksbury...18th Day of January A.D. 1790

Betty Washer of Amherst...New Hampshire...18th Day of January A.D. 1790

Wid^w Betty Gordard of Boston...26th Day of January A.D. 1790

Hannah Hutchinson of Middleton...26th Day of January A.D. 1790

Wid^w Mary Nick, her Children, Mary, Rebecca & Sally; also the Wid^w Ruth Gro, her Children, Lydia & Ruth, all of Marblehead...26th Day of January A.D. 1790

William Burs of Boston...Carpenter...with his Wife...with their Children, Jesse, William, John, Joseph, Rebecca & Polly - & also...John Parker of Salem...Innholder...with his Wife Lucy...with his Children Lucy & John...8th Day of February A.D. 1790

Mrs Sarah Pope of Lynnfield...with her Son Oliver & Daughter Betsey...22d Day of February A.D. 1790

Wid^w Phebe Nichols of Salem...with her Family Viz Thomas & Benjamin Nichols...22d Day of February A.D. 1790

Deaⁿ Daniel Green of Stoneham...with his Wife Ruth & Children viz; Ruth, Abigail, Rhoda, Polly & Charles; also Daniel Green Junr & Wife Sally & Children viz Daniel & Ezra...22d Day of February A.D. 1790

Timothy Lewis of Lynn...Labourer...with his Wife Martha, & their Children, viz, Martha, Timothy, Ede, William, Pierson, Charles, Mary & Lydia...22d Day of February A.D. 1790

Darius Harvey Gentleman of Cambridge...with his Wife Polly & Child Polly...22d Day of February A.D. 1790

John Sweetser of Lynn...Gentleman...with his Wife Elisabeth & Chidren viz John & Elisabeth and Jonathan Pratt, Joseph Cheever, Ezra & Moses Sweetser...22^d Day of February A.D. 1790

John Hart of Ipswich...Physician...with his Wife Mary, & Children, viz, Polly, Abraham, John, William, Sally & Child...22^d Day of February A.D. 1790

May 6th 1790...Sarah Raynard of Marblehead Spinster and Ebenezer Russel Labourer and Mehitable his wife and their Children of Danvers

Sharper Freeman...of Lynn...Labourer and Philis his wife and Children Sharper Doss Sherburn and Jenne...Thirteenth Day of January [1791]

John Johnson...of Andover...Cordwainer and Ede his wife and Children Polly & Betsey and Samuel Brown of Dunstable...Cordwainer and Amos Prescott of Groton...Cordwainer and Nathan Mason of Marblehead...Labourer and wife Rebecka and Children Rebecka and Larkin and Phineas Sweetser of Stoneham...Cordwainer and wife Rebecka and Children Rebecka and Sukey...Thirteenth Day of January A.D. 1791

Mary [Conaway?] of Salem...Spinster and Betsey [Sentor?] of woburn...Spinster and Joseph Holden...of Stoneham...Labourer and Jenne his wifee and Son Ebenezer and George Brown of Stoneham...and Wife Sarah and Son George and family Janes Willey Thadeous Symond Duke Hay Jaohn Poland and Abial Brown of Stoneham...Cordwainers and James Newhall and Ruben Newhall and Joseph Newhall and wife Susanah all of Lynnfield...Cordwainers and Rhoda Brown of Stoneham...Spinster and Thomas Sweetser of Stoneham...Labourer and Mary Sweetser of Stonhame...Spinster and Mary Whitterage of Danvers...Spinster and Anna Edes and Anna Edes Junr and Lydia Boyington all of Harvard...Spinsters and Timothy Bryant Junr of Stoneham...Labourer and Lucy his wife and Oliver Pope of Danvers...Cordwainer and Lowis his wife...thirteenth Day of January [1791]

David Pratt of Lynn...Cordwainer and Elizabeth his wife and Thomas Myles of Worsester...Cordwainer and wife Mary and Children Joseph and Polly and Joseph [Ranydal?] of Lynn...Cordwainer...Twentyfourth Day of January [1791]

Ebenezer Abbot of Andover...Cordwainer and wife Sarah and Children Ebenezer Ephraim Eliab and Robert Mason of Marblehead...Labourer and wife Elizabeth and Children Daniel and Thomas and Cesar Mayson of Westford...Labourer & Elizabeth Goodall Spinster to the Town from which She Last came and Mary Gilman of Andover...Spinster...Twenty fourth Day of January [1791]

Silas Wiman of Woburn...Cordwainer and Jeremiah Rea of Lynnfield...Labourer and wife Bridget and Jermiah and Peleliah his sons and Samson Whiting of Parkerburg...Labourer and John Bancroft of Lynnfield...Cordwainer and Abigail Fitch of Boston...Spinster and Hannah Tucker of Salem...Spinster and Adino Carter of Woburn...Labourer and wife Abigail and Chidren Elijah and Abigail - Thomas Carter of Woburn...Blacksmith and wife Thankfull and Children Nancy Ephraim Thiomas Eliab and polly and Joseph Adams of Lynnfield...Housewright and Elizabeth Bowden and Sarah Tibbet both of Marblehead...Spinsters and Ephraim Flagg of Wilminton...Labourer and his wife Ruth and Children Josiah Theoder and Ruth and Ebenezer Flagg of wilminton...Labourer and wife Rebecka and John Newhall of Charlstown...Labourer...Twenty fourth Day of January [1791]

Widow Molly Holden and Daughter Fanny and Neomi Holden and Son Thomas all of Stoneham...Twenty first Day of February [1791]

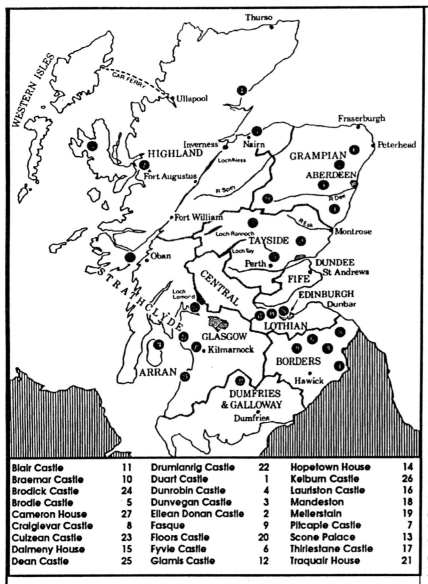

Blair Castle	11	Drumlanrig Castle	22	Hopetown House	14
Braemar Castle	10	Duart Castle	1	Kelburn Castle	26
Brodick Castle	24	Dunrobin Castle	4	Lauriston Castle	16
Brodie Castle	5	Dunvegan Castle	3	Mandeston	18
Cameron House	27	Eilean Donan Castle	2	Mellerstain	19
Craigievar Castle	8	Fasque	9	Pitcaple Castle	7
Culzean Castle	23	Floors Castle	20	Scone Palace	13
Dalmeny House	15	Fyvie Castle	6	Thirlestane Castle	17
Dean Castle	25	Glamis Castle	12	Traquair House	21

The High Road to Scotland
by Sherrill Yates

This article was compiled from personal experience, excerpts from "Scottish Roots" by Alwyn James and information leaflets handed out by the Scottish Record Office.

Last June, with barely a week's notice, Marianne Sheldon and I made a two week trip to Great Britain. Landing in Edinburgh, Scotland, we immediately checked out the available genealogy records. We spent the first part and the last part of our stay in Edinburgh. In between, we zipped around the countryside in a British auto playing Russian roulette with the lorries! Scotland had a feel all its own as we "soaked" in the Scottish mists and terrain. We saw as many castles and abbeys as we could fit into our tight schedule (tight by our own making). We checked out the Lake District, the Cotswalds, Warwick Castle, Yorkminster, Holy Island, Hadrian's Wall, Durham, Berwick upon Tweed, and even managed to visit Marianne's sister who lives south of London. Although I could write a book about our two weeks, it is genealogy about which I must focus.

But first, a little history: The history of the Scottish records over eight centuries is almost as engrossing as the history of the country itself. Shortly after the earliest recorded mention of a custodian of the royal records in 1288, the records were removed to London by Edward I ('Hammer of the Scots') as a preliminary to the bitter Wars of Independence whereby Scotland under Robert the Bruce secured its independence from England. The records were to suffer the same fate at the hands of Oliver Cromwell in 1651, but were returned (not without loss) on the restoration of Charles II in 1660.

Apart from these two great dispersals, the nation's archives suffered most from centuries of inadequate accommodation, and from fire, damp, vermin, carelessness and neglect. Stored originally in Edinburgh Castle as the strongest fortress in the kingdom, they were gradually transferred in the later 17th century to the Laigh (or Low) Parliament House in Edinburgh's High Street, close to the High Kirk of St. Giles', where they were more accessible to the lawyers of the Court of Session. This accommodation was, however, far from satisfactory. The clerks petitioned for a cat to keep the mice under control! Even the Treaty of Union of 1707, which laid down that the public records of Scotland should remain in Scotland 'in all time coming', made no financial provision for their proper custody.

It was not until 1765 that a grant from public funds was made for the erection of a proper record office. The foundation stone was laid in 1774 and a further 15 years were to elapse before the staff and records could start moving into His Majesty's General Register House, designed by Robert Adam, the distinguished Scottish architect. Since 1789, this gracious edifice—believed to be the first custom-built archive repository in Europe—has been the headquarters of the Scottish Record Office. In 1971, its 13 miles of shelving were virtually doubled by the conversion of a former city center church (first completed in 1814) to be an additional repository. The West Register House in Charlotte Square houses the records of modern government departments, the Scottish railway records, the large collection of maps and plans, and the microfilm collection. The Scottish Record Office today is thus able to provide a full range of modern records services from two of Edinburgh's finest Georgian buildings.

The Scottish Record Office recommends the following printed works which might be helpful in researching your Scottish ancestry. They are:

Scottish Family History
by Margaret Stuart and Sir James Balfour Paul, (Edinburgh, 1930).

Scottish Family Histories Held in Scottish Libraries, (Edinburgh, 1960).

Introducing Scottish Genealogical Research by Donald Whyte, (Edinburgh, 1982).

The Pursuit of Pedigree,
by Hector McKechnie, (Edinburgh, 1928).

Sources for Scottish Genealogy and Family History,
by D.J. and A.E.F. Steel, (London and Chichester, 1970).

In Search of Scottish Ancestry,
by Gerald Hamilton-Edwards, (London and Chichester, 1972).

Wills and where to find them,
by J.S.W. Gibson, (London and Chichester, 1974), pp. 197-207.

Scottish Roots,
by Alwyn James, 1981.

Issues of *The Scottish Genealogist* (Journal of the Scottish Genealogy Society).

THE NEW REGISTER HOUSE (also known as the General Register Office) sits back from and to the left of the General Register House (also known as The Scottish Record Office). In "*Scottish Roots*," Alwyn James proudly boasts, "There lies the most comprehensive collection of genealogical source material to be found in Britain and maybe even the world. In England, the equivalent information is dispersed through St. Catherine's House, London, the Public Records Office, hundreds of parish churches and scores of local libraries, archives and repositories." The New Register House contains records of every birth, marriage and death in Scotland since 1st January 1855, census lists of every person living in Scotland on the relevant day in 1841, 1851, 1861, 1871, 1881, 1891, and 4,000 volumes of old pre 1855 records from more than 900 parishes.

1) Births, Marriages and Deaths: From 1st January 1855, all births, marriages and deaths had to be registered with the civil authorities. The wonderful news is not only do these records contain more information than usually found in similar U.S. records, but they are ALL indexed! There are nearly 1,000 volumes of index arranged by year and in three groups and color coded: Births (red), Marriages (green), and Deaths (black - what else!). More great news is that in both marriages AND in deaths, the woman is listed by both maiden and married name.

Once you have found your ancestor, you may order a copy. However, that takes several days and is expensive. You may prefer to request to see the record and copy down the information. (Be sure to note any addresses you find--you will need them for the Census Returns.) Access to the registers is limited to 30 minutes or 6 entries at a time. To gain access, after you have found the place and entry number, look it up on the wall chart in the room and note the reference number. Then you put your name down on a waiting list and wait to be called. This could take a few minutes to half an hour depending on tourist season. Once called, a Repository Assistant will take you to the area where the records are kept, bring the volume and open it at the correct entry. You may take down the details (in pencil).

2) The Census Returns 1841-1891: The second group of records in the New Register House is the Census Returns. June 7, 1841 was the first door-to-door, person-to-person census. These carry the name, occupation and age of everyone living in Scotland at that time. Unfortunately, there is no index. Instead, the census returns are listed by town, and then by street. Addresses are a must and can usually be obtained from the Birth, Marriage & Death Records, or from trade directories (more on them later). Once you find a town and street, there is a correlated Census District # and enumerator book #. The Census Returns will give you names, birthplaces, and family information such as occupation and education if degreed. You might want to note the neighbors for future reference.

3) The Old Parochial Records (OPR) is the last category of special interest to genealogists. These are 4,000 volumes of records kept by the churches before the 1855 law forcing the keeping of records. Births, Marriages and Deaths become Baptisms, Banns and Burials! Unfortunately, there was no standard for keeping these records. Also, these were church records kept solely at the discretion (and dependant upon the efficiency) of the parishes. Therefore, there are gaps in them and not all parishes are represented.

In order to tap into this reservoir of information, you MUST know the parish. Then you must have an idea of what year or years you need. First, there are two volumes listing the parishes for which the Registrar-General holds records. There is an index at the back of these volumes. By referring to the correct volume, you will be able to find the OPR identification number. With this information, you can request the book containing the record. Unfortunately, these records are unindexed. If you are lucky, the clerk may have put the records down in a "rough" alphabetic system. Also if you are lucky, you will be able to read the clerk's handwriting. If you are very, very lucky, some fine soul has produced an index for that particular set of records. If that is so, a reference mark in the two volume index will tell you. The Church of Christ's Latter Day Saints has started work preparing a comprehensive county-by-county index of the Old Parochial Registers dealing with Baptisms and Marriages.

Other records available in New Register House include:

1. Register of Neglected Entries:
Births, marriages and deaths known to have occurred in Scotland between 1801 and 1854, but not included in the Old Parochial Registers.

2. Marine register of births and deaths after 1855:
Births and deaths on British merchant vessels if Scottish.

3. Service records after 1881:
Births, marriages and deaths of Scottish persons serving overseas in the Armed Forces.

4. War registers from 1899:
Three registers for the South African War (1899-1902), the 1914-18 War and the 1939-45 War.

5. Consular returns: Births (from 1914), marriages (from 1917) and deaths (from 1914) registered by British consuls.

6. Foreign countries: Births of children of Scottish parents, marriages and deaths of Scottish subjects, from information supplied by the parties concerned.

COSTS: (It ain't cheap!) Daily rates depend upon the records you want to search and are subject to change. (Amounts noted here were for 1988 and are in pounds - at present the exchange rate is about $1.60 per pound.)

Indexes to the Post 1855 BMDs	5.50
Census Returns	4.50
Parish Registers pre 1855	4.50
To search all three, daily	8.50
per week	25.50
per month	70.00
per quarter	140.00

One other very important item. You can and should pre-register for a spot in the New Register House. This is especially wise if it is during May - September. People line up at 8:30 for the 9:00 opening. If you have come a long way in great anticipation, pre-registering by mail is a must. Otherwise, you may be turned away disappointed.

GENERAL REGISTER HOUSE
(or Scottish Record Office)

Now that we have exhausted the New Register House, it is time to move next door to the "FREE" Register House. The Historical Search Room is the place you want to be. The information there is as follows:

1) RECORD OF WILLS
Commissary Court Records, Testaments and Inventories: Up until 1822, all testaments were confirmed by the Commissary Courts of Scotland. The origin of these courts lay within the Church, therefore, you need to know the dioceses. Fortunately, all testaments are indexed in volumes according to the relevant Commissary Court, from the earliest recorded examples (ranging from 1514 in Edinburgh to 1700 in Wingtown) up to the year 1800.

The Sheriff Courts took over responsibility for confirmation of testaments from 1823 onwards. From that date until 1876, there are some confirmations that are still kept by the sheriff clerks. From 1876, the annual tax list provides a simple means of tracking down the testaments.

The Register of Deeds: from 1554, indexed from 1770 and some earlier periods often contain genealogical information.

2) RECORDS RELATING TO PROPERTY AND SUCCESSION

Registers of Sasines: (Land Records) begun in 1617 and still current, record the transfer of heritable property. Indexes are available from 1781 and to parts of older registers. Earlier transfers of land were recorded in notaries' protocol books. Although incomplete, these date from 1510.

Burgh Registers of Sasines: for royal burghs only, 1681-1963. Some are indexed.

Retours and Services of Heirs: record succession to heritable property, from 1545. Abstracts

have been printed to 1699 and decennial indexes thereafter.
Registers of Tailizies:
Entails and disentails, 1688 to present. Indexes, 1688-1904. [NOTE: *Webster's New Collegiate Dictionary* defines entail: "to restrict property by limiting the inheritance to the owner's lineal descendants or to a particular class thereof (as to his male children)"]

3) RECORDS WHICH LIST INDIVIDUALS

Diligence Records: Legal processes for enforcement of obligations. Not indexed.
Court of Session Records: Particularly for bankruptcies. Indexed from 1839.
Court of Justiciary (Criminal) Records: Can be useful for transportations to Australia.
Hearth Tax and Poll Tax Records: Compiled in the 1690s, arranged under counties, may list names of farms, villages and settlements.
Taxation Schedules: Dating from the middle of the 18th century in the case of the window tax. Information varies from one county to another. Records are not indexed.
Valuation rolls: Assessments of counties, cities and burghs, 1855-1975, listing proprietors, tenants and occupiers. Earlier volumes not indexed.
Church Records: The most useful are the kirk session records of the parish churches, dating mainly from mid-17th century. These contain communion rolls, lists of heads of families, and lists of baptisms, marriages and burials before 1855.
Burgh records: Older records from a number of former burghs, can include lists of inhabitants.
Estate records: Archives of landed families cover many parts of Scotland, but mainly after mid 17th century.

4) USING RECORDS BEFORE 1600:
Since there are virtually no statistical records for this period, it is vital to know locations.
Register of the Great Seal (in print 1306-1688): Royal grants of land and major offices.
Register of the Privy Seal (in print 1488-1584): Warrants for Great Seal Grants.
Register of the Privy Council of Scotland (in print 1545-1691): Administrative and judicial info.
Exchequer Rolls (in print 1264-1600) **the Treasurers Accounts** (in print 1473-1580): entries for persons who came into a monetary relationship with the crown.
Cartularies: Estate records of ecclesiastical and lay landlords of the medieval and early modern period. May contain tenants.

QUERIES BY POST: The Scottish Record Office cannot undertake detailed research, but are always glad to advise on the use of the records and to answer specific inquiries or requests for photocopies when supplied with sufficient information for the documents to be readily identifiable. Postal inquiries should be addressed to:

**The Keeper of the Records of Scotland,
Scottish Record Office,
HM General Register House,
Edinburgh EH1 3YY.
Telephone 031-556-6585.**

❖ ❖ ❖ ❖ ❖

After you have finished with the Register House, don't forget:
REFERENCE LIBRARIES: Marianne and I worked a few hours in an excellent one in Edinburgh, The National Library of Scotland on George IV Bridge Street. They claim to have a copy of every book ever written about Scotland and its people.
Trade Directories: Started in the larger urban centers in the second half of the eighteenth century, trade directories supply occupations and addresses.
School Directories: From Grammar School to Universities - often give detailed information.
The Ministers of Scotland: If you are lucky enough to have a minister in the Church of Scotland, their ministers are fully documented in *Fasti Ecclesiae Scotiae*, which reads like a Whos Who and goes back to the 1600s.
Session Books: Usually pre 1855 contains the "goings-on" of the church community.
Statistical Account: Also prepared by the Church, gives a sketch of what was happening in the community - how much the laborers were paid, what equipment was used on the farms, crops grown, what factories existed, etc.

❖ ❖ ❖ ❖ ❖

SCOTLAND is a fastinating place. The Scots are a people of paradox. From earliest history they have been wanderers, but no matter where they have gone, they have taken a deep-rooted devotion to their native land. Every year thousands of people, speaking many languages and with many different accents, make sentimental journeys to Scotland to see the places where their forebears were born. **It is well worth the trip!**

GLAMIS CASTLE

MAKING OF A NATION - A Report on My Ancestors

By Tammy Terry, age 13

The United States of America was the first great nation to be formed from the families of every other nation on earth. It has been called the melting pot of the world because of the diversity of people who come here and live and build. My first ancestor to come to America was Francis Eaton. And my family tree grew to send out many branches and many roots to bear much fruit. It is interesting how God wove all of the different families together, each with its own contribuition, to make a great nation to glorify Him.

Frances Eaton came to America on the Mayflower, but was considered a stranger. He signed the Mayflower Compact which was the first document of law in America. He came with his wife Sarah Eaton and his son. But, during their first winter, she died. He remarried, but she died also. The next year Christian Penn arrived. They married and had four children one of which was Ebenezer Eaton. Later Francis died.

Because many of my ancestors lived in Massachusetts and Maine in the 1600s, they were often found in battles and skirmishes with the Indians. My ancestor, Joseph Rice, owned a garrison which offered shelter and protection from the warlike Indians. On a cold Fall day in about 1680 in New Hampshire, two of our Rice ancestor boys were kidnapped, at the age of nine and eleven, by a band of Indians. When they grew up, one married a chief's daughter and later became a chief, with no recollection of his childhood, language, or home. The other, remembering some of his childhood family, returned to visit, but could not remember the language, so he returned to live with the Indians, his people.

On October 15, 1667, Elizabeth (King) Rice and Samuel Rice had a son named Samuel. Two weeks after Samuel's birth, Elizabeth died leaving Samuel with six children including a two-week old baby son. He gave the infant to Elizabeth's "brother and sister King" to be raised as their own. When he grew up he was known as Samuel King alias Rice, and that name (King alias Rice) followed for at least three generations. Samuel King alias Rice had a son named Ezra King alias Rice in 1797, who was killed in the French and indian wars on January 14, 1746, in Cape Breton, Canada.

Abraham Pettingell was born in 1707 in Newbury. He was enrolled in Captain George Berry's Company in 1747. He also was in Lieut. Benjamin Morgridge's Company in 1749. He was captured by Indians while in service and was taken to Louisburg. Later, he was brought, with other exchange prisoners, to Boston in the schooner "Britannia." One of the other prisoners was Benjamin Lake, who will be discussed later. In 1729 he bought a lot in North Yarmouth, Maine. He was a juryman in North Yarmouth in 1760.

In September 1634, Abraham's son David was born. On November 23, 1758, David married Mercy Lake, daughter of Benjamin and Mercy (Eaton) Lake. Benjamin was, you'll remember, a prisoner with David's father, Abraham, and Mercy Eaton was descended from Francis Eaton, who arrived on the Mayflower.

David served in the colonial wars. He resided at North Yarmouth, Maine, and was in the squad of scouts under Sergt. Jacob Parsons, at New Gloucester. He also was on a roll dated at Boston, March 15, 1757 and 1758. He also served under Capt. Joshua Freeman in 1758 and Capt. Leissner in 1759. Later he served in the Revolution in Capt. Nicholas Blaisdell's Co. and under Col. Edward Wigglesworth, Feb. 26 1777 and 1778, and was killed at the battle of Saratoga January 6, 1778.

December 10, 1761, a son Benjamin was born to David and Mercy Pettingell. He was, no doubt, named for his grandfather Benjamin Lake. He served in Wimmam Cobb's Co. in the Revolution and was discharged in 1779. He later served until 1783 and was in the Battle of Kingsbridge. Following his service, he moved "west" to western New York. He died in 1844 and the following was taken from his obituary:

> "...at the age of twenty enlisted into the United States Service as a soldier, where he performed with fidelity and courage the severest hardships and trials during three long years of bloody warfare, in Colonial

defence against British cruelty and tyrannical oppression without compensation for his service. The unequal contest being gloriously ended, and America declared free and independent, he returned in joy to his native Province, with the precious boon of freedom spreading over our delightful country, and destined to encircle a world in its embrace. Up to his seventy-eighth year he gave his ballot as a free citizen to support that government he had so faithfully defended in his youth. Not only did he serve his country in her struggle for liberty, but, when called upon to defend our northern frontier in the last war, (the war of 1812) he left his family and friends to preserve our national honor and teach Great Britain that the same spirit that inspired the fighters of '76 was still remembered by themselves and their patriotic sons...While blessed with reason he was unwavering in the cause of Christianity and virtue, beloved in society and a sincere devoted member of the Methodist Church."

In 1790, a daughter, Mercy (Polly) was born to Benjamin and Mercy (Briggs) Pettingell. And in 1814, Polly married William King Rice, the great grandson of Ezra King alias Rice, previously described as having died in the Colonial Wars in 1746. They then moved to Ohio where Horace was born in 1829. Some time later, they moved further west to Illinois where William died and then moved into Iowa where Polly married Mr. Cook. It was there too that Horace married Eliza Jane Bolton in 1849.

Eliza Jane Bolton had come from Virginia where her grandfather Henry Bolton, had fought in the Revolutionary War. Henry and his brother Conrad lived in Liverpool England. One day, in their teens, the two boys went to the docks to see the ships come in. They were invited to see the inside of the ship. When they came back up on deck, they had sailed out to sea. When they arrived in America, a Mr. Moore agreed to pay their passage in return for 7 years of indentured service. One day a man came to ask if Henry would come and tend his horses. After permission was granted by Mr. Moore, Henry was released to go with the man who turned out to be General George Washington. In this service, Henry was hit by a musket ball in the hip. He was carried off the field, strapped to a cannon, as a stretcher, and he limped from then on.

Conrad tried to return to England but he never reached there. The boys did not know how to read or write, so they did not know the proper spelling for their last name, so their line cannot be traced farther back. Henry had two wives and fathered 20 children.

In January, 1850, a son George was born to Horace and Eliza, and early in the spring of 1851 they started west for Oregon, arriving late in 1851. Eliza Jane walked most of the way to make it easier for the oxen. She carried little George in her arms.

"In 1851, with his own family... (Horace, Eliza, Polly, Mr. Cook, and little George) made the trip across the plains to Oregon. They used ox teams until arriving at Bridger Wyoming, where they traded them for horses. The trip was continued with much hardship and suffering. Their food was exhausted and at Ft. Boise, they traded a portion of their bedding for dried salmon skins prepared by the Indians. They were obliged to dig roots, eat hazel brush and roseballs. At Umatilla the Indians gave them beef. From the Dalles to the Cascades the trip was made by steamer ship "Flint," and from there to the mouth of the Big Sandy, they traveled in a flat boat. Judge Taylor drove them from there to Milwaukee. Eliza worked there for $1.00 per day cooking in a boarding house, and her husband made $2.50 per day in a sawmill. Later he made excellent wages, from $10 to $40 per day in handling wood and timber. Typhoid fever attaced his family and they finally journeyed back to the Dalles where he bought a railroad homestead on 15 mile creek.

He was the first man to plant grain there. He was the butt of ridicule until they saw the excellent crops. They too took up land and commenced to raise wheat."

Horace and Eliza Jane Rice were my great, great, great grandparents.

When my grandmother was researching our family history she discovered that there is a Rice organization in the east and they thought that when the Rices headed for Oregon that they had been killed by Indians. But with some research it turned out that they did make it to Oregon and we are their descendants.

It took many people with many talents, gifts, and abilities to make this country great. Some were leaders of great reputation. Some were soldiers. Some were politicians. Some were farmers. Some were obscure. Some were famous, but all were Americans, and all were important. Their lives worked together to form the fabric of this nation. I am proud to be part of the story of America.

BIBLIOGRAPHY

1. An Illustrated History of Central Oregon (Spokane, WA: Western Historical Pub. Co., 1905).

2. Interview with Verda E. Cornutt, Genealogist. Interviewed by Tammy Terry October 28, 1987.

3. Pedigree Charts.

4. Edmund Rice Assn. Inc. A Genealogical Register of Edmund Rice Descendants (Rutland, VT): Charles E. Tuttle, 1970).

5. Pettingill, Charles I., A Pettingell Genealogy (Boston, MA: Fort Will Press, 1906).

(Tammy Terry, age 13, is the granddaughter of ESOGer Verda E. Cornutt, 1751 S.W. Turner Road, West Linn, OR 97068.)

THE CHARM OF RESEARCH

To weave together the fading dates of old manuscripts with the traditions that have survived sleeping generations, until the joy and the tears, the quaint speech and early piety, stand out upon the tapestry in the semblance of a living man - this gives a pleasure which he only who has stood at the loom can feel and understand.

Charles Knowles Bolton

Quoted in *The Essex Antiquarian*, I:150

Research in Progress

HENRY COLLINS OF LYNN AND HIS DESCENDANTS

By Caroline Martino and Marcia Lindberg

There were at least five Collins "Heads of Families" in the Massachusetts Bay Colony in the 17th century: Christopher Collins, shoemaker, of Boston and Braintree (1639); Edward Collins, merchant, of Cambridge and Medford (1636); John Collins, shoemaker, of Boston (1639); John Collins of Salem and Gloucester (1642) and Henry Collins, starchmaker, of Lynn (1635) (Charles H. Pope, *Pioneers of Massachusetts* [Boston, 1900], 112). There is no evidence to suggest any connection between these families. This paper will trace five generations of descent from Henry Collins of Lynn.

A few accounts of Henry Collins have been published. Anna L. P. Collins and Charles Henry Pope wrote a 19-page treatise entitled *Henry Collins of Lynn; and Some of His Descendants in Southborough, Massachusetts and Fitzwilliam, New Hampshire* (Cambridge, Mass., 1910); hereafter "Collins and Pope." This work is limited to one line from Henry^1, Joseph^2, Ezekiel^3, William^4, Ezekiel.^{5} It may be consulted at New England Historic Genealogical Society in Boston or at the Lynnfield Public Library. *Descendants of John Collins of Charlestown, R.I,. and Susannah Daggett, His Wife*, by Capt. George Knapp Collins, 1901; hereafter, "G. K. Collins," lists the 16 children of John^2 as well as the 10 children of John^3. A copy is at NEHGS and the Lynnfield Library. A brief biography of Henry^1 Collins is given in Dana Converse Backus's *The English Ancestry of Dana Converse Backus* (Salem, Mass., 1949); hereafter "Backus"), 73-74. Finally, an unpublished manuscript of 20 pages, by Winifred Lovering Holman was consulted at the New England Historic Genealogical Society. No complete 5-generation study of all the descendants of Henry Collins is known to exist. This paper will attempt to bring together the accounts mentioned above and will add new data discovered through research into court records.

The English roots of Henry Collins have been partially determined. Although his birth, parentage and marriage have not been found, the baptisms of his first three children, who accompanied Henry to New England, are recorded in the parish records of Stepney, St. Dunston, County Middlesex, England (Mormon Microfilm, # 0595417):

> "Henry Collins, Jr., son of Henry, christened November 4, 1629 at 5 days old.
> John Collins, son of Henry, christened January 22, 1631 at 8 days old.
> Margery Collins, dau. of Henry, christened November 13, 1633 at 7 days old."

Also in the parish records of Stepney is a christening record for a Henry Collins, son of Thomas, 19 December 1599, but this is probably not Henry of Lynn, who was born in 1606 (see below), and the name Thomas never appears in this Collins family. "The parish of Stepney, in the eastern part of the present city of London, is dedicated to St. Dunston, and is one of the oldest in London" (letter of A. Chalkey Collins of Great Barrington, Mass., dated 10 Aug 1900, cited in G. K. Collins, 8).

HENRY^1 COLLINS was born in England, probably at Stepney Parish, county Middlesex, in 1606, according to his age given as 29 on the passenger list of "The Abigail" in 1635 (Charles Edward Banks, *Planters of the Commonwealth* [Baltimore, MD, 1975], 164). He was buried at Lynn in the Massachusetts Bay Colony, as "Henry, Sr., grandfather of Henry, 3rd," 20 February 1687, age 81 (*Lynn Vital Records to 1850*; hereafter LVR). But in Henry's will, dated 10 February 1686/7, he calls himself "82 or thereabouts" (Suffolk Probate, 1532). Henry married, about 1628, probably at Stepney Parish, ANN ---- (perhaps RIALL/RYALL/ROYAL), who was born in 1605, according to her age of 30 on the passenger list of "The Abigail" in 1635. She died at Lynn, 29 September 1691, as "mother of Henry, 3d" (LVR).

The reasons for supposing that Ann Collins's maiden name was Riall (or Ryall or Royal) are three-fold: one, Henry and Ann Collins gave the unusual name of Riall to a daughter who died young (LVR). Secondly, Isaac Ryall (or Royal), a carpenter of Dorchester, Mass., married Ruth Tolman, daughter of Thomas Tolman. Two children of Henry Collins also married children of Thomas Tolman. Thirdly, William Ryall, of Salem/Beverly, Mass., is thought to have been born at Stepney Parish (Henry F. Waters, *Genealogical Gleanings in England* [Baltimore, 1969], II:738).

Henry and Ann Collins, with their first three children, came to New England in 1635 aboard "The Abigail" of London, Richard Hackwell, Master. "The Abigail" sailed from Plymouth, England about 1 August, 1635, with 220 persons and many cattle. She arrived at Boston about 8 October, infected with smallpox. Among those coming in this ship, but not listed, were Sir Henry Vane, son and heir of Sir Henry Vane, Comptroller of the King's Household, traveling incognito; the Reverend Hugh Peter, pastor of the English Church at Rotterdam, and the Reverend John Wilson, who was returning to Boston, with his wife, her first appearance in New England. The list of passengers in the Public Record Office, cited in Banks, *Planters*, 161, 164, includes:

"Henry Collins [age] 29, Starchmaker, certified at Stepney [settled at] Lynn;
Mrs. Anne Collins, 30;
Henry Collins, 5;
John Collins, 3;
Margery Collins, 1"

Although Henry Collins was called a starchmaker on the above list, on all subsequent deeds in Essex County, he is called husbandman or yeoman.

Henry became a freeman on 9 March 1636/7 (Massachusetts Archives, 35:351). In October of 1637, he served on a jury for Essex County (*Records and Files of the Quarterly Courts of Essex County*; hereafter *EQCR*, I:6); and for most of his life, the name of Henry Collins, Sr. appears on lists for Juries of Trials and Grand Juries (ibid., various pages).

In 1638, Lynn's petition to the General Court for more land, resulted in the so-called "six mile grant" into the country. In the general allotment to residents of the town, Henry Collins received "80 acres and ten," one of the larger amounts granted. This indicates that he had contributed to the colony. The lands distributed were in the outlying areas that later became Reading (the part that is now Wakefield) and Lynnfield (Loea Parker Howard, *The Beginnings of Reading and Lynnfield* [Reading, Mass., 1937], 5-10).

In 1645, Henry was one of the signers of a petition to the General Court for a reduction in rates, or Colony Taxes, due to the "removal of so many families to Reading, Long Island, and other places" (Mass. achusetts Archives, 100:14; Alonzo Lewis and James R. Newhall, *History of Lynn* [Lynn, 1898], 214-215). On the 24th of February 1657, he was one of seven men chosen to lay out Nahant in planting lots, "each household to have an equal share" (Mass. Archives, cited in Lewis, *Hist. of Lynn*, 240).

On 1 September 1661, Henry Collins, husbandman, purchased 30 acres of land for 25 pounds from Daniel King, gentleman (Essex Deeds, 2:19).

Henry Collins was a Selectman for Lynn in 1664 and 1666, having previously served as Constable in 1642 and later as Tithingman in 1677 (EQCR, I:42, 45; III:162, 373; VI:289). He was frequently called upon to take inventories of estates; for William Tilton's estate in 1653, William Hacker's and George Farr's in 1662, Richard Johnson's in 1666 and Edward Ireson's in 1675 (*Historical Collections of Essex County* [Salem, 1859-60]; hereafter, *EIHC*, I:10, 96, 144; II:15, 231).

He was mentioned in the will of Daniel King, 7 February 1671/2 (Mass. Archives, 16:98).

On the 12th of March 1671/2, Henry Collins, Sr., yeoman, sold to Andrew Mansfield, for 16 pounds, 10 shillings, 5 1/2 acres in Reedy Meadow. This land lies in present-day Lynnfield and Wakefield, and was probably part of his 80-acre grant from the town of Lynn. The deed was recorded on 27 April 1677 (Essex Deeds, 4:154). Previously published accounts of Henry Collins, state that his homestead was off Essex Street in what is now the eastern part of Lynn, but the records show that he lived and died in the western part of the town (the part that is now Saugus) near the border of Rumney Marsh. All of his sons continued in that part of Lynn.

When an Oath of Allegiance to the King was required in 1678, listed among those taking the oath at Lynn were: Henry Collins, Sr., Henry Collins, Jr., and Henry, son of Henry, Jr., as well as John Collins, John, Jr., Benjamin and Joseph Collins (*EQCR*, VII:158). In June of 1681, when a country rate (tax) was taken, Henry Collins was assessed 14 shillings, 10 d. This was the third highest rate among the forty assessments at that date. Only "Mr. King" and "Mr. Burrill" had higher assessments (ibid., VIII:122).

Henry made his will on 10 February 1686/7. Although he died in Lynn, in Essex County, the will was probated in Boston in Suffolk County. "This was during the administration of Sir Edmond Andros, at which time...[if a man's estate] amounted to more than fifty pounds, probate had to be acted upon in Boston" (*The American Genealogist*, 12:175).

WILL OF HENRY COLLINS

dated 10 Feb 1686/7; probated 31 Mar 1687 (Suffolk Probate, 1532)

In the name of God Amen. I, Henry Collins, Senior, of Lynn, New England, aged 82 or thereabouts, being weak and infirm in body yet God granting me my reason and understanding in good measure so that I find myself in a good capacity to settle the affairs of my family not knowing how soon my great change may come and being at present apprehensive of the imminent danger I am in in regard of prevailing distempers on my body have observed the providence of God in this present opportunity which God hath granted me to dispose of myself and that outward estate which God of his bounty and goodness hath bestowed upon me. As for my poor precious immortal soul, I resign it up unto the hands of my Dear Redeemer the Lord Jesus Christ who hath ransomed it by his precious blood looking to be justified freely by his grace and through his redemption exercising faith in him alone and trusting and relying upon him for righteousness and salvation having a well-ground assurance of his everlasting love and rich grace...as having a poor frail body I command it to the dust out of which it was taken willing a decent interment thereof suitable to my rank and quality, and I die in the belief of the resurrection of my body, knowing that my redeemer lives and shall stand at the latter day upon the earth and though the worms may destroy this body yet in my flesh shall I see God. Job 19.26.27.

As for the disposal of my outward estate, my will is that all my honest debts be duly and truly paid out of my estate.

Item: That what ever lands or estate I have already given to any of my children whether my own natural children or those that stand related to me by marriage with any of my daughters that the said estate and every part of it be confirmed to them, with those parcels of land and meadow which I have given to my son Johnson upon marriage with my daughter; viz: three acres of meadow in the country, two acres of salt marsh in Rumney Marsh next to John Burrills, and two acres of upland in my son Joseph Collins' field, to be confirmed to my son Johnson and his heirs for ever.

Item: My will is that my dear and loving wife, who hath ever been tender of me and industrious in her place in procuring what outward estate God hath bestowed upon us, my will is that my whole personal estate that I am now possessed of, both housing and lands, etc., be and abide to be my wife's during her natural life; for her comfortable maintenance.

Item: I give to my wife all my movables, chattels, cattle, etc. to be at her disposal either to my own children or my grandchildren as she shall see cause at her decease.

Item: My will is that after my wife's decease all my lands and meadows (excepting four score acres of land lying up in the country near goodman Gowans) otherwise all my lands and meadows wheresoever to be divided equally among my three sons, Henry, Joseph and Benjamin, only my eldest son Henry have 30 pounds worth of land more than his other two brothers, and this together with his proportion of lands with Joseph and Benjamin and what I have formerly bequeathed to him that he accept of as a double portion.

Item: My will is that my son Benjamin have 10 acres of land in my planting field towards his proportion.

Item: I bequeath to my daughter Margery 30 pounds, and to my daughters Hannah and Elizabeth 20 pounds apiece to be paid out of my whole estate. As for my son John deceased his portion he received in his life time and so that his children do greatly and peaceably enjoy the same.

Finally my will is that my children may carry it dutifully and tenderly toward their aged mother and that they may live in the fear of God, improving their interest in the covenant; and that they may live in love and peace one with another all their days, that so the God of their father, the God of love and peace may be with them and bless them and grant them many prosperous days here and heaven hereafter.

I do constitute my loving wife and eldest son, Henry Collins, to be executors of this my last will and testament, and Mr. Oliver Purchase and Mr. Jeremiah Shepard to be overseers, and to this my last will and testament I have set my hand and seal this 10th day of February in the year of our Lord 1686/7.

The witnesses were Jeremiah Shepard, Paul Mavericke, Matthew Farrington, Jr. The will was probated on 31 March 1687. Recorded on the same date, was the inventory of "Henry Collins, Senior," which was presented to the court by Henry Collins, Executor. It included the dwelling house and barns with all other housing with the orchard and land therein, 70 pounds; upland, pasture lands, meadows and salt marsh, 315 pounds; 80 acres of wilderness land up in the country, so-called, but sold, 21 pounds; cows, 2 heffers, a bull, 4 sheep, 3 shoats, a horse and mare, 32 Pounds, 5 shillings. Moveables, outside and in, linens, clothing, etc., 33 pounds. Total estate, 474 pounds, 10 shillings (Suffolk Probate Record Books, 9:184).

On the 13th of December 1687, Henry's widow, Ann Collins, with her son Henry "now Sr.," sold to John Bancroft, for 6 pounds, 13 shillings, 4 pence, 10 acres of land between Reedy Meadow and Stone Meadow. Both parcels were part of the six-mile grant to Lynn. The deed was recorded on 4 December 1693 (Essex Deeds, 10:117; 9:171).

WILL OF ANN COLLINS

dated 8 Sept. 1690, probated 24 Nov, 1691 (Essex Probate 6028)

I, Ann Collins of Lynn...widow and relict of Henry Collins Sr... deceased... being very aged and my time of departure out of this world most uncertain and may be very sudden as I have cause to think by reason of some late providences of God visiting me with some touches of his hand upon my frail body and hath taken away my natural sight... and being free from pain... and in perfect memory... and clear understanding, do make this my last will and testament and dispose of what estate... was left unto me by the last will of my husband...

As for my temporal estate that God of his mercy hath vouchsaved to me to dispose of I give and bequeath to be divided and disposed of after my decease as hereafter followeth renouncing all former wills, I give to my eldest son, Henry Collins, my horse. I give to my grandson Nathaniel Collins, a cow and a young mare, and after my decease, twenty shillings out of my estate then left if it will reach to do it, and so I leave that to my Executors. I give to my grandchildren, viz: the children of my son John Collins, deceased and not named in my will before, viz: Elizabeth, Mary, Daniel, Hannah, Lois, the sum of three pounds to be paid to each... as a testamony of my love to them who were suddenly deprived of their father and of his estate. I give to my two grandsons, the sons of John Collins deceased, viz: Samuel and Joseph Collins, the sum of five shillings each after my decease. Also to Abigail, now Townsend. I give to Susannah Collins, the daughter of Benjamin Collins, twenty shillings. I... appoint my sons Henry Collins and Joseph Collins to be my two Executors... and to make me a comely and decent burial... Moreover, I give unto my granchildren Johnsons viz: Mary, Richard, Ruth, Samuel, each the sum of twenty shillings after my decease... I desire my well respected and trusty friends, Mr. Jeremy Shepard, pastor of the Church of Christ in Lynn, and Oliver Purchass to be my overseers... I set my own hand and seal hereunto. As also that I have paid unto Elizabeth Collins, now alias Basset so much of my legacy to her in Indian corn the sum of 21 shillings.

Ann Collin's will was witnessed by Henry Silsbey, Oliver Purchase, Henry Collins, Jr. and was presented by one of the executors, Joseph Collins, who renounced the trust, the other son, Henry Collins, accepted.

Three years after the death of Ann Collins, on 27 November 1694, the three surviving sons of Henry and Ann Collins, namely: Henry Collins (now called "Senior"), Joseph Collins and Benjamin Collins, made an agreement to divide the lands left to them by their father:

AGREEMENT BETWEEN HENRY, JOSEPH AND BENJAMIN COLLINS

dated 27 Nov 1694 (Essex Probate, 6057)

"This indenture, covenant and agreement made between Henry Collins, senior, Joseph Collins and Benjamin Collins, sons to Henry Collins

deceased of Lynn in the County of Essex.... Witnesseth that whereas our Honored father in his Last Will and Testament left us our several portions of land and meadow or marsh undivided, leaving also his solemn dying charge that love and unity and peace may be maintained and continued amongst his children to avoid therefore any differences that may for the future arise either among ourselves or posterity in succeeding generations with reference to the divisions or bounds of the several tracts or parcels of land or meadow willed and bequeathed to us by our honored father; we have therefore mutually agreed and consented to and accepted of our several divisional parts and parcels of land and meadow or marsh with their limits and bounds that we settled and firmly agreed upon forever therewith, to rest satisfied and contented. And we do therefore by these presents firmly and forever bind ourselves, our heirs, executors and administrators to accept of and forever to rest satisfied....

HENRY COLLINS SENIOR, *his divisional part. Eighteen acres of upland, lying on or being on his father's land or pasture, bounded southeast by his own land and so butting upon the ten acre lots eastwardly; west by an apple tree; southwest to a stake in the field and so on to a heap of stones in the fence westerly, and from thence to a walnut tree marked in the mill pasture with a heap of stones about it, and so from thence east noreast to a heap of stones at the corner of a swamp, the said tract of land containing in it the 5 acres toward payment of said Henry Collins 30 pounds willed to him by his father.*

Item: one third part of the meadow in Rumney Marsh staked out and bounded on the river west and northeast; bounded on the marsh of his brother Joseph Collins as it is staked out.

Item: Three acres in the fresh meadow, bounded on Crispus Brewer on the southeast; northwardly on the brook; west norwest upon the meadow of Joseph Collins; southwest on the common as it is staked out. Also in the Town Marsh 2 acres toward his thirty pounds willed him and one acre more as his divisional part bounded south upon the river; west upon the marsh of Benjamin Collins as it is staked out. Also to said Henry is alloted 2/3 of the westerly end of the old barn with the orchard adjoining.

JOSEPH COLLINS, *his divisional part alloted to him; fifteen acres of upland; from the ten-acre lots westerly to three rocks and so along to his cousin Joseph Collins's land and southwardly bounded upon Benjamin's line. Also 1/3 part of the marsh in Rumney Marsh bounded on the marsh of his brother Henry southwardly; westerly on the River; northwardly on Benjamin Collins's marsh; eastwardly to a stake. Also in the Town Marsh one acre adjoining northwardly to Benjamin; southward bounded by the River as it is staked out; west on Mr. Cobbett's marsh. Also in the fresh meadow 3 acres... bounded southwardly on Henry Collins's meadow; norward upon the brook; west upon the common as it was staked out.*

BENJAMIN COLLINS, *his divisional part alloted to him: 28 acres bounding his 10 acres by his deed of gift; bounded south by the land of his brother Henry, norward by the ten-acre lots; norwest upon his brother Josephs land to 3 rocks and so along to his kinsman Collins's land. Also all (tailors?) rocks in land of the (coues coast ?) and from thence to*

Henry Collins's land and from thence to a heap of stones in the fence adjoining Henry Collins. Thence westward to a Walnut tree in the mill pasture and all the land of Henry Collins deceased, his pasture; on the norwest side of his brother Henry's bounds and so down to the fresh marsh; except the highway through the said pasture. Also 8 acres of fresh meadow containing (?) acres given to him by his father; southward bounded by the highway, north by the brook, n (?) by Crispus Brewer; westward by the town common. Also allotted to Benjamin in rumney Marsh 1/3 of his father's marsh as it is staked out, bounded upon the river west; south on the marsh of Joseph Collines, east upon the marsh of John Burrill Sr. Also in the town marsh one acre bounded on the River southward; upon the marsh of his brother Henry westward; upon the marsh of his brother Joseph and as it is now staked out. Also the orchard adjoining Benjamin's dwelling house with liberty of carting to the barn through the yard only care to be taken for putting up the fence for the security of the yard.

And we the said Henry Collins Sr, Joseph Collins and Benjamin Collins, sons of Henry Collins deceased do by these present freely, truly and really covenant, indent. bind and oblige ourselves and our heirs for ever to stand to these promises, these divisional tracts and parcels of land and marsh and meadow and whatever else according to herein bounded and stated and never to molest each other in the free enjoyment thereof. Whereof, we set our hands and seals, 27 November 1694.

The witnesses were Jeremiah Shepard, John Floyd and Mary Shepard. Written across the side of the document: "Memorandum: [We] mutually agree that whereas there is about 2 acres of land within the bounds of Benjamin Collins over and above his share and division of true intent and meaning is that said 2 acres being near the saw mill in Lynn shall be common for free use of all parties hereunto subscribing."

Children of Henry and Ann Collins, first 3 born in England, others probably at Lynn:

2. i. HENRY^2, b. 29 Oct 1629; m. MARY TOLMAN.
3. ii. JOHN, b. 14 Jan 1631; m. ABIGAIL JOHNSON.
   iii. MARGERY, b. 6 Nov 1633; d. at Salem, Mass., betw. 3 & 12 Oct 1702 (when her will was written & probated; Essex Probate, 30028). She m. ca 1659, ISAAC WILLIAMS of Salem. Isaac appointed "my brother Henry Collins" an overseer of his will on 9 Nov 1696 (Essex Probate, 30003). Children, in order named in wills of Isaac and Ann, born at Salem, bpt. at 1st Church, Salem (surname Williams): 1. Sarah, b. ca 1653; bpt. 5 June 1664; m. --- Lander. 2. Deborah, b. ca 1655; bpt. 5 June 1664; ;m. (1) 10: 6m: 1675, Joseph Gray (Salem VR); m. (2) 14 June 1690, Dr. James Holgrave (SVR; Backus, 187-88). 3. Elizabeth, b. 23: 6m: 1660; m. at Salem, 1 Apr 1678, Joseph Mansfield (ibid.). 4. Isaac, b. 20 Dec 1662 (ibid.); m. 2 Aug 1685, Mary Endicott (ibid.). 5. Benjamin, b. 18 Mar 1664. 6. Jonathan, bpt. 14: 5m: 1667; d. y. 8. Jonathan, bpt. 6 June 1669. 9. John, bpt. 21 July 1672. 10. Ebenezer, bpt. Dec 1675; m. 26 Dec 1698, Elizabeth Trott (ibid.).
   iv. HANNAH, b. ca 1635; m. 25 Mar 16--, Deacon NATHANIEL INGERSOLL (Salem VR), b. 1632-3; d. at Salem, 27 Jan 1718 (ibid.), s. of Richard & Ann/Agnes (Langley) Ingersoll (Sidney Perley, *History of Salem* [Salem, 1924], I:131). They had a dau. who died before her father (ibid.). Nathaniel's will left all to his wife during her lifetime, then to his adopted son, Benjamin Hutchinson (ibid.; Lillian Drake Avery, *A Genealogy of the Ingersoll Family in America* [New York, 1926]).

	v.	MARY, b. ca 1640; d. at Lynn, 9 Feb 1682 (LVR); m. at Lynn, 22: 11m: 1663, SAMUEL JOHNSON, b. prob. at Lynn, in 1640 (figured from age at death); d. there 1 Nov 1723, in his 83rd year (ibid.), son of Richard and Alice Johnson. Samuel prob. m. a 2nd wife and had a son David, b. "son of Samuel, last of Jan 1688/9" (ibid.). Ann Collins made a bequest of 1690 pounds each to Mary, Richard, Ruth and Samuel Johnson (see will above). Children of Samuel & Mary (Collins) Johnson, b. at Lynn (surname Johnson): 1. Mary, b. 19: 11m: 1664; d. at Lynn 13: 2m: 1665 (ibid.). 2. Samuel, b. 18: 9m: 1666; d. 14: 4m: 1669 (ibid.). 3. Mary, b. 25 May 1669 (named in grandmother's will in 1690). 4. Hannah, b. 15 May 1671; d. bef. 1690. 5. Elizabeth, b. 6: 10m: 1672; d. bef. 1690. 6. Richard, b. 8 Nov 1674 (named Ruth, b. 6 Mar 1678 (named in will); m. (int.) at Lynn, 26 Oct 1699, Parker Kendall (ibid.). 8. Samuel, b. 18 Mar 1678/9.
4.	vi.	JOSEPH, b. ca 1642; m. (1) SARAH SILSBEE; m. (2) MARIAH SMITH.
	vii.	RIALL, b. 1644; d. at Lynn, 14: 3m: 1681, in her 37th year (Bible Record of Charles S. Viall, cited in LVR). The Lynn Vital Records do not say that she was the daughter of Henry, but this was the only Collins family in Lynn at the time, and her birth age fits.
	viii.	ELIZABETH, b. ca 1648; d. at Dorchester, Mass., 7 Oct 1690 (Dorchester VR); m., as his 1st wife, "last 9br; 1666" JOHN TOLMAN (DVR), b. ca 1635; d. at Dorchester, 1 Jan 1724/5, age 82, son of Thomas & Elizabeth (Johnson) Tolman ("Tolman Genealogy," *New England Historical and Genealogical Register*, hereafter *Register*, XIV [1860]: 247). John Tolman m. (2) at Dorchester, 15 June 1692, wid. Mary Paul. No children (ibid.). Children of John & Elizabeth (Collins) Tolman, b. at Dorchester (surname Tolman): 1. Elizabeth, b. 14: 10m: 1667; m. at Dorch. 28 Oct 1692, Moses Heirse (Hewes?). 2. John, b. 8: 2m: 1671; m. (1) at Dorch., Feb 1696/7, Susanna Breck; m. (2) at Dorch., Elizabeth White. 3. Joseph, b. 6: 7m: 1674. 4. Benjamin, b. 6 Dec 1676; went to Scituate (ibid., 248). 5. Henry, b. 13 Mar 1678/9; m. at Dorch., Hannah ---; nine children, b. at Dorch.; fam. rem. to Attleboro, Mass. (ibid.). 6. Ann, b. 2m; 1st d. 1681. 7. Ebenezer, b. 27 Mar 1683. 8. Ruth, b. 1 July 1685; m. at Dorch. 18 Jan 1711/12, Joseph Burt. 9. William, b. 2 Sept 1687 (ibid.).
5.	ix.	BENJAMIN, b. ca 1650; m. (1) PRISCILLA KIRTLAND; m. (2) ELIZABETH (LEACH) PUTNAM.

(To be continued)

WILLIAM IVORY OF LYNN AND HIS DESCENDANTS - continued

By Eleanor Tucker

7. **JOHN[4] IVORY** (Theophilus[3], Thomas[2], William[1]) was born at Charlestown, Mass., 26 July 1705 and died there before 21 June 1737, when his wife remarried (Thomas Bellows Wyman, *The Genealogies and Estates of Charlestown, Massachusetts*, 545). He married at Boston, 4 February 1728/9, MARTHA THWING (ibid.), who was born at Boston, 26 March 1699 (*Reports of the Record Commissioners of Boston*; hereafter, *BRC*, 9:253), and died there, as Martha Newell, 27 October 1784, in her 86th years (gravestone at King's Chapel, cited in Wyman, 699), daughter of John and Martha (Drew) Thwing. Martha (Thwing) Ivory married, second, at Boston, 21 June 1737, Andrew Newell, who died at Charlestown, 11 March 1739/40, age 48 (gravestone, cited in Wyman, 699).

John Ivory was a seaman on the brigantine "Sarah" from Boston to Jamaica and back early in 1727 (ibid., 545). His estate was taxed in 1727, 1729 and 1730, and his taxes were abated in 1730/31 (ibid.).

Child, born at Charlestown:

   i. JOHN[5], b. 19 Dec 1729; d. at Shirley, Mass., 12 Nov 1789, in his 60th year (gravestone at Shirley Centre Cemetery); m. at Charlestown, 22 Aug 1751, SARAH HUSSING, b. 22 July 1733; d. at Shirley, Nov 1789, dau. of Charles and Hannah Hussin (Shirley, Mass. VR). John Ivory was admitted to the church at Charlestown, 5 Aug 1764. He became a resident of Shirley in 1765 when he purchased an estate in the village. He was a cooper and an agriculturist, working at both vocations in their seasons. He was a deacon of the church and for many years the Town Clerk. He proved his scholarship to be above the common level of the time by the way his records were kept and by his penmanship (Seth Chandler, *History of the Town of Shirley from its Early Settlement*). Children of John and Sarah (Hussing) Ivory, first two born at Charlestown, others at Shirley: 1. <u>John</u>, b. 17 May 1756; d. 1 Mar 1818; m. (int.) 14 Mar 1778, Lucy Russell, b. at Littleton, Mass., 6 May 1759, dau. of William and Lucy Russell. John was a Private in the Revolution. 2. <u>Theophilus</u>, b. 7 Nov 1759; d. in the service of his country at New York, 29 Sep 1776. 3. <u>Martha</u>, b. 15 Aug 1766; m. at Shirley, 27 Nov 1788, John Campbell. 4. <u>Thomas</u>, b. 10 Aug 1769; d. 1 Mar 1772 (all dates from Shirley VR).

8. **SILAS[4] IVORY** (Benjamin[3], Thomas[2], William[1]) was born at Lynn, about 1716. He married, first, at Charlestown, 26 September 1734, HANNAH MORGAN, who was baptised at Charlestown, 27 July 1712, the daughter of John and Hannah Morgan (Wyman, 685). Silas Ivory married, second, 14 December 1752, ELIZABETH HUNNEWELL, b. at Charlestown, 21 April 1723, daughter of Charles and Amy Hunnewel (ibid., 527).

Silas was a joiner, or carpenter, by trade. On 12 January 1773, he sold to Ephraim Breed, chairmaker, and Aaron Newhall, cordwainer, a common lot in Lynn Town Common, awarded to widow Mary Ivory, being the 14th lot, 2nd Division and second range, bounded east by the lot of John Ivory and west by John Newhall and his son John. Elizabeth, wife of Silas, relinquished her right of dower. Witnesses were Edmond Quincy and Roddphus Faye (Essex Deeds, 122:273). Silas's estate was taxed at Charlestown, 1732 and 1737 (Wyman, 545).

Children, by first wife, Hannah (Morgan), first three born at Charlestown, the fourth at Boston:

    i.   HANNAH^5, b. 25 May 1735.
    ii.   KATHERINE, b. 19 Dec 1736.
    iii. NATHANIEL, b. Dec 1736.
    iv. WILLIAM, b. 16 Jan 1739.

Children, by second wife, Elizabeth (Hunnewell), b. at Boston (Boston VR):

    v.   BENJAMIN, b. 4 Nov 1753.
    vi. LUCY, b. 24 Apr 1757.
    vii. CHARLES, b. 20 June 1759.

****

IVORY NOTES

Benjamin Ivory, Private in Capt. Bliss's company (*Massachusetts Soldiers and Sailors in the Revolutionary War*, 651).
Benjamin Ivory received wages for April on 29 June 1776 (*New England Historical and Genealogical Register*, 50:198).
Benjamin Ivory received wages for the month of July, dated 14 Aug 1776, NY (ibid., 50:199).
Benjamin Ivory was attached to the briganteen "Angelica" when it was captured. He was committed to Forton Prison, England, 7 July 1778 (ibid., 33:38).
Benjamin Ivory is listed in the 1790 census.

Charles Ivory of Shirley is listed in Capt. Samuel Kelton's company (S&SRW, 651).
Charles Ivory received wages for Apr & June 1776 (*Register*, 50:198-99).
Charles Ivory is listed in the 1790 census.

IVORY ADDITIONS

Additional children of DEBORAH (IVORY) PERRY (dau. of Benjamin^3 Ivory):

    8. <u>Moses</u>, 3d., b. 25 Nov 1755; d. 2 Mar 1819; m. Mary Sanger. He was a cooper and resided in Sherborn. 9. <u>Nathaniel</u>, b. 16 Sept 1757; moved to South Carolina. 10. <u>Deborah</u>, b. 15 June 1759; m. 4 Sept 1783, Deac. Joseph Dows (Dowse). 11. <u>Benjamin</u>, b. 15 Sept 1761; moved to South Carolina.

Additional child of SARAH (IVORY) WITT (dau. of Benjamin^3 Ivory):

    7. <u>Joseph</u>, b. 3 Jan 1757 (Balcomb, *Witt Genealogy*, 5).

(Conclusion)

THE STOCKER FAMILY OF MASSACHUSETTS

By Marcia Wiswall Lindberg, C.G.

The name "Stocker" is not a common one in the records of colonial New England. There was an Edward Stocker who fathered a family in Lyme, Connecticut, but there appears to be no connection with him and the Massachusetts Stockers. The first of the name to appear in Massachusetts was Thomas Stocker, who, in 1640, became a tenant on the farm of John Cogan of Rumney Marsh (*Notebook Kept by Thomas Lechford, Esq.* [Repr. Camden, ME, 1988], 241). Rumney Marsh was then an outlying district of Boston, but later became part of Chelsea, and still later, part of Saugus (which was then a section of Lynn). Families who lived in this section could go to the church of their choice; to Lynn (in Essex County), to Malden (in Middlesex County), or to Boston (in Suffolk County). Previous Stocker researchers have claimed the family moved from Rumney Marsh to Lynn or to Boston, but the records indicate that they stayed in the same location, with land boundaries and church affiliations changing.

There are no birth, marriage or death records for Thomas Stocker, and his name does not appear on any known ship's passenter list. Nor did he leave a will. The births of only two of his probable five or more children appear in the records of Boston and Lynn. This paucity of early records necessitates a reconstruction of the family by using other sources. Taking into account the rarity of the surname, it is probable that the four Stocker males who appear between 1640 and 1655 in Massachusetts are all sons of Thomas and Martha Stocker. Three of these sons left known progeny. One daughter, Elizabeth, was recorded, and there may have been more, but no others have been found.

Thomas Stocker's place of birth is presumed to be England, although no mention of the name is found in available published works such as Thomas Waters' *Genealogical Gleanings in England*. The name "Stocker" is occasionally found as Stalker, Stoker, and once Striker, but Stocker will be used here unless a direct quote gives otherwise. Surnames of families who married into the Stocker family of Massachusetts include Bachelder, Ballard, Berry (3 times), Breed (twice), Burrill (twice), Farrington, Hathorn, Ingalls, Lewis (twice), Mansfield (5 times), Newhall (3 times), Norwood, Osgood, Potter, Rhodes, Richards and Witt - all names associated with Lynn.

1. **THOMAS[1] STOCKER** was born, probably in England, in 1620, according to a deposition taken on 29 March 1675, in which he stated his age as "about 55 years" (*Records and Files of the Quarterly Courts of Essex County, Massachusetts*; hereafter *EQCR*, IX:10). His death date is unknown, but he was probably still living on 28 May 1698 when Thomas Skinner of Malden testified at Court that "Mr. Cogan's farm at Rumney Marsh, within the bounds of Boston, where Capt. Floyd now lives, has been possessed by John Doolittle, Thomas Stocker and John Floyd, by plowing and fencing quite to the sea or the Sandy beach and so along to the Pines River that goes to Lynn...and they hath peacably enjoyed it for above forty-seven years" (Mellin Chamberlain, *History of Chelsea...* [Cambridge, Mass., 1908], I:173). In documents of that period, a man was referred to as "deceased" if he were no longer living. Thomas Stocker married, before 1645, MARTHA ----. Her family name is unknown. A possible clue to her identity is found in the will of James Browne of Boston, dated 9: 3: 1651, which states:

> "It is my will that my wife GRACE BROWNE, have my house and land during her life ... or till my sonne James comes to age of 21 .... In case God take away my sonne ere he come to 21, then **the children of thomas stocker of rumney marsh** shall have 10 pounds out of my sonnes halfe ... the rest to service of Christ in this Church of Boston whereof I am a member...." Signed James Browne, James Penn & William Aspinwall. (Suffolk County Wills [Baltimore, MD: 1984], 110).

In 1652 and 1654, Thomas Stocker was named "surveyor" and in March of 1655, was a member of the committee to run the line between Lynn and Boston and between Charlestown and Boston. He was a

Constable in Boston in 1660/61 and 1661/62, and was again named "Surveyor" in 1669/70 (*7th Report of the Record Commissioners of Boston* [Boston, 1881]; hereafter *BRC*, 1, 5, 52).

In October of 1665, Thomas Stocker brought the body of a dead man to the Constable of Lynn, on a cart "lying in such a way as to cause bruises, which puzzled the inquest jury" (*EQCR*, III:297). On 3: 9: 1673, "Thomas Stocker and his son Ebenezer," appeared as witnesses at a jury trial in Lynn (ibid., V:259). In 1674, Thomas Stocker, Sr. was taxed at Rumney Marsh, 16 shillings; his son Thomas Stocker, Jr. was taxed 3 shillings (*BRC*, I:59).

On 6 December 1673, Samuel Bennett of Rumney Marsh, sold to William Bartholomew, all his farm of 150 acres "now or late in the tenure and occupation of Thomas Stocker." This farm was bounded on the northeast by the Iron Works Farm, southeast by Joseph Jenks, southwest by Elisha and John Bennett, and northwest by the Lynn town line (Suffolk Deeds, VIII:432-433).

On 21 February 1676, "Quartermaster Thomas Stocker" and Robert Burges presented an inventory of the estate of Mr. John Hathorn" (*EQCR*, VI:311). At Lynn, on 19 October 1676, "Quatermaster Thomas Stocker" is listed as owing four or five pounds to John Hawthorne's estate (ibid.). When Captain Thomas Marshall was sued for cutting and carrying off wood from the land of Samuel Appleton in 1682, Thomas Stocker and his son Ebenezer Stocker were then said to live at Captain Marshall's home (ibid., VIII:416-17). Ebenezer was married to Captain Marshall's daughter Sarah (see below).

On 15 January 1679, Thomas served on a jury at an inquest into the death of William, son of Joseph Edmonds. The verdict was "accidental drowning in a hole of water about 4 ft deep near a great rock" (ibid., VIII:61).

Probable children, the last two recorded in Boston Vital Records:

2.   i.   SAMUEL^2, b. about 1645; m. (1) MARY ----; m. (2) MARY WITT; m. (3) DORCAS ----.
3.   ii.   JOSEPH, b. 1647; m. ANN SHEFFIELD.
4.   iii.   EBENEZER, b. 1650; m. SARAH MARSHALL.
      iv.   THOMAS, a twin, "of Church of Linn," b. 6d: 3m: 1655 ("Boston VR" in *BRC*, 9:53). Thomas Stocker, Jr. was taxed three shillings at Rumney Marsh in 1674. (see above). No further information found.
      v.   ELIZABETH, twin, b. 6d: 3m: 1655 (ibid.). Nothing further known. Twins occur in the 4th and 5th generations of the Stocker family.

(Note: James Savage, in his *Genealogical Dictionary of the First Settlers of New England* [IV:198] gives a Daniel Stocker marrying in 1672 Margery Salmon, but this is certainly an error. Margery Salmon, on 22 June 1672, complained that her husband, Daniel Salmon, spent too much money at John Hathorne's brewhouse in Lynn [*EQCR*, V:63]).

2. **SAMUEL^2 STOCKER** (Thomas^1) was born, probably at Rumney Marsh, about 1645, and died after 24 May 1682/3 when he was paid 15 shillings for work at the County Bridge in Lynn (*EQCR*, IX:40). He appears to have married three times; first to MARY (----), whose last name is unknown, and by whom he had one recorded child. His second marriage was recorded in both Boston and Lynn VR on 6 June 1666, to MARY WITT. Mary was born MARY DIVAN, daughter of John and Hester (or Ester) Divan (ibid., 412). She had married, first, at Lynn, 23 March 1663, Jonathan Witt, who died before 11 January of 1665, when an inventory was taken of his estate (*The Probate Records of Essex County* [Salem, Mass., 1917], II:8). A child, Hester (or Ester) Witt, born at Lynn, 5 February 1665 (LVR), married, 26 December 1683, Ebeniezur Hathorn (ibid.). In 1674, Hester chose [her step-father] Samuel Stocker as her guardian (*EQCR*, V:428). The will of John Divan, Sr., dated 20 August 1684, bequeathed to "my four grandchildren, as namely; Samuel Stoker and Martha Stoker, both children to my son in lawe Samuel Stoker; to Elizabeth Divan ... one cow a piece as they arrive at one and twenty years of age ... and Hester Hathorne, twenty shillings

after my wife's decease" (ibid., IX:411, 412). Samuel Stocker married, third, probably at Boston, before 1680, DORCAS (----). Her surname has not been found.

On 27 February 1671, Samuel Stocker was witness to a transfer of 10 acres of land in Lynn from Samuel and Sarah Bennett of Rumney Marsh to Benjamin Muzzey and Huson Leverett of Boston (ibid., VIII:196).

Samuel Stocker "of Medford" is listed as wounded in King Phillips War in 1675/76. He was in Capt. Nathaniel Davenport's regiment (George M. Bodge, *Soldiers in King Philip's War* [Baltimore, 1976], 171. It is assumed that this is the Samuel Stocker given here as no other by that name has been found in the records. In the list of those who took the Oath of Fidelity and were sworn [in] by Captain Thomas Marshall of Lynn, on 26 February 1677, Samuel Stocker is listed in Thomas Bancroft's squadron, and his brother Ebenezer is listed in Edward Baker's and William Merriam's squadron (*EQCR*, VI:399-400).

Samuel was, at least part-time, a mariner by occupation. On 14 March 1677/78, a letter of Attorney was given by Samuel Stocker of Boston, mariner, to John Keene of Boston, Innholder, whereas John Lee, for five shillings, withdrew his action against Samuel Stocker (ibid., VII:100).

On 19 September 1681, Samuel Stocker, of Boston, mariner, mortgaged, for 100 pounds, to John Nelson of Boston, Merchant, "all my messuage [dwelling house] and tenement lying ... at the northerly end of Boston, butted southwest by the street, southeast by land of Matthew Armstrong, deceased, northwest by Ephraim Hunt and northeast by Joseph Shaw. One year later, on 11 September 1682, Samuel redeemed the mortgage and Mr. John Nelson acknowledged that he was fully paid and released the estate over to Samuel (Suffolk Deeds, XII:110). Seven days later, on 18 September 1682, Samuel, with his wife Dorcas, once again mortaged his property, including "the houses, outhouses, buildings, shops, fences, yards and gardens," for 54 pounds, to William Hewes (ibid., 303). There is no record of this mortgage being redeemed, and shortly thereafter, Samuel appears to be living at Capt. Marshall's house near the Iron Works with his brother Ebenezer and father Thomas.

On 24 March 1682/83, Samuel Stocker was paid 15 shillings for work at the County Bridge. Ebenezer was paid four pounds (*EQCR*, IX:40). Also on 28: 9: 1682, Samuel was paid six shillings for two days work (ibid., VIII:264). Samuel appears on the Tax Lists for Rumney Marsh in 1681, 1687 and 1688 (*BRC*, I:69, etc.).

On 28 June 1683, "Naomi Flanders, age 24, testified that one night when she dwelt with her master Samuel Stocker, Priscilla Wilson gave birth to a child on a bed in his house." Hester Witt, age 18, also testified that "when she lived at the Old Iron works, with her father Stocker, Priscilla Wilson had a child ... and the child was the image of Mr. Samuel Appleton" (*EQCR*, IX:65).

No records have been found for Samuel Stocker and his family after December 1683, when daughter Sarah's birth was recorded at Boston.

Child by Mary (----):

i. MARY^3, b. 25 Apr 1666 (Boston VR). She is prob. the Mary Stocker who m. 22 Jan 1685, SAMUEL CHADWICK (Woburn, Reading & Boston VRs). Children, rec. in Woburn VR (surname Chadwick): 1. <u>Mary</u>, b. 2 Nov 1685; m. at Reading, 27 Dec 1704, Joel Jenkins. 2. <u>Martha</u>, b. 1 Oct 1687; d. at Woburn, 15 Mar 1688. 3. <u>Martha</u>, b. 5 June 1689; m. at Reading, in Mar 1716, Robert Trevitt of Charlestown (Readng VR; Lilley Eaton, *Genealogical History of the Town of Reading* [Boston, 187], 58).

Children by Mary (Divan) Witt:

   ii. SAMUEL, b. about 1668; named in grandfather John Divan, Sr.'s will in 1684. No further record found.
   iii. MARTHA, b. 12 Sept 1670 (Boston VR); named in grandfather Divan's will in 1684. She was perhaps the Martha Stocker whose intentions of marriage to SAMUEL BREDEAN were published at Lynn, 10 Mar 1695/6 (LVR); or perhaps the Martha Stocker who m. 4 Jan 1699, ISAAC ADAMS (Boston VR). Nothing further has been found.

Children by Dorcas (----), recorded in Boston VR:

   iv. JANE, b. 1 July 1680.
   v. ELIZABETH, b. 9 May 1682.
   vi. SARAH, b. 8 Dec 1683. Boston VR give Sarah's parents as Samuel and Elizabeth Stocker, but this appears to be an error. Samuel's wife in 1683 was Dorcas. Sarah is perhaps the Sarah Stocker whose marriage is recorded in Boston VR on 1 Sept 1704 to CHARLES RENOUF.

****

3. **JOSEPH^2 STOCKER** (Thomas^1) was born, probably at Rumney Marsh, in 1647, according to his deposition in September of 1677, saying he was "age about 30 years" (*EQCR*, VI:329). He died after 1695, when he was listed as an inhabitant of Boston (*BRC*, I:158). Joseph married, about 1669, ANN SHEFFIELD, who was born at Braintree, Mass., 1 April 1649, daughter of Edmund and Mary (Woodie) Sheffield (*New England Historical and Genealogical Register*; hereafter, *Register*, LXXVII [1923]:193). This marriage does not appear in the Vital Records, but is stongly indicated by the fact that a son is given the unusual name of Sheffield, and the Ann Sheffield given here is the right age.

Joseph Stocker was a carpenter and seaman, as was his brother Samuel. On 17: 5: 1665, he is mentioned in a court case concerning timber carried to Captain Marshall's house (*EQCR*, III:285), and on 22 September 1677, he deposed in court that "he was a carpenter aboard the 'John and Ann' and at sea between Madeira and Lisbon, when Richard Knott left the ship" (ibid., VI:329). Joseph appears on the tax lists of Rumney Marsh in 1681, 1685, 1687 and 1688 (*BRC*, I:74, 81, 123, 143). He is listed as an inhabitant of Boston in 1695 (ibid., 158).

Children, recorded in *BRC*, Vols. 9 & 24:

   i. MARY^3, b. 10 Apr 1671; m. at Boston, 12 May 1692, BENJAMIN HALLOWELL. Children, b. at Boston (VR) (surname Hallaway/Hollowell): 1. <u>Mary</u>, b. 17 Mar 1692. 2. <u>Ann</u>, b. 29 Jan 1694. 3. <u>Benjamin</u>, b. 20 Jan 1698. 4. <u>William</u>, b. 11 Nov 1700. 5. <u>Joseph</u>, b. 22 Nov 1702. 6. <u>Sarah</u>, b. 1 Sept 1705. 7. <u>Samuel</u>, b. 25 Nov 1707.
   ii. ANN, b. 26 July 1677; perhaps m. at Boston 23 Nov 1704, WILLIAM BRIGGS (Boston VR).
   iii. JOSEPH, b. 18 Sept 1681; m. at Marlboro, Mass., 1713, (----) HALL (Marlboro VR). Possible children: 1. <u>Joseph</u>, m. at Boston, 22 Dec 1732, Mary Hunt (or Mercy Holland) (Boston VR). 2. <u>Ann</u>, m. (1) 25 Nov 1742, Anthony Brown; m. (2), 21 Jan 1746, William Sanders (Boston VR).
   iv. SHEFFIELD, b. 12 Jan 1685.
   v. HANNAH, b. 27 Sept 1687.

4. **EBENEZER² STOCKER** (Thomas¹) was born, probably at Rumney Marsh, in 1649, according to his deposition on 27 Apr 1685, giving his age as 35 years (*EQCR*, IX:465), and died at Lynn, 2 November 1704 (Lynn VR). He married at Lynn, 15 July 1674, SARAH MARSHALL (Ibid.), who was born at Reading, Mass., 14 February 1654, and died after 1705. She was the daughter of Captain Thomas and Rebecca Marshall of Reading and Lynn (Lynn VR; Louis Effingham DeForest, *Our Colonial and Continental Ancestors*, 175).

On 3: 9: 1673, Ebenezer Stocker and his father, Thomas Stocker, appeared as witnesses at a jury trial in Lynn (*EQCR*, V:259). He took the Oath of Fidelity on 26 February 1677 (ibid., VI:400), and was listed as a Freeman on 18 April 1691 (Lucius R. Paige, *List of Freemen of Massachusetts, 1630-1691* [Baltimore, 1978], 40).

On 31 August 1680, Ebenezer Stocker, of Lynn, husbandman, purchased from John Doolittle of Boston, yeoman, with consent of his wife, Sarah, for 240 pounds, a parcel of land that Doolittle had purchased from Samuel Bennett of Rumney Marsh, formerly of Lynn, containing the dwelling house and barn "where said Stocker now lives," bounded north on the Country Highway and Rumney Marsh, west on Capt. Marshall, John Divan and John Edmunds, and east on the Town Commons, called "Noemans's Swamp," also 9 acres of salt marsh in the 1st Division of Rumney Marsh, bounded east on John Witt, west on Joseph Mansfield, north on John Edmunds, and south on Allen Breed and William Merriam. Witnesses were John Fuller and John Lewis (*Essex Deeds*, 5:90). Ebenezer was to pay 20 pounds yearly for eleven years. But, on 3 March 1700, John Floyd of Rumney Marsh, executor of the Last Will and Testament of John Doolittle, received 240 pounds from Ebenezer Stocker, and signed a quitclaim to the above deed (ibid., 14:101). The will of Abraham Doolittle of Wallingford (New Haven), Connecticut, witnessed by John Richards and Ebenezer Stocker on 22 September 1681, left to his son-in-law, John Floyd of Malden, "that 200 pounds that Ebenezer Stocker is to pay me..." (Suffolk Probate, 6:358).

On 24 May 1682/3, Ebenezer Stocker was paid 4 pounds for "work at the County Bridge." His brother, Samuel, received 15 shillings (*EQCR*, IX:40). When Henry Collins of Lynn presented an account of the charges and disbursements about repairing the bridge at Lynn in August of 1682, Ebenezer Stocker was credited with 6 oxen for 6 days; 2 oxen for 2 days; 2 "hands" for 4 days; 1 "hand" for 4 days; and for 18 trees out of his own land, for a total of 2 pounds, 34 shillings (ibid., VIII:365). On 16 May 1692, Ebenezer requested the Selectmen of Lynn to resolve a difference between him and Clerk Ballard concerning their lot line (*Records of ye Towne Meetings of Lyn*, I:12).

Ebenezer served the town of Lynn in many capacities. From 1692 to 1704, he was chosen Constable; served on the Superior Court; was chosen to collect for the Minister's pay, and "to see that no family takes on persons belonging to another town." He also was one of five to see that no one cut any green trees on the common, and to preserve "wood, shells and lime" (ibid., I:12, 25, 45, 67, 68; II:17, 24). On 30 May 1699, he was voted "four poles of land where his new house now stands" for 20 shillings (ibid., I:62). In 1697, 1698, 1700 and 1701, he was one of four men chosen "to collect the heads of 12 blackbirds to be killed by every household in town." A bounty of 8 pence per dozen was offered in 1701 (ibid., I:73).

Ebenezer Stocker died intestate, in 1704, at the age of 52 years. Bonds were posted by Sarah Stocker, "Relict," and Thomas Stocker, Jr., "Esquire," and Samuel Rogers. The court appointed John Burrill, Joseph Halsey and Thomas Baker as a Committee "to appraise the estate and to apportion it amongst Ebenezer's children or heirs without spoiling or prejudicing of the whole" (Essex Probate, 26609). The inventory included a dwelling house and barn, a parcel of land adjoining the house, nine acres of Salt Marsh, one piece of upland, "the house that Thomas now lives in, i.e., so much of it as his father did own," and one negro boy. The total estate was valued at 328:1:06 pounds, and debts against the estate totaled 37:14:07 pounds (ibid.).

Sarah Stocker received her widow's thirds, and Thomas Stocker, Jr., eldest son, received a double portion of the remaining two-thirds of the estate. Acknowledging receipt of their shares in their father's estate, were:

John Hathorn of Lynn, brewer, and Rebecka his wife, 21 October 1712
    Witnesses: William Merriam and John Lewis
Samuel Stocker of Lynn, husbandman, 4 March 1714
    Witnesses: Jonathan Mansfield and Grover Pratt
Martha Stocker, 4 March 1714
    Witnesses: Samuel Stocker and Jonathan Mansfield
John Ballord of Boston, shipwright, and Sarah his wife, 15 March 1714
    Witnesses: John Stocker and Rebeckah Hathorn
John Stocker of Boston, 12 December 1717
    Witnesses: Mary Lewis and Sarah Mors

Children, all dates recorded in Lynn Vital Records, unless stated:

5.   i.   THOMAS^3, b. 24 Apr 1675; m. SARAH BERRY.

    ii.   EBENEZER, b. 31 July 1677; d. at Lynn, 29 Dec 1702.

    iii.   SARAH, b. 11 Dec 1679; d. at Lynn, 17 Dec 1679.

    iv.   SARAH, b. 27 Feb 1680; d. at Lynn, 20 Oct 1744; m. (int.) at Lynn, 30 Oct 1703, JOHN^3 BALLORD, JR.; b. at Lynn, abt. May 1682; d. there, 23 Oct 1765, son of John^2 (William^1) and Rebecca Ballord (Lynn VR:Charles Frederic Farlow, *Ballard Genealogy* [Boston, 1911], 23). Children (surname Ballord): 1. Sarah, b. 26 Oct 1704; m. (int.) 30 Nov 1729, Alexander Douglas (or Duggles). 2. Rebecca, m. 27 Jan 1729/30, Thomas Berry. 3. John, res. at Danvers; estate adm. by Joseph Ballord, 27 Aug 1801. 4. William, b. 1719; d. at Lynn, 25 Aug 1794 "age 75 years;" m. at Lynn, 24 June 1751, Anna Sprague of Billerica. 5. Ebenezer, b. 28 Oct 1716; m. at Boston, 21 Dec 1738, Mary Hunting. 6. Martha, m. (as Martha Bullard) at Salem, Mass., 21 Nov 1752, John Work. 7. Jane, m. (1) 15 Dec 1740, Joseph Hunting; m. (2) (int.) 15 Apr 1756, Deacon John Lewis. 8. Mary, m. 11 Dec 1754, Ephraim Rhodes (ibid., 23-24).

6.   v.   SAMUEL, b. 29 Nov 1684; m. HANNAH LEWIS.

    vi.   REBEKAH, b. 29 July 1687; m. (int.) at Lynn, 10 Nov 1711, JOHN HATHORN, b. at Lynn, 1 May 1688, son of Ebinezur and Ester (Witt) Hathorn. On 21 Oct 1712, Rebekah & John Hathorn agreed with "brother Thomas's division of her father Ebenezer Stocker's estate (Essex Probate, 26609).

    vii.   MARTHA, b. 13 Jan 1689; d. aft. 1720; m. at Lynn, 4 Mar 1713/14, JONATHAN MANSFIELD, b. at Lynn, 26 Feb 1690/91; d. there, 1 Mar 1728, son of Joseph and Elizabeth (Williams) Mansfield) (Lynn VR; Geneva A. Daland and James S. Mansfield, *Mansfield Genealogy* [Hampton, NH, 1980], 14, 18). Children, b. at Lynn (surname Mansfield): 1. Joseph, b. 22 Jan 1714/15; m. at Lynn, 14 Jan 1738/9, Sarah Stocker (his 1st cousin), b. 6 Mar 1716/7, dau of Thomas & Sarah (Berry) Stocker. 2. Jonathan, b. 29 Apr 1717; d. at Salem, 9 Mar 1791; m. (1) at Lynn, 5 June 1737/8, Dorcas Ramsdell; m. (2) at Lynn, 19 Feb 1756, Elizabeth Burchstead, b. 1730; d. 20 June 1785. 3. Martha, b. 9 July 1719; m. at Lynn, 11 May 1738, Thomas Brown. 4. John, b. 19 Feb 1721/2; d. 20 Apr 1809; m. 14 Oct 1747, Sarah Cheever, b. 1730; d. 15 Mar 1780. 5. Ebenezer, b. 14 Mar 1724/5; m. 15 Oct 1747, Mary Norwood. 6. Matthew, b. 22 Nov 1726; d. 29 Oct 1800; m. 14 June 1750, Hannah Proctor. 7. Robert, b. 4 July 1729; d. Feb 1795; m. 19 Aug 1751, Mary Newhall, dau. of Daniel & Mary (Breed) Newhall (ibid., 18-19); Lynn VR).

7.   viii.   JOHN, b. 13 Nov 1693; m. ABIGAIL LEWIS.

(to be continued)

Miscellaneous Notes

THE LYNN ALBUM: A PICTORIAL HISTORY, by Elizabeth Hope Cushing, is a new publication of the Lynn Historical Society. This book, sponsored by The Century North Shore Bank and the Lynn Daily Evening Item, consisting of approximately 200 pages and more than 300 photographs of Lynn's history, will be published in November of 1990. The photographs and artifacts chronicle Lynn places, events and people from 1840 to the beginning of the first World War, sharing with the reader the extraordinary collection of the Society and the rich history of the people of Lynn. To reserve your copy, send a check to the Lynn Historical Society, 125 Green St., Lynn, MA 01902. Pre-publication Cost: $29.95 plus $1.50 sales tax. Post-publication prices will be $32.95 plus $1.65 sales tax. For mailing, include address and $2.50 postage and handling for each copy.

THE SANBORN FAMILY ASSOCIATION REUNION will be held Sunday, August 26, 1990, from 9:00 a.m. to 4:30 p.m., at Owl's Head Development, Mansonville, Quebec, Canada (close to the Quebec/Vermont border). Contact: Arthur H. Sanborn, Pres., 312 Chester Rd., Candia, NH 03034. Tel: (603) 483-2227.

NEW ACQUISITIONS AT THE NEW ENGLAND ARCHIVES (at Waltham). (from the New England Branch National Archives Newsletters):
- Rolls 1 to 80 of microfilm publication M-265, Index to Passenger Lists of Vessels Arriving in Boston 1848-1891, arranged alphabetically by name. Rolls 1 to 80 cover A to Far.
- T-843 - Boston Passenger Arrival rolls numbers 300 to 332, covering the dates June 1, 1925 through March 11, 1928.
- NARA Microfilm Publication "Petitions and Records of Naturalization of the U.S. District and Circuit Courts of the District of Massachusetts, 1906-1929" (330 rolls). These rolls are in the Reference Room cabinets. Researchers wanting copies will make their own from microfilm at 80 cents per page. The large books will no longer be handled and copied.

THE FIRST UNITED STATES PASSPORT was issued 8 July 1796, to Francis Maria Barrere, "a citizen of the United States having occasion to pass into foreign countries about his lawful affairs." It was signed by Thomas Pickering, Secretary of State." (from "Ask the Globe," quoted in the National Archives Newsletter). Passports are another source of genealogical information.

THIS IS THE YEAR OF THE 1990 CENSUS. The following information on censuses was given in the Old Farmer's Almanac:
- In 1980 there were 26 Eskimos living in Nebraska.
- In 1980 the average person received 266 letters, 45 periodicals, 134 circulars, and three parcels through the mail.
- In 1870, 473 Americans recorded their occupation as "mule packer."
- During World War II the census bureau predicted that the U.S. population would stop growing by 1980, peaking at 153 million.
- In 1989 the Census Bureau predicted that the U.S. population would stop growing by 2038, peaking at 302 million.

CENSUS INDEX BOOKS FOR NEW ENGLAND at the New England Branch of the National Archives

Maine	1790 through 1850
New Hampshire	1800 through 1860
Vermont	1800 through 1850
Massachusetts	1790 through 1850
Rhode Island	1800 through 1870
Connecticut	1790 through 1860

(The New England Archives also has many census indexes for every state in the U.S.)

The Ahnentafel

The Ahnentafel is an Ancestor Table, or list. It follows the numbering system of standard Ancestor Charts; i.e.: yourself is number 1; your father and mother are numbers two and three. A father's number is always double that of the child; 13 is a child of 26 (his father) and 27 (his mother). Ahnentafels preserve in print what is known of your ancestors. They also serve as an exchange column for those working on the same surnames or lines. TEG will accept current Ahnentafels and also those of earlier ancestors. If submitting an Ahnentafel for a great grandfather, etc., the numbering must begin with that ancestor as number one. In other words, a submitter cannot use a computer printout starting with a great grandfather as number eight, because the doubling numbers mentioned above will not correspond. Therefore, the great grandfather's Ahnentafel must be renumbered for submission for this column in TEG. As an example, see the last two Ahnentafels printed below.

****

Ahnentafel of Clair Everet Wyman, La Coquina #102E, 2820 No. Beach Rd, Englewood, FL 34223

I	1	Clair Everet Wyman	1916-	Manchester, NH
II	2	Fred Darling Wyman	1865-1938	Clinton, ME; Keene, NH
	3	Delia Hersey Woodbury	1871-1942	Lincoln, ME; Nashua, NH
III	4	Seth Fish Wyman	1829-1894	Benton-Mattawamkeag, ME
	5	Exsah Augusta Thompson	1838-1920	Waldo, ME; Manchester, NH
	6	Tyler Chandler Woodbury	1838-1890	Lincoln, ME
	7	Anna Maria Estes	1841-1900	China, Lincoln, ME
IV	8	Zebedee Wyman	1794-1879	Vassalboro, Clinton, ME
	9	Martha Osborn	1795-1886	Winslow, Canaan, ME
	10	James Clements Thompson	1808-1838	Montville, Waldo, ME
	11	Esther C Farnham	1808-1875	Jefferson, Augusta, ME
	12	Tyler Marsh Woodbury	1803-1889	Charlton, MA; Anoka, MN
	13	Sophronia Tolman	1808-1860	Augusta, Lincoln, ME
	14	John Estes	1811-1855	China, Lincoln, ME
	15	Elizabeth Kennedy	c1813-1841	Malta?, Chilna, ME
V	16	Francis Wyman	1750-1834	Lunenburg, MA; Vassalboro, ME
	17	(2) Mary Fall (Cross)	1760-1819	Walpole, Vassalboro, ME
	18	Ephraim Osborn	c1750-1814+	CT/LI?, Winslow, ME
	19	(3) Lydia Wyman	c1770-1864	Bowdoinham?, Shawmut, ME
	20	Joshua Thompson	1785-1870	So Bristol, Walso, ME
	21	Deborah Clements	1785-1835	Sanford, Waldo, ME
	22	Daniel Farnham	1751-1837	Wolwich, Jefferson, ME
	23	(2) Mary McCurdy	1769-1837?	Bristol, Jefferson, ME
	24	Aaron Woodbury	1771-1840	Sutton, MA; Groton, NY
	25	Rebecca King	1774-1808	Sutton, MA; Bangor, ME
	26	Jeremiah Tolman	1779-1854	Augusta, Lincoln, ME
	27	Martha Babcock	1789-1880	Augusta, Lincoln, ME
	28	Caleb Estes	1778-1821	Durham, China, ME
	29	Charlotte Day	1780-1821	Durham, China, ME
	30	Bolton? Kennedy	c1785-c1814	Jefferson? Windsor? ME
VI	32	Ezekiel Wyman	1712-1784+	Woburn, Lunenburg, MA
	33	Abigail Wyman	1713-1784+	Woburn, Lunenburg, MA
	34	Zebedee Fall	1724-?	Kittery, Walpole? ME

38	William Wyman	1731-1783	Falmouth, Winslow, ME
39	Love (Chick?)	c1735-c1819	Falmouth? Winslow, ME
40	Joshua Thompson	1758-1843	Bristol, ME
41	Martha Coombs	1761-1843	New Meadows, Bristol, ME
42	Jeremiah Clements	1758-1841	Dover, NH; Knox, ME
43	Experience Yeaton	1764-1828	Berwick, Knox, ME
44	Joshua Farnham	1728-1803	York, Woolwich, ME
45	Mary Grow	1732-1813?	York, Woolwich, ME
46	John McCurdy	1736-1807?	Bristol, Windsor, ME
47	Anna Hilton	1741-1786?	Manchester, MA; Windsor, ME
48	John Woodbury	1749-1831	Sutton, MA
49	Mary Chase	1748-1799	Sutton, MA
50	William King	1734-1825	Sutton, MA
51	Silence Dwight	1736-1798	Sutton, MA
52	Samuel Tolman	1740-1832+	Dorchester, MA; Augusta, ME
53	Martha Babcock	1746-1823	Boston, MA; Augusta, ME
54	Henry Babcock	1750-1824	Roxbury, MA; Augusta, ME
55	Sarah Fisk	1761-1803	Providence, RI; Augusta, ME
56	Caleb Estes	1747-1822	Hanover, MA; Durham, ME
57	Lydia Bishop	1749-1815	Pembroke? MA; Durham, ME
58	Josiah Day	c1742-1837	Gloucester, MA; Durham, ME
59	Wealthy Blethen	c1750-1849?	Georgetown, Durham, ME
60	Robert Kennedy	c1740-c1812	Boothbay? Augusta, ME
61	Elizabeth (Bolton)?	c1743-1815+	Bridgewater, MA? Augusta, ME

Ahnentafel of Charles S. Brack Jr., PO Box 2473, Hendersonville, Tennesee 37077

I	1	Charles S. Brack Jr	1933-	Hartford, CT
II	2	Charles S. Brack	1910-1959	Somerville, MA; Miami, FL
	3	Esther J. Tompkins	1912-	Cambridge, MA; Miami, FL
III	4	Samuel C. Brack	1890-1951	Roxbury, MA; Miami, FL
	5	Margaret Cargill	1891-1962	Boston, MA
	6	Henry Tompkins	1891-1965	Cambridge, MA
	7	Grace G. Blevins	1893-1982	Boston, MA; Miami, FL
IV	8	Charles S. Brack	1871-1916	Altenbamberg, Germany; Somerville, MA
	9	Emma Bohlman	1873-1946	Bavaria, Somerville, MA
	10	William J. Cargill	1863-1897	Boston, MA
	11	Catherine H. Sullivan	1864-1933	Charlestown, MA
	12	Henry Tompkins	1866-1944	Ringabella (Cork) Ireland; Cambridge, MA
	13	Esther Gray	1869-1929	Ballykeenan (Carlow) Ireland; Cambridge, MA
	14	John F. Blevins	1861-1934	Cambridge, MA
	15	Ellen Fitzgerald	1856-1911	Boston, MA
VI	16	Frederick Brack		Germany
	17	Elisabeth Graves		Germany
	18	John von Poehlman		Germany
	19	Margaretha Oertile	1852-1939	Bavaria, Hartford, CT
	20	Daniel W. Cargill	1839-1883	Boston, MA
	21	Catherine Green	-----1923	County Cork, Ireland; Boston, MA
	22	Timothy P. Sullivan		County Cork, Ireland; Charlestown, MA
	23	Mary E. McCarthy		County Cork, Ireland; Charlestown, MA
	24	Thomas Tompkins		County Cork, Ireland
	24	Margaret Scanlon	-----1911	County Cork, Ireland; Cambridge, MA

	26	Martin Gray		County Carlow, Ireland
	27	Susan Vynard		County Carlow, Ireland
	28	John Blevins	1829-1871	County Armagh, Ireland; Cambridge, MA
	29	Mary Halpin	1832-1913	Ireland; Cambridge, MA
	30	William Fitzgerald		Ireland; Boston, MA
	31	Margaret Quinlan		Ireland; Boston, MA
VI	38	Johan Oertle		Germany
	40	Daniel Dole Cargill	1818-1839	Newcastle, ME; Boston, MA
	41	Elizabeth D. Ripley		Jefferson, ME; Boston, MA
	42	Matthew Green	-----1853	County Cork, Ireland; Boston, MA
	50	John Scanlon		Ireland
	56	William Blevins		County Armagh, Ireland
	57	Mary Ann McElroy	-----1873	County Armagh; Boston, MA
	58	Bartlett Halpin		Ireland
	59	Margaret Sellery		Ireland
	60	Edmund Fitzgerald		Ireland

Ahnentafel of Haffield Gould, Ancestor of Paul A. Hillman, Lynnfield, MA 01940

I	1	Haffield Gould	1779-1856	Milbury, Hardwick, MA
II	2	Capt. Jonathan Gould	1749-1781	Sutton, MA; killed at war.
	3	Hannah Singletary	1753	Sutton, MA
III	4	Thomas Gould	1720-1769	Danvers, Sutton, MA
	5	Hannah Masters	1717-	Manchester, Sutton, MA
	6	Amos Singletary	1721-1806	Sutton, MA
	7	Mary Curtis	1726-1799	Topsfield, Sutton, MA
IV	8	Thomas Gould	1694-1732	Salem Village (Danvers) MA
	9	Margaret ----		
	10	Nathan Masters	1699-	Salem, MA
	11	Hannah Woodbury	1694-1771	Manchester, MA
	12	John Singletary	1675-1826	Haverhill, Sutton, MA
	13	Mary Greele	1678-1733/5	Salisbury, Sutton, MA
	14	Samuel Curtis	1698-	Boxford, Sutton, MA
	15	Hannah Dodge	1692-1782	Beverly, Sutton, MA
V	16	Thomas Gould	1667-	Salem Village, MA
	17	Abigail Needham	1671-1731	Salem Village, MA
	20	Abraham Masters		
	219	Ablgall Ormes	1660-	Salem, MA
	22	Joseph Woodbury	1657-1714	Salem, Manchester, MA
	23	Elizabeth West	1663-	Beverly, MA
	24	Nathaniel Singletary	1644-1689	Salisbury, Haverhill, MA
	25	Sarah Belknap	1655-	Haverhill, MA
	26	Andrew Greele	1646-	Salisbury, MA
	27	Sarah Brown	1654-1727	Salisbury, MA
	28	John Curtis	1649-1718	Boxford, MA
	29	Mary Look	1654-1745	Lynn, Topsfield, MA
	30	Edward Dodge	1645/51-1727	Beverly, MA
	31	Mary Haskell	1660-1737	Gloucester, Beverly, MA
	32	Thomas Gould	1639-1689	England; Salem Village, MA
	33	Elizabeth ----		
	34	Anthony Needham	1628/31	England; Peabody, MA
	35	Ann Potter		England; Salem, MA
	40	John Masters	-----1639	England; Cambridge, MA
	417	Jane ----	-----1639	England; Cambridge, MA

	42	John Ormes	-----1693	England; Salem, MA
	43	Mary ----		
	44	Nicholas Woodbury	1618-1686	England; Beverly, MA
	45	Anne Palgrave	1626-1791	England; Beverly, MA
	46	Thomas West	-----1678	England; Beverly, MA
	47	Phebe Waters	-----1674	Salem, MA
	48	Richard Singletary	1595-1662	England; Haverhill, MA
	49	Susanna Cook	1616-1682	England; Haverhill, MA
	50	Samuel Belknap	1627-c1701	England; Haverhill, MA
	51	Sarah Jones	c1631-1689	England; Haverhill, MA
	52	Andrew Greele	1697	England; Salisbury, MA
	53	Mary Moyse	1703	England; Salisbury, MA
	54	Henry Brown	1615-1701	England; Salisbury, MA
	55	Abigail ----	-----1702	Salisbury, MA
	56	Zaccheus Curtis	-----1682	England; Topsfield, MA
	57	Mary Cortwithen		
	58	Thomas Look		England; Lynn, MA
	60	Richard Dodge	1602-1671	England; Salem, Beverly, MA
	61	Edith ---	c1603-1678	England; Beverly, MA

Ahnentafel of Dana Mills Walcott's paternal ancestry, mostly Essex Co. He was the great-grandfather of Helen (Schatvet) Ullman, 713 Main St., Acton, MA 01720. (* means not verified)

I	1	Dana Mills Walcott	1840-1919	Natick, MA; Rutherford, NJ
II	2	Jonathan P. Walcott	1817-1850	Danvers, Natick, MA
III	4	John Walcott	1788-1862	Danvers, Natick, MA
	5	Rebecca Newhall	1789-1866	Pepperell, Natick, MA
IV	8	Jonathan Walcott	1762-1844	Danvers, MA
	9	Lydia Gale	1757-1830	Salem, Danvers, MA
	10	Oliver Newhall	1749-1839	Lynn, Pepperell, MA
	11	Abigail Phillips	1732-1811	Pepperell, MA
V	16	John Walcott	1732-1811	Salem, Danvers, MA
	17	Sarah Gardner	1740-1813	Salem, Danvers, MA
	18	Samuel Gale*	1726-	Salem, MA
	19	Mary Hooper*	1724-1814	Salem, MA
	20	Jeremiah Newhall	1708-1780	Lynn, MA
	21	Sarah Bates	1709-1794	Lynn, Lynnfield, MA
	22	Isaac Phillips	1717-1760	Groton, Pepperell, MA
	23	Abigail Nutting	1718-175?	Groton, Pepperell, MA
VI	32	Jonathan Walcott	1700-1737?	Salem, MA
	33	Elizabeth Smith	1704?	Salem, MA
	34	Thomas Gardner	1705-1753	Salem, MA
	35	Eunice Waters	1706-	Salem, MA
	36	William Gale*	1699-	Salem, MA
	37	Elizabeth Grant*	1702-	Salem, MA
	38	Charles Hooper*	1689-1759	Salem, MA
	39	Hannah Neal*		Salem, MA?
	40	Thomas Newhall	1680-1738	Lynn, MA
	41	Mary Newhall	1689- Lynn, MA	
	42	John Bates	1686-1708	Lynn, MA
	43	Annice Gowing	1683-1716	Lynn, MA
	44	Seth Phillips	-----1757	----, Groton, MA
	45	Lydia ---		
	46	Ebenezer Nutting	1686-1769	Groton, MA

	47	Ruth Shattuck	1694-176-	Watertown, Groton, MA
VII	64	John Walcott	1666-1738	
	65	Mary ----		
	66	Abraham Smith*		
	67	Mary Perkins*		
	68	Abel Garner	1673-1739	Salem, Peabody, MA
	69	Sarah Porter	1676-1728	Peabody, MA
	70	John Waters*	1665-1742	Salem, MA
	71	Mary ----	1674?	
	72	Abraham Gale*	1674-	Beverly, MA
	73	Lydia Ropes*	1672-1750?	Salem, MA?
	74	Daniel Grant*	----1718	Scotland; Salem, MA
	75	Mary (Glover) Driver*	----1737+	Salem, MA
	76	Benjamin Hooper*	1672-1718	Salem, MA
	77	Eleanor Clark*	----1702+	
	78	Jeremiah Neal*	1645-1722	Salem, MA
	79	Mary Buffum	-1692	
	80	Joseph Newhall	1658-1706	Lynn, MA
	81	Susanna Farrar	1659-	Lynn, MA
	82	John Newhall	1655-1738	Lynn, MA
	83	Esther Bartram	1658-1728	Lynn, MA
	84	Robert Bates	----1727	----, Lynn, MA
	85	Sarah		
	86	John Gowing	1645-1720	Dedham, Lynn, MA
	87	Johanna Darling?*		
	92	John Nutting	1651-1731	Woburn, Groton, MA
	93	Mary Lakin	1652-171-	Reading, Groton, MA
	94	William Shattuck	1670-1717?	Watertown, Groton, MA
	95	Hannah Underwood	165--1717?	London, Eng; Groton, MA

Book News

BOOKS ADDED TO THE LYNNFIELD PUBLIC LIBRARY AUGUST 1989 - JULY 1990

- a selective list -

FAMILY HISTORIES

BRAINERD	*The Genealogy of the Brainerd Family in the United States*, by David D. Field. 1857.
BUCKNAM BUCKMAN	*A Bucknam-Buckman Genealogy; Some Descendants of William Bucknam of Charlestown and Malden, and John Buckman of Boston*, by Ann Theopold Chaplin, 1988.
BURRILL	*The Burrell/Burrill Genealogy; Descendants of George Burrill of Lynn, Mass. & Descendants of John Burrill of Weymouth*, by Ruth Burrell-Brown. 1990.
FLINT	*Genealogical Register of the Descendants of Thomas Flint of Salem*, by John Flint and John H. Stone, 1860.
GILLEY	*The Gilley Family of Marblehead, Massachusetts*, by Dorothy Briggs Houtz. 1989.
GRAVES	*Samuel Graves, 1630 Settler of Lynn, Massachusetts and his Descendants*, (Graves Family Genealogies - Volume 5), by Kenneth Vance Graves. 1985.
HILLS	*The Hills Family in America* (2 vols), by William Sanford Hills & Thomas Hills, 1906.
HOLWAY-RICH	*Holway-Rich Heritage; a History & Genealogy of Two Cape Cod Families*, by Richard Thomas Holway, 1988.
HOOPER	*Hooper Genealogy*, by Charels Henry Pope and Thomas Hooper, 1908.
HOWARD	*A Howard Family History; the Howards of Lynn & Saugus*, by William C. Howard.
KEYES	*Genealogy of Robert Keyes of Watertown*, by Asa Keyes, 1880.
KINGSBURY	*Genealogy of the Descendants of Henry Kingsbury of Ipswich and Haverhill, Massachusetts*, by Frederick John Kingsbury, 1905.
LEIGHTON	*A Leighton Genealogy; Descendants of Thomas Leighton of Dover, New Hampshire*, 2 vols., by Perley M. Leighton. 1989.
LEIGHTON	*Leighton Genealogy; an Account of the Descendants of Capt. William Leighton of Kittery, Maine*, by Tristam Frost Jordan, 1885.
LUNT	*Lunt: A History of the Lunt Family in America*, by Thomas S. Lunt, 1914.
MERRILL	*A Merrill Memorial; An Account of the Descendants of Nathaniel Merrill, an early Settler of Newbury, Massachusetts* (2 vols), by Samuel Merrill, 1917-1928
MITCHELL	*Some Descendants of Michael & Sarah (Catlin) Mitchell of Connecticut & Massachusetts 1694-1988*, by Marilyn Jordan-Solari, 1988.
MORRILL	*Morrill Kindred in America*, by Annie Morrill Smith, 1914.
PIERCE	*Pierce Genealogy; the Record of the Posterity of Thomas Pierce, an Early Inhabitant of Charlestown Village (Woburn)*, by Frederick Beech Pierce. 1882.
POTTER	*Genealogies of the Potter Families & Other Descendants in America*, by Charles Edward Potter. 1888.
PERLEY	*History and Genealogy of the Perley Family*, by M. V. B. Perley, 1906.
PROCTOR	*John Proctor of Ipswich and Some of his Descendants*, by Leland H. Proctor, 1985.
PUTNAM	*The Direct Line: Putnam Family History*, by Read H. Putnam. 1982.

RAND	*A Genealogy of the Rand Family in the United States*, by Florence Osgood Rand. 1898.
RICHARDSON	*The Richardson Memorial* (2 vols), by John Adams Vinton, 1876.
ROGERS	*Ancestry & Descendants of Cassie Matilda Rogers*, by Janet Ireland Delory. 1989.
RUSSELL	*Descendants of William Russell of Salem, Mass., 1674*, by George Ely Russell. 1989.
RUSSELL	*Russells in America 1640-1988; Ancestors & Descendants of William David Russell 1821-1876*, by Mary Russell Stetson Clark. 1988.
THURSTON	*Thurston Genealogies (1635-1892)*, by Brown Thurston, 1892.

MASSACHUSETTS

CAMBRIDGE	*Proprietors' Records of Cambridge, Massachusetts, 1635-1829*, by Edward J. Brandon.
DEDHAM	*The Vital Records of Dedham, Massachusetts*, by Robert Brand Hanson.
IPSWICH	*Memento Mori; Tombstone Inscriptions from the Old North Burial Yard in Ipswich, 1935.* *Mass., 1634-1934*, by Arthur W. Johnson.
NASHAWAY TOWNS	*Inscriptions from Burial Grounds of the Nashaway Towns; Lancaster, Harvard, Bolton, Leominster, Sterling, Berlin, West Boylston and Hudson*, Lancaster League of Historical Societies, 1989.
SHREWSBURY	*History of the Town of Shrewsbury, Massachusetts*, by Andrew H. Ward, 1847.
SWANSEA	*In a Place Called Swansea*, by John Raymond Hall.
WESTFORD	*History of the Town of Westford*, by Rev. Edwin R. Hodgman, 1803.
WILMINGTON	*Wilmington Records of Births, Marriages and Deaths, from 1730 to 1898*, by James Kelley, 1898.
WOBURN	*Woburn Records of Births, Deaths, and Marriages from 1640-1873*, by Edward F. Johnson & William R. Cutter, 1890.

MISCELLANEOUS

The American Genealogist; the complete Jacobus Years, 1932-1965 (33 volumes bound in 11).
Delaware Genealogical Research Guide, by Thomas P. Doherty.
Early History of Southhampton, Long Island, by George Rogers Howell, 1887.
Founders & Patriots of America Index, Nat'l Soc. of Dau. of Founders & Patriots of America.
The Genealogical Quarterly Magazine, ed. by Eben Putnam (9 vols bound in 4).
Genealogical Resources in English Repositories, by Joy Wade Moulton.
New England Historic Genealogical Society Book Loan Catalogs.
New Loyalist Index, by Paul J. Bunnell.
Public Records - Report on the Custody and Condition of the Public Records of Parishes, Towns, and Counties for Massachusetts, by Carroll D. Wright, 1889.
Scotia Heritage, by Edith L. Fletcher (Every-name index by Earle C. Hazelwood, Jr.).
The Search for Missing Friends: Irish Immigrant Advertisements Placed in the Boston <u>Pilot</u>; Vol. I.

MICROFILM/MICROFICHE

Quaker Meeting Records; New England Yearly Meetings, Quarterly and Monthly Salem Meetings (Microfilm; 18 rolls).
Hartford Times Index, by Marion Ryan Donoghue (Microfiche of index and newspaper pages).

Society News

FORTHCOMING MEETINGS

September 15, 1990
>Centre Church, Lynnfield; Social Hour 12:00; Program 1:00
"KNIGHTS OF THE WHIP" - COACH TRAVEL IN NEW ENGLAND", a program about Life in Colonial America, by the husband and wife team of Elaine and Robert Dow of Topsfield, Mass. The program takes stage travel from its earliest reference in 1712 to its demise after the birth of the railroad. In the skit that follows, a coach driver stops at a tavern for a change of horses and ale and tells the barmaid anecdotes from his "personal experiences."

October 20, 1990
>Centre Church, Lynnfield; Social Hour 12:00; Program 1:00
"SCOTS-IRISH RESEARCH: RESOURCES IN IRELAND", by Robert C. Starratt, B.A., M.P.H., M.P.A., Family History Consultant from Edinburgh, Scotland, formerly from New Hampshire. This lecture will be illustrated with slides and handouts. Bob will be traveling from Scotland to New England on a lecture tour of the U.S.

November 17, 1990
>Centre Church, Lynnfield; Social Hour 12:00; Program 1:00
"USING LAND RECORDS EFFECTIVELY", by Yvonne H. P. Silva, Title Examiner/Paralegal, who has been in the field for 30 years. Yvonne teaches at Bentley College, lectures for the New England Law School, and has served on a Panel Discussion with the Massachusetts Bar Association.

December 15, 1990
>Centre Church, Lynnfield
CHRISTMAS COVERED DISH LUNCHEON - 12:00
SHOW AND TELL - 1:00

January 19, 1991
>Lynnfield Public Library
All day work meeting
BOOK TALK - 12:00, by Marcia Lindberg
USED BOOK AUCTION - 1:00, with Donald Doliber

****

NOTE: THERE WILL BE NO GENEALOGY CLASSES SPONSORED BY ESOG THIS FALL, DUE TO INTERIOR RENOVATIONS TO THE LYNNFIELD PUBLIC LIBRARY

WALTHAM ARCHIVES THREATENED

U. S. Congressman Silvio O. Conte of Pittsfield, Mass. has announced the approval of his amendment to CLOSE THE NEW ENGLAND BRANCH OF THE NATIONAL ARCHIVES AT WALTHAM AND OPEN A NEW FACILITY AT PITTSFIELD, at a cost to the taxpayers of several million dollars. This amendment was included as part of the Treasury, Postal Service and General Government Appropriations bill of fiscal 1991. Genealogists in New England are outraged at the political maneuvering to move a Federal facility to a politicians back yard without proper studies or justification. Thousands of genealogists and historians in Metropolitan Boston will be deprived of convenient access to these important records. The present location in Waltham is admirably located, 10 miles from downtown Boston and just inside the Rte 128 beltway, providing easy access to several million people in eastern Mass., New Hampshire, maine, Rhode Island and Connecticut. To move this facility would be unconscionable.

WRITE TO YOUR CONGRESSMEN NOW!

Example: Senator Edward M. Kennedy, 315 Russell Building, U.S. Senate, Washington, DC 20510
Representative Chester G. Atkins, 504 Cannon, House Office Building, Washington, DC 20515

MASSACHUSETTS
* Senator Edward M. Kennedy (D), SR-315
* Senator John F. Kerry, SR-421
Repr. Silvio O. Conte (R-1st), 2300 RHOB
Repr. Richard E. Neal (D-2nd), 2426 RHOB
* Repr. Joseph D. Early (D-3rd), 2349 RHOB
Repr. Barney Frank (D-4th), 1030 LHOB
* Repr. Chester G. Atkins (D-5th), 504 CHOB
Repr. Nicholas Mavroules (D-6th), 2432 RHOB
Repr. Edward J. Markey (D-7th), 2133 RHOB
* Repr. Joseph P. Kennedy II (D-8th), 1208 LHOB
Repr. John Joseph Moakley (D-9th), 221 CHOB
Repr. Gerry E. Studds (D-10th), 237 CHOB
Repr. Brian J. Donnelly (D-11th), 2229 RHOB

NEW HAMPSHIRE
Senator Gordon J. Humphrey (R), SH-531
* Senator Warren B. Rudman (R), SH-530
Repr. Robert C. Smith (R-1st), 115 CHOB
Repr. Chuck Douglas (R-2nd), 1338 LHOB

MAINE
Senator William S. Cohen, SH-322
Senator George J. Mitchell, SR-176
Repr. Joseph E. Brennan (1st), 1428 LHOB
Repr. Olympia J. Snowe (2nd), 2404 RHOB

CONNECTICUT
Senator Christopher J. Dodd, SR-444
Senator Joseph I. Lieberman, SH-123
Repr. Barbara B. Kennelly (1st), 204 CHOB
Repr. Sam Gejdenson (2nd), 1410 LHOB
Repr. Christopher Shays (4th), 1531 LHOB
Repr. Nancy L. Johnson (6th), 119 CHOB
Repr. Bruce A. Morrison (3rd), 330 CHOB
Repr. John G. Rowland (5th), 329 CHOB

RHODE ISLAND
Senator Claiborne Pell (D), SR-335
Senator John H. Chafee (R), SD-507
Repr. Ronald K. Matchley (1st), 1123 LHOB
Repr. Claudine Schneider (2nd), 1512 LHOB

VERMONT
* Senator Patrick J. Leahy, SR-433
Senator James M. Jeffords, SD-530
Repr. Peter Smith, 1020 LHOB

KEY
Address for Senate: (Room # given above), United States Senate, Washington, DC 20510
Address for House: (Room # given above), Bldg name) House Office Building, Washington DC 20515

SR = Russell Building
SH = Hart Building
SD = Dirksen Building

RHOB = Rayburn House Office Building
LHOB = Longworth
CHOB = Cannon

* = Most important names to contact:

Queries

GUIDELINES FOR SUBMITTING QUERIES

Readers may submit free queries. No query to exceed 50 words. No limit on number of queries. Ask specific questions re parentage, birthplace, marriage, children, etc. Use identifying detail such as name, date, or place. *Type* or *print* on 3x5 card. Use abbreviations listed at end of February Query section. Deadlines for queries: Jan 1, Apr 1, July 1, Oct 1. Send queries to: Teg query editor, Lynnfield Public Library, 18 Summer St., Lynnfield, MA 01940

MELCHER
Need data mo Sarah MELCHER b Kensington, NH, 1782, dau Jonathon & Polly ----.

CHURCH/SAWYER/FOSTER
Need data anc John CHURCH b 1802, NH, mov Clarenden, NY; m 26 Mar 1829 Louisa SAWYER b 24 Nov 1806, NH, dau Jacob & Anne FOSTER of Sharon, NH.

CADMAN/FORD
Seek data par Lydia CADMAN b 23 Sep 1758; d 9 July 1802 prob Middleville, NY. She m Benoni FORD b 17 May 1758, CT; d 8 Apr 1825.

FOSTER/WETHERBEE/SAWYER/BARNARD
Seek data anc Anne FOSTER b Pepperel, MA, 9 July 1781, dau Leonard & Lucy WETHERBEE. She m Jacob SAWYER b Sharon, NH, 1779, s Josiah & Lydia BARNARD. E. W. Crutchley, Greystone 16 Route 4, Boone, NC 28607.

****

EATON/POPE
Need par, bdt, bpl Mary EATON, m John POPE b 1713/14.

HANEVER/BLAKE
Seek anc Anne HANEVER b 7 Jan 1698; d 21 Nov 1790 Taunton, MA; m Edward BLAKE.

TEAGUE/ADDITON (ATHERTON)
Seek all data Mary TEAGUE m 1723 Samuel ADDITON (ATHERTON).

DOUNTON
Need info William DOUNTON, gaol-keeper of Salem 1686 & w Mary ----.

KNIGHT/PATASHALL
Seek anc, bdt both Daniel KNIGHT m/int 1734 Manchester, MA, Martha PATASHALL.

LOWELL/WEBBER
Seek par, bdt, bpl Abner LOWELL & 2/w Sarah WEBBER of Bucksport, ME. His will pro 1803.

SAXTON (SEXTON)/BISHOP
Need any info Patience SAXTON (SEXTON) m William BISHOP b 18 Oct 1714 s John BISHOP (1655-1731); liv Guilford & Durham, CT. Mrs. John F. Calvert, 20 Flower Ln, Marcellus, NY 13108.

****

HOLBROOK/DOANE
Seek names ch Thomas HOLBROOK of Wellfleet, m Margaret DOANE 1734/5. Was Jane HOLBROOK gdau?

ROWE/ROUSE
Who were par Anthony ROWE, Portsmouth, & w Joanna ROUSE?

NOBLE/JACKSON
Seek any info Christopher NOBLE b ca 1680, Portsmouth, m Lydia JACKSON. Also info her f John b 1637.

FIFIELD/SANBORN
Rachel FIFIELD b 25 Jan 1740/1, dau Samuel of Hampton, NH & Ruth ----. Was she a SANBORN?

WRIGHT/MCKENNEY
Margaret WRIGHT m John MCKENNEY. Was she dau Thomas WRIGHT 1724 Exeter & Elizabeth ----? Helen D. Dotts, 7501 Palm Ave. #127, Yucca Valley, CA 92284.

****

BROWNING
Thomas BROWNING b Essex Co 1671. Need par & maiden name w Mary ----.

HADLOCK/HUTCHINGSON
Seek par James HADLOCK, m Rebecca HUTCHINGSON Salem 1658. Who was James' 1/w?

PASCO/PEASE
Need anc Hugh PASCO b ca 1645, poss Salem; m Mary PEASE, d Enfield, CT 1706/7.

SIMONS/HADLOCK
Need par William SIMONS b ca 1659; m Sarah HADLOCK of Salem. William & Sarah mov Enfield, CT; d 1738 & 1739. Mary Louise Gossum, 201 Court Dr., Fulton, KY 42041.

***

ROBINSON
Need anc Rebecca ---- w/ John ROBINSON of Boston. Was Rebecca b 8 May 1748 their dau? Need all ch & later data.

DICKERSON/TAPLEY
Seek par Judith DICKERSON b ca 1780 & He-man DICKERSON of Salem? Elizabeth TAPLEY m a DICKERSON 20 Jan 1664, Salem. Who was he?

PITMAN/BOWLES/LOCKE
Seek info fam William PITMAN m ca 1680 wid Elizabeth BOWLES LOCKE of Portsmouth.

PITMAN/SHORTBRIDGE/ABBOTT
Who was 2/hus PITMAN of Susannah SHORTBRIDGE ABBOTT of Portsmouth?

PITMAN
Who m Sarah PITMAN b 1679 & Mary PITMAN b 1684? Miss Elizabeth C. Westcott, RFD 2, Box 920, Apt. 202, Bucksport, ME 04416.

***

ALLEN/STORY/WHITE
Seek info Lucy ALLEN b 6 May 1752 Gloucester, m Nehemiah STORY, Jr. 7 Apr 1771, Manchester. Was she dau Deacon David ALLEN & Mary WHITE, both b 1722 Gloucester?

EMERSON/WOLCUTT
Need par Hannah/Joanna EMERSON, m John WOLCUTT 4 Jan 1684 Newbury.

HOOPER/ALLEN/GALE
Was Lydia HOOPER who m Azariah ALLEN 15 Jan 1735/6 Manchester, dau William HOOPER & Abigail GALE?

JACKSON/WEST
Seek info John JACKSON[1] d Ipswich 1648. Dau Elizabeth m Thomas WEST 1661.

ADAMS/GATES
Seek par Thankful ADAMS 3/w Oldham GATES, m 5 Sep 1759 in Brookfield. Was she dau Jonathan & Mary ADAMS of Grafton?

BURR
Seek info Mercy/Mary --- m Samuel BURR, Jr. He b 1667 Hartford, CT, m 1690 Hartford.

COMEY (COMEE)
Seek info Mary ---- m David COMEY (COMEE) prob b ca 1700 Lexington area.

BARTON
Seek anc Ann ---- m Joshua BARTON, m 19 Aug 1718 Framingham, MA. He b 24 Dec 1697 Framingham.

BERRY/BEACH
Seek info Robert BERRY, mov Amherst, NS, 1765. Had ch: Nancy, Thomas, Jenny, Margaret, Elizabeth m Isaac BEACH, Ketley, Robert, Andrew.

GRAVES/BANKS
Seek par Joseph GRAVES b ca 1730 CT (?), mov New Brunswick ca 1760. Ch: George, Elias, John m Elizabeth BANKS, Rachel, Elizabeth.

COLE/GOULD
Seek info Rebecca COLE m Henry GOULD, Jr. 19 Mar 1712 Ipswich. He b 1688/9 Ipswich.

PIERCE/ALLEN
Seek par Mary PIERCE m Jonathan ALLEN 1709 Manchester, MA. She d. 1762 Manchester. Not dau Daniel PIERCE & Eliz MILWARD.

BUTLER/MORGARIDGE/HEARD/OSGOOD
Seek info John BUTLER b 7 Nov 1735 Ipswich & w Mary MORGARIDGE b 6 July 1740 Salisbury. Was he s John BUTLER & Hannah HEARD? Was she dau JOHN MORGARIDGE & Betty OSGOOD?

WHIPPLE/BISHOP
Seek par Rebecca WHIPPLE b ca 1710, m John BISHOP 20 May 1731 New London, CT.

RICHARDSON/TURNER/BARTON
Seek anc Thomas RICHARDSON b ca 1740 & w Elizabeth TURNER. Had dau Unity b 3 Apr 1782 Attleboro, MA, m Nathan BARTON, Jr. 3 Feb 1802 Wrentham, MA. Betty Andrews Story, 5515 S. Bonnie Ln., Hales Corners, WI 53130.

***

DEERING/DOWNS/SAWYER/CONNOR/LOWE/LYNCH

Need info fam Samuel DEERING & Mary Ann H. DOWNS of Brewer, m 25 Nov 1841 Brewer & raised fam there. Ch: Flora m Charles William SAWYER - Need all dts, pls; Mary Wilma b 7 Oct 1853 m Frank CONNOR - need all dts; Charles B. - need all info; Rose Etta m Fred LOWE of Winterport, ME - need all dts, pls; Samuel H. b ca 1862 - need exact bdt, ddt, dpl, he m 14 Apr 1904 Mary LYNCH of Grand Falls, NB. Merle Grant Graffam, 2827 Westbrook Dr., Bldg 3/4 Apt 513, Fort Wayne, IN 46805.

****

BENSON/HAMMOND

Need all info Charity BENSON m Sylvanus HAMMOND (int 19 Feb 1785) poss Rochester, MA.

CURTIS/RANDALL

Need all info Elizabeth CURTIS b 18 May 1750 Hanover, MA. Par believed to be Ebeneazer CURTIS & Elizabeth RANDALL.

FORD/STETSON

Need all info Joseph FORD b Marshfield, MA; m Lois STETSON 28 Mar 1691, Scituate, MA. Also need all info Lois. Helen E. Palmer, Royal Greens, 2075 NE 19th, Gresham, OR 97030.

****

THORNDIKE/OBER

Need all info John THORNDIKE m 13 Nov 1723 Elizabeth OBER, Beverly, MA. Also need info Elizabeth.

GARDNER/WELD

Need all info Elizabeth WELD dau Daniel WELD & Bethia ---; m John GARDNER 11 Jan 1704 Salem, MA.

APPLETON/GLOVER

Need all info Priscilla APPLETON b 25 Dec 1657, dau John APPLETON & Priscilla GLOVER. Harwood G. Palmer, Royal Greens, 2075 NE 19th, Gresham, OR 97030.

****

STONE/LONG

Who were par Elias STONE, m Abigail LONG 1686 Charlestown? Was he a seaman on one of the Norton ships? From London?

SNOWMAN/COOPER

Need all dts Christian SNOWMAN m Boston, 25 Dec 1712, Mary COOPER b 1693. Who were her par?

STAPLES/SNOWMAN

Need anc Sarah STAPLES b 18 Nov 1723, m 1 Jan 1755 Boston, MA, John SNOWMAN.

HORNE/RANDLE/SNOWMAN

Need all info Elisha HORNE & w Tamesin RANDLE, par Comfort b 4 Aug 1762 Penobscot, ME. She m 21 Dec 1780 John SNOWMAN.

DUDLEY/WHEELER

Need par Frances DUDLEY, m Sarah WHEELER. Both of Concord, MA.

FELT/WILKENSEN

Need all vitals George FELT & w Elizabeth WILKENSEN, m 1633, ME.

HOUGHTON/NORTON

Need all info Mary HOUGHTON, m Francis NORTON.

RANDLE (RANDOLF)/BUSH

Need all info Sarah RANDLE (RANDOLF) m Jonathan BUSH 24 July 1715 Marlboro, MA.

NORTON

Are John NORTON, Francis NORTON, Henry NORTON related? How? Howard E. Wescott, Jr., 3031 Fairfield St., Ontario, CA 91761.

****

DAVIS/DOW

Wish corr with anyone researching desc Ephraim DAVIS, Jr. of Amesbury; m Haverhill, MA, 7 May 1803 Polly DOW. Postage returned. S. Cook, 3600 Lester Ct., Lilburn, GA 30247.

****

CHESMORE/GIBSON/WHITTEMORE

Need par Daniel CHESMORE Henniker, NH & Troy, VT, d 1816 NY, m 1800 Mary GIBSON, b 1777, d 1848. Dau Elizabeth (Betsey) b 1804, d 1864 Fitchburg, MA, m 1825 Fitchburg, Jonathan WHITTEMORE. Walter R. Whittemore, 1815 Sycamore Valley Dr., Apt. 304, Reston, VA 22090.

****

SANDBERG
Seek info bro & sis Sven Edward SANDBERG b 1 Apr 1864 Laholm Halland Sweden, d 17 Aug 1936 Malden, MA.

BROOKS/BRISCALL
Need par Oliver BROOKS b Chelsea, MA, 1832; d Charlestown 1873; m Elizabeth E BRISCALL Boston 1860. Poss Calvin/Betsey or Oliver/Hannah.

BROOKS/FIFIELD
Need bp & par Dudley BROOKS of Lempster, NH, m Betsey FIFIELD 1820 of Plainfield, NH. Jane M. Atherton, 9 Sunnyside Ave., Saugus, MA 01906.

****

HARPER/HENDERSON
Need data William & Rachel --- HARPER. Dau Sarah d Rutland, MA 25 June 1751, m Sudbury 16 Dec 1736 James HENDERSON b ca 1715 Ireland, d Rutland 1 Mar 1776.

HEALD/CHANDLER
Need par Hannah ----, m Timothy HEALD b Concord MA 7 June 1696; d there 28 Mar 1736, s John & Mary (CHANDLER) HEALD.

TUTTLE/HOLYOKE/FLOYD
Need par Martha ----, m John TUTTLE b 22 Apr 1666; d Chelsea, MA 10 Apr 1744, s John & Mary (HOLYOKE) TUTTLE; s Samuel m Boston 1713 Abigail FLOYD.

DARVILL/NOYES
Robert DARVILL d Sudbury, MA 26 Feb 1662; m Esther ---- who d Feb 1661. Dau Mary m Joseph NOYES of Newbury. Need par Esther.

BATCHELDER/DENNIS
Joseph BATCHELDER b Wenham MA 1662; d there June 1720, s John & Mary (DENNIS) BATCHELDER; m ca 1686 Sarah ---- who d 1740, ae 76y. Need par Sarah.

SAVORY/SAWYER/MITCHELL
Robert SAVORY d Bradford, MA 9 Apr 1685; m Newbury 8 Dec 1656 Mary (SAWYER) MITCHELL d Newbury 23 Dec 1704. Need par both.

GOODSPEED/KING/WOODING (WOODEN)
Stephen GOODSPEED b Rochester, MA 17 Sep 1706; d Scituate, RI 1 June 1763, s Nathaniel & Sarah (KING) GOODSPEED; m Rochester, MA 1 Mar 1730 Bethiah WOODING (WOODEN) d Scituate Oct 1763, dau Peter. Need data par Bethiah. Mrs. Margaret S. Rose, 2011-20th St., Portsmouth, OH 45662.

****

MOULTON/WILLIAMS
Seek info ch Stephen & Abigail (WILLIAMS) MOULTON m 8 Aug 1754 Newbury. Esp s Samuel & s Stephen, Jr., heirs of Stephen, Sr.'s bro Joseph in 1795. Where did they settle? Did they m? Clayton R. Adams, 6 Laurel Rd., Brusnwick, ME 04011-3420.

****

FINSON/GOSS/WITHAM
Tammy FINSON m Thomas GOSS 25 Nov 1777 Gloucester, MA. Need her bdt, bp & par. Believe she m/2 Ebenezer WITHAM, Jr., poss d Danville or Levant, ME.

GOSS/HARRADEN
Need info Thomas GOSS who m Patience HARRADEN bef 1730. Her dts & par also. Liv Gloucester, MA.

TARR/WALLIS/GOSS
Need any info Caleb TARR & Martha WALLIS. Par of Mary TARR m Thomas GOSS 30 Nov 1751 Gloucester, MA.

WITHAM/PATEE
Need dts & pls Ebenezer WITHAM & w Elizabeth PATEE both of Gloucester, m 14 Jan 1734/5 Goucester. Her par?

HOOL/WITHAM
Sarah HOOL w Ebenezer WITHAM, Jr., b 1 Sep 1755 poss Gloucester, MA. She d 10 July 1810 poss New Gloucester, ME. Need her par.

WITHAM/GOSS
Seek ddt & dpl Elizabeth WITHAM GOSS poss Hermon or Levant, ME, aft 1809. Harriette Wyman, Sawyer's Crossing Rd, PO Box 27, West Swanzey, NH 03469.

****

ALLEN/BROWN
Seek par of James BROWN, b Manchester, MA ab. 1750; m. there, 11 Dec 1770, Lydia ALLEN. Betty Andrews Storey, 5515 South Bonnie Lane, Hales Corners, Wisconsin 53130.

The Essex Genealogist

VOLUME 10, NUMBER 4   **AUGUST 1990**

CONTENTS

Letter from the Editor	176
TEG FEATURE ARTICLE: "The Beginnings of Lynn Re-examined," by Robert Charles Anderson, F.A.S.G.	177
IT HAPPENED IN ESSEX COUNTY: "Frank the Firefighter," by Richard C. Howland	186
"Those People [that] Were Buried in the Friend's Burying Ground"	187

RESEARCH IN PROGRESS

"Peter Twiss of Salem, Mass.," by Harriet Dietrich	192
"Henry Collins of Lynn" - continued, by Carolyn Martino and Marcia Lindberg	198
"The Stocker Family" - continued, by Marcia Lindberg	208
"The Ramsdell Family" - continued, by Roselyn Listernick	213
TOOLS OF THE TRADE: *"The Records and Files of the Quarterly Courts of Essex County*	217
THE AHNENTAFEL	220
SOCIETY NEWS	225
QUERIES	226
INDEX TO QUERIES IN VOLUME 10	230
MOMENTS IN HISTORY: *"Bradford's Journal Lost and Found"*	Back Cover

---

THE ESSEX GENEALOGIST is published quarterly: February, May, August and November for $13 per year, by the Essex Society of Genealogists, Lynnfield Public Library, 18 Summer Street, Lynnfield, MA 01940. Second Class Postage paid at Lynnfield, MA 01940. ISSN: 0279-067X USPS: 591-350. POSTMASTER: Send address changes to ESOG, Lynnfield Public Library, 18 Summer Street, Lynnfield, MA 01940.

Letter from the Editor

This issue brings to a close ten years of publishing *The Essex Genealogist*. From the beginning, it has been a labor of love. During these ten years, we have witnessed many changes. Physically, *TEG* has progressed from typewritten pages, to a "letter quality printer" then to our present laser-jet printer. In size, *TEG* has grown from 32 pages per issue to 60 pages per issue. The first volume in 1981 contained 146 pages. This 10th volume has 234 pages. In 1981, the cost of a year's subscription to *TEG* was $6.00; this year it is $13.00. The quality of articles and of research has improved also; one has only to look at the four issues of 1981 to see the difference.

Over the years, we have added features and lost features, but the main ones have remained. For the first seven years, Lyman Tucker provided us with a **CREST AND SHIELD** column that added graphic interest to the journal. At his untimely death in October of 1987, Lyman bequeathed his collection of books on heraldry to the Lynnfield Library, where they have been greatly appreciated.

Many of us looked forward every issue to Sid Russell's original poems that appeared inside the back cover. When Sid died of cancer in August of 1988, it was a great loss. We have replaced Sid's poetry with **MOMENTS IN HISTORY**, and we are hoping that one of our readers will offer to take charge of this interesting and informative feature.

Donald Doliber started **IT HAPPENED IN ESSEX COUNTY** in the very first issue, in February of 1981, and he continued until last year, when responsibilities of teaching and family demanded more of his time. In this issue, we are pleased to present a new author for this column. We know our readers will enjoy Dick Howland's story, "Frank the Firefighter."

TOOLS OF THE TRADE was a regular column for awhile, with well-known contributors, such as David Dearborn, Roger Joslyn, Ann Lainhart, and many others. We still include that heading now and then. In this issue, you will find an article on *Records and Files of the Quarterly Courts of Essex County*, a description of one of the most important research tools for tracing families in Essex County.

Three to four **AHNENTAFELS** have appeared in almost every issue, starting in the second issue of 1981. Many of our readers have found "connections" through this medium.

MISCELLANEOUS NOTES has appeared in most issues, bringing to our readers news of regional and national happenings. **OUR READERS WRITE** and **THE MAIL BAG** were former headings used, but now that ESOG has a well-established Research Committee, correspondence is handled through that group.

Every August issue, except this year, has included a **SPECIAL FEATURE** that describes the resources available at one of the wonderful libraries and/or historical societies in Essex County towns. Starting in 1981, TEG has presented Lynn Historical Society (1981), Andover Historical Society (1982), The Treasures of Newburyport (1983), Beverly Historical Society (1984), Ipswich Historical Society (1985), York County, Maine (1986), The Essex Institute at Salem (1987), The Treasures of Marblehead (1988), and Lynn's Satelite Town's - Saugus, Lynnfield, Swampscott and Nahant (1989).

At the end of the May, 1986, issue, there was an eleven-page index to articles and authors for the first five volumes. We hope to incorporate that index into a new 10-volume index that will be sold as a separate item.

As Editor, I am proud of the fact that every issue (40 in all) has arrived at the printers on the first day of each publishing month. We are also grateful to Steve Cramp of *Printcraft*, in Wilmington, Mass., our faithful printer from the beginning.

Our former "collaters" miss their quarterly gatherings to collate and staple each issue of TEG. It was a nice "happening" that has gone the way of progress. The collating and stapling is now done by *Printcraft*, and the mailing is done by Helen Bosworth, Jan and Earle Hazelwood and 5 other volunteers, who affix the mailing stickers. Helen, too, is proud that they have not missed a mailing deadline in these 10 years.

Now we go into our 11th year, with no changes in price or size. We hope our 700 subscribers will continue to "read each issue from cover to cover."

Marcia Lindberg

TEG Feature Article

THE BEGINNINGS OF LYNN RE-EXAMINED

By Robert Charles Anderson, F.A.S.G.

(A lecture presented to ESOG at Haverhill, Mass., April, 1990)

Today I'm going to talk to you about some very preliminary thoughts I have on the earliest days of the town of Lynn. But before that, let me tell you about the project that I have been involved with for a year now - the Great Migration Study Project, which is being sponsored by the New England Historic Genealogical Society. I'll be giving another lecture this week at that society, and I'm going to start the lecture with a library "trolley" beside me with all the basic reference tools we use and all the things we look at - Savage, Pope, Libby, Noyes & Davis, Colket's guide, and so forth. I personally became tired of having to look at these sources - as good as they are (Savage's work, after all, is 125 years old, and for his day he was spectacular and is still usefull), but so much has been done since his time. I want a single reference work, which, at least for the earliest settlers, will present what is known, right now, of their English origins. When did they make the migration? Where did they first settle? Did they move on when they were in New England? Were they married? Did they have children, and so forth. There is no such reference work.

It would be impossible for any one person in a lifetime to do that for the range of time that Savage covered, so I have chosen the period from the arrival of the Mayflower to 1643. I won't go through a long song and dance about why I chose 1643 as the cutoff date for this study, but I will say that any of you that might happen to subscribe to the *Great Migration Newsletter* (which is part of the project) will find out about that in the second issue. The project is one year and a quarter into its 3-year period. So I'm hoping that in early 1992, I will have a two-volume set that will cover all those people that came on the Mayflower, and Endicott's group in 1628, and Higginson's in 1629, and the Winthrop Fleet, and a few that came after that, before the heavy part of the migration in the latter part of the 1630s.

The Newsletter is just eight pages, but I think it is interesting. It's a way to generate some income and to generate interest in the project, and to keep people informed and interested in what is going on. I should have some copies with me, but I'm happy to say the first run of the first issue is gone. I do not have a sample to show you. But if you look in the *Register* or in *Nexus*, you'll see information on how you can subscribe to the *Great Migration Newsletter* if you're interested.

In that Newsletter, in the middle section, pages 3-6, my intention is to focus each issue on one of the early settlements - try to come up with some new ideas, to look at the sources that are available for that town and see if we can squeeze any new information about them - to look at what's known about where the immigrants came from - what can be said about the transatlantic connections - anything of interest - and try to give an overview of the exact time it was settled, when the church was established, and anything unusual about that town - with a strong emphasis on the nature of the land granting process.

The first issue I did was Watertown because it happened to be the one I had done the most work in. In the 2nd issue, the focus is on Cambridge, which is similar to Watertown, but there are some interesting differences. One of the next issues which I'll be preparing will focus on Lynn, because I've come up with what I think are some interesting things, and it's a challenge, because, as you well know, the records in the early years "aren't," whereas Watertown and Cambridge are just overflowing with town meeting minutes and land records, and vital records, etc. (no church records for either of them either, only civil records). So Lynn is a very special challenge. You have to come at it indirectly.

Over the years, I have made use of Lewis and Newhall's *History of Lynn*, and I don't know when I became dubious about it, but it dawned on me that there was something wrong with the year-by-year list of immigrants. There were just far too many people they were claiming were in Lynn by 1630. I know these town histories were done in a different way in the 19th century than they are now. Perhaps they did have access to information we no longer have. I'm always dubious of traditions that have been passed down through the centuries. But there are things that were known in the 19th century that have been lost today. So it's not good enough just to be doubtful about it. I have to have good reasons for saying that I am not going to accept everything that's in Lewis and Newhall. So that's what I'm going to do today. I'm going to survey the first six or eight years of Lynn history from a viewpoint that I've developed and I'll be interested to see what some of you might think about it.

We start with a concept of "establishment" - one of those places where the language has shifted a little bit over 100 years. As we drive down the highways of Massachusetts, we see these nice signs that are supposed to look like an open book, and they tell us the town was established in such and such a time. It doesn't always say "incorporated" or "established." Sometimes it says "settled." I think for all of us, in our modern usage, when applied to a town, "settled" means when people set down roots in that town. It didn't mean that in the 1630s. I'm not sure exactly what it meant, but it was different. Let me give you an example from a very famous letter, written by James Cudworth in December of 1634, from Scituate, not long after his arrival, to his father-in-law, Rev. John Stoughton back in London. He's giving, in the style of many of the other early writers, a survey of all the towns he is aware of in New England at that time. I read from his letter:

> "and to relate to you that which yet I have not concerning the estate of New England. Here are these churches...
>
> Plymouth, where Mr. Smith is Pastor; no teacher
> Boston, Mr. Wilson, Pastor; Mr. Cotton, teacher"

(I'm not sure you're all aware of this, but the New England churches tended to have a pastor who tended to the duties of the church, that is, to administer the sacraments - he was the senior minister - and a teacher, who generally was not responsible for administering the sacraments, but who was responsible for preparing the sermon.)

I will not give all the towns, but as we go on through the list, number eight is:

> "At Saugus, where Mr. Humphrey lives, Mr. Bachiler, Pastor."

Then we have Salem and Ipswich. In the next paragraph, Cudworth says:

> "Now those plantations that are not yet settled and are newly begun are three:
>
> Duxbury, where Mr. Collier dwells, no pastor nor teacher
> Ours (Scituate) to whom the Lord has been very gracious and his providence has been admirably seen to bring us our pastor whom we have so long expected, Mr. Lathrop, who the Lord has brought to us in safety.
> And the other is Bear Cove (Hingham), where is no Pastor nor teacher."

Read that first sentence... "Now those plantations that are not yet settled and are newly begun" - clearly here, settlement did not mean that people had arrived and had started to build houses. Settlement was a later stage. So what we would call settlement, they would call plantation - the planting of the town physically.

So a settled town, to the Puritans in the 1630s, was something else - it was a state beyond a few houses and a few families. And as we go through my points, I'll try to work out that a part of a settled town was having a minister. But I think it was more than that. I think we'll see, as I go through the details for Lynn what the elements of a settled town were in the 1630s.

The earliest reliable mention of anyone at Saugus (or Lynn) that I can find - many of you have seen this and looked at it - is the deposition by William Dixey, in a court case of 1657. Actually, the deposition was presented in 1678, when the 1657 suit was being renewed at the Essex Quarter Court. And quoting here from the published version that you've all seen in the *Records and Files* (I do want to go to Essex County and see the original deposition - and there are dozens of depositions - it may be possible to winkle out a little more information about this...). But I'll just read the transcript for this in July 1657:

> "Ens. William Dixy, aged about fifty years, deposed that about twenty-eight years ago, Mr. Isaack Johnson, his master, wrote to the Hond. Governor, Mr. Endecott 'for a place to sitt downe in,' whereupon Mr. Endecott gave them leave to go wherever they would. They went to Saugust, now Linne, where they met with Sagamore James and some other Indians, who gave them leave to dwell thereabouts, and they and the rest of his Master's company cut grass for their cattle, keeping them on Nahant, and had quiet possession. Sworn, 1:5:1657, before Elias Stileman, cleric. Copy made by Hilliard Veren, cleric."

Then all these little depositions carry on and on about the fencing of Nahant to keep the cattle in, and then arguments later on to see if Nahant was part of Lynn, or was owned by private individuals - a feast for the lawyers, I'm sure.

I'm sure that any of you who have dealt with depositions know that ages and dates given in multiples of five and ten, can be very unreliable. Now, they're especially unreliable, because it's very clear in most cases that the person doesn't have a precise memory and is just estimating. But in this case, we're told, not that it was 25 or 30 years ago, but 28 years ago. And 28, obviously from 1657, gets us back to 1629. Now, if you're dubious even about that - we have something better. Isaac Johnson had written in 1630, to the Hon. Gov. Mr. Endicott. And after the arrival of Winthrop, Endicott was not governor. So Isaac Johnson could only have written to Endicott as Governor prior to the arrival of Winthrop in 1630. That's why I believe that this is reliable. The advance party of servants to Isaac Johnson were using part of Lynn for agricultural purposes, if nothing else, and presumably living in some primitive form of housing at that time. So that date of 1629, I'm perfectly willing to accept. But was it a town as such? First of all, we have some corroboration of this situation in Winthrop's Journal. In October of 1630, he states, "the wolves killed some swine at Saugus." All this indicates again that Nahant at least, was being used for those purposes.

But there are other things about Lynn in these first two years, and I'm talking about a very narrow span of time - 1629-1632. There are a number of things you can look at - at least by comparison with other towns that are clearly called settled. I speak of Boston, Charlestown, Watertown, Dorchester and Salem. There was the institution of Freemanship. The first group of Freemen requested admittance in October of 1630, but the court did not deem fit to admit them until May of 1631. That first group was admitted more or less upon application, as I understand it. At that same session, May of 1631, it was also made a requirement that in order to be a Freeman, from that day forward, you had first to be a member of a church. Although it was not too difficult to become a member of the church in the first years, it became a bit more difficult. So it was a difficult two-step process. But after that May 1631 group, if your name appears as a Freeman, the implication is that you had to have earlier, and maybe just a day or two earlier, been admitted to a church.

At any rate, examining the 1631 list of Freemen, which has about 120 or so, for most of the towns, in Boston, Dorchester, Salem and Watertown, Cambridge and so on, you'll find about 15 to 20 individuals named in that list. As best as I can make out, from the 1631 list, there are only three who settled in Saugus. Mr. Edward Tomlins, Mr. John Dillingham and Thomas Dexter. Then there was a fourth that I would add, although he was not admitted until 3 July 1632. He had applied with the others in 1631, Mr. Nathaniel Turner. I have four names only that I can attach to Lynn through the period I'm talking about - down to March of 1633.

Of course there was no church at Lynn at that time, but that's no excuse, because Cambridge had no church at that time either. But I think it can be demonstrated that the earliest Cambridge residents, those of Thomas Hooker's party, arrived in 1632, prior to Hooker himself coming in 1633. Those men settled in Cambridge, but I find about ten of them as Freemen. And my assumption is, that they joined the Watertown Church, which would be the nearest church. Certainly not Boston or Charlestown, because the records for those towns still exist.

So there's one problem right there - only four names for Lynn, whereas the other towns were up to 20 or 30 families at least being made freemen. That's a serious discrepancy.

Another indicator is in the tax records. Within this period, we find in the published Massachusetts Bay General Court Records, "A tax shall be levied out of the several plantations - the sum of 30 pounds for the making of the creek at the New Town" (Cambridge), and there are assessments against 10 towns, including Boston, 5 pounds; Dorchester, 4 pounds 10 shillings; Watertown, 5 pounds; Salem, 3 pounds 5 shillings; Charlestown, 4 pounds 10 shillings. Then you have these places: Nantasket (Hull), 10 shillings, Winnissimet (Chelsea), 15 shillings, Wessaguscus (the early name for Weymouth), 30 shillings, and Saugus, 20 shillings.

So that Saugus is down there in what Cudworth would have called unsettled, or not settled plantations, and one-fifth or one-fourth of the rate of towns such as Boston or Dorchester that were fully organized.

A third indication is what I would call social extremes - that's sort of an extreme statement. The point is, for all those other towns, the bulk of the population were yeoman families. They were neither that high up on the social structure or that low down. They were good, solid yeomen, good middle-class farmers. They came as groups. They came with wives and children and so forth.

When you look at the few records that survive for Lynn, for that period, you see only two things. You see gentlemen and you see servants. You see none of this in-between social stratum that forms the core of these other towns. Notice again, the four names I listed as Freemen, Mr. Edward Tomlins, Mr. John Dillingham, Thomas Dexter, Mr. Nathaniel Turner. "Mr." was, at least for early New England, the most elevated stratum there was. The ordinary yeoman was "goodman."

Notice also, when I read from William Dixey's deposition, he said, "for my master, Isaac Johnson." Isaac had married the daughter of the Earl of Lincoln and he was the wealthiest man who had come on the Winthrop Fleet. William Dixey, when he finished his servitude, had a family, became Ensign, and so forth, and joined that yeoman class. But in 1629, as a 22-year old man, he was a single servant and that's repeated again and again in the various depositions that you see.

The first reference to Saugus in the Colony Records is 3 May 1631 for "John Legge, servant to Mr. Humphrey." (Now Mr. Humphrey, in 1631, was not even in the country. He, like Johnson, had sent an advanced party of servants over.) So you have this atypical social split, with the few people we know of in Lynn, being of "gentle" or near "gentle" status, very wealthy, or single servants. No yeoman families - none of the intermediate gradation you find in all the other towns.

Another indication that's slighter than these. On 9 May 1632, after Watertown had raised questions about taxation (the first documentable protest of taxation without representation) - the first steps towards the development of the lower house of the General Court, when deputies were appointed from the towns to meet with the Assistants to discuss the problems about taxation, all the other towns - Boston, Dorchester, and so forth - had two deputies. Saugus had only one, Richard Wright. So this tells me that Lynn at this period was in an intermediate stage. It certainly wasn't settled in a modern sense. It didn't have a church. It didn't have the social structure as the other towns. And for some reason it was not thought proper for them to have two deputies, as all the other towns did. That's 1629-1632.

Then in 1632, we have a change. That was when Rev. Stephen Bachiler and his company of husbandmen arrived, with Richard Dummer and a number of others. (I find Rev. Stephen Bachiler one of the most fascinating people in this whole period. He was already approaching his 70s, I believe. He brought large numbers of his family with him - grandchildren. Those of you who know his career, know that he went all over the map in this country, then went back to England in the 1650s and began to stir up trouble there when he was in his 80s. A remarkable man.) At any rate, he arrived with the company of husbandmen in June of 1632, and this is the next stage in the growth of Saugus. And almost immediately he gets in trouble here. Quoting from the Records of the General Court for 3 October 1632 (He's been in the country for three months):

"Mr. Bachiler is required to forbear exercising his gifts as a Pastor or a Teacher publicly in our patent (jurisdiction) unless it be to those he brought with him, for his contempt of authority, and until some scandals be removed"

(Mr. Bachiler always had scandals brewing about him.) The "unless it be for those he brought with him," refers to his immediate family - the Husseys, the Wings, the Sanborns, and his Bachiler son, and to some other members of the company of husbandmen, like Richard Dummer. A very few came in 1631, and the bulk of them came in 1632. This indicates to me, first of all, that the church had not yet been organized, contrary to some statements in print, and furthermore, there was already a dispute between the nucleus that Bachiler had clearly formed in England and brought with him, and those few families that were already there ahead of him - Dexter and Dillingham, the Tomlins and so on. What we don't know and we don't have records to show one way or another, is whether there were other families that came in with Bachiler or if that was the totality of the individuals to be dealt with. At any rate, this was in October 1632. The winter passes, and at the court on 4 March 1632/3, again, "The court has reversed the last act against Mr. Bachiler, which restrained him from further gathering a church within this patent." He must have convinced them somehow that he would no longer be contentious and that the scandals were not scandals. But I also infer that the church had still not yet been organized by this date, March 4, 1632/3. Bachiler certainly wanted it to have been, and I have no doubt that he was lecturing at least to those he brought with him. In the formal way they went about things at that time, at least in New England, I don't believe there was a church in Saugus at that date.

On that same 4 March 1632/3, the date the court set Bachiler free to complete the organization of the church, there are two other names in the Freemen's list attached to Lynn - John Kerman, who I take to be the John Kerman who came on the "Plough" in 1631, in the advanced party of the company of husbandmen, and Timothy Tomlins, the brother of Mr. Edward Tomlins, who possibly had been here with Edward from the beginning and was just getting around to this. But the court ordered that these men be made Freemen at this date, so they must have been admitted to some other other church - perhaps Salem.

We don't really hear of anything during the next year or so, during 1633. Bachiler, at least by the records, doesn't get into any more trouble. Then on 14 May 1634, at the General Court, the following year, we have four more Lynn persons becoming Freemen: Thomas Talmage, Daniel Howe, Christopher Hussey, and Thomas Coldham. (Christopher Hussey was Bachiler's son-in-law). I don't know about the other three men, but here we at least see the beginning of those that Bachiler brought with him, being admitted as Freemen. It's peculiar that Bachiler himself was not made Freeman at this time, but I'm satisfied at least that Bachiler had his church organized by this time. I suggest that this Bachiler church, if you can call it that, was formally organized in 1633. There were still problems with it. it was probably not done to the standards of the other churches in the Bay.

On 14 May 1634, the lower house of Deputies is fully established, and by this time, Saugus has its full quota of three deputies at the court. So, at least at that level, the population has increased. There is a church. The central government is now admitting Lynn (Saugus) as apparently a full-fledged member with the other settled towns. Not long after, December 1634, Cudworth writes the note I started with, and includes Lynn (Saugus) as one of the settled plantations where Mr. Humphrey lives, with Mr. Bachiler, pastor. Still, the next year, there are only 2 more names that I can associate with Saugus, being made

Freemen. September 1634, Joseph Redknap; March 1634/5, Thomas Stanley. But in these months, as it was late in the year, very few men were admitted Freemen. At the General Court in May, 90% of the Freemen were admitted in one bunch. And I think, but I haven't got the evidence firmly in hand about this, but I'm quite sure they were admitted prior to the opening of the court. So they were immediately eligible to vote at the Court of Assistants, which was the main purpose of being a Freeman in the first place. In October of 1633, we have a Tax List of 400 pounds, collected over several plantations to defray public charges - a general country rate: Boston, Roxbury, New Town, Watertown, Charlestown, 48 pounds apiece; Dorchester, 80 pounds - by far the wealthiest town in the colony - but now Saugus is 36 pounds, still less then the others - not one-fifth, but three-fourths - and well ahead of Salem, and way ahead of Winnissimet, Medford and Agawam (Ipswich). So that in the tax rate also, we see that Saugus has developed wealth, which would be a combination of the estate of the very wealthiest people, such as Humphrey, Dillingham, and so forth, and then the broad spectrum of the yeoman families, which largely had come with Bachiler. So, in this aspect too, Saugus had moved into the company with the rest of those towns.

Now, at this point, we begin to see the problems again that Bachiler is capable of having. This is from Winthrop's Journal, 15 March 1634/5, just after that last Freemanship record I gave you for Thomas Stanley, and before the 1635 General Court:

> "Two of the Elders of every church met at Saugus and spent there three days. The occasion was the members of that church, not liking the conduct of the pastor, and "withal making a question whether they were a church or not," did separate from church communion. The Pastor and other brethren desired the advice of the rest of the churches, who, not thinking fit to judge of the cause without hearing the other side, offered to meet at Saugus about it. Upon this, the Pastor (Bachiler), etc. required the separate members to deliver their grievances in writing which they refusing to do, the Pastor, etc. wrote to all the churches that for this cause they were proposed to proceed against them as persons excommunicated; and therefore desired them to stay their journey. This letter being read at a lecture at Boston where some of the elders of every church were present, they all agreed with consent of their churches to go presently to Saugus, to stay this hasty proceeding. Accordingly, being met, and both parties, after much debate, being heard, it was agreed that they were a true church though not constituted a first in due order, yet, after [i.e., later], consent and practice of a church estate had supplied that defect. So all were reconciled."

Now that again was an optimistic conclusion on Winthrop's part. But at the General Court of elections in May of 1635, we at last have our good long list of Lynn Freemen, which is comparable to what we have had for other towns for as much as four years before. And I don't know that every one of these was from Lynn, but generaly the colony clerk entered them by the town, because the list had to be sent in by the minister to verify church membership before they could be Freemen. But there's no indication on the list of Freemen whether they are from Salem, or Ipswich, or whereever. This is the list in the order it sits on the published Massachusetts Bay Freemen's list:

Boniface Burton, Robert Bodfish, Robert Driver, William Edmunds, John Ravensdale, John Legg, George Farr, Robert Cotty, and Mr. Stephen Bachiler. So, Bachiler, at last, becomes a Freeman, and at least six of these other names are well-connected with Lynn. I'm not so convinced of Bodfish and Cotty. At any rate, this is the first large group of Saugus people joining as Freemen that can be found in the records. And I think it's related in some way with that reconciliation brought about two months before by the elders of the other churches.

Well, as I say, they were a little overly optimistic in that year in making that decision, because, as Winthrop records, in January of 1635/6, less than a year later, there is again a dispute in the Saugus church. Bachiler was requested to remove himself within 3 months, and we know he did. He goes very briefly to Cape Cod, then again very briefly to Newbury, and finally to Hampton where he stayed for some years.

There is another reference to the Saugus dispute in Winthrop's Journal of 1635/6. Bachiler has gone and a number of his family members certainly move along with him to these other places, including some of those that had been with him as part of the company of husbandmen right along. Then on 8 November 1636, according to the discussion of the early churches by Harold Worthley, a new church was gathered at the coming of the second minister, to allay any fears concerning Lynn's ecclesiastical organization. That second minister, of course, was Samuel Whiting. So, they did finally, in November of 1636, orgainize a church in the accepted and proper way.

Now there's a little more to it than Worthley lets on there, because there was virtually a total revolution in the church structure in 1636. Remember that some of the towns, virtually lock, stock and barrel, had moved off to Connecticut; large numbers from Watertown, the entire population of Cambridge, large numbers from Dorchester, and Roxbury, had all gone off to the Connecticut River Valley. The church in Watertown continued its corporate existence, but the churches at Dorchester and Cambridge (the churches themselves) went to Connecticut, and new churches had to be established in those two towns. Similarly, Salem is reorgainzed after Roger Williams left, and you find a new covenant in Salem. And there's another thing going on which was the last crowning development in the so-called New England Way, in the Congregational Church - the development of what was called the "confession of faith," which was the requirement that not only did the prospective member have to be able to show knowledge of Christian doctrine, but they had to be able to give satisfactory evidence of having actually experienced "saving grace." That would be the equivalent, at that time, of being "born again," I presume - the standard stage in any Evangelical Church experience. So, many of the churches rewrote their covenants in 1636 to incorporate this development. It wasn't just, as Worthley says, to allay any fears concerning Lynn's ecclesiastical organization, although it certainly had that effect.

And so the upshot is that finally, in the fall of 1636, I think then Lynn had all the elements of a settled plantation. It had the proper number of deputies; it had a full range of social classes, with the solid yeoman middle class; it had a properly organized church. And you would have to say that Saugus suffered not only from Mr. Bachiler's peculiar activities, it was also a desired feature that these towns have one of the prominent members of the colony present - a man who could sit as local Justice of the Peace. That man for Saugus should have been John Humphrey, who was so well regarded that he was elected as an Assistant every year, even though he didn't come until 1634. So Lynn hobbled along wihout a proper church, without the guidance, which they felt they needed, of a great man such as John Humphrey - which I think was also a disappointment to the town. But finally Humphrey had arrived in 1634, two years later Mr. Bachiler was gone, and a settled minister was in place. Saugus could fully join the company of the other towns that had had this establishment for some time.

To summarize: We've discussed two periods, 1629-1632, when Saugus was an outpost of the agricultural activities of a few prominent men in England, and had no settled church, and none or very few of the solid middle class. And then a period - 1632-1636, when it had most of the elements of a settled town, but didn't quite. Things didn't quite fit. Things weren't quite up to the standards of the General Court and people like John Winthrop, who made these decisions.

A little indication to me that what I've said, is close to being correct is this record, again from the General Court - this entry: 15 November 1637, "Saugus is called Lynn." Now, virtually every one of the plantations from its earliest days had a name that the Indians had used for it. Boston was Shawmut, Dorchester was Mattapan, Ipswich was Agawam, Salem was Naumkeag, and Lynn was Saugus. All those other towns had their names changed in 1630, and other towns later that were settled which had Indian names, had their names changed at an early time by the court. I don't know whether it was a conscious act on the part of the General Court, but I think that was part of their acceptance of a town, when it was given an English name. Then it met all the criteria. So, November 15, 1637, one year after the Samuel Whiting church was established, the General Court finally says to Saugus, "You're one of us now."

I think all of this is very instructive. Because, without a case like this, you wouldn't know any of this. All the others were so cut and dried. People come to Boston, they "sit down" and they're organized; people come to Watertown, they "sit down" and are organized. It wasn't like that in Lynn. And that unusual situation, by reflection, tells us a great deal about the settlement of all the towns in Massachusetts Bay.

That's as far as I've gone to this point. This is a work in progress. It's tentative. It's meant to be provocative. I'd like to have your reaction.

(Further notes generated by questions from the floor...the questions were inaudible on tape)

To take the "Oath of Fidelity" (to the King) you had to be 16 and up. Freemen had to be 21. It was essentially the same, but the Fidelity Oath omitted the part about voting - it was a lesser stage and didn't have that benefit.

****

I have the list of land grantees of 1638 for Lynn and have annotated it as to when they came - including the Newhalls, who came much later then Lewis and Newhall say. You can take the 1630 list of Lynn settlers that Lewis and Newhall give and knock a lot of names out of it, because we have English records of them after that date. I'll give just one example. They give four or five people in 1629, including the Ingalls brothers, and we know from Threlfall's work, that they came much later.

****

There were, of course, some people who did not take up their Freemanship, and they were constantly being "beat upon" about it. I think in the earliest years, it hadn't been settled yet as to whether you had to be a Freeman to receive a land grant from the proprietors. That was established by 1640, that you did not have to be a Freeman to get a grant of land from the town. But, I think in the earliest days, people still had that concern - if they didn't take up their freemanship, they wouldn't be able to join in the standard land grants.

****

There were no Quakers at that time. Quakerism didn't begin until after 1650. A Catholic, if there had been a stray one at the time, couldn't become a Freeman. The church wasn't called the Congregational Church. Let me make this point. The settlers in Plymouth were Separatists and had rejected the Church of England, and were establishing a new church. For political reasons, this was very dangerous. That's why they went to Holland in the first place. The Massachusetts Bay colonists, I think were deluding themselves when they claimed they were not Separatists. The effect of what they did was to separate, but they claimed, so as to attempt not to affect their political status, not to be Separatists. What they thought they were doing was "cleansing" the established Church of England. They would not have permitted anyone else to join but those who followed their particular way. The fact is, there were a few people around who tried to support the King's Church - the Church of England - which was an unregenerate church. Virtually everything that the Massachustts Bay Puritans did was schizophrenic, you might say, in that they claimed not to be separatists, but, everything they did, had separatist tendencies. In the Church of England at that time, in fact many of the ministers who had been ministers in England who came over, had been ordained by their Bishops, usually shortly after they had graduated University. These non-separatist Puritans didn't believe in the Bishops. So there were great arguments as to whether those past ordinations had to be revoked in a sense, and they were then ordained here. For the best account of that - look in the published volume of Dedham, Massachusetts, church records, about Rev. John Allin. There's a very detailed discussion of how the church members were selected, and then step by step, how they decided who would be minister, who would be elder. So it was a community operation and community based. That is, the surrounding ministers came in - Richard Mather came in from Dorchester, and George Phillips came over from Watertown, and so on, and, as a group, they ordained by laying on of hands, John Allin, and they abjured the Bishops of England. This, of course was quite different from what was going on in Virginia, where the Bishop of London sort of had an extension of his diocese. Virginia was an extension of his church. He ordained ministers to go to Virginia. None of that in New England. They sort of plucked this procedure out of thin air (practically everything they did was out of thin air, and the ordination was one of the things they did). Now there's probably a precedent for it in some of the separatist churches in Holland, but there were very few, and very few records kept. But I think there was a tradition for that sort of thing. I definitely recommend you look at the published Dedham church records. It has about 25 to 30 pages of very dense reading. But at least you'll get a feeling for what happened in Haverhill later. A teacher preached but he couldn't administer any sacraments. As things developed, in towns like Haverhill, and some of the later towns, like Billerica and Chelmsford, a Harvard graduate, a young man out of Harvard - would be invited in by the new settlement, and he would be invited to preach for a year, and then they would decide whether they wanted to keep him or not. Then he'd go through the proper steps. But before that he would be a teacher but not a pastor.

****

The problem with servants is, that's not a good term. That's not really what it was. These people were servants at a certain stage in their lives - it does not mean they were a lower level. In their late teens, that term "domestic servitude" was really just an undifferentiated form of apprenticeship. And when they had served their five to seven years, they would then become eligible to marry their master's daughter, or someone from a family of similar status, and then they would get their grants of land and would join the class they had been serving. It's part of the migration process.

****

Indenture was any legal instrument that involved two or more parties.

****

John Humphrey is a man I would like to know more about. He was obviously a man Winthrop thought highly of and put great hope in. They needed men of stature to give themselves stature, and also to provide money, and Humphrey had it. Also, he was Isaac Johnson's brother-in-law. They had both married daughters of the Earl of Lincoln. Winthrop's Journal, and General Court records, and the Winthrop Papers, all expect Humphrey. They keep electing him as an Assistant each year. Of course, he had his servants in the land already here, raising cattle. He finally does come in 1634, but I think his sympathies really lay elsewhere. As a result, Saugus certainly did not have one of the magistrates like Saltonstall of Watertown, Dudley of Cambridge, and so on, that stabilized the town.

Robert Charles Anderson is a native of Bellows Falls, Vermont. He earned his A.B. at Harvard (1971), his M.S. at California Institute of Technology (1973). He is a Fellow of the American Society of Genealogists, and a member of the Board for Certification of Genealogists. He is also a member of many genealogical societies, including the New England Historic Genealogical Society, The National Genealogical Society and The Essex Society of Genealogists. In 1976, he published *Directions of a Town; a History of Harvard, Massachusetts*. He resides in Salt Lake City, Utah. **THE GREAT MIGRATION STUDY PROJECT**, of which he is Director, will examine everything in print on the 20,000 English men, women and children who crossed the Atlantic to settle in New England between 1620 and 1643.

It Happened in Essex County

FRANK THE FIREFIGHTER

By Richard C. Howland

Frank was a firefighter who joined the Gloucester Fire Department in 1905, arriving by train from Albany, New York. It is believed by some he was recruited because his reputation for strength, dependability and public relations had reached all the way to the North Shore. He was first assigned to Engine 2 at the East Gloucester station and quickly lived up to his advance publicity. He was not only the biggest firefighter there, but always the first or second out the door. Aerobics and weight lifting were hardly the popular prescription for getting and keeping in shape in the early part of the century. However, Frank and his colleagues, in keeping with an exercise regimen and municipal needs, had to spend at least one hour a day hauling trash or water wagons. Frank, approaching middle age, got stronger and stronger.

Frank's tenure in East Gloucester was surprisingly brief. The department's administration felt he was needed more at the Prospect Street Fire House which, because of its central location, reponded to more alarms than any other station. They also felt he'd be more efficient assigned to a ladder truck than a steamer. Here is where Frank's reputation really took off, where he became a national, then international figure. Frank, you see, caught the eye of sculptress Anna Hyatt Huntington (1876-1973), a summer resident of Annisquam village. Anna was the daughter of Gloucester marine scientist Alpheas Hyatt. She married philanthropist Archer Huntington. She died at the age of 97, leaving behind a full creative life, recognition as a world famous sculptress, and an unexpected immortaility for Frank the Wonder Horse.

In 1911, a New York Joan of Arc Statue committee commissioned Anna to create the original object d'art, a statue of the Maid of Orleans, in historically correct armored dress with eyes to the sky, brandishing a sword in her right hand, and mounted on an equally imposing steed, the model for which was Frank. This statue was unvelied on Riverside Drive, New York City in 1915. According to Gloucester auther-historian, Joseph E. Garland, this earned the sculptress the Purple Rosette of the French government. Replicas were sent to Blois, France, southwest of Orleans in 1921, to San Francisco, to Quebec City's Plains of Abraham, and of course to Legion Square, Washington Street, Gloucester.

Paul Kenyon, former associate editor of the Gloucester Daily Times reported years ago in a column he wrote about Frank, that former Deputy Fire Chief Fitz Robinson had himself written a remembrance account in 1953. Deputy Robinson recalled that once Anna spotted Frank around town, she felt he'd make the fitting model for Joan of Arc's mount. "She had been to other countries and had looked at other horses, but they did not suit her. To think that after all her travels she should come home and find what she wanted in her own back yard!"

Anna visited the station two or three times a week to study the steed's bearing, determine his height and weight and make friends with him. Frank would respond with happy whinnies and clomping hooves and no wonder, for "every time she came she brought lumps of sugar or candy."

On July 4, 1921, the bronze replica of the World War I Memorial statue was dedicated, but the sculpture itself, reportedly a present to the Gloucester post of the American Legion, was not put in place until the following Labor Day weekend. Robinson noted that Frnk was ridden in that Fourth of July parade by a Miss Melba Proctor dressed as Joan of Arc, that "It was a very hot day. The next morning Frank was found dead ... thus ending his career in a blaze of glory - willing to do his part at all times." So Joan of Arc's martyrdom, Anna Hyatt Huntington's artistry, and Frank's noble service, all came together here in Essex County - and also in four other cities, three countries, and two continents.

And why not? After all, we are one world.

"THOSE PEOPLE [THAT] WERE BURIED IN THE FRIEND'S BURYING GROUND"

(A handwritten booklet owned by The Essex Institute. Only 1/3 of these burials appear in the published *Lynn Vital Records*. Those records not in Lynn VRs are starred below.)

* Mark Estes Wife, Died the 23rd of the 4th mo 1781

* 1781 Jacob Colinses Child Died ye 11: of ye 6th m - (a son)

* Abijah Newells Child Died ye 21st of ye 8th mo (a son), 1781

  1781 William Estes Died ye 19th of ye 10 m

  Elihu Goold Died ye 19th of ye 11th mo 1781

  Hannah Silsbe Died ye 23rd of ye 11th mo 1781 (Henery Silsbe's wife)

* Hannah Newhall (Daniel Newhall's wife) Died ye 27th of ye 11th 1781

* John Bassets son John Died ye 8th of ye 1st mo 1782

* Lydia Collins Died the 27th of the 8th m 1784 (Jacob Collins wife)

  Nehemiah Johnson Died the 1st of the 11th mo 1784

* Matthew Estes Died the 16th of the 11th mo 1784

* Abigail Silsbe Sampson Silsbes wife Died the 23rd of the 3rd mo 1785

  Deliverance Purinton Died the 15th of the 5th mo 1785 James' daughter

  David Oliver Died (Drowned) the 11th of the 6th mo 1785

* Hannah Cutter Died the 1st of the 9th mo 1785

* Deliverance Breed Died the 25th of the 10th mo 1785 (an old woman)

* Richard Hood Died the 6th of the 1st mo 1786

* A Man taken upon the Beach the 11th of the 5th mo Buried the 12 1786 Suposed to be Drowned

* Martha Hawkes Child Died the 2nd of the 9th mo 1786

* Agnes Hood Died the 4th of the 9th mo 1786

* William Graves Died the 20th of the 10th mo 1786

* Ruth Breed (Amos Breed's Wife) Died the 2nd of the 3rd mo 1787

* Elizabeth Hood Sarah Hood's Daughter, Died the 13th of the 7th mo 1787

* Widow Elizabeth Hood Died the 29th of the 9th mo 1787

* Lydia Farrington Died the 10th of the 8th mo 1787 (Daniel Farrington's daughter)

* Ephereham Silsbe Died the 25th of the 9th mo 1787

* Philadelphia Hawkes Died the 13th of the 10th mo 1787

Francis Newhall died the 11th mo 29th 1787

Elizabeth Estes Died the 6th of ye 4th mo 1788

Rebeckah Breed Died the 20th of 4th mo 1788 (Richd Breeds daughter)

* Widow Lidia Basset Died the 1 of the 12 m 1788

* Sarah Hood Died the 23rd of the 5th mo 1789 - Widow Sarah Hoods daughter

Richard Breed Died the 28th of the 6th mo 1789

* Benj^a Phillips Child Died 11th mo 1789

* Benj^a Breed's Child Died the 21st of the 1st mo 1790

Hannah Breed, James Breed's Daughter died the 6th of the 5th mo 1790

* Theodate Alley's Child Died the 25th of the 3rd mo 1790, an <u>illegetimate</u> Child - -

* Jacob Collin's Child Died the 2nd of the 7th mo 1790

Simeon Breed Died the 21st of the 9th mo 1790 (Simeon Breed's Son) abought 2 yrs old

Anna Breed Died the 23rd of the 9th mo 1790 (the Widow Anna Breed's Daughter)

Content Collins Died the 24th of 9th mo 1790 - Sam^{ll} Collins's Daughter

* Joseph Basset Died the 14th of the 12th mo 1790

* Joanna Graves Died the 5th of the 2nd mo 1791

* Agnes Richards Died the 18th of the 5th mo 1791

Ebenezer Hawkes Died the 21st of the 8th mo 1791

Elizabeth Basset Died the 29th of the 8th mo 1791

John Chase Saml Chases Son Died the 12th of the 10th mo 1791

* Ephereham Collins Died the 25th of the 2nd mo 1792
  & Daniel Newhall 3rd's Child Died the Same Day - a Daughter

* Mary Breed Died the 9th of the 3rd mo 1792 - (Jabez Breed's wife)

* Mary Gaile Died the 28th of the 3rd mo 1792

Content Purinton Died the 7th of the 4th mo 1792 (Pelatiah Purinton's Wife)

Abigail Newhall died the 10th of the 7th mo 1792 (Abijah Newhall's wife)

* The Widow Elizabeth Phillips Died the 11th of the 12th 1792 - She was one Hundred Years of Age - When she died

Elener Breed Died the 4th of the 2nd mo 1793 Ezra Breed's Daughter

Abigail Phillips Died the 4th of the 4th mo 1793 (William Phillips Wife)

Abigail Newhall Died the 29th of 4th mo 1793 (Abijah Newhall's Daughter)

Ruth Breed Died the 22nd of the 6th mo 1793 (Amos Breed's Daughter)

* The Widow Mary Breed Died the 24th of the 6th mo 1793

* Fortin Phillips James Phillips Negro man Died the 14th of the 9th mo 1793

* Amos Phillips Died the 14th of 10th mo 1793 (James Phillips Son)

* Jacob Purinton son of Moses Purinton of Barwick Died the 24th of 10th mo 1793

* Henry Olivers Child Died the 28th of the 10th mo 1793

Daniel Newhall Died the 15th of 11th mo 1793

* Benjn Chase's Childe Died the 22nd of 11th mo 1793 - a Daughter --

Benj^a Chase's Son Benj^a Died the 6th of 12th mo 1793

* Nathan Breed 3rd Died the 10th of 1st mo 1794 - (son of Nathan Breed --)

Benj^a Chase's Son Phillip Died tthe 12th of the 3rd mo 1794

* Nancy Phillips Died the 19th of 5th mo 1794

* Widdow Eunice Basset Died the 4th of 10th mo 1794

* Jacob Collins's Child - the 21 of 10 mo 1794 - daughter

Joshua Collins Died the 8 of 1 mo 1795

Sarah Oliver Died the 19 of 1 mo 1795 with a Still Born Child a twin at the same time Wife of Henry Oliver

* Zacheus Collins Child Died the 5 of 1 mo 1795 Daughter

James Breed 4 son of James Breed Died 28 of 3 mo 1795

* Enoch Stickney Child Died 16th of 3 mo 1797

This Fall [of 19]97 - 1 or 2 small infants Died

Tacey Pratt was born the 16th of 6th mo 1781 & Died the 23 of 9 mo 1797 at Past 11 oclock Fore Noon

* Eben^r Mansfield's Wife Died the 4th of 10 mo 1797

* Saml Chase's Child a Daughter Died the 8th of 10 mo 1797

* Benj^a Newhall Breed Child Died 10 mo 8 - a son

  Gideon Phillips Died the 16 of 10 mo 1797

* The Widow Abigail Newhall (Granny) Newhall Died 2 m 2 1798

  Sarah Johnson Died 9th of 2 mo 1798 Saml Johnson's wife

* John Mower's Child Died 3 mo 30 1798

* Nathan Breed's Child Born & Died the same day about 4 mo [17]98

* Zacheus Phillip's Child Died abought 4 mo [17]98

  Benj^a Breed Died the 6 of 7 mo 1798 an old man of Breed's End

* Judeth Collins Died the 23 of 7 mo 1798 Saml Collins' Wife

  Saml Silsbe Died the 27 of 7 mo 1798

  James Phillips Died the 25th of 8 mo [17]98

* Moses Alley's Child Died the 29 of 8 mo 1798

* Pharoah Johnson's Child Died the 6 of 9 mo 1798

* Nehemiah Collins Died the 8 of 9 mo 1798

* Nathan^ll Jones' Child Died abought the 10th of 9 mo 1798

  Hugh Alley Died the 29th of 12 mo 1790

  Lydia Breed Wm Breed's Wife Died the 12 of 1 mo 1799

* Anna Estes Died 15th of 3 mo 1799

* Phareoh Johnson Died 1st of 5 mo 1799

* Winthrop Newhall's Child Died in 6 mo 24 1799

* John Curtin Died 7 mo 23 - 1799 -

* Isaac Burril Child Died in 9th mo - 1799 -

* Ezra Baker's Child Died in 10 mo 1799

* Nathan Jones Child Died 10 mo 1799

* Patience Silsbe Died 12 mo 12 1799

  Rubin Collins Died 3 mo 11 1800

  Walter Philips Died 3 mo 18th 1800

* James Breed's Child Died 4th mo 10th 1800

* Jonathan Phillips Died abought 6 mo 6th 1800 & his Child Died 7th mo 12 1800

   Judeth Breed - Died - 9th mo 2 1800 Anne Breed's Daughter

* Lydia Jones Died the 8th of 10th mo 1800

* Estes Newhall's Child Died 11th mo 4th 1800 - a Son

* Saml Johnson's Child Born & Died 11th mo 11 1800

* Charles Chases Child Died 12th mo 1800

* James Breed 3rd lost a Child (Me?) 1801

   John Mower's Wife Hannah Died 7th mo 13 1801

   Previous to the Last Deborah Oliver Died - Henry Oliver's Wife 6th mo 1801

   Moses Alley Died 8 Mo 7th 1801

   Benj^a H Phillips Son Nathan Died 8 mo 18 1801

* Nathan Jones Child Died 8 mo 27 - 1801

* James Breed Jr - Twins - the first Died 7 m 9 - 1801
         the other 10 m 9 1801

* Widow Ellis Alley - Moses Alley Wife Died 10 m 23 1801

* Lucy Collins Died 10 mo 25 1801 Zachary Collins Wife

   James Purinton Died 10 Mo 26 1801

* Zacheus Phillips Child a Twin Died 2 mo 21 1802

* Zacheriah Collins Died 4 mo 29 1802

* Abigail Phillips Died 6 mo 23 1802 - W$\underline{m}$ Phillps Daughter

   Hannah Breed Died James Breed's Wife 7 mo - 13 - 1802

* Thomas Riches Child Died 7 mo - 18 - 1802

* Isaac Burril Child Died 9 mo 3 - 1802 -

* Abner Alley's Child Died a Son 10th mo 1802

* Manuel Austins Child 11 mo 20 1802

(To be continued)

Research in Progress

PETER TWISS OF SALEM, MASSACHUSETTS

By Harriet Dieterich

Twiss or Twist was certainly not a common name among the early immigrants. Of the most well-known sources, it appears only in Frank R. Holmes's *Directory of the Ancestral Heads of New England Families 1620-1700* (2nd Edition, Baltimore, 1964). He mentions four immigrant Twisses: Daniel, Nathan and William, who were the sons of Dr. William Twiss of England (They were said to have come to New England before 1660, and they may have gone to Connecticut, as there were several Twiss families there); the fourth was Peter, the subject of this article, who is first on record in Marblehead, Massachusetts about 1680. No connection between Peter and the others is known.

The only known account of Peter's family consists of two paragraphs in Sidney Perley's *History of Salem* (Salem, Mass., 1924), III:157), listing Peter's children and those of his sons, John and Daniel, as they appear in the published Salem Vital Records. The Mormon *Family Register* identifies Peter Twiss as the Peter born 1654, who, in the *International Genealogical Index* (hereafter *IGI*), is said to have been christened in Old Alresford, County Hampshire, England, where quite a large number of Twistes are listed. There are also a great many Twisses, Twists, etc. listed for this period in Lancashire, but none for Edinburgh, from which city Dr. Bentley says Peter set sail (see below).

Throughout the records of this family for the first three or four generations, the spelling of the name can be Twist, Twiss, Twisse, Twese, Twis - often several spellings in one document. In later generations the families in a given region may have settled on one way to spell the name; Twist in Woburn, Twiss in Charlton and in New Hampshire. Except in direct quotations, "Twiss" will be used throughout this account. All places mentioned are in Massachusetts, except where specifically labelled and all dates of births, baptisms, marriages and deaths are taken from the published series of vital records unless otherwise noted.

1. **PETER[1] TWISS** was probably the Peter Tweist, christened at Old Alresford, County Hampshire, England, 17 June 1654, the son of Thomas Twiest (*IGI* and *Mormon Family Register*). He died about 1743 in Massachusetts. Peter married at Salem, 26 October 1680 (Salem VR), ANNE CALLUM, who was christened at Lynn, 25 June 1659 (Court Record, *New England Historical and Genealogical Register*, 5:95), the eldest of the three children of Mackum and Martha Callum.

The Diary of William Bentley, D.D. (Gloucester, Mass., 1962), II:203, states:

> *Oct. 24, 1796, Mr. Twisse tells me that he is 63 years of age, & that about his tenth year his G. grandfather died. Peter Twisse died about 70 years of age so that coming young into our country from Edinburg in Scotland he must have come at the close of the last century. His son Peter died in Danvers & the grand Son John, father of the present Jonathan. Mr. Chapman his wife's Father died last week aged 87*

On the 27th of June 1677, a warrant was issued for the appearance of Peter Twist, "servant to Capt. Marshall." Peter was presented for rescuing some horses driving to the pound. He was fined, but the fine was later respitted (*Records and Files of the Quarterly Courts of Essex County, Massachusetts*; hereafter *EQCR* (VI:294-95). Peter was a witness to the beating of John Pudney Jr. by Henry Cook (ibid., VIII:145). He was later presented for fornication with Prisilla Vinton, but Jeremiah Rogers, constable of Salem, "could not find them" (ibid., 147, 237, 372).

Peter was a yeoman and farrier by trade, as shown by deeds on file at Essex County Registry of Deeds. In September of 1700, he and Samuel Pudney paid 80 pounds for one whole fifth part of a tract... being the north east division of Humphrey's farm lying in Salem and part in Lynn (Essex Deeds, 15:61). Peter Twiss, Senior, was clearly a respected member of the community by 1711, when he was assigned a seat in the 2nd row of the meeting house, the South Church of Peabody (*Essex Institute Historical Collections*; hereafter *EIHC*, 87:59).

Children, born at Salem, Mass.:

2.	i.	PETER^2, bpt. 1 Sept 1681; m. SARAH NURSE.
	ii.	ANNE, b. 22 May 1683.
3.	iii.	EDWARD, b. 29 June 1685; m. HANNAH ABORN.
4.	iv.	JOHN, b. 24 Jan 1687/8; m. ABIGAIL PUDNEY.
5.	v.	DANIEL, b. 9 June 1690; m. MARY ABORN.
	vi.	MARY (twin), b. 11 Jan 1693/4.
	vii.	SARAH (twin), b. 11 Jan 1693/4; m. 8 Oct 1719, THORNDIKE VERY, bpt. 1 Oct 1704, son of Thomas and Elizabeth (Proctor) Very (Jones Very, "The Very Family", *EIHC* [II:34]). On 30 Oct 1729, Joseph Very, admin. of the estate of his father, Thomas, lists himself as eldest and Thorndike, Elizabeth and Alice [not clear] (Essex Probate, 28581).
	viii.	MARTHA, b. June 1697; m. (int.) at Salem, 13 Mar 1713/14, JONATHAN NURSE, b. at Salem, 3 May 1682; living in 1743 (Perley, *Hist. of Salem* [II:143]), s. of John & Elizabeth (Very) Nurse.
6.	ix.	WILLIAM, b. 9 Mar 1700/1; m. (1) LYDIA MARSH; m. (2) MARY DOUTY.

2. **PETER^2 TWISS, JR.** (Peter^1), was born at Salem, Mass., in September of 1681. He died after 29 September 1757, when he acknowledged a deed to his sons (see below). He married at Salem, 20 December 1699, SARAH NURSE, born at Salem, 10 November 1680, the daughter of John Nurse and his second wife, Elizabeth Very. Sarah's grandmother was Rebecca Nurse, who was hanged as a witch at age 71.

Peter was a husbandman and housewright by trade. He was listed for rates in 1753 (*Collections of the Danvers Historical Society*, 37:85).

On 6 June 1757, when they were 76 and 77 years of age, Peter Twiss and Sarah Twiss, his wife, for 100 pounds, granted to their two sons, Jonathan and Peter Twiss, both of Danvers "and to their respective heirs in equal shares All my Real Estate in Danvers, Lynn and Elsewhere as well as all my Buildings Upland medow wood Land Pasture Land." In September of the same year, they sold 20 acres to their son Benjamin.

Probable children (order of birth unknown):

> (Rev. Bentley's Diary makes it clear that John belongs here, and Jonathan, Benjamin and Peter are identified in deeds as Peter's sons. The others are placed here because they are of the right ages, with no duplication of names, and they do not fit into any other family.)

7.	i.	JONATHAN^3, b. c1700; m. (1) ABIGAIL TRASK; m. (2) ELIZABETH NURSE.
8.	ii.	JOHN, b. c1703; m. (1) ELIZABETH TRASK; m. (2) MARY (NURSE) WALDEN.
9.	iii.	JOSEPH, b. c1706; m. SARAH LASKIN.

iv. SARAH, b. c1709; m. at Salem, 16 July 1735, JOSEPH GOULD. (It has not been determined which Joseph Gould this is. None of the Josephs listed in Benjamin Apthorp Gould's *The Family of Thadeus Gould of Topsfield* (Lynn, Mass., 1895), fits the dates for this Joseph. Children of Joseph and Sarah (Twiss) Gould, listed in Sutton, Mass. VR (Surname Gould): 1. Daniel, b. 19 Oct 1735; m. at Sutton, 9 Dec 1762, Mary Putnam. 2. Sarah, b. 5 Dec 1743; m. at Sutton, 22 Dec 1763, Solomon Holman 3rd. 3. Molly, b. 19 July 1751. 4. Bettey, b. 26 Feb 1759; m. at Oxford, Mass., 3 Dec 1778, Daniel Carriel. 5. Gideon, b. 26 Apr 1762; m. at Douglas, Mass., 5 Dec 1782, Hannah Marsh (Sutton VR).

v. BENJAMIN, b. c1712. Recived land in Lynn from his parents in 1757 (Essex Deeds, 120:166). He was perhaps the Benjamin Twiss who served in the War of Jenkins' Ear, 7/15 - 8/11/42, for 4 weeks under Capt. Arthur Noble (Myron O. Strachin, *Massachusetts Officers and Soldiers 1723-1743*). He is also perhaps the Benjamin Twiss who was assesed in the North Parish in 1760 and died 16 Nov 1761 (Howard K. Sanderson, *Lynn in the Revolution*, II:452-53).

vi. MARY, b. c1715; m. at Salem, 5 Aug 1739, EDWARD NORRIS, JR., s. of Edward and Remember (White) Norris. He m. (2) 16 Nov 1743, Elizabeth (West) Neal; had children by second wife, none by Mary Twiss (Perly, *Hist. of Salem*, II:82).

10. vii. PETER, b. c1718; m. (1) JUDITH TOWN; m. (2) EUNICE UPTON.

viii. ANNE, b. c1721; d. at Lynn, 9 Feb 1806 ("Descendants of Thomas Brown of Lynn" *Essex Antiquarian* [XII:103]); m. at Salem, 15 Feb 1742/3, Capt. EPHRAIM BROWN of Lynn, son of John & Mary (Paul) Brown (ibid.). Children, b. at Lynn (surname Brown): 1. Ephraim, b. 19 June 1743; prob. d. bef. 1788. 2. Rufus, b. 17 Sept 1744; m. at Lynn, Lydia Burrill. 3. John, b. 19 Nov 1746; prob. m. at Lynn, Elisabeth Huchinson. 4. Peter, b. 27 Mar 1749. 5. Ezra, b. 2 Nov 1750; m. (1) at Lynn, Jane Stocker; m. (2) at Lynn, Mary Mansfield. 6. Sarah, b. 22 Sept 1753; m. Joseph Barrett. 7. Jonathan, liv. in 1793. 8. Benjamin, b. 17 Nov 1757, liv. in Merrimac, NH 1792. 9. Hannah, b. 28 Nov 1759; m. 26 May 1786, Thomas Mansfield, Jr. 10. James, b. 11 Mar 1762; d. Jamaica, VT 1833; m. (int.) 19 May 1787, Catherine Berry of Chelsea. 11. Rachel, b. 2 Sept 1764; m. 3 May 1786, Samuel Boardman, Jr. (ibid.).

ix. DEBORAH, b. c1723; m. at Salem, 5 Dec 1745, MICHAEL CHAPMAN; perhaps m. (2) at Ipswich, 17 May 1758, John Henderson.

x. ELIZABETH, b. c1725; m. at Salem, 28 July 1747, JOSEPH DOUGHTY, JR.

xi. ABIGAIL, b. c1728; m. at Salem, 6 Apr 1748, DANIEL MARSH, s. of Ezekiel and Rebecca (Gould) Marsh. He m. (2) Mary Chudd/Judd, the mother of his children (Col. Lucius B. Marsh, *The Genealogy of John Marsh of Salem* [Amherst, MA, 1888], 71).

3. **EDWARD² TWISS** (Peter¹) was born at Salem, 29 June 1685, and died at Tewksbury, Mass., 20 August 1748 "of consumption" (Tewksbury VR). He married, first, at Salem, 3 February 1708/9, HANNAH ABORN (Eborne, in Salem VR), the daughter of Moses Aborn of Lynn, and his second wife, Abigail Gilbert of Ipswich (*Essex Antiquarian*, I:162). She was born at Lynn, 26 August 1684, and died at Tewksbury, a widow, on 22 November 1767. She is mentioned in the will of her father, Moses Aborn of Lynn, who left her and her sister Mary (who married Edward's brother, Daniel) each twenty pounds (Essex Probate, 175).

Children, listed in administration of Edward Twiss's estate, all but John probably born at Salem:

- 11. i. EBENEZER[3], b. c1713; m. HANNAH HARWOOD
- ii. HANNAH, b. c1715; bpt. at Danvers, 31 Dec 1727 ("Baptisms by Rev. Messrs Prescott & Holt of Salem, Middle Precinct, now South Danvers," *EIHC*, 7:40). She is perhaps the Hannah Twiss, schoolteacher, who was buried at Salem, 9 Aug 1805, aged 90. (There were 3 Hannah Twisses, the daughters of Edward, John and Daniel, and no clue, except dates, as to which is which.)
- 12. iii. EDWARD, b. c1717; m. HANNAH WYMAN.
- 13. iv. JAMES, b. c1719; m. LYDIA FARLEY.
- 14. v. JOHN, b. at Tewksbury, 25 May 1722; m. (1) SARAH PATTEN; m. (2) SARAH HOPKINS.

4. JOHN[2] TWISS (Peter[1]), was born at Salem, 24 January 1687/8. He married at Salem, 20 November 1718, ABIGAIL PUDNEY (or PUTNEY), who was born at Lynn, 28 February 1693, the daughter of John, Jr. and Mary (Jones) Pudney (*EIHC*, III:16).

Children baptized at Salem:

- i. ABIGAIL[3], bpt. 12 June 1720; m. at Salem, 3 Jan 1739/40, RICHARD PHILLIPS. He was perhaps the son of Walter and Ruth Phillips. Walter signed the Quakers' list at Lynn, 22th 4mo. 1703 (Albert M. Phillips, *Phillips Genealogies* (Auburn, MA, 1885], 160).
- ii. HANNAH, bpt. 6 June 1725 (see note under Hannah, dau. of Edward[2]); m. at Oxford (Worcester County) Mass., 16 June 1748, ELIAS JENNISON, b. 23 Sept 1724, s. of Robert and Dorothy Jennison. Children, listed in Sutton, Mass. VR (surname Jennison): 1. <u>Abigail</u>, b. 20 Jan 1749; m. 21 Sept 1769, William Dike, bpt. at Sutton, 3 Dec 1747, s. of Daniel. 2. <u>Olive</u>, b. 20 Aug 1751; m. 1 June 1770, Reuben Barton. 3. <u>Mary</u>, b. 18 Nov 1754; m. 24 Sept 1776, Ezra Lovell. 4. <u>Elias</u>, b. 4 July 1756. 5. <u>Robert</u>, b. 18 May 1758. 6. <u>William</u>, b. 18 Jan 1760; m. 7 July 1784, Judith Kenney (all data from Sutton VR).

5. DANIEL[2] TWISS (Peter[1]) was born at Salem, 9 June 1690, and married there, 22 December 1714, MARY ABORN, who was born at Lynn, 19 April 1686; was living in 1723, the younger sister of Hannah Aborn who married Daniel's brother, Edward. They lived in Salem.

Children, born at Salem:

- 15. i. DANIEL[3], b. 5 Feb 1718/9; m. LYDIA CALLUM.
- ii. HANNAH, prob. b. c1721; bpt. 5 Apr 1730 (see note under Hannah, dau. of Edward[2]; m. at Billerica, 30 Aug 1737, THOMAS MANNING, b. at Billerica, 11 June 1718, s. of Eliphelet & Rebeckah Manning. They lived in Tewksbury. Children, b. at Billerica (surname Manning): 1. <u>Thomas</u>, b. 2 Sept 1738; d. 24 Aug 1749. 2. <u>Hannah</u>, b. 21 Dec 1740; d. 10 Aug 1749. 3. <u>Mary</u>, b. 20 Feb 1744. 4. <u>Thomas</u>, b. Nov 1750.
- iii. MARY, bpt. 5 Apr 1730; m. (int.) at Salem, 13 July 1751, THOMAS NEEDHAM, bpt. at Salem, 27 Oct 1728, s. of George & Rachel (Gould) Needham. He m. (2) 17 Feb 1754, Seeth Phippeny; (3) 4 Aug 1779, Lydia Lefavour. No children by Mary Twiss (Perley, *Hist. of Salem*, II:210).

6. **WILLIAM² TWISS** (Peter¹) was born at Salem, 9 March 1700/1 and died at Danvers, in July of 1772 (source). He married at Salem, 9 January 1722/3, LYDIA MARSH, who was born at Salem, 2 April 1702, the daughter of Ebenezer and Alice (Booth) Marsh (ibid., I:235). He married, secondly, at Salem, 6 June 1728, MARY DOUGHTY or DOUTY (Salem VR). William nentions in his will her inheritance from her father Douty.

Will of William Twiss, written 6 July 1758, probated 4 May 1773 (Essex Probate, 28424):

> *I William Twiss of Danvers in the County of Essex... Being weak of Body but of sound mind & memory Do for the Settlement of what worldly Estate God has graciously given me make & ordain my Last will and Testament in form & manner following. Imp. I will that my just debts & the charges of a decent Funeral be well paid & Discharged.*
>
> *Item I Give & bequeath to **my Beloved wife Mary Twiss** the whole of my Household Goods and what yet remains in her Brothers hand of the Legacy to her left by **Her Father Douty** to be to her and at her disposal forever. I also give unto her, my 2nd wife, the one third part of the income and improvement of my Real Estate, to be yearly to her paid by my **Son William Twiss**, For her comfortable subsistance during her natural life and one third part of the produce of the ? or that shall be raised upon the Estate, yearly to be to her rendered by my said son during the term of her life.*
>
> *Item I give to **my three Daughters, Ruth, Mary & Charity** Five Pounds Lawful money Each, to be paid by my Executor hereafter named the one half within two years after my decease and the other half two years after my wifes decease.*
>
> *Item I give to my **Two Daughters, Jane & Lydia** Seven Pounds Lawful money, Each, that Fourteen Pounds Lawfull money in equal shares To be to them paid the one half within two years after my decease and the other half within two years after my wifes Decease.*
>
> *Item I give unto **my Son William Twiss** the Whole Remainder of my estate Reall and personall to be to him and his heirs forever, the rendering to his mother as above provided, and paying to his sisters the Legacies above expressed, and twenty shillings lawful money to **my grandaughter Lydia Flint**.*
>
> *Item I do hereby constitute and appoint my Son William Twiss above named to be the sole executor of this my last will and testament. In Witness whereof I have hereunto set my hand & seal the Twenty sixth day of July Anno Dom. 1758.*
>
> *Signed Seald & declared by William Twiss to be his last will & Testament, in presence of Joseph Purdy, Peter Twiss, Benjamin Twiss. Signed, William Twiss & seal.*

Children, by first wife, Lydia (Marsh), from will and Salem VR

    i.   JANE^3, b. c1724; named in father's will in 1758.

    ii.   LYDIA, b. c1726; m. at Salem, 25 Jan 1745/6, WILLIAM FLINT, husbandman, b. at Reading, Mass., 14 Apr 1714, s. of Dea. William & Abigail (Nichols) Flint of Reading (Perley, *Hist. of Salem*, II:277). Daughter Lydia named in grandfather, William Twiss's will in 1758.

Children by second wife, Mary (Douty), named in will:

16.   iii.   WILLIAM, JR, bpt. 17 Mar 1729; m. ELIZABETH COOK, JR.

    iv.   RUTH, b. c1730; m. at Salem, 10 July 1749, JOHN NEEDHAM, bpt. at Salem, 27 July 1729, s. of George & Rachel (Gould) Needham (ibid., II:210).

    v.   MARY, b. c1731; perhaps the Mary Twiss who m. (1) at Danvers, 2 Nov 1762, ISAAC KNAPP, b. at Salem, 9 Nov 1730, s. of Ebenezer & Jane (Hanover) Knapp (Arthur Mason Knapp, *The Knapp Family in America* [Boston, 1909], 12); m. (2) Isaac Very, b. 1745, s. of Isaac & Elizabeth (Giles) Very; d. 1831. He m. (2) Margaret Brown; (3) Rachel Jones (Vinton, *Giles Memorial*, 47). Child of Mary (Twiss) and Isaac Very, surname Very: 1. Isaac, b. 31 Oct 1766; d. at Guadaloupe, West Indies, 1 May 1805; m. Hannah Twiss (?).

    vi.   CHARITY, b. c1733; m. (int.) at Danvers, 19 Feb 1756, JOHN TWISS, JR., son son of John^3 Twiss (see, #8 below).

(To be continued)

LIBRARY RENOVATIONS

In December, the Lynnfield Public Library will begin a major renovation project, that is expected to continue for about a year. These renovations are part of a 4.4 million dollar town-wide project to upgrade and repair its public buildings.

Due to state statutes, all buildings will be completely accessible to handicapped persons. The renovations at the library will inclue a 3-story elevator in the center of the building, with two lavatories beside it. A long ramp will traverse the front of the building. The basement level will be converted to public use, with a new exit at the rear out to the parking lot. Adult fiction and biography will be placed in that lower level, which will have carpeting and new lighting. The present work room, or book-processing area, and the Library Director's office will be moved upstairs to where the Genealogy Room is now. The Genealogy Room will be moved downstairs where the director's office is now. There will be new carpeting throughout, new lighting, and the entire building will be centrally air-conditioned. See page 220 for "Good News and Bad News."

HENRY COLLINS OF LYNN AND HIS DESCENDANTS - continued

By Carolyn Martino and Marcia Lindberg

2. **HENRY^2 COLLINS** (Henry^1) was born at Stepney Parish, county Middlesex, England, 29 October 1629 and was baptized there 4 November 1629 at "5 days old" (Stepney Parish Register [Mormon Microfilm, #0595417]). He died at Lynn, in the Massachusetts Bay Colony, as "father of Henry, 3d," on 14 October 1722, at the age of 92 (Bible of Charles S. Viall, cited in LVR). His wife, whom he married about 1650, was probably MARY TOLMAN, who was born about 1632/3, either in England or in Dorchester, Mass., the youngest child of Thomas and Katherine Tolman. Thomas Tolman's will names "daughter Mary Collins" ("Tolman Genealogy," *New England Historical and Genealogical Register*; hereafter, *Register*, XIV [1860]:247). There are two deaths given in Lynn Vital Records for Mary Collins: one gives "Mary, w. Henry, Feb 27, 1713/4" (Bible Record of Charles S. Viall); the other gives "Mary, mother of Henry, 3d, Feb 14 1723." These dates seem to be irreconcilable, but there was no other known Mary Collins in Lynn at this time.

Henry Collins, Jr. (so-called until the death of his father when he became Henry, Sr.) was a carpenter by trade. He was active in the Town affairs of Lynn, working his way up from Constable in 1691, Fence Viewer in 1693/4, Surveyor of Highways in 1696-8, Collector of Rates in 1697, and finally to the position of Selectman (*Records of Ye Towne Meetings of Lyn*; hereafter *Lynn Town Records*, Vols. I and II, various pages).

On the 6th of November 1663, Henry Collins, Jr. and his brother John Collins, "carpenters," bought for 50 pounds sterling, from Robert Rand, 9 acres of land, including a house and orchard. Witnesses were Andrew Mansfield and Joseph Collins. The deed was recorded at Salem, 17: 10: 1667 (Essex Deeds, 3:23). On the 7th of April 1692, Henry^2 Collins (by then called Henry, Sr.) and his wife Mary, gave by deed to his son, Henry, 3rd (then called Henry, Jr.), 10 acres of land "on which son Henry's house now stands," bounded by Chadwell's lot, Henry, Sr.'s lot and the county highway; also 3 acres of salt marsh that Henry bought from Capt. Thomas Marshall, bordered by Laughton's Lane and Pines River (ibid., 10:154).

On the 27th of November 1694, Henry^2 Collins made an agreement with his brothers Joseph and Benjamin, to divide the lands that their father had given them in common. Henry received 28 acres (see transcription under Henry^1 [*TEG*, X:149-151]).

At a town meeting of Lynn, on 26 September 1717, Henry Collins was allowed to enlarge his pew in the church:

> *"Whereas a pew formerly granted to Henry Collins Jr... and the town now being informed he had given the same to his sons, Henry Collins, Eleazer Collins, and his sons in law, viz. Moses Hudson and John Newhall amongst them and there being 4 families, therefore voted; that said Henry Collins, Eleazer Collins, Moses Hudson and John Newhall hath liberty to enlarge that pew beginning at the back part of the "sque" next the window and so upon a square formed so far as to leave a suitable allowance as the Committee for the Meeting House shall order and to maintain the windows against it"* (Lynn Town Records, III:5).

There is no will on file for Henry^2 Collins at Essex Probate Court or at Suffolk Probate Court.

Children, recorded in Lynn Vital Records, as children of Henry, Jr. Dates in parentheses are those given in the Essex County Court Records (*Register*, VI [1851]:95).

6. i. HENRY³, b, 2:8m:1651 (Oct 2, 1651); m. (1) HANNAH LAMSON; m. (2) SARAH HEIRES (AYERS).

ii. HANNAH, b. 1:12m:1659 (Feb 1, 1660); d. at Stonington, CT, 27 Dec 1723; m. at Lynn, 8 Jan 1677, THOMAS BROWN, JR. (LVR), b. c1657; d. at Stonington, CT, 27 Dec 1723, s. of Thomas & Mary (Newhall) Brown of Lynn (Cyrus Henry Brown, *Brown Genealogy*, II Part I:15, 17; LVR). [Cyrus Brown is in error when he says Hannah was dau. of John Collins. John's dau. Hannah was born in 1674.] Children, b. at Stonington (surname Brown): 1. <u>Samuel</u>, b. 8 Dec 1678. 2. <u>Hannah</u>, b. 5 Dec 1680. 3. <u>Mary</u>, b. 26 May 1683; m. at Stonington, Thomas York (ibid.). 4. <u>Sarah</u>, b. 8 July 1686; d. y. 5. <u>Jerusha</u>, b. 25 Dec 1688. 6. <u>Sarah</u>, b. 11 July 1689. 7. <u>Thomas</u>, b. 14 Feb 1692; m. at Stonington, Deborah Holdredge . 8. <u>Elizabeth</u>, b. 9 May 1694; m. at Stonington, James Pendleton. 9. <u>Daniel</u>, b. 9 Oct 1694; m. at Ston., Mary Breed. 10. <u>Priscilla</u>, b. 30 Jan 1699. 11. <u>Humphrey</u>, b. 16 Sept 1701; m. at Stonington, Tabitha Holdridge (ibid.).

iii. JOHN, b. 19:6m:1662 (Aug. 19, 1662).

iv. SARAH, b. 9:11m:1665 (Jan. 9, 1666); m. at Lynn, 12 Nov 1685, MOSES HUDSON, b. at Lynn, 15:5m:1658; d. there 27:7m:1738, s. of Jonathan Hudson (LVR). Children, b. at Lynn (surname Hudson): 1. <u>Sarah</u>, b. 29 Aug 1687; bur. at Lynn, 15 Sept 1687 (ibid.). 2. <u>Sarah</u>, b. 12 Oct 1688; m. at Lynn, 8 Aug 1711, Jonathan Norwood (ibid.). 3. <u>Ruth</u>, b. 12 May 1690; d. bef. 1693. 4. <u>Jonthan</u>, b. 15 Sept 1681; m. at Lynn, 14 Nov 1720, Mary Hathorn (ibid.). 5. <u>Ruthe</u>, b. 4 Mar 1693/4; d. 22 Apr 1694 (ibid.). 6. <u>Moses</u>, b. 8 Sept 1695; d. 20 Jan 1695/6 (ibid.). 7. <u>Moses</u>, b. 29 Sept 1696. 8. <u>Mary</u>, b. 27 May 1699; m. at Lynn, 27 Nov 1722, Ralph Hartt (ibid.). 9. <u>Thomas</u>, b. 14 Apr 1702; m. 5 Jan 1725/6, Mary Mils (ibid.). 10. <u>Joseph</u>, b. 15 Oct 1704. 11. <u>Elizabeth</u>, b. 14 July 1707; m. 7 May 1727, Joshua Pratt (ibid.). 12. <u>John</u>, b. 27 Sept 1709.

v. REBECCA, b. 9 June 1668; d. at Lynn, 3 Feb 1742/3 (LVR); m. there, 4 Mar 1691, JOHN NEWHALL, 4th (LVR), b. at Lynn, 11 Oct 1664; d. there, 3 May 1718, s. of John & Elizabeth (Normanton) Newhall (LVR: *Essex Institute Historical Collections*, 18 [1881]:32). John Newhall's will names "wife Rebecca, and a legacy of about 20 lbs, given by honored father Henry Collins, yet in revertion" (Essex Probate, 19321). Children, b. at Lynn (surname Newhall): 1. <u>John</u>, b. 22 Dec 1692; m. at Lynn, 7 Jan 1719/20, Lydia Scarlet of Malden (LVR). 2. <u>Henry</u>, b. 7 June 1695; m., as "Henry Newel of Boston", 22 Nov 1722, Susannah Swift of Dorchester (Dorchester VR in *21st Report of the Record Commissioners*; hereafter BRC, 110). 3. <u>Eleazer</u>, b. 20 Apr 1698; m. as Eliezer Newel, 15 Mar 1721, Mary Grice of Boston (*BRC*, 20:102). 4. <u>Increase</u>, b. 19 Mar 1699/1700; d. 31 May 1713 (LVR). 5. <u>Sarah</u>, b. 19 July 1703. 6. <u>Nathaniel</u>, b. 7 Oct 1706; d. at Lynn, 29 July 1737, age 31 y, 10 m (LVR). 7. <u>David</u>, b. 29 Aug 1710; m. (1) (int.), 14 May 1738, Mary Burchstead; m. (2), April 1745, Elizabeth Merchant? (ibid.).

7. vi. ELEAZER, b. 9:8m:1673 (Oct 9, 1673); m. REBECKA NEWHALL.

3. **JOHN² COLLINS** (Henry¹) was born at Stepney Parish, county Middlesex, England, on 14 January 1631, and was baptized there, 22 January 1631 at 8 days old (Stepney Parish Register [Mormon Microfilm, #0595417]). He died "being cast away at sea" about 22 December 1679 (*Probate Records of Essex County*, III:372-3; *EQCR*, VII:412). He married, at Lynn, about 1655, as her first husband, ABIGAIL JOHNSON, daughter of Richard and Alice Johnson. Richard Johnson bequeathed 5 pounds to his daughter Abigail Collins (*Probate Records of Essex County*, II:77). After John Collins's death, his widow Abigail Collins married, at Lynn, 3 March 1680/1, as his second wife, THOMAS FARRAR, who died at Lynn 23 February 1694 (LVR; Thomas Farrar's will, Essex Probate 9263). Thomas Farrar's first wife was Elizabeth (surname unknown).

Little is recorded about John Collins, except for the births of his sixteen children. His name appears, with his brothers, Benjamin, Henry and Joseph, as "Troopers of Lynn" on 29 May 1679 (Mass. Archives, 69:228). A trooper was a member of the elite horsemen of the local militia.

Although there are no deeds registered at the Essex County registry, some inferences may be made from the inventory of John's estate, which consisted of houses, orchards, 36 acres of land, part of a saw mill and linen and woolen cloth.

Administration on John's estate was granted 29:4m:1680 to Abigail Collins, widow. An inventory was brought in and allowed, and an agreement was drawn up by the widow with the consent of the children and relations of the father and mother:

> "Inventory of the estate of John Collins of Lynn, who departed this life about Dec. 22, 1679, as being cast away at sea, and dyed intestate, taken Mar. 27, 1680, by Andrew Mansfield and Ralph King and presented by Abigail the widow of the deceased: waring apparel that was not lost at sea, 3 pounds, 8 shillings; Bedding, bedsteads, sheets, curtains, valance, 17 pounds, 1 shillings; cupboard, cloth & a chest, 3 pounds, 5 shillings; tables & joined stools, 1 pound, 12 shillings; an old cupboard, cradle, chairs and wheels, l pound, 5 shillings; 5 cows, 2 oxen, 2 steers, 33 pounds, 10 shillings; 19 sheep, 9 pounds, 10 sh., pewter and a lattin pan, l pound, 15 shillings; brass, 2 pounds, iron pot and kettles, frying pan and a morter, 1 pound, 14 shillings, 3 pounds, 14 shillings, dog irons, pot hooks, a pot hanger, 1 pound, 5 shillings; armes, 4 pounds; stiliard, 10 shillings, scythes & sickles, 10 shillings, 5 pounds; smoothing iron, 3 shillings; wooden ware, 10 shillings; tools and old iron, 1 pound, 15 shilling, 2 pounds, 8 shillings; a hat, cupboard and a box, 12 shillings; plows, carts, yokes, chain, 2 pounds, 2 shillings, 2 pounds, 14 sh. woolen and linen yarn, l pound, 6 shillings; cards, 3 shillings; Bibles, 8 shillings; l pound, 17 shillings; pair of tongs & a fire shovel, 3 shillings; Pork, l pound, 10 shillings; barrels, 12 shillings, 2 pounds, 5 shillings; grain, 3 pounds, a fan, sadle, old boots & flax, l pound, 4 pounds; loom, harnice & sleighs, 2 pounds, an hour glass & a sieve, 2 shilling, 2 pounds, 2 sh. the land the houses stand upon with the houses & orchard, 80 pounds, 32 acres of land and meadow, 160 pounds, 4 acres and a half of meadow in Wigwam meadow, 13 pounds, 10 shillings; pair of scales, weight and adz, 5 shillings; money, 5 pounds. a 6th part in the saw mill, 5 pounds; woolen cloth, 2 pounds, more linen cloth, 10 shillings, 2 pounds, 10 sh; an old chest & a box & and inkhorn, 3 shillings, 6 pence; 2 mares, l pound, 10 sh. one grindlestone, 10 shillings; a warming pan, 2 shillings, 12 shillings. Total, 365 pounds, 1 sh, 6 d." (*EQCR*, 33:78).

The inventory was attested at Salem court on 30:4:1680, by Abigail Collins, who was appointed administratrix of her husband's estate.

ADMINISTRATION OF THE ESTATE OF JOHN[2] COLLINS

> "*John Collins of Lynn who died, intestate, having been cast away at sea, and leaving a wife and twelve children, the widow with her relations, judging it most meet, desired **Abigail Collins, Samuel Collins, Joseph Collins, Andrew Mansfield, Henry Collins, sr., and Henry Collins, Jr.**, to divide his estate, which they have do as follows: to the widow, all the movable estate, both stock and store within doors and without as her free estate, 111 pounds, 11 shillings, 6 pence, which being taken out of the sum of the inventory, the houses, lands and meadow remain to be disposed, which amount to 253 pounds, 10 shillings, of which one third part goes to the widow during her life and the other two thirds to the two eldest sons, Samuel and Joseph Collins, equally, as they come to age. Samuel having a good trade as a gunsmith, maketh up to him his double portion; and this to be understood, the widow to have the use of the whole estate until the two said sons come of age, and then to have only her thirds, and at her death the whole estate to the two sons, they to pay to each of their brothers and sisters, namely, **Benjamin, Daniel, Nathaniel and John, Elizabeth, Mary, Hannah, Lois, and Alice Collins**, ten pounds in current pay, as they come to age, their sister **Abigail Townsend** having already received her portion. If any of the children should die before they come of age, then their portion [is to be divided] equally to the surviving children, also that Samuel and Joseph Collins are not to leave their mother, but to live with her and carry on her business for her upon the consideration of their having the housing and lands as aboresaid, the house and lands to stand bound for the payment of the children's portions.*
>
> *The eldest son giving his consent to the above agreement in the Salem court 30:4:1680, it was allowed and confirmed*" (EQCR, 33:11, 101).

The son, John Collins, named in the settlement of John Collins, Sr.'s estate above, was christened William at birth, but after the death of his father and brother John, Jr., by drowning at sea, William appears to have changed his name to John.

John Collins's mother, Ann, bequeathed 3 pounds each to her grandchildren, children of "my son John Collins, deceased and not named in my will before, viz: Elizabeth, Mary, Daniel, Hannah, Lois... as a testimony of my love to them who were suddenly deprived of their father and of his estate." And to her two grandsons, sons of John Collins deceased, viz.: Samuel and Joseph Collins.. 5 shillings each...(Essex Probate, 6028).

Children, recorded in Lynn VR; dates in parentheses are from Essex County Court Records in *The Register*, V [1851]:95):

    i.   MARY[3], b. 26:9m:1656 (Nov 26); d. 27:12m:1656
    ii.   JOHN, b. 17:10m:1657 (Dec 17); d. 27:10m:1657
8.   iii.   SAMUEL, b. 19:3m:1659 (May 19); m. (1) HANNAH ----; m. (2), REBECCA (HUSSEY) HOWLAND.
    iv.   ABIGAIL, b. 23:1m:1660/61 (March 23, 1661); d. at Lynn, 22 Feb 1693; m. at Lynn, 18 July 1678, ANDREW TOWNSEND (LVR), b. 1654 (deposition); d. at Lynn, 10 Feb 1692/3, s. of Thomas & Mary (Newgate?) Townsend (Charles Henry Townshend, *The Townsend Family of Lynn*, Rev. 3d ed. [New Haven, c1875], 93-4). Children, b. at Lynn (surname Townsend):
        1. <u>Thomas</u>, b. 12 June 1679; m. (1) Elizabeth ----; m. (2), Elizabeth Orris.

                      2. Abigail, b. 23 Jan 1680; m. Nathaniel Evens of Malden. 3. Elizabeth, b. 21 May 1683. 4. Mary, b. 7 July; d. 10 Dec 1685. 5. Andrew, b. 13 Feb 1686/7. 6. Daniel, b. 6 Dec 1688; m. a wife who m (2) a Mr. Farmer; no descendants. 7. David, b. 6 Apr 1692; m. 1 July 1714, Mabel Shippee (Information on children from Henry F. Waters, "Sketch of Townsend Families of Lynn, *EIHC*, XX [1883]:37, 40; and C. H. Townsend, *The Townshend Family*; 55-56; 93, 99).

	v.	JOHN, b. 10:7m:1662 (LVR erroneously gives 1762); was shipwrecked at sea with his father in 1679 ("Collins Family," 8).
9.	vi.	JOSEPH, b. 6:4m:1664 (6 June); m.? MARGARET (DOWNING?).
	vii.	ELIZABETH, b. 8 Apr 1666; d. prob. at Pilesgrove Twp, Salem, N.J.; m. c1688, ELISHA BASSETT, b. at Lynn, c1649; d. prob. at Pilesgrove Twp (Catherine Soleman Chandler, *The Bassett Family, Lynn, Mass. to Salem County, NJ* [Salem, NJ, 1964], 14). Children, b. at Lynn (surname Bassett): 1. Hannah, b. 15 Dec 1689. 2. Elizabeth, b. 15 Apr 1691; named in grandmother Ann Collin's will in 1694; m. Peter Keene (*Report of the Reunion of the Bassett Family* [Woodmont, CT, 1902], 15). 3. Elisha, b. 21 Aug 1692; m. at Pilesgrove Twp, c1717/18, Abigail Davis (Chandler, 14). 4. Danell, b. 20 Oct 1694; m. Mary Lawrence (ibid., 33). ?6. Zebedee, b. 1680 (*Report of Reunion*, 15). ?7. William, b. 1685; m. Rebecca (ibid.).
	viii.	BENJAMIN, b. 19:7m:1667; named in adm. of father's estate, 1680.
	ix.	MARY, b. 20:12m:1669; m. (1) at Marblehead, MA, 24 Jan 1688, JOSEPH NORMAN; m. (2), at Marblehead, HENRY HOOPER, s. of Robert & Elizabeth (Fletcher) Hooper (*Compendium of American Genealogy*, III:147).
10.	x.	DANIEL, b. 3;1m;1670/71; m. REBECCA CLEMENT.
11.	xi.	NATHANIEL, b. 1:12m:1672; m. MARY SILSBEE.
	xii.	HANNAH, b. 26 Apr 1674.
	xiii.	SARAH, b. 26 Dec 1675; d. at Lynn 6 Jun 1676; named in widow Sarah Collins will in 1673.
	xiv.	LOIS, b. 12 May 1677; m. (1) at Boston, MA, 15 Dec 1698, DAVID ADAMS, b. at Boston, 23 May 1676; d. bef. 1705, s. of David & Hannah (Gannett?) Adams. Lois (Collins) Adams m. (2), at Boston, 8 Jan 1705, WILLIAM WATERS (Boston VR). Children by 1st husband, b. at Boston (surname Adams): 1. Hannah, b. 21 Feb 1699. 2. Nathaniel, b. 29 Oct 1701; m. ?19 July 1727, Elizabeth Hughes. Children by 2nd husband, b. at Boston (surname Waters): 3. William, b. 10 Apr 1707; 4. Lois, b. 15 June 1715.
	xv.	ALICE, b. 30 Apr 1678.
12.	xvi.	WILLIAM (renamed JOHN), b. 28 June 1679; m. SUSANNAH DAGGAT.

4. JOSEPH² COLLINS (Henry¹) was born, probably at Lynn, Mass., in 1642/3, according to a court deposition (see below). He died there, between 16 May and 2 November of 1724, the dates of the writing and recording of his will (Essex Probate, 6082). He married, first, at Lynn, about 1668, SARAH SILSBEE, born probably at Salem, Mass., about 1646, and died at Lynn, 25 February 1682 (LVR). She was the daughter of Henry and Dorothy Silsbee ("Henry Silsbee and Some of His Descendants," *EIHC*, XVII [1880]:258). Joseph Collins married, second, at Lynn, 15 Oct 1684, MARIAH SMITH. Mariah was born at Ipswich, Mass., 28 February 1664, as "Moriah Smith," daughter of John and Martha (Colley?) Smith, (Court Record cited in Ipswich VR; Abraham Hannett, *The Hammett Papers* (Baltimore, MD, 1980), 336). Clarence Torrey's *New England Marriages before 17* gives Cooley as the probable maiden name of Mariah's mother. Mariah died after 1724, when Joseph's will was probated (see below).

Joseph Collins was a housewright, or carpenter and builder, by trade, as described on deeds at the Essex County Registry of Deeds at Salem. He owned considerable property, and was called "Senior" after his son Joseph, came of age. He served the town of Lynn in many capacities: as perambulator in

1694, surveyor in 1697-98, and fence viewer in 1700. He also served on the grand jury in 1700 and 1708 (*Lynn Town Records*, I & II, various pages).

As a young man, on 25 June 1672, Joseph Collins was brought before the court for drinking "17 quarts of Rum." It was stated that his wife also drank. At the same court, Henry Collins, John Collins, Henry Collins, Jr. and Joseph Collins petitioned the court against John Hathorne for abuses of over drinking at his house (*EQCR*, V:60). It appears that the close-knit Collins family blamed the innkeeper rather than their own brother and son. Joseph apparently learned his lesson, as he later adopted the Quaker religion. His wife, at this time, was Sarah Silsbee, who died after 1679 and before 1685.

Joseph served in King Philip's War, being credited with one pound, ten shillings, on 24 June 1676, for service under Capt. Nicholas Manning (George Madison Bodge, *Soldiers in King Philips War* [Baltimore, 1976], 278). On 4 June 1685, he was one of 25 soldiers from Lynn who petitioned the General Court for land promised them for service in Nipmugg country and at the Narragansett Fort (ibid., 406).

On the 24th of March 1689, Joseph deposed in a case concerning Edward Richard's estate in Lynn, that he was about 47 years of age, which would make his birth date 1642/3.

In 1713, the town of Lynn voted that Joseph Collins, Sr.'s two daughters have liberty to set up seats in the Meeting House (*Lynn Town Records*, II:71). In 1716/17, Joseph Collins, Sr. and his brother Samuel, were listed as Quakers, and had their taxes for repairing the Meeting House abated (ibid., II:93).

During his life time, Joseph made gifts of land to his three eldest sons, William, Joseph and Ezekiel, as stated in his will of 1724 (see below).

On 20 February 1721/2, Joseph Collins signed a deed of gift to his son Ezekiel. The deed was recorded at the Essex County Registry the same day:

> *I, Joseph Collins, Senior, of Lynn, housewright, for love and good will and affection, to my son Ezekiel Collins of Lynn, yeoman, also in consideration that my said son, Ezekiel Collins, re his heirs, executors and administrators shall and do comfortably maintain me and his mother my* **wife Merriah** *during our and each of our natural lives with all things necessary for our comfortable subsistance and we to live in the dwelling house we now live in and at mine and my wives decease to afford us a decent burial at his own cost and charge, and also that my said son, Ezekial Collins shall do well and truly pay or cause to be paid within 3 years after my and my wives decease unto my children hereafter named, the several sums hereafter described and set forth in such money as shall then at which time of said payment thereof pass from man to man, viz: to my* **son Ebenezer Collins**, *10 pounds, to my* **son Daniel Collins**, *10 pounds, to my* **daughter Ann Ingalls**, *11 pounds, to my* **daughter Dorothy Gray**, *7 pounds, to my* **daughter Sarah Richards**, *7 pounds, to my* **daughter Mary Farrar**, *15 pounds, to my* **daughter Elizabeth Graves**, *15 pounds, to my* **daughter Martha Odell**, *15 pounds to my* **granddaughter Ruth Graves**, *10 pounds... and unto my* **son Ezekiel** *his heirs etc. all my housing and lands, both upland, meadow, salt marsh, and pasture... in Lynn, with all my moveable estate except what is within my dwelling house the which is moveable to be my said wife to give and dispose as she shall see fit. But my said son Ezekiel Collins not to come into the actual or full posession of said above granted premises in his own right until after my and my said wife's decease, neither do I debar myself from selling any part of my estate if I have occasion. But in the meantime, my said son to have the improvement thereof as he shall think best and after my and my wife's decease all shall be to my said son Ezekiel Collins, his heirs and*

assigns forever. Signed, 20 February 1721/2. Witnesses: Edward Thompson, Benjamin Sewall (Essex Deeds, 40:121).

WILL OF JOSEPH COLLINS

Dated 16 May 1724; probated 2 November 1724 (Essex Probate, 6082)

Calling himself a house carpenter, aged and weak, but of perfect memory, he instructed his heirs to pay his funeral charges. Bequests were:

> *...to my beloved **wife Merryah Collins**, all my moveables and improvement of all the rest of my estate during her natural life.*
> *... to my **3 sons, William, Joseph & Ezekiel**, 1 shilling, they having received their portions in times past.*
> *... to **son Daniel**, 10 pounds and what I've alread given him.*
> *... to **daughter Ann Ingols**, 12 pounds*
> *... to **daughter Dorothy Gray**, 6 pounds*
> *... to **daughter Sarah Richards**, 6 pounds*
> *... to my other **3 daughters, Mary Farrar, and Elizabeth Graves and Martha ODell**, each 12 pounds*
> *... to my **granddaughter Ruth Graves**, 1 shilling, having given her deceased mother her portion in times past*
> *... to my **son Ebenezer**, all my estate except that mentioned above, and I appoint son Ebenezer to be my sole executor.*

Witnesses: Theophilus Burrill, John Lewis and Joseph Mansfield.

Attached to the above will, are the following receipts:

10 Nov 1727
Samuel & Elizabeth (her mark) Graves
    Witnesses: James Brown, Jn Fuller
Robard (his mark) & Dority (her mark) Gray
    Witnesses: James Browne, Jn Fuller
Crispus (mark & seal) and Sarah (mark & seal) Richards
    Witnesses: James Browne, Jn Fuller
Nahemiah (Mark & Seal) and Ann (mark & seal) Inguls
    Witnesses: James Browne, Jn Fuller
15 Nov 1727
John (seal) and Mary (seal) Farrar
    Witnesses: Samuel Webber, Moriah Collins
William and Martha Odell
    Witnesses: Samuel Webber, Moriah Collins

On the 2nd of November, Ebenezer Collins, as Principal, Francis Norwood and Jacob Collins as sureties, posted a bond of 1000 pounds for the last will and testament of Ebenezer's father, Joseph Collins, late of Lynn (ibid.).

On 10 November 1724, 8 days after Joseph Collins's will was probated, Ebenezer Collins mortgaged "the homestead of my honored father Joseph Collins, Sr." for 400 pounds, to his great-nephew, Jacob Collins, son of John Collins (see details under account of Ebenezer Collins, following). This was evidently undertaken so that Ebenezer could pay off the legacies stated in his father's will, receipts for which are given above.

On 16 June 1729, Daniel Collins quitclaimed to Jacob Newhall, for 10 pounds, real estate "a legacy of my father Joseph Collins, late of Lynn." Witnesses were Ezekiel Collins and Samuel Graves (ibid.).

Children, by first wife, Sarah (Silsbee), b. at Lynn (dates in parentheses from Essex County Court records):

i. SARA^3, b. 18:6m:1669; d. 19:7m:1669.

ii. JOSEPH, b. 16:7m:1671; d. bef. 1695, when 2nd Joseph born.

iii. HENRY, b. 23:9m:1673 (23 Nov 1672); d. bef. 1721 (not in father's deed).

iv. ANN, b. 13:12 m:1673 (13 Feb 1674); bur. at Lynn, 19 June 1754 (Zaccheus Collins Diary, cited in LVR); m. c1691, NATHANIEL INGALLS, b. prob. at Lynn, c1660; d. there 4:10m:1737 (LVR), s. of Robert & Sarah (Harker) Ingalls (Charles Burleigh, *Genealogy & History of the Ingalls Family in America* [Malden, 1903], 23). Children, as given in Burleigh, 1st 3 b. at Lynn (surname Ingalls): 1. Nathaniel, b. 25 Dec 1692; m. 1 Jan 1722, Tabitha Lewis (LVR). 2. Sarah, b. 14 Apr 1693; d. at Lynn, 25 Nov 1761 (LVR); m. at Lynn, 1 Nov 1715, Samuel Ingalls (ibid.). 3. Ruthe, b. 29 Jan 1695; m. at Lynn, 22 Mar 1711/12, John Berry of Salem (ibid.). 4. Tabitha, b. c1700; m. (int. at Lynn), 8 Sept 1723, John Williams. 5. Meriah, b. c1702; ;m. (int. at Lynn), 25 Jan 1723/4,Samuel Berry of Salem. 6. Joseph, b. c1705; m. at Lynn, 3 Nov 1726, Rebecca Collins, b. 4 Apr 1706, dau. of Eleazer & Rebecca (Newhall) Collins (ibid.). 7. William, b. c1708; m. at Lynn, 13 Nov 1729, Zeruiah Norwood. 8. Henry, b. c1712; m. at Lynn, 26 Dec 1734, Sarah Richards. 9. Hannah, b. c1715; m. at Lynn, 30 Mar 1735, Daniel Hitchings. 10. Jacob, b. c1717; m. at Lynn, 17 Nov 1737, Mary Tucker.

v. DOROTHY/DORATY, b. 6 Mar 1675/6; d. at Lynn, "wife of Robert Gray," 23:11m:1729/30 (Z. Collins Diary; LVR). She m. at Lynn, 19 Oct 1700, ROBERT GRAY (ROBERD GREAY), who d. at Lynn, 28:7:1731. Robert & Dorothy Gray signed a release on her father's estate. Children, b. at Lynn (surname Gray): 1. Dorothy, b. 23 Aug 1701; m. at Lynn, 30 Oct 1723, John Tarbox. 2. Deborah, b. 24 Nov 1704; m. (int.) at Lynn), 21 June 1724, Benjamin Tarbox. 3. Robert, b. 27 June 1708; m. (1) at Lynn, 22 May 1732, Elizabeth Allen; m. (2) at Lynn, 11 Dec 1755, Anna Newhall. 4. Sarah, b. 25 Nov 1713.

vi. SARAH, b. 10 Aug 1678; d. "old" 23 June 1757 (Z. Collins Diary; LVR); m. at Lynn, 21 Dec 1702 CRISPUS (CRISPAS) RICHARDS (LVR), b. at Lynn, 30 Oct 1681; d. there 17 May 1763, s. of John & Mary (Brewer) Richards (LVR). Sarah & Crispus signed release on her father's estate 1727. Children, from Manuscript of Winifred Lovering Holman, at New England Historic Genealogical Society in Boston (surname Richards): 1. Joseph, b. c1703; m. Mary Bowden. 2. Esther, b. c1705; m. at Lynn, 7 June 1723, Aaron Estes, "a stranger." 3. John, b. c1707; ?m. at Lynn 25 Jan 1732/33, Lydia Phillips. 4. Sarah, b. c1709; m. 26 Dec 1734, Henry Ingalls. 5. Hannah, b. c1711; d. at Lynn, 25 Mar 1740; m. there, 30 Mar 1738, John Stocker. 6. Mary, b. c1713; d. at Lynn, 30 June 1758. 7. Deborah, b. c1715; alive unm. 1756. (Note: Rev. A. Morse, in his *Genealogical Register of the Descendants of Several Puritan Families*, lists only 4 children for Crispus and Sarah (Collins) Richards: Joseph, John, Richard & Ester).

vii. ESTER, b. 2 Jan 1679; d. bef. 1721 (not named in deed of gift).

Children by 2nd wife, Mariah (Smith), b. at Lynn:

    viii.   RUTH, b. 26 Oct 1685; d. bef. 1715; m. at Lynn, 9 Jan 1710, as his 1st wife, THOMAS GRAVES, b. at Lynn, 16 Dec 1686, s. of Samuel and Sarah (Brewer) Graves. Thomas m. (2) at Lynn, 22 Feb 1715, Ruth Taylor of Andover, Mass., by whom he had 2 children. child of Thomas and Ruth (Collins) Graves, b. at Lynn (surname Graves): 1. Ruth, b. 10 Jan 1710; m. 3 Dec 1729, Isaak Buck of Woburn, Mass. (Kennth Vance Graves, *Samuel Graves, 1630 Settler of Lynn, Massachusetts and his Descendants* [Wrentham, Mass., 1985], 15). Ruth was named in grandmother Ann Collins's will.

    ix.   MARY, b. 16 Jan 1687/8; m. at Lynn, 2 Oct 1715, JOHN FARRAR "of Great Britain" (LVR). John was no doubt connected with Thomas Farrar of Lynn who m. (2) Abigail (Johnson) Collins, widow of John^2 Collins (see above). Mary and John Farrar signed release to her father's estate, 1727. Child, b. at Lynn (surname Farrar): 1. John, b. 19 July 1716.

13.   x.   WILLIAM, b. 14 Jan 1689/90; m. ABIGAIL RICHARDS.

    xi.   ELIZABETH, b. 23 Dec 1692; m. (int. at Lynn), 7 Oct 1716, SAMUEL GRAVES, b. at Lynn, 1 June 1692; s. of Mark & Rebecca Graves (ibid.). Samuel & Elizabeth Graves signed release of her father's will 1727. K. V. Graves gives 2 children: 1. Desire, b. at Lynn 1724, and 2. Samuel, b. at Reading, 8 Mar 1736 (12 years apart!).

14.   xii.   JOSEPH, b. 26 Mar 1695; m. PATIENCE BENIGHTON.

15.   xiii.   EZEKIEL, b. 17 Feb 1697/8; m. REBECCA GRAVES.

    xiv.   MARTHA, b. 1 Apr 1700; d. at Lynn, 29:6m:1731 (Z. Collins Diary; LVR); m. (int. at Lynn), 10 Dec 1720, WILLIAM ODELL of Marblehead, Mass. He prob. m. (2) at Marblehead, 6 Aug 1733, Rachel Merry (Marblehead Vital Records). Children of William & Martha (Collins) Odell, b. at Marblehead (surname Odell): 1. William, b. 30 Aug 1724. 2. William, bpt. 4 Sept 1726. William & Martha Odell signed a release to her father's estate 1727.

16.   xv.   EBENEZER, b. c1702; m. (1) MARY CHADWELL; m. (2) MARY MERREY.

    xvi.   DANIEL, b. c1704; named in father's deed of gift in 1721 and father's will in 1724. On 16 June 1729, Daniel signed a release for the ten pounds "a legacy of my father, Joseph Collins," witnessed by Ezekiel Collins and Samuel Graves (Essex Probate, 6082). No further record found.

5. **BENJAMIN^2 COLLINS** (Henry^1) was born, probably at Lynn, about 1650, and died at Colchester, Connecticut about 1711 (see below). He married, first, at Lynn, 25 September 1673, PRISCILLA KIRTLAND, b. probably on Long Island c1645-50 (Mary Walton Ferris, *Dawes-Gates Ancestral Lines*, [1931], II:518-521). She died at Lynn, 28 October 1676 (LVR), probably the daughter of Nathaniel and Parnell Kirtland (Ferris, 521). Priscilla had been betrothed to Daniel Knight. In November of 1672, Priscilla was granted by the court a 10 pound bequest from the estate of her deceased fiance, Daniel Knight who died intestate (ibid.). Benjamin Collins married, second, at Lynn, 5 September 1677, widow ELIZABETH (LEACH) PUTNAM, b. at Salem, Mass., daughter of Richard Leach of Salem, who named "daughter Elizabeth, wife of Benjamin Collins" in his will of 17 June 1685 (Essex Probate, cited in *EIHC*, IV [1867]:174). Elizabeth had married first, Samuel Putnam.

In 1678, Benjamin Collins took the "oath of allegiance" to the King, with his father and brothers (*EQCR*, VII:158). He was a Trooper (horseman) of Lynn with his brothers Henry, John and Joseph. Their names appeared on a petition to the General Court on 29 May 1679, to appoint Richard Walker as their leader (Mass. Archives, 69:228). He served in King Phillips War, under Capt. Nichols, 24 June 1676, and again under Captain Hunting and Capt. George Curwin, 23 September 1676; was credited with a total of 4 pounds, 29 shillings, 11 pence (Bodge, *King Philip's War*, 260, 290, 291).

On the 24th of February 1690/91, Benjamin Collins of Lynn, "was judged by the Selectmen to be of orthodox religeon and enough property and so was made Freeman by the General Court" (Mass. Archives, 37:11).

He served the town of Lynn as Haward, in 1693/4, Overseer of cutting of wood in 1694/5, Fence Viewer in 1698/9, Surveyor in 1701/2, and Constable in 1705/6. He also served on a jury of trials in 1691, 1692 and 1709 (*Lynn Town Records*, I & II, various pages). In 1706, Benjamin Collins, with his brother Joseph was listed with those who seized Quaker property for the ministerial rate (Mass. Archives, 11:236 A, 236B).

Children by first wife, Priscilla (Kirtland), born at Lynn:

i. SUSANNA^3, b. 9 July 1674; named in grandmother Ann Collins's will in 1690.
ii. WILLIAM, b. 14 Oct 1676; d. at Lynn, 26 Oct 1676 (LVR).

Children by second wife, Elizabeth (Leach Putnam), b. at Lynn:

iii. PRISCILLA, b. 2 May 1679; d. at Colchester, CT?; m. at Colchester, CHARLES WILLIAMS (*Boston Transcript* [4 May 1927], 465). "Charles Williams and w. Priscilla, Thomas Adams & w. Sarah, all of Colchester, sell to Jonathan Silsbee, land which belonged to our honored father, Benjamin Collins of Colchester" (Colchester Deeds, 5:272/3).
iv. ELIZABETH, b. 3 Jan 1681.
v. BENJAMIN, b. 5 Dec 1684; d. 1720; m. SARAH COLLINS, dau. of Henry^3. Henry died intestate, and his estate was administered on 7 March 1720, with Sarah Collins, relict and widow, of Benjamin Collins, husbandman, as principle, and Henry Collins, husbandman and Nathaniel Collins, weaver, of Lynn as sureties. A return of the widow's dower was made 17 October 1720. A list of debts and division of estate is given but is impossible to read (Essex Probate, 6033). Sarah Collins, widow of Benjamin, was buried at Lynn, 19 Dec 1770 (*Commonplace Book of Richard Pratt*, LVR). Sarah left a will leaving her estate to her brother Jonathan and her neices Lydia Bowdon, Sarah Clark, and Martha Curtin (see account under Henry^3).
vi. RICHARD, b. 2 Apr 1689.
vii. SARAH, b. 28 Aug 1692; d. at Colchester, CT (recorded also at Lynn); m. 6 Aug 1715, THOMAS ADAMS (see account under sister Priscilla).
viii. ANNA, b. 29 May 1695.

(To be continued)

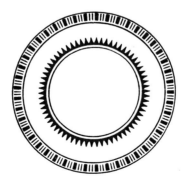

THE STOCKER FAMILY OF MASSACHUSETTS - continued

By Marcia Wiswall Lindberg, C.G.

5. **THOMAS^3 STOCKER** (Ebenezer^2, Thomas^1) was born at Lynn, 24 April 1675, and died there "old" about 27 January 1753 (Zacheus Collin's Diary, cited in Lynn VR). He married at Lynn, 29 November 1700, SARAH BERRY (Lynn VR), who was born, probably at Rumney Marsh, about 1674, the daughter of Thadeus and Hannah (Farrar) Berry (Marcia Wiswall Lindberg, "Thadeus Berry of Rumney Marsh, Massachusetts," *The Essex Genealogist*, 8 [February 1988]:17). She died between 6 March 1716/17 and 5 June 1718 (ibid., 21).

Thomas Stocker was a husbandman, according to deeds (see below). He lived and died in Lynn, where he served the town for many years in various capacities: as surveyor of highways (1703, 1709, 1712, 1723-25), perambulator of boundaries (1708, 1709) and fence viewer of Rumney Marsh, with brother Samuel Stocker (1714/15). He served at the Court of Pleas at Salem in 1702, on a Committee to see that the town was properly supplied with good bulls (1715), and on a Committee to see that work was done on the Meeting House (1716). He served as Constable from 1717 to 1719. In 1720, he was on a Committee to tell Mr. Henchman he had been chosen Minister, and to advise him about his "settlement;" then later was on the entertainment committee for the ordination. He served as tithingman from 1721 to 1724. In 1723 and 1724, he was called "Lieutenant" (*Records of the Towne Meetings of Lynn*; hereafter, *Lynn Town Records*, various pages).

When his father, Ebenezer Stocker, died on 2 November 1705, Thomas Stocker (called "Thomas Stocker, Jr., Esquire"), as the eldest son, was named Administrator of the estate, and received a double portion, after his mother's "widow's thirds" were settled (Essex Probate, 26609).

On 19 May 1720, Thomas quitclaimed to his brother Samuel Stocker, several parcels of land in Lynn "whereas my brother Samuel Stocker of Lynn, husbandman, has paid the half of all that was to pay to the other children of my father as was agreed upon by me and my said brother." The parcels totaled over 40 acres and included Samuel's barn (Essex Deeds, 37:128).

In 1730, Thomas Stocker's sister, Martha Mansfield, "widow of Lynn," and Daniel Mansfield, "clothier of Lynn," joint Executors of the last will and testament of Jonathan Mansfield, sold to Thomas Stocker, for 60 pounds, several parcels of land; one lot laid out on Lynn Commons to Nathaniel Newhall's successors, one acre, 58 poles in the 6th Division; 4 acres, 20 poles laid out on the Town Common in the 5th Divison to Dr. Burchstead, now deceased; one acre, 58 poles on the Town Common in the 6th Division, laid out to John Moor's successors; 2 acres, 28 poles laid out to Joshua Rhoads; 29 poles laid out to Mark Graves and his successors; 25 poles in the 6th Division laid out to Thomas Stocker, the whole lot containing 123 poles; and one-half of the lot in the 5th Division, containing 6 acres, 10 poles; and one-half of the lot in the 5th Division, containing 6 acres, 10 poles; laid out to Isaac Wheeler; said lot conveyed by Smith, Boyce and Trask to the said Jonathan Mansfield, deceased, by deed dated 8 January 1728. The deeds were witnessed on 5 August 1730 by Theophilus Burrill and Elizabeth Townsend. On the 6th of August, Martha and Daniel Mansfield acknowledged the deeds, which were recorded on the 11th of that month (ibid., 57:76).

In 1743/4, Martha Breed, "widow woman" and John Wyer, "sadler," both of Charlestown, sold to Thomas Stocker and Thomas Stocker, Jr., both of Lynn, husbandmen, for 210 pounds, 13 acres of salt marsh and uplands, joining together in Lynn in the 2nd Division of Rumney Marsh, being part of Breed's Island, formerly Capt. John Breed's and Joseph Merriam's and partly on Newell's upland. Martha Breed and John Wyer appeared in Charlestown on 15 February 1743 and acknowledged the deed, which was witnessed by Edward Miriek and John Jenks, and was recorded on the 27th of February 1743/4 (ibid., 86:266).

On the 13th of July 1747, Nathan Breed, cordwainer, of Lynn, sold to Thomas Stocker, husbandman, for 80 pounds, three acres of salt marsh and one acre of upland on Breed's Island, bounded southwest on Thomas Stocker; southeast by Richard Johnson and Daniel Mansfield, northeast on marsh formerly Winters, northwest on marsh lately Joseph Burrill's and Benjamin Potter's. Witnesses were Nathaniel Henchman and John Jenks. Nathan Breed acknowledged the deed on 20 July 1747 and it was recorded on the 22nd of April 1748 (ibid., 90:188).

WILL OF THOMAS STOCKER

Thomas Stocker's will was written on 6 August 1745, eight years before his death. After payment of just debts, he bequeathed **to his** *"****beloved wife Sarah****" all his indoor moveable estate, and improvement of his Real Estate during her natural life.* **To his son, Ephraim** *and his heirs, he gave six acres of upland and salt marsh on Breed's island, "being one full and equal half" of that which he and his son Thomas, Jr. purchased from Breed; the whole lot containing 12 acres in Rumney Marsh, 4 acres and 12 of Salt Marsh in Chelsea and 4 acres of upland at the NW corner of "my pasture land," plus one common lot laid out to Thomas on Vinegar Hill pasture in the 4th Range, between Ebenezer Hathorn and Jacob Newhall, containing 3 acres, 30 poles, together with what he had already given him.*

To his son Thomas Stocker *and his heirs, he gave all the remaining part of his Real Estate, both housing and lands in the Township of Lynn..." he or his heirs paying the several sums of money to his brother and sisters as hereafter expressed..."* **To his son Ebenezer,** *the sum of 150 pounds old tenor equal to silver at 30 shillings per ounce, to be paid by son Thomas one year after his mother's death.* **To his daughter Mary Breed,** *50 pounds old tenor to be paid two years after her mother's death, with what he had already given her.* **To the heirs of his daughter Hannah Bacheler,** *50 pounds old tenor to be paid by son Thomas 3 years after her mother's death in equal shares to each of them.* **To his daughter, Sarah Mansfield,** *50 pounds, with what he had already given her.*

He named his "truly and well-beloved friend," Capt. John Jenks and his beloved wife Sarah Stocker to be his Executors. Witnesses were William and Job Collins and John Ferris. On the 26th of March 1753, the three witnesses all appeared at Ipswich court and swore they were present and saw Thomas Stocker, late of Lynn, sign said will. An inventory was brought in by John Jenks, Jonathan Hawks, Jonathan Wayt and Joseph Edmunds:

The inventory of Thomas Stocker's estate, included: "2 adjoining lots of salt marsh; buildings and two acres of land by the barn; 20 acres in the Acorn Pasture; 6 acres in Vinegar Hill pasture; 4 1/2 acres salt marsh in Chelsea; 6 acres of upland at Breed's Island; 11 acres in the "600 acres;" 4 acres of marsh in Rumney Marsh. Totals: about 60 acres, valued at 332.8 pounds. Personal estate included six cows and one horse, indoor moveables "not disposed of by his will" and "8 dollars in the house." The total estate was valued at 370 pounds, 12 shillings, 4 pence" (Essex Probate, 26626).

Children, born at Lynn (all VRs in published series, unless noted):

    i.   MARY^4, b. 22 Oct 1701; m. at Lynn, 11 Dec 1723, MATTHEW BREED, b. at Lynn, 31 Jan 1698/9, son of Joseph & Sarah (Farrington) Breed. Children, b. at Lynn (surname Breed): 1. <u>Mary</u>, b. 10 Oct 1724; m. at Lynn, 4 Mar 1742, Benjamin James. 2. <u>Sarah</u>, b. 23 Aug 1726. 3. <u>Mehitabel</u>, b. 12 Mar 1728/9; m. at Lynn, 22 Sept 1747, Samuel Hallowell. 4. <u>Hannah</u>, b. 18 Jan 1730; m. at Lynn, 6 Mar 1755, Samuel Bachelder. 5. <u>Mathew</u>, b. 16 Aug 1733; d. 8 Sept 1733. 6. <u>Ruth</u>, b. 1 Aug

		1734; m. at Lynn, 26 Jan 1758, Joseph Breed (*Breed Family Association Papers*, 130).
	ii.	HANNAH, b. 19 May 1703; d. bef. 1747; m. at Lynn, 24 Mar 1723/4, HENRY BACHELDER. He m. (2) at Lynn, 18 Apr 1747, Sarah Johnson (*Essex Antiquarian*, VII [1903]:134). Children by Hannah (Stocker), b. at Lynn (surname Bachelder): 1. Samuel, b. 11 Oct 1725; d. 1766; m. 6 Mar 1755, Hannah Breed. 2. Lydia, b. 16 Jan 1726/7; m. 21 Oct 1756, Richard Johnson. 3. Hannah, b. 1 Jan 1728/9. 4. Henry, b. 31 Jan 1732/3; m. 4 Apr 1758, Jerusha Breed. 5. Sarah, b. 1 Oct 1734; m. 8 May 1766, Daniel Needham. 6. Mary, b. 2 Apr 1738; d. unm. 6 Aug 1757, age 19. 7. Theophilus, b. Feb 1742/3; d. young. Henry Bachelder had five children by his second wife, Sarah (Johnson): Lois, Theophilus, Rufus, Anna & Jonathan (ibid.). (All information from LVR)
	iii.	EBENEZER, b. 27 May 1705.
8.	iv.	THOMAS, JR., b. 20 Apr 1708/9; m. ELIZABETH MANSFIELD.
9.	v.	EPHRAIM, b. 4 Apr 1713; m. LYDIA NEWHALL.
	vi.	SARAH, b. 6 Mar 1716/17; m. at Lynn, 4 Jan 1738/9, JOSEPH MANSFIELD, b. 22 Jan 1714/15, son of Jonathan & Martha (Stocker) Mansfield. Children, b. at Lynn (surname Mansfield): 1. Rufus, b. 28 Dec 1739; d. 8 Feb 1810; m. 1 Sept 1763, Lydia Merritt. 2. Sarah, b. 26 July 1741. 3. Martha, b. 10 June 1744. 4. John, b. 16 Oct 1748. 5. Hannah, b. 24 Dec 1753. 6. Joseph, b. 8 Mar 1758; d. at Salem, Mass., 23 Oct 1827; m. 17 May 1783, Lucretia Derby (All info. from LVR and Geneva A. Daland & James S. Mansfield, *Mansfield Genealogy* [Hampton, NH, 1980], 26).

6. **LT. SAMUEL^3 STOCKER** (Ebenezer^2, Thomas^1) was born at Lynn, 20 November 1684, and was buried there on 9 February 1755 (*Commonplace Book of Richard Pratt*, cited in LVR). He married at Lynn, 13 November 1711, HANNAH LEWIS, who was born at Lynn, 22 January 1685/6, and was buried at Lynn, 16 December 1760 (ibid.), the daughter of John^3 (John^2, Edmund^1) and Elizabeth (Brewer) Lewis (LVR; George Harlan Lewis, *Edmund Lewis of Lynn, Massachusetts and Some of His Descendants* [Salem, Mass., 1908], 18).

Samuel Stocker was a husbandman by occupation, inheriting part of his father's farm. Like his father and brother Thomas, Samuel served the Town of Lynn in many capacities - from 1710, when he was granted leave to set up a seat in the Meeting House, rising to the position of Selectman from 1733 to 1736. He was a fence viewer (1714-19); a swineherd (1709-13); a surveyor of highways (1719-28); and a tithing-man (1721-24). He also served on a Jury of Trials in 1718 (*Lynn Town Records*, various pages). In these Town Meeting records, Samuel is at times referred to as Samuel, Jr., to distinguish him from his Uncle Samuel. In 1736, he is referred to as Ensign Samuel Stocker, and from 1733 on, he is called Lieutenant.

In 1718, after Samuel paid the "one-half of all that he was to pay" to the other children of his father, as was agreed upon by him and his older brother Thomas, he received a quitclaim from Thomas for 12 acres of land in Lynn, bounded north on the road to Boston, east on John Ballord, south on Rumney Marsh, and west on his own land; also 20 acres, including land his own barn was on, bounded north on the highway, east on his brother Thomas's and Thomas Berry's land, and land that was Joseph Hitchen's; also 4 acres, 95 poles, and one acre, 120 poles of land laid out to his father Ebenezer Stocker in the 1st Division, called the "600 acres;" land in the Ox Pasture; a strip next to Samuel Jencks in the 3rd Division; and three acres laid out to Joseph Rhoads. The deed was signed by Thomas Stocker and Sarah his wife, who renounced all right of dower. On 25 December 1718, Thomas appeared and acknowledged the deed, which was witnessed by Jonathan Mansfield and Grover Pratt. The deed was recorded on 19 May 1720 (Essex Deeds, 37:128).

At the same time, a partition of land was recorded between Thomas and Samuel Stocker, stating that they purchased between them in equal halves, land laid out on the Town Common to Joseph Merriam (between Baker's and Thomas Lewis) in the 4th Division and part of the 3rd Division, a lot laid out to Alexander Duggle (Douglas) lying on one side and Josiah Rhoads, Jr. on the other side. This deed was signed on 30 December 1718 and was witnessed by Jonathan Johnson and Grover Pratt. On 27 April 1719, Thomas and Samuel acknowledged the deed, and it was recorded on 19 May 1720 with the aforementioned deed (ibid.).

On 31 July 1723, Joseph Edmonds, husbandman of Lynn, and his wife Mary, signed a deed of land to Samuel Stocker of Lynn, for 230 pounds; land including dwelling house and barn thereon; said barn excluded, lying in Lynn, between Boston bounds, Baker's Hill and Rumney Marsh; said homestead divided into two parts by a highway. The land was bounded on the lower part of French's land, East on Thomas Stocker's the lower part of the homestead now conveyed to John Bullard, northeast on Samuel Stocker's land. The description includes timber trees, fruit trees, water and herbage. This deed was witnessed by John Bullord and Richard Mower, and was recorded 20 September 1725 (ibid., 49:59).

On the 23rd of June 1730, Samuel Stocker was one of ten men who paid a total of three pounds ten shillings to Divan Berry, "lawful owner of the premises" for land bounded west on the road to Reading, north on Thomas Berry's land, east and south on Divan's land. The ten men were Richard Mower, Jrs., Innholder, Thomas Berry of Boston, Samuel Stocker, Henry Rhoads and Hezekiah Rhoads, husbandmen, John Ballord, shipwright, Jacob Newhall, cordwainer, Samuel & Ebenezer Harthorn, blacksmiths, and Thomas Cheever, Jr., miller, all of Lynn. This deed was witnessed by Ebenezer Burrill and Zacheus Collins and was recorded on 21 August 1730 (ibid., 57:78).

Samuel Stocker died intestate in February of 1755 (Lynn VR); and on the 7th of July that year, a bond was posted by John Stocker, shipwright, Ebenezer Burrill, Jrs., husbandman, and Jonathan Hawkes, cordwainer, all of Lynn on the estate of John's father, Samuel Stocker. An inventory was brought in, listing a dwelling house and 3/4 acres, a barn, 20 acres between the road and the salt marsh, 20 acres below Ballards to the house where Hill lives, 15 acres formerly Edmonds's, 12 acres in the Ram Pasture, six acres of salt marsh on Oak Island in Chelsea, 4 acres of salt marsh and three common lots. The total acreage was over 78 acres, and this, together with a personal estate, was valued at 16 pounds, 11 shillings, seven pence. in the distribution of the estate, one third, including the dwelling house, was set aside to the widow Hannah. The remaining two-thirds of the estate was divided into three parts, with elder son, John Stocker, receiving a double portion, and younger son Samuel receiving a single portion. The inventory and division was signed by William and Zaccheus Collins, John Jenks and John Mansfield. In actual acreage, widow Hannah (Lewis) Stocker received 22 acres, John received 28 acres, and Samuel received 23 1/2 acres, with the value of the building being taken into account (Essex Probate, 26622).

Children, born at Lynn (Lynn VR):

10.	i.	JOHN^4, b. 15 Feb 1712/13; m. (1) HANNAH RICHARDS; m. (2) RUTH BREED.
11.	ii.	SAMUEL, twin, b. 28 July 1717; m. (1) ELIZABETH GRIFFIN; m. (2) PRISCILLA RHODES.
	iii.	JOSEPH, twin, b. 28 July 1717; died young.

7. **JOHN^3 STOCKER** (Ebenezer^2, Thomas^1) was born at Lynn, on 13 November 1693 (Lynn VR), and died, probably at Newbury, Mass., after 1742, when he deeded a warehouse to his son Thomas (Essex Deeds, 83:221). His intentions of marriage were published at Lynn on 30 September 1716 to ABIGAIL LEWIS (Lynn VR), who was born on 14 October 1696, and was perhaps the "widow Stocker" who died at Newburyport in April of 1774, age 73 years (Newburyport VR), although Abigail Lewis Stocker would have been 78 years old. She was the daughter of Thomas^3 (John^2, Edmund^1) and Mary (Breed) Lewis.

John Stocker was a shipwright by trade and resided in Boston, Mass., until 1727 when he removed to Newbury. Positive proof has not been found to identify John Stocker of Newbury as the John Stocker of Boston, but John Stocker, "shipwright" and Abigail (Lewis) Stocker, his wife, were of Boston between 1715 and 1726 when six children were recorded to them in the Boston Vital Records. Then the Boston records become silent, and the following year, a John Stocker, "shipwright" appears in Newbury records where six (more) children are born (Newbury VR). No mother is given in these Newbury birth records. There is no duplication of names for these two sets of children, and both sets of names are familiar to the Stocker family. The dates of births in Boston and in Newbury, continue right along in the usual 2-year sequence. Also, the marriage of John, Jr. in 1743, was recorded both in Lynn and Newbury; and the marriage of son Joseph was recorded in both Marblehead and Newburyport (see below).

In Newbury, Zachariah Nowell, boatbuilder of Newbury, sold to John Stocker, shipwright, of Newbury, for 253 pounds "good currant money" a certain piece of land in Newbury with one dwelling house, bounded by Joseph Titcomb's and Ordway's land. The deed was recorded 2 January 1730 (Essex Deeds, 58:25).

On the 23rd of August 1738, William Dunn, lawyer, of Newbury, deeded to John Stocker, shipwright of Newbury, for 220 pounds, "my now dwelling house in Newbury, with its appurtenances, where I now dwell, which stands on land formerly owned by John Ordway of Newbury, which I had by absolute state of inheritance." The deed was recorded on 25 August 1738 (ibid., 77:76). At the same time, John Ordway, housewright, for 80 pounds, deeded to John Stocker, 14 square rods of land, bounded by Ordway Lane, Stephen Jackson and Joseph Hoyt (ibid.).

On 28 August 1742, John Stocker deeded to his son, Thomas Stocker of Newbury, shipwright, for 196 pounds, Warehouse #4 on Queen's Warf, and also a new #38 near the steeple door in the Meeting House at Newbury (ibid., 83:221).

No probate or death records have been found for John Stocker of Newbury.

Probable children, the first six recorded in Boston VR, the last six recorded in Newbury VR:

	i.	THOMAS^4, b. 25 Mar 1715 (before parent's marriage); d. young (Lewis, *Edmund Lewis*, 22).
	ii.	JOHN, b. 1 Oct 1717; prob. m., as John Jr., 29 Oct 1743, ANNE (ANNIE) STEVENS of Kittery. The marriage was recorded in Lynn and Newbury.
12.	iii.	THOMAS, b. 25 Mar 1719; m. SARAH TITCOMB.
	iv.	ABIGAIL, b. 29 Mar 1721; m. at Boston, 2 Apr 1740, JAMES VISCOUNT.
	v.	SARAH, b. 1 Dec 1723; perhaps the Sarah Stocker who m. at Newbury, 28 Jan 1750, JOHN ROPES of Falmouth (Newbury VR).
	vi.	WILLIAM, b. 30 July 1726.
13.	vii.	EBENEZER, bpt. at Newbury, 24 Mar 1727/8; m. HANNAH THORLA.
	viii.	JOSEPH, bpt. at Newbury, 25 Oct 1730; d. young.
	ix.	JOSEPH, bpt. at Newbury, 12 Mar 1731/32. A Joseph Stocker m. 25 May 1762, JOANNA BURCHSTEAD (recorded at Marblehead & Newburyport VR).
	x.	MICHAEL, bpt. at Newbury, 7 July 1734.
14.	xi.	SAMUEL, bpt. at Newbury, 16 Jan 1735/36; m. (1) -----; m. (2) HANNAH WOODMAN.
	xii.	MARSHALL, bpt. at Newbury, 3 June 1739. This was probably the Marshall Stocker of Amesbury, who served in the Revolutionary War as a Private, from the alarm of April 19, 1775 (9 days) until he was furloughed in 1782.

(To be continued)

JOHN RAMSDELL OF LYNN, MASSACHUSETTS - continued

By Roselyn Listernick

11. **JONATHAN[4] RAMSDELL** (Isaac[3-2], John[1]) was born at Lynn on 16 September 1690 and died prior to 4 April 1769 according to the administration of his estate (Essex Probate, 23191). He married at Lynn, 27 November 1710, SARAH HATHORN, born 26 October 1684, daughter of Ebenezer[2] (John[1]) and Hester, or Esther (Witt) Hathorn (Rev. Charles N. Sinnett, *The Sturdy Families of Maine* (1922).

Jonathan was a yeoman, and was probably the Jonathan who was chosen a fence viewer at the Lynn Town Meetings, held 6 March 1726/7, 29 January 1730/1 and 6 March 1731/32. Jonathan Ramsdell, Isaac Ramsdell and Isaac Ramsdell, Jr. were given permission by liberty of the selectmen to keep a dog or bitch. (*Records of Ye Town Meetings of Lynn*; hereafter, *Lynn Town Records*, III:76, IV:8, 10, 14).

Jonathan died intestate, and on 4 April 1769, Zacheus Curtis, Ebenezer Burrill and Moses Hudson were chosen to appraise the estate. An inventory, taken on 24 April 1769, showed a total value of 77 pounds, 6 shillings, twopence. The property was divided on 31 July 1769 as follows:

> "We, the subscribers, have divided 1/3 of the real estate of Jonathan Ramsdell unto his widow, Sarah Ramsdell, as her right of dower. To her, the lower rooms of the dwelling house and that part of the cellar under the same with the privilege to the road." Also a 1/3 part of the half acre adjacent, northeast, to Joseph Mansfield's land, and 1/3 part of a four acre lot northeast to land belonging to heirs of John Fuller, and land belonging to Timothy Ramsdell. Likewise, another four acre lot near Pine Hill was a third divided out. Finally, one hundred six poles of woodland lying in the place called, "the six-hundred acres" was 1/3 divided out, this land lying between land owned by the heirs of David Hutchinson, deceased, and Moses Hawkes.

Isaiah Ramsell, eldest son, was appointed administrator of the estate on 3 April 1769. A total of 7 pounds, 18 shillings and 5 pence were paid in debts to individuals. Isaiah received 5 pounds, 4 shillings, "for looking after and nursing his mother in her last sickness." Other expenses listed were funeral charges, expenses of the appraisal committee, and "time and trouble" of the administrator. The grand total was 26 pounds, 9 pence (Essex Probate, 23191).

Children, born at Lynn:

i. KEZIA[5], b. 5 June 1711; m. at Lynn, 9 Nov 1732, DAVID DUNNELL. Children, born at Lynn (surname Dunnell): 1. <u>Ruth</u>, b. 31 Dec 1732; d. at Lynn, 15 Dec 1814, age 84; m. at Lynn, 29 Oct 1751, Isaac Meachum, b. in 1726, d. 6 Nov 1794, age 68 (LVR; Howard Kendall Sanderson, *Lynn in the Revolution* [Boston, 1909], 354-55). 2. <u>Mary</u>, b. 2 July 1734; m. at Lynn, 29 Jan 1754, John Wayt (Wait). 3. <u>Solomon</u>, b. 13 Dec 1736/37. <u>Rubin</u>, b. 12 Jan 1739/40. 5. <u>Sarah</u>, b. 4 Mar 1741/2; m. at Lynn, 27 Nov 1760, Ebenezer Merriam. 6. <u>Jacob</u>, b. 5 Dec 1743; m. at Lynn, 12 Dec 1771, Rebecca Flurence (Florence). 7. <u>David</u>, b. 15 Sept 1745. 8. <u>Jonathan</u>, b. 4 May 1759.
ii. ISAIAH, b. 3 Apr 1713.
iii. ISAIAH, b. 27 Jan 1714/15; d. at Lynn, 8 Aug 1796, at 81 years; m. at Lynn, 13 May 1734, HANNAH EAST.

    iv.   JONATHAN, b. 7 June 1721.
    v.   EPHRAIM, b. 15 Jan 1723/24; m. (int.) at Boston, 28 Mar 1745, ELIZABETH WILLS (Boston VR).

12. **NATHANIEL^4 RAMSDELL** (Isaac$^{3-2}$, John^1) was born at Lynn, 14 September 1694, and died after 1740, the date when his last child was born. His intention of marriage to Sarah Farrington was published at Lynn, on 6 April 1729. It is probable that this marriage did not take place, or perhaps they did marry and Sarah died soon thereafter, although there is no death record for her at Lynn. At any rate, ten months later, on 26 February 1729/30, Nathaniel Ramsdell married JOANNA DOWNING, possibly a descendant of MacCullum More Downing, "who came from Scotland and worked at the Forge" ("General Items Relative to Lynn," *Register*, V [1851]:207). She was probably the Joanna Ramsdell who was buried at Lynn, 23 January 1763 (LVR).

Very little is known about this Nathaniel. There are no deeds on file at Essex County Registry of Deeds, and no will or settlement of estate is recorded at the Essex Probate Court.

Children of Nathaniel and Joanna (Downing) Ramsdell, born at Lynn:

    i.   NATHANIEL^5, b. 5 Nov 1730; living in 1790 (1790 U. S. census); m. at Lynn, 4 Dec 1755, by Rev. Nathaniel Henchman, TABITHA RAMSDELL, b. at Lynn, 27 May 1729, and was probably the "Tabitha, w. of Nathaniel," who died of apoplexy, 21 Dec 1801, age 74 y. (LVR), although there is a 2 year discrepancy. She was the daughter of Ebenezer^4 and Tabatha (Rhodes) Ramsdell (Sanderson, 415). Children, b. at Lynn: 1. "child of Nathaniel" d. 30 Nov 1756 (LVR). 2. <u>Joanna</u>, b. 1 Nov 1757. 3. <u>Eunis</u>, b. 20 Mar 1760. 4. <u>Ebenezer</u>, b. 21 July 1763; m. (int.) at Lynn, 6 Nov 1785, Mary Ramsdell. (For further information on this line, write to: Mary Jane E. McArthur, 35 Scofield Rd., Cohasset, MA 02025). 5. <u>Gideon</u>, b. 10 Mar 1766; m. (int.) at Lynn, 20 May 1791, Paty (Martha) Loachem. 6. <u>William</u>, b. 7 May 1768. 7. <u>Rebecca</u>, b. 25 June 1771.
    ii.   DANIEL, b. 13 Aug 1734.
    iii.   DANIEL, b. 12 Aug 1736.
    iv.   ANNIS, b. 16 Feb 1739/40.

13. **EBENEZER^4 RAMSDELL** (Isaac$^{3-2}$, John^1) was born at Lynn, 9 April 1705 and died sometime before 30 December 1756, at which time his widow Tabitha, was made executrix of his estate (Essex Probate, 23181). He married (int.) at Lynn, 15 March 1724/5, TABITHA RHODES, who was born at Lynn, 7 March 1705, the daughter of Henry^3 (Josiah^2, Henry^1) and Elizabeth Rhoades (*Register*, V [1851]:341).

The first reference for Ebenezer in town affairs, was at the 3 March 1734/5 Town Meeting, when he was chosen "tithing man." In 1735/6, 1737 and 1738, the town leased to Ebenezer, Sedg Island for 10 shillings. On 25 March 1739, the town sold to Ebenezer, 3 poles at the north end of his land for 10 shillings (*Lynn Town Records*, IV:various pages). On 3 March 1746, Ebenezer Ramsdell, Jonathan Hudson and Jacob Burrill were chosen to see "that the fish have passage" (ibid., V:20).

There are no deeds on file at the Essex County Registry of Deeds for Ebenezer Ramsdell. He died intestate in 1756, and on 30 December of that year, the Essex County Probate Court appointed Tabitha Ramsdell, widow, administratrix of her husband's estate, and ordered that an inventory be taken of Ebenezer's effects, by the first Monday of September 1757. The inventory was presented by William Collins, Daniel Mansfield and Ebenezer Burrill Jr. and consisted of:

"*Dwelling house and barn, 66 pounds, 13 shillings, 4 pence*
The homestead about 12 acres, 80 pounds

One lot of Salt Marsh by Bear Creek, 4 1/2 acres, 20.18.8
One piece of upland & meadow, 11 acres, 20 pounds
One piece of land north of fresh meadow, 7 acres, 13.6.8
One lot laid out to widow Chadwell, 4 acres, 40 poles, 4 pounds
90 poles in the "600 acres" so called, 16 shillings
One acre at Choose Hill, 16 shillings
One common lot at Sheep Hill, 3 acres, 60 poles, 1.12.00
A schooner of about 20 tons, 160 pounds
1 heifer, 2 yearlings, a grey mare, 1 swine...
...farm equipment and household furnishings
Total inventory, 424 pounds, 9 shillings, 1 pence."

Debts against the estate were itemized and included personal debts to more than 40 persons, as well as advancements to the widow for "necessaries", 20 pounds; loss on sale of schooner, 40 pounds, and the administrator for time and trouble, 5 pounds. Total debts were 291 pounds, 18 shillings, 2 pence. William Collins, Esq., Daniel Mansifeld, Wsq., Ebenezer Burrill, Jr., Samuel Johnson and John Mansfield were named the committee to divide out 1/2 part of the estate for the widow Tabitha. Her third consisted of:

"The lower room of the garret in the east end of the dwelling house with 1/2 of the cellar under it, and also the west-remaining 2/3 of the estate.
Also about 4 acres of land, part of the homestead, lying on the easterly side, bounded on land of Jonathan Ramsdell and Moulton's land.
Also one common lot lying on Burrill Hill (so called) and the way laid out to the widow Chadwell, containing 4 acres, 14 poles.
Also a piece of Salt Marsh lying above Bear Creek, bounded on Nathaniel Collins, about 1 acre.
Also 4 acres, 40 poles of upland and meadow, bounded by Timothy Ramsdell and Ebenezer Burill. (Essex Probate, 32181; Record Books, 334:210; 335:135-137)

Children, born at Lynn:

i. EBENEZER[5], b. 26 July 1726.
ii. TABITHA, b. 27 May 1729; m. at Lynn, NATHANIEL RAMSDELL (see above).
iii. SARAH, b. 27 May 1732; m. (int.) at Lynn, 16 Aug 1761, WILLIAM SHILLABER, bpt. at Salem, 22 Sept 1734, s. of William and Sarah Shillaber (Salem VR).
iv. LIDIA, b. 19 Sept 1732; m. (int.) at Lynn, 25 Mar 1759, JAMES GREEN of Boston.
v. JOHN,, b. 18 Dec 1736; m. at Lynn, 1 June 1758, MARY DOWNING.
vi. REBECCA, b. 26 Feb 1739/40; m. at Lynn, 18 Sept 1761, JOHN DOWNING.
vii. WILLIAM, b. 9 Apr 1742; d. bef. 18 Nov 1817, when "an order asking for guardianship of children of William Ramsdell was filed at Essex Probate Court ... he having lately deceased" (Sanderson, 417). He m. (1) at Lynn, 29 Nov 1769, Mrs. Polly White, and (2) at Lynn, 25 Aug 1774, Sarah Newhall (LVR). Children: 1. Mary. 2. Williiam. 3. Sally. 4. Catherine. 5. Betsy. 6. Peggy. Sally, Betsy and Peggy were under order for guardianship in 1817 (ibid.).
viii. GIDEON, b. 31 Jan 1743/4; ? d. at Lynn, 6 Sept 1760.
ix. TIMOTHY, b. 16 July 1745; m. at Lynn, 10 Dec 1765, ABIGAIL NEWMAN.

14. **JONATHAN**[4] **RAMSDELL** (Jonathan[3], Isaac[2], John[1]) was born at Lynn, 23 March 1698/9, and died at Nantucket, Mass., 15 December 1777. He married, at Charlestown, Mass., around 1721/22, probably 4 May 1721, ANNA FOSDICK of Charlestown, born 9 November 1701 at Charlestown, and died at Nantucket, 2 April 1749. She was the daughter of Jonathan and Sarah (Sprague) Fosdick. Sarah had a brother who went to Nantucket, and later we find that Jonathan and Anna are in Nantucket before 1744 when their first-born son, Jonathan, married there (Lynn, Charlestown and Nantucket VR). Jonathan married, second, at Nantucket, 7 October 1753, JANE BUNKER, widow of William Bunker, and daughter of Ebenezer[4] (James[3], Tristam[2], Peter[1]) and Eleanor (Barnard) Coffin, who was born on 14 April 1714, and died in 1786 (Nantucket VR; "The Coffin Family," *Register*, XXIV [1870]:305, 306).

Children, born at Charlestown, Mass.

    i.   JONATHAN[5], b. 1 Sept 1722; d. at Nantucket, 17 July 1799; m. there, 22 Nov 1744, PRISCILLA COFFIN. She was b. at Nantucket, 24 May 1724, and d. there, 26 Sept 1806, dau. of George[5] and Ruth (Swain) Coffin (ibid., 306). Children, b. at Nantucket: 1. <u>William</u>, b. 18 Jan 1748; d. there 29 Jan 1819; m. there 15 Oct 1771, Ruth Gardner. 2. <u>Anna</u>, b. 21 Aug 1751; d. there, Dec 1822; m. there, 15 Feb 1770, Seth Folger. 3. <u>Jonathan</u>, b. 13 Sept 1753; d. at St. Johns, Newfoundland, 25 Dec 1778 "single, carpenter's mate on board the Martin 'Sloop of War' ... perished in a snowstorm" (NVR). 4. <u>Benjamin</u>, m. Susanna of England. 5. <u>George</u>, m. Eunice Burnell; removed to Maine. 6. <u>Lydia</u>, b. 24 Jan 1767; m. at Nantucket, 4 Sept 1788, Cromwell Bunker. 7. <u>Mary</u>, d. at Nantucket 13 Mar 1791; m. there 2 May 1782, George Coleman.

    ii.   WILLIAM, b. 4 July 1724.

    iii.   ANNA, b. 16 Jan 1725; d. at Nantucket, 1 July 1775; m. (int.) there, 25 Dec 1746, PELEG GARDNER, b. 31 Nov 1722/3, s. of Ebenezer & Judith (Coffin) Gardner.

    iv.   SARAH, b. 17 or 19 Nov 1727; d. at Charlestown, 25 Dec 1729.

    v.   JOHN, b. 7 Sept 1729; d. at Nantucket, 9 Sept 1782; m. there, 3 Jan 1750, RACHEL SWAIN. She was b. at Nantucket, 12 May 1729 and d. there 6 Oct 1790, dau. of Eliakim & Elizabeth (Arthur) Swain (NVR). Children, b. at Nantucket: 1. <u>Sarah</u>, b. 25 Aug 1752; d. there Feb 1831; m. there, 3 Jan 1771, William Myrick. 2. <u>James</u>, b. 5 Oct 1755; d. at Nantucket, 6 June 1833; m. (1) there, 14 Nov 1782, Jedidah Folger; m. (2) there, 22 Mar 1794, Mary Foy. 3. <u>Peggy, or Margaret</u>, d. at Nantucket, 7 Nov 1781; m. there, 29 June 1775, Reuben Fitch. 4. <u>John</u>, b. 20 Jan 1761; d. there, 15 May 1816; m. there, betw. 25 April 1800 & 25 Apr 1801, Phebe Ellis, widow of David Ellis. 5. <u>Elizabeth</u>, b. abt. 1763; d. at Nantucket, 24 Aug 1781, age abt. 18. 6. <u>William</u>, d. at Nantucket, 11 Jan 1811; m. there, 3 Aug 1790, Sylvia Coleman. 7. <u>Eunice</u>, d. at Nantucket, 31 Mar 1797; m. there, 24 Nov 1791, James Clark.

    vi.   SARAH, b. 22 Sept 1731.

    vii.   MARY, b. 21 Sept 1733; bpt. 16 June 1734; d. at Nantucket, 11 Oct 1807, as Mary Folger; m. (1) (int.) 21 Dec 1752, NATHANIEL PINKHAM; m. (2) 2 Dec 1764, RUBEN FOLGER.

    viii.   ABIGAIL, b. 1736; bpt. 4 July 1736 at Charlestown; d. at Nantucket, 12 May 1819, age 83 y. 5 m.; m. at Nantucket, 4 Dec 1755, TRISTAM BUNKER. He was b. at Nantucket, 13 Feb 1733; d. there, 26 Aug 1831, s. of Reuben & Mary (Chase) Bunker. A child, b. at Nantucket (surname Bunker): 1. <u>Abigail</u>, b. 12 Aug 1762; d. at Nantucket, 26 Aug 1831; m. there, Simeon Hussey (Charlestown, Nantucket VR).

(to be continued)

Tools of the Trade

RECORDS AND FILES OF THE QUARTERLY COURTS OF ESSEX COUNTY

By Marcia Wiswall Lindberg

One of the most important publications for those doing research on early Essex County, is the multi-volume *Records and Files of the Quarterly Courts of Essex County, Massachusetts*. Eight volumes, encompasing 1636-1685, were published by the Essex institute from 1911 to 1921. An additional ninth volume, edited by Mary Thresher of our society, was published in 1974, bringing the printed records up to 1688.

To some, the *Records and Files* may appear dull and uninteresting. But often, these records provide the only clue to an individual's age (as given in copious depositions), or to a person's very existence in Essex County. Relationships are often established as well. Wills and inventories are tucked in here and there, and lists of Freemen and Tax rolls are among the treasures included. For those interested in life as it actually was in colonial New England, there is no better source; some of the "cases" are actually salacious.

As with all published sources for research, the introduction is important. It explains the scope and background of the work itself. However, few researchers are fortunate enough to own this set of books, and the limited time allotted for research at libraries is too precious to spend on "introductions." That introduction is given here in its entirety.

INTRODUCTION

"The Charter of "The Governor and Company of Massachusetts Bay in New England," granted March 4, 1628-9, provided that annually there should be chosen from among the freemen of the Company, a Governor, Deputy-Governor and eighteen Assistants. Among the duties presribed for this governing body was that of holding *"Upon every last Wednesday in Hillary, Easter, Trinity and Michelmas terms respectively for ever, one great, general and solemn Assembly, which four General Assemblies shall be stiled and called the Four Great and General Courts of the said Company."*

For a number of years this Court exercised the entire judicial powers of the Colony but with the increase of population there came a necessity for additional tribunals, and at a session of the General Court held in Boston on March 3, 1635-6, the following law was adopted:

*"Further, it is ordered, that there shall be 4 courts kept every quarter, **1 at Ipswich**, to which Newbury shall belong; **2 at Salem**, to which Saugus shall belong; **3 at New Towne** [Cambridge], to which Charlton, Concord, Meadford, & Watertown shall belong; **4th at Boston**, to which Roxbury, Dorchester, Weymouth & Hingham shall belong. All of their Courts shall be kept by such magistrates as shall be dwelling in or near the said towns, & by such other persons of worth as shall from time to time be appointed by the General Court, so as no Court shall be kept without one magistrate at the least, & that none of the magistrates be excluded, who can & will intend the same; yet the General Court shall appoint which of the magistrates shall specially belong to each of the said Courts. Such persons as shall be joined as Associates to the Magistrates in the said Court shall be chosen by the Generall Court, out of a greater number of such as the several towns shall nominate to them, so as there may be in each of the said Courts many magistrates as may make five in all. These Courts shall **try all civil causes, whereof the debt or damage shall not excede ten pounds, & all criminal causes, not concerning life, member, or banishment**. And if any person shall find himself grieved with the sentence of any of the said Courts, **he may appeal to the next great Quarter Court** [at Boston] provided that he put in sufficient cause to present his appeal with effect, & to abide the sentence of the magistrates in the said great Quarter Court, who shall see that all such that shall bring any appeal without just cause be exemplarily punished.*

***There shall be four great Quarter Courts kept yearly at Boston**, by the Government and the rest of the magistrates; the first, the first Tuesday in the 4th month, called June; the second, the first Tuesday in September; the third, the first Tuesday in December; the fourth, the first Tuesday in the 1st month called March. The inferior Courts shall be kept the 1st, the last Tuesday in June, & the rest the last Tuesday in each of the said months.*

All actions shall be tried at that Court to which the defendant belongs. All offenders which shall be in the prison at Boston at the time of any Court there holden, shall be tried at that Court, except in the war^t of his commitm^t he be reserved to *the great Quarter Court. And it shall be lawful for the Governor, or Deputy-Governor, or any two magistrates (upon special & urgent occasion), to appoint Courts to be kept upon other days then in this order are appointed."*

The first session of this Court in Essex County was held June 27. 1636, at Salem. With the continued increase of population there came a demand for more frequent sessions of the Courts, and on June 2, 1641, the General Court established four quarter-annual courts as follows:

*"Whereas it is desired by this Court to ease the country of all unnecessary travels & charges, it is ordered, that there shall be 4 Quarter Courts kept yearly by the Magistrates of Ipswich & Salem, with such others to be joined in commission with them as this Court shall appoint, not hindering any other magistrates that will help them; this order to take effect after these next Quarter Courts shall be ended at Salem & Ipswich, two of these Quarter Courts to be kept at Salem & the other 2 at Ipswich, the first Court to be kept the last third day of the 7th month at Ipswich, (& the rest at the same time the former Courts were), the next quarter at Salem, the 3rd quarter at Ipswich, the 4th at Salem, & the magistrates of Ipswich & Salem to attend each of these Courts, but no jurymen to be warned [called] from Ipswich to Salem, nor from Salem to Ipswich; to each of these places, a grand jury shall be warned once a year, & these Courts to have the same power, both in civil and criminal causes, the Court of Assistants hath at Boston, except trials for life, limbs or banishment, which are wholly reserved to Boston Court; provided, it shall be lawful to appeal from any of these Courts to Boston. **And it shall be in the liberty of any plaintiff that hath an action of above one hundred pounds principal debt to try his cause in any of these Courts or at Boston**; the fines of these Courts to defray the charges of the same, & the overplus to be returned to the Treasurer for the public. And Salisbury & Hampton are joined to the jurisdiction of Ipswich, & each of them to send a grand juryman once a year to Ipswich."*

Massachusetts Bay was divided into shires or counties by a law passed May 10, 1643. The territorial limits of Essex County were much as they are at the present time, save that all the towns lying north of the Merrimack river were established as the county of Norfolk, thereby including the towns of Haverhill and Salisbury. Norfolk County was divided, with Dover and Portsmouth, forming the northern and the remaining towns the southern part.

The Quarterly Courts in the southern jurisdiction were held at Salisbury and Hampton and the records of these sessions are included in the following pages until Feb 4, 1679-80, when the towns of Haverhill, Amesbury and Salisbury were placed within the jurisdiction of the Essex County Courts.

These County Courts or Inferior Quarterly Courts had jurisdiction in civil and criminal cases except in cases of divorce and crimes involving life, limb or banishment. They had power to summon grand and petit jurors, to appoint their own clerks and other necessary officers, to lay out highways, license ordinarys to see that a proper ministry was supported, to prove wills, to grant adminstrations and to have general control of matters in probate. In 1664, they were authorized to admit freemen. In general, they had jurisdiction in all matters not reserved to the Court of Assistant, which was the Court of Appeal. The writs, declarations, and other pleadings, complaints, indictments, and course of proceedings in the courts were simple, brief and informal. For the first twenty years the testimony in a trial was written down by the clerk of the court and became a part of the records in the case. But in 1650, on account of "the inconvenience of taking verbal testimonyes in Court by reason of many intimacies in their relations, so that the clerk cannot well make a perfect record thereof," it was ordered that henceforth all testimony be given in writing to be attested in court if the witness lived within ten miles of it, and before a magistrate, if the witness lived at a greater distance. These statements or depositions went to the jury who returned them to the court with their verdict.

The records of the Essex County Quarterly Courts fo the colonial period (1636-1692) are now preserved in seventeen volumes. There are also copies of Norfolk County records (southern jurisdiction), in two volumnes, made in 1852 by David Pulsifer. The originals from which these copies were made are not in the custody of the clerk at the present time (1911) and seem to have disappeared.

ESSEX COUNTY QUARTERLY COURT RECORDS

	Inclusive dates of records		Vol
Salem,	27:4:1636-25:11:1641,	58 p.	(1)
	7:1638-1:1:1647-8	232	(2)
	14:9:1648-26:4:1655	77	(3)
	29:9:1655-19:9:1666	178	(4)
	June 25:1667-24:4:1679	135	(5)
	25:9:1679-Apr 24:1692	81	(6)

30:4:1674-29:9:1681	90	(7)
June 27:1682-Nov 24:1685	155	(8)

Ipswich

Mar 31:1646-25:7:1666 158	11	
4:9:1645-May 5:1663	75	(12)
29:4:1664-Sept 29:1674	134	(13)
Sept:1682-Apr 20:1656	63	(14)
April:1666-June 20:1682	382	(-)
Sept:26:1682-Mar 29:1692	89	(15)
Births, marriages and deaths, 1654-1691	60	(19)
Births, marriages and deaths, 1658-1701	98	(-)
Births, marriages and deaths, 1663-1786	128	(-)

Salisbury and Hampston Courts

26:7:1648-Apr 12:1670	79	(16)
8:8:1672-Nov 11:1679	112	(17)
Births, marriages and deaths, intentions of marriage, ear marks and strays		
1670-1747	375	(-)

Supplementing the record books kept by the clerks of the courts is a large collection of original papers consisting of presentments, depositions upon almost every conceivable subject, correspondence and documents of greatly varied character, deeds, wills, inventories of estates, contracts, attested copies of records, papers connected with the witchcraft trials, apprentices' indentures, inquests, writs, executions, and papers of every kind connected with the various cases. These papers or files, connected with the Salem and Ipswich courts, are arranged and mounted in fifty-four folio volumes and there are two volumes of papers relating to Norfolk County. "Waste books" or books of preliminary records were kept by the clerks and when the entries were transcribed into the books of permanent records, not infrequently a word or a phrase was overlooked or omitted. Such omissions are here included within brackets with proper indications as to their source.

The records and files are here printed in abstracted form, free from needless verbiage, but every essential particular is retained so that the historian, genealogist and sociologist may be assured that nothing of value has been omitted. The subject matter in leaded type above the line is taken from the clerk's books of records. That below the line, set in solid type, is found in the files. The footnotes appear below. But little attempt has been made to elucidate the text or the obsolete spelling by means of footnotes, but autograph signatures and seals are always noted. Names and words are spelled exactly as the appear in the original records or files, but they have been indexed under modern spelling when the modern form could be determined. Nearly all of the contractions used appear in the original record and are easily understood.

In modernizing the early dates it should always be remembered that previous to the adoption of the Gregorian calendar by Act of Parliament to take effect Sept. 1752, the month of March was the first month in the year and "double-dating" prevailed between Jan. 1st and March 24th inclusinve, in each year, so that 21:12 mo:1656-7, when modernized, should read Feb. 21, 1657.

Cordial acknowledgment is due to the Board of County Commissioners for the County of Essex, who, appreciating the present and future value of these records, have heartily co-operated by assuming the larger part of the cost of abstracting. Thanks are alos due to Edward B. George, Esq., Clerk of Courts for Essex County, and to his corps of assistants, for facilitating the progress of the work in every way. The work of abstracting the frequently obscure originals and of arranging the copy has been done by Miss Harriet S. Tapley, but the final proofs have always received the careful inspection of Sidney Perley, Esq., who at all times has encouraged and aided the work.

George Francis Dow, Editor
Salem, Mass., November 1st, 1911."

END OF INTRODUCTION

Essex Institute in Salem, Mass. has the original Quarterly Court Records, and also "W.P.A." Transcripts of those Court Records (57 volumes, covering 1636-1651). They also have a 3-volume index, but Volume 1 is missing. The Mormon Church has the 3-volume index on microfilm (evidently filmed before the loss). Yale University has now filmed the index also, and plans to film the remaining court records held at Essex Institute, according to Jane Ward, Curator of Manuscripts at Essex Institute.

In 1692, the General Court was divided into the Court of General Sessions (for minor criminal cases) and the Court of Common Pleas (for civil cases). Essex Institute also has these records from 1692 to 1820.

The $3 fee for non-members using the library at Essex Institute, is waived if a researcher is just consulting these public court records.

The Ahnentafel

The Ahnentafel is an Ancestor Table, or list. It follows the numbering system of standard Ancestor Charts; i.e.: yourself is number 1; your father and mother are numbers two and three. A father's number is always double that of the child; 13 is a child of 26 (his father) and 27 (his mother). Ahnentafels preserve in print what is known of your ancestors. They also serve as an exchange column for those working on the same surnames or lines. TEG will accept current Ahnentafels and also those of earlier ancestors. If submitting an Ahnentafel for a great grandfather, etc., the numbering must begin with that ancestor as number one. In other words, a submitter cannot use a computer printout starting with a great grandfather as number eight, because the doubling numbers mentioned above will not correspond. Therefore, the great grandfather's Ahnentafel must be renumbered for submission for this column in TEG. As an example, see the last three Ahnentafels printed below.

****

Ahnentafel of Catherine M. Robertson, 8 Melvin Avenue, Lynn, MA 01902

I	1	Catherine M. Robertson	1965-	Lynn, MA
II	2	John K. Robertson	1925-	Swampscott, Lynn, MA
	3	Irene P. Casey	1928-	Boston, Lynn, MA
III	4	Ralph H. Robertson	1887-1957	Lynn, MA
	5	Marguerite L. Kelley	1888-1964	Lynn, MA
	6	Thomas F. Casey	1887-1958	Boston, MA
	7	Josephine F. Sullivan	1892-1964	Boston, MA
IV	8	Walter Bloomfield Robertson	1852-1941	Nova Scotia, New Brunswick; Lynn, MA
	9	Annie A. Rogers	1857-1952	New Brunswick; Lynn, MA
	10	John Z. Kelley	1859-1933	Newburyport, Lynn, MA
	11	Agnes T. McLoaughlin	1858-1942	Newburyport, Lynn, MA
	12	Michael Casey	1853-1923	Galway, Ireland; Boston, MA
	13	Bridget M. Lyons	----- 1887	Galway, Ireland; Boston, MA
	14	John B. Sullivan	1848-1925	Boston, MA
	15	Mary A. Hanlon	1867-1941	Cork, Ireland; Boston, MA
V	16	William J. Robertson	----- 1890	Nova Scotia
	17	Elizabeth S. Street	----- 1886	New York; Nova Scotia
	18	Willlam Rodgers		Ireland; New Brunswick
	19	Catherine E. Harrison	1828-1895	New Brunswick; Lynn, MA
	20	Michael Kelley	1840-1910	Sligo, Ireland; Newburyport, MA
	21	Margaret Poer (Powers)	1841-1913	Ireland; Newburyport, MA
	22	John McLoughlin	1822-1873	Mayo, Ireland; Newburyport, MA
	23	Winifred A. Burke	----- 1873	Galway, Ireland; Newburyport, MA
	24	Martin Casey		Galway, Ireland
	25	Honora (Bridget) Guardiner		Galway, Ireland
	26	John Lyons		Galway, Ireland
	27	Bridget -----		Galway, Ireland
	28	Daniel F. Sullivan	----- 1894	Cork, Ireland; Boston, MA
	29	Catherine Horgan	----- 1869	Ireland; Boston, MA
	30	William Hanlon	----- 1910	Cork, Ireland
	31	Johannah Coleman	----- 1915	Cork, Ireland; Boston, MA
VI	34	Samuel Street	----- 1838	Halifax, Nova Scotia
	35	Sarah S. Smith	----- 1831	Halifax, Nova Scotia
	38	Morris Harrison	----- 1856	Carlow, Ireland; New Brunswick

	39	Sarah O'Neil		
	40	John Kelley		Ireland
	41	Catherine McGlonne		Ireland
	42	Patrick Poer (Poore)		Ireland
	43	Elizabeth (Lydia) Kennedy		Ireland
	44	Henry McGloughlin		Ireland
	45	Ellen ----		Ireland
	46	Patrick G. Burke		Galway, Ireland; Newburyport, MA
	47	Bridget Fighely	----- 1866	Galway, Ireland; Newburyport, MA
	56	William Sullivan		Ireland
	57	Julia Murray	----- 1869	Ireland; Boston, MA
	58	Jeremiah Horgan		Ireland
	59	Mary -----		Ireland
	62	Daniel Coleman		Ireland
	63	Mary McCarthy		Ireland

****

Ahnentafel of Florence (Ramsey) Sutherland, mother of Donald Ramsey Sutherland, 162 Foxwook Road, Guilford, CT 06437

I	1	Florence Josephine Ramsey	1882-1956	Haverhill, MA
II	2	William Henry Ramsey	1845-1918	Amesbury, Haverhill, MA
	3	Rosina Jane Gilman	1843-1916	Newburyport, Haverhill, MA
III	4	Charles C. Ramsey	1804-1867	Amesbury, Haverhill, MA
	5	Hannah Goodwin	1824-1900	Newton, NH; Haverhill, MA
	6	Lewis Gilman	1805-1877	Springfield, Kingston, NH: West Newbury, MA
	7	Mary Jane Farrington	1807-1895	West Newbury, MA; Kingston, NH
IV	8	Charles Ramsey	1775-1865	Newburyport, Amesbury, MA
	9	Anna Miriam Pressey	1775-	Amesbury, MA
	10	Daniel B. Goodwin	1786-1875	Newton, Brentwood, NH
	11	Sarah F. Heath	1796-1883	Newton, Haverhill, MA
	12	Joel Gilman	1778-	Springfield, Salisbury, NH
	13	Polly (or Molly) Elliot	1773-	Newton, Lebanon, NH
	14	Ebenezer Farrington	1775-1857	Fryeburg, ME; West Newbury, MA
	15	Ruth Bartlett	c1781-1860	West Newbury, MA
V	16	William Ramsey	c1740-1777	Newburyport, MA
	17	Elizabeth Sargent	1741-1799	Amesbury, MA
	18	Hezekiah Pressey	1752-1802	Amesbury, MA
	19	Mary Challis	1754-	Amesbury, MA
	20	Daniel Goodwin	1748-1834	Amesbury, MA; Newton, NH
	21	Miriam Blaisdell	1756-1819	Amesbury, MA; Newton, NH
	22	Nehemiah Heath	1763-1831	Amesbury, MA; Newton, NH
	23	Mary Peaslee	1771-1815	Newton, NH
	24	Daniel Gilman	1754-1835	Kingston, Springfield, NH
	25	Mehitable Judkins	1758-1838	Kingston, Springfield, NH
	26	Thomas Elliot		Amesbury, MA; Newton, NH
	27	Anna Challis	1752-	Amesbury, MA; Newton, NH
	30	Isaac Bartlett	1749-	Newbury, MA
	31	Rebecca Sargent	1750-1828	Haverhill, Newbury, MA
VI	34	Charles Sargent	1694-1754	Amesbury, MA

	35	Hepzibah Heath	1698-1754	Haverhill, Amesbury, MA
	36	Joseph Pressey	1719-1781	Amesbury, MA
	37	Judith Challis	1728-c1807	Amesbury, MA
	38	William Challis, Jr.	1711-	Amesbury, MA
	39	Hannah Weed	1713-	Amesbury, MA
	40	Daniel Goodwin	1714-	Amesbury, MA
	41	Hannah Colby	1717-	Amesbury, MA
	42	Samuel Blaisdell	c1716-1769	Amesbury, MA
	43	Dorothy Barnard	1713-1756	Amesbury, MA
	44	Sargent Heath	1719-	Amesbury, MA
	45	Judith Hoyt	1722-	Amesbury, MA
	46	John Peaslee	1735-1807	Haverhill, Amesbury, MA
	47	Mary Huntington	1739-1814	Amesbury, MA
	48	Steven Gilman	1713-	Kingston, NH
	49	Mary French	1720-	Kingston, NH
	50	Samuel Judkins	1736-	Kingston, Salibury, NH
	51	Sarah Bohonon	1736-	Boscawen, Salisbury, NH
	60	Benjamin Bartlett	1708-	Newbury, MA
	61	Jemima Parkhurst	1715-	Weston, Newbury, MA
	62	Henry Sargent	1723-1773	Amesbury, Haverhill, MA
	63	Anna Smith	1720-1801	Haverhill, Newbury, MA

****

Ahnentafel of Candace Porter Ladd, paternal grandmother of Linda B. Hastings, 17545 Wheat Fall Drive, Rockville, MD 20855

I	1	Candace Porter Ladd	1875-1950	Belmont, New Hampton, NH
II	2	Arthur Stuart Ladd	1838-1912	Belmont, NH
	3	Ellen Mariah Porter	1841-1907	Lyman, Belmont, NH
III	4	Langdon Ladd	1811-1887	Belmont, NH
	5	Sylvania Colby	1818-1882	Sanbornton, Belmont, NH
	6	Irad Porter	1807-1892	Lyman, Belmont, NH
	7	Letta Knapp	1811-1882	Lymna, Belmont, NH
IV	8	Edward Ladd	1773-1820	Belmont, NH
	9	Hannah Hoyt	1776-1856	Amesbury, MA; Belmont, NH
	10	Barnard Hoyt Colby	1789-1862	Sanbornton, NH
	11	Grace Brown	1791-1880	Deerfield, Sanbornton, NH
	12	Joseph Porter	1780-1856	; Lyman, NH
	13	Emma Parker	1788-1861	Lyman, NH
	14	Elijah Knapp	1769-1869	Norton, MA: Lyman, NH
	15	Sally Eliot	1776-1868	Hinsdale, Lyman, NH
V	16	Samuel Ladd	1744-1801	Belmont, NH
	17	Abigail Flanders	1747-1803	Exeter, Belmont, NH
	18	Barnard Hoyt	1730-1810	Amesbury, MA; Sanbornton, NH
	19	Annah Stuart	1736-1832	; Sanborton, NH
	20	Ebenezer Colby	1761-1840	Haverhill, MA; Sanbornton, NH
	21	Anna Hoyt	----- 1825	; Bradford, MA
	22	Enoch Brown	1753-1838	; Deerfield, NH
	23	Abigail Stuart	1759-1840	; Deerfield, NH
	26	Samuel Parker	1755-1834	Groton, MA; Lyman, NH
	27	Candace Hand		
	28	Abial Knapp	1738-1832	Norton, MA; Lyman, NH

	29	Keziah Cheney	1743-	Norton, MA; Lyman, NH
VI	32	Edward Ladd	1707-1787	Exeter, Belmont, NH
	33	Catherine Thing	1711-1773	; Belmont, NH
	34	Thomas Flanders	1721-	Salisbury, MA; Gilmanton, NH
	35	Margaret Lawrence		Stratham, NH;
	36	John Hoyt	1689-	Amesbury, MA;
	37	Sarah Barnard	1700-	Amesbury, MA;
	38	Robert Stuart	1701-1781	Rowley, MA; Newton, NH
	39	Ann Adams	1705-1787	Newbury, MA; Newton, NH
	40	Ebenezer Colby	1717-1795	Amesbury, Sandown, NH
	41	Mary Chase	1728-	Haverhill, MA
	42	same as #18		
	43	same as #19		
	44	Enoch Brown	1725-1796	; Deerfield, NH
	46	Samuel Stuart	1728-1767	Bradford, MA
	47	Grace Hubbard	1737-1784	
	52	Solomon Parker	1722-1798	Groton, MA; Lyman, NH
	53	Hepzibah Douglas	1727-1820	; Lyman, NH
	56	Jonathan Knapp	1709-1793	Taunton, Norton, MA
	57	Mehitable Tucker	1707-1795	Norton, MA
	58	Benjamin Cheney	1725-	

I welcome any comments, additions, corrections, and particularly any help with any of the missing names.

****

Ahnentafel of Ella Maud Brown, maternal grandmother of Linda B. Hastings, 17545 Wheat Fall Drive, Rockville, ME 20855

I	1	Ella Maud Brown	1873-1955	Haverhill, MA; Middletown, NY
II	2	John Henry Brown	1842-1923	Bradford, Haverhill, MA
	3	Julia O'Neil	1839-1918	Ontario, Canada; Haverhill, MA
III	4	Charles Henry Brown	1820-1900	Bradford, Haverhill, MA
	5	Sarah Phillips	1823-1913	Bradford, Haverhill, MA
	6	Arthur O'Neil	1808-1848	Ireland; Ontario, Canada
IV	8	Benjamin Brown	1791-1835	Where?; Bradford, MA
	9	Parthenia Peabody	1797-1873	Bradford, MA
	10	Leonard Phillips	1792-1832	Bradford, MA
	11	Sally Head	1796-1881	Bradford, Haverhill, MA
V	18	Andrew Peabody	1748-1812	Bradford, MA
	19	Mary Morse	1760-	Bradford, MA
	20	Samuel Phillips	1760-1829	Bradford, MA
	21	Mehitabel Haggett	----- 1825	; Bradford, MA
	22	Reuben Head	1759-1819	Bradford, MA
	23	Lydia Day	1765-1848	Bradford, MA
VI	36	John Peabody	1714-1765	Bradford, MA
	37	Mary Chadwick	1713-	Bradford, MA

	38	Thomas Morse		
	39	Elizabeth Bartlett		
	40	John Phillips		
	41	Elizabeth Haggett		
	44	John Head	1721-1785	; Bradford, MA
	45	Mehetabel	----- 1789	; Bradford, MA
	46	Abraham Day	1738-1819	Bradford, MA
	47	Elizabeth Little	1744-1777	Newbury, Bradford, MA
VII	72	David Peabody	1678-1726	Boxford, Bradford, MA
	73	Sarah Pope	1683-1756	; Boxford, MA
	80	James Phillips		Ipswich, Bradford, MA
	81	Molly Lord		
	88	James Head	1683-1743	Newcastle, NH;
	89	Elizabeth Atwood	1700-	Bradford, MA;
	92	Abraham Day	1738-1819	Bradford, MA
	93	Mary Bailey	1719-1780	Newbury, Bradford, MA
	94	Nathan Little	1717-1745	Newbury, MA
	95	Hannah Mighill	1719-1753	Rowley, Newbury, MA

I welcome any comments, addition,, corrections, and particularly any help with the ancestry of Benjamin Brown, #8.

****

GOOD NEWS AND BAD NEWS

What does the Lynnfield Library renovation project mean to researchers using the genealogy room? The good news is that the library will try to remain open to the public during the renovations, with perhaps the exception of six weeks in late May, early June. The bad news is that it will be very noisy (from 7 a.m. to 3 p.m., Monday through Friday) and will probably be very dusty.

The Genealogy Room is in Phase One, which means the entire collection has to be moved out in December. The good news is that the collection will be moved to the open balcony, where it can be consulted. However, it will be a reduced collection. The "lesser-used" items will be boxed (and unavailable) during the construction period. Only two tables will be available, and, because of fire codes, the number of people on the balcony at any one time, must be kept at a minimum. The present staircase will be unavailable, and only the stairway at the far end of the balcony will be usable. Every effort will be made by ESOG to provide basic service for researchers.

Further bad news is that, when the new Genealogy Room is opened downstairs, it will be a great deal smaller than the present one, in fact, about 2/3 the size. However, all film readers will be outside the room, leaving more space for books, and we are looking into condensed, rolling stacks to better utilize the space available. Meanwhile, genealogy librarian, Marcia Lindberg, is "weeding" the collection, discarding items not used or not pertinent to the collection policy she established in 1970. These books will be offered at ESOG's Book Auction in January.

To recap, basically, the core of the collection will be available throughout the year of renovations, and a slightly reduced collection will be housed on the main floor of the library when the work is finished, making easier access to copying machines. That is Good News.

Society News

FORTHCOMING MEETINGS

November 17, 1990 - Centre Church, Lynnfield; Social Hour 12:00; Program 1:00
    USING LAND RECORDS EFFECTIVELY, by Yvonne H. P. Silva,

December 15, 1990 - Centre Church, Lynnfield
    CHRISTMAS COVERED DISH LUNCHEON - 12:00; SHOW AND TELL - 1:00

January 19, 1991 - Centre Church, Lynnfield
    BOOK TALK - 12:00; USED BOOK AUCTION - 1:00

February 16, 1991 - Centre Church, Lynnfield; Social Hour 12:00; Program 1:00
    WORCESTER COUNTY; ITS PEOPLE AND THE RECORDS, by Kay Sheldon

March 16, 1991 - Centre Church, Lynnfield; Social Hour 12:00; Program 1:00
    COLLECTING ANCESTORS, by Noreen Pramberg

April 20, 1991 - **HAVERHILL PUBLIC LIBRARY - ALL DAY WORK MEETING**

May 18, 1990 - Centre Church, Lynnfield; Social Hour 12:00; Program 1:00
    ADVANCED GENEALOGY; A MINI-COURSE, by Marcia Lindberg

REPORTS OF PREVIOUS MEETINGS

15 September was a lovely, mild, sunny day but only 65 came to launch our 1990/91 season. Those who came to enjoy the social hour had fun swapping tales about research experiences and findings during their summer activities. At 1:00 p.m., Pres. Marcia Lindberg called the meeting to order with her usual enthusiastic welcome, and brought us up-to-date about ESOG happenings during our summer recess, after which Elaine and Bob Dow took us along the old post roads so full of history (the forerunner of many of our present state and interstate highways). There was never a dull moment when traveling in those days, for most always the unexpected lay within or just ahead - coaches swayed and jolted along rutty, rocky "roads" and could overturn from the shifting of weight, companions could be from "sophisticated" outlaws to noted dignitaries, highway robbers and unfriendly Indians lurked in the shadows, wheels came off or broke, a horse could break a leg and have to be shot, and to be mired in deep mud ruts or upset in swollen streams after heavy rain, was all part of the ride. Drivers and out-riders were rugged, weather-beaten, individuals who rode "shot-gun" for they often carried mail, cash and important documents too, and could tell many interesting and humorous tales. The Dows have a delightful way of telling stories and those of us who attended this meeting enjoyed an educational and entertaining program.

20 October. We were lucky again for it was a nice fall day and it was good to see 95 members in attendance, including those from Maine, New Hampshire, and a number of once-in-awhiles and Nick Marks on his annual visit from California. We got word that our speaker would be late, so Pres. Marcia Lindberg called the meeting to order at 1:00, was pleased to see so many present. She told about the Cemetery Project, to be published in December, and about the renovations at the Lynnfield Library. Bob Canney told about his manuscript on the early Marriages of Strafford County, NH, that Heritage Books will publish. Nick Marks told about the portrait of a noted person he had found and rescued from the trash heap. By that time our speaker, Bob Starrett, had arrived. Bob is a local resident, transplanted in Scotland, and involved in Scots-Irish research. Using graphic slides, he gave us an interesting first-hand "lesson" in tracing Scots-Irish ancestry in northern Ireland. As is our custom, this lecture will appear in a forthcoming issue of TEG.

Queries

> **GUIDELINES FOR SUBMITTING QUERIES**
>
> Readers may submit free queries. No query to exceed 50 words. No limit on number of queries. Ask specific questions re parentage, birthplace, marriage, children, etc. Use identifying detail such as name, date, or place. *Type* or *print* on 3x5 card. Use abbreviations listed at end of February Query section. Deadlines for queries: Jan 1, Apr 1, July 1, Oct 1. Send queries to: Teg query editor, Lynnfield Public Library, 18 Summer St., Lynnfield, MA 01940

GREEN/POOL/LYON
Seek info William GREEN, Jr. b ca 1788, s William Sr & Betsy (POOL) GREEN of Reading, MA & Peru, VT; William, Jr. m 1812 Peru, VT Dorcas LYON; had large fam, mov in 1830's to OH? Nova Scotia? Seek names & bdt.

CARTER/BOUDRO/DAVISON
Seek info Charles CARTER of Nova Scotia; s George b Sep 1833 Nova Scotia, fr Point Pleasant Halifax 1865, m 1865 at Clare, NS Mary Eunice/Louisa BOUDRO dau of Patrick BOUDRO. Charles m Adazilla DAVISON. Would like to corr with anyone researching CARTER and/or BOUDRO.

GREEN/GHAFNEY
Seek info William GREEN b VT, m 1 June 1837 Jane GHAFNEY spinster of Shipton, Richmond Co, Que. Ch: Thomas E. b 1839, James A. b 1842, Henry H., George W., maybe more. Who are par William & Jane?

PAYSON/CARTER
Seek info Hanley PAYSON merchant-fisherman Westport, Digby Co, N. S. 1866-81, b ca 1825. Seek rel to Charles & George CARTER etc.

GHAFNEY
Seek info Thomas GHAFNEY b ca 1766-85. In 1825 census Shipton, Richmond Co., Que. had 6 ch. Need names, bdts, etc.

BOUDREAU/COMEAU/GAUDET/BELLIVEAU/TULL
Seek info H. BEAUDREAU m N. COMEAU prob of Church Point, N.S.; s Elias Victor BEAUDREAU b 15 Aug 1839 Church Point. Elias m 3 times, w/1 d childbirth 1863, w/2 Mary Vitaline Otil GAUDET wid Wm. BELLIVEAU, w/3 Jessie Maud TULL. He d Mar 1924 Clementsport, N.S. Carol A. Carter, 10 Timothy Rd., W. Peabody, MA 01960.

****

JOHNSON/MACOMBER
Mehitable JOHNSON b ca 1746-7 m 14 July 1766 Elijah MACOMBER Middleboro, MA. Need par/anc Mehitable.

SMITH/MACOMBER
Seek info Chloe SMITH m Middleboro, MA 22 Dec 1796 Elijah MACOMBER.

ROADS/GREEN
Need par Elizabeth ROADS b 1745, m 17 Nov 1767 Marblehead, MA Samuel H. GREEN. She d 24 Oct 1826 Marblehead.

WASHBURN/LE BARON/RUSSELL
Need info Elizabeth WASHBURN Middleboro, MA, m 9 May 1781 James LE BARON; dau Hannah b 24 Dec 1788 Hebron, ME. Elizabeth d bef. Feb 1791 when James m/2 Jane RUSSELL of Gray, ME.

DOWNS/THOMAS/JACKSON
Need info Jane DOWNS b Mar 1770 Cape Cod, m/1 19 May 1791 Robert JACKSON at Boston; m/2 1 July 1796 Nathaniel THOMAS. Jane d 22 Dec 1850 Plymouth, MA. Betty Lenth, 39 Merriwold Ln., Deep River, CT 06417.

****

STEVENS/HOYT/RAND
Seek iden Hannah STEVENS m/1 Thomas HOYT, m/2 22 Jan 1806 at Hampstead, NH Moses RAND of Barnstead, NH. She d 1842 Barnstead. Clayton R. Adams, 6 Laurel Rd., Brunswick, ME 04011.

****

HURD/POND
Need anc Charles W. HURD b ca 1820-25 & w Emmeline POND. He d ca 1900 bur Pondville, MA. They had many ch; John b ca 1862 Pondville, MA (now Foxboro?)

RHOADES/JORDAN/RUSSELL/COBB
Cecil RHOADES m Lucy A. JORDAN, dau Carrie b 5 Feb 1867 d 29 June 1945 m Edwin C. COBB of ME. Lucy m/2 6 July 1891 in Lynn, MA L. Octavius RUSSELL. May have liv Saugus. Need anc RHOADES & JORDAN. Earl C. Pike, 271 N. Gorham Rd., Gorham, ME 04038.

****

PEVERLY/WALFORD
Welcome any data par Thomas PEVERLY & w Jane WALFORD; Portsmouth 1650s. Helen D. Dotts, 7501 Palm Ave., Yucca Valley, CA 92284.

DUNHAM
John^2 DUNHAM Jr of Plymouth, MA was b where? (1615 Leyden, Holland or 1620 England?) He m Mary ----. Need her dts.

BUFFINGTON/LUTHER
Need all data William^4 BUFFINGTON, Jr & w Phebe^5 LUTHER m 1746/7 Freetown, MA. Ch: Royal, Commings, Phebe, Cynthia, Noah.

GARNSEY/MUNNINGS
Need all data Henry^1 GARNSEY Dorchester, MA m Hannah^2 MUNNINGS. Dr. Dorothy Branson, 10505 E. 42nd St. #D, Kansas City, MO 64133.

WIDGER/HOWE
Seek par Sarah WIDGER w of Daniel HOWE (1719-1797) m 1739 res Ipswich & Andover, MA.

JONES/OSGOOD
Seek par Robert JONES of Amesbury, MA, b ca 1633 m Joanna OSGOOD ca 1658 Salisbury, MA.

COCHRAN/CARTER
Seek par Hannah COCHRAN b ca 1790 m Henry CARTER of Andover, MA. Donald M. Chaffee, 19 Columbia St., Wellesley Hills, MA 02181-1602.

KEIZER/POORE/MITCHELL
Need VR John Jesse KEIZER b Canterbury, NH ca 1791 m/1 May 1812 Portland, ME Nancy POORE, m/2 Nancy MITCHELL (where?) Liv E. Corinth, ME ca 1818. Desc liv OH. Leon Keyser, 22 Tamarland, Portland, ME 14103.

BADGER/WARREN/McIVER
Seeking desc 2 BADGER fam researchers: the late Phelps WARREN (liv 955 Lexington Ave, NY, NY 10021 in 1970) & Mrs. Edward H. McIVER of Charlestown, SC. Marie Green Bryant, 6 Cornus Ct., Savannah, GA 31406.

FOSTER/WOODFORD
Seek par David FOSTER & Ursula WOODFORD both b ca 1800 Hartford, CT; m there ca 1824.

HILL/TILTON
Seek par Elizabeth HILL m Daniel TILTON ca 1708 Stratham, NH.

SMITH/TILTON
Seek par Rachel SMITH m Abraham TILTON ca 1758 Rockingham Co., NH. Elizabeth Tilton, 3425 Madrona Dr., Santa Barbara, CA 93105.

NICHOLS (NICALS)/STONE/EATON
Seek par Mary NICHOLS (NICALS) b ca 1714 poss Hingham, MA, m 28 Apr 1734 Gloucester, MA Benjamin STONE b 1714 Andover, MA; dau m Jonathan EATON b 1736 Haverhill, MA. Would like to corr with anyone researching these fam.

STONE/FOSTER
Seek anc Benjamin STONE b 1714 Andover, MA. Were par Hugh Jr. b 1682 & Dorothy ---- ? Were gpar Hugh Sr & Hannah FOSTER? Was Hannah dau of Andrew FOSTER?

EATON/STONE/WOOD
Seek w of Jonathan^6 EATON b 7 May 1768 Atkinson, Rockingham Co. NH s of Jonathan^5 EATON & Mary STONE. He m ca 1794 Lucinda ----; s Benjamin b 23 Apr 1795. Fam in Steuben Co, NY early 1800s with bro Benjamin. Sis Mary (Molly) m Gideon WOOD 4 Jan 1784. Bonnie Venneberg, Box 1048, Syracuse, KS 67878.

BARTLETT
Need anc Lydia BARTLETT (1690-1720) of MA. Whom did she m?

DURKEE/CROSS
Need proof William DURKEE & Martha CROSS (1650-1727) m 20 Dec 1664 Ipswich, MA. They d Hampton, CT.

MORRISEY
Who was w Richard MORRISEY b 1793 England? He arr Boston 24 Dec 1823 on ship George Henry.

STEVENS/PEARL
Need proof Elizabeth STEVENS (1697-1736) m Nathan PEARL. Richard Morrissey, 28656 Murrieta Rd., Sun City, CA 92381.

BUTCHER/BATES
Seek info John BUTCHER & fam, b VA m Nancy BATES. Mov OH early 1800s. Known ch: George

Washington b 1850, William, Claude. Later mov Ventin, Benton Co., IA. Sylvia R. Braswell, 10904 Ada Ave., Stockton, CA 95205.

****

FITCH/STRONG
Need anc Eleanor STRONG m Coventry, CT 24 Jan 1736/7 Stephen FITCH.

CLARK
George & Sarah CLARK, Milford, CT, had dau Sarah b 26 Oct 1706. Who did Sarah m?

KNOWLTON/AUSTIN
Deborah KNOWLTON of Ipswich & Wenham, MA b 1723 m 24 Sept 1754 John AUSTIN; dau Mary m 1784 Edmund KNOWLTON. Need anc Deborah & John.

CURTIS/ABELL
Henry CURTIS m Elizabeth ABELL 13 May 1645 CT; ch: Samuel b 1649, Nathaniel b 1651. Did Samuel or Nathaniel have dau Sarah b ca 1686 Northampton, MA?

BURKE
Would someone with *American Families with British Ancestry*, by Burke, be willing to copy some pages for me? Mrs. Gilbert Tatro, 1700 Ben Franklin Dr., #4C, Sarasota, FL 34236.

****

RYLEY (RILEY)
Who was Thomas RYLEY m Sedgwick ME 16 June 1824? What became of this couple?

STEWART/GRAY/BUNKER
Who was Charles STEWART "from Duxbury" (ca 1800) Sedgwick, ME? Were par Charles & Mary? Who w/1? Others bel Esther GRAY & Mary BUNKER. 4 known ch. Need all dates.

DODGE/BROWN/FLOWERS
Did John DODGE b Gloucester 26 July 1747 d 1829 m/2 Lydia BROWN 1805? Was she wid of James? Or did Lydia m/2 int 1798 Bartholomew FLOWERS?

AVERY/BARNES/STOVER
Solomon AVERY b 15 Jan 1749/50 m 25 Dec 1772 Hannah BARNES. Did he or son m 1801 Eunice STOVER of York? Who were Elizabeth b 12 Nov 1769 & Robert int 22 Oct 1796?

BORTHRICK
Seek ident Dolly, w Abel BORTHRICK, d Sedgwick, ME 6 May 1786. Need anc & ch.

CALEF
Need data on ch Dr. John CALEF, Loyalist of Castine, ME & NB. Miss Elizabeth C. Wescott, RFD 2, Box 920, Apt. 202, Bucksport, ME 04416.

****

RAYNER/GILBERT
Need anc William RAYNER m 1658 Ipswich, MA Elizabeth, wid Humphrey GILBERT.

GILBERT/KIMBALL/KILHAM/BLACK
Was Elizabeth --- wid Humphrey GILBERT, dau John & Susanna BLACK as alleged in *Gilberts of New England?* She m/3 Henry KIMBALL, m/4 Daniel KILHAM.

FOSSEY/RAYNER
Need par Thomas FOSSEY d 1700, m 1685 Ipswich Elizabeth RAYNER, dau William & Elizabeth RAYNER.

QUESTED/KENNETT/SHARPLES/SWEENY/COOPER
Seek desc William QUESTED (1796-1873) & w Ann ---- (1798-1888); arr W. Newbury, MA fr Co Kent, Eng. 1843. Ch all b Eng: George m Charlotte KENNETT, James m Ann KENNETT, Mary Ann m John SHARPLES, William m Mary SWEENY, Maria m ---- COOPER, John, Elizabeth, Alice.

GORMAN/FURBUSH/GREEN/HENDREHAN/COY (McCOY)
Seek anc/desc Peter GORMAN (s Patrick & Mary?) m 1855 Newburyport, MA Ellen GREEN or HENDREHAN; m/2 1867 Sarah FURBUSH of Bradford, ME wid --- COY or McCOY. Peter & Sarah res Haverhill aft 1887.

RAMSEY/GOODWIN/PRESSEY/SARGENT/EDDY
Charles C. RAMSEY (1804-1867) m/1 Lucy EDDY 1828, m/2 1843 Haverhill, MA Hannah GOODWIN (1824-1900). Was he s Charles RAMSEY & Anna PRESSEY; grs William RAMSEY & Elizabeth SARGENT? Daniel H. Burrows, RD 1, Box 211A, Otisville, NY 10963.

****

WARNER/HOVEY
Who was Priscilla WARNER w James HOVEY (1650-1675) of Ipswich & Brookfield, MA? Need dts & par. Was she wid John WARNER of RI or John of Ipswich?

PETERS/LEWIS/CUTLER
Who were 4 dau Philip PETERS b 1753 of Woburn & Wilmington & w Susanna LEWIS other than Susannah (1771-1775) & Eunice m 1804 Samuel CUTLER?

LOOMER (LUME)/MILLER/LOOMIS
Stephen LOOMER (LUME) m New London, CT by 1684 Mary MILLER of Groton dau George MILLER. Any rel Joseph LOOMIS who purch land Windsor, CT 1638?

LINTON (LETTIN) WATERS
Robert LINTON (LETTIN) d 1665 Lancaster, w Elizabeth ---; had 3 kwn ch. Need all data. Dau Ann m 1634-45 Lawrence WATERS of Charlestown.

HOWLETT/FRENCH
Thomas HOWLETT (ca 1606-1678) Ipswich m 1640 Alice FRENCH wid Thomas of Boston. Need Alice's par & ch.

HOUSE/BROWN/CUTTING
Need par Hannah HOUSE b ca 1650 m 1670 at Charlestown James BROWN, travelling glazier fr Ipswich, s James & Sarah (CUTTING); settled Newbury.

HOUSE/LINNELL (LARNETT)
Need all dat Jemima/Peninah HOUSE dau Rev. John, m ca 1627 Robert LINNELL (LARNETT) of Scituate. Also dau Abigail & 1/w Robert.

HOLLIS/WHITMAN
Who was Abigail HOLLIS m ca 1663 John WHITMAN of Weymouth, MA? Was she sis John (1645-1700)?

BEARD (BEIRD)/WILLIAMS/BAKER
Need par Andrew BEARD (BEIRD) b Eng d 1717 Billerica, m ca 1696 Mary WILLIAMS b 1672 dau Thomas. Also need ddts of s Ebenezer & w Esther BAKER of Woburn, Arlington, Wilmington, MA.

GOODRICH/GOODRIDGE/BAILEY
Need ddts Francis Bowman GOODRICH b 1800 Bedford & w Mary S. b 1810, m/2 1855 James BAILEY. Need all data dau Lucy A. & Martha E. & fa Capt. William GOODRIDGE b 1757 of Newbury, RevW. & VT.

WILLIAMS/LORD
Need all data Daniel WILLIAMS b NY or VT m 1819 Mary LORD at Wakefield, mov Westbrook, ME. Had 3 s & maybe dau Mary.

HANDS (HANNES) BELL/BULFINCH
John HANDS (HANNES) b 10 Sep 1654 s Mark (1609-1664) & Mary ----, m Boston Mary BELL b ca 25 Dec 1653 Charlestown, "servant to Jones 1671." Was Mary dau Abraham BELL & Katherine BULFINCH? Need dau Katherine's bdt & 1/w Mark. M. J. Lewis, Box 676, Balboa, CA 92661.

****

MERRYFIELD/WHITE
Seek anc Bonnel MERRYFIELD m 10 Oct 1709 Marblehead, MA Susanna WHITE.

JONES/GAMMON
Seek info Thomas JONES, Gloucester, MA & New London, CT, m 26 June 1677 Catherine GAMMON.

BAKER
Seek par & gpar of the Ebenezer BAKER, h of Polly & fa of Ebenezer, bpt 4 Oct 1807 Sandy Bay/Gloucester/Rockport, MA.

BAKER/ANNABLE
Seek par of the Ebenezer BAKER, Manchester & Ipswich, m 20 Feb 1765 Jemima ANNABLE.

CEELY (SEELEY)/MERRYFIELD
Seek anc Benjamin CEELY (SEELEY) m 30 Aug 1742 Marblehead Susannah MERRYFIELD. Douglas A. Wenny, 1124 Windon Drive, Wilmington, DE 19803.

****

MUSSMACHER/DRISCOLL
Need any info MUSSMACHER/DRISCOLL fam, arr America 1847-57, liv Brooklyn area, NY. Kathy Mussmacher, RD #1 Box 248, Dolgeville, NY 13329.

****

GRANT/MORTON
Seek info Abraham GRANT & w Sarah MORTON New Germany, NS. Most ch em to Lynn & Brockton, MA, 1894, shoe work. Poss Abraham & Sarah d in New Eng.

BEAL/WILSON
Seek any info Phoebe Anne WILSON b 1836? Minot, ME? m Hiram BEAL 1854? Was in Wisc. 1855-61; in Newburyport 1898. American Indian?

BEAL/WENDELL/WILD BROTHER
Wish corr with anyone with info Gordon's Camp, a lumber camp Winn, ME ca 1903. Camp cook Albert BEAL. WENDELL name in book WILD BROTHER pseudonym for Albert & Effie BEAL. Robert A. Beal, Jr., 91 Prospect St., #2, Newburyport, MA 01950.

INDEX TO QUERIES IN VOLUME X

ABBOTT, Elizabeth, 57; Family, 115; John Bennett, 113; Susannah Shortbridge, 172
ABELL, Elizabeth, 228
ADAMS, Jonathan, Mary, Thankful, 172
ADDITON (ATHERTON), Samuel, 171
AD(E)SHADE FAMILY, 55
ALLEN, Lydia, 116, 174; Azariah, David, Jonathan, Lucy, 172
ANDERSON, Betsey, Jacob, Joseph, 54
ANDREWS, Dorcas, Elizabeth, Hulda, Jerusha, John, Stephen, 56
ANNABLE, Jemima, 229
APPLETON, John, Priscilla, 173
ATKINS, Alice, 57
ATWOOD, Abigail, 56; Isaac, Orsamus, 55
AUSTIN, John, Mary, 228
AVERILL (AVERY), Lydia, Solomon, 54
AVERY, Solomon, 228
BADGER FAMILY, 227, John, 57
BAILEY, Caleb, David, Mary, 112; James, Lucy, Martha, 229
BAKER, Cynthia, Isaac, 55; Ebenezer, Esther, 229
BALLARD, William, 114
BANCROFT, Timothy, 116
BANKS, Elizabeth, 172
BARETO, Nicholas, 113
BARNARD, Hannah, 57; John, 55; Lydia, 171
BARNES, Hannah, 228
BARNS, Hannah, 54
BARKER, John, 116
BARTLETT, Miriam, Nathan, 57; Perley, 113; Lydia,
BARTON, Mehitable, 115; Joshua, Nathan, Jr., 172
BARTRAM, Esther (Estar), William, 56
BATCHELDER, John, Joseph, 174
BATES, John, 55; Nancy, 227
BEACH, Isaac, 172
BEAL, Albert, Effie, Hiram, 229
BEARD (BEIRD), Andrew, Ebenezer, 229
BEAUDREAU, Elias Victor, H., 226
BECK, Mary, 54
BELL, Abraham, Mary 229
BELLIVEAU, William, 226
BENSON, Charity, 173
BERRY (BARRY), Thadeus (Teague), 116
BERRY, Henry, Isaac, John, 116; Andrew, Elizabeth, Jenny, Ketley, Margaret, Nancy, Thomas, Robert, 172
BISHOP, John, William, 171; John, 172
BIXBY, Anna (Nancy), 116
BLACK, John, Susanna, 228
BLAISDELL, Molly, 57
BLAKE, Edward, 171

BLETHEN, Elizabeth, Joseph, Miriam, 54
BODFISH, Thankful, 55
BODWELL, Henry, 112
BORTHRICK, Abel, Dolly, 228
BOSTON (BASTON), Sophia, 116
BOSWORTH, Susanna, 55
BOUDRO, Louisa, Mary Eunice, Patrick, 226
BOWLES, Elizabeth, 172
BOWMAN, Hannah, 114
BOYCE, Benjamin, Sarah, 55
BRAINARD, Daniel, 56
BREED, Allen, 114
BRISCALL, Elizabeth E., 174
BROOKS, Dudley, Oliver, 174
BROWN, Emily, 113; James, 54, 174, 228; John, 54; Lydia, 228
BROWNING, Thomas, 171
BUFFINGTON, Commings, Cynthia, Noah, Phebe, Royal, William, 227
BULFINCH, Katherine, 229
BULLARD (BULLOCK), Anna, 54
BUNKER, Mary, 228
BURNAP, Benjamin, 56
BURR, Samuel, Jr., 172
BURTON, Hannah, 116
BUSH, Jonathan, 173
BUTCHER, Claude, George Washington, John, William, 227
BUTLER, John, 172
BUTTERFIELD, Ebenezer, 54
CODMAN, Lydia, 171
CALEF, Dr. John, 228
CAMMITT, Abraham, Ann, David, Hannah, Isaac, Judith, Mary, Paul, Peter, Robard, Silas, Thomas, 55
CARLETON, Richard A., 113
CARTER, Mary, 114; Charles, George, Henry, 226
CEELY (SEELEY), Benjamin, 229
CHADWICK, John, Jonathan, 114
CHALLIS, Mary, 116
CHAMBERLIN, Elizabeth, John, William, 54
CHANDLER, Mary, 114, 174; William, 114
CHESMORE, Daniel, Elizabeth (Betsey), 173
CHILTON FAMILY, 115
CHURCH, John, 171
CHURCHILL FAMILY, 115
CLARK, George, Sarah, 228
CLARKE, Stephen, 112
CLEVELAND, Jerusha, 115
CLOUGH, Daniel, Jabez, Marshall, 56
COBB, Bethia, 55; Edwin C., 226; Helen Elizabeth, 113; Martha, 115

230

COCHRAN, Hannah, 227
COLBY, Anthony, Thomas, 114
COLE, John, 114; Rebecca, 172
COMEAU, N., 226
COMEY (COMEE), David, 172
CONNOR, Frank, 173
COON, W. H., 56
COOPER FAMILY, 228; Mary, 173
COY, Matthew, Sarah, 114
CROSS, Martha, 227
CUNNINGHAM, Mary, 57
CURTIS FAMILY, 114; Ebenezer, Elizabeth, 173; Henry, Nathaniel, Samuel, Sarah, 228
CUTLER, Samuel, 229
CUTTING, Sarah, 229
DANA, Hannah, 54
DARVILL, Mary, Robert, 174
DAVIS, Alice, 112; Ephraim, 173; Jonathan, 57
DAVISON, Adazilla, 226
DEERING, Lydia, Charles B., Flora, Mary Wilma, Rose Etta, Samuel, 173
DELANO FAMILY, 115; Joshua, Lydia, 57
DENNIS, Mary E., 112; Mary, 174
DENNISON, Mehitable, 113
DICKERSON, Judith, He-man, 172
DINGLEY, Susannah, 112
DOANE, Margaret, 171
DODGE, John, 228
DOUGLASE, James, John, 54
DOUNTON, William, 171
DOW, Polly, 173
DOWNS, Mary Ann H., 173; Jane, 226
DREW, Ebenezer, 115; Job, 57
DRISCOLL FAMILY, 229
DUDLEY, Frances, 173
DUNHAM, Thomas, 115; John, 227
DUNN, Lydia, 57
DURKEE, Pearl, Phineas, 57; William, 227
DUSTIN, Samuel, Timothy, 112
DYKE, Jonathan, 54
EATON, Daniel, 114; Mary, 171; Jonathan, 227
EDDY, Lucy, 228
ELKINS, Thomas, 55
EMERSON, Hannah (Joanna), 172
EMERY, Bethia, 112
FARRAR, Hannah, 116
FARREN (FARRIN), Aquilla, Jonathan, Sarah, 112; Zebulon, 113
FARRINGTON, John William, 54; Abigail, 112
FELLOWS, Samuel, 55
FELT, George, 173
FELTON, Daniel, 113
FIFIELD, Betsey, 174; Rachel, Samuel, 171
FINSON, Tammy, 174
FISHER, Molly, 112

FITCH, Stephen, 228
FLOWERS, Bartholomew, 228
FLOYD, Abigail, 174
FORD, Benoni, 171; Joseph, 173
FORTUNE FAMILY, 55
FOSSEY, Thomas, 228
FOSTER, Experience, 54; Anne, Leonard, 171; Andrew, David, Hannah, 227
FOWLER, Mary, 114
FRENCH, Joseph, 54; John, Thomas, 114; Alice, Thomas, 229
FRIZZELL, John, John Allen, 112
FULLER, Abigail, 54; Susanna, 112
FURBUSH, Sarah, 228
GALE, Abigail, 172
GAMMON, Catherine, 229
GARDNER, John, 173
GARNSEY, Henry, 227
GATES, Oldham, 172
GAUDET, Mary Vitaline Otil, 226
GETCHEL, Nathaniel, 54
GHAFNEY, Jane, Thomas, 226
GIBSON, Mary, 173
GILBERT, Elizabeth, Humphrey, 228
GLOVER, Priscilla, 173
GOODELL, Alfred, William, 115
GOODRICH (GOODRIDGE), Charlotte, Francis Bowman, Sophia, 114; William, 114, 229
GOODRIDGE, Mehitabel, 116
GOODSPEED, Nathaniel, Stephen, 174
GOODWIN, James, Lois, 55; Hannah, 228
GORMAN, Mary, Patrick, Peter, 228
GOSS, Elizabeth Witham, Thomas, 174
GOULD, Henry, Jr., 172
GRACIE FAMILY, 55
GRAFFAM, Elias, Elmira, Hannah, Sarah, Samuel, 57
GRANT, Abraham, 229
GRAVES, Elias, Elizabeth, John, Joseph, George, Rachel, 172
GRAY, Esther, 228
GREEN, Laomi, Russell, 115; Ellen, Henry, George, James, Samuel, Thomas, William, 226
GROE, Hannah, 113
GROVER, Jane, 56; James, Thomas, 113
GUNNISON, Eunice, John, Rebecca, 55
GUTCH, Sarah, Robert, 56
HADLOCK, James, 171; Sarah, 172
HALE, Adolphus, E.M., F.D., Sarah Jane, 56
HALLAHAN, Johanna, 57
HALLOWELL, Margaret, 55
HAMMOND, Sylvanus, 173
HANDS (HANNES), John, Mark, Katherine, 229
HANNEVER, Anne, 171
HANKEY, Mary, 57
HARPER, Sarah, William, 174

HARRADEN, Patience, 174
HARWOOD, Jonathan, 55
HASKINS, William, 55
HASTINGS, Solomon, 114
HATCH, Jeremiah, 112
HAWKES, Jonathan, Sarah, 112
HEALD, John, Timothy, 174
HEARD, Hannah, 172
HEELEY, Mary, 57
HEMINGWAY, Samuel, 113
HENDERSON, James, 174
HENDREHAN, Ellen, 228
HENDRICKSON (HENRICKSON, HENRIKSSON), Carl Wilhelm, 55
HILL, Elizabeth, 227
HILTON, Hannah, Mary, William, 113
HOLBROOK, Jane, Thomas, 171
HOLGRAVE, Lydia, 56
HOLLIS, Abigail, John, 229
HOLMES, Elizabeth, 57
HOLT, Alice, 55
HOLYOKE, Mary, 174
HOOL, Sarah, 174
HOOPER, Lydia, 172; William, 116, 172
HORNE, Comfort, Elisha, 173
HOUGHTON, Mary, 173
HOUSE, Hannah, Jemima, John, Peninah, 229
HOVEY, James, 228
HOWE, Daniel, 227
HOWLETT (HOLLET, HALLET), Martha Manning, 113; Thomas, 229
HOYT, Thomas, 226
HURD, Charles W., John, 226
HUSE, Abel, 112
HUSSEY, Lydia, 115
HUTCHINGSON, Rebecca, 171
HYDE, Jonathan, Samuel, 54
INGALLS, Edmund, Mary, 114
ISHAM, Abigail, 55
JACKSON, Elizabeth, John, 172; John, 171; Robert, 226; Lydia, 171
JACOB, Elizabeth, 114
JENKINS, Obidiah, 114
JEWETT, Sally, Spofford, 116
JOHNSON, Sally, William, 54; Sarah, 112; Mehitable, 226
JOHNSTON, James, Jane, 54
JOLLS, Sarah, 115
JONES, Hannah, Mary, 114; Robert, 114, 227; Thomas, 229
JORDAN, Lucy A., 226
KEITH, Achsah, 56
KEIZER, John Jesse, 227
KEMP, Esther, 115
KENNETT, Ann, Charlotte, 228
KILBURN, Lucy, 115
KILHAM, Daniel, 228
KIMBALL, Babgail, Christopher, 115; Henry, 228
KING, Sarah, 174
KNIGHT, Martha, Mary, Robert, William, 114; Daniel, 171
KNOWLTON, Deborah, Edmund, 228
KRAMER, Johanna, 57
LE BARON, Hannah, James, 226
LEE (LEIGH), Richard, Thomas, 114
LEWIS, Edmund, Joseph, 114; Susanna, 229
LINCOLN, Rebecca, 55
LINNELL (LARNETT), Robert, 229
LINTON (LETTIN), Ann, Robert, 229
LOCKE, Elizabeth Bowles, 172
LONG, Abigail, 173
LOOMER, Stephen, 229
LOOMIS, Lucy, 114; Joseph, 229
LORD, Mary, 56, 114, 229
LOW, Elizabeth (Betsy), 112
LOWE, Fred, 173
LOWELL, Mary, 112; Percival, Richard, 114; Elijiah O., 115; Abner, 171
LUMBERT, David, 55
LUME, Stephen, 229
LUTHER, Phebe, 227
LYNCH, Mary, 173
LYON, Dorcas, 226
MACOMBER, Elijah, 226
MANSFIELD, Lydia, 54; Andrew, 116
MASON, John L., 115
MASURY, Susanna, 54
McIVER, Mrs. Edward H., 227
McKENNEY, John, 171
McLEOD FAMILY, 55
McREYNOLDS, Andrew, Eliza, Esther, Hugh, Isabella, John, Matthew, Robert, Samuel, 56
MEARS FAMILY, 113; Alexander, 114
MELCHER, Jonathon, Sarah, 171
MERRILL, Bela, Eliza, John, Joseph, Paul, 115
MERRYFIELD, Bonnel, Susannah, 229
MILLER, George, Mary, 229
MILLET, Joseph, 113
MILLS, Jane, 54
MILWARD, Eliz, 172
MIRES, Mary, 113
MITCHELL, Mary Sawyer, 174; Nancy, 227
MOORE, Betsey, Martha, Patricia, 115
MORGARIDGE, John, Mary, 172
MORRISEY, John, 57; Richard, 57, 227; Michael, 115
MORTON, Sarah, 229
MOULTON, Abigail, 112; Joseph, 112, 174; Mary, 113; Samuel, Stephen, 174
MUNNINGS, Hannah, 227
MUSSMACHER FAMILY, 229

NASH, Sarah, 55
NEWHALL, John, Thomas, 56; Mary, 115; Sarah, 112
NICHOLS, Ebeneazer, Thomas, 113; Mary, 227
NOBLE, Christopher, 171
NORTON, Samuel, 55; Francis, John, Henry, 173
NOYES, Joseph, 174
NURSE, Mary, 116
OBER, Elizabeth, 173
OSBORN(E), Anna, Eliza, James L., Hannah, John Simpson, Mehitable, 115; William, 116
OSGOOD, Jacob Dyer, Patricia, 115; Betty, 172; Joanna, 227
PARKER, Elizabeth, 57
PARSONS, Ann, 113
PASCO, Hugh, 172
PATASHALL, Martha, 171
PATEE, Elizabeth, 174
PAYSON, Hanley, 226
PEARL, Timothy, 57; Nathan, 227
PEASE, Mary, 172
PEDRICK, John, 113
PENNOCK, Albert, Alice, Anna, Charles, Emma, Franklin, George, Mary, William, 56
PETERS, Eunice, Philip, Susannah, 229
PETERSON, Hopestill, 57
PEVERLY, Thomas, 227
PHILBRICK, Hannah, 113
PHILLIPS, James, 114
PICKERING, Elizabeth, 54
PIERCE, Daniel, Mary, 172
PITMAN, Mary, Sarah, William, 172
POLAND, Martha, 114
POND, Emmeline, 226
POOL, Elizabeth, 56; Betsy, 226
POOR(E) (POWER), Thomas, 113; Nancy, 227
POPE, John, 171
POTTER, Elizabeth, Robert, 56
POWER, Hannah, Richard, 113
PRATT, Joseph, Margaret, 113
PRESSEY, Anna (Miriam), Hezekiah, 116; Anna, 228
PRINCE, Thankful, 57
PROCTOR, Martha, 54
PURRINGTON, Charles, 57
PUTNAM, Ephraim, 112
QUESTED, Allice, Elizabeth, George, James, Maria, Mary Ann, John, William, 228
RAMSEY, Charles, William, 116, 228
RAND, Moses, 226
RANDALL, Elizabeth, 173
RANDLE (RANDOLF), Sarah, Tamesin, 173
RAYNER, Elizabeth, William, 228
REVIL (RAVELL, ROWEL), Mary, William, 113
RHOADES, Carrie, Cecil, 226
RICHARDSON, Mary, 56; Thomas, Unity, 172
RIDER, Ann, 112

RILEY, Thomas, 228
RING, Molley, 55
ROADS, Elizabeth, 226
ROBERTS, Elizabeth, 114
ROBINSON, Daniel, 56; John, Rebecca, 172
ROPES, John, George, Mary, Ruth, 116
ROSS, Mary, 54
ROUSE, Joanna, 171
ROWE, Anthony, 171
RUSSELL, Louis, 113; Jane, L. Octavius, 226
SANBORN, Louisa Hoyt, 114; Ruth, 171
SANDBERG, Sven Edward, 174
SARGENT, Elizabeth, 116, 228
SAVAGE, Hannah, John, Mary, 113
SAVORY, Robert, 174
SAWYER, Alan, Humphrey, 115; Jacob, Josiah, Louisa, 171; Charles William, 173; Mary, 174
SAXTON (SEXTON), Patience, 171
SEARS, Mary, 112
SEELEY, see CEELY
SHARPLES, John, 228
SHATSWELL, Theophilus, 55
SHEARER, Nancy, 55
SHEPARD, Mark, 113
SHORTBRIDGE, Susannah, 172
SIMONS, William, 172
SMITH, Chloe, Rachel, 226
SNODDY, Elizabeth, 56
SNOWMAN, Christian, John, 173
SOANE FAMILY, 114
SOUTHWICK, Ebenezer, Samuel, 54; William, 115
SPENCER, Gerrard, Hannah, Jared, 56
STAPLES, Sarah, 173
STETSON, Lois, 173
STEVENS FAMILY, 115; John, Nathan 57; Sarah, 113; Hannah, 226; Elizabeth, 57, 226
STEWART, Charles, Mary, 228
STODDARD (STODDER), Abner, Rachel, 112
STONE, Elias, 173; Benjamin, Hugh, Mary, 227
STORY, Nehemiah, Jr., 172
STOVER, Eunice, 228
STRONG, Eleanor, 228
SWEENY, Mary, 228
SWIFT, Betsey, Dean, Elnathan, Enoch, Hasadiah, Mary, Rebecca, Rufus, Sarah, 56
TAPLEY, Elizabeth, 172; Francis, Margaret, Mary, Samuel, 56
TARBELL, David, Jesse, Sally, 115
TARR, Caleb, Mary, 174
TEAGUE, Mary, 171
THOMAS, Nathaniel, 226
THOMPSON, Annie, 112
THORNDIKE, John, 173
TILTON, Daniel, Abraham, 227
TOLBERT (TALBERT), James C., 114

TUCKER, Benjamin, 112; Benoni, 113
TULL, Jessie Maud, 226
TURNER, Elizabeth, 172
TUTTLE, Trueworthy, 54; John, Samuel, 174
VARNUM, Abigail, 56
WALFORD, Jane, 227
WALLIS, Martha, 174
WANTON, Joseph, 57
WARNER, John, Priscilla, 228
WARREN, Phelps, 227
WASHBURN, Elizabeth, 226
WATERHOUSE, Sargent, 57
WATERS, Lawrence, 229
WEBB, Francis, 114
WEBBER, Sarah, 171
WELD, Daniel, Elizabeth, 173
WELLS, Sarah, 112
WEST, Thomas, 172
WETHERBEE, Lucy, 171
WHEELER, Frances, Isaac, Thomas, 54; Sarah, 173
WHIPPLE, Rebecca, 172
WHITE, Mary, 172; Susannah, 229
WHITMAN, Mary, 54; John, 229
WHITTEMORE, Jonathan, 173
WIDGER, Sarah, 227
WILEY, Alice, Charles, Emily, Mary, Ruth, 114
WILKENSEN, Elizabeth, 173
WILLIAMS, Abigail, 174; John, 57, 114; Thomas, 112, 229; Daniel, Mary, 229
WILSON, Phoebe Anne, 229
WITHAM, Ebenezer, Jr., Elizabeth, 174
WOLCUTT, John, 172
WOODFORD, Ursula, 227
WOODING (WOODEN), Bethiah, Peter, 174
WOODMAN, Ruth, 112
WRIGHT, Margaret, Thomas, 171

Compiled by Marilyn R. Fitzpatrick

Edited by Dorothea R. Griebel

ABBOT See also ABBOTT
   Ebenezer, 106, 137
   Eliab, 137
   Elizabeth (Harnden), 106
   Ephraim, 137
   George, 106
   Hannah, 106
   Hannah (Abbot), 106
   Hannah (Chandler), 106
   Hannah (Furman), 106
   John, 106
   Joseph, 106
   Lois (Bennett), 106
   Sarah (Barker), 106
   Sarah (___), 137
ABBOTT, 115 See also ABBOT
   Clarissa (Sizer), 78
   Elizabeth, 57
   George, 77
   Hannagh, 77
   Hannah (___), 77
   John, 77-78
   John Bennett, 77-78, 113
   Joseph, 77
   Lavanda Laura, 77
   Lois (Bennett), 77
   Martha Manning (Howlett), 113
   Susannah (Shortbridge), 172
ABELL
   Elizabeth, 228
ABORN
   Abigail (Gilbert), 194
   Hannah, 193-195
   Mary, 193-195
   Moses, 194
ACIE
   Elizabeth, 20
ADAM
   Robert, 138
ADAMS, 74
   Abigail, 27, 90
   Amanda (Hall), 47
   Ann, 223
   Clayton R., 107
   Clayton Rand, 47
   David, 202
   Dorcas, 27
   Elizabeth, 27, 106
   Elizabeth (Hughes), 202
   Elizabeth Trask (Rand), 47
   Ernest Clayton, 47

   Franklin, 47
   Hannah, 27, 202
   Hannah (Gannett), 202
   Harriet Moulton (Pettingell), 47
   Isaac, 158
   James, 27
   John, 27, 47, 104
   Jonathan, 172
   Joseph, 137
   Lois (Collins), 202
   Mark, 47
   Martha (Stocker), 158
   Mary (Hill), 47
   Mary (Perry), 47
   Mary (___), 172
   Nathaniel, 27, 202
   Praesilla (Ramsdell), 27
   Priscilla (Shore), 27
   Sarah, 108
   Sarah (Collins), 207
   Sarah Ann, 9
   Thankful, 172
   Thomas, 47, 207
ADDITON
   Mary (Teague), 171
   Samuel, 171
ADSHADE/ADESHADE, 55
ALIOUS
   Betty, 130
ALLEN
   Azariah, 172
   David, Dea., 172
   Elizabeth, 48, 205
   Jonathan, 172
   Lucy, 172
   Lydia, 116, 174
   Lydia (Hooper), 172
   Mary (Pierce), 172
   Mary (White), 172
   Tabitha, 132
   Timothy, 35
ALLEY
   Abner, 191
   Ellis (___), 191
   Hugh, 85, 190
   Moses, 190-191
   Theodate, 188
ALLIN
   John, 185
   John, Rev., 184

ALWYN
   James, 139
AMOS
   Sarah (Youngman), 29
   William, 29
ANDERSON
   Agnes (___), 54
   Betsey, 54
   Hannah, 47
   Jacob, 54
   Joseph, 54
   Robert Charles, 177, 185
ANDREWS
   Ann Elizabeth, 48
   Deborah (___), 56
   Dorcas, 56
   Elizabeth, 56
   Grace (Melburn), 106
   Hulda, 56
   Jerusha, 56
   John, 56
   John, Jr., 56
   Robert, 106
   Ruth, 106
   Stephen, 56
ANDROS
   Edmond, Sir, 147
   Elizabeth (Papoon), 87
   John, 87
   Sarah, 131
ANNABLE
   Jemima, 229
ANNIS
   Sin, 135
APPLETON
   John, 89, 173
   Priscilla, 173
   Priscilla (Glover), 173
   Samuel, 156-157
ARCHER
   Samuel, 37
ARCULARIUS
   George, 43
ARMSTRONG
   Matthew, 157
ARNOLD
   James N., 128
   James Newell, 121
   Noah J., 9
ARTHUR
   Elizabeth, 216

Sarah, 164
Sarah (Jones), 165
BELL
    Abraham, 229
    Charles H., 21
    Dorothy C., 24
    Katherine (Bulfinch), 229
    Mary, 229
BELLIVEAU
    Mary Vitaline Otil (Gaudet), 226
    Wm., 226
BELONG
    Agnes, 48
BENIGHTON
    Patience, 206
BENNET
    David, 135
    Susanna (___), 135
    Thomas, 135
    William, 135
BENNETT
    Bathsheba (Phelps), 106
    Elisha, 106, 156
    George, 106
    John, 106, 156
    Lois, 77, 106
    Lois (Wilder), 106
    Lydia (Kibby), 106
    Mary (___), 106
    Samuel, 34, 106, 156, 157, 159
    Sarah, 50, 75
    Sarah (___), 157
BENSON
    Charity, 173
BENTLEY
    William, Dr., 192
BENTLY
    ___, Rev., 193
BERRY, 155 See also BARRY
    Andrew, 172
    Anna/Nancy (Bixby), 116
    Catherine, 194
    Divan, 211
    Elizabeth, 50, 172
    Elizabeth (Divan), 50
    George, Capt., 142
    Hannah (Farrar), 116, 208
    Henry, 116
    Isaac, 116
    Jenny, 172
    John, 116, 205
    Ketley, 172
    Margaret, 172
    Meriah (Ingalls), 205

    Nancy, 172
    Rachel (___), 116
    Rebecca (Ballord), 160
    Robert, 172
    Ruthe (Ingalls), 205
    Sally (Jewett), 116
    Samuel, 205
    Sarah, 160, 208-209
    Thadeus, 208
    Thadeus/Teague, 116
    Thomas, 50, 160, 172, 210-211
BEUEREDGE
    Susanna, 131
BISHOP
    C. Nelson, 13, 16
    Eleanor, 16
    Eleanor C., 13
    John, 172
    Lydia, 163
    Patience (Saxton/Sexton), 171
    Rebecca (Whipple), 172
    William, 171
BIXBY
    Anna/Nancy, 116
BLACK
    Elizabeth, 228
    John, 228
    Susanna (___), 228
BLACKSTONE
    William, 119
BLAINE
    Joseph, 127-128
BLAISDELL
    Dorothy (Barnard), 222
    Miriam, 221
    Molly, 57
    Nicholas, Capt., 142
    Samuel, 222
BLAKE
    Anne (Hanever), 171
    Dearborn, 94-95
    Edward, 171
    Jeremiah, 91
    John, 99
    Joseph, 92
    Sherburne, 92
BLANEY
    Elizabeth (Purchis), 87
    Hannah (Rand), 87
    Henry, 39, 41, 86-87
    Ivory, 87
    John, 87
    Lois (Ivory), 86-87
    Lois (___), 39

    Mary (Browne), 87
BLETHEN
    Elizabeth (___), 54
    Joseph, 54
    Miriam, 54
    Wealthy, 163
BLEVINS
    Ellen (Fitzgrerald), 163
    Grace G., 163
    John, 164
    John F., 163
    Mary (Halpin), 164
    Mary Ann (McElroy), 164
    William, 164
BLIGH See also BLY
    Lois (Ivory), 36
    Ruth, 85
BLISS
    ___, Capt., 154
BLODGETT
    Martha, 108
BLODGETTE
    George B., 17
    George Brainard, 17
BLOWERS
    Jerusha, 126
BLY See also BLIGH
    Lois (Ivory), 39
    Samuel, 39
    Theophilus, 39
BOARDMAN
    Aaron, 87
    Abiah, 87
    Abiah (Sprague), 87
    Eunice, 87
    Eunice (Ivory), 87
    Ivory, 87
    John, 87
    Lois, 87
    Mary, 87
    Mary (Cheever), 87
    Mary (Jenks), 87
    Rachel (Brown), 194
    Samuel, Jr., 194
    Sarah, 87
    Susanna (Norwood), 87
    William, 87
BOCLEA
    William, 7
BODFISH
    Robert, 182
    Thankful, 55
BODGE
    George M., 157

ASH
  Eliza, 93
ASPINWALL
  William, 155
ATHERTON See ADDITON
ATKINS
  Alice, 57
ATKINSON
  Mary, 108
ATWELL
  Anna (Ramsdell), 81
  Elisabeth, 135
  Hannah, 135
  John, 81, 135
  Joseph, 135
  Margaret (Max), 81
  Mary (Stone), 81
  Nathan, 81
  Pann (___), 135
  Rebecca, 135
  William, 81
ATWOOD
  Abigail, 56
  Cynthia (Baker), 55
  Elizabeth, 224
  Isaac, 55
  Nancy (Shearer), 55
  Orsamus, 55
AUSTIN
  Deborah (Knowlton), 228
  John, 228
  John O., 128
  John Osborn, 121, 126
  Manuel, 191
  Mary, 228
AVERY, 74
  Elizabeth, 228
  Eunice (Stover), 228
  Hannah (Barnes), 228
  Hannah (Barns), 54
  Lillian Drake, 151
  Lydia, 54
  Robert, 228
  Solomon, 54, 228
AYERS See HEIRES

BABCOCK
  Henry, 163
  Martha, 162-163
  Sarah (Fisk), 163
BACHELDER, 155 See also
      BACHELER
  Anna, 210
  Hannah, 210

Hannah (Breed), 209-210
Hannah (Stocker), 210
Henry, 210
Jerusha (Breed), 210
Jonathan, 210
Lois, 210
Lydia, 210
Mary, 210
Rufus, 210
Samuel, 209-210
Sarah, 210
Sarah (Johnson), 210
Theophilus, 210
BACHELER See also BACHELDER
  Hannah (Stocker), 209
BACHILER, 182-183
  ___, Mr., 178
  Stephen, 182
  Stephen, Rev., 181
BACKUS
  Dana Converse, 145
  Dana Converse, 80
  Mary E. N., 80
BADGER, 227
  John, Rev., 57
  Samuel, 130
BAILEY
  Caleb, 112
  David, 112
  Eunice (Walker), 104
  James, 229
  Jane, 104
  Mary, 112, 224
  Mary (___), 112
  Mary S. (___), 229
  Ruth (Ivory), 36
  Susanna (Dingley), 112
  Theophilus, 35-36
  Thomas, 104
BAILY
  Ruth (Ivory), 34
BAKER, 211
  Cynthia, 55
  Ebenezer, 229
  Edward, 28, 157
  Esther (___), 229
  Ezra, 190
  Isaac, Rev., 55
  Jemima (Annable), 229
  Mary, 109
  Polly (___), 229
  Thomas, 159
BALCOMB
  Frank W., 86

BALLARD, 155 See also BULLARD
  Clerk, 159
  Deborah (Tobey), 89
  Elizabeth (Jacob), 114
  Nathaniel, 89
  Rebecca (Hudson), 89
  Sarah (Burrill), 89
  Susanna, 84
  William, 89, 114
BALLORD
  Anna (Sprague), 160
  Ebenezer, 160
  Jane, 160
  John, 160, 210
  John, Jr., 160
  Joseph, 160
  Martha, 160
  Mary, 160
  Mary (Hunting), 160
  Rebecca, 160
  Rebecca (___), 160
  Sarah, 160
  Sarah (Stocker), 160
  William, 160
BANCROFT, 85
  Abigail, 135
  Alice, 135
  Alpheus, 135
  James, 13
  John, 49, 137, 148
  Joshua, 130
  Lydia, 49
  Mary (Newhall), 116
  Nathaniel, 136
  Ruth (Newhall), 49
  Samuel, Jr., 133
  Sarah, 131
  Thaddeas, 130
  Thomas, 157
  Timothy, 116
BANKS
  Charles Edward, 27, 33, 83, 145
  Elizabeth, 172
BARETO
  Eliz. (___), 113
  Nicholas, 113
BARKER
  Joannah (___), 106
  John, Jr., 116
  Mehitebel (Goodridge), 116
  Richard, 106
  Sarah, 106
BARNARD
  Alice (Holt), 55

Dorothy, 222
Edward T., 42, 46
Edward Townsend, 46
Eleanor, 216
Everett L., 46
Hannah, 57
John, Jr., 55
Lydia, 171
Sarah, 223
Therina (Townsend), 46
BARNES
　Hannah, 228
　Rebecca, 22
BARNS
　Hannah, 54
BARRETT
　Joseph, 194
　Sarah (Brown), 194
BARRIT
　James, 131
BARROW
　George, 88
　Hannah (Chandler), 88
　Katherine (Ivory), 88
　Relief (Rows), 88
BARRY See BERRY
BARSTOW See BARETO
BARTHOLOMEW
　William, 156
BARTLETT
　Benjamin, 222
　Elizabeth, 224
　Hannah (Philbrick), 113
　Isaac, 221
　Jemima (Parkhurst), 222
　Josiah, Col., 96
　Lydia, 227
　Miram, 57
　Molly (Blaisdell), 57
　Nathan, 57
　Norton, 113
　Perley, 113
　Rebecca (Sargent), 221
　Ruth, 221
BARTON
　Ann (___), 172
　Joshua, 172
　Mehitable, 115
　Nathan, Jr., 172
　Olive (Jennison), 195
　Reuben, 195
　Unity (Richardson), 172
BARTRAM
　___, Mrs., 56

Esther, 166
Esther/Estar, 56
William, 56
BASS
　Hannah, 109
　Joseph, 39
　Lois (Ivory), 39
BASSET
　Elizabeth, 188
　Elizabeth (Collins), 149
　Eunice (___), 189
　John, 187
　Joseph, 188
　Lidia (___), 188
BASSETT
　Abigail (Davis), 202
　Danell, 202
　Elisha, 202
　Elizabeth, 202
　Elizabeth (Collins), 202
　Hannah, 202
　Mary (Lawrence), 202
　Rebecca (___), 202
　William, 202
　Zebedee, 202
BASTON See BOSTON
BATCHELDER
　Abigail, 91
　Andrew, 49
　Bethiah (Woodbury), 49
　Charles H., 66
　Ephraim, 91
　Esther (___), 91
　Ezra, 49
　Jemina (Conant), 49
　Joanna, 91, 98
　John, 49, 91, 174
　John, Capt., 13
　Joseph, 174
　Margaret, 49
　Mary (Dennis), 174
　Mary (Woodbury), 49
　Molly/Mary, 94
　Oliver Felton, 49
　Sally (Felton), 49
　Sally (Osborn), 49
　Sarah, 95
　Sarah (___), 174
　Stephen, Rev., 66
　William Oliver, 49
BATES
　Annice (Gowing), 165
　Elizabeth, 32
　Elizabeth (Chadwell), 29, 37

Elizabeth (Proctor), 32
Elizabeth (Ramsdell), 32
Hannah (Cammitt), 55
John, 55, 165
Joseph, 29, 32, 37
Nancy, 227
Robert, 32, 166
Sarah, 32, 165
Sarah (___), 32, 166
BATT
　Mary, 100
BAXTER
　Hannah (Ivory), 39
　Samuel, 28, 39
BAYLEY
　Theophilus, 85
BEACH
　Elizaeth (Berry), 172
　Isaac, 172
BEAL
　Albert, 229
　Effie (___), 229
　Hiram, 229
　Phoebe Anne (Wilson), 229
BEAMAN
　Alden G., 122, 128
BEAN
　Mary, 22
BEARD
　Abel, 135
　Andrew, 229
　Mary (Williams), 229
　Mary (___), 135
BEAUDREAU
　Elias Victor, 226
　H., 226
　Jessie Maud (Tull), 226
　Mary Vitaline Otil (Gaudet), 226
　N. (Comeau), 226
BECK
　Mary, 54
BEERS
　Jesse, 134
　John, 134
　Joseph, 134
　Mary, 134
　Mary (___), 132
　William, 132, 134
BEESON
　Abigail, 32
BEIRD See BEARD
BELCHER, 85
BELKNAP
　Samuel, 165

George Madison, 19, 32, 203
BODWELL
    Bethia (Emery), 112
    Henry, 112
BOHLMAN
    Emma, 163
BOHONON
    Sarah, 222
BOLTON
    Charles Knowles, 144
    Conrad, 143
    Eliza Jane, 143
    Elizabeth, 163
    Henry, 143
BOOTH
    Alice, 196
BORTHRICK
    Abel, 228
    Dolly (___), 228
BOSTON
    Sophia, 116
BOSWORTH
    Susanna, 55
BOUDRO
    Mary Eunice/Louisa, 226
    Patrick, 226
BOULANGER
    Matilda, 48
BOURWELL
    Ruben, 130
BOUTILIER
    Melissa, 48
BOUTTELL
    Caleb, 136
BOWDEN
    Elizabeth, 137
    Mary, 205
BOWDON
    Lydia, 207
    Michall, 41
BOWEN
    Richard LeBaron, 129
BOWERS
    Mary, 109
BOWLES
    Elizabeth, 172
BOWMAN
    Hannah, 114
BOYCE, 208
    Benjamin, 55
    Sarah, 55
    Susannah (___), 55
BOYINGTON
    Lydia, 137

BOYNTON
    Anne, 102
    Benjamin, 102
    Caleb, 19
    Ebenezer, 19
    Elizabeth, 102
    Ellen/Ellenor (Pell), 19
    Ellenor, 102
    Enoch, 75
    Hannah, 19, 75
    Hannah (Harriman), 19
    Jeremiah, 19
    John, 19, 102
    Jonathan, 100, 102
    Joseph, Capt., 102
    Margaret, 19, 102
    Margaret (Harriman), 100, 102
    Mary, 102
    Ruth, 19
    Sarah, 102
    Sarah (Swan), 102
BRACK
    Charles S., 163
    Charles S., Jr., 163
    Elisabeth (Graves), 163
    Emma (Bohlman), 163
    Esther J. (Tompkins), 163
    Frederick, 163
    Margaret (Cargill), 163
    Samuel C., 163
BRADBURY
    Jerusha, 47
BRADSTREET
    Margaret (Gordon), 22
    Samuel, 22
BRAGDON
    Arthur, 83
BRAGG
    Bridget, 131
    Elizabeth, 131
    John, 131
    Sarah, 131
    Sarah (___), 131
BRAINARD
    Daniel, 56
    Hannah (Spencer), 56
BRASIER
    Hannah (Ivroy), 88
    Hannah (Webb), 88
    Thomas, 88
BRAY
    Abigail, 132
BREAD See also BREED
    Allen, 26

BRECK
    Susanna, 152
BREDEAN
    Martha (Stocker), 158
    Samuel, 158
BREED, 155 See also BREAD
    ___, Capt., 80
    Allen, 36, 114, 159
    Amos, 187, 189
    Anna, 188
    Anna (___), 188
    Anne, 191
    Banjamin, 188, 190
    Benjamin Newhall, 190
    Deliverance, 187
    Elener, 189
    Elizabeth (Jacob), 114
    Ephraim, 153
    Ezra, 189
    Hannah, 188, 209-210
    Hannah (___), 191
    Jabez, 188
    James, 188, 191
    James, 3rd, 191
    James, Jr., 191
    Jerusha, 210
    John, 36, 41
    John, Capt., 208
    Joseph, 209-210
    Judeth, 191
    Lydia (___), 190
    Martha (___), 208
    Mary, 50, 160, 199, 209, 211
    Mary (Stocker), 209
    Mary (___), 188-189
    Mathew, 209
    Matthew, 40-41, 89, 09
    Mehitabel, 209
    Nathan, 189-190, 209
    Rebeckah, 188
    Richard, 188
    Ruth, 87, 189, 209, 211
    Ruth (Breed), 210
    Ruth (___), 187
    Sarah, 209
    Sarah (Brown), 37
    Sarah (Farrington), 209
    Simeon, 188
    Timothy, 37
    William, 190
BREWER
    Crispus, 150-151
    Elizabeth, 210
    Mary, 205

BUTTERFIELD
    Ebenezer, 54
    Sally (Johnson), 54
BUTTERS
    Benjamin, 132
    Elizabeth, 132
    Elizabeth (___), 132
    Mahetable, 132
BUZZY See BUSS

CADE
    Ammaziah, 131
CADMAN
    Lydia, 171
CAIN
    George, 81
CALEE
    Mary, 19-20, 23
CALEF
    John, Dr., 228
CALL
    Ann (Wharff), 88
    Ann/Anne, 88
    Caleb, 88
    Elizabeth, 88
    Esther, 133
    Esther (___), 133
    Samuel, 133
CALLUM
    Anne, 192
    Lydia, 195
    Mackum, 192
    Martha (___), 192
CAMMITT
    Abraham, 55
    Ann, 55
    David, 55
    Hannah, 55
    Isaac, 55
    Judith, 55
    Margaret (Hallowell), 55
    Mary, 55
    Paul, 55
    Peter, 54
    Robard, 55
    Silas, 55
    Thankful (Bodfish), 55
    Thomas, 55
CAMPBELL
    John, 153
    Martha (Ivory), 153
    Olivia, 90
CARGILL
    Catherine (Green), 163
    Catherine H. (Sullivan), 163
    Daniel Dole, 164
    Daniel W., 163
    Elizabeth D. (Ripley), 164
    Margaret, 163
    William J., 163
CARLETON
    Richard A., 113
CARNEY
    John, 126
CARPENTER
    Anna, 109
    Esther, 109
    Oliver, 109
    Sarah (French), 109
CARR
    Agnes D., 75-76
CARRIEL
    Bettey (Gould), 194
    Daniel, 194
CARTER
    Abigail, 131, 137
    Abigail (___), 137
    Abigal (___), 131
    Adazilla (Davison), 226
    Adino, 131, 137
    Amaziah, 136
    Amos, 130
    Benjamin, 130
    Charles, 226
    Eliab, 137
    Elijah, 131, 137
    Enock, 130
    Ephraim, 131, 137
    George, 226
    Hannah (Cochran), 227
    Henry, 227
    Isaac, 131
    Jabez, 130, 136
    Kezia, 130
    Keziah, 136
    Lydia, 130
    Lydia (___), 130
    Martha, 130, 136
    Mary, 114
    Mary, 130
    Mary Eunice/Louisa (Boudro), 226
    Nancy, 137
    Polly, 137
    Sarah, 131
    Thankfull (___), 137
    Thomas, 137
CARY
    Martha, 88

CASE
    Asa, 133
    Betsey, 132
    Elisabeth (___), 132
    Hulda (___), 133
    Humphry, 132
CASEY
    Bridget M. (Lyons), 220
    Honora/Bridget (Guardiner), 220
    Irene P., 220
    Josephine F. (Sullivan), 220
    Martin, 220
    Michael, 220
    Thomas F., 220
CASIE
    John, 131
CASTLE
    Jane, 135
CASWELL, 74
CATHERCOLE
    Lydia, 37
CAZNEAU
    Pax, 10
CEELY
    Benjamin, 229
    Susannah (Merryfield), 229
CHADBOURNE, 74
CHADDLE
    Ruth, 130
CHADWELL
    ___, Mrs., 215
    Anna, 29, 37, 80-81
    Benjamin, 37
    Elizabeth, 29, 37, 80-81
    Hannah (Smith), 37
    Lois, 37
    Margaret, 37
    Margaret (___), 37
    Mary, 206
    Moses, 29, 35, 37, 80
    Ruth, 37, 50
    Sarah, 37, 132
    Sarah (Brown), 37
    Sarah (Ivory), 29, 35-37, 80
    Thomas, 29, 36-37, 80
CHADWICK
    Hannah (___), 114
    John, 114
    Jonathan, 114
    Martha, 157
    Mary, 157, 223
    Mary (Stocker), 157
    Samuel, 157

Sarah, 206
BRIDGES
    ___, Capt., 34
BRIGGS
    Ann (Stocker), 158
    Mercy, 143
    William, 158
BRINTNALL
    John, 28, 85
    William, 85
BRISCALL
    Elizabeth E., 174
BRITTON
    Lois (Rogers), 39
    Phillip, 39
BROAD
    Kaziah, 90
BROCKLEBANK
    John, 102
BROCKLEBROOK
    Hannah, 103
BROOK
    Samual, 7
    Thomas, 7
BROOKS
    Betsey (___), 174
    Calvin, 174
    Dudley, 174
    Elizabeth E. (Briscall), 174
    Hannah (___), 174
    Oliver, 174
BROWN, 49
    Aaron, 108
    Abial, 131
    Abial, 137
    Abigail, 108
    Abigail (Stuart), 222
    Abigail (___), 165
    Ann (Stocker), 158
    Anthony, 158
    Benjamin, 99, 194, 223
    Catherine (Berry), 194
    Charles Henry, 223
    Cyrus Henry, 199
    Daniel, 98, 199
    Deborah (Holdredge), 199
    Elisabeth, 130
    Elisabeth (Huchinson), 194
    Elizabeth, 199
    Elizabeth (Pickering), 50, 54
    Ella Maud, 223
    Emily H. F., 113
    Enoch, 222-223
    Ephraim, 194

Ephraim, Capt., 194
Esther/Easter (Ramsdell), 79
Ezra, 194
George, 137
Grace, 222
Hannah, 108, 194, 199
Hannah (Collins), 199
Hannah (House), 229
Hannah (Tilton), 93
Henry, 165
Humphrey, 199
J., 41
James, 50, 54, 94, 174, 194, 228-229
Jane, 115
Jane (Stocker), 194
Jedidiah, 135
Jephtha, 135
Jerusha, 199
Jesse, 135
Joe, 6
John, 50, 54, 108-109, 131, 194
John C. J., 29
John Henry, 223
Jonathan, 194
Joseph, 79
Josiah, 135
Judith, 135
Judith (___), 135
Julia (O'Neil), 223
Lydia, 228
Lydia (Allen), 174
Lydia (Burrill), 194
Margaret, 197
Martha (Mansfield), 160
Mary, 23, 99, 108, 199
Mary (Breed), 199
Mary (Burnham), 108
Mary (Mansfield), 194
Mary (Newhall), 199
Mary (Paul), 194
Mary (___), 99
Mehetabel, 135
Olive (Mitchell), 108
Parthenia (Peabody), 223
Patience, 135
Peter, 194
Priscilla, 199
Rachel, 194
Rhoda, 137
Rufus, 194
Sally, 98
Samuel, 137, 199
Sarah, 37, 164, 194, 199
Sarah (Cutting), 229

Sarah (Emmerson), 109
Sarah (Phillips), 223
Sarah (___), 137
Stephen, 93
Susanna (Masury), 50, 54
Susannah, 50
Tabitha (Holdridge), 199
Thankful (___), 131
Thomas, 160, 194, 199
Thomas, Jr., 199
BROWN/BROWNE
    James, 204
BROWNE
    David, 85
    Grace (___), 155
    James, 155
    Mary, 87
BROWNING
    Mary (___), 171
    Thomas, 171
BRYANT
    Abraham, 10
    Lucy (___), 137
    Timothy, Jr., 137
BUCK
    Cleaveland, 135
    Dolley, 130
    Dorcas (___), 135
    Ebenezer, 130
    Elisbeth, 130
    Ephraim, 135
    Isaak, 206
    Lydia, 130
    Ruth (Graves), 206
    Samuel, 130
    Willard, 130
BUFFINGTON
    Commings, 227
    Cynthia, 227
    Noah, 227
    Phebe, 227
    Phebe (Luther), 227
    Royal, 227
    William, Jr., 227
BUFFUM
    Mary, 166
BULFINCH
    Katherine, 229
BULL
    John, 126
BULLARD See also BALLORD
    Anna, 54
    John, 38, 211

William, 135
BULLOCK See BULLARD
BULLORD See BULLARD
BUNKER
    ___, Mr., 75
    Abigail, 216
    Abigail (Ramsdell), 216
    Cromwell, 216
    Hannah (Hadlock), 76
    Jane (Coffin), 216
    John, 76
    Lydia (Ramsdell), 216
    Mary, 228
    Mary (Chase), 216
    Mary (Graham), 75
    Reuben, 216
    Tristam, 216
    William, 216
BURCHAM
    Edward, 34
BURCHSTEAD
    ___, Dr., 208
    Elizabeth, 160
    Joanna, 212
    Mary, 199
BURGES
    Robert, 156
BURGESS
    Beulah, 48
    Flora (Williams), 48
    Lillian (Dorey), 48
    Reginald, 48
BURGIS
    Robert, 25
BURK
    Abigal, 132
BURKE
    Bridget (Fighely), 221
    Patrick G., 221
    Winifred A., 220
BURLEIGH
    Charles, 205
BURLINGAME, 25
BURNAP
    Abigail, 14
    Abigail (___), 14-15
    Benjamin, 56
    Cyrus, 14
    Elizabeth (Newhall), 56
    George, 14
    Isaac, 13-14
    Jacob, 14
    Joseph, 14-15
    Joseph, Capt., 13-14
    Joseph, Jr., 14
    Joseph, Sr., 14
    Robert, 13
    Sarah, 13
    Susanna, 14
    Susannah (Emerson), 13
    Susannah (___), 13-14
    Tabitha, 13
    Zoraday, 14
BURNELL
    Eunice, 216
BURNHAM
    Mary, 108
    Mary (Lane), 109
    Thomas, 109
BURPEE
    Sarah, 103
BURR
    Mercy/Mary (___), 172
    Samuel, Jr., 172
BURRAGE
    John, 41, 89-90
    John, Dea., 40, 89
    Susanna, 88
    Thomas, 85
BURRELL
    Francis, 37-38
BURRELL-BROWN
    Ruth, 81
BURRIL
    Isaac, 191
BURRILL, 86, 155
    ___, Maj., 80
    ___, Mr., 147
    Anna, 37
    Ebenezer, 37, 85, 211, 213, 215
    Ebenezer, Jr., 211, 214-215
    Ellen Mudge, 37
    Eunice/Unis (Ramsdell), 81
    Francis, 36
    Francis, Sr., 38
    George, 34, 36
    Hannah (Holyoke), 37
    Isaac, 190
    Jacob, 81, 214
    John, 26, 28, 35-36, 147, 159
    John, Capt., 37
    John, Sr., 151
    Joseph, 209
    Lois, 37
    Lydia, 194
    Lydia (Cathercole), 37
    Margaret (Jarvis), 37
    Martha (Farrington), 37
    Mary, 37
    Mary (Cooper), 36
    Mary (Stower), 37
    Mary (___), 28
    Nathaniel, 41
    Ruth, 37
    Samuel, 37
    Sarah, 37, 89
    Theophilus, 28, 37, 204, 208
    Thomas, 37
BURROUGH
    Peleg, 126, 128
BURS
    Jesse, 136
    John, 136
    Joseph, 136
    Polly, 136
    Rebecca, 136
    William, 136
BURT
    Edward, 34
    Joseph, 152
    Ruth (Tolman), 152
BURTON
    Boniface, 182
    Hannah, 116
BUSH
    Jonathan, 173
    Mary, 109
    Sarah (Randle/Randolf), 173
BUSHBY
    (Brown), 49
    Asa, 49
    John, 49
    Lydia (Willson), 49
    Sally, 49
BUSS
    John, 72
BUSWELL
    Isaac, 72
BUTCHER
    Claude, 228
    George Washington, 227-228
    John, 227
    Nancy (Bates), 227
    William, 228
BUTLER
    Abigail (Ramsdell), 79
    Benjamin, 94
    Hannah (Heard), 172
    James, 79
    John, 172
    Mary (Morgaridge), 172
    Polly, 134

CHALLIS
- Anna, 221
- Hannah (Weed), 222
- Judith, 222
- Mary, 116, 221
- William, Jr., 222

CHAMBERLAIN
- Experience (Foster), 54
- George Walter, 29
- Jacob, 54
- Mellin, 155
- William, 54

CHAMBERLIN
- Elizabeth, 54

CHANDLER
- Catherine Soleman, 202
- Hannah, 88, 106
- James, 102
- Mary, 114, 174
- Mary (Carter), 114
- Mary (Fowler), 114
- Mary (Lord), 114
- Seth, 153
- William, 114

CHAPMAN
- ___, Mr., 192
- Deborah (Twiss), 194
- Michael, 194

CHARLES II, 138

CHARNOCK
- Hannah, 37
- Hannah (Holyoke), 37

CHASE
- Benjamin, 189
- Charles, 191
- John, 188
- Mary, 163, 216, 223
- Phillip, 189
- Samuel, 188, 190

CHEEVER
- Elizabeth, 87
- Eunice (Ivory), 86-87
- Eunice (___), 39
- Ezekial, 87
- Joseph, 137
- Mary, 87
- Mary (Boardman), 87
- Mary (___), 87
- Sarah, 132, 160
- Thomas, 86-87
- Thomas, Jr., 39, 211

CHENEY
- Benjamin, 223
- Ebenezer, 108
- Hannah (Gould), 108
- Joanna, 107
- Joanna (Pike), 108
- Joanna (Thayer), 109
- John, 108
- Keziah, 223
- Susannah, 108
- William, 109

CHESMORE
- Daniel, 173
- Elizabeth/Betsey, 173
- Mary (Gibson), 173

CHICK
- Love, 163

CHILD
- Susanna, 90

CHILTON, 115

CHISEMORE
- Abigail, 108
- Jacob, 108
- Martha (Smith), 108

CHISIMORE
- Abigail, 107

CHIVERS
- Arthur, Rev., 67

CHUDD
- Mary, 194

CHURCH
- John, 171
- Louisa (Sawyer), 171

CHURCHILL, 115

CILLEY
- Deborah, 93

CLARK
- Eleanor, 166
- Eunice (Ramsdell), 216
- George, 228
- James, 216
- Sarah, 207, 228
- Sarah, 228
- Sarah (___), 228

CLARKE
- Abigail (___), 112
- Stephen, 112

CLEMENT
- Rebecca, 202

CLEMENTS
- Deoborah, 162
- Experience (Yeaton), 163
- Jeremiah, 163

CLEMMONS
- Abigal (___), 131
- Eli, 131
- Hannah, 131
- John, 131
- Jonathan, 131
- Ruth, 131

CLEVELAND, 90
- Elizabeth (Perry), 90
- Jerusha, 115

CLIFFORD
- Hannah, 98
- Rachel, 96-97

CLINTON
- Catherine, 52

CLOUGH
- Abigail (Atwood), 56
- Abigail (Varnum), 56
- Daniel, 56
- Jabez, 56
- Marshall H., 56
- Miriam, 99

COATES
- Hopestill (Eliot), 81
- Joseph, 81
- Margaret (Ramsdell), 81
- Mary (Hodgkins), 81
- Robert, 81

COBB
- Bethia, 55
- Blanche Gordon, 21
- Carrie (Rhoades), 226
- Edwin C., 226
- Helen/Nellie Elizabeth, 113
- Martha, 115
- Wimmam, 142

COBBET
- ___, Mr., 35

COBBETT
- ___, Mr., 150

COBBITT
- ___, Mr., 26

COCHRAN
- Hannah, 227

COFFIN
- Ebenezer, 216
- Eleanor (Barnard), 216
- George, 216
- James, 216
- Judith, 216
- Peter, 216
- Priscilla, 216
- Ruth, 81
- Ruth (Swain), 216
- Tristam, 216

COGAN
- ___, Mr., 155
- John, 155

DAVIS, 10
   Abigail, 202
   Alice, 112
   Amasa, 6
   Elizabeth, 108
   Ephraim, Jr., 173
   Jenken, 25
   Jenkin, 37
   John, 38
   Jonathan, 57
   Juliette G., 10
   Jynkin, 38
   Mary, 36, 37, 39
   Mary (Calee), 20
   Mary (Tilton), 98
   Mary (___), 37-38
   Miram (Bartlett), 57
   Polly (Dow), 173
   Samuel, 98
   Walter Goodwin, 82
   William, 20
DAVISON
   Adazilla, 226
DAY
   Abraham, 224
   Charlotte, 162
   Elizabeth (Little), 224
   Josiah, 163
   Lydia, 223
   Mary (Bailey), 224
   Wealthy (Blethen), 163
DEALON
   Ebenezer, 131
DEARBORN, 74
   David, 77
   Sarah, 95
DEDMAN
   Lydia, 136
   Mary, 136
   Mary (___), 136
   Nancy, 136
   William, 136
DEERING
   Charles B., 173
   Flora, 173
   Lydia, 57
   Mary (Lynch), 173
   Mary Ann H. (Downs), 173
   Mary Wilma, 173
   Rose Etta, 173
   Samuel, 173
   Samuel H., 173
DeFOREST
   Louis Effingham, 33, 159

DELANO, 115
   Joshua, 57
   Lydia, 57
DEMCY
   Mary (Smith), 31
   Thomas, 31
DENNIS
   Mary, 174
   Mary E., 112
DENNISON
   Mehitable, 113
DERBY
   Lucretia, 210
DEXTER, 181
   John Haven, 10
   Thomas, 179-180
DICKERSON
   Elizabeth (Tapley), 172
   He-man, 172
   Judith, 172
DICKINSON
   James, 19
DIETERICH
   Harriet, 192
DIKE
   Abigail (Jennison), 195
   Daniel, 195
   William, 195
DILLINGHAM, 181-182
   John, 179-180
DINGLEY
   Jacob, Jr., 112
   Susanna, 112
   Susanna (Fuller), 112
DINON
   John, 134
DIVAN
   (H)ester (___), 156
   Elizabeth, 50, 156
   John, 156, 159
   John, Sr., 156, 158
   John, Sr., 158
   Mary, 156
DIXEY
   William, 179-180
DIXY
   William, Ens., 179
DOANE
   Margaret, 171
DODGE
   Anna, 31
   Edith (___), 165
   Edward, 164
   Eunice, 94

   Hannah, 164
   Hannah (Raymond), 49
   Joanna, 49
   John, 228
   Joshua, Dea., 49
   Lois, 131
   Lydia (Brown), 228
   Mary (Haskell), 164
   Nancy, 71
   Richard, 165
   Winifred Lovering Holman, 72
   Winthrop, 131
DOGE
   Elisabeth, 130
DOLIBER
   Donald, 52
DOLTON
   Micael, 130
DOOLITTLE
   Abraham, 159
   John, 155, 159
   Sarah (___), 159
DOREY
   James, 48
   Lillian, 48
   Melissa (Boutilier), 48
DOUGHTY
   Elizabeth (Twiss), 194
   Joseph, Jr., 194
   Mary, 196
DOUGLAS See also DUGGLE
   Alexander, 160
   Hepzibah, 223
   Sarah (Ballord), 160
DOUGLASE
   James, 54
   John, 54
DOUNTON
   Mary (___), 171
   William, 171
DOUTY
   Mary, 193, 197
DOUTY See DOUGHTY
DOW, 74
   Ebenezer, 98
   George Francis, 83
   Martha, 21
   Nathaniel, 98
   Polly, 173
DOWNING
   Hannah, 84
   Joanna, 79, 214
   John, 215
   MacCullum More, 214

COLBY
    Anna (Hoyt), 222
    Anthony, 114
    Barnard Hoyt, 222
    Ebenezer, 222-223
    Frances (Webb), 114
    Grace (Brown), 222
    Hannah, 222
    Mary (Chase), 223
    Sylvania, 222
    Thomas, 114
COLDHAM
    Thomas, 181
COLE
    John, 114
    Mary (Knight), 114
    Rebecca, 172
    William, 131
COLEMAN
    Daniel, 221
    George, 216
    Johannah, 220
    Mary (McCarthy), 221
    Mary (Ramsdell), 216
    Sylvia, 216
COLEMEN
    Benjamin, 104
COLINS
    Jacob, 187
COLLEGE
    Tom, 120
COLLEY
    Martha, 202
COLLIER
    ___, Mr., 178
COLLIN
    Jacob, 188
COLLINS, 85
    A. Chalkey, 145
    Abigail, 149, 201
    Abigail (Johnson), 151, 200-201, 206
    Abigail (Richards), 206
    Alice, 201-202
    Ann, 203-205
    Ann (Riall/Ryall/Royal), 145-146, 148-149, 151-152
    Ann (___), 201-202, 206-207
    Anna, 207
    Anna L. P., 145
    Benjamin, 147-152, 198, 200-202, 206-207
    Christopher, 145
    Content, 188
    Daniel, 149, 201-206
    Dorothy, 203-205
    Ebenezer, 203-204, 206
    Edward, 145
    Eleazer, 198-199, 205
    Elizabeth, 148-149, 152, 201-204, 206-207
    Elizabeth (Leach), 152, 206-207
    Ephereham, 188
    Ester, 205
    Ezekiel, 145, 203-206
    George Knapp, Capt., 145
    Hannah, 148-149, 151, 199, 201-202
    Hannah (Lamson), 199
    Hannah (___), 201
    Henry, 145-151, 159, 198-200, 203, 205-207
    Henry, 3rd., 145, 198
    Henry, Jr., 145, 147, 149, 198-199, 201, 203
    Henry, Sr., 37, 145-151, 198, 201
    Jacob, 187, 189, 204
    Job, 209
    John, 145-149, 151, 198-204, 206
    John, Jr., 147, 201
    John, Sr., 201
    Jonathan, 207
    Joseph, 86, 88, 145, 147-152, 198, 200-207
    Joseph, Sr., 203-204
    Joshua, 189
    Judeth (___), 190
    Lois, 149, 201-202
    Lucy (___), 191
    Lydia (___), 187
    Margaret (Downing), 202
    Margery, 145-146, 148, 151
    Mariah (Smith), 152, 202, 206
    Martha, 203-204, 206
    Mary, 149, 152, 201-204, 106
    Mary (Chadwell), 206
    Mary (Merrey), 206
    Mary (Silsbee), 202
    Mary (Tolman), 151, 198
    Merriah (Smith), 203
    Merryah (Smith), 204
    Moriah, 204
    Nathaniel, 149, 201-202, 207, 215
    Nehemiah, 190
    Patience (Benighton), 206
    Priscilla, 207
    Priscilla (Kirtland), 152, 206-207
    Rebecca, 199, 205
    Rebecca (Clement), 202
    Rebecca (Graves), 206
    Rebecca (Hussey), 201
    Rebecca (Newhall), 205
    Rebecka (Newhall), 199
    Riall, 146, 152
    Ruth, 190, 206
    Samuel, 149, 190, 201, 203
    Samuell, 188
    Sarah, 199, 202-205, 207
    Sarah (Collins), 207
    Sarah (Heires/Ayers), 199
    Sarah (Silsbee), 152, 202, 205
    Sarah (___), 202
    Susanna, 207
    Susannah, 149
    Susannah (Daggat), 202
    Susannah (Daggett), 145
    Thomas, 145
    William, 86, 145, 201-204, 206-207, 209, 211, 214-215
    Z., 205-206
    Zaccheus, 79
    Zachary, 191
    Zacheriah, 191
    Zacheus, 85-86, 189, 208, 211
COLMAN
    Eunis, 131
    Jane, 104
    John, 131
    Joseph, 131
    Lois (___), 131
    Phebe (Pearson), 104
    Thomas, 104, 131
COMEAU
    N., 226
COMEE See COMEY
COMEY
    David, 172
    Mary (___), 172
CONANT
    Bethiah (Mansfield), 49
    Jemina, 49
    John, 49
CONAWAY
    Mary, 137
CONLEY
    Benja, 130
    Catherine (___), 130
    Neholis, 130
    Solomon, 130
CONNERS
    Ebenezer, 135
    Josiah, 135
    Mary (___), 135

Rebecca, 135
Robert, 135
CONNOR
    Frank, 173
    Mary Wilma (Deering), 173
COOK
    ___, Mr., 143
    David, 119
    Elizabeth, Jr., 197
    Henry, 192
    Polly (Pettingell), 143
    Ruth (Sanford), 119
    Susanna, 165
    Tom, 123
COOKE
    Harriet Ruth (Waters), 85
    Thomas, 119, 127
COOMBS
    Joann, 77
    Laura, 77
    Lyman, 77
    Lyman Drewry, 106
    Martha, 163
COON
    Achash S. (Keith), 56
    W. H., 56
COOPER, 228
    Emm/Ame (___), 19
    Hannah, 19
    Leonard, 19
    Maria (Quested), 228
    Mary, 19, 36, 173
    Mary (Harriman), 19
    Moses, 19
    Peter, 19
    Ruth T., 93
    Samuel, 19
    Samuel, Jr., 19'
COREY
    Deloraine Pendre, 27
CORNUTT
    Verda E., 144
CORTWITHEN
    Mary, 165
COTTON
    ___, Mr., 178
    Seaborn, 71
COTTY
    Robert, 182
COY, 228
    Elizabeth (Roberts), 114
    Matthew, 114
    Sarah, 114
    Sarah (Furbush), 228

CRAFTS See CROFTS
CRAM
    Elmer H., 72
    Jonathan, Jr., 91
CRANDALL
    Ralph J., 128
CRICHTIN
    John, 40
CROCKER
    John, 131
    Mary, 131
    Sarah, 131
CROFTS
    Ann (South), 33-34, 36, 38
    William, 33-34, 36, 38
CROMWELL
    Oliver, 27, 138
CROSBY, 115
CROSS
    Abigail, 130
    Margaret (Northend), 100
    Martha, 227
    Mary (Fall), 162
CROUCH
    Harriet M., 15
CUDWORTH
    James, 178
CUMMINGS
    Abigail, 105
CUNNINGHAM
    Mary, 57
CURRIER
    Daniel, 95
    Meribah (Tilton), 95
CURTICE
    James, 84
CURTIN
    John, 190
    Martha, 207
CURTIN See CRICHTIN
CURTIS
    Ebeneazer, 173
    Elizabeth, 173
    Elizabeth (Abell), 228
    Elizabeth (Randall), 173
    Hannah (Dodge), 164
    Henry, 228
    John, 164
    Mary, 164
    Mary (Cortwithen), 165
    Mary (Look), 164
    Nathaniel, 228
    Samuel, 164, 228
    Sarah, 228

Zaccheus, 165
Zacheus, 213
Zacheus, Jr., 30
CURWIN
    George, Capt., 206
CUTLER
    Eunice (Peters), 229
    John, 132-133
    Lydia, 133
    Lydia (___), 133
    Samuel, 229
CUTTER See also CUTLER
    Hannah, 187
CUTTING
    Sarah, 229

DAGGAT
    Susannah, 202
DAGGETT
    Susannah, 145
DAKIN
    John, 35
DALAND
    Geneva, 210
    Geneva A., 29. 81, 160
    Robert, 130
DALTON
    Abigail, 23
    Dorothie (Swan), 23
    Joseph, 132
    Samuel, 23
DANA
    Anna (Bullard/Bullock), 54
    Hannah, 54
    Richard, 54
DANFORTH
    Benjamin, 134
    Elisabeth, 134
    Joshua, 130, 133-134
    Keziah (___), 134
    Lydia (___), 133-134
    Piercy, 134
    Polly, 134
    Sarah, 134
DANIELS
    Sarah, 79
DARLING
    Johanna, 166
DARVILL
    Esther (___), 174
    Mary, 174
    Robert, 174
DAVENPORT
    Nathaniel, Capt., 157

Margaret, 202
Mary, 215
Rebecca (Ramsdell), 215
DOWNS
Jane, 226
Mary Ann H., 173
DOWS
Deborah (Perry), 154
Joseph, Dea., 154
DOWSE See DOWS
DRESSER
John, 17
DREW
Ebenezer, 115
Job, Sgt., 57
Martha (Cobb), 115
Thankful (Prince), 57
DRISCOLL, 229
DRIVER
Mary (Glover), 166
Robert, 35, 182
Ruth, 85
DUDLEY, 185
Abigail (Tilton), 93
Eunice, 133
Frances, 173
Sarah, 39, 133
Sarah (Wheeler), 173
Stephen, 93
DUGGLE See also DOUGLAS
Alexander, 211
DUGGLES See DOUGLAS
DUMMER
Richard, 181
DUNBAR
Edith Flanders, 94
DUNHAM
John, Jr., 227
Mary (___), 227
Sylvina/Sarah (___), 115
Thomas, 115
DUNN
Lydia, 57
William, 212
DUNNELL
David, 213
Hannah (East), 213
Jacob, 213
Jonathan, 213
Kezia (Ramsdell), 213
Mary, 213
Rebecca (Flurence/Florence), 213
Rubin, 213
Ruth, 213

Sarah, 213
Solomon, 213
DURFEE, 123
DURKEE
Martha (Cross), 227
Mary (Hankey), 57
Pearl, Capt., 57
Phebe (Pearl), 57
Phineas, 57
William, 227
DUSTIN
Hannah (___), 20
Ruth (___), 112
Samuel, 112
Sarah (Johnson), 112
Thomas, 20
Timothy, 112
DWIGHT
Silence, 163
DYKE
Experience (Foster), 54
Jonathan, 54

EAST
Hannah, 213
EASTMAN
Abigail (Harriman), 23
John R., 93
Sarah, 22
William, 23
EATON
Aaron, 130
Anna (Rand), 107
Anna/Hannah (Rand), 39
Benjamin, 39, 107, 130, 227
Christian (Penn), 142
Daniel, 114
Ebenezer, 142
Francis, 142
Hannah, 48, 107
Hannah (Pearson), 107
Jonathan, 227
Lilley, 157
Lucinda (___), 227
Mary, 171
Mary (Ingalls), 114
Mary (Stone), 227
Mary/Molly, 227
Mercy, 142
Nathan, 130
Sarah (___), 142
Thomas, Capt., 13
ECCLES
Mary (___), 10

William, 10
EDDY
Lucy, 228
EDES
Anna, 137
Anna, Jr., 137
EDMONDS
Joseph, 156, 211
Mary (___), 211
William, 156
EDMUNDS
John, 159
Joseph, 209
William, 182
EDWARD I, 138
ELIOT
Hopestill, 81
Sally, 222
ELITHORP
Margaret, 100-102
Mary (Batt), 100
Nathaniel, 100
ELITHORPE
Margaret, 19
ELKINS
Henry, 64
Sarah (Gutch), 56
Thomas, 55-56
ELLIOT
Anna (Challis), 221
Polly/Molly, 221
Thomas, 221
ELLIS
Anna, 108
David, 216
Elizabeth (Rawson), 108
Emma Jane (Hale), 108
Frederick O., 108
John, 109
Mary (Baker), 109
Mary (Brown), 108
Orin, 108
Phebe (___), 216
Seth, 108
Seth, Jr., 108
Susannah (Cheney), 108
ELWELL
David, 76
Mary (Graham), 76
EMERSON
Hannah/Joanna, 172
Sarah, 22
Susannah, 13

FURBUSH
  Sarah, 228
FURMAN
  Hannah, 106

GAGE
  Daniel, 102
  Margaret (Harriman), 102
  Sarah (Kimball), 102
GAILE
  Mary, 188
GALE
  ___, Col., 95
  Abigail, 172
  Abraham, 166
  Elizabeth (Grant), 165
  Lydia, 165
  Lydia (Ropes), 166
  Mary (Hooper), 165
  Samuel, 165
  William, 165
GAMMON
  Catherine, 229
GANNETT
  Hannah, 202
GARDNER
  Anna (Ramsdell), 216
  Ebenezer, 216
  Elizabeth (Weld), 173
  Eunice (Waters), 165
  Frank A., 36
  Grindal, 81
  Jeremiah, 81
  John, 173
  Joseph, 81
  Judith (Coffin), 216
  Lois (Ramsdell), 81
  Peleg, 216
  Perhas, 131
  Ruth, 216
  Ruth (Coffin), 81
  Sarah, 165
  Thomas, 165
GAREY
  Anne, 134
  Joanna (___), 134
  Reuben, 134
  Robert, 134
GARLAND
  Joseph E., 186
GARNER
  Abel, 166
  Sarah (Porter), 166

GARNSEY
  Hannah (Munnings), 227
  Henry, 227
GASTON
  Alexander, 10
GATES
  Oldham, 172
  Thankful (Adams), 172
GAUDET
  Mary Vitaline Otil, 226
GEARE
  Sarah, 31
GEISSENHAINER
  ___, Pastor, 46
  Frederick William, 43
GETCHELL
  Miriam (Blethen), 54
  Nathaniel, 54
GHAFNEY
  Jane, 226
  Thomas, 226
GIBSON
  J. S. W., 139
  Mary, 173
  Roland, 120
GILBERT
  Abigail,
  Elizabeth (Black), 228
  Humphrey, 228
GILES
  Elizabeth, 197
GILL
  Jane, 131
GILLOW
  John, 26
GILMAN
  Daniel, 221
  Joel, 221
  Lewis, 221
  Mary, 137
  Mary (French), 222
  Mary Jane (Farrington), 221
  Mehitable (Judkins), 221
  Polly/Molly (Elliot), 221
  Rosina Jane, 221
  Steven, 222
GILYAN
  Mary, 135
GLOVER
  Mary, 166
  Priscilla, 173
GODDARD
  Simon, 9

GODFREY
  Betty (Tilton), 96-97
  Jonathan, 96-97
GOING
  Mary, 132
GOLDTHWAITE
  Benjamin, 87
  Lois (Boardman), 87
GOODALL
  Elizabeth, 137
GOODELL
  Alfred, 115
  Jerusha (Cleveland), 115
  William, 115
GOODRICH
  Charlotte, 114
  Francis Bowman, 114, 229
  Hannah (Bowman), 114
  Lucy A., 229
  Martha E., 229
  Mary S. (___), 229
  Sophia, 114
  William, Capt., 114
GOODRIDGE
  Joanna, 108
  Mehitebel, 116
  William, Capt., 229
GOODRIDGE See also GOODRICH
GOODSPEED
  Bethia (Wooding/Wooden), 174
  Nathaniel, 174
  Sarah (King), 174
  Stephen, 174
GOODWIN
  Amos, 107
  Daniel, 221-222
  Daniel B., 221
  Esther (Pierce), 107
  Hannah, 48, 107, 221, 228
  Hannah (Colby), 222
  James, 55
  Judeth (___), 55
  Lois, 55
  Major, 108
  Mary (Atkinson), 108
  Miriam (Blaisdell), 221
  Sarah F. (Heath), 221
GOOLD
  Elihu, 187
GORDARD
  Betty (___), 136
GORDON
  Abigail, 21
  Abner, 22

EMERY
  Bethia, 112
EMMERSON
  Sarah, 109
EMMONS
  Mary, 92
ENDECOTT
  ___, Gov, 179
ENDICOTT
  Mary, 151
ENSLOW
  Ann E. (Williams), 48
  Clayton Nehemiah, 48
  Diana Marie (Houde), 48
  Elizabeth (Pool), 48
  Hannah I. (Williams), 48
  James Cox, 48
  Jonathan David, 48
  William David, 48
  William Howard, 48
ESTES
  Aaron, 205
  Anna, 190
  Anna Maria, 162
  Caleb, 162-163
  Charlotte (Day), 162
  Elizabeth, 188
  Elizabeth (Kennedy), 162
  Esther (Richards), 205
  John, 162
  Lydia (Bishop), 163
  Mark, 187
  Matthew, 187
  William, 187
EUSTIS
  Matthew, 85
EVANS
  Betsey, 108
  Betsey (Walker), 108
  Eli, 109
  Hannah (Larcum), 109
  Helen F., 23
  Peter, 109
  Randall, 108
  Ruth (Petty), 109
EVENS
  Abigail (Townsend), 202
  Nathaniel, 202

FAIRBANK
  Jonas, 107
  Jonathan, 106
  Lydia (Prescott), 107
  Mary, 106

  Mary (Hayward), 106
FAIRFIELD
  Sarah (Geare), 31
FALL
  Mary, 162
  Zebedee, 162
FARLEY
  Lydia, 195
FARLOW
  Charles Frederic, 89, 160
FARMER
  ___, Mr., 202
FARNHAM
  Daniel, 162
  Esther C., 162
  Joshua, 163
  Mary (Grow), 163
  Mary (McCurdy), 162
FARR, 85
  George, 146, 182
  Mary, 85
FARRAR
  Abigail (Johnson), 200
  Elizabeth (___), 200
  Hannah, 116, 208
  John, 204, 206
  Mary (Collins), 203-204, 206
  Susanna, 50, 166
  Thomas, 200, 206
FARREN
  Aquilla, 112
  Desire (Hemingway), 113
  Hannah (___), 112
  Jonathan, 112
  Sarah, 112
  Sarah (Wells), 112
  Zebulon, 113
FARRINGTON, 28, 155
  Abigail, 112
  Abigail (Fuller), 50, 54
  Daniel, 188
  Dorothy, 28
  Ebenezer, 221
  John, 50, 54
  Lydia, 50, 188
  Lydia (Mansfield), 54
  Martha, 37
  Mary Jane, 221
  Matthew, 85
  Matthew, Jr., 148
  Ruth (Bartlett), 221
  Sarah, 209, 214
  Sarah (Potter), 35-36
  William, 54

FARWELL
  Jonathan, 134
FAVOUR
  John, 135
FAYE
  Roddphus, 153
FAYERWEATHER, 126
  John, 89
FELLOWS
  Molley (Ring), 55
  Samuel, 55
FELT
  Elizabeth (Wilkensen), 173
  George, 173
  Joshua, 82
FELTON
  Benjamin, Capt., 49
  Daniel, 113
  Hepsibah (Shelton), 49
  Joseph, 49
  Margaret, 113
  Mary (Trask), 49
  Ruth (Hamilton), 49
  Sally, 49
  Sarah (Stevens), 113
  Skelton, 49
FERRIN See FARREN
FERRIS
  John, 209
  Mary Walton, 206
FIFIELD
  Betsey, 174
  Rachel, 171
  Ruth (___), 171
  Samuel, 171
FIGGIES
  Harriett Babson, 48
FIGHELY
  Bridget, 221
FINSON
  Tammy, 174
FISH
  Hephezibah, 132
FISHER
  Anna, 29
  Deborah (Witt), 90
  John, 90
  Leonard, 45
  Molly, 112
FISK
  Samuel, 133
  Sarah, 163
FISKE
  Jane Fletcher, 119, 127-128

FITCH
    Abigail, 137
    Eleanor (Strong), 228
    Peggy/Margaret (Ramsdell), 216
    Reuben, 216
    Stephen, 228
FITZGERALD
    Edmund, 164
    Ellen, 163
    Margaret (Quinlan), 164
    William, 164
FLAGG, 85
    Ebenezer, 137
    Ephraim, 137
    Josiah, 137
    Rebecka (___), 137
    Ruth, 137
    Ruth (___), 137
    Theoder, 137
FLANDERS
    Abigail, 222
    Margaret (Lawrence), 223
    Naomi, 157
    Sarah, 93
    Thomas, 223
FLETCHER
    Elizabeth, 202
FLINT
    Abigail (Nichols), 197
    Hezekiah, 131
    Lydia, 196-197
    Lydia (Twiss), 197
    William, 197
    William, Dea., 197
FLOOD
    Alles, 130
FLORENCE See FLURENCE
FLOWERS
    Bartholomew, 228
FLOYD
    ___, Capt., 155
    Abigail, 174
    John, 151, 155, 159
FLURENCE
    Rebecca, 213
FOGG
    Jeremiah, Rev., 74
FOLGER
    Anna (Ramsdell), 216
    Jedidah, 216
    Mary (Ramsdell), 216
    Ruben, 216
    Seth, 216

FOLSOM
    Elizabeth Knowles, 64
FORD
    Benoni, 171
    Joseph, 173
    Lois (Stetson), 173
    Lydia (Cadman), 171
FORTUNE, 55
FOSDICK
    Anna, 81, 216
    Jonathan, 216
    Sarah (Sprague), 216
FOSSEY
    Elizabeth (Rayner), 228
    Thomas, 228
FOSTER
    Andrew, 227
    Anne, 171
    David, 227
    Experience, 54
    Hannah, 227
    Judith (___), 15
    Leonard, 171
    Lucy (Wetherbee), 171
    Nancy, 15-16
    Rachel, 49
    Samuel, 15
    Susann (Orr), 49
    Ursula (Woodford), 227
FOULD
    Jacob, 130
FOWLER
    Mary, 114
FOY
    Mary, 216
FRASER
    Collins, 100
FREEMAN
    Anna, 136
    Chloe, 135-136
    Chloe (___), 134, 136
    Dinah (___), 135
    Dos, 134
    Doss, 137
    Jenne, 137
    Jenney, 134, 136
    Joshua, Capt., 142
    Kemer, 135
    Lucy, 136
    Peggy, 134
    Peter, 134, 136
    Phebe, 134, 136
    Philis (___), 137
    Phillis (___), 134

    Sharper, 134, 137
    Sherburn, 137
FRENCH, 211
    Alice (___), 229
    Edward, 66
    Elizabeth, 22, 33
    Elizabeth (Davis), 108
    Elizabeth (___), 114
    Experience (Foster), 54
    Harry Dana, 66
    Jacob, 108
    John, 54, 114
    Joseph, 22, 54
    Mary, 22, 31, 222
    Mary (Harriman), 20, 22
    Mehitable, 22
    Rebecca, 107
    Ruth, 22
    Sarah, 22, 109
    Sarah (Eastman), 22
    Susanna, 22
    Thomas, 114, 229
    Timothy, 22
FRIZZELL
    Annie (Thompson), 112
    John, 112
    John Allen, 112
    Molly (Fisher), 112
FROST
    Gilman D., Dr., 67
    Rebecca, 31
FROTHINGHAM
    Catherine, 89
    Elizabeth, 88
    Elizabeth (Call), 88
    Hannah, 36
    Hannah (Rand), 88
    Joseph, 88
    Joseph, Jr., 88-89
    Mary, 89
    Mary (Ivory), 88
    Mercy (Stearns), 88
    Nathaniel, 36, 88
    Peter, 36
    Samuel, 36
    William, 36
FULLER
    ___, Ens., 26
    Abigail, 32, 50, 54, 84
    Benjamin, 84
    Jn, 204
    John, 27, 159, 213
    Susanna, 112
    Susanna (Ballard), 84

Alexander, 21-22
Benjamin, 21
Benoni, 20-21
Daniel, 20-22
Dinah, 21
Elizabeth, 22
Elizabeth (Harriman), 20-22
Hannah, 21
James, 21
Margaret, 22
Margaret (Harriman), 20, 22
Mary, 22
Mary (Lissen), 21-22
Nathaniel, 21
Rebecca (Heard), 21
Thomas, 20-22
Thomas, Jr., 20
Timothy, 21
GORHAM
   Henry S., 25
GORMAN
   Ellen (Green/Hendrehan), 228
   Mary (___), 228
   Patrick, 228
   Peter, 228
   Sarah (Furbush), 228
GORTON
   Samuel, 120
GOSS
   Elizabeth (Witham), 174
   Mary (Tarr), 174
   Patience (Harraden), 174
   Tammy (Finson), 174
   Thomas, 174
GOTT
   Daniel, 26
GOULD
   ___, Mrs., 9
   Abigail (Needham), 164
   Benjamin Apthorp, 194
   Bettey, 194
   Daniel, 194
   Elizabeth (___), 164
   Gideon, 194
   Haffield, 164
   Hannah, 108
   Hannah (Learned), 109
   Hannah (Marsh), 194
   Hannah (Masters), 164
   Hannah (Singletary), 164
   Henry, Jr., 172
   John, 31, 84, 109
   John, Capt., 84
   Jonathan, Capt., 164

   Joseph, 84, 194
   Margaret (___), 164
   Mary (Putnam), 194
   Molly, 194
   Rachel, 195, 197
   Rebecca, 194
   Rebecca (Cole), 172
   Samuel, 84
   Sarah, 194
   Sarah (Twiss), 194
   Thadeus, 194
   Thomas, 84, 164
   Zacheus, 84
GOULETTE
   Anne Merrill, 50
GOWING
   Annice, 165
   Johanna (Darling), 166
   John, 166
GRACIE, 55
GRAFFAM
   Elias, 57
   Elmira, 57
   Hannah, 57
   Lydia (Deering), 57
   Lydia (Dunn), 57
   Samuel, 57
   Sarah, 57
GRAHAM
   Andrew, 76
   Hannah, 76
   Mary, 75-76
   Mary (___), 76
GRANT
   Abraham, 229
   Daniel, 166
   Elizabeth, 165
   John, 18
   Mary (Glover), 166
   Sarah (Morton), 229
GRAVES
   Desire, 206
   Elias, 172
   Elisabeth, 163
   Elizabeth, 172
   Elizabeth (Banks), 172
   Elizabeth (Collins), 203-204, 206
   George, 172
   Hannah (Rand), 87
   Joanna, 188
   John, 172
   Joseph, 172
   K. V., 206
   Kennth Vance, 206

   Mark, 206, 208
   Rachel, 172
   Rebecca, 206
   Rebecca (___), 206
   Ruth, 203-204, 206
   Ruth (Collins), 206
   Ruth (Taylor), 206
   Samuel, 204-206
   Sarah (Brewer), 206
   Thomas, 206
   William, 187
GRAY
   Anna (Newhall), 205
   Deborah, 205
   Deborah (Williams), 151
   Dorothy, 205
   Dorothy (Collins), 203-205
   Elizabeth (Allen), 205
   Esther, 163, 228
   Joseph, 151
   Martin, 164
   Robard/Robert, 204
   Robert, 205
   Sarah, 205
   Susan (Vynard), 164
GREELE
   Andrew, 164-165
   Mary, 164
   Mary (Moyse), 165
   Sarah (Brown), 164
GREELEY
   Jane, 94
   Jonathan, 94
   Martha, 94
GREEN
   Abigail, 136
   Betsy (Pool), 226
   Catherine, 163
   Charles, 136
   Daniel, Dea., 136
   Daniel, Jr., 136
   Dorcas (Lyon), 226
   Eliza (Osborn), 115
   Elizabeth (Roads), 226
   Ellen, 228
   Ezra, 136
   George W., 226
   Hannah (Osborn), 115
   Henry H., 226
   James, 215
   James A., 226
   Jane (Ghafney), 226
   Jonas, Jr., 131
   Joshua, 122

Ester/Hester (Witt), 156, 213
Ebenezer, 209, 213
Ebeniezur, 156
Ebinezur, 160
Ester (Witt), 160
John, 156, 160, 213
Mary, 199
Nathaniel, 79
Rebecka (Stocker), 160
Rebeckah, 160
Sarah, 79, 213

HATHORNE
John, 203
Wm., 27

HAVEN
Richard, 26

HAWKE
Abigail (Farrington), 112
Ebenezer, 188
Hannah, 87
Jonathan, 112, 211
Martha, 187
Moses, 213
Philadelphia, 188
Sarah (Newhall), 112

HAWKS
Ebenezer, 79
Jerusha (Merriam), 79
John, 79
Jonathan, 209

HAWTHORN
Mary, 85

HAWTHORNE See HATHORN

HAY
Abigal, 131
Anna, 131
Duke, 137
Elizabeth (___), 131
James, 131
John, 131
Luce, 131
Lucrece, 131
Phebe, 133
Sarah, 131
Thomas, 131
Thos, 131

HAYES
John, 72

HAYWARD
Abigail (___), 134
Hannah (Hosmer), 107
Joseph, 107
Mary, 106

HAYWOOD
Hannah, 131
Seth, 9

HAZARD
"Nailer" Tom, 126
Thomas, 121
Thomas Robinson, 120

HAZEN
Benjamin, 104
Edward, 103-104
Israel, 104
Jane (Pickard), 103
Margaret, 103
Samuel, 103-104
Sarah, 104
Sarah (Harriman), 103
Unice/Eunice, 104

HAZLTON
Rebecca, 81

HAZZEN
Sarah (Harriman), 102

HEAD
Elizabeth (Atwood), 224
James, 224
John, 224
Lydia (Day), 223
Mehetabel (___), 224
Reuben, 223
Sally, 223

HEALD
Hannah (___), 174
John, 174
Mary (Chandler), 174
Timothy, 174

HEALEY
Levi, 91

HEARD
Hannah, 172
Rebecca, 21

HEATH
Anna (Fisher), 29
Hepzibah, 222
Judith (Hoyt), 222
Martha (Dow), 21
Mary (Peaslee), 221
Nehemiah, 221
Sarah F., 221
Sargent, 222

HEELEY
Mary, 57

HEIRES
Sarah, 199

HEIRSE
Elizabeth (Tolman), 152

Moses, 152

HEMINGWAY
Desire, 113
Mehitable (Dennison), 113
Samuel, 113

HENRICKSON/HENDRICKSON See HENRICKSSON

HENCHMAN
___, Mr., 208
Nathaniel, 209
Nathaniel, Rev., 214

HENDERSON
Deborah (Twiss), 194
James, 174
John, 194
Sarah (Harper), 174

HENDREHAN
Ellen, 228

HENLEY
Berkley, 24

HENRICKSSON
Adolph Herman, 55
Carl Wilhelm, 55
Hulda Marie, 55

HERIMAN See HARRIMAN
HERREMEN See HARRIMAN
HERRIMAN See also HARRIMAN

HEUREUX
Julianna, 48

HEWES
William, 157

HEWES See HEIRSE

HILL
Abraham, 85
Abraham, Capt., 88
Amy (___), 9
Elizabeth, 227
Hannah (___), 85
Jonathan, 9
Martha (Cary), 88
Mary, 47, 88

HILLIARD
Ann, 96

HILTON
Ann (Parsons), 113
Anna, 163
Frances (___), 113
Hannah, 113
Mary, 112
William, 113

HITCHEN
Joseph, 210

HITCHENS
May, 130

Josiah, 130
Lidia (Ramsdell), 215
Loami, 115
Mary, 50
Mary (Parker), 122
Matthew, 164
Nathaniel, Gen., 126
Polly, 136
Rhoda, 136
Russell, 115
Ruth, 136
Ruth (___), 136
Sally (___), 136
Samuel H., 226
Thomas E., 226
William, 226
William, Jr., 226
William, Sr., 226
GREENLEAF
    Mary (___), 132
    Samuel, 133
    Stephen, 132
GRICE
    Mary, 199
GRIFFIN
    Elizabeth, 211
GRIMES See GRAHAM
GRO
    Lydia, 136
    Ruth, 136
    Ruth (___), 136
GROVER
    ___, Mr., 56
    Emily H. F. (Brown), 113
    Helen/Nellie Elizabeth (Cobb), 113
    James, 113
    Mary (Richardson), 56
    Thomas, 113
GROW
    Mary, 163
GUARDINER
    Honora/Bridget, 220
GUNNISON
    Eunice, 55
    John, 55
    Rebecca (___), 55
GUTCH
    Lydia (Holgrave), 56
    Robert, 56
    Sarah, 56

HACKER
    William, 146
HACKWELL
    Richard, 146
HADLEY
    John, 135
    Thomas, 134
HADLOCK
    Hannah, 76
    Hannah (Ral/Rall), 76
    James, 171
    Lucy, 76
    Mary, 76
    Mary (Graham), 75
    Mary (Lurvey), 76
    Mary (Marshall), 76
    Nathaniel, 76
    Rebecca (Hutchingson), 171
    Sarah, 172
    William Nathaniel, 75-76
HAES
    Ana/Anne (Harriman), 23
HAGGETT
    Elizabeth, 224
    Mehitabel, 223
HAINES
    Elizabeth, 22
    Hannah, 22
    Hannah (Harriman), 20-21
    Jonathan, 21-22
    Joseph, 22
    Lydia/Lidiah, 22
    Mehitable, 22
    Sarah, 22
    Sarah (Moulton), 21
    Thomas, 20-21
HALE
    Achsah S. (Keith), 56
    Adoolphus, 56
    Betsey (Evans), 108
    E. M., 56
    Edna, 47
    Elizabeth (Holman), 109
    Emma Jane, 108
    F. D., 56
    Jacob, 103, 109
    John Waldron, 108
    Joseph, 103
    Lydia (Stow), 108
    Mary (Harriman), 103
    Mary (Watson), 103
    Sarah Jane, 56
    Silas, 108
    Stephen, 108
    Susan (Waldron), 108
    Thomas, 103

HALL, 158
    Abigail (Dalton), 23
    Abigail (Hutchinson), 47
    Abigail (Parker), 93
    Amanda, 47
    Ebenezer, 47
    Hannah (Anderson), 47
    Israel, 47
    Joseph, 35
    Martha, 50
    Richard, Jr., 23
    Sarah, 23
HALLAHAN
    Johanna (Kramer), 57
HALLAWAY See HALLOWELL
HALLET See HOWLETT
HALLOWELL
    Ann, 158
    Benjamin, 158
    Joseph, 158
    Margaret, 55
    Mary, 158
    Mary (Stocker), 158
    Mehitabel (Breed), 209
    Samuel, 158, 209
    Sarah, 158
    William, 158
HALPIN
    Bartlett, 164
    Margaret (Sellery), 164
    Mary, 164
HALSEY
    Joseph, 159
HAMILTON
    Nathan, 49
    Ruth, 49
    Ruth (Wheeler), 49
HAMILTON-EDWARDS
    Gerald, 139
HAMMOND
    Charity (Benson), 173
    Elizabeth, 27
    Isaac W., 99
    Priscilla, 21-22
    Sylvanus, 173
HANAFORD
    Elizabeth (Tilton), 93
    Guy, 93
HANBURY
    Luke, 33
    Peter, 33
HAND
    Candace, 222

HANDS
    John, 229
    Mark, 229
    Mary (Bell), 229
    Mary (___), 229
HANEVER
    Anne, 171
HANKEY
    Mary, 57
HANLON
    Johannah (Coleman), 220
    Mary A., 220
    William, 220
HANNES See HANDS
HANNETT
    Abraham, 202
HANOVER
    Jane, 197
HARDY
    Susanna (Tilton), 92
HARKER
    Sarah, 205
HARNDEN
    Elizabeth, 106
    Mary (___), 106
    Richard, 106
HARPER
    Rachel (___), 174
    Sarah, 174
    William, 174
HARRADEN
    Patience, 174
HARRIMAN
    Abigail, 20, 22-24, 103
    Abigail (Tilton), 92-93
    Abner, 20-21, 23-24
    Abraham, 101
    Alta, 17
    Ana/Anne, 23
    Ann, 23-24
    Ann (Stevens), 23
    Anne/Anna, 104
    Asa, 104-105
    Ashael, 23
    Dudley, 105
    Elizabeth, 20-21, 23
    Elizabeth (Swan), 19-21, 24
    Enoch, 104
    Ezekiel, 23
    Hannah, 19-21
    Harold, 24
    Iva, 17
    Jaasiel, 23
    Jane, 104-105
    Jane (Bailey), 104
    Jane (Colman), 104
    Jeremiah, 101-102, 105
    Jesse, 93
    Joab, 23
    Joanne, 24
    Joel, 23
    John, 17, 19-20, 22-24, 101, 104-105
    Jonathan, 18-20, 24, 100-102, 105
    Joseph, 21
    Joshua, 21
    Leonard, 17-20, 22-24, 100-101, 104
    Leonard, Capt., 102-103
    Lucy, 105
    Margaret, 20, 22, 100, 102-104
    Margaret (Elithorp), 19, 100-102
    Margaret (___), 17-19
    Martha (Page), 21, 24
    Martha (Plummer), 102
    Mary, 19-24, 102-103
    Mary (Calee), 19-20, 23
    Mary (___), 21
    Matthew, 18-21, 23-24
    Matthew, Jr., 19-21
    Matthew, Sr., 20
    Mehetabel, 22
    Mehetable, 20-21
    Mehetible, 23
    Mehitable, 23, 103
    Mehitable (Spofford), 103
    Moses, 23-24, 103
    Naomi, 23
    Nathaniel, 20-21, 23-24, 101, 103, 105
    Nathaniel, Lt., 103
    Patience (Perley), 105
    Peter, 23
    Phebe, 105
    Philip, 21, 24
    Richard, 20-21, 23-24
    Rossamon/Rosamond, 103
    Ruth, 23
    Samuel, 23, 101-104
    Sarah, 23, 102-103
    Sarah (Hall), 23
    Sarah (Merrill), 23
    Sarah (Morrill), 22
    Sarah (Page), 24
    Sarah (Palmer), 19, 100, 102
    Solomon, 104
    Stephen, 21, 24
    Susanna, 21
    Thomas, 104
    William, 105
HARRIS
    John, 18
HARRISON
    Catherine E., 220
    Morris, 220
    Sarah (O'Neil), 221
HART
    Abraham, 137
    Isaac, 26
    John, 32, 137
    John, Dr., 131
    Joseph, 37, 50
    Mary (___), 137
    Phebe (Ivory), 50
    Polly, 137
    Ruth (Chadwell), 37, 50
    Sally, 137
    Samuel, 26, 50
    Sarah, 50
    William, 137
HARTHORN
    Ebenezer, 211
    Samuel, 211
HARTT
    Mary (Hudson), 199
    Ralph, 199
HARVEY
    Darius, 136
    Polly, 136
    Polly (___), 136
HARWOOD
    Hannah, 195
    Jonathan, 55
    Sarah (Boyce), 55
HASKELL
    Caleb, Jr., 47
    Edna (Hale), 47
    Mary, 47, 164
HASKINS
    Rebecca (Lincoln), 55
    William, 55
HASSAM
    John T., 87
HASTINGS
    Linda B., 222-223
    Harriet E. (___), 114
    Solomon C., 114
HATCH
    Ann (Rider), 112
    Jeremiah, 112
HATHAWAY, 123
HATHORN, 155
    ___, Maj., 30

HITCHINGS
    Daniel, 205
    Hannah (Ingalls), 205
HITCHINSON
    Elisabeht, 133
HOBSON
    William, 18
HODGKINS
    Mary, 81
HOLBROOK
    Jane, 171
    Margaret (Doane), 171
    Thomas, 171
HOLDEN
    Ebenezer, 137
    Fanny, 137
    James, 132
    Jenne (___), 137
    Joseph, 137
    Molly (___), 137
    Naomi (___), 132
    Neomi, 137
    Thomas, 137
HOLDIN
    Joseph, 132
    Mary (___), 132
HOLDREDGE See also HOLDRIDGE
    Deborah, 199
HOLDRIDGE See also HOLDREDGE
    Tabitha, 199
HOLGRAVE
    Deborah (Williams), 151
    James, Dr., 151
    Lydia, 56
HOLLAND
    Bathsheba (Ivory), 90
    Deborah, 90
    Elizabeth (Park), 90
    Elizabeth (Spooner), 90
    Esther, 90
    Hannah (Spooner), 90
    Ivory, 90
    John, 90
    Jonas, 90
    Luther, 90
    Martha (Rogers), 90
    Mercy, 158
    Park, 90
    Vashti, 90
HOLLET See HOWLETT
HOLLIS
    Abigail, 229
    John, 229
HOLLOWELL See HALLOWELL

HOLMAN
    Elizabeth, 109
    Mary Lovering, 17, 100
    Sarah (Twiss), 194
    Solomon, 194
    Winifred Lovering, 25, 145, 205
HOLMES
    Elizabeth, 57
    Frank R., 25, 192
HOLT
    ___, Rev., 195
    Alice, 55
HOLYOKE
    Mary, 174
HOOD
    Agnes, 187
    Elizabeth, 187
    Elizabeth (___), 187
    Richard, 26, 26
    Sarah, 187-188
    Sarah (___), 188
    Vernon, 67
HOOKER
    Thomas, 180
HOOL
    Sarah, 174
HOOPER
    Abigail (Gale), 172
    Benjamin, 166
    Charles, 165
    Eleanor (Clark), 166
    Elizabeth (Fletcher), 202
    Elizabeth (Harriman), 23
    Hannah (Neal), 165
    Henry, 202
    Lydia, 172
    Lydia (Allen), 116
    Mary, 165
    Mary (Collins), 202
    Robert, 202
    William, 116, 172
HOPKINS
    Sarah, 195
HOPKINSON
    John, 19
    Jonathan, 104
HORGAN
    Catherine, 220
    Jeremiah, 221
    Mary (___), 221
HORNE
    Comfort, 173
    Elisha, 173
    Tamesin (Randle), 173

HORTON
    Sarah, 40, 89
HOSMER
    Hannah, 107
HOUDE
    Alfred, 48
    Anthony, 48
    Beulah (Burgess), 48
    Diana Marie, 48
    Hector H., 48
    Julianna (Heureux), 48
    Matilda, 48
    Matilda (Boulanger), 48
    Matilda (Houde), 48
    Roland M., 48
HOUGHTON
    Mary, 173
HOUSE
    Hannah, 229
    Jemima/Peninah, 229
    John, Rev., 229
HOVEY
    Dorcas (Ivory), 33
    James, 228
    John, Sgt., 33
    Priscilla (___), 228
HOW
    Benjamin, 90
    John, 18
    Persiluh, 131
    Vashti (Holland), 90
HOWARD
    Abijah, 9
    Loea Parker, 33, 146
    Lorie A., 15
    Thomas, 28
HOWE
    Daniel, 181, 227
    Nehemiah, 74
    Sarah (Widger), 227
HOWLAND
    Rebecca (Hussey), 201
    Richard C., 186
HOWLETT
    Alice (___), 229
    Martha Manning, 113
    Thomas, 229
HOWS
    Joseph, 35
HOYT
    Anna, 222
    Annah (Stuart), 222
    Barnard, 222
    David, 52

Elizabeth L., 22
Joel, 22
John, 22
Mary, 22
Mary (Bean), 22
Mehitable, 221
Samuel, 22, 222
Sarah (Bohonon), 222

KEASER
   George, 34-35
KEENE
   Elizabeth (Basset), 202
   John, 157
   Peter, 202
KEITH
   Achsah S., 56
KEIZER
   John Jesse, 227
   Nancy (Mitchell), 227
   Nancy (Poore), 227
KELLEY
   Agnes T. (McLoaughlin), 220
   Catherine (McGlonne), 221
   David, 78
   John, 221
   John Z., 220
   Margaret (Poer/Powers), 220
   Marguerite L., 220
   Michael, 220
KELTON
   Samuel, Capt., 154
KEMBAL
   Lucy, 82
KEMP
   Esther, 115
KENDALL
   Parker, 152
   Ruth (Johnson), 152
KENISTON
   John, 67
KENNEDY
   Bolton, 162
   Elizabeth, 162
   Elizabeth (Bolton), 163
   Elizabeth/Lydia, 221
   Robert, 163
KENNETT
   Ann, 228
   Charlotte, 228
KENNEY
   Jethro, 132
   Judith, 195

KENYON
   Paul, 186
KERMAN
   John, 181
KEYES
   Mary, 39
KEZER
   Abigail (Harriman), 103
   Samuel, 103
KIBBY
   Lydia, 106
KIDDAR
   Calatine, 134
   Jonathan, 134
   Mary (___), 134
   Nancy, 134
   Sarah, 134
   William Lambert, 134
KILBURN
   Lucy, 115
KILBURNE
   George, 18
KILCUP
   Dudson, 39
   Lois (Rogers), 39
KILHAM See also KILLUM
   Alice, 31
   Anna, 31
   Anna (Dodge), 31
   Austin D., 31
   Elizabeth, 31
   John, 31
   Mary (Poland), 31
   Rebecca (Frost), 31
   Sarah (Patch), 31
KILLUM See also KILHAM
   Austin, 31
   Daniel, 31
   Elizabeth (Ramsdell), 31
   Sarah (Geare), 31
KIMBALL See also KEMBAL
   Babgail, 115
   Christopher, 115
   John, 95
   Sarah, 102
   Sarah (Harriman), 23
   Sarah (Jolls), 115
KING
   ___, Mr., 147
   Ardis, 72
   Daniel, 34, 146
   Elizabeth, 142
   Ezra, 142-143
   Ralph, 200

   Rebecca, 162
   Samuel, 142
   Sarah, 174
   Silence (Dwight), 163
   William, 163
KINNEY
   Mary, 133
KIRTLAND
   Nathaniel, 206
   Parnell (___), 206
   Priscilla, 152, 206-207
KNAPP
   Abial, 222
   Arthur Mason, 197
   Ebenezer, 197
   Elijah, 222
   Isaac, 197
   Jane (Hanover), 197
   Jonathan, 223
   Keziah (Cheney), 223
   Letta, 222
   Mary (Twiss), 197
   Mehitable (Tucker), 223
   Sally (Eliot), 222
KNIGHT
   Daniel, 171, 206
   Martha, 114
   Martha (Patashall), 171
   Mary, 114
   Robert, 114
   Wm., 114
KNOTT
   Richard, 158
KNOWLTON
   Deborah, 228
   Edmund, 228
   Mary (Austin), 228
KRAMER
   Johanna, 57

LADD
   Abigail (Flanders), 222
   Arthur Stuart, 222
   Candace Porter, 222
   Catherine (Thing), 223
   Edward, 222-223
   Ellen Mariah (Porter), 222
   Hannah (Hoyt), 222
   Langdon, 222
   Samuel, 222
   Sylvania (Colby), 222
LAINHART
   Ann S., 130
   Ann Smith, 3, 10

David W., 22
Hannah, 222
Hannah (Stevens), 226
John, 223
Joseph, 212
Judith, 222
Sarah (Barnard), 223
Thomas, 226
HUBBARD
   Grace, 223
HUDSON
   Elizabeth, 199
   John, 199
   Jonathan, 199, 214
   Jonthan, 199
   Joseph, 199
   Mary, 199
   Mary (Hathorn), 199
   Mary (Mils), 199
   Moses, 198-199, 213
   Rebecca, 89
   Ruth, 199
   Ruthe, 199
   Sarah, 199
   Sarah (Collins), 199
   Thomas, 199
HUGHES
   Elizabeth, 202
HUMPHREY, 182
   ___, Mr., 178, 180-181
   John, 183, 185
HUNNEWEL/HUNNEWELL
   Amy (___), 153
   Charles, 153
   Elizabeth, 153-154
HUNT
   Eliphalet, 97
   Ephraim, 157
   Mary, 158
HUNTING
   ___, Capt., 206
   Jane (Ballord), 160
   Joseph, 160
   Mary, 160
HUNTINGTON
   Anna (Hyatt), 186
   Archer, 186
   Mary, 222
HURD
   Charles W., 226
   Emmeline (Pond), 226
   John, 226
HUSE
   Abel, 112

   Mary (Hilton), 112
HUSSEY
   Abigail (Bunker), 216
   Christopher, 181
   Lydia, 115
   Rebecca, 201
   Simeon, 216
HUSSIN/HUSSING
   Charles, 153
   Hannah (___), 153
   Sarah, 153
HUTCHINGSON
   Rebecca, 171
HUTCHINSON
   Abigail, 47
   Anne, 120
   Benjamin, 32, 151
   David, 213
   Elisabeth, 194
   Francis, 133
   Hannah, 136
   Sarah (Sawyer), 47
   Stephen, Jr., 47
   Timothy, 130
HYATT
   Alpheas, 186
   Anna, 186
HYDE, 39
   Hannah (Dana), 54
   Jonathan, 54
   Mary (Beck), 54
   Samuel, 54
   William, 39

IDES
   ___, Dr., 9
INGALLS, 155, 184
   Ann (Collins), 203-205
   Anna (___), 114
   Edmund, 114
   Francis, 34
   Hannah, 205
   Henry, 205
   Jacob, 205
   Joseph, 205
   Mary, 114
   Mary (Tucker), 205
   Meriah, 205
   Nahemiah, 204
   Nathaniel, 205
   Rebecca (Collins), 205
   Robert, 205
   Ruthe, 205
   Samuel, 205

   Sarah, 205
   Sarah (Harker), 205
   Sarah (Ingalls), 205
   Sarah (Richards), 205
   Tabitha, 205
   Tabitha (Lewis), 205
   William, 205
   Zeruiah (Norwood), 205
INGERSOLL
   Ann/Agnes (Langley), 151
   Hannah (Collins), 151
   Mary, 108
   Nathaniel, 109
   Nathaniel, Dea., 151
   Richard, 151
INGOLS See INGALLS
INGULS See INGALLS
IRESON
   Edward, 146
ISHAM
   Abigail, 55
   Abigail (___), 55
   Isaac, 55
IVERY See IVORY
IVES
   Ruth, 78
IVORY
   Ann (South), 33-34, 36
   Anne (Ann/Anne), 88
   Bathsheba, 90
   Benjamin, 39-41, 86-87, 89, 153-154
   Charles, 154
   Deborah, 89-90, 154
   Deborah (Tobey), 40, 89
   Deborah (___), 39
   Dorcas, 33
   Ebenezer, 89
   Edmond, 33
   Elizabeth, 86-88
   Elizabeth (Hunnewell), 153-154
   Esther, 89
   Eunice, 86-87
   Hannah, 88, 154
   Hannah (Morgan), 153
   Hannah (Morgan), 154
   Hannah (Morgan), 90, 153-154
   John, 33, 39-40, 85-89, 153
   John, Jr., 89
   Joseph, 33, 89
   Katherine, 88, 154
   Katherine (Mitchell?), 88
   Katherine (___), 40
   Lois, 34, 36, 39, 86-87

Lucy, 154
Lucy (Russell), 153
Luke, 33
Martha, 153
Martha (Thwing), 88, 153
Mary, 39-40, 86, 88-89
Mary (Davis), 36-39
Mary (Hill), 88
Mary (___), 153
Nathaniel, 89, 154
Phebe, 50
Robert, 33
Ruth, 34, 36, 86-87, 89
Ruth (Ivory), 86-87, 89
Ruth (Potter), 40, 85, 89
Ruth (___), 39
Sarah, 29, 34-35, 37, 39-41, 80, 89, 154
Sarah (Horton), 40, 89
Sarah (Hussing), 153
Sarah (___), 89
Silas, 39, 90, 153
Stephen, 89
Sylvanus, 89
Talithcumy/Tabitha, 39
Theophilus, , 39-40, 88, 153
Thomas, 33-39, 85, 88-89, 153
Timothy, 89
William, 33-34, 36-37, 40-41, 85, 88-90, 153-154
Zaccheus, 89

JACKSON
Caleb, 19
Elizabeth, 172
Jane (Downs), 226
John, 171-172
Lydia, 171
Robert, 226
Stephen, 212
JACOB
Elizabeth, 114
JACOBS
Joseph, 85
JAMES
Alwyn, 138
Benjamin, 209
Mary (Breed), 209
Sagamore, Indian, 179
JARVIS
Margaret, 37
JEFFORDS
Mary, 85

JENCKS
Samuel, 210
JENKINS
Joel, 157
Mary (Chadwick), 157
Mary (Jones), 114
Obadiah, 114
Sarah, 79
JENKS
Elizabeth (Berry), 50
John, 50, 108-109, 211
John, Capt., 209
Joseph, 28, 156
Mary, 87
Sarah, 50, 84
Sarah (Merriam), 50
JENNISON
Abigail, 195
Dorothy (___), 195
Elias, 195
Hannah (Twiss), 195
Judith (Kenney), 195
Mary, 195
Olive, 195
Robert, 195
William, 195
JERRILL
Gamaliel, 133
Jemima (___), 133
Rebecca, 133
JEWELL
Erastus Perry, 63
JEWETT
Amos E., 17
Joseph, 19
Maximillian, 18
Nehemiah, 19
Sally, 116
Sophia (Boston), 116
Spofford, 116
JOAN OF ARC, 186
JOHNSON, 147
Abigail, 136, 151, 200, 206
Alice (___), 152, 200
Benjamin, 132
Betsey, 137
David, 131, 152
Ede (___), 137
Elizabeth, 152
Francis, 83
Hannah, 135, 152
Isaac, 179-180, 185
John, 137
Jonathan, 82, 211

Lydia (Bachelder), 210
Margret, 131
Martha (Proctor), 54
Mary, 149, 152
Mary (Collins), 152
Mehitable, 226
Nehemiah, 187
Phareoh, 190
Pharoah, 190
Polly, 137
Rebecca (___), 134
Richard, 41, 80, 85, 146, 149, 152, 200, 209-210
Ruth, 149, 152
Sally, 54
Samuel, 86, 149, 152, 190-191, 215
Sarah, 112, 210
Sarah (___), 190
William, 54
JOHNSTON
Abigail, 134
James, Jr., 54
Jane (___), 54
JOLLS
Sarah, 115
JONES, 229
___ (Curtis), 114
___ (Soane), 114
Catherine (Gammon), 229
Hannah, 114
Joanna (Osgood), 227
John, Sr., Col., 90
Lydia, 191
Mary, 114, 122, 195
Nathan, 190-191
Nathaniel, 190
Rachel, 197
Robert, 114, 227
Sarah, 165
Sylvanus B., 8
Thomas, 229
JONSON
Abigal, 131
Ephraim, 131
Obed, 131
JORDAN
Lucy A., 226
Miriam, 109
JUDD See CHUDD
JUDKINS
Abigail, 22
Abigail (Harriman), 20, 22
Catherine, 22
Elizabeth, 22

LAITON
   Thomas, 38
LAKE
   Benjamin, 142
   Mercy, 142
   Mercy (Eaton), 142
LAKIN
   Mary, 166
LAMBERT
   Thomas, 101-102
LAMSON
   Hannah, 199
LANDER, 151
   Sarah (Williams), 151
LANE, 73
   Ann Elizabeth (Andrews), 48
   Anna E., 48
   George W., 48
   Huldah (Tilton), 96-97
   Jeremiah, 91
   Joseph, 90
   Levi, 91
   Mary, 109
   Rebecca (Witt), 90
   Simeon, 96-97
LANGLEY
   Ann/Agnes, 151
LARABEE
   Elener, 130
LARCUM
   Hannah, 109
   Job, 109
   Mary (Bush), 109
LARNETT See LINNELL
LARRABEE
   Betsey, 136
   Hannah, 136
   Hannah (___), 136
   John, 136
   Nancy, 136
   Polly, 136
   Samuel, 136
   Sarah, 136
   Thomas, 136
   William, 136
LASKIN
   Sarah, 193
LATHROP
   ___, Mr., 178
LATON
   Swain, 130
LAUGHTON
   ___, Mr., 28
   ___, Mrs., 34

Thomas, 38
Thomas, Sr., 38
LAWRENCE
   Margaret, 223
   Mary, 202
LAYTHE
   Benjamin, 133
LEACH
   Elizabeth, 152, 206-207
   Richard, 206
LEARNED
   Hannah, 109
LEAVITT
   James, Capt., 99
LeBARON
   Elizabeth (Washburn), 226
   Hannah, 226
   James, 226
   Jane (Russell), 226
LECHFORD
   Thomas, 155
LEE
   John, 157
   Richard, 114
   Sarah (Coy), 114
   Thomas, 114
LeFAVOR
   John, 135
   Lydia, 195
LEGG
   John, 182
LEGGE
   John, 180
LEIGH See LEE
,
LEISSNER
   ___, Capt., 142
LEONARD
   Henry, 30
   James, 30
LETTIN See LINTON
LEVERETT
   Huson, 157
LEWIS, 155
   Abigail, 160, 211-212
   Alonzo, 33, 146
   Charles, 134, 136
   Ede, 134-136
   Edmund, 114, 210, 212
   Elizabeth (Brewer), 210
   George Harlan, 210
   Hannah, 134, 160, 210-211
   Hannah (Jones), 114
   James, 114

Jane (Ballord), 160
John, 50, 86, 159-160, 204, 210
John, Dea., 160
Joseph, 114
Lydia, 134, 136
Martha, 134, 136
Martha (___), 134, 136
Mary, 136, 160
Mary (Breed), 211
Mary (Jones), 114
Pearson, 134
Pierson, 136
Polly, 134
Sarah (Lindsey), 50
Susanna, 229
Susannah, 50
Tabitha, 205
Thomas, 211
Timothy, 134, 136
William, 134, 136
LIBBY
   Charles Thornton, 82
LINCOLN
   ___, Earl, 180, 185
   Rebecca, 55
LINDBERG
   Marcia, 145, 198
   Marcia Wiswall, 155, 208
LINDSEY, 85
   Eleazar, 50
   Lydia (Farrington), 50
   Mary (Breed), 50
   Ralph, 50
   Sarah, 50
LINNELL
   Abigail, 229
   Jemima/Peninah (House), 229
   Robert, 229
LINSCOTT
   John, 82-83
   Lydia (Milbury), 82
   Mary, 31, 82-83
LINTON
   Ann, 229
   Elizabeth (___), 229
   Robert, 229
LISSEN
   Mary, 21-22
LISTERNICK
   Roselyn, 25, 79, 213
LITTLE
   Elizabeth, 224
   Hannah (Mighill), 224
   Nathan, 224

Ruth (Harriman), 23
Samuel, 23
Sarah, 23
MERRITT
   Lydia, 210
MERRY
   Elizabeth, 87
   Rachel, 206
MERRYFIELD
   Bonnel, 229
   Susanna (White), 229
   Susannah, 229
METCALF
   Stephen, 9
MIDDLETON
   Alice Chester, 48
   Anna E. (Lane), 48
   Charles W., 48
   Watson, 48
MIDDLETON
   Elizabeth (Allen), 48
MIGHILL
   Hannah, 224
MIGILL
   Benjamin P., 17
MILBURY
   Lydia, 82
MILES
   Byrd E., Mrs., 67
MILLER
   George, 229
   Mary, 229
MILLET
   Hannah (Power), 113
   Joseph, 113
   Margaret (Felton), 113
MILLS
   James, 82
   Jane, 54
MILS
   Mary, 199
MILWARD
   Eliz., 172
MIRES
   Mary, 113
MIRIAM See MERRIAM
MIRIEK
   Edward, 208
MITCHELL
   Alexander, 88
   Joanna, 47
   John, 57
   Katherine, 88
   Mary (Ingersoll), 108

Mary (Morrissey), 57
Mary (Sawyer), 174
Miriam (Jordan), 109
Nancy, 227
Olive, 108
Phebe (___), 125
Robert, 108-109
Susanna (Burrage), 88
MONTAGUE
   Abigail, 90
MOOR
   John, 208
MOORE
   ___, Mr., 143
   Betsey, 115
   Martha/Patricia, 115
MORGAN
   Hannah, 90, 153-154
   Hannah (___), 153
   John, 153
MORGARIDGE
   Betty (Osgood), 172
   John, 172
   Mary, 172
MORGRIDGE
   Benjamin, Lt., 142
MORRELL See MORRILL
MORRILL
   Moses, 22
   Rebecca (Barnes), 22
   Sarah, 22
MORRISEY
   Richard, 57, 227
MORRISSEY
   Edmund, 57
   Johanna (Kramer), 57
   John, 57
   Mary, 57
   Mary (Cunningham), 57
   Mary (Heeley), 57
   Michael, 115
MORS
   Sarah, 160
MORSE
   A., Rev., 205
   Abner, Rev., 90
   Augusta, 15
   Elizabeth (Bartlett), 224
   Joanna (Tilton), 91
   Mary, 223
   Moses, 15
   Thomas, 224
MORTON
   Sarah, 229

MOSHER
   Nellie Beaman, 122, 128
MOULTON, 215
   Abigail (Williams), 107, 174
   Abigail (___), 112
   Elizabeth (Winn), 47, 107
   Elizabeth Maria, 47, 107
   Hannah (Eaton), 48, 107
   Joseph, 48, 48, 107, 112, 174
   Mary, 113
   Mary (Noyes), 107
   Mary E. (Dennis), 112
   Moses Benjamin, 47, 107
   Moses Emerson, 47, 107
   Ruth (Somerby), 47, 107
   Samuel, 174
   Sarah, 21, 93
   Stephen, 107, 174
   Stephen, Jr., 174
   Stephen, Sr., 174
MOWER
   Hannah (___), 191
   John, 190-191
   Richard, 80, 211
   Richard, Jr., 211
MOYSE
   Mary, 165
MUDGETT, 74
MUGOON
   Dinah (Gordon), 21
MUNNINGS
   Hannah, 227
MURRAY
   Julia, 221
MUSSMACHER, 229
MUZZEY
   Benjamin, 157
MYLES
   Joseph, 137
   Mary (___), 137
   Polly, 137
   Thomas, 137
MYRICK
   Sarah (Ramsdell), 216
   William, 216

NAILER
   Tom, 120
NASH
   Ephraim, 48
   James, 47
   Keziah (Lockwood), 47
   Mary, 47
   Mary (McDonald), 48

LOACHEM
  Paty/Martha, 214
LOCKE
  ___, Mrs., 74
  Elizabeth (Bowles), 172
  Samuel, 73
LOCKWOOD
  Benjamin, 48
  Keziah, 47
  Keziah (Springer), 48
LONG
  Abigail, 173
LOOK
  Mary, 164
  Thomas, 165
LOOMER
  Mary (Miller), 229
  Stephen, 229
LOOMIS
  Joseph, 229
  Lucy, 114
LORD
  Mary, 56, 114, 229
  Mary/Molly/Elinor, 114
  Molly, 224
LOTHROP
  ___, Capt., 19
LOVELL
  Ezra, 195
  Mary (Jennison), 195
LOVERING
  Leah, 93
LOW
  Elizabeth/Betsy, 112
LOWD
  Mary, 93
LOWE
  Fred, 173
  Rose Etta (Deering), 173
LOWELL
  Abner, 171
  Elijah O., 115
  Mary, 112
  Mary (Chandler), 114
  Mehitable (Osborn), 115
  Percival, 114
  Richard, 114
  Sarah (Webber), 171
LUCAR
  Catherine (Clinton), 52
  John, 52
  Mary, 52
LUIS, 131

LUMBERT
  Abigail (Isham), 55
  David, 55
LUME See LOOMER
LURVEY
  Hannah (Boynton), 75
  Jacob, 75-76
  Mary, 76
  Mary (Graham), 75
  Samuel, 75
  Sarah (Bennett), 75
LUTHER
  Phebe, 227
LUTZ
  Melinde Laura, 74
LUVEY
  Samuel, 76
LYNCH
  Mary, 173
LYON
  Dorcas, 226
LYONS
  Bridget (___), 220
  Bridget M., 220
  John, 220

MACGOON
  Dinah, 20
MACKENTIRE
  Deborah, 132
MACKINTIER
  Asa, 133
  Polly, 135
  Sarah (___), 133
  Solomon, Jr., 135
MACKINTIRE
  Ebenezer, 131
MACKSFIELD
  William, 130
MACOMBER
  Chloe (Smith), 226
  Elijah, 226
  Mehitable (Johnson), 226
MAKEFASHION
  Ambrose, 30
MANNING
  Eliphelet, 195
  Hannah, 195
  Hannah (Twiss), 195
  Mary, 195
  Nicholas, Capt., 203
  Rebeckah (___), 195
  Thomas, 195
MANSFIELD, 155

Amos, 81
Andrew, 27, 36, 116, 146, 198,
  200-201
Anna (Ward), 81
Bethiah, 49
Daniel, 79, 86, 208-209, 214-215
Debora, 81
Deborah, 29
Dorcas (Ramsdell), 160
Dorcas/Dakis (Ramsdell), 81
Ebenezer, 160, 189
Elizabeth, 29, 210
Elizabeth (Burchstead), 160
Elizabeth (Williams), 29, 81, 151,
  160
Hannah (Brown), 194
Hannah (Proctor), 160
Hannah (___), 81
James, 81, 210
James S., 29, 160
John, 160, 210-211, 215
Jonathan, 81, 160, 208, 210
Joseph, 26, 29, 32, 81, 151, 159-160,
  204, 210, 213
Joseph, Jr., 28, 79, 81
Joseph, Sr., 80
Lucretia (Derby), 210
Lydia, 54
Lydia (Merritt), 210
Martha, 160, 210
Martha (Stocker), 81, 160, 208, 210
Mary, 194
Mary (Newhall), 116, 160
Mary (Norwood), 160
Mary (Palmer), 81
Matthew, 160
Robert, 29, 81, 160
Rufus, 210
Sarah, 210
Sarah (Cheever), 160
Sarah (Stocker), 160, 209-210
Thomas, Jr., 194
William, 81
MARDEN
  Barbara B., 91
MARROW
  Anna (Youngman), 29
  Daniel, 29
MARSH
  Abigail (Twiss), 194
  Alice (Booth), 196
  Daniel, 194
  Ebenezer, 196
  Ezekiel, 194

Hannah, 194
John, 194
Lucius, Col., 194
Lydia, 193, 196-197
Mary (Chudd/Judd), 194
Rebecca (Gould), 194
MARSHALL
   ___, Capt., 158-159, 192
   John, 135
   Mary, 76
   Rebecca (___), 159
   Sarah, 156, 159
   Thomas, Capt., 32, 37, 156-157, 159, 198
MARTINO
   Caroline, 145
   Carolyn, 198
MASON
   ___, Mr., 7
   Abigail, 32
   Ann, 79
   Cesar, 134, 137
   Daniel, 137
   Deborah, 132
   Elizabeth, 132
   Elizabeth (Hammond), 27
   Elizabeth (___), 137
   Hanna (Ramsdell), 27
   Hugh, 27
   Hugh, Capt., 27
   John, 27
   John L., 115
   Larkin, 137
   Mary, 132
   Mary Eliza, 27
   Nathan, 131, 137
   Rebecka, 137
   Rebecka (___), 137
   Richard, 132
   Robert, 132, 137
   Sally (Tarbell), 115
   Thomas, 137
MASSEY
   Benjamin, 50
   Jane (Vining), 50
   John, 50
   Nathaniel, 50
   Rebecca (Tomkins), 50
   Sarah, 50
   Sarah (Hart), 50
MASTERS
   Abigail (Ormes), 164
   Abraham, 164
   Hannah, 164

Hannah (Woodbury), 164
Jane (___), 164
John, 164
Nathan, 164
MASURY
   Susanna, 50, 54
MATHER
   Richard, 185
MAVERICKE
   Paul, 148
MAX
   Margaret, 81
McARTHUR
   Mary Jane E., 214
McCARTHY
   Mary, 221
   Mary E., 163
McCOY See COY
McCURDY
   Anna (Hilton), 163
   John, 163
   Mary, 162
McDONALD
   Mary, 48
McELROY
   Mary Ann, 164
McGLONNE
   Catherine, 221
McGLOUGHLIN
   Ellen (___), 221
   Henry, 221
McIVER
   Edward H., Mrs., 227
McKECHNIE
   Hector, 139
McKENNEY
   John, 171
   Margaret (Wright), 171
McLEOD, 55
McLOAUGHLIN
   Agnes T., 220
McLOUGHLIN
   John, 220
   Winifred A. (Burke), 220
McREYNOLDS
   Andrew, 56
   Eliza, 56
   Elizabeth (Snoddy), 56
   Esther, 56
   Hugh, 56
   Isabella, 56
   John, 56
   Matthew, 56
   Robert, 56

Samuel, 56
MEACHUM
   Isaac, 213
   Ruth (Dunnell), 213
MEAD
   Eli, 136
   John, 131
MEARS, 113
   Alexander, 114
   Martha (___), 114
MELBURN
   Grace, 106
MELCHER
   Jonathon, 171
   Polly (___), 171
   Sarah, 171
MELLENDY
   Abigail (___), 134
   Daniel, 134
   Nabby, 134
   William, 134
MELLINDY
   Patience, 134
MERCHANT
   Elizabeth, 199
MERREY
   Mary, 206
MERRIAM
   Abigail, 79
   Abigail (Ramsdell), 79
   Ann (Mason), 79
   Charles Pierce, 79
   Ebenezer, 79, 213
   Esther/Easter, 79
   Ezekiel, 79
   Jerusha, 79
   John, 79
   Joseph, 79, 208, 211
   Sarah, 50, 79
   Sarah (Daniels), 79
   Sarah (Dunnell), 213
   Sarah (Jenkins), 79
   Theophilus, 79
   William, 79, 157, 159-160
MERRILL
   Bela, 115
   Eliza, 115
   Hannah (Osborn), 115
   John, 115
   Jonathan, 23
   Joseph, 115
   Margaret (Osborn), 115
   Mary (Brown), 23
   Paul, 115

Sarah, 55
NEAL
    Elizabeth (West), 194
    Hannah, 165
    Jeremiah, 166
    Mary (Buffum), 166
NEEDHAM
    ___, Mr., 35
    Abigail, 164
    Ann (Potter), 164
    Anthony, 164
    Daniel, 210
    George, 195, 197
    John, 197
    Lydia (Lefavour), 195
    Mary (Twiss), 195
    Rachel (Gould), 195, 197
    Ruth (Twiss), 197
    Sarah (Bachelder), 210
    Seeth (Phippeny), 195
    Thomas, 195
NELSON
    Ann (___), 135
    Elisabeth, 135
    Esther, 135
    Hannah, 103
    Hannah (Brocklebrook), 103
    Jacob, 103
    James, 135
    Jane, 135
    Jeremiah, 103
    John, 135, 157
    Joseph, 103
    Mary (Harriman), 102-103
    Phillip, Lt., 101
    Sarah, 135
NEWEL See NEWHALL
NEWELL
    Abijah, 187
    Andrew, 153
    Martha (Thwing), 153
NEWGATE
    Mary, 201
NEWHALL, 155, 184
    Aaron, 153
    Abigail, 189
    Abigail (Phillips), 165
    Abigail (___), 189-190
    Abijah, 189
    Andrew, 50
    Anna, 205
    Benjamin, 132
    Daniel, 160, 187-189
    David, 199
    Eleazer, 199
    Elinor (Ramsdell), 29
    Elisabeth, 133
    Elizabeth, 56
    Elizabeth (Merchant), 199
    Elizabeth (Normanton), 199
    Elizabeth (Potter), 50, 56
    Elizabeth (___), 29
    Estes, 191
    Esther (Bartram), 166
    Esther/Estar (Bartram), 56
    Francis, 188
    Hannah (___), 187
    Henry, 199
    Increase, 199
    Isabella, 50
    Jacob, 205, 209, 211
    James, 137
    James R., 33, 146
    Jeremiah, 165
    John, 56, 134, 137, 153, 166, 198-199
    John Brown, 50
    John, Jr., 28
    Joseph, 50, 137, 166
    Lydia, 210
    Lydia (Scarlet), 199
    Mary, 87, 116, 160, 165, 199
    Mary (Breed), 160
    Mary (Burchstead), 199
    Mary (Grice), 199
    Mary (Newhall), 165
    Nathaniel, 29, 199, 208
    Oliver, 165
    Phebe, 29
    Phebe (Towne), 29
    Rebecca, 165, 205
    Rebecca (Collins), 199
    Rebecka, 199
    Ruben, 137
    Ruth, 49
    Sarah, 112, 199, 215
    Sarah (Bates), 165
    Susanah (___), 137
    Susanna (Farrar), 50, 166
    Susannah (Brown), 50
    Susannah (Lewis), 50
    Susannah (Swift), 199
    Thomas, 26, 29, 35, 56, 165
    Winthrop, 190
NEWMAN, 85
    Abigail, 215
    Abigail (Ramsdell), 84
    Hannah (Downing), 84
    John, 84
    Mary (Ramsdell), 84
    Thomas, 84
NICALS See NICHOLS
NICHOLAS
    ___, Capt., 206
NICHOLS
    Abigail, 197
    Benjamin, 136
    Benoni (Tucker), 113
    Ebeneazer, 113
    Ebenezer, 132
    Ebenezer, Capt., 7
    James, 7
    John, 130
    Joshua, 7
    Mary, 132, 227
    Phebe (___), 136
    Sarah, 132
    Sarah (___), 132
    Susanna, 132
    Thomas, 113, 136
NICK
    Mary, 136
    Mary (___), 136
    Rebecca, 136
    Sally, 136
NOBLE
    Arthur, Capt., 194
    Christopher, 171
    Lydia (Jackson), 171
NORMAN
    Joseph, 202
    Mary (Collins), 202
NORMANTON
    Elizabeth, 199
NORRIS
    Edward, 194
    Edward, Jr., 194
    Eleanor, 96
    Elizabeth (West), 194
    Mary (Twiss), 194
    Remember (White), 194
    William, Maj., 96
NORTHEND
    Margaret, 100
NORTON
    Eunice (Gunnison), 55
    Francis, 173
    George, 37
    Henry, 173
    John, 173
    Mary (Houghton), 173
    Samuel, 55

Elizabeth (Adams), 106
Ruth (Andrews), 106
PHILBRICK
    Hannah, 113
PHILIP
    King, 32
PHILIPS
    Walter, 190
PHILLIP
    Zacheus, 190
PHILLIPS
    ___, Mr., 77
    Abigail, 165, 191
    Abigail (Nutting), 165
    Abigail (Twiss), 195
    Abigail (___), 189
    Albert M., 195
    Amos, 189
    Benjamin, 188
    Benjamin H., 191
    Elizabeth (Haggett), 224
    Elizabeth (___), 189
    Fortin, 189
    George, 185
    Gideon, 190
    Isaac, 165
    Israel, 125
    James, 114, 189-190, 224
    John, 224
    Jonathan, 191
    Leonard, 223
    Lois (Ivory), 39
    Lydia, 205
    Lydia (___), 165
    Mary/Molly/Elinor (Lord), 114
    Mehitabel (Haggett), 223
    Molly (Lord), 224
    Nancy, 189
    Nathan, 191
    Richard, 195
    Ruth (___), 195
    Sally (Head), 223
    Samuel, 223
    Sarah, 223
    Seth, 165
    Stephen, 39
    Walter, 195
    William, 189, 191
    Zacheus, 191
PHIPPENY
    Seeth, 195
PHIPPS
    Jedediah, 9

PICKARD
    Hannah (Nelson), 103
    Jane, 103
PICKERING
    Elizabeth, 50, 54
    John, 37
    Sarah (Burrill), 37
PIERCE
    Abigail (Brown), 108
    Daniel, 172
    Eliz. (Milward), 172
    Esther, 107
    Heman, 78
    Jacob, 78
    James, 78
    Mary, 172
    May Lizzie, 78
    Moses, 108
    Thomas, 78
    Thomas, Jr., 78
    William H. H., 78
PIERSON
    Hannah, 132
    Jonathan, 132
    Kendal, 132
    Lois, 132
    Lois (___), 132
    Samuel, 132
    Timothy, 132
PIGEON
    Henry, 89
PIKE
    Joanna, 108
    Naomi (Harriman), 23
    Rebecah, 132
PILLSBURY
    Charles Stinson, 17, 100
    John Sargent, 17, 100
PINKHAM
    Mary (Ramsdell), 216
    Nathaniel, 216
PITCHER
    Andrew, 125
    John, 125
PITMAN
    Elizabeth (Bowles), 172
    Mary, 172
    Sarah, 172
    Susannah (Shortbridge), 172
    William, 172
PITTS
    Henry, 8
    John H., 8
    Sarah (___), 8

PLACE
    Enoch Hayes, Elder, 67
PLUMER
    Abner, 23
    William, 67
PLUMMER
    Ann (Wood), 102
    Benjamin, 102
    Jonathan, 103
    Martha, 102
    Mehitable (Harriman), 103
    Nathaniel, 103
POER
    Elizabeth/Lydia (Kennedy), 221
    Margaret, 220
    Patrick, 221
POLAND
    Jaohn, 137
    Martha (___), 114
    Mary, 31
POND
    Emmeline, 226
POOL
    Alice Chester (Middleton), 48
    Ann Eliza, 48
    Benjamin, 135
    Betsy, 226
    Elizabeth, 48, 56
    Harriett Babson (Figgies), 48
    James, 131
    Mary, 130
    Mehetabel (___), 135
    Thomas Saville, 48
    Waldo E., 48
POOR See also POWER
    Enoch, Col., 95
    Mary (Revil), 113
    Thomas, 113
POORE
    Nancy, 227
POPE
    Betsey, 136
    Betsy, 132
    Charles H., 145
    Ebenezer, 132
    Gould, 132
    Jesse, 132
    John, 132, 171
    Lowis (___), 137
    Lucy, 132
    Mary (Eaton), 171
    Oliver, 132, 136-137
    Polly, 132
    Ruth (___), 132

NORWOOD, 155
   Francis, 204
   Jonathan, 199
   Mary, 160
   Sarah (Hudson), 199
   Susanna, 87
   Zeruiah, 205
NOWELL
   Peter, 83
   Zachariah, 212
NOYES
   Harriette, 24
   Harriette Eliza, 23
   Joseph, 174
   Mary, 107
   Mary (Darvill), 174
   Sybil, 82
NUDD
   Abigail, 95
NURSE
   Elizabeth, 193
   Elizabeth (Very), 193
   John, 193
   Jonathan, 193
   Martha (Twiss), 193
   Mary, 116, 193
   Rebecca, 193
   Sarah, 193
NUTTING
   Abigail, 165
   Ebenezer, 165
   John, 166
   Mary (Lakin), 166
   Ruth (Shattuck), 166

O'NEIL
   Arthur, 223
   Julia, 223
   Sarah, 221
OBER
   Elizabeth, 173
   Mary (Woodbury), 49
ODELL
   Martha (Collins), 203-204, 206
   Rachel (Merry), 206
   William, 204, 206
ODLIN
   Patty, 92
   Winthrop, 92
OERTILE
   Margaretha, 163
OERTLE
   Johan, 164

OLIVER
   David, 187
   Deborah (___), 191
   Henry, 189, 191
   Sarah (___), 189
ORDWAY
   John, 212
ORMES
   Abigail, 164
   John, 165
   Mary (___), 165
ORR
   John, 49
   Susan (Skofield), 49
   Susann, 49
ORRIS
   Elizabeth, 201
OSBORN
   Anna, 115
   Betsey (Moore), 115
   Eliza, 115
   Eliza (Merrill), 115
   Ephraim, 162
   Green, 115
   Hannah, 49, 115
   Jacob, 115
   James L., 115
   Jane (Brown), 115
   John Simpson, 115
   John, 3rd, 49
   Joseph, 49
   Kendall, 49
   Lydia (Hussey), 115
   Lydia (Southwick), 49
   Lydia (Wyman), 162
   Margaret, 115
   Martha, 162
   Mary (Proctor), 49
   Mehitable, 115
   Mehitable (Barton), 115
   Sally, 49
   Sally (Bushby), 49
   Thomas F., 115
OSBORNE
   Hannah (Burton), 116
   Joseph, 49
   Rachel (Foster), 49
   William, 116
OSGOOD, 155
   Betty, 172
   Jacob Dyer, 115
   Joanna, 227
   Martha/Patricia (Moore), 115
   Rebecca, 107

PAGE
   Joseph, 21
   Martha, 21, 24
   Martha (Dow), 21
   Sarah, 24
PAIGE
   Lucius R., 159
   Lucius R., Rev., 18
PALGRAVE
   Anne, 165
PALMER
   John, Sgt., 100
   Margaret (Northend), 100
   Mary, 81
   Sarah, 19, 100, 102
PAPOON
   Elizabeth, 87
   Elizabeth (Ivory), 87
   Joseph, 87
   Mary, 87
   Mary (Newhall), 87
   Richard, 87
PARK
   Elizabeth, 90
PARKER
   Abigail, 93
   Bethiah, 107
   Candace (Hand), 222
   Edmund, 15
   Elisabeth (___), 134
   Elizabeth, 39, 57, 122
   Elizabeth (Wright), 108
   Emma, 222
   Ephraim, 7
   George, 122
   Hepzibah (Douglas), 223
   John, 134, 136
   Jonathn, 130
   Lucy, 134, 136
   Lucy (___), 134, 136
   Mary, 122
   Mary (___), 122
   Nathan, 13
   Nathaniel, 108
   Peter, 122
   Phinehas, Capt., 134
   Samuel, 222
   Solomon, 223
PARKHURST
   Jemima, 222
PARSONS
   Ann, 113
   Jacob, Sergt., 142

PARTRIDGE
- Mary (Perry), 90
- Reuben, 90

PASCO
- Hugh, 172
- Mary (Pease), 172

PATASHALL
- Martha, 171

PATCH
- Abigail (___), 136
- Maho Greenleaf, 133
- Mayo Greenleaf, 136
- Polly, 136
- Sarah, 31, 133

PATEE
- Elizabeth, 174

PATTEN
- Sally, 90
- Sarah, 195

PAUL
- James Balfour, Sir, 139
- Mary, 194
- Mary (___), 152

PAYSON
- Hanley, 226

PEABODY
- Andrew, 223
- David, 224
- John, 223
- Mary (Chadwick), 223
- Mary (Morse), 223
- Parthenia, 223
- Sarah (Pope), 224

PEALE
- Benjamin, 130

PEARL
- Elizabeth (Holmes), 57
- Elizabeth (Stevens), 57, 227
- John, 57
- Nathan, 227
- Phebe, 57
- Timothy, 57

PEARSOHN
- Moses, 132

PEARSON
- Hannah, 107
- John, 26, 26
- Phebe, 104
- Rebecca (Osgood), 107

PEASE
- Mary, 172

PEASLEE
- John, 222
- Mary, 221

Mary (Huntington), 222

PEDRICK
- John, 113

PEIRCE
- William Macbeth, 20

PELL
- Ellen/Ellenor, 19

PENDLETON
- Elizabeth (Brown), 199
- James, 199

PENN
- Christian, 142
- James, 155

PENNOCK
- Albert, 56
- Alice, 56
- Anna, 56
- Charles, 56
- Elizabeth (Pool), 56
- Emma, 56
- Franklin, 56
- George, 56
- George Merle, 56
- Mary, 56
- William, 56

PEPPERALL
- ___, Justice, 83

PERKINS
- Abiather, 131
- Elizabeth, 27, 29-30
- Elizabeth (Wooten), 30
- James, 96
- Jonathan, 73
- Josiah, 31
- Mary, 166
- Shuah, 96
- Shuah (___), 96
- William, 30
- William, Rev., 30

PERLEY
- Abigail (Cummings), 105
- Patience, 105
- Samuel, 19, 105
- Sidney, 30, 84, 151, 192

PERRY
- Abigail, 90
- Abigail (Adams), 90
- Abigail (Perry), 90
- Benjamin, 154
- Deborah, 90, 154
- Deborah (Ivory), 90, 154
- Elizabeth, 90
- Ivory, 90
- John, 47

Kaziah (Broad), 90
Mary, 47, 90
Mary (Runnells), 47
Mary (Sanger), 154
Moses, 90, 154
Nathaniel, 90
Phebe, 90
Susanna (Child), 90

PERVEAR
- Mary (Emmons), 92
- Phillip, 92

PETER
- Hugh, Rev., 146

PETERS
- Benjamin, 135-136
- Benjamin, Jr., 136
- Eunice, 229
- Hannah, 135-136
- Hannah (___), 135
- Patty, 136
- Patty (___), 136
- Philip, 229
- Samuel, 135-136
- Susanna (Lewis), 229
- Susannah, 229

PETERSON
- Hopestill, 57

PETTINGELL
- Abraham, 142
- Andrew Haskell, 47
- Benjamin, 142-143
- David, 142
- Eleazer, 47
- Elizabeth Maria (Moulton), 47
- Harriet Moulton, 47
- Mary (Haskell), 47
- Mary (Nash), 47
- Mercy (Briggs), 143
- Mercy (Lake), 142
- Mercy/Polly, 143
- Moses, 47
- William Fisher, 47

PETTINGILL
- Charles I., 144

PETTY
- Ruth, 109

PEVEAR/PERVEAR
- Mary, 92

PEVERLY
- Jane (Walford), 227
- Thomas, 227

PHELPS
- Bathsheba, 106
- Edward, 106

Sarah, 224
Sarah (___), 132, 136
PORTER
   Dudley, 133
   Elizabeth, 39
   Ellen Mariah, 222
   Emma (Parker), 222
   Irad, 222
   Joseph, 222
   Letta (Knapp), 222
   Sarah, 166
   Sarah (___), 133
POTE, 74
   Miriam, 47
POTTER, 155
   ___, Mrs., 56
   Ann, 164
   Bathia, 86
   Benjamin, 79, 82, 209
   Benjamin, Capt., 37
   Elizabeth, 50, 56
   Ephraim, 85
   Martha (Hall), 50
   Robert, 26, 35, 50, 56, 85
   Ruth, 40, 85, 89
   Ruth (Burrill), 37
   Ruth (Driver), 85
   Sarah, 35-36
   Sarah (___), 85
POWELL
   Comfort, 96
POWER See also POOR
   Hannah, 113
   Margaret (Felton), 113
   Mary (Mires), 113
   Richard, 113
   Thomas, 113
POWERS See POER
PRATT
   David, 137
   Elizabeth (Hudson), 199
   Elizabeth (___), 137
   Grover, 160, 210-211
   Jonathan, 137
   Joseph, 113
   Joshua, 199
   Margaret (Felton), 113
   Richard, 207, 210
   Tacey, 189
PREBLE
   ___, Capt., 83
   Abraham, 82
PRESCOTT
   ___, Rev., 195

Amos, 137
Benjamin, Hon., 94
Huldah, 96
John, 94
Jonathan, 96-97
Lucy, 96-97
Lydia, 107
Mary, 107
Rachel (Clifford), 96-97
Rebecca, 94
Rebecca (Prescott), 94
Sarah, 97
PRESCUTT
   James, Jr., 91
PRESSEY
   Anna, 228
   Anna Miriam, 221
   Anna/Miriam, 116
   Hezekiah, 116, 221
   Joseph, 222
   Judith (Challis), 222
   Mary (Challis), 116, 221
PRESTON
   Mary (Ivory), 88
   Samuel, 88
PRICHARD
   William, 34
PRINCE
   Lydia (DeLano), 57
   Thankful, 57
   Thomas, 57
PROCTOR
   Elizabeth, 32, 193
   Hannah, 160
   John, 49
   Lydia (Waters), 49
   Martha, 54
   Mary, 49
   Melba, 186
PUDNEY
   Abigail, 193, 195
   John, Jr., 192, 195
   Mary (Jones), 195
   Samuel, 193
PURCHAS See also PURCHASE
   Oliver, 28
PURCHASE See also PURCHAS
   Oliver, 148
   Oliver, 149
PURCHIS
   Elizabeth, 87
PURDY
   Joseph, 196

PURINTON
   Content (___), 188
   Deliverance, 187
   Jacob, 189
   James, 187, 191
   Moses, 189
   Pelatiah, 188
PURRINGTON
   Charles, 57
   Elmira (Graffam), 57
PUTNAM
   Elizabeth (Leach), 152, 206-207
   Ephraim, 112
   Mary, 194
   Rachel (Stoddard), 112
   Samuel, 206
PUTNEY See PUDNEY

QUESTED
   Alice, 228
   Ann (Kennett), 228
   Ann (___), 228
   Charlotte (Kennett), 228
   Elizabeth, 228
   George, 228
   James, 228
   John, 228
   Maria, 228
   Mary (Sweeny), 228
   Mary Ann, 228
   William, 228
QUIMBY
   David, Capt., 96
QUINCY
   Edmond, 153
QUINLAN
   Margaret, 164
QUINT
   Alonzo H., 20

RADLOFF
   Herman, 45
RADULSKI
   George, Lt., 15
RALFE
   Abigal, 131
   Jesse, 131
   Luse, 131
   Luse (___), 131
   Patte, 131
   Steeven, 131
RALL/RAL/RALLS
   Hannah, 76
   Hannah (Graham), 76

Fitz, 186
Jemima, 107
John, 172
Leah (Youngman), 29
Rebecca, 172
Rebecca (___), 172
Richard, 29
RODGERS
    Catherine E. (Harrison), 220
    William, 220
ROGERS
    ___ (Hyde), 39
    Abigail, 48, 107
    Abigail (Chisemore), 108
    Abigail (Chisimore), 107
    Abigail (Winn), 108
    Annie A., 220
    Daniel, 108
    Elizabeth (Kilham), 31
    Elizabeth (Porter), 39
    Ezechi, 17-18, 101
    Ezekial, Capt., 39
    Ezekiel, Rev., 17
    Hannah (Brown), 108
    Hannah (Turner), 107
    Jeremiah, 192
    John, 108
    John, 31
    Jonathan, 108
    Lois, 39
    Lois (Ivory), 39
    Martha, 90
    Mary, 47, 107
    Miriam, 48, 107
    Miriam (Rogers), 48, 107
    Nathaniel, 39
    Paul, 48, 107
    Rebecca (French), 107
    Samuel, 159
    Silas, 107
    Simeon, 107
    Theophilus, 39
    Timothy, 107
ROOTEN
    Edmund, 37
ROOTON
    Richard, 34
ROPES
    George, 116
    John, 116, 212
    Lydia, 166
    Mary (___), 116
    Ruth (___), 116
    Sarah (Stocker), 212

ROSS
    Mary, 54
ROTHERMET
    Catherine, 43-44
ROUSE
    Joanna, 171
ROWE
    Anthony, 171
    Hannah, 93
    Joanna (Rouse), 171
    Mary, 93
    Nancy, 93
ROWELL
    Hugh Grant, 21
    Joanna, 52
ROWS
    Relief, 88
ROYAL See RIALL
RUCKE
    John, 37
RUCKS
    Samuel, 132
RUNNELLS
    Mary, 47
RUSSEL
    Ebenezer, 137
    Mehitable (___), 137
RUSSELL
    Jane, 226
    Jedediah, 132
    L. Octavius, 226
    Louis, 113
    Lucy, 153
    Lucy (___), 153
    Lucy A. (Jordan), 226
    Mary (Savage), 113
    Sarah (___), 132
    Stephen, 132
    William, 153
RUST
    Abigail, 87
RYALL See also RIALL
    Isaac, 146
    Ruth (Tolman), 146
    William, 146
RYLEY
    Thomas, 228

SALMON
    Daniel, 156
    Margery (___), 156
SALTONSTALL, 185
SANBORN, 171, 181
    Abigail, 93

Ann (Tilton), 96-97
Edward J., 99
George Freeman, Jr., 61, 74
Jeremiah, 99
Louisa Hoyt, 114
Melinde L., 22
Phebe, 93
Theophilus, 96-97
SANDBERG
    Sven Edward, 174
SANDBROOKE
    Thomas, 18
SANDERS
    Ann (Stocker), 158
    William, 158
SANDERSON
    Howard K., 194
    Howard Kendall, 213
SANFORD
    Ruth, 119
SANGER
    Mary, 154
SARGENT
    ___, Mr., 69
    Anna (Smith), 222
    Benjamin, 50
    Charles, 221
    Elizabeth, 116, 221, 228
    Henry, 222
    Hepzibah (Heath), 222
    Isabella (Newhall), 50
    Joseph, 50
    Mary (Green), 50
    Mary (Viall), 50
    Mary Hawkes, 50
    Nathan, 50
    Nathaniel, 50
    Rebecca, 221
    Sarah (Jenks), 50
    Sarah (Massey), 50
SAVAGE
    Hannah (___), 113
    James, 25, 33, 156
    John, 113
    Mary, 113
SAVORY
    Mary (Sawyer), 174
    Robert, 174
SAWTELLE
    William Otis, 76
SAWYER
    ___, Rev., 74
    Alan, 115
    Anna (Osborn), 115

Mangel, 76
RAMSDELL
    Abigail, 84, 216
    Abigail (Beeson), 32
    Abigail (Fuller), 32, 84
    Abigail (Mason), 32
    Abigail (Newman), 215
    Abigail (Towne), 31, 83
    Abigail (___), 29, 79
    Anna, 79, 81, 216
    Anna (Chadwell), 29, 37, 80-81
    Anna (Fosdick), 81, 216
    Annis, 214
    Aquilla, 25-27, 31-32, 84
    Benjamin, 31-32, 84, 216
    Betsy, 215
    Catherine, 215
    Daniel, 214
    Debora (Mansfield), 29, 81-82
    Dorcas, 29, 160
    Dorcas/Dakis, 81
    Ebenezer, 80, 214-215
    Eleanor (Vinton), 27-28
    Elizabeth, 27, 30-32, 83-84, 216
    Elizabeth (Chadwell), 29, 37, 80-81
    Elizabeth (Mansfield), 29
    Elizabeth (Perkins), 27, 29-31
    Elizabeth (Wills), 214
    Elner/Elliner, 29
    Ephraim, 80, 214
    Ester, 80
    Eunice, 216
    Eunice (Burnell), 216
    Eunice/Unis, 81
    Eunis, 214
    George, 216
    Gideon, 214-215
    Hanna, 27
    Hannah, 32
    Hannah (___), 27, 31-32
    Hepseba, 81
    Isaac, 26-30, 32, 79-81, 213-214, 216
    Isaac, Jr., 79, 213
    Isaac, Sr., 28
    Isaiah, 213
    Jacob, 81
    James, 216
    Jane (Coffin), 216
    Jedidah (Folger), 216
    Joanna, 214
    Joanna (Downing), 79, 214
    John, 25-32, 37, 79-84, 213-216
    John, Sr., 26-27
    Jonathan, 25, 27, 29, 32, 37, 79-81, 213-216
    Jonathan, Sr., 80
    Joseph, 29, 40-41, 81-82, 84
    Katherine, 84
    Kezia, 213
    Lidia, 215
    Lidiah (___), 32
    Lois, 81
    Lucy (Kembal/Kimball), 82
    Lydia, 83, 216
    Lydia (___), 27, 31, 84
    Margaret, 81
    Margerity (Williams), 80
    Mary, 30-31, 81, 84, 214-216
    Mary (Downing), 215
    Mary (Foy), 216
    Mary (Linscott), 31, 82-83
    Mary (Ramsdell), 214
    Mary (Rhoades), 80
    Mary (Rich), 80
    Mary (Wares), 84
    Moses, 32, 84
    Nathaniel, 29-32, 79, 82-84, 214-215
    Paty/Martha (Loachem), 214
    Peggy, 215
    Peggy/Margaret, 216
    Phebe (___), 216
    Polly (___), 215
    Praesilla, 27
    Priscilla, 31-32
    Priscilla (Coffin), 216
    Priscilla (___), 25
    Rachel (Swain), 216
    Rebecca, 214-215
    Rebecca (Hazlton), 81
    Ruth (Gardner), 216
    Sally, 215
    Samuel, 32
    Sarah, 29, 81, 215-216
    Sarah (Hathorn), 79, 213
    Sarah (Newhall), 215
    Sarah (Wittum), 83
    Silas, 82
    Susanna (___), 216
    Sylvia (Coleman), 216
    Tabatha (Rhodes), 214
    Tabitha, 214-215
    Tabitha (Ramsdell), 214-215
    Tabitha (Rhoades), 80
    Tabitha (Rhodes), 215
    Timothy, 31, 80, 83-84, 213, 215
    William, 214-216
RAMSDEN See also RAMSDELL
    Joseph, 25
RAMSEY
    Anna (Pressey), 228
    Anna/Miriam (Pressey), 116, 221
    Charles, 116, 221, 228
    Charles C., 221, 228
    Elizabeth (Sargent), 116, 221, 228
    Florence Josephine, 221
    Hannah (Goodwin), 221, 228
    Lucy (Eddy), 228
    Rosina Jane (Gilman), 221
    William, 116, 221, 228
    William Henry, 221
RAND
    Anna, 107
    Anna/Hannah, 39
    Daniel, 39
    Elizabeth, 39
    Elizabeth (Parker), 39
    Elizabeth (Woodbury), 47
    Elizabeth Richason, 39
    Elizabeth Trask, 47
    Florence Osgood, 39
    Hannah, 39, 87-88
    Hannah (Stevens), 226
    Hannah/Anna (Ivory), 39
    Jerusha (Bradbury), 47
    John, 39, 47
    Joseph, 88
    Lois, 39
    Lucy Ann (Small), 47
    Mary, 39-41
    Mary (Hill), 88
    Mary (Keyes), 39
    Moses, 226
    Robert, 39, 89, 198
    Robert, Jr., 39
    Roland, 47
    Sarah (Dudley), 39
    Talithcumy/Tabitha (Ivory), 39
    Thomas, 39
    Woodbury, 47
    Zachariah, 39, 41
RANDALL
    Elizabeth, 173
RANDLE
    Sarah, 173
    Tamesin, 173
RANDOLF See RANDLE
RANYDAL
    Joseph, 137
RAVENSDALE
    John, 182

RAWSON
- Elizabeth, 108
- Hannah (Bass), 109
- Josiah, 109

RAYMOND
- Hannah, 49

RAYNARD
- Sarah, 137

RAYNER
- Elizabeth, 228
- Elizabeth (Black), 228
- William, 228

REA
- Bridget (___), 137
- Jeremiah, 137
- Peleliah, 137

READ
- Elisabeth, 133
- Samuel, 130

REDDINGTON, 21

REDKNAP
- Benjamin, 36
- Joseph, 182
- Joseph, 26

RENOUF
- Charles, 158
- Sarah (Stocker), 158

REVERE
- Paul, 6

REVIL
- Mary, 113
- Mary (___), 113
- William, 113

RHOADES
- Carrie, 226
- Cecil, 226
- Henry, 80
- Joseph, 80
- Josiah, 80
- Lucy A. (Jordan), 226
- Mary, 80
- Priscilla (Smith), 80
- Tabitha, 80

RHOADS
- Anna (Burrill), 37
- Henry, 211
- Hezekiah, 211
- Joseph, 210
- Joshua, 208
- Josiah, 37
- Josiah, Jr., 211
- Samuel, 79
- Sarah (Merriam), 79

RHODEAMILLE
- ___, Mr., 46
- Catherine, 46
- Catherine (___), 44

RHODES, 155
- Elizabeth (___), 214
- Ephraim, 160
- Henry, 81, 214
- Hepseba (Ramsdell), 81
- Josiah, 81, 214
- Mary (Ballord), 160
- Mary (Ivory), 39
- Priscilla, 211
- Priscilla (Smith), 81
- Tabatha, 214-215
- Thomas, 39

RIALL
- Ann, 145-146

RICE
- David, 39
- Edmund, 144
- Eliza Jane (Bolton), 143-144
- Elizabeth (King), 142
- Elizabeth (Rand), 39
- Ezra, 142-143
- George, 143
- Horace, 143-144
- Joseph, 142
- Polly (Pettingell), 143
- Samuel, 142
- William King, 143

RICH
- Mary, 80

RICHARD
- Edward, 203
- Joseph, 87
- Lydia (Witt), 87

RICHARDS, 155
- Abigail, 206
- Agnes, 188
- Crispus, 204
- Crispus/Crispas, 205
- Deborah, 205
- Esther, 205
- Hannah, 205, 211
- John, 159, 205
- Joseph, 205
- Lydia (Phillips), 205
- Mary, 205
- Mary (Bowden), 205
- Mary (Brewer), 205
- Richard, 205
- Sarah, 205
- Sarah (Collins), 203-205

RICHARDSON
- Beulah, 7
- Bradbury, 63
- Elizabeth (Turner), 172
- Grover, 135
- Jane, 56
- Loammi, 135
- Mary, 135
- Mary, 56
- Patty, 135
- Peace, 130
- Peter, 135
- Thomas, 130, 172
- Unity, 172
- William, 135

RICHASON
- Elizabeth, 39

RICHERDSON
- Ebenzer, 131

RICHES
- Thomas, 191

RICHMOND
- Katharine Hayes, 72

RIDER
- Ann, 112

RING
- Molley, 55

RIPLEY
- Elizabeth D., 164

ROADS
- Elizabeth, 226

ROBARDS
- Abigail (Gordon), 21

ROBERT THE BRUCE, 138

ROBERTS See also ROBARDS
- Abigail, 20
- Elizabeth, 114
- Gary, 121

ROBERTSON
- Annie A. (Rogers), 220
- Catherine M., 220
- Elizabeth S. (Street), 220
- Irene P. (Casey), 220
- John K., 220
- Marguerite L. (Kelley), 220
- Ralph H., 220
- Walter Bloomfield, 220
- William J., 220

ROBIE
- Hannah, 97-98

ROBINSON
- Abraham, 90
- Daniel, 56
- Esther (Holland), 90

Anne (Foster), 171
Charles William, 173
Flora (Deering), 173
Humphrey, 115
Jacob, 171
James, 98
James, Jr., 98
Josiah, 94, 171
Louisa, 171
Lydia (Barnard), 171
Mary, 106, 174
Mary (Prescott), 107
Mary (___), 115
Roland, 64
Roland D., 97
Sarah, 47
Thomas, 107
SAXTON
   Patience, 171
SCALES
   William, 18
SCANLON
   John, 164
   Margaret, 163
SCARLET
   Lydia, 199
SCHAEFFER
   Frederick Christian, Rev., 43
SCHATVET
   Helen, 165
SCHERER See also SHERER
   Anna, 45
   Anna Catharina, 45
   Anna Catharine (Steinhauser), 45
   Catharina, 45
   Elizabetha, 45
   Heinrich, 42, 45-46
   Henry, 45
   Jacob, 45
   Johann Christian, 45
   Johann Conrad, 45
   Johann Heinrich, 45
   Johann Jost, 45
   Margaretha, 45
   Margaretha (___), 46
SCHOEFFLER
   Bill, 119
SCHULPZE
   Paul, Rev., 43
SCHWALM
   Mark, 45
SCOTT
   Roger, 34

SCRIBNER
   John, 98
SEARS
   Mary (Hilton), 112
SEDG
   Ebenezer, 214
SEELEY See CEELY
SELLERY
   Margaret, 164
SENTOR
   Betsey, 137
SEWALL
   Benjamin, 204
SEXTON See SAXTON
SHACKFORD
   S. B., 72
   Samuel Burnham, 72
SHADUCKE
   Samuell, 37
SHARPLES
   John, 228
   Mary Ann (Quested), 228
SHATSWELL
   Susanna (Bosworth), 55
   Theophilus, 55
SHATTUCK
   Hannah (Underwood), 166
   Lemuel, 27
   Ruth, 166
   William, 166
SHAW
   Elijah, 97
   Elizabeth (Ramsdell), 27
   Hannah (___), 27
   John, 27
   Joseph, 157
   Moses, 97
   William, 27
SHEARER
   Nancy, 55
SHEFFIELD
   Ann, 156, 158
   Edmund, 158
   Joseph, 122
   Martha, 122
   Mary (Woodie), 158
SHELDEN
   Anna, 133
   Francis, 133
SHELDON
   Mariannne, 138
SHELTON
   Hepsibah, 49

SHEPARD
   Hannah (Hilton), 113
   Jeremiah, 148, 151
   Jeremy, 149
   Mark, 113
   Mary, 151
SHEPHERD
   Jeremy, 36
   Tom, 120
SHERE See SHERER
SHERER
   Ann (___), 44
   Catherine, 42, 44, 46
   Catherine (Sherer), 42-43
   Elizabeth (___), 43
   Henry, 42-44, 46
   Henry Martin, 43
   Henry, Jr., 42-44, 46
   Jacob, 43
   John, 43
   John Henry, 42-43
   Julia, 43
   Louisa, 43-44
   Louisa Emeline, 42, 46
   Lucretia (___), 44
   Margaret, 43
   Margaretha/Margaret (___), 43
   Margaretta/Margaret (___), 44
   Martin, 43
   Peter, 43-44
   William, 42, 46
SHERMAN
   ___, Mrs., 128
SHERRER
   Elizabeth (___), 42
SHERRON
   Andrew, 130
SHILLABER
   Mary, 49
   Sarah (Ramsdell), 215
   Sarah (___), 215
   William, 215
SHIPPEE
   Mabel, 202
SHORE
   Priscilla, 27
SHORTBRIDGE
   Susannah, 172
SILSBE
   Abigail (___), 187
   Ephereham, 188
   Hannah (___), 187
   Henery, 187
   Patience, 190

Florence (Ramsey), 221
SWAIN
   Eliakim, 216
   Elizabeth (Arthur), 216
   Rachel, 216
   Ruth, 216
SWAN
   Dorothie, 23
   Elizabeth, 19-21, 24
   Elizabeth (Acie), 20
   Robert, 20
   Sarah, 102
SWEENY
   Mary, 228
SWEET
   Betsey, 135
   David, 135
   Sarah (___), 135
SWEETSER
   Cornelius, 131
   Elisabeth, 137
   Elisabeth (___), 137
   Ezra, 137
   John, 137
   Mary, 137
   Moses, 137
   Phineas, 137
   Phinehas, 132
   Rebecka, 137
   Rebecka (___), 137
   Sukey, 137
   Thomas, 137
SWIFT
   Betsey, 56
   Dean, 56
   Elnathan, 56
   Enoch, 56
   Hasadiah, 56
   Mary, 56
   Mary (Lord), 56
   Rebecca, 56
   Rufus, 56
   Sarah, 56
   Susannah, 199
SYMES
   Mary (Ivory), 88
   Thomas, Dea., 88
SYMOND
   Thadeous, 137
SYMONDS
   Otis P., 15
   Rose, 15

TALBERT See TOLBERT

TALMAGE
   Thomas, 181
TAPLEY
   Elizabeth, 172
   Francis, 56
   Margaret Howard, 56
   Mary (___), 56
   Samuel, 56
TARBELL
   David, 115
   Esther (Kemp), 115
   Jesse, 115
   John, 116
   Mary (Nurse), 116
   Sally, 115
TARBOX
   Benjamin, 205
   Deborah (Gray), 205
   Ebenezer, 39
   John, 205
   Mary (Rand), 39
TARR
   Caleb, 174
   Martha (Wallis), 174
   Mary, 174
TATE
   ___, Master, 71
TAY
   Mary, 134
TAYLOR
   ___, Judge, 143
   ___, Mrs., 35
   Ruth, 206
TEAGUE
   Mary, 171
TEFFTS
   James, 121
   Martha (Sheffield), 122
   Martha (___), 121
TERRY
   Tammy, 142, 144
THAYER
   Joanna, 109
THING
   Catherine, 223
THOITS
   Lydia, 133
THOMAS
   Jane (Downs), 226
   Joanna (___), 133
   Nathaniel, 226
   Richard, 133
THOMPSON
   Abijah, 13

Annie, 112
Deborah (Clements), 162
Edward, 204
Esther C. (Farnham), 162
Exsah Augusta, 162
James, 36
James Clements, 162
Joel, 9
Jonathan, 36
Joshua, 162-163
Leonard, 135
Martha (Coombs), 163
Timothy, 14
THOMSON
   Dorcis, 131
   Steephan, 131
   William, 131
THORLA
   Hannah, 212
THORNDIKE
   Elizabeth (Ober), 173
   John, 173
THORNTON
   Nell, 76
THURSTON
   Lois Ware, 17, 24, 100
THWING
   John, 153
   Martha, 88, 153
TIBBET
   Sarah, 137
TILDEN
   Bill, 46
TILTON
   Aaron, 94
   Abigail, 92-93, 98
   Abigail (Batchelder), 91
   Abigail (Nudd), 95
   Abigail (Parker), 93
   Abigail (Sanborn), 93
   Abraham, 95-97, 227
   Abraham Hayward, 93
   Ann, 96-97
   Ann (Hilliard), 96
   Benjamin, 96-97
   Betty, 92, 96-97
   Bridget (___), 92
   Caleb, 91, 93
   Caleb Morse, 93
   Comfort (Powell), 96
   Daniel, 91-99, 227
   David, 91-92, 94, 98-99
   Deborah (Cilley), 93
   Dolly, 98

Sampson, 187
Samuel, 190
SILSBEE, 41
    Dorothy (___), 202
    Henry, 202
    Jonathan, 207
    Mary, 202
    Sarah, 152, 202-203, 205
SILSBEY
    Henry, 149
SIMONS
    Sarah (Hadlock), 172
    William, 172
SIMPSON
    Jonathan, 93
    Molley (Tilton), 93
SINGLETARY
    Amos, 164
    Hannah, 164
    John, 164
    Mary (Curtis), 164
    Mary (Greele), 164
    Nathaniel, 164
    Richard, 165
    Sarah (Belknap), 164
    Susanna (Cook), 165
SINNETT
    Charles N., Rev., 213
SIZER
    Clarissa, 78
SKILLINS
    Eleanor (Youngman), 29
    Joseph, 29
SKINNER
    Thomas, 155
SKOFIELD
    Susan, 49
SLEEPER
    Ann (Tilton), 96
    Daniel, 96
    Elizabeth (Tilton), 96
    John, 96
SLOCUM
    Giles, 123
SMALL
    Anna (Staples), 47
    Bethia (Wyman), 47
    James, 47
    John, 47
    Lucy Ann, 47
SMALLIDGE
    Robert, 76
SMITH, 208
    ___, Mr., 178
    ___, Mrs., 6
    Abigail, 109
    Abraham, 166
    Amos, 133, 136
    Anna, 222
    Asahel, 31
    Chloe, 226
    Elizabeth, 31, 165
    Ephraim, 31
    Ethel Farrington, 72
    Francis, Dea., 133, 136
    George, 122
    Hannah, 31, 37, 109
    Hannah (Gordon), 21
    Hephzeba, 31
    Hugh, 17
    Isaac, 41, 134
    John, 31, 122, 202
    John, Dea., 130
    Joseph F., Jr., 31
    Louisa, 92
    Mariah, 152, 202, 206
    Martha, 108
    Martha (Colley), 202
    Mary, 31
    Mary (French), 31
    Mary (Jones), 122
    Mary (Perkins), 166
    Mary (Ramsdell), 31
    Merriah, 203
    Merryah, 204
    Phebe, 83
    Priscilla, 31, 80-81
    Rachel, 227
    Robert, 31
    Samuel, 100
    Sarah, 31, 134
    Sarah (___), 133-134, 136
    Sarah S., 220
SNODDY
    Elizabeth, 56
SNOWMAN
    Christian, 173
    Comfort (Horne), 173
    John, 173
    Mary (Cooper), 173
    Sarah (Staples), 173
SOMERBY
    Hannah (Goodwin), 48, 107
    Henry, 48, 107
    Joanna (Cheney), 107
    Ruth, 47, 107
    Samuel, 107
    Sarah (Adams), 108
SOUTH
    Ann, 33-34, 36
    Thomas, 33
SOUTHWICK
    Ebenezer, 49, 54
    Lucy (Kilburn), 115
    Lydia, 49
    Margaret Batchelder, 49
    Mary (Ross), 54
    Mary (Whitman), 49
    Mary (Whitman), 54
    Samuel, 54
    Susann (Orr), 49
    William, 115
SPENCER
    Hannah, 56
    Hannah (___), 56
    Jared/Gerrard, 56
SPENSER
    Gerard, 34
SPERRY
    Kip, 128
SPOFFORD
    John, 18
    Mehitable, 103
    Samuel, 103
    Sarah (Burpee), 103
SPOONER
    Elizabeth, 90
    Hannah, 90
SPRAGUE
    Abiah, 87
    Anna, 160
    Lois (Burrill), 37
    Samuel, 37
    Sarah, 216
SPRINGER
    Keziah, 48
STALKER See STOCKER
STANLEY
    Thomas, 182
STANTON
    Benjamin, 84
    Henry, 84
    Sarah (Jenks), 84
STAPLES
    Anna, 47
    Joseph, 47
    Miriam (Pote), 47
    Sarah, 173
STARK
    John, Gen., 93
STEARNS
    Mercy, 88

Sarah (___), 134
Timothy, 134
STEEL
   A. E. F., 139
   D. J., 139
STEINHAUSER
   Anna Catharine, 45
STEPHENS
   Polly, 134
STETSON
   Lois, 173
STEVENS, 115
   Alice (Atkins), 57
   Ann, 23
   Anne/Annie, 212
   Elizabeth, 57, 227
   Elizabeth (Abbott), 57
   Elizabeth (Parker), 57
   Hannah, 226
   Hannah (Barnard), 57
   Hannah (Graffam), 57
   John, 57
   John, Jr., Left., 57
   Jonathan, 96
   Nathan, 57
   Sally (Tilton), 96
   Sarah, 113
   William H., 57
STEWART
   Anne (Winchurst), 102
   Charles, 228
   Duncan, 102
   John, 102
   Margaret (Harriman), 102
   Mary (___), 228
STICKNEY
   Enoch, 189
STILEMAN
   Elias, 179
STOCKER
   ___ (Hall), 158
   Abigail, 212
   Abigail (Lewis), 160, 211-212
   Ann, 158
   Ann (Sheffield), 156, 158
   Anne/Annie (Stevens), 212
   Charles, 16
   Charles, Mrs., 16
   Daniel, 156
   Dorcas (___), 156-158
   Ebenezer, 156-157, 159-160, 208-212
   Edward, 155
   Elizabeth, 155-156, 158

Elizabeth (Griffin), 211
Elizabeth (Mansfield), 210
Enoch, 135-136
Ephraim, 209-210
Hannah, 158, 209-210
Hannah (Lewis), 160, 210-211
Hannah (Richards), 205, 211
Hannah (Thorla), 212
Hannah (Woodman), 212
Hannah (___), 136
James, 155
Jane, 158, 194
Joanna (Burchstead), 212
John, 160, 205, 211-212
John, Jr., 212
Joseph, 156, 158, 211-212
Lydia (Newhall), 210
Marshall, 212
Martha, 81, 156, 158, 160, 208, 210
Martha (___), 155
Mary, 157-158, 209
Mary (Divan), 156, 158
Mary (Hunt), 158
Mary (___), 156
Mercy (Holland), 158
Michael, 212
Priscilla (Rhodes), 211
Ruth (Breed), 211
Sally, 136
Samuel, 156-160, 208, 210-212
Samuel, Ens., 210
Samuel, Jr., 210
Samuel, Lt., 210
Sarah, 157-158, 160, 209-210, 212
Sarah (Berry), 160
Sarah (Berry), 208, 209
Sarah (Marshall), 156, 159
Sarah (Titcomb), 212
Sarah (___), 210
Sheffield, 158
Thomas, 155-157, 159-160, 208-212
Thomas, Jr., 156, 159, 208-210
Thomas, Sr., 156
William, 212
STODDARD
   Abner, 112
   Elizabeth/Betsy (Low), 112
   Rachel, 112
STODDER See STODDARD
STOKER See STOCKER
STON
   William, 131
STONE
   Abigail (Long), 173

Benjamin, 227
Dorothy (___), 227
Elias, 173
Hannah (Foster), 227
Hugh, Jr., 227
Hugh, Sr., 227
Mary, 81, 227
Mary (Nichols), 227
STORY
   Nehemiah, Jr., 172
STOUGHTON
   John, Rev., 178
STOVER
   Eunice, 228
STOW
   Abigail (Smith), 109
   Lydia, 108
   Stephen, 109
STOWER
   Mary, 37
STRACHIN
   Myron O., 194
STRATON
   Samuel, 131
STREET
   Elizabeth S., 220
   Samuel, 220
   Sarah S. (Smith), 220
STRIKER See STOCKER
STRONG
   Eleanor, 228
STUART
   Abigail, 222
   Ann (Adams), 223
   Annah, 222
   Grace (Hubbard), 223
   Margaret, 139
   Robert, 223
   Samuel, 223
STUTZ
   Jean, 123
SULLIVAN
   Catherine (Horgan), 220
   Catherine H., 163
   Daniel F., 220
   John B., 220
   Josephine F., 220
   Julia (Murray), 221
   Mary A. (Hanlon), 220
   Mary E. (McCarthy), 163
   Timothy P., 163
   William, 221
SUTHERLAND
   Donald Ramsey, 221

Dorothy, 96
Ebenezer, 91-93, 96-97
Eleanor (Norris), 96
Eliza (Ash), 93
Elizabeth, 93, 96, 98
Elizabeth (Hill), 227
Esther, 92
Eunice (Dodge), 94
Hannah, 93, 98
Hannah (Clifford), 98
Hannah (Robie), 97-98
Hannah (Rowe), 93
Horatio Gates, 95
Hulda, 93, 95
Huldah, 96-97
Huldah (Prescott), 96
Isaac, 98
Jacob, 94
James, 96-97
Jane (Greeley), 94
Jeremiah, 98-99
Jesse, 92
Jethro Batchelder, 92
Joanna, 91-92
Joanna (Batchelder), 91, 98
John, 91-93, 96-99
John Lowd, 93
Jonathan, 93-94, 96-97, 99
Joseph, 91-99
Joseph C., 97
Joseph, Jr., 94-95
Josiah, 92-96, 98
Judith, 98
Leah (Lovering), 93
Levi, 92-93, 95
Levi R., 93
Lucy (Prescott), 96-97
Margaret, 99
Martha (Greeley), 94
Mary, 91-92, 98
Mary (Brown), 99
Mary (Lowd), 93
Mary (Lucar), 52
Mary (Pevear), 92
Mary (Rowe), 93
Mary (___), 97
Mehitable, 93
Mercy, 97
Meribah, 95
Miriam (Clough), 99
Molly/Molley, 99
Molley, 93
Molly, 92, 95
Molly/Mary (Batchelder), 94

Nancy (Rowe), 93
Nanny, 92
Nathan, 95
Nathaniel, 95, 98-99
Olly, 92
Patty (Odlin), 92
Peter, 91
Phebe (Sanborn), 93
Phillip, 94-95
Phillip, Capt., 99
Rachel (Smith), 227
Rebecca, 96
Rebecca (Prescott), 94
Reuben, 92
Richard, 94, 98
Ruth T. (Cooper), 93
Sally, 95-96
Samuel, 91-96, 98
Samuel, Jr., 91, 93
Sarah, 96, 98
Sarah (Batchelder), 95
Sarah (Dearborn), 95
Sarah (Flanders), 93
Sarah (Moulton), 93
Sarah (Prescott), 97
Sarah (True), 95
Sherburne, 96-97
Shuah (Perkins), 96
Silas Barnard, 93
Susanna, 92-93
Theophilus, 96
Thomas, 52
Timothy, 96-97
William, 146
William, 91-99, 146
TITCOMB
   Joseph, 212
   Sarah, 212
TOBEY
   Deborah, 40, 89
TODD
   John, 18
TOLBERT
   James Clinton, 114
   Lucy (Loomis), 114
TOLMAN
   Ann, 152
   Benjamin, 152
   Ebenezer, 152
   Elizabeth, 152
   Elizabeth (Collins), 152
   Elizabeth (Johnson), 152
   Elizabeth (White), 152
   Hannah (___), 152

   Henry, 152
   Jeremiah, 162
   John, 152
   Joseph, 152
   Katherine (___), 198
   Martha (Babcock), 162-163
   Mary, 151, 198
   Mary (___), 152
   Ruth, 146, 152
   Samuel, 163
   Sophronia, 162
   Susanna (Breck), 152
   Thomas, 146, 152, 198
   William, 152
TOMKINS
   Rebecca, 50
TOMLINS, 181
   Edward, 179-181
   Timothy, 181
TOMPKINS
   Esther (Gray), 163
   Esther J., 163
   Grace G. (Blevins), 163
   Henry, 163
   Margaret (Scanion), 163
   Thomas, 163
TOPPAN
   Jane (Colman), 104
   Timothy, 104
TORNER
   ___, Capt., 25
TORREY
   Clarence, 202
   Clarence Almon, 52
TOWN
   Edwin Eugene, 83
   Judith, 194
TOWNE
   Abigail, 31, 83
   Jacob, 83
   Jacob, Jr., 30
   Phebe, 29
   Phebe (Smith), 83
   William, 83
TOWNSEND
   Abigail, 126, 202
   Abigail (Collins), 149, 201
   Adelaide Louise (Turner), 46
   Andrew, 201-202
   Anna, 126
   C. H., 202
   Charles Henry, 201
   Daniel, 202
   David, 202

WHEELER
    Elizabeth (Chamberlin), 54
    Frances (___), 54
    Isaac, 54, 208
    Ruth, 49
    Sarah, 173
    Thomas, 26, 54
WHIPPLE
    Rebecca, 172
WHITE
    Elizabeth, 152
    Mary, 172
    Polly (___), 215
    Remember, 194
    Susanna, 229
WHITING
    Sampson, 136
    Samson, 137
    Samuel, 183
WHITINGS, 85
WHITMAN
    Abigail (Hollis), 229
    John, 229
    Mary, 49, 54
WHITNEY
    Ichabod, 130
WHITTAKER
    Ann, 22
    David, 22
    Jonathan, 22
    Joseph, 22
    Mehetabel (Harriman), 22
    Mehetable, 22
    Mehetable (Harriman), 20
    Ruth, 22
    Sarah, 22
    Sarah (Emerson), 22
    Thomas, 22
    William, 22
    William, Jr., 22
WHITTEMORE
    Elizabeth/Betsey (Chesmore), 173
    Jonathan, 173
WHITTERAGE
    Mary, 137
WHYTE
    Donald, 139
WIDGER
    Sarah, 227
WIGGLESWORTH
    Edward, Col., 142
WILD BROTHER, 229
WILDER
    Ann/Anna/Hannah (___), 106
    Lois, 106
    Mary (Fairbank), 106
    Mary (Sawyer), 106
    Nathaniel, 106
    Oliver, 106
    Thomas, 106
WILEY
    Alice Jennie, 114
    Charles Edwin, 114
    Emily Louisa, 114
    Louisa Hoyt (Sanborn), 114
    Mary Sanborn, 114
    Ruth Benton, 114
WILKENSEN
    Elizabeth, 173
WILLEY
    Janes, 137
WILLIAM
    John, 130
WILLIAMS
    Abigail, 107, 174
    Agnes (Belong), 48
    Ann E., 48
    Benjamin, 107, 151
    Charles, 207
    Daniel, 130, 229
    Deborah, 151
    Ebenezer, 151
    Elizabeth, 29, 81, 131, 151, 160
    Elizabeth (Trott), 151
    Flora, 48
    Hannah, 131
    Hannah I., 48
    Isaac, 151
    Jemima (Robinson), 107
    John, 57, 114, 151, 205
    Jonathan, 151
    Margerity, 80
    Margery (Collins), 151
    Martha (Knight), 114
    Mary, 229
    Mary (Endicott), 151
    Mary (Lord), 229
    Mary (Lowell), 112
    Paul, 48
    Peter, 57
    Priscilla (Collins), 207
    Roger, 119, 183
    Ruth (Woodman), 112
    Sarah, 151
    Sarah (Graffam), 57
    Tabitha (Ingalls), 205
    Thomas, 112, 229
WILLS
    Elizabeth, 214
WILLSON
    Benjamin, 49
    Lydia, 49
    Lydia (Bancroft), 49
WILSON
    ___, Mr., 178
    John, Rev., 146
    Mary (Shillaber), 49
    Phoebe Anne, 229
    Priscilla, 157
    Robert, 49
WIMAN
    Silas, 137
WINCHURST
    Anne, 102
WING, 181
WINK
    Aaron, 8
    Frank, 8
    Katy (___), 8
WINN
    Abigail, 108
    Abigail (Rogers), 48, 107
    Bethiah (Parker), 107
    Elizabeth, 47, 107
    George, 15
    Hezekiah, 107
    James, 132
    Jeremiah, 132
    John, 15, 48, 107
    Joseph, 108
    Martha (Blodgett), 108
    Mary, 109
    Mary (Bowers), 109
    Mary (Rogers), 47, 107
    Mehetabel (___), 132
    Moses, 47, 107
    Susanna, 16
    Susanna (___), 15
    Timothy, 109
WINSHIP
    Hannah, 133
WINTERS, 209
WINTHROP, 179, 182, 185
    John, 183
WISE
    Anna (Ellis), 108
    Robert E., 108
WISWALL
    Marcia Wilson, 29, 37, 80
WITHAM
    Ebenezer, Jr., 174

Edward, 46
Elizabeth, 202, 208
Elizabeth (Orris), 201
Elizabeth (___), 201
Jerusha, 126
Jerusha (Blowers), 126
John, 32
Kendall, 130
Lydia, 126
Mabel (Shippee), 202
Mary, 202
Mary (Newgate), 201
Therina, 46
Thomas, 201
William, 126
TRASK, 208
   Abigail, 193
   Elizabeth, 193
   Hannah (Osborn), 49
   John, 49
   Mary, 49
TREVITT
   Martha (Chadwick), 157
   Robert, 157
TROTT
   Elizabeth, 151
TRUE
   Abraham, Dea., 95
   Sarah, 95
TRULL
   Dorothy (___), 52
TUCKER
   Alice (Davis), 112
   Benjamin, 112
   Benoni, 113
   Eleanor, 33, 85, 153
   Hannah, 137
   Mary, 205
   Mehitable, 223
TULL
   Jessie Maud, 226
TURNER
   Adelaide Louisa, 46
   Elizabeth, 172
   Hannah, 107, 132
   Joanna (Goodridge), 108
   Juliette Amanda, 42
   Louisa Emeline (Sherer), 42, 46
   Myron, 42, 46
   Nathaniel, 179-108
   William, 108
TUTTELL
   Elisabeth, 130

TUTTLE
   Abigail (Floyd), 174
   John, 174
   Martha (___), 174
   Mary (Holyoke), 174
   Samuel, 174
   Trueworthy, 54
TWEIST See TWISS
TWISS
   Abigail, 194-195
   Abigail (Pudney), 193
   Abigail (Pudney/Putney), 195
   Abigail (Trask), 193
   Anne, 193-194
   Anne (Callum), 192
   Benjamin, 193-194, 196
   Charity, 196-197
   Charity (Twiss), 197
   Daniel, 192-195
   Deborah, 194
   Ebenezer, 195
   Edward, 193-195
   Elizabeth, 194
   Elizabeth (Cook), Jr., 197
   Elizabeth (Nurse), 193
   Elizabeth (Trask), 193
   Eunice (Upton), 194
   Hannah, 195, 197
   Hannah (Aborn), 193-195
   Hannah (Harwood), 195
   Hannah (Wyman), 195
   James, 195
   Jane, 196-197
   John, 192-193, 195, 197
   John, Jr., 197
   Jonathan, 192-193
   Joseph, 193
   Judith (Town), 194
   Lydia, 196-197
   Lydia (Callum), 195
   Lydia (Farley), 195
   Lydia (Marsh), 193, 196-197
   Martha, 193
   Mary, 193-197
   Mary (Aborn), 193-195
   Mary (Doughty/Douty), 196
   Mary (Douty), 193, 197
   Mary (Nurse), 193
   Nathan, 192
   Peter, 192-194, 196
   Peter, Jr., 193
   Peter, Sr., 193
   Ruth, 196-197
   Sarah, 193-194

   Sarah (Hopkins), 195
   Sarah (Laskin), 193
   Sarah (Nurse), 193
   Sarah (Patten), 195
   Thomas, 192
   William, 192-193, 196-197
   William, Dr., 192
   William, Jr., 197
TWIST See also TWISS
   Ephraim, 130

ULLMAN
   Helen (Schatvet), 165
UNDERWOOD
   Hannah, 166
UPTON
   Abraham, 133
   Edmond, 133
   Elias, 133
   Eunice, 194
   Eunis, 131
   George, 131
   Hezekiah, Capt., 7
   Isaac, 133
   Jeduthan, 131
   Joshua, 132
   Molly, 133
   Rebecca, 133
   Sarah, 133
   Susanna (___), 133

VAN ARSDALE
   Peter, 44
VANE
   Henry, Sir, 146
VARNUM
   Abigail, 56
VEREN
   Hilliard, 179VERY
   Alice, 193
   Elizabeth, 193
   Elizabeth (Giles), 197
   Elizabeth (Proctor), 193
   Hannah (Twiss), 197
   Isaac, 197
   Jones, 193
   Joseph, 193
   Margaret (Brown), 197
   Mary (Twiss), 197
   Rachel (Jones), 197
   Sarah (Twiss), 193
   Thomas, 193
   Thorndike, 193

VIALL
    Charles S., 152, 198
    Mary, 50
    Nathaniel, 50
    Sarah (Bennett), 50
VINING
    Jane, 50
VINTON
    Ann (___), 28
    Eleanor, 27-28
    John, 28, 30
    John Adams, 28
    Prisilla, 192
VISCOUNT
    Abigail (Stocker), 212
    James, 212
VON FUCHS
    Marrh., Lt., 45
VON POEHLMAN
    John, 163
    Margaretha (Oertile), 163
VYNARD
    Susan, 164

WADE
    Amelia (___), 8
    Edward E., 8
    John P., 8
    Nathaniel, Capt, 75
WAIT See WAYT
WALCOTT
    Dana Mills, 165
    Elizabeth (Smith), 165
    John, 165-166
    Jonathan, 165
    Jonathan P., 165
    Lydia (Gale), 165
    Mary (___), 166
    Rebecca (Newhall), 165
    Sarah (Gardner), 165
WALDEN
    Mary (Nurse), 193
WALDRON
    Hannah (Smith), 109
    John, Col., 108
    Mary (Winn), 109
    Richard, 109
    Susan, 108
WALFORD
    Jane, 227
WALKER
    Aaron, 109
    Anna (Carpenter), 109
    Betsey, 108

    Esther (Carpenter), 109
    Eunice, 104
    Joseph B., 24
    Richard, 206
    Samuel, 109
    Timothy, Rev., 24
WALLIS
    Abigail (Tilton), 93
    Martha, 174
    Stephen, 93
WANTON
    Joseph, 57
WARD
    Anna, 81
WARDWELL
    Hannah, 133
    Jonathan, 133
WARES
    Mary, 84
WARNER
    John, 228
    Priscilla (___), 228
WARREN
    Phelps, 227
WASHBURN
    Elizabeth, 226
WASHER
    Betty, 136
WASHINGTON, 75, 126
    George, Gen., 143
WATERHOUSE
    Sarah (Graffam), 57
    Sargent, 57
WATERS
    Ann (Linton), 229
    Eunice, 165
    Harriet Ruth, 85
    Henry F., 146, 202
    John, 166
    Lawrence, 229
    Lois, 202
    Lois (Collins), 202
    Lydia, 49
    Mary (___), 166
    Phebe, 165
    Thomas, 29, 155
    William, 202
WATKINS
    Walter K., 25
WATSON
    Mary, 103
WAYT
    John, 213
    Jonathan, 209

    Mary (Dunnell), 213
WEARE
    Mesach, 66
    Nathaniel, 66
    Nathaniel, Judge, 66
WEBB
    Frances, 114
    Hannah, 88
WEBBER
    Samuel, 204
    Sarah, 171
WEBSTER
    James, 72
    John, 72, 72
    Jonathan, 94
    Thomas, 72
WEED
    Hannah, 222
WELD
    Bethia (___), 173
    Daniel, 173
    Elizabeth, 173
WELLS
    Dorothy (___), 52
    Joanna (Rowell), 52
    Luke, 52
    Sarah, 112
    Thomas, Rev., 52
    Titus, 52
WELMAN
    Artemus, 26
WENDELL, 229
WENNER
    G. U., 43
WEST
    Elizabeth, 164, 194
    Elizabeth (Jackson), 172
    Henry, 80, 133
    Phebe (Waters), 165
    Ruth (___), 80
    Thomas, 165, 172
WESTFALL
    Frederick, 43
WESTON
    Jonathan, 13-14
    Jonathan, Capt., 13, 15
    Jonathan, Jr., 13
WETHERBEE
    Lucy, 171
WHARFF
    Ann, 88
WHEAT
    Moses, 81

Elizabeth, 174
Elizabeth (Patee), 174
Sarah (Hool), 174
Tammy (Finson), 174
WITHERS, 85
WITT, 155
   Abigail (Montague), 90
   Abigail (Rust?), 87
   Bathia (Potter), 86
   Benjamin, 87, 90
   Daniel, 87
   Deborah, 90
   Elizabeth (Cheever), 87
   Elizabeth (Merry), 87
   Ester, 160
   Ester/Hester, 156, 213
   Gedney, 87
   Hannah (Hawkes), 87
   Hester, 157
   Ivory, 87, 90
   John, 86-87, 89-90, 159
   John, Lt., 89
   Jonathan, 35, 156
   Joseph, 154
   Lydia, 87
   Mary, 87
   Mary (Divan), 156, 158
   Mary (Ivory), 39, 86
   Olivia (Campbell), 90
   Rebecca, 90
   Ruth (Breed), 87
   Sally (Patten), 90
   Sarah, 90
   Sarah (Ivory), 89-90, 154
   Stephen, 90
   Thomas, 39-40, 86
   Thomas, Capt., 86
WITTUM
   John, Jr., 83
   Lydia (Ramsdell), 83
   Sarah, 83
WOLCUTT
   Hannah/Joanna (Emerson), 172
   John, 172
WOOD
   Albert G., 97
   Ann, 102
   Gideon, 227
   Joseph G., 97
   Margaret (Elithorpe), 19, 100

   Mary/Molly (Eaton), 227
   Samuel, 100-101
   Thomas, 100-101, 104
WOODBRIDGE
   Dudley, 134
   Sarah (___), 134
WOODBURY
   Aaron, 162
   Andrew, Capt., 49
   Anna Maria (Estes), 162
   Anne (Palgrave), 165
   Bethiah, 49
   Delia Hersey, 162
   Elizabeth, 47
   Elizabeth (West), 164
   Hannah, 164
   Joanna (Dodge), 49
   Joanna (Mitchell), 47
   John, 47, 163
   Joseph, 164
   Mary, 49
   Mary (Chase), 163
   Nicholas, 165
   Rebecca (King), 162
   Sophronia (Tolman), 162
   Tyler Chandler, 162
   Tyler Marsh, 162
WOODEN See WOODING
WOODFORD
   Ursula, 227
WOODIE
   Mary, 158
WOODING
   Bethiah, 174
   Peter, 174
WOODMAN
   Hannah, 212
   Ruth, 112
WOODMANSEE
   Patience, 121
WOODS
   Aaron, 90
   Sarah (Witt), 90
   Thomas, 9
WOOTEN
   Elizabeth, 30
WORK
   John, 160
   Martha (Ballord), 160
WORTHLEY
   Harold, 183

WRIGHT
   David, 131
   Elizabeth, 108
   Elizabeth (___), 171
   Margaret, 171
   Richard, 180
   Sally, 133
   Sarah, 131
   Sarah (___), 131
   Thomas, 171
WYER
   John, 208
WYMAN
   Abigail, 162
   Abigail (Wyman), 162
   Bethia, 47
   Clair Everet, 162
   Delia Hersey (Woodbury), 162
   Exsah Augusta (Thompson), 162
   Ezekiel, 162
   Francis, 162
   Fred Darling, 162
   Hannah, 195
   Love (Chick), 163
   Lydia, 162
   Martha (Osborn), 162
   Mary (Fall), 162
   Seth Fish, 162
   Thomas Bellows, 87, 153
   William, 163
   Zebedee, 162

YATES
   Sherrill, 138
YEATON
   Experience, 163
YORK
   Mary (Brown), 199
   Thomas, 199
YOUNGMAN
   Anna, 29
   Anna (Fisher), 29
   Daniel, 29
   Eleanor, 29
   Francis, 29
   John, 29
   Jonathan, 29
   Leah, 29
   Mary, 29
   Sarah, 29
   Sarah (Ramsdell), 29

MOMENTS IN HISTORY

Making Money in Colonial Days

"Currency was a problem in the Massachusetts Bay Colony, as it was in all new countries. Pirates and honest traders alike were bringing in specie in every conceivable form: Spanish doubloons; Portuguese johannes and moidores; French crowns; Dutch ducats; silver bars from the mines of Peru. Yet there was no proper currency to be had. For want of a staple, the balance of trade with England was so adverse that whatever sterling money came with the immigrants went back for remittances; the foreign coin was confusing and much of it proved counterfeit or clipped. Most of the business in the colony was done by barter, taxes paid in kind, and small change made by 'muskett bulletts of a full boare' at a farthing apiece; white wampum at four a penny, etc., the rate being lowered from time to time. So in 1652 the General Court, in pursuance of its steadfast policy of building up a prosperous, self-sufficient commonwealth, decided to exercise the sovereign prerogative of coining money. By coining shillings that weighed only three-quarters of the sterling standard, they hoped both to supply the want of currency, and to keep it at home. Accordingly, the Colony provided a mint-house sixteen foot square and ten foot stud, with tools, implements for melting, refining, and coining of silver. John Hull of Boston was appointed Master of the Mint, and directed to coin bullion, plate or Spanish coine into shillings, sixpences and three-penny bits...taking a suitable seigniorage for his pains. Hull called into partnership his friend Robert Sanderson.... Together they took an oath to coin all moneys by 'the just allay of English coine,' and to give true weight... The simple and irregularly shaped coins made under this act lent themselves so readily to clipping and washing that the act was changed the same year, providing an inscription and a tree design, within two concentric rings. Under this law Hull and Sanderson began the coinage of what are generally known as the pine-tree shillings. The act, however, said nothing about the tree being a pine, and the earliest coins, bearing the closest resemblance to the official design, show a tree which is anything but a pine. In fact there are three different types of Massachusetts shillings, known to collectors as the willow-tree, the oak-tree, and the pine-tree coins.... After the restoration, attention of the English government was called to the fact that Massachusetts Bay had usurped an unchallenged royal prerogative by coining money. Sir Thomas Temple was deputed by the General Court to placate offended Majesty. He began the interview apologetically. The colonists did not know they were doing wrong; they needed currency and had to make it themselves, since His Majesty, to their great grief, had been in no position to supply them. A shilling was produced and showed to the King. Charles inquired what tree that was. Sir Thomas had the wit to declare it to be the royal oak, which the good people of the Bay had placed on their coins as token of loyalty, daring not to incur the usurper's displeasure by using the royal name! The King was greatly pleased, called the New Englanders 'a parcel of honest dogs,' and allowed the Boston mint to continue operations" (Samuel Eliot Morison, Builders of the Bay Colony [Boston: Houghton Miflin, 1964, 150-153).

MOMENTS IN HISTORY

The Perils of Disease in the 17th Century

"The impressive toll of death which followed the voyages of the Mayflower and the Winthrop Fleet, claiming half the passenger list of the Pilgrims in the first winter and about a third of the emigrants who settled the Bay Colony, brings clearly to the reader of the early settlement of New England one of the worst features of ocean travel in that day. The rovers of the of the Seven Seas who put out from English ports in the sixteenth century had learned by bitter experience that long, deep-water voyages...became a question of proper food, and it gradually came to their knowledge that man could not survive indefinitely on dried or salted meats.

The Pilgrims were the first to feel the heavy hand of scorbutic starvation, and when, after nearly ten weeks at sea, their vessel dropped anchor inside the tip of Cape Cod, ...there were not many seaworthy men left to navigate the craft. Bradford called it the 'general sickness' for want of definite information, but in reality they were all suffering from scurvy, the crew as well as passengers, and for weeks many were unable to leave the ship...Only one thing enabled them to keep going - the casks and hogsheads of English beer.... Added to the perils of the deep, was the lack of fresh vegetables to be obtained from the land, as they arrived [in] winter when not a green thing was left to supply their starved blood with the vitamins of health. Bradford himself was a scorbutic victim as were all the leaders.

The Winthrop Fleet suffered the same experience only in lesser degree... The Lady Arbella Johnson was among the first to go, and she was soon followed by her husband, then by Edward Rossiter, and then Winthrop's family physician, [whose] death is a striking instance of the helplessness of the profession in that period in the face of outraged Nature. Neither Giles Heale, the ship's surgeon on the Mayflower, nor William Gager, on the Arbella could cope with this situation. As a result the slopes of Charlestown Neck became a hospital camp during the autumn and winter after the landing of Winthrop. The aged and weakly went first until, as Dudley states, 'there dyed by estamacon about two hundred at least so lowe hath the Lord brought us.'

It was not until Captain William Pierce of the Lyon [brought] lemons, the remedial palliative of scurvy, that its ravages began to abate in the following spring. Winthrop [advised his wife] to bring 'a gallon of Scurvy grasse to drinke a little 5 or 6 mornings...with some saltpeter disolved in it and a little grated nutmege.'"

(William Banks, Planters of the Commonwealth [Boston, 1930], 24-28)

MOMENTS IN HISTORY

Wandering Bones

In 1826, Estes Newhall of Boston, petitioned the General Court of Massachusetts to have the bodies in Boston's Quaker Cemetery removed to Lynn, Mass., which was New England's second largest Quaker Community. The Boston Cemetery was in disrepair due to dwindling numbers. Newhall's petition was granted and 99 people (72 adults and 37 children) were removed from Boston to Lynn.

According to Quaker custom, these graves were left unmarked at Lynn, and over the years they were forgotten. In 1924, the Lynn Quaker Meeting decided to build two apartment houses on the site, and when bulldozers began digging, human bones began to appear. These remains of Boston's Quakers were once again removed and sent to Salem's Quaker Burial Ground where they remain.

Today the Lynn Quaker Cemeteries are hidden from view by the Harrington School, apartment buildings of Broad and Friend Street, and the current Quaker Meeting House.

In 1953, the Pine Grove Cemetery Commission took over care of the cemeteries, but lack of funding has left the historic site a victim of vandalism and neglect. The Department of Community Development, led by State Representative Timothy Bassett, is working to find funding to save this public landmark.

(Janet Lane, "Lynn's Quaker cemetery lives on," [Lynn] *Daily Evening Item*)

MOMENTS IN HISTORY

A Great Book Disappears

In 1620, the Pilgrims landed at Plymouth, having undergone a long and difficult passage across the ocean. Their years in Holland, their voyage, the landing at Plymouth, and the years that followed, were faithfully chronicled by William Bradford, Governor of the small colony. That journal of Governor Bradford's, which he humbly called his "scribbled writings," is now recognized as one of the great books of the seventeenth century. But for a period of 150 years, it was "lost."

The manuscript had been handed down from Governor William Bradford, to his son Major William Bradford, and then to his son John Bradford, who loaned it to Judge Sewall. Thomas Prince next had it in his "New England Library" at Boston. Its whereabouts from that time until it was discovered, quite by accident, in 1855, is an unsolved mystery.

In 1844, Samuel Wilberforce, Bishop of Oxford, published *The History of the Protestant Episcopal Church in America*. It contained extracts from manuscripts he had discovered in the library of the Bishop of London at Fulham. Years later, in 1855, John Wingate Thornton happened to pick up a copy of the book, and took it to his friend, Mr. Barry, who was then writing his *History of Massachusetts.*. Mr. Barry, in looking through the church history, was struck by the fact that here was a clue to the precious Bradford manuscript, so long lost. He went to Charles Deane, "a master of historical investigation in this country," and Mr. Deane at once saw the importance of the discovery. Deane wrote to Joseph Hunter, an eminent English scholar, who visited the palace at Fulham and established beyond a question the identity of the manuscript, comparing the writing with an original letter in Bradford's hand. "How the manuscript got to Fulham nobody knows. Whether it was carried over by Governor Hutchinson in 1774; whether it was taken as spoil from the tower of the Old South Church in 1775; whether, with other manuscripts, it was sent to Fulham at the time of the attempts of the Episcopal churches in America, just before the revolution, to establish an episcopate here, nobody knows." The manuscript was put in print in 1856 by the Massachusetts Historical Society, which secured a transcript of the document from London, and printed it in the Society's Collections.

Many attempts were made to have the manuscript returned to America. Mr. Robert Charles Winthrop, in 1860, urged the Bishop of London to give it up, but the Bishop refused. Again, in 1869, John Lothrop Motley, Minister to England, tried, but his appeal had the same fate. In 1881, Benjamin Scott, Chamberlain of London, proposed again in the newspapers that restitution should be made, but nothing came of it. In 1895, Senator George F. Hoar went abroad, determined to see the original manuscript, writing in advance to the Bishop at Fulham, who agreed to show Hoar "The Log of the Mayflower." Senator Hoar told the Bishop, "I think this book ought to go back to Massachusetts." The Bishop said, "I think myself it ought to go back... and I think I ought to speak to the Queen [Victoria] about it." When Senator Hoar returned home, he and Mr. Thomas Francis Bayard, Ambassador to the Court of St. James, brought the matter to the attention of the American Antiquarian Society, The Massachusetts Historical Society, The Pilgrim Society of Plymouth and the New England Society of New York. These societies formed a committee, and with Governor Roger Wolcott of Massachusetts, dispatched a letter through Mr. Bayard. "The rarest good fortune attended every step of the transaction." On the 29th of April 1897, the Honorable Thomas F. Bayard, "with all due diligence," conveyed the original, delivered to him by the Lord Bishop of London, to the City of Boston. At a special ceremony, attended by both the Senate and the House of Representatives, he presented the treasured manuscript to Governor Wolcott.

The original "Journal" is now preserved at the Massachusetts State Library in the State House at Boston. It was published in 1928, as *Bradford's History "Of Plimouth Plantation,"* and this edition is found in most libraries today, where it continues to be an inspiration to all Americans.

(From the introductory material in the 1928 edition of *Bradford's History "Of Plimouth Plantation*.)

Printed in the United States
151685LV00001B/10/P